T0188898

IFIP Advances in Information and Communication Technology 398

IFIP – The International Federation for Information Processing

IFIP was founded in 1960 under the auspices of UNESCO, following the First World Computer Congress held in Paris the previous year. An umbrella organization for societies working in information processing, IFIP's aim is two-fold: to support information processing within its member countries and to encourage technology transfer to developing nations. As its mission statement clearly states,

> IFIP's mission is to be the leading, truly international, apolitical organization which encourages and assists in the development, exploitation and application of information technology for the benefit of all people.

IFIP is a non-profitmaking organization, run almost solely by 2500 volunteers. It operates through a number of technical committees, which organize events and publications. IFIP's events range from an international congress to local seminars, but the most important are:

- The IFIP World Computer Congress, held every second year;
- Open conferences;
- Working conferences.

The flagship event is the IFIP World Computer Congress, at which both invited and contributed papers are presented. Contributed papers are rigorously refereed and the rejection rate is high.

As with the Congress, participation in the open conferences is open to all and papers may be invited or submitted. Again, submitted papers are stringently refereed.

The working conferences are structured differently. They are usually run by a working group and attendance is small and by invitation only. Their purpose is to create an atmosphere conducive to innovation and development. Refereeing is also rigorous and papers are subjected to extensive group discussion.

Publications arising from IFIP events vary. The papers presented at the IFIP World Computer Congress and at open conferences are published as conference proceedings, while the results of the working conferences are often published as collections of selected and edited papers.

Any national society whose primary activity is about information processing may apply to become a full member of IFIP, although full membership is restricted to one society per country. Full members are entitled to vote at the annual General Assembly, National societies preferring a less committed involvement may apply for associate or corresponding membership. Associate members enjoy the same benefits as full members, but without voting rights. Corresponding members are not represented in IFIP bodies. Affiliated membership is open to non-national societies, and individual and honorary membership schemes are also offered.

Christos Emmanouilidis   Marco Taisch
Dimitris Kiritsis (Eds.)

Advances in Production Management Systems

Competitive Manufacturing for Innovative Products and Services

IFIP WG 5.7 International Conference, APMS 2012
Rhodes, Greece, September 24-26, 2012
Revised Selected Papers, Part II

 Springer

Volume Editors

Christos Emmanouilidis
ATHENA Research and Innovation Centre
in Information Communication and Knowledge Technologies
ATHENA RIC Building, University Campus, Kimeria, 67100 Xanthi, Greece
E-mail: chrisem@ceti.athena-innovation.gr

Marco Taisch
Politecnico di Milano
Department of Management, Economics, and Industrial Engineering
Piazza Leonardo da Vinci, 32, 20133 Milano, Italy
E-mail: marco.taisch@polimi.it

Dimitris Kiritsis
École Polytechnique Fédérale de Lausanne (EPFL)
STI-IGM-LICP, ME A1 396, Station 9, 1015 Lausanne, Switzerland
E-mail: dimitris.kiritsis@epfl.ch

ISSN 1868-4238   ISSN 1868-422X (electronic)
ISBN 978-3-642-44637-5   ISBN 978-3-642-40361-3 (eBook)
DOI 10.1007/978-3-642-40361-3
Springer Heidelberg Dordrecht London New York

CR Subject Classification (1998): J.1, J.7, I.2, H.1, H.4, C.2, K.4.3

Typesetting: Camera-ready by author, data conversion by Scientific Publishing Services, Chennai, India

Printed on acid-free paper

Springer is part of Springer Science+Business Media (www.springer.com)

Preface

Since the first conference that took place in Helsinki back in 1990, APMS is one of the major events and the official conference of the IFIP Working Group 5.7 on Advances in Production Management Systems. Recently, APMS successfully took place in Washington (USA, 2005), Wroclaw (Poland, 2006), Linköping (Sweden, 2007), Espoo (Finland, 2008), Bordeaux (France, 2009), Cernobbio (Italy, 2010), and Stavanger (Norway 2011).

APMS 2012 was sponsored by the IFIP WG 5.7 and co-sponsored by the ATHENA Research & Innovation Centre and the Hellenic Maintenance Society in Greece. In an era of increased globalization and ever-pressing needs for improved efficiency, the APMS 2012 theme was "Competitive Manufacturing for Innovative Products and Services." In this setting, among the key elements of success in modern manufacturing and production management are:

- **Resource Efficiency**: the ability to perform in a resource-efficient manner throughout the lifecycle of a production process, product use or offered services.
- **Key Enabling Technologies**: the exploitation of the latest materials, manufacturing and production control technologies to support competitive and sustainable production.
- **Networked Enterprise and Global Manufacturing and Supply Chains**: the ability to operate as a globally interconnected organization and perform at a global scale, both at an intra- and inter-organizational scale.
- **Knowledge Intensity and Exploitation**: the efficient use of enterprise and human resources tangible and intangible knowledge, including efficient knowledge lifecycle management.
- **Innovation**: the ability to efficiently port R&D results into competitive new forms of production, products or services.

The APMS 2012 conference brought together leading experts from industry, academia and governmental organizations. They presented the latest developments in production management systems and debated how to shape up the future of competitive manufacturing. It comprised seven keynote talks and 36 sessions, including a dedicated Industry Panel Session, to offer the practitioners' view on linking research to industry, thus efficiently supporting the innovation process. The keynotes offered insight into cutting-edge issues of production management and its future, comprising the following talks:

- "A Business Perspective for Manufacturing Research," Jochen Rode, SAP
- "ICT-Driven Innovation in the Factories of the Future," Rolf Riemenschneider, European Commission
- "Sustainable Manufacturing: Towards a Competitive Industrial Base in Europe," Filip Geerts, CECIMO

- "ICT Integration Challenges in Manufacturing: From the Device to the Enterprise Level," Thilo Sauter, Austrian Academy of Sciences
- "The IMS Global Platform Services for Manufacturing Research and Innovation," Dan Nagy, IMS
- "Energy Management Operations in Shipping Industry," Takis Varelas, DANAOS
- "The FoF PPP Call in WP2013 and Future Opportunities for Manufacturing R&I in Horizon2020," Andrea Gentili, European Commission

Industry and academia converged in a stimulating Industry Panel Session, organized by Prof. Hermann Loedding and Dr. Gregor Alexander von Cieminski. The session theme was "Linking Research to Industry: The Practitioner's view on Competitive Manufacturing for Innovative Products and Services." The following panellist talks introduced the session discussion:

- "Leadership in Electronics Operations @Continental," Wolfgang Menzel, Continental
- "Integrating Industrial Needs with Academic Perspectives — Concept and Realization of the RWTH Aachen High Tech Campus," Volker Stich, RWTH Aachen

Wolfgang Menzel and Volker Stich were joined in the panel by Paul Schönsleben (ETH), Dan Nagy, IMS and Filip Geerts, CECIMO and debated about the crucial linkage between research and industry in order to shed light on what constitutes successful practices in bringing forward R&D from the lab to industry-relevant innovation. The panel argued that higher education institutions should offer opportunities to students to undertake part of their studies in industry, with this being acknowledged and recognized as a formal part of education. Furthermore, industry could have more active presence within public research and educational campuses and FIR-RWTH Aachen was presented as an example of such an endeavor. Emphasis was placed on the industrial relevance of research, which would depart from theoretical solutions for "non-relevant" problems to conducting "relevant" research offering pragmatic and innovative solutions to industry.

Several special sessions were organized and ongoing research initiatives and projects presented their progress and results. A PhD Workshop was held prior to the conference, chaired by Sergio Cavalieri (University of Bergamo) and offered the opportunity to PhD researchers to present their research plans, objectives, and results to scientific discussants and gain valuable feedback to strengthen their research plan and activities.

At the conclusion of the conference, following the APMS tradition, the conference offered the following awards:

- Burbidge award for best paper to Dimitris Mourtzis (University of Patras)
- Burbidge award for best presentation to Morten Lund (University of Aalborg)

– Best PhD workshop paper award to Elzbieta Pawlik (University of Strathclyde)

Approximately 240 academics, researchers, practitioners and scientists from 31 countries joined the APMS 2012 conference, sharing their expertise and providing insight into what constitutes the currently best practice in manufacturing and production management, while also projecting into the future of competitive manufacturing for innovative products and services. The conference involved a high-quality International Steering and a Scientific Committee of acknowledged excellence, while the review process involved 73 experts, all making key contributions to the conference success. The conference program included 196 regular presentations and 11 PhD workshop presentations. The review process involved pre-conference extended abstracts reviews and a post-conference full paper review process, followed by a final paper submission by the authors, addressing the review comments. The result of this process is the present two-volume edited proceedings, comprising 182 full papers, organized under the following sections:

– Part I, Sustainability, including Energy Efficient Manufacturing, Sustainable Value Creation, Business Models and Strategies
– Part II, Design, Manufacturing and Production Management, including Mass Customization, Products of the Future and Manufacturing Systems Design, Advanced Design, Manufacturing and Production Management, as well as Robotics in Manufacturing
– Part III, Human Factors, Learning and Innovation, including Modern Learning in Manufacturing and Production Systems, Human Factors, Quality and Knowledge Management, as well as Innovation in Products and Services in Developing Countries
– Part IV, ICT and Emerging Technologies in Production Management, including Emerging Technologies in Production and the Lifecycle Management of Products and Assets, Enterprise Integration and Interoperability, as well as ICT for Manufacturing, Services and Production Management
– Part V, Product and Asset Lifecycle Management, including Product Lifecycle Management, Asset Lifecycle Management, as well as Performance and Risk Management
– Part VI, Services, Supply Chains and Operations, including Services, Managing International Operations, Supply Networks and Supply Chain Management, as well as Production Management, Operations and Logistics

We wish to acknowledge the support of **Intelligent Manufacturing Systems (IMS)** for the USB sticks and Lanyards for badges, as well as **Prisma Electronics SA** for sponsoring the APMS 2012 Welcome Reception.

We wish to thank the active members of the IFIP WG 5.7 community for their contribution and support of the conference, their support in the papers review process and the promotion of APMS 2012 through their networks and collaborating partners. Particular thanks are due to the **ATHENA Research and Innovation Centre** and the **Hellenic Maintenance Society** in Greece for co-sponsoring and supporting the conference and Zita Congress SA for their professional conference management services.

The conference was hosted on the island of Rhodes, Greece, a world-class destination, boasting a unique mixture of ancient and modern with holiday attractions and a continuing history of well over three millennia. According to mythology, Rhodes was created by the union of Helios, the Titan personalizing the sun, and the nymph Rhode. The ancient city of Rhodes hosted one of the ancient wonders of the world, the Colossus of Rhodes, a giant statute of Helios. Manufacturing and production management have made giant strides and continue to contribute toward a world of smart, sustainable and inclusive growth, but much more needs to be done and a global effort is needed to continue pushing toward such ends. The APMS 2012 conference constituted a focused effort and contribution in supporting such aims. We hope that the present two-volume set will be of interest to the industrial and academic communities working in the area of manufacturing and production management and the associated enabling technologies.

February 2013   Christos Emmanouilidis
                                                 Marco Taisch
                                                 Dimitris Kiritsis

Organization

The APMS 2012 conference was sponsored by the IFIP WG 5.7 Advances in Production Management Systems, co-sponsored by the ATHENA Research & Innovation Centre, in Information, Communication and Knowledge Technologies, Greece, and co-sponsored by the Hellenic Maintenance Society (HMS), Greece.

Conference Chair

Christos Emmanouilidis ATHENA Research & Innovation Centre,
  Greece

Conference Co-chairs

Marco Taisch Politecnico di Milano, Italy
Dimitris Kiritsis Ecole Polytechnique Fédérale de Lausanne,
  Switzerland

APMS 2012 International Advisory Board

Christos Emmanouilidis ATHENA R.I.C., Greece
Jan Frick University of Stavanger, Norway
Dimitris Kiritsis EPFL, Switzerland
Vidosav Majstorovich University of Belgrade, Serbia
Riitta Smeds Aalto University, Finland
Volker Stich FIR - RWTH Aachen, Germany
Marco Taisch Politecnico di Milano, Italy
Bruno Vallespir University of Bordeaux, France

APMS 2012 Doctoral Workshop Chair

Sergio Cavalieri University of Bergamo, Italy

APMS 2012 Local Organizing Committee

Christos Emmanouilidis ATHENA R.I.C, Greece
Athanassios Kalogeras ATHENA R.I.C, Greece
Zacharias Kaplanidis Zita Congress, Greece
Irini Katti Zita Congress, Greece
Christos Koulamas ATHENA R.I.C, Greece
Dimitris Karampatzakis ATHENA R.I.C, Greece
Nikos Papathanasiou ATHENA R.I.C, Greece
Petros Pistofidis ATHENA R.I.C, Greece

APMS 2012 Conference Secretariat

Zita Congress SA   Attica, Greece

International Scientific Committee

Bjørn Andersen	Norwegian University of Science and Technology, Norway
Abdelaziz Bouras	University of Lyon, France
Luis M. Camarinha-Matos	New University of Lisbon, Portugal
Sergio Cavalieri	University of Bergamo, Italy
Stephen Childe	University of Exeter, UK
Alexandre Dolgui	Ecole des Mines de Saint-Etienne, France
Guy Doumeingts	University Bordeaux, France
Heidi C. Dreyer	Norwegian University of Technology and Science, Norway
Christos Emmanouilidis	ATHENA Research & Innovation Centre, Greece
Peter Falster	Technical University of Denmark, Denmark
Rosanna Fornasiero	ITIA-CNR, Italy
Jan Frick	University of Stavanger, Norway
Susumu Fujii	Sophia University, Japan
Marco Garetti	Politecnico di Milano, Italy
Antonios Gasteratos	Democritus University of Thrace, Greece
Bernard Grabot	Ecole Nationale d'Ingénieurs de TARBES, France
Robert W. Grubbström	Linköping Institute of Technology, Sweden
Thomas Gulledge	George Mason University, USA
Hans-Henrik Hvolby	University of Aalborg, Denmark
Harinder Jagdev	National University of Ireland, Ireland
Athanassios Kalogeras	ATHENA Research & Innovation Centre, Greece
Dimitris Kiritsis	EPFL, Switzerland
Christos Koulamas	ATHENA Research & Innovation Centre, Greece
Andrew Kusiak	University of Iowa, USA
Lenka Landryova	VSB Technical University Ostrava, Czech Republic
Ming Lim	Aston University, UK
Hermann Lödding	Technical University of Hamburg, Germany
Vidoslav D. Majstorovic	University of Belgrade, Serbia
Kepa Mendibil	University of Stratchclyde, UK
Kai Mertins	Fraunhofer IPK, Germany
Hajime Mizuyama	Kyoto University, Japan
Irenilza Nääs	Universidade Paulista, Brazil
Gilles Neubert	ESC Saint-Etienne, France

Jan Olhager	Linköping University, Sweden
Jens Ove Riis	University of Alborg, Denmark
Henk Jan Pels	Eindhoven University of Technology, Netherlands
Selwyn Piramuthu	University of Florida, USA
Alberto Portioli	Politecnico di Milano, Italy
Asbjorn Rolstadas	Norwegian University of Science and Technology, Norway
Paul Schoensleben	ETH Zurich, Switzerland
Dan L. Shunk	Arizona State University, USA
Riitta Smeds	Aalto University, Finland
Vijay Srinivasan	National Institute of Standards and Technology, USA
Kenn Steger-Jensen	Aalborg University, Denmark
Kathryn E. Stecke	University of Texas, USA
Volker Stich	FIR RWTH Aachen, Germany
Richard Lee Storch	University of Washington, USA
Jan Ola Strandhagen	SINTEF, Norway
Stanisław Strzelczak	Warsaw University of Technology, Poland
Marco Taisch	Politecnico di Milano, Italy
Ilias Tatsiopoulos	National Technical University of Athens, Greece
Sergio Terzi	University of Bergamo, Italy
Klaus-Dieter Thoben	University of Bremen/BIBA, Germany
Mario Tucci	University of Florence, Italy
Bruno Vallespir	University of Bordeaux, France
Agostino Villa	Politecnico di Torino, Italy
Gregor Alexander von Cieminski	ZF Friedrichshafen AG, Germany
Dan Wang	Harbin Institute of Technology, China
J.C. Wortmann	University of Groningen, The Netherlands
Iveta Zolotová	Technical University of Košice, Slovakia

External Reviewers

Alexander von Cieminski, Gregor	ZF Friedrichshafen AG, Germany
Andersen Bjorn	Norwegian University of Science and Technology, Norway
Battaïa Olga	EMSE, France
Bouras Abdelaziz	Lumière University Lyon 2, France
Camarinha-Matos Luis M.	New University of Lisbon, Portugal
Cavalieri Sergio	University of Bergamo, Italy
Childe Stephen	University of Exeter, UK
Corti Donatella	Politecnico di Milano, Italy
Dolgui Alexandre	Ecole des Mines de Saint-Etienne, France

Dreyer Heidi C.	Norwegian University of Technology and Science (NTNU), Norway
Emmanouilidis Christos	ATHENA Research & Innovation Centre, Greece
Errasti Ander	TECNUN University of Navarra, Spain
Evans Steve	University of Cambridge, UK
Eynard Benoit	Université de Technologie de Compiègne, France
Falster Peter	Technical University of Denmark, Denmark
Fornasiero Rosanna	ITIA-cnr, Italy
Frick Jan	University of Stavanger, Norway
Garetti Marco	Politecnico di Milano, Italy
Gasteratos Antonios	Democritus University of Thrace, Greece
Grabot Bernard	Ecole Nationale d'Ingenieurs de TARBES, France
Grubbstrom Robert W.	Linkoping Institute of Technology, Sweden
Hvolby Hans-Henrik	Aalborg University, Denmark
Jagdev Harinder	National University of Ireland, Galway, Ireland
Kaihara Toshiya	Kobe University, Japan
Kalogeras Athanasios	ATHENA Research & Innovation Centre, Greece
Karampatzakis Dimitris	ATHENA Research & Innovation Centre, Greece
Kiritsis Dimitris	EPFL, Switzerland
Koulamas Christos	ATHENA Research & Innovation Centre, Greece
Krüger Volker	Aalborg University, Denmark
Landryova Lenka	VSB - Technical University of Ostrava, Czech Republic
Lim Ming	University of Derby, UK
Loedding Hermann	Technical University of Hamburg, Germany
Macchi Marco	Politecnico di Milano, Italy
Majstorovic Vidosav D.	University of Belgrade, MEF, Serbia
Mandic Vesna	University of Kragujevac, Serbia
May Gökan	Politecnico di Milano, Italy
Mendibil Kepa	University of Strathclyde, UK
Mertins Kai	Fraunhofer IPK/TU Berlin, Germany
Mizuyama Hajime	Aoyama Gakuin University, Japan
Nääs Irenilza	Paulista University-UNIP, Brazil
Netland Torbjoern H.	Norwegian University of Science and Technology, Norway
Neubert Gilles	Ecole Supérieure de Commerce, France
Olhager Jan	Lund University, Sweden
Oliveira Manuel F.	SINTEF, Norway

Pels Henk Jan   Eindhoven University of Technology,
                               The Netherlands
Piramuthu Selwyn   University of Florida, USA
Pistofidis Petros   ATHENA Research & Innovation Centre,
                               Greece
Portioli Alberto   Politecnico di Milano, Italy
Pourabdollahian Borzoo   Politecnico di Milano, Italy
Pourabdollahian Golboo   Politecnico di Milano, Italy
Riis Jens Ove   Aalborg University, Denmark
Sauter Thilo   Austrian Academy of Sciences, Austria
Schoensleben Paul   ETH Zurich, Switzerland
Shunk Dan L.   Arizona State University, USA
Smeds Riitta   Aalto University, Finland
Srinivasan Vijay   National Institute of Standards and
                               Technology, USA
Stahl Bojan   Politecnico di Milano, Italy
Stecke Kathryn E.   University of Texas at Dallas, USA
Steger-Jensen Kenn   Aalborg University, Denmark
Stich Volker   FIR RWTH Aachen, Germany
Storch Richard Lee   University of Washington, USA
Strzelczak Stanislaw   Warsaw University of Technology, Poland
Taisch Marco   Politecnico di Milano, Italy
Tatsiopoulos Ilias   National Technical University of Athens,
                               Greece
Terzi Sergio   University of Bergamo, Italy
Thoben Klaus-Dieter   BIBA - Bremer Institut für Produktion und
                               Logistik, Germany
Tucci Mario   Università di Firenze, Italy
Uusitalo Teuvo   VTT Technical Research Centre of Finland,
                               Finland
Vallespir Bruno   Bordeaux University, France
Vasyutynskyy Volodymyr   SAP Research Dresden, Germany
Villa Agostino   Politecnico di Torino, Italy
Wortmann J.C.   University of Groningen, The Netherlands
Zolotova Iveta   Technical University of Kosice, Slovakia

Table of Contents – Part II

ICT for Manufacturing, Services and Production Management

Part V: Product and Asset Lifecycle Management

Product Lifecycle Management

Asset Lifecycle Management

Performance and Risk Management

Part VI: Services, Supply Chains and Operations

Services

Managing International Operations

Supply Networks and Supply Chain Management

Production Management, Operations and Logistics

Table of Contents – Part I

Part I: Sustainability

Energy Efficient Manufacturing

Sustainable Value Creation, Business Models and Strategies

Part II: Design, Manufacturing and Production Management

Mass Customization

Products of the Future and Manufacturing Systems Design

Advanced Design, Manufacturing and Production Management

Robotics in Manufacturing

Part III: Human Factors, Learning and Innovation

Modern Learning in Manufacturing and Production Systems

Human Factors, Quality and Knowledge Management

Innovation in Products and Services in Developing Countries

Analysis of Manufacturing Process Sequences, Using Machine Learning on Intermediate Product States (as Process Proxy Data)

Thorsten Wuest[1], Christopher Irgens[2], and Klaus-Dieter Thoben[1]

[1] Bremer Institut für Produktion und Logistik GmbH (BIBA), Hochschulring 20,
28359 Bremen, Germany
{wue,tho}@biba.uni-bremen.de
[2] University of Strathclyde, Glasgow, G1 1XQ, UK
chris.irgens@dmem.strath.ac.uk

Abstract. Quality and efficiency increased in importance over the last years within the manufacturing industry. To stay competitive companies are forced to constantly improve their products and processes. Today's information technology and data analysis tools are promising to further enhance the performance of modern manufacturing. In this paper, at first, the concept of the product state based view in a distributive manufacturing chain is presented, followed by a brief introduction of relations between product states along the chain. After showing that a in detail description based on cause-effect models is not economical viable today, the possibilities of using machine learning on intermediate product states to analyze the process sequence is introduced and discussed. Providing a chance to analyze large amounts of data with high dimensionality and complexity, machine learning tools combined with cluster analysis are perfectly suited for the task at hand within the product state based concept.

Keywords: Manufacturing processes, machine learning, product state, proxy data, quality.

1 Introduction

Today's global manufacturing environment is increasingly becoming more complex and competitive [1]. Quality is considered a consequential key factor of success for manufacturing companies due to this development [2]. Successful manufacturing companies have to improve constantly to meet increasingly rigorous customer requirements on product and service quality [3, 4]. A number of companies have chosen to focus on their core competencies [5] and collaborate in production networks in order to meet these challenging customer requirements [6].

These developments, especially networked production, lead to an increase of complexity of a company's business processes. The quality of business processes on the other hand, has a major influence on the company's business success [7]. Thinking of manufacturing companies, the manufacturing processes are key as they directly add

C. Emmanouilidis, M. Taisch, D. Kiritsis (Eds.): APMS 2012, Part II, IFIP AICT 398, pp. 1–8, 2013.
© IFIP International Federation for Information Processing 2013

value to the product and define the company's reception on the market through the product's quality [8, 9]. In recent years, the importance of looking at the complete manufacturing chain instead of isolated single process steps in order to reduce scrap and rework and thus, increase quality was slowly recognized by industry and academia [10].

All these mechanisms and developments add to the complexity modern companies face today. One lever to help these companies cope with the complexity is to take a closer look at the value adding manufacturing processes and the information/data involved. Understanding the mechanisms of the manufacturing processes and how the product changes along the whole manufacturing process and the single process steps can help to identify improvement potential and finally to realize better product and process quality. To do so, there is a need for a new perspective on the processes, focusing on the products state, its state and state characteristic change, and the process parameters involved along the manufacturing chain [11]. During the development of this product state based view, the importance of cross process relations and (inter-) dependencies surfaced. In a complex manufacturing process chain, different causes trigger various effects and the connection between cause and effect is not necessarily clear. For example, the cause can be triggered at an early stage of the process during an operation carried out by company A. The connected effect triggered at these early stages might surface at the final process step carried out by company D. The connection, especially in a networked production, is neither obvious nor easy to analyze. But in order to optimize the manufacturing process as a whole and thus the final product quality, the connection is nevertheless important.

In the following chapter, the product state based view will be introduced briefly as a basic framework for the following considerations. Based on that, possible relations of states over the manufacturing process are presented and the challenges/complexity of describing such relations e.g. through cause-effect diagrams are elaborated. Following, machine learning in combination with cluster analysis is introduced as a possible solution to grasp the complexity and high dimensionality and generate results usable from a product state perspective.

2 Product State

The advantage of the product state based view is the focus on the product itself to structure the information and data involved throughout the process. Using the intermediate product states as proxy data for this purpose, a product can at any time throughout its life cycle be described by its product state. Within this paper, the focus will be on the Beginning-of-Life (BOL) phase of the lifecycle, the manufacturing processes.

The product state describes a product at a certain time during the production process or after through a combination of (selected) state characteristics (see Fig. 1). State characteristics are definable and ascertainable measures, which can be described in a quantitative or qualitative way, e.g. weight or chemical composition of the material. The product state changes due to external influence, for example machining or corrosion from t=0 to t=1 when at least one descriptive state characteristic changes [11].

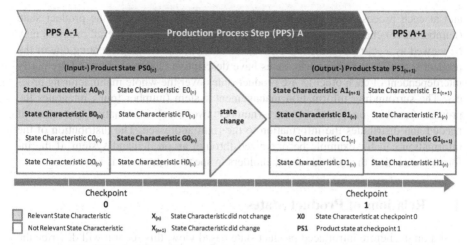

Fig. 1. Product State Change during Manufacturing Process Step [12]

The product state can be derived theoretically at all times during the manufacturing process. In order to develop a manageable and sufficiently detailed model, the points when the product state should be derived have to be defined. The number of defined product state checkpoints during the manufacturing process affect the complexity of the model and the amount of data/information generated. It makes sense to choose at least as many check points (plus one) as there are process steps to grasp the major (intentional) product state changes.

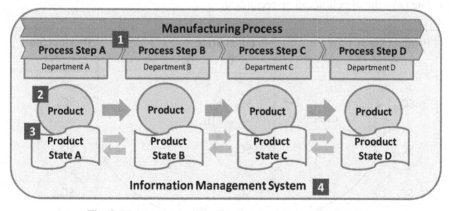

Fig. 2. Main Aspects of the Product State Based View [13]

Fig. 2. provides an overview on how the information and data can be structured through the product state based view. Number one in the figure indicates that the whole manufacturing process has to be considered even so not all process steps take place in one location. In that case, it is necessary to think about physical and virtual interfaces between department or company boarders. The physical product (number two) is in the center of the concept. The flow of the physical product is one directional and at each process step value is added to the product and such the product state (number three) changes by definition. In this way, the product's overall progress may be viewed as a set of concatenated 'state vectors', each vector representing one of the product states [14]. The product states have descriptive characteristics and are partly interdependent of each other as are product states over the whole manufacturing process. The surrounding information management system (number four), integrates the process (number one) and product (number two/three) information processes if needed and distributes the information to the right addressee. The distribution of the information can for example be organized through an on demand system, if the information need of the individual stakeholders in specific situations is known.

3   Relations of Product States

Based on the before introduced product state based view, this section will describe the relations along the manufacturing process between the different product states and state characteristics, which are helpful to provide some understanding the complexity of a modern manufacturing process chain. The term relations will be used throughout this paper compromising other terms like dependency or interdependencies to help the understanding even so the alternative terms might theoretically be more appropriate at different times. Within a complex manufacturing chain there can be a lot of different relations (see Fig. 3). They can be within a certain product state (a/b), between two directly following product states (c) or even between random product states (d). In the cases of c/d, the direction of the relation is one-directional whereas in within a product state (a/b) the direction can be reciprocal.

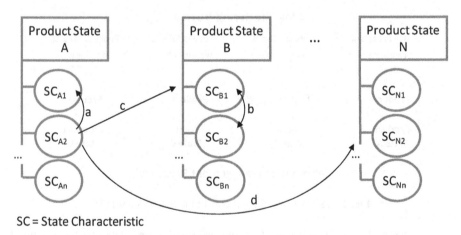

SC = State Characteristic

Fig. 3. Schematic Illustration of Possible Relations of State Characteristics

In theory, it would be ideal, if all relations along the manufacturing chain could be described in great detail so a prefund forecast of the products final state could be made with exact results. That way, in case of a deviation to the originally planned product state, certain adjustments could be executed accordingly to meet the customer requirements. But practically, due to the high complexity and dimensionality of the task, it is unlikely that all or even most relations can be identified and described in the needed detail. This is due to different factors e.g. too expensive, time-consuming, lack of knowledge or extensive to analyze. Therefore the chance to develop a functional and practical tool (e.g. cause-effect-diagram), based on the existing (known) product state relations, is not very likely today. A main question in this context is how relevant drivers (causes) of certain product state changes can be identified in a practical and efficient way without having to analyze the relations in such great detail. Prescriptive data processing/algorithm will find this sort of complexity hard/impossible to handle because cause-effect mechanisms may be hidden and unknown by all the relations, some of which are in themselves unknown. By basing the manufacturing process chain analysis on a 'growing' state-vector and pushing this into a machine learning process the idea is to identify the state characteristics that are likely to drive the product to success/failure.

It is thus assumed that the finished product quality, 'fitness for purpose', can be envisaged as driven by all the 'drivers' which come into play during the complete manufacturing of the product. It is clearly impractical to capture all influencing process data that is likely to contribute to the final product quality. It is thus assumed that proxy data would be useful in this context. Proxy data may be seen as two sets of parameters likely to be captured to a greater or lesser extent during the manufacturing cycle. S = the set of product states, such that

$$S = \{s_i\}, \ i = 0,1,..........m$$

and P = the set of recorded process parameters, such that

$$P = \{p_i\}, \ i = 1,2,........m$$

where m = number of manufacturing steps and step = 0 represents the raw material/blank product input.

The proxy data sets S and P are represented by sets of vectors, matrices, such that at any stage k, $C_k = S_k + P_k$ represents the complete product proxy information at k.

It should be noted that $difference(C_k)$ represents the incremental proxy state progression from stage k-1 to stage k. Both C_k and $difference(C_k)$ may be used as inputs to combined supervised and un-supervised machine learning so that analysis may be performed to determine which are the product quality driving parameters at any stage. C_k and $difference(C_k)$ will imply a degree of cluster behaviour and the dynamics of such clustering may be used to observe the quality dynamics of the product through the manufacturing cycles. In this manner it may be possible to capture cause-effect mechanisms that influence the product quality through observing the product state progression in conjunction with the practically recorded process information.

4   Machine Learning

The initial discussion points above are seen as pertinent to a number of recent methodologies used in handling large multi-variate data sets. Traditional methods and techniques may be unsuitable due high dimensionality and heterogeneous, distributed nature of the data. It is therefore considered relevant to draw on ideas from machine learning/AI, pattern recognition, statistics, and database systems.

Cluster analysis (CA) classifies unknown groups while discriminator function analysis classifies known groups. CA allows many choices about the nature of the algorithm for combining groups. Each choice may result in a different grouping structure.

In short, clustering analysis is about defining groups of data matching certain requirements as e.g. given a set of data points, each having a set of attributes, and a similarity measure among them, find clusters (see Fig. 4).

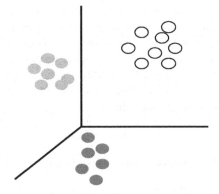

Fig. 4. Examples of Data to be Clustered [16]

When trying to establish the characteristics of a process state or regime, a clear division between the different regimes/states is required. Therefore some form of classification method would be useful.

Support Vector Machine (SVM) has received considerable attention. This classification technique has its roots in statistical learning theory and has shown promising empirical results in a number of practical applications and works very well with high-dimensional data. Another unique aspect of this approach is that it represents the decision boundary using a subset of the training examples, known as the **support vectors.**

The basic idea behind SVM, is the concept of a maximal margin hyper plane. A linear SVM can be trained explicitly to look for this type of hyper plane in linearly separable data, the method can be extended to non-linearly separable data.

Fig. 5 shows a data set containing examples that belong to two different classes, represented as squares and circles. The data set is also linearly separable; i.e., there is a hyper plane such that all the squares reside on one side of the hyper plane and all the circles reside on the other side. Inevitably such clear cut results are not always available in real applications and suitable compromise solutions are used in order to allow a certain amount of mis-classification.

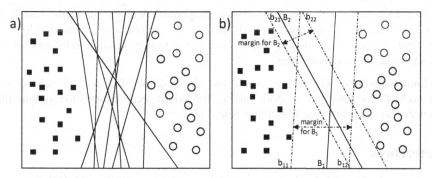

Fig. 5. Possible Decision Boundaries for a Linear Separable Data Set b) Margin for Decision Boundary [16]

There are infinitely many hyper-planes possible. Although their training errors may be zero, there is no guarantee that the hyper-planes will perform equally well on previously unseen examples. The classifier must choose one of these hyper-planes to represent its decision boundary, based on how well they are expected to perform on test examples. The problem with SVM classifiers is, being able to establish relevant training/learning data for the case at hand so that the computation of the support vectors can be completed. Given that most process control and analysis task display a degree of dynamism, the use of SVM is not immediately clear for such applications as it is likely that the generation of support vectors will have to be done frequently and without knowledge of detailed performance results of the process.

Through an application of suitable tools like Cluster-Analysis combined with Support Vector Machines, it is considered likely to determine which process parameters are the product state drivers based on process or even proxy data. This way, the relevant information for adjusting the manufacturing process to reach the customers quality requirements of the individual product can be derived and put to use.

5   Conclusion

The paper presented an approach to derive information of the manufacturing process sequence using intermediate product states using a combination of cluster analysis and machine learning. This approach is capable of handling the complexity and high dimensionality of modern production whereas describing the actual relations between state characteristics along the manufacturing chain (through e.g. cause-effect models) soon reaches its limits of being applicable efficiently.

The introduced approach seems well suited for the tasks within the product state based view. The perspective on the product by its time-dependent state over the manufacturing process corresponds directly with the requirements of machine learning tools. Thus, the time and effort to match the (product state) data to the requirements of the machine learning tools will be within an acceptable range and can possibly even be automated in a later step.

In a next step the theoretically presented approach will be put to the test with manufacturing process data and an in depth analyses and discussion of the results will offer the chance to evaluate its prospects in an industrial application to increase quality and reduce rework and scrap.

Acknowledgement. The authors would like to thank the "Deutsche Forschungsgemeinschaft" for financial support via the funded project "Informationssystem für werkstoffwissenschaftliche Forschungsdaten" (InfoSys).

References

1. Levitt, T.: The globalization of markets. Harvard Business Review, 92–102 (May/June 1983)
2. Enderwick, P.: Globalization and Labor. Chelsea House Publications, New York (2005)
3. Kovacic, M., Sarler, B.: Application of the Genetic Programming for Increasing the Soft Annealing Productivity in Steel industry. Materials and Manufacturing Processes 24, 369–374 (2009)
4. Ellram, L.M., Krause, D.R.: Supplier Partnerships in Manufacturing Versus Non-Manufacturing Firms. International Journal of Logistics Management 5(1), 43–54 (1994)
5. Hamel, G., Prahalad, C.K.: The Core Competence of the Corporation. Harvard Business Review 1990(33), 79–91 (1990)
6. Seifert, M.: Unterstützung der Konsortialbildung in Virtuellen Organisationen durch perspektives Performance Measurement. Dissertation Universität Bremen (2007)
7. Linß, G.: Qualitätsmanagement für Ingenieure. Hanser Verlag, München/Wien (2002)
8. Brinksmeier, E.: Prozeß- und Werkstückqualität in der Feinbearbeitung. Fortschritt-Berichte VDI Reihe2: Fertigungstechnik Nr. 234. VDI Verlag, Düsseldorf (1991)
9. Jacob, J., Petrick, K.: Qualitätsmanagement und Normung. In: Schmitt, R., Pfeifer, T. (eds.) Masing Handbuch Qualitätsmanagement, pp. 101–121. Carl Hanser Verlag, München (2007)
10. Zoch, H.-W., Lübben, T.: Verzugsbeherrschung - Systemorientierter Ansatz als wesentliche Voraussetzung für den Erfolg. Stahl Strukturen - Industrie-, Forschungs-, Mikro- und Bauteilstrukturen, vol. 26. Aachener Stahlkolloquium, Verlagshaus Mainz (2011)
11. Wuest, T., Klein, D., Thoben, K.-D.: State of steel products in industrial production processes. Procedia Engineering 10(2011), 2220–2225 (2011)
12. Wuest, T., Klein, D., Seifert, M., Thoben, K.-D.: Method to Describe Interdependencies of State Characteristics Related to Distortion. Mat.-wiss. u. Werkstofftech. 43(1-2), 186–191 (2012)
13. Wuest, T., Thoben, K.-D.: Exploitation of Material Property Potentials to Reduce Rare Raw Material Waste - A Product State Based Concept for Manufacturing Process Improvement. Journal of Mining World Express (MWE) 1(1) (2012)
14. Irgens, C., Wuest, T., Thoben, K.-D.: Product state based view and machine learning: A suitable approach to increase quality? In: Proceedings of the 14th IFAC Symposium on Information Control Problems in Manufacturing, Bucharest, Romania, May 23-25 (2012)
15. Mirkin, B.: Clustering for Data Mining, A Data Recovery Approach. Chapman & Hall/CRC, London (2005)
16. Pang-Ning, T., Steinbach, M., Kumar, V.: Introduction to Data Mining. Pearson/Addison Wesley, Old Tappan (2005)

Improving Tree-Based Classification Rules
Using a Particle Swarm Optimization

Chi-Hyuck Jun[*], Yun-Ju Cho, and Hyeseon Lee

Department of Industrial and Management Engineering
Pohang University of Science and Technology, Pohang, 790-784, Korea
{chjun,jyj0729,hyelee}@postech.ac.kr

Abstract. The main advantage of tree classifiers is to provide rules that are simple in form and are easily interpretable. Since decision tree is a top-down algorithm using a divide and conquer induction process, there is a risk of reaching a local optimal solution. This paper proposes a procedure of optimally determining the splitting variables and their thresholds for a decision tree using an adaptive particle swarm optimization. The proposed method consists of three phases – tree construction, threshold optimization and rule simplification. To validate the proposed algorithm, several artificial and real datasets are used. We compare our results with the original CART results and show that the proposed method is promising for improving prediction accuracy.

Keywords: Classification, Data mining, Decision tree, Particle swarm optimization.

1   Introduction

Decision tree is a popularly used data mining tool for classification and prediction. A decision tree usually handles one variable at a time and so it provides the classification rule that is easily interpreted. Decision tree has been widely used in many areas such as medical diagnosis, customer churn prediction, quality prediction and so on. Among many algorithms, CART (Breiman et al. 1984) and C4.5 (Quinlan, 1993) are the most famous and popularly used ones.

Over the years, however, some studies show that constructing the optimal decision tree belongs to a non-deterministic polynomial-time complete problem (Hyafil and Rivest, 1976; Naumov, 1991). Therefore, most algorithms are greedy top-down approach (Lior and Oded, 2005). When the algorithm searches for the splitting criteria, it considers only one variable at a time without considering the potential interaction between other attributes or variables. This approach has a risk of reaching a local optimal solution. To overcome this problem, multivariate splitting criteria are proposed by many researchers. However, the problem of finding the optimal linear split is more difficult and intractable than that of finding the optimal univariate split (Murthy, 1998; Lior and Oded, 2005). In the problem of finding the optimal univariate

---

[*] Corresponding author.

C. Emmanouilidis, M. Taisch, D. Kiritsis (Eds.): APMS 2012, Part II, IFIP AICT 398, pp. 9–16, 2013.
© IFIP International Federation for Information Processing 2013

split, Athanasios and Dimitris (2001) proposed the use of a genetic algorithm to directly evolve classification decision trees. The computational burden for genetic algorithms is substantially bigger than that for other algorithms. Saher and Shaul (2007) introduced a framework for anytime induction of decision tree, which generates the best answer up to the allowed time. However, it also suffers from the computational burden. Recently, Cho et al. (2011) developed an optimization procedure of a decision tree using a particle swarm. But, they only optimize threshold values of variables chosen by the CART.

If we combine an existing efficient decision tree algorithm and an evolutionary optimization algorithm, computational burden can be reduced and more efficient decision tree can be obtained. This paper extends the work by Cho et al. (2011) by considering an iterative way of finding better combination of variables and thresholds. The proposed algorithm consists of three phases; constructing a decision tree, optimizing the decision tree and rule simplification. First phase is to construct a preliminary decision tree by using well-known CART (classification and regression tree) proposed by Breiman et al. (1984). Second phase is to optimize the preliminary decision tree by determining the optimal thresholds of splitting variables using an adaptive particle swarm optimization (PSO). The last phase is to simplify the rules by combining the regions having same class.

2   Adaptive Particle Swarm Optimization

Particle swarm optimization (PSO) is one of evolutionary computation techniques developed by Kennedy and Eberhart (1995). As birds fly through a three-dimensional space, this algorithm makes use of particles moving in n-dimensional space to search for the optimal solution. PSO is a population-based iterative algorithm. The population consists of many particles, where each particle represents a candidate solution and moves toward the optimal position by changing its position according to a velocity.

Let x_{ik}^t and v_{ik}^t be the position and the velocity, respectively, in the k-th variable of the i-th particle at the t-th iteration. Then, the updating formula for the position and the velocity of the i-th particle are as follows.

$$x_{ik}^{t+1} = x_{ik}^t + v_{ik}^{t+1} \tag{1}$$

$$v_{ik}^{t+1} = w \times v_{ik}^t + c_1 \times rand_1 \times (pbest_{ik}^t - x_{ik}^t) + c_2 \times rand_2 \times (gbest_k^t - x_{ik}^t) \tag{2}$$

where $rand_1$ and $rand_2$ are random numbers between 0 and 1. Here, $pbest_{ik}^t$ is the previous best position in the k-th variable of the i-th particle and $gbest_k^t$ is the previous best position in the k-th variable among the entire population. We may omit the subscripts and the superscripts later if there is no risk of confusion. The parameter w is the inertia weight, and c_1 and c_2 are called acceleration coefficients which in the directions of pbest and gbest, respectively.

All the particles are evaluated by the fitness function at every iteration. The fitness function is used to evaluate the quality of the candidate solution. In the classification problem, accuracy, or mixture of sensitivity and specificity is usually used as the fitness function.

Like other evolutionary computation algorithms, the PSO requires some parameters as inputs. The size of the population, inertia weight (i.e., w), acceleration coefficients (i.e., c_1 and c_2), and the maximum number of iterations are parameters. To overcome the difficulty of parameter selection, Clerc (1999) first proposed an adaptive process. Several papers report that adaptive PSO enhances the performance of PSO in terms of convergence speed, global optimality, solution accuracy, and algorithm reliability (Clerc, 1999; Shi and Eberhart, 2001; Xie et al. 2002). In this paper, the algorithm developed by Zhan et al. (2009) is used for optimizing the decision tree. It identifies the current population state and proposes a control strategy of w, c_1 and c_2. The current population state is classified into four evolutionary state based on the evolutionary factor: exploration, exploitation, convergence, and jumping out. Before defining the evolutionary factor, the mean distance of the i-th particle to all other particles at each iteration is calculated by

$$d_i = \frac{1}{N-1} \sum_{j=1, j \neq i}^{N} \sqrt{\sum_{k=1}^{D} (x_{ik} - x_{jk})^2} \tag{3}$$

where D is the number of variables and N is the number of population. Then, the evolutionary factor is obtained by

$$f = \frac{d_g - d_{min}}{d_{max} - d_{min}} \in [0,1] \tag{4}$$

where d_g is the mean distance of the globally best particle, d_{max} is the maximum and d_{min} is the minimum mean distance. The evolutionary state will be assigned by the fuzzy membership function and the control strategy for w, c_1 and c_2 is determined according to the rules of each evolutionary state in Zhan et al. (2009).

3   Proposed Algorithm

As mentioned before, most decision tree algorithms are greedy approach. They usually consider only one variable at a time when growing the tree. This approach may reach a local optimal solution. Most desirably, splitting criteria should be searched simultaneously. However, searching every possible combination requires a huge computation time. To avoid it, a three-phase hybrid procedure is proposed. First phase is to construct a preliminary decision tree by CART and to determine the splitting variables. But, the threshold values from CART are not used in the proposed method. Only the number of threshold values will be maintained and the threshold values of each splitting variable will be re-determined in the second phase.

Second phase is to optimize the preliminary decision tree by determining the optimal thresholds of splitting variables simultaneously using the adaptive PSO in Zhan et al. (2009). The positions of particles in the adaptive PSO represent thresholds of splitting variables. However, there are some differences in the way of classification between CART and the proposed method using the adaptive PSO.

Suppose that there are K splitting variables involved in the preliminary tree and that there are J_k threshold values for the k-th splitting variable (k=1,...,K). Then, the number of variables to be considered in the proposed method is

$$D = \sum_{k=1}^{K} J_k \tag{5}$$

Also, the total number of cells to be partitioned in the adaptive PSO is $(J_1 + 1)$ $(J_2 + 1) ... (J_K + 1)$. The training data should be partitioned accordingly and the class prediction should be made in each cell. The class of a cell is predicted as the one having the largest observations among the training data partitioned. If there is no training data partitioned in a cell, predicted class may be determined randomly.

Basically, we may draw a separate classification rule for each cell partitioned in the proposed method. But, the classification rules can be simplified if some adjacent cells have the same predicted class. The third phase performs this. Based on this simplified rule, a new decision tree can be drawn if needed. It should be noted that the new decision tree may not have the same structure as the preliminary tree. The proposed algorithm can be summarized as follows.

Phase 1. Construct a preliminary decision tree by CART. Breiman et al. (1984) provide the detailed algorithm of CART, which consists of two steps.

Step 1-1. Grow the tree by splitting variables based on Gini impurity function until every node has a single (pure) class.
Step 1-2. Prune the tree based on cost-complexity and select the best pruned tree to obtain the preliminary tree.

Phase 2. Optimize the preliminary decision tree by the adaptive PSO.

Step 2-0. Initialize the positions and the velocities of particles at random. Set the initial gbest to the thresholds of the preliminary decision tree.
Step 2-1. Evaluate particles according to the selected fitness function.
Step 2-2. If the current fitness value of each particle is better than pbest, then update pbest value. If the current fitness value of population's overall best is better than gbest, then update gbest value.
Step 2-3. Update the parameters adaptively.
Step 2-4. Change the velocity and position of the particles according to the equations (1) and (2).
Step 2-5. If the maximum number of iterations is reached, stop. Otherwise, go to Step 2-1.

Phase 3. Simplify the rules by combining the adjacent cells having the same class.

Step 3-1. Represent each partitioning cell in terms of binary D-digits. Sort all cells in the ascending order of digits.

Step 3-2. Starting from the smallest digit cell, find the adjacent cells having the same class.
Step 3-3. Combine the adjacent cells having the same class
Step 3-4. If there are no remaining cells for combining, stop. Otherwise, go to Step 3-1.

Note that the Phase 1 and Phase 2 may be repeated several times by selecting different variables to generate various trees.

4   Experiments and Results

To validate the proposed algorithm, numerical experiments are performed with an artificial data and a real data. Each data set is separated into two: the two thirds of the observations are used as a training set and the rest of one thirds are set aside as the test set. The number of particles and the maximum number of iterations are set to 100 and 500, respectively in the adaptive PSO. The initial values of (w, c_1, c_2) are set to (0.9, 2, 2). We compare our results against the original CART results using 5-fold cross validation to see the performance improvement through the proposed optimization method. In the proposed method, we use the classification accuracy as the fitness function.

4.1   Artificial Data Sets

The artificial data sets having three classes and three attributes are generated from 3-dimensional multivariate normal distributions. Three different mean vectors and variance-covariance matrices are chosen as in Table 1. Three cases having different number of observations and different value of σ^2 are considered. Case 1 includes 100 observations for class 1, 150 observations for class 2, and 50 observations for class 3 (total of 300 observations), whereas σ^2 is set to 0.1. Case 2 includes 500 for class 1, 750 for class 2, and 250 observations for class 3 (total of 1500), whereas σ^2 is again set to 0.1. Case 3 is composed of the same class observations as Case 1, where σ^2 is set to 0.2.

Table 1. Mean vectors and variance-covariance matrices for generating artificial data

	Class 1	Class 2	Class 3
Mean	$\begin{bmatrix} 0.1 \\ -1.0 \\ 0.3 \end{bmatrix}$	$\begin{bmatrix} 1.5 \\ 0.1 \\ 1.2 \end{bmatrix}$	$\begin{bmatrix} -0.5 \\ 1.5 \\ 0.5 \end{bmatrix}$
Variance-Co variance	$\sigma^2 * \begin{bmatrix} 2 & 0 & 2 \\ 0 & 4 & 1 \\ 2 & 1 & 3 \end{bmatrix}$	$\sigma^2 * \begin{bmatrix} 4 & 1 & 1 \\ 1 & 3 & 3 \\ 1 & 3 & 4 \end{bmatrix}$	$\sigma^2 * \begin{bmatrix} 5 & 0 & 0 \\ 0 & 1 & 0 \\ 0 & 0 & 5 \end{bmatrix}$

Table 2 compares the classification accuracies of the CART and the proposed procedure in the training and test sets for each of three cases. We randomly selected 2/3 of observations as the training set and the rest 1/3 as the test set. In fact, each number in a cell represents the average over 50 repetitions of experiments. It shows that the proposed method generally improves the classification accuracy as compared with CART. When the number of observations is increased as in Case 2 or σ^2 is increased as in Case 3, the proposed method outperforms the CART. The results are not reported here, paired t-tests were performed, which showed significantly difference in accuracies between the proposed method and the CART.

Table 2. Comparison of Accuracy for Training and Test Data (in percentage)

	Case 1		Case 2		Case 3	
	train	test	train	test	train	test
CART	95.86	**93.41**	92.57	89.61	89.28	81.52
Proposed	**97.43**	92.59	**96.18**	**93.32**	**94.53**	**83.98**

4.2   Real Data Sets

Three real data sets, that is, Parkinson's, Pima Indians Diabetes (Diabetes), and Blood Transfusion Service Center (Blood), were chosen for the application, which are available from UC Irvine Machine Learning Repository (http://archive.ics.uci.edu/ ml/). Table 3 shows the outline of these data sets.

Table 3. Outline of Three Real Data Sets

	Parkinson's	Diabetes	Blood
# classes	2	2	2
# observations	195	393	748
in training set	130	262	499
in test set	65	131	249
# attributes	22	8	4

Table 4. Classification Accuracy in Three Data Sets

	Parkinson's	Diabetes	Blood
Proposed method			
Training set	**100**	**91.6**	**83.0**
Test set	**89.2**	**72.5**	**77.1**
CART			
Training set	96.9	86.6	81.2
Test set	84.6	67.9	76.7

Table 4 shows the classification accuracy for each of the above three data sets. Performance of the proposed method is compared with that of the CART. We clearly see that the proposed method outperform the CART in all data sets. Particularly for Parkinson's and Diabetes data sets the proposed method significantly outperforms the CART.

5   Concluding Remarks

In this paper, we proposed the three-phase procedure of optimizing the decision tree. Combining the CART algorithm and an adaptive PSO as the optimization tool, computational burden can be reduced and an improved decision tree can be obtained with the increased the classification performance. Particularly, we consider an iterative way of finding optimal combination of variables and thresholds as well as rule simplification. The performance was demonstrated through numerical experiments with artificial and some real data sets.

The proposed method can be applied to many quality classification problems in the area of production management. The quality of products from a manufacturing process can be classified into several grades and so a classification model can be built using the operation data from the manufacturing process. Using this type of model we can predict the quality of the final product in advance.

To improve the decision tree further, we may optimize the fully grown tree instead of a pruned if the computation cost is not severe. After optimizing the fully grown tree, we may eliminate redundant splitting criteria and prune the decision tree to get the user-specific size of tree. Furthermore, other variable selection method can be adopted when generating the preliminary tree instead of CART. If we can get a good set of variables critical to predict classes, then this will lead to a better classification rule. In this sense, combining random forest and the adaptive PSO may be a good alternative. Similarly, other optimization algorithm such as genetic algorithm, ant colony optimization, or simulated annealing, may be used. Optimization of decision tree having multiway splits is also an interesting future area for study.

Acknowledgement. This work was supported by Basic Science Research Program through the NRF funded by the MEST. (Project No. 2011-0012879)

References

1. Athanasios, P., Dimitris, K.: Breeding Decision Trees Using Evolutionary Techniques. In: Proceedings of the Eighteenth International Conference on Machine Learning, pp. 393–400 (2001)
2. Breiman, L., Friedman, J.H., Olashen, R.A., Stone, C.J.: Classification and Regression Trees. Chapman & Hall/CRC, London (1984)
3. Cho, Y.-J., Lee, H., Jun, C.-H.: Optimization of Decision Tree for Classification Using a Particle Swarm. Industrial Engineering & Management Systems 10, 272–278 (2011)
4. Clerc, M.: The Swarm and the Queen: Towards a Deterministic and Adaptive Particle Swarm Optimization. In: Proceedings of the 1999 Congress on Evolutionary Computation, pp. 1951–1957 (1999)
5. Hyafil, L., Rivest, R.L.: Constructing Optimal Binary Decision Trees is NP-Complete. Information Processing Letters 5, 15–17 (1976)
6. Kennedy, J., Eberhart, R.C.: Particle Swarm Optimization. In: Proceedings of IEEE International Conference on Neural Networks, pp. 1942–1948 (1995)

7. Lior, R., Oded, M.: Top-Down Induction of Decision Trees Classifiers-A Survey. IEEE Transactions on Systems, Man, and Cybernetics—Part C: Applications and Reviews 35, 476–487 (2005)

8. Murthy, S.K.: Automatic Construction of Decision Trees from Data: A Multidisciplinary Survey. Data Mining and Knowledge Discovery 2, 345–389 (1998)

9. Naumov, G.E.: NP-Completeness of Problems of Construction of Optimal Decision Trees. Soviet Physics 36, 270–271 (1991)

10. Quinlan, J.R.: C4.5: Programs for Machine Learning. Morgan Kaufmann Publishers Inc., San Francisco (1993)

11. Saher, E., Shaul, M.: Anytime Learning of Decision Trees. Journal of Machine Learning Research 8, 891–933 (2007)

12. Shi, Y., Eberhart, R.C.: Fuzzy Adaptive Particle Swarm Optimization. In: Proceedings of the 2001 Congress on Evolutionary Computation, pp. 101–106 (2001)

13. UCI (University of California - Irvine) data repository: University of California, Irvine. Center for Machine Learning and Intelligent Systems, http://archive.ics.uci.edu/ml/

14. Xie, X.F., Zhang, W.J., Yang, Z.L.: Adaptive Particle Swarm Optimization on Individual Level. In: International Conference of 2002 6th on Signal Processing, pp. 1215–1218 (2002)

15. Zhan, Z.H., Jun, Z., Yun, L., Chung, H.S.: Adaptive Particle Swarm Optimization. IEEE Transactions on Systems, Man, and Cybernetics—Part B: Cybernetics 39, 1362–1381 (2009)

Profiling Context Awareness in Mobile and Cloud Based Engineering Asset Management

Petros Pistofidis and Christos Emmanouilidis

ATHENA Research & Innovation Centre, 58 Tsimiski St., Xanthi, 68100, Greece
{pistofid,chrisem}@ceti.gr

Abstract. This paper presents an analysis of the potential and a methodology for handling context events and adaptations in maintenance services. A significant number of industrial IT systems employ data models and service frameworks whose design specifications where drafted on the basis of functional requirements for non context-aware systems. Such systems were modular in nature but little care was taken for providing data fusion in a context-aware manner. Though system intelligence might have been a feature for a subset of such systems, two major requirements kept implementations away from wider adoption: (i) refactoring and reengineering of the system's base services (ii) customising and modifying the structure of a data model tightly connected with inter-process organisation. This paper discusses a methodology for injecting industrial asset management systems with modelling semantics and software mechanisms that enable context awareness via portable clients and application-agnostic data fusion services.

Keywords: Context Awareness, Asset Modeling, Mobile & Intelligent Services.

1 Introduction

Increasingly computational logic is aggregated inside IT systems that serve industrial processes to enhance their capacity for offering adaptive services. Their corresponding platforms exhibit an aggressive shift to embody and exploit intelligent mechanisms for the organization, correlation and fusion of field data into application knowledge [1]. Both tasks introduce high-capacity processing and require a capable infrastructure to serve them. Such requirements become a costly overhead especially when involving scaled semantics and rich parameter-lists for capturing highly focused contexts. Engineering asset management constitutes a domain containing several systems that already benefit from such mechanisms, many of which currently advertise services ranging from smart condition monitoring to enterprise-level decision support. The question at hand is whether such complexity can be easily handled by rigidly implemented systems and how recent software trends that decouple intelligence from the application context, can facilitate a more modular implementation.

This paper proposes an operational shift of focus for the above systems, addressing the feasibility and potential of adopting components that exploit the dynamics of modern IT technologies. After building a case for the versatility and scalability of

C. Emmanouilidis, M. Taisch, D. Kiritsis (Eds.): APMS 2012, Part II, IFIP AICT 398, pp. 17–24, 2013.
© IFIP International Federation for Information Processing 2013

contextualized services, we explain how a simple semantics framework can facilitate legacy systems to annotate their existing model and compose functionally beneficial contexts. This simple enrichment can fuel mobile components that track and detect context events, and respond to them with application oriented calibration of maintenance services. Such a modeling evolution can lead to the identification of simple context patterns and binding rules that offer elevated knowledge of the process. At the same time, a new meta-context can emerge and become available for monitoring and system-adaption. Computational and operational challenges of multi-site and multi-industry contexts point at the exploitation of cloud services. The features of modern cloud frameworks are discussed and specific interfacing components are analyzed to provide a conceptualization of how cloud's adoption is feasible by maintenance IT.

2   Context Awareness in Engineering Asset Management

From a system's design perspective, the semantics of context awareness in engineering asset management, though tightly connected with the data model, essentially derive from functional and non-functional specifications of the information system. Positioning assets and personnel, as well as any ICT smart agent, in a scaled manufacturing shop-floor, constitutes part of the asset management context. Indirect and direct localization options offer effective detection, introducing highly capable components within tools already available in mobile maintenance practice [2]. Location awareness brings added value to positioning events and translates their impact in the system. This impact may involve a wide range of functional adaptations and reconfigurations, irrespective of the flat semantics defining the underlying legacy system.

As with most context aware systems, the design of a maintenance-oriented one should follow a few essential steps. As a first step, serving a practical understanding of the maintenance context, its semantics should be associated with three core concepts: location (spatial locality), identity (actor locality), and time (time locality). In order to build a more focused context and extend its semantics, an extraction of functional dynamics must result from defining the desired system's response.

Context awareness is not limited to location awareness, nor is it bound by limitations to sensed parameters. The concept of context is addressed by semantics of any direct, computed or inferred factors [3]. The practice of data analytics on large volumes of maintenance records has gradually revealed that the fusion of new parameter sets may result in discovering new meta-contexts [4][5]. The importance of each new context is assessed by the correlation of events with maintenance semantics. The fusion of machinery condition parameters can fuel the identification of new context instances, such as the machinery states. On a different level, fusion of a maintenance plan's Key Performance Indicators (KPIs) with maintenance personnel expertise, can lead to discovering contexts that optimally balances performance with utilization of human resources. Scenarios of context awareness addressed in our research include:

- A technician's route during inspection tracked directly or indirectly through GPS or RFid beacons. Machinery proximity can be inferred, enabling system to adapt the mobile interface, providing instant access to maintenance history and a list of pending tasks associated with the specific units.

- When abnormal readings are taken and unknown conditions are inferred, the monitoring agents switch to "alarm" status. A gateway reports to personnel, while sensor monitoring is adapted/ calibrated to a new collective operation profile.
- When an engineer edits the maintenance plan with a corrective task, he may also allocate spare parts and assign a task to personnel. The system captures the session path and presents equipment parts, recommending available personnel and actions.

There are three basic constituents in the described cases: (a) the context, (b) the context event and (c) the system's response. The data schema should define the participation of each maintenance data type in context-related events, as well as map a response or response rule to the identified context. The internal components should incorporate or facilitate processes and services responsible for compiling the context states, detecting the events and executing the system's adaptation. These context interpretation and calibration services are integrated in mobile and server side components respectively, providing the final set of "smart" maintenance services.

3   A Context Aware E-Maintenance Architecture

The majority of recent IT architectures are developed with the modularity required for fast and effective adoption of the aforementioned mechanisms. The service-oriented nature of modern condition monitoring, asset tracking and maintenance management systems enables context awareness to be achieved by the hosting of a supplementary pool of services and data entities. Our research studies the extent at which legacy and modern systems can facilitate and tune federated services for mobile and cloud-based context awareness. We propose the semantics of a context-organizing sub-schema template that can be easily customized and imported in existing models of industrial systems. We discuss how mobile applications can serve a context identification/adaptation engine that captures and responds to context events, occurring in a complex shop-floor or a multi-site enterprise. Finally the role of cloud computing is assessed by evaluating emerging frameworks offering application-agnostic services for data clustering and classification [7].

3.1   WelCOM Maintenance Platform and Piloting Testbed

The conducted research constitutes part of the WelCOM (Wireless sensor networks for Engineering asset Life-Cycle Optimal Management) project [8]. The WelCOM platform utilizes a smart sensor infrastructure for machinery condition monitoring, while interfacing with a CMMS (Computerized Maintenance Management System), to deliver a context aware asset management tool (Fig. 1). An Intelligent Maintenance Advisor client handles context aware operations by exploiting the mobility of portable devices with mechanisms able to record the user's location, environment and system session. The client adapts visually and functionally to changes in the apparent context of a service request. The same client enables maintenance staff to select parameter semantics that profile new monitored contexts. These contexts are processed by the

Knowledge Management sub-System, utilizing a set of local or remotely accessed data fusion services. The Intelligent Maintenance Advisor offers an abstraction layer between maintenance practice and computations, by providing a profiling tool that translates maintenance engineering and management specifications into appropriate method invocation for modeling services. Context modeling and identification, as well as context-based adaptation are key elements in the WelCOM approach.

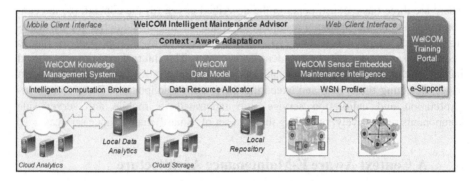

Fig. 1. WelCOM e-Maintenance Architecture

The development of WelCOM's mobile client drives an assessment of direct and indirect methods for inferring maintenance related contexts. One of our main testbed sites is the Kleemann's lift testing tower. This tower is equivalent to a seventeen floor building, and comprises four testing units. The WelCOM intelligent advisor should be able to monitor, map and analyze a set of condition parameters related to lift operational parts and components (Fig. 2). The lift testbeds themselves are technical structures composing an integrated lift machinery installation.

Fig. 2. WelCOM Testbed Planning

3.2   Context in Mobile Maintenance

A range of context models have been investigated by research initiatives and development processes. While the first seek to explore the depth and breadth of context semantics, the later battle their way through implementations that can deliver functionality to facilitate handling of these contexts. Maintenance related models are connected with indicators of operational performance and descriptive power, providing a solid base for context aware systems. The extensibility of these models is achieved through compliance to established schemas (MIMOSA [9]) and the native importing (multi-inheritance) features of the modeling technology (XML schemas). While earlier and recent models, address context modeling with respect to a single application or application class, engineering asset management constitutes a problem space that allows scaling of semantics at a generic level. This derives from the ranged scope of the corresponding services that start from shop-floor maintenance tasks to strategic level KPI analysis. The WelCOM maintenance advisor is designed to be configured by a context engine that detects and adapts to the following context types (Fig. 3):

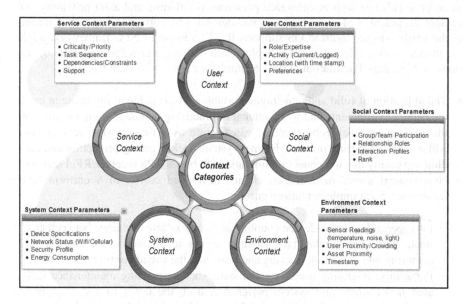

Fig. 3. Context in Mobile Maintenance

- <u>User Context</u> – It maps the semantics behind the information included in user profile, system preferences and logged activity. Profile information designates personnel's expertise, maintenance roles and system credentials. Preferences express a set of property values that allow user-defined adaptation of services and console personalisation. Logged activities contain a list of both completed and pending tasks, along with checked/unchecked notifications.
- <u>System Context</u> – It holds the semantics for describing device features, along with other non-functional information, such as the connection status and network

availability (e.g. availability of Wi-Fi networks and/or 3G signal strength), power level and system performance/status, etc.

- Environment Context – It addresses the location coordinates or code of the personnel proximate position (asset/segment => position), along with a timestamp of his presence there. It also includes a set of property values that describe constituents of the sensed industrial environment (temperature, noise, humidity, light).
- Service Context – The context of the user assigned functions and services. It contains the semantics about the service participation in a larger workflow (sequence number in maintenance plan), its criticality/priority and its dependences with other services/functions. A set of property values that define maintenance specific task parameters, such as constraints and available supporting material.
- Social Context – This context describes the dynamics of group participation and collaboration between industrial agents such as personnel. The semantics here draw a constantly updated linked graph, where flow of knowledge and authority identify individual skills for co-operative efficiency and effective supervision.

In order to enhance both maintenance personnel positioning and asset proximity, we explore the potential of using NFC-enabled devices with corresponding tags. Currently the vastly adopted android OS supports the 3rd version of NFC framework, while the mobile market offers a range of tablets with native features for read/write operations on NFC-tags. Facilitation of such technologies can lead certain benefits:

- The utilization of solid and non-fragile portable units, capable of operating in harsh industrial environments and by maintenance practicing hands. Introducing state-of-the-art features, such robust tablets can operate as a final product/service host, without strict handling policies. Former systems lacked casing protection and handling versatility due to connection limitations (tablet + GPS receiver/RFid reader).
- New context aware maintenance clients, developed on-top of a uniform NFC framework. Such implementations ensure:

  - Interoperability: cross device coupling and context data exchange between proximate personnel. Technicians passing reports to engineers, for collaborative authoring and validation, serving and powering the **social context**.
  - Portability: migrating users' session state, such as pending maintenance tasks, alert notifications and system preference, from the tablet to his smartphone. Synchronizing a single rich session between shop-floor tablet, the client pc and the personal smartphone, serving and powering the **user context**.
  - Compliance: exploiting the wide range of supported tags, offered by the NFC framework to program multiple associations. One tag to multiple assets and multiple tags to one asset. Optimal collaboration with the driver-set of other sensors can detect and map a detailed **environment context**.
  - Scalability: NFC framework is integrated with state-of-the-art devices driven by the latest versions of Android (and Windows8) operating system. Such versions include the most recent libraries for data presentation, UI composition and wireless coupling. They effectively incorporate the features capable of performing unique client adaptation for the maintenance **service context**.

3.3   Context Aware Maintenance Cloud

The concept of cloud and its serving technologies have only recently found application in the engineering asset management field. The term "sensor cloud" has emerged to offer the first maintenance cloud tool in modern IT architectures [10]. A sensor cloud is introduced as the method to outsource storage of maintenance data, supported also by proper tools that semantically annotate and organise the collected volumes. A cloud approach comes to offer two main advantages: (i) the provision of scalable storage and service instances, hosted in (ii) third party infrastructures. In maintenance systems, scalable resources may become crucial when multiple diagnostics and modelling services are invoked by different monitoring agents (software/personnel). Aggregating the execution of such complex tasks demands high availability of resources. Few of them can easily dominate the capacity of a limited infrastructure. To address such a challenge many industries overtook the indoor development of custom distributed diagnostics, operating them on top of enterprise-owned/maintained servers/clusters and backup systems. The multifold cost of such an investment is where the second cloud feature comes to serve. Cloud providers enable enterprises to escape the cost of running their maintenance system on top off owned storage and processing facilities. The Quality of Service (QoS) defined in a cloud Service Level Agreement (SLA) has proven to be much more reliable and cost-efficient than most self-maintained centres. The question then is how secure is for a competitive industry to outsource such core functions that support its manufacturing edge, i.e. the maintenance process.

Cloud services have evolved to deal with security issues of data analytics, by supporting the abstraction layer of application-agnostic frameworks. This means that cloud providers can now efficiently host generic modelling services, whose analytic power can be extensively configured to provide highly focused results. In this scenario, apart from the service hosting/handling infrastructure, the development cost of base services is also escaped by the client industry. Such a cloud-based maintenance system only requires the following components:

- The Intelligent Computation Broker – Knowing and analysing the capabilities of the employed cloud services, this subsystem is responsible for orchestrating an appropriate workflow of service invocations that eventually returns the desired results. It operates as an engine that profiles specialised tasks of maintenance intelligence into sequenced calls of application agnostic analytics.
- The Data Resource Allocator – This subsystem handles the encryption, wrapping and exchange of maintenance data. Such tasks ensure that the output of one cloud service is properly formatted and securely passed to lead the input of the next one in the workflow. It is also responsible for monitoring and imposing the data caching, replication and migration policies between the cloud storage sites.

The target of the WelCOM's cloud side is to assess how thin and modular our maintenance advisor can be, by exploiting cloud instead of local resources. Currently, frameworks such as Mahout offer ready-to-use cloud services, addressing core tasks in context analytics (classification, clustering and batch-based collaborative filtering).

Our goal is to calibrate and facilitate such services in order to provide, consume and/or extend maintenance services.

4   Conclusions

Context awareness is a design methodology that promotes adaptation in customised IT services and content. In the last few years, many field adoptions have been studied and evaluated, while enabling technologies and techniques progressed to enable new context dimensions for maintenance management and condition monitoring. By employing them, modern maintenance systems can offer advanced adaptive services build upon application-agnostic cloud frameworks. This paper described the Wel-COM-platform's semantics, design and implementation plan for a contextualised mobile client of a distributed model that constitutes a maintenance mobile cloud.

Acknowledgement. The collaboration with all project partners and especially Kleemann Lifts for providing the application case, as well as Atlantis Engineering and Prisma Electronics for contributing to the application scenario setup, within the context of the GSRT projectt 09SYN-71-856, 'WelCOM', are gratefully acknowledged.

References

1. Samanta, B., Nataraj, C.: Prognostics of machine condition using soft computing. Robotics and Computer-Integrated Manufacturing 24, 816–823 (2007)
2. Emmanouilidis, C., Liyanage, J.P., Jantunen, E.: Mobile Solutions for Engineering Asset and Maintenance Management. Journal of Quality in Maintenance Engineering 15, 92–105 (2009)
3. Emmanouilidis, C., Koutsiamanis, R.-A., Tasidou, A.: Mobile Guides: Taxonomy of Architectures, Context Awareness, Technologies and Applications. Journal of Network and Computer Applications 36(1), 103–125 (2013)
4. Roy, N., Gu, T., Das, S.K.: Supporting pervasive computing applications with active context fusion and semantic context delivery. Pervasive and Mobile Computing 6, 21–42 (2010)
5. Chen, G., Li, M., Kotz, D.: Data-centric middleware for context-aware pervasive computing. Pervasive and Mobile Computing 4, 216–253 (2008)
6. MIMOSA, CRIS, Common relational information schema specification, v3.2.1 (2008), http://www.mimosa.org
7. Owen, S., Anil, R., Dunning, T., Friedman, E.: Mahout in Action. Manning (2011)
8. Pistofidis, P., Emmanouilidis, C., Koulamas, C., Karampatzakis, D., Papathanassiou, N.: A Layered E-Maintenance Architecture Powered by Smart Wireless Monitoring Components. In: IEEE Conference on Industrial Technologies, ICIT 2012, Athens, Greece, May 19-21, pp. 390–395 (2011)
9. MIMOSA, Machinery Information Management Open Systems Alliance, http://www.mimosa.org
10. Melchor, J., Fukuda, M.: A design of flexible data channels for sensor-cloud integration. In: Proc. 21st International Conference on System Engineering, ICSEng 2011, Las Vegas, USA, August 16-18, pp. 251–256 (2011)

Seamless Access to Sensor Networks for Enhanced Manufacturing Processes

Kostas Kalaboukas[1], Borislav Jerabek[2], Rok Lah[2], and Freek van Polen[3]

[1] SingularLogic, N. Ionia, Attica, Greece
kkalaboukas@singularlogic.eu
[2] Gorenje, Partizanska cesta 12, 3320, Velenje, Slovenia
{boro.jerabek,rok.lah}@gorenje.si
[3] Sense B.V., Lloydstraat 5, Rotterdam, Netherlands
freek@sense-os.nl

Abstract. WSNs are largely deployed nowadays in "smart factories". However, their smooth operation is hindered by device heterogeneity and lack of integration with the current IT systems. The SIMPLE project aims at seamless inter-working of sensors, actuators, tags and devices with business IT systems and distributed control systems towards simpler integrated manufacturing processes. SIMPLE delivers a novel hierarchical network architecture, based on the envisioned manufacturing processes and reflecting the functional hierarchy of aggregations of goods or production processes found in the manufacturing use case.

Keywords: integrated manufacturing processes, network design, sensor networks, smart factories.

1 Introduction

Wireless Sensor Networks (WSNs) have been identified as one of the most important technologies for the 21st century. The deployment of WSN in "smart factories" applications is already a fact and has attracted the interest of the research community and the electronics development giants worldwide. In a medium sized manufacturing plant over an area of 10000m^2, 5000 pressure sensors, 1000 temperature sensors and 500 sensors of other types exist on average [1]. However, significant problems hinder their wide exploitation: this great number of sensors includes sensors of different type (e.g. temperature, pressure, RFID reader), operating on different device platforms with different capabilities and communication characteristics. This heterogeneity prevents the simple, uniform access of information throughout the sensor cloud and its seamless integration with the business IT systems, which will be more and more needed, as the number of cheap multi-purpose sensors proliferates and even more reconfigurable sensor nodes are under development [2].

The seamless inter-working of sensors, actuators, tags and devices with business IT systems (e.g., ERP, WMS, MES) and distributed control systems towards "simpler" integrated manufacturing processes is at the core of the SIMPLE[1] project [3].

---

[1] Self-organizing Intelligent Middleware Platform for manufacturing and Logistics Enterprises.

C. Emmanouilidis, M. Taisch, D. Kiritsis (Eds.): APMS 2012, Part II, IFIP AICT 398, pp. 25–32, 2013.
© IFIP International Federation for Information Processing 2013

SIMPLE aims at designing and developing a flexible sensor network architecture and a middleware solution in order to compensate for the current lack of open-source and commercial solutions capable of monitoring the state of shipments at different grouping levels (e.g. at the crate and case levels) and, more generally, of tracing goods along the whole supply chain. The vision is to enable information collection from all over the manufacturing plant in a uniform way without having to consider the heterogeneity of the underlying infrastructure.

The present paper starts from the analysis of the current manufacturing processes (in section 2), which was carried out to create a concrete list of requirements, and reports the improvements, that an integrated solution can bring in section 3.To achieve these objectives and meet the identified requirements, a hierarchical network architecture has been designed and is presented in section 4. It reflects the functional hierarchy of aggregations of goods or production processes found in the manufacturing use case. Conclusions are drawn in section 5.

2   Manufacturing "As-is" Situation

To capture the functionality that can significantly simplify the manufacturing process, first the currently adopted white goods manufacturing process was analysed, based on input provided by Gorenje[2]. Currently, white goods manufacturing consists of 4 main phases:

Phase A: Framework Construction. All mechanic parts of the product are being assembled. The parts are picked from the warehouse and transferred to the production centre. There, a fully automated assembly line is responsible for putting together all parts to create the framework of the product.

Phase B: Electronic parts assembly. The framework goes to the second phase, where all electronic parts, circuits, accessories, control mechanisms, etc. are manually inserted. Similar to the mechanic parts, the electronics, are picked by the warehouse, exit it and transferred to the production center. Once assembled, the final product enters the testing phase.

Phase C: Testing. According to the results and the severity of the failures (if found), the product may have one of the following paths:

- *The product has no failures and ready to be released.* The product goes to the warehouse of final products for further delivery.
- *The product has minor failures.* In this case, the technical team disassemblies the product. All parts then are returned to the materials warehouse.
- *The product has severe failures.* The product is being disassembled and the technical team checks all parts separately. Those that are reusable go to the materials warehouse and the damaged ones are destroyed.

Phase D: After Sales Support. When the product has been sold, automated management support can still be provided. Within regular intervals, the appliances perform self-testing and upon detecting a malfunction, an alert message is sent or an error code

---

[2] Gorenje is one of the partners of the SIMPLE project consortium and the largest Slovenian manufacturer of white goods (larger home appliances).

appears on the built-in led display. The after-sales support office is informed either by the client or automatically, so that the problem gets fixed.

3 Manufacturing "To-be" Situation

Through SIMPLE the manufacturing process is being automated in various phases allowing for easy monitoring of incoming/outgoing goods in the warehouse, as well as better tracking of the production and product-in-use phases. The modifications that were considered necessary for each manufacturing phase are described next:

Phase A: Framework Construction. A visual camera could test the position of the part to be assembled, the part type, as well as any possible anomalies.

Phase B: Electronic Parts assembly. Parts will be RFID-tagged in the warehouse and RFIDs will be registered in the SIMPLE server. A motion sensor will register parts transportation to the production center. After assembly, the final product is being tagged and the aggregated RFID is registered in the SIMPLE server.

Phase C: Testing. Depending on the testing result, the following SIMPLE intersection points can be triggered:

- The product has no failures. The product will be released, while a motion sensor will register the event of the product being ready for delivery.
- The product has minor failures. All parts will contain this information and enter the warehouse. A motion sensor will also register this event.
- The product has severe failures. The product is disassembled and the aggregated tag is being destroyed. The reusable parts are led to the warehouse and this event is recorded through a motion sensor. Each (tagged) part also contains the severe failures history and "reusable" status. The tags of the non-reusable parts are also deleted from SIMPLE. Additionally, integration with the ERP system can lead to automatic creation of material consumption reports and warehouse documents (when a part enters or leaves it, as well as automatically tracking the production process).

Phase D: After Sales Support. The product has an embedded Automated Testing Tool (ATE), which is beyond the scope of SIMPLE.

According to the envisioned manufacturing scenario, a number of system requirements have been derived. The requirements, related to the network architectural design, which is at the focus of this paper, are the following:

- Collection, filtering and processing of the readings from a variety of sensors, tags and sensor networks (e.g., RFID, temperature, pressure, humidity), and accordingly delivering them as reports.
- Mapping and correlation of the above reports to business events associated with user-defined business contexts and processes for integrated manufacturing. RFID tags will allow for accurate and automated association of manufacturing processes and items with wider business processes.
- Enabling configuration and invocation of actuating services in machines, devices and actuators.
- Provision of techniques and graphical tools for managing sensors, devices, as well as business contexts and processes.

4   The SIMPLE Solution

SIMPLE is understood as a middleware platform and as such, it shall be a software layer operating on every device that is part of a SIMPLE application, and form the bridge among these devices capitalizing on emerging works on programming sensor nodes [4]. To efficiently face the diversity of devices mainly with respect to their hardware (processing and storage) capabilities, we have reviewed the devices usually involved in a manufacturing plant and we have organized them in classes, prior to designing the overall SIMPLE network and node architecture. Then, to address the scalability issues arising in such systems, we have designed a hierarchical network architecture that discriminates different hierarchy layers and specifies the functionality (including the middleware, networking and application functionality) that the device belonging to each layer should execute. It is worth stressing that there is no one-to-one relation between device class and layers, since a device belong to a specific class depending on its hardware capabilities while it plays the role of a layer –x device depending on the functionality it supports. Finally, to guide the development of the SIMPLE system, based on the network architecture and the specified functionality per layer, the SIMPLE node architecture is drawn.

4.1   SIMPLE Nodes Classification

The SIMPLE devices are classified according to hardware limitations as follows:
Class 0 Devices: RFID Tags. Radio-frequency identification (RFID) makes use of radio signals to exchange data between a reader and an electronic tag attached to an object, for the purpose of identification and tracking. RFID tags can be read by the RFID reader, in case of short distance, antenna matching and possible signal propagation. The RFID tags contain an integrated circuit for storing and processing information, modulating and demodulating a radio signal and an antenna for receiving and transmitting the signal. RFID tags can either just have a fixed ID or they could in addition also have a read-write memory from and to which the reader is able to read and write information.

In case of RFID tags the RFID readers that communicate to the individual tags are the interfaces to the rest of the SIMPLE system. The RFID readers collect the information from the tags, store it locally and, if required, communicate the information to the rest of the SIMPLE system and write new information to the RFID tags via the middleware interface. The main functions that these tags types support are tag inventorying and optimizing, reading/writing, locking and killing.
Class 1 Devices: WSN Nodes. WSNs are distributed networked systems composed of embedded computing nodes, each one being equipped with a processing unit (typically a microcontroller), a wireless communication interface, sensor(s) board and a battery. The wireless sensor networks typically make use of ad-hoc multi-hop networking schemes, which means that all nodes operate as routers, as well as they should be able to join and leave the network without any disruptions to the network operation.

Class 2 Devices: Hand-held RFID Readers. While RFID readers by themselves may be very small and attached to WSN nodes, hand-held RFID readers are included in a separate class, mainly due to their specific role in the SIMPLE systems. This class will typically be able to engage in user interaction, while also being able to read RFID devices, and thus be a powerful tool in a SIMPLE system for configuring installations. This type of device shall typically be used to add RFID tags to the system, to aggregate groups of devices, and to attach RFID tags to objects that need to be represented in the system.

Class 3 Devices: Hand-held and Embedded Devices. Hand-held and embedded devices, even personal and general-purpose devices, such as smartphones, are expected to be present in manufacturing environments. Devices of this type are marked by a high degree of connectivity. In SIMPLE, this class of devices could fulfill several different functions. First, their ubiquitous presence and high connectivity gives them the potential to be powerful ad-hoc routing hops. Second, they could operate as mobile sinks for any WSNs in the vicinity, as well as gather their own sensor data, with any sensors they might have equipped themselves. Third, these devices typically are designed for user interaction, and so could be used by any SIMPLE application.

Class 4 Devices: Desktops and Laptops. Desktops and laptops feature great processing power and memory, which allow them to sit in the background behind a sink node and operate on data that have been collected by a WSN. Within SIMPLE, desktops and laptops will be a readily available source of computing power and user interaction. Therefore, they could store and process large amounts of data in a local fashion. Additionally, they will be the most obvious choice for SIMPLE applications to interface with users, allowing them to monitor processes and configure a SIMPLE installation.

Class 5 Devices: Servers and "The Cloud". With recent developments in cloud computing and the increase in cloud computing services being offered, a virtually unlimited amount of computing power and storage room becomes available. Recently, however, services have become available that focus specifically on the storage and processing of sensor data. Within SIMPLE, this class of devices will be able to store and backup all data gathered in an installation. While the capabilities of this class of devices are virtually unlimited, they do have their limitations in that the amount of communication required may introduce lag in the system. Therefore, a the kind of data being stored and processed locally (typically recent data that may become relevant very quickly), as well as the kind of data being transported to the cloud for storage and processing should be carefully chosen.

4.2   The SIMPLE Network Architecture for the Manufacturing Use Case

The SIMPLE hierarchical network architecture can be applied to a variety of cases and is specifically useful for large and heterogeneous WSN systems. However, as the focus of this paper is on the enhancement of the manufacturing process, we concentrate on its operation for the manufacturing ("to-be") use case. The SIMPLE layered network architecture is presented in Fig. 1.

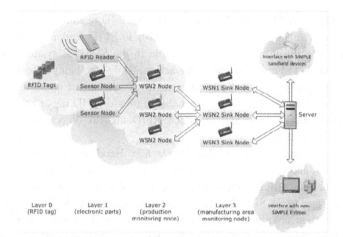

Fig. 1. The SIMPLE high level network architecture for the manufacturing case

In Phase A, the RFID reader and the camera or other visual inspection devices are considered as layer-1 devices. A layer-2 node (acting as information aggregator) receives the sensed data and can create a list of the mechanical parts that will be used for a specific good and their condition. This list is created either periodically or upon user request.

In Phase B, the RFID reader and the camera are regarded as layer-1 nodes.

In Phase C, testing, once a new device has been produced, a layer-2 node or another layer -1 node inspects the product. The result is announced to the layer-2 node, which has also collected information about the parts that the product consists of. This node now creates a product ID, associates it with the RFIDs of the parts it consists of and creates a message towards the server to inform that a new product is ready providing the details of its sub-parts. In the case of failure, the product is disassembled and the layer-2 node generates a different message providing the list of RFIDs of the parts. If any of them is no longer reusable, its RFID is sent to the server marked as "to be destroyed".

In Phase D, after sales support, it is the embedded Automated Testing Tool (ATE) that assists in problem fixing and SIMPLE is not involved.

From *a communication perspective*, layer-3 nodes are assumed to be installed in large manufacturing areas and are responsible for collecting information from sensor nodes regarding one or multiple production lines, as well as area-related information (e.g. temperature, humidity, light). Layer-3 nodes are also acting as gateways to the enterprise server.

Layer 1, 2 and 3 nodes are either in one or multi-hop distance between them, thus the need for realizing a WSN routing protocol arises. As regards the location, all nodes will most probably be placed in fixed locations, thus the exact coordinates can be statically configured.

As regards functionality,

1. layer-1 nodes sense data (RFID reader, anomaly detection, visual inspection),
2. layer-2 nodes generate product IDs and associate them with the IDs of the parts that form the product,
3. layer-3 nodes aggregate information regarding one or more production lines and areas and connects the layer 2 nodes to the server.

4.3   The SIMPLE–Node Architecture

The high level architecture of the SIMPLE node following an OSI approach is shown in Fig. 2. The SIMPLE research efforts are focused on the layers above the MAC layer.

At the network layer, a location manager module will exist which will either become aware of the nodes location through GPS or will execute a localization technique.

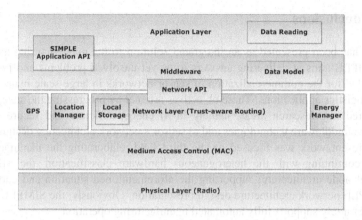

Fig. 2. The SIMPLE OSI-aligned node architecture

At the same OSI layer, the trust-aware routing block will undertake the responsibility to define the path of any message from any SIMPLE node towards the SIMPLE sink node. In addition, a trust management system will guarantee the detection and avoidance of malicious nodes. The trust information will be kept in the Local Storage block per one-hop neighbor and will be combined with the location information to define the next-hop node.

The Energy manager monitors the remaining energy of the node for two purposes: first, to inform the upper layers in case the remaining energy is running low and second to inform any layer (e.g. routing) about the current energy level so that it takes this information into account to reduce the overall energy consumption.

The middleware layer contains the data model, containing all necessary data for the manufacturing case. The data fields specified in this model are a listing of the data type stored in the middleware layer. Consequently, all functionality offered to the SIMPLE applications shall ultimately operate on these data fields. The data model provides functionality to store sensor data, as well as device IDs and aggregations between devices. Also, the data model is able to represent real world objects, which are not SIMPLE devices, and associations between SIMPLE devices and objects. For the manipulation of these basic data fields, low-level data manipulation functions are defined, which are part of this data model.

The SIMPLE Application API forms the bridge between the SIMPLE middleware layer and SIMPLE applications. The API allows applications to pose queries and subscribe to specific events. Moreover, the API allows the application to set certain conditions on the validity of the data that are to be returned. These conditions can be on the value of data itself, but also on the geographic region from which the data originate, the time at which the data were gathered, or the confidence the middleware layer has that indeed it is valid data.

5   Conclusions

SIMPLE has been presented as an integrated solution to the manufacturing automation. SIMPLE aims at delivering answers to as yet unsolved problems and products long needed for the commercialization of sensor networks in large-scale manufacturing and logistics applications. These objectives are met by progressing the state-of the art in three key research areas, namely in a) energy efficient and secure sensor routing, b) middleware technologies and c) sensor's network architecture design.

The present work was focused on the third field, elaborating the manufacturing process, continuing with the heterogeneous hardware classification, the SIMPLE high-level node architecture, supporting the aforementioned situation and ending in the SIMPLE network architecture design presentation. Obviously, the SIMPLE architecture definitely supports fully automated manufacturing operation.

The designed architecture, along with the defined functionality, will be mapped to a real-life test-bed, demonstrating the complete functionality of the SIMPLE system. The proposed developments will be able to provide traceability of the components and the products, store the history of each product and provide monitoring and transparent trace data to the manufacture plants, the warehouse, the distribution stores and the final customers. The test-bed will be set up in the Gorenje premises.

Acknowledgement. The work presented in this paper was partially funded by the ARTEMIS SIMPLE project.

References

1. Mols, D.: Making Measurement Count. Control Engineering Europe Journal, 24–26 (June/July 2009)
2. http://www.artemis-smart.eu/home.aspx
3. http://www.simple-artemis.eu/
4. Mottola, L., Picco, G.: Programming Wireless Sensor Networks: Fundamental Concepts and State of the Art. ACM Computing Surveys (2011)

Wireless Sensor Network Technologies for Condition Monitoring of Industrial Assets

Spilios Giannoulis[1], Christos Koulamas[1], Christos Emmanouilidis[2],
Petros Pistofidis[2], and Dimitris Karampatzakis[2]

"ATHENA" Research and Innovation Center in
Information, Communication and Knowledge Technologies
[1] Industrial Systems Institute, Patras, Greece
{sgiannoulis,koulamas}@isi.gr
[2] Institute for Language and Speech Processing, Xanthi, Greece
{chrisem,pistofidis,karampatzakis}@ceti.gr

Abstract. Systematic and robust condition monitoring of crucial equipment is the cornerstone of any successful preventive maintenance policy in the industrial environment. Recent advances in low-cost wireless sensor network (WSN) technologies and products indicate a promising future for a cost-effective, wider and more permanent deployment of a distributed sensing and processing infrastructure. This paper aims to provide a comprehensive assessment of main WSN technology alternatives available today, based on a qualitative and quantitative analysis of the typical range of requirements in the specific application domain of industrial machine condition monitoring.

Keywords: Industrial Wireless Sensor Networks, Asset Management.

1   Introduction

Over the last years numerous advancements have boost the use of wireless communications in many areas of the industry. Wireless communications have become standardized and can provide many options to the industry engineer to choose from, in order to design and deploy a wireless communication infrastructure. With speeds ranging from few Kbps to more than 100 Mbps and the cost of a wireless node dropping every day, wireless technologies look even more appealing. Then the notion of wireless sensor networks (WSN's) came into play to provide the wireless node with intelligence and upgrade it from a typical routing/transmitting mechanism to an intelligent sensing device. Every node in a WSN can now control autonomously a set of transducers or composite sensors, execute complex data processing techniques to the sensor data and organize, support and manage distributed applications in cooperation with other nodes in the network.

The paper is structured as follows. In the first part, the focus is on the definition of the most important application specific characteristics, the requirements on the services that a WSN infrastructure has to provide, as well as the main trade-offs in the

C. Emmanouilidis, M. Taisch, D. Kiritsis (Eds.): APMS 2012, Part II, IFIP AICT 398, pp. 33–40, 2013.

design process. In the second part, the dominant wireless communication technologies and standards are presented, pointing out the pros and cons against each requirement and trade-off axis based on the requirements of Industrial Asset Management applications. The goal of this paper is mainly to pinpoint the possible characteristics of each technology that provide specific advantages within the Application Domain and try to point in the direction of a technology that should exhibit most of these characteristics in the future.

2   Domain Characteristics

Looking into the wider industrial monitoring and control systems supporting the application domain of scope, the mostly cited efforts on addressing important specific requirements can be structured in: a) the real-time performance and dependability axis, and b) the seamless integration and interoperability axis.

Regarding the first axis, systems and networks needed for condition monitoring applications used in the context of a preventive maintenance policy implementation may be safely categorized under the SP100 classes 5 and/or 4, that is, logging, downloading/uploading and alerting systems. Typical periodicities of sampling simple, one-dimensional sizes, such as temperatures, pressures etc. do not introduce really strict real-time requirements, since the machine wear – which is the main monitoring objective - usually evolves in a wider time scope. However, more complex measurements such as vibration monitoring may pose stricter real-time requirements, when it comes to certain architectural and design decisions over the handling of the time series that constitutes one "sample". This depends on the needed size of the sample and the complexity of the applied algorithmic processing (e.g. for novelty detection and/or fault diagnosis), which, in turn, define alone a design space with certain decisions on computation / storage / bandwidth trade-offs. As an indicative order of magnitude, consider that a 16-bit/80kHz vibration sample produces 160kByte/sec that needs to be handled. The approach of data preprocessing in the wireless node reduces the volume of data that need to be transmitted to the data server, however in some cases the raw sample data is required to be transferred, either for simple data logging purposes or for more complex data processing, leading to extensive networking transmission load and increased latency if the networking technology is not able to handle effectively the volume of the raw data set.

Furthermore, synchronization requirements may also exist between measurements at different sensing points when for example collaborative sensor applications are the case at hand. Adding into the picture the wireless nature, related to medium behavior aspects - especially in the noisy industrial environment - as well as to energy related constraints, it is also obvious that the trade-off space may drastically increase.

Finally, the demand for seamless integration and interoperability clearly indicates a necessary focus on established international standards for any large scale industrial investment to be justified. These standards mainly have to address the networking and inter-networking layer, as well as the application level protocols, data definition and architectural layers. Since in this paper the focus is on networking technologies, the main relevant standards and industrial specifications are presented and discussed in the following sections.

3   WSN Technologies and Standards

Three main standardized wireless technologies exist today that can be used in the context of WSN's to provide the required connectivity mechanisms. These include IEEE 802.11 [1], IEEE 802.15.1[2] and IEEE 802.15.4 [3]. Based on these standards several enhancements/related standards or products have been presented like the WirelessHART [7] and ISA 100.11a [8] standards that are based partially on the IEEE 802.15.4, as well as Bluetooth [5] and   WISA [9],   that are based fully or partially on IEEE 802.15.1 respectively.   The characteristics of each standard/solution shall be presented in this section and the pros and cons of each protocol shall be exposed with respect to the application domain characteristics and requirements.

The IEEE 802.11x family of standards defines the physical and MAC layer protocols that can match perfectly to the design and organization of a wireless local area network (WLAN). Various transmission speeds are supported from 2 Mbps up to hundreds of Mbps with the latest 802.11n standard that introduces MIMO techniques to mitigate the effect of the multipath problem, as well as a range of transmission up to hundreds of meters outdoors and approximately 50-60m indoors. This technology can still be used in WSN's with the disadvantage of relatively high power consumption opposed to the low power requirements of a WSN. Even more, IEEE 802.11x family suffers from interference issues and exhibits reduced robustness especially in the presence of Bluetooth/IEEE 802.15.4 that both use the same ISM 2.4 GHz band as well as possible interference from industrial processes present in close proximity of the transceiver. The use of a CSMA based MAC algorithm provides non-deterministic timing behavior and therefore cannot support strict real time application requirements especially if the typical state of the network in terms of data load is anything else than low.

The IEEE 802.15.1 standard on the other hand came at first to fulfill the need for wireless connectivity in the range of a few meters, hence it was characterized as a personal area network protocol (PAN).   Its main target was to replace wires connecting devices like keyboards and mice to a pc, speakers to any kind of sound source, and in general any low-range, low-bandwidth wired solution until that day. The idea of using IEEE 802.15.1 as a wireless solution to enable wireless networking came together with Bluetooth, an enhancement of IEEE 802.15.1 focusing mainly on upper layers of a wireless network providing advanced routing and application specific profiles as well as 3 classes of possible transmitting power that provide different communication range from few meters (class 3 device) up to 100m maximum (class 1 device). The maximum supported theoretical throughput is 3 Mbps in Bluetooth v2.0 standard although it has been found that in practice no more than 2.1 Mbps can be achieved due to protocol overhead. For Bluetooth v1.x the maximum theoretical throughput is 1 Mbps but it has been shown in [11] that it cannot surpass the 700 kbps barrier for the same reason as stated before, protocol overhead. The main disadvantage of IEEE802.15.1/Bluetooth, which hinders its wider adoption in WSN's, is its small range and restricted support of scalability since it supports only a few nodes per Piconet, the proposed cluster of devices in Bluetooth standard employing a single master-multiple slaves stations architecture. Its main advantage is its real time behavior based on the MAC layer used, as well as in the application profiles defined by Bluetooth for time critical applications.

The WISA solution that is based on IEEE 802.15.1 offers re-usability of wireless frequencies forming cells much like in the mobile telephony networks. Using TDMA as well in the MAC layer, WISA provides deterministic behavior as well as advanced interference deterrent techniques like frequency division duplex and frequency hopping to minimize interference in the industrial environment. It should also be noted that in addition to the wireless communication solution, WISA also provides a wireless power provisioning solution based on long-wave radio frequencies that takes advantage of the inductive magnetic coupling phenomenon. This technology could render WISA a completely wireless and free from power constraints solution for the industrial environment.

The IEEE 802.15.4 standard provides wireless communication speeds up to 250 kbps and communication range up to 60-80m outdoors as well as low power characteristics that make it an ideal candidate for use in the context of wireless sensor networks. It can be considered a middle solution between IEEE 802.11 and IEEE 802.15.1 standards in terms of range but not in terms of power and throughput, since it exhibits the lowest power consumption making it ideal for WSN but also the lowest link throughput. Based on the IEEE 802.15.4, several standards exist that focus on providing higher layer services like routing, application profiles etc. These standards include ZigBee [4]/ZigBee Pro, an analogous of what Bluetooth is for IEEE 802.15.1, as well several other standards that try to provide enhanced services like the 6LowPAN standard from IETF.

ZigBee provides on top of the IEEE 802.15.4 PHY and MAC layers, the Network and Application layer as well as security services. The most important characteristic that ZigBee adds is the mesh networking capabilities combining Tree Routing with on demand nonTree (mesh) Routing based on the well-known AODV routing algorithm [13]. It also natively supports both star and tree typical networks topologies. Besides adding two high-level network layers to the underlying structure, another significant improvement is the introduction of ZigBee Device Objects (ZDOs). These are responsible for a number of tasks, which include keeping of device roles, management of requests to join a network, device discovery and security. Compared to IEEE 802.15.4 it improves greatly the possible selection of topologies to enable the deployment of a ZigBee based network as well as adding security mechanism on top of IEEE 802.15.4. and vendor specific ZDOs to enable interoperability between different vendor devices. ZigBee Pro enhances transmission range up to hundreds of meters by increasing the transmission power and receiver sensitivity.

6LowPAN enables the use of IPv6 addressing over IEEE 802.15.4 based WSN's hence enabling the Internet of Things notion where every node in a WSN is visible as a device from any connected IP based network machine transparently. Its main advantages are the reuse and interoperability of already known and tested services and application data models like HTTP, HTML and XML as well as the transport sub-protocols of IP, TCP and UDP. Furthermore, all existing IP based security and network management infrastructure already established in Industrial Environments can be used with minimal integration efforts.

WirelessHART on the other hand focuses in providing interoperability with wired Hart networks. Using frequency hopping combined with the DSSS modulation of the 802.15.4 radios, it increases the resistance of the WSN to common interference sources such as 802.11x when operating in the 2.4GHz band, and Bluetooth as well as several industrial processes and devices. Also the use of TDMA instead of CSMA/CA MAC algorithm as defined in IEEE 802.15.4, results in deterministic behavior of the WirelessHART in the time domain. Finally, the ISA 100.11a standard is also based on the IEEE 802.15.4 PHY. It also adds support for TDMA like WirelessHART, but also supports Channel Hopping and Mesh Routing in the lower layers while providing reliable and secure operation for critical monitoring, alerting, supervisory control, open loop and closed loop control applications.

4   Comparing the Alternatives

IEEE 802.11x family of standards offers high bandwidth that may be needed for continuous data logging purposes but suffers from interference from other devices in the 2.4 GHz ISM band as well as from typical industrial operations. The use of a CSMA based algorithm in MAC layer results in non-deterministic timing behavior, hindering the usage of IEEE 802.11x in time critical applications. The fact that it supports high bandwidth modes of operation lessens the impact of the CSMA algorithm when low network data load is the case. Its wide transmission range provides efficient and less challenging deployment methodologies to be used with few nodes being able to provide coverage to a large industrial area. This characteristic is also the reason that IEEE 802.11x is not able to provide a dense network solution for WSN's, since its wide range and the CSMA MAC algorithm used are a poor combination when dense wireless networking topologies is one of the requirements. It must be also noted that the maximum throughput obtained most of the times is far from the theoretical optimal especially if the wireless data load is high, due to CSMA based MAC, and also if there is interference of any kind.

IEEE 802.15.1 offers low bandwidth, low transmission range, does not scale well, but offers good real time support at all times. This is mainly due to the TDMA MAC algorithm used, as well as because of the requirement imposed from the standard that only 7 active slave nodes can coexist per master node at all times. This behavior results in IEEE 802.15.1/Bluetooth to be a good candidate for alarm/condition monitoring in critical industrial systems where conditions change frequently and in a matter of seconds. On the other hand it is not suitable to be used for data logging/continuous data transfer since the bandwidth offered is low and cannot fulfill the needs imposed by the data logging application.

WISA provides deterministic behavior by using a TDMA based MAC algorithm, further optimized to provide up to 120 sensors/actuators per Base Station as well as short cycle times up to 2048µs. Furthermore, it adds advanced interference mitigation techniques to minimize interference in the harsh industrial environment and there is no need for frequency planning in case of multiple cells since the FH sequences are constructed to guarantee adequate separation between consecutive hops and low correlation. In all cases, all operating cells use the entire available ISM band of 80 MHz at 2.2GHz [9].

The IEEE 802.15.4 standard offers medium transmission range, medium bandwidth, and good scalability but suffers from time characteristics due to the CSMA based MAC layer used in IEEE802.15.4 and all standards based on it like ZigBee and ZigBee Pro. Only ZigBee Pro supports communication ranges up to few hundreds of meters duo to increased transmission power that results in lower power aware characteristics. As it was shown in [12], IEEE 802.15.4 performance is substantially lower in terms of throughput in comparison with the throughput defined in the standard. In fact no more than 140Kbps can be achieved in any case when the standard states that the theoretical speed of IEEE 802.15.4 is 250Kbps. This difference is based mainly in the small packet size defined in the standard that in conjunction with the required protocol data overhead present in each packet results in a 44% reduction of actual application data throughput.

ISA100.11a and WirelessHART on the other hand provide real time characteristics since they are based on a TDMA MAC as well as robust operation, increasing the resistance of the WSN to common interference sources by the usage of frequency/channel hopping combined with the DSSS modulation. The above characteristics result in proclaiming ISA100.11a and WirelessHART better candidates than standard IEEE802.15.4/ZigBee/ZigBee Pro, while the main disadvantage is the lack of wide availability of products, so far.

Comparing all families of standards, it seems that IEEE 802.15.4 provides today a middle-level solution capable to support the wider possible range of related trade-offs, excluding the extreme cases of high-bandwidth, continuous data logging scenarios. Combined with 6LoWPan it may also offer superior interoperability and scalability since it provides IPv6 addressing and so direct communication with IP based backbone infrastructures, eliminating the usage of application level gateways and protocol translators. It should also be noted that in general, low power wireless solutions like IEEE 802.15.4/ZigBee and /IEEE 802.15.1/Bluetooth are well suited for low data rate industrial applications duo to their low power characteristics that result in maximized longevity of the provided solution. But for high data rate applications, solutions like the IEEE 802.11x should be considered since they offer lower normalized power consumption per transmitted byte compared to IEEE 802.15.1 and IEEE 802.15.4 as it has been shown in [10].

In Table 1, a qualitative comparison of the aforementioned protocols and products is presented with respect to the requirements imposed by the applications of the Condition Monitoring for Industrial Assets domain.

Table 1. Comparison of the presented Wireless Communication Standards based on the requirements of Industrial Asset Management

Wireless Technology	Robustness	Real Time Performance	Range	Link Throughput	Network Scalability	Power awareness
IEEE 802.11	*	*	***	***	**	*
IEEE 802.15.4	**	*	**	*	**	***
ZigBee	**	**	**	*	***	***
ZigBee Pro	**	**	***	*	***	**
IEEE 802.15.1	**	***	*	**	*	**
Bluetooth	**	***	*	**	*	**
WirelessHART	***	***	**	*	**	***
ISA 100.11a	***	***	**	*	**	***
Bluetooth	**	***	*	**	*	**
WISA	***	***	*	**	**	***

5   Conclusion

This paper presents the requirements imposed by the applications of Industrial Asset Management and Preventive Maintenance. It then focuses on the standardized wireless technologies available today and presents their advantages and disadvantages resulting in a qualitative assessment of each wireless technology with respect to the requirements of Industrial Asset Management applications. It is evident that each technology has its specific advantages and disadvantages and can be used for specific applications of Asset Management but no one-fits-all solution exists at this time. As a final conclusion, it seems that in a future wireless standardization effort, several advantages could and should coexist like IP based communication, physical layer robustness due to the use of frequency division duplex and/or frequency hopping as well as possible MIMO antenna techniques to reduce the multipath effect. Last but not least TDMA based MAC protocol could be supported to provide real time performance which is so critical for most Industrial Applications. In this context, the two standards focusing in Industrial environment applications, the WirelessHart and ISA100.1a seem promising and it is our intention to evaluate them through extended benchmarks and QoS testing when several of-the-self products become available in order to have a detailed view of their behavior and QoS performance.

Acknowledgements. The financial support received through GSRT (grant 09SYN-71-856, project WelCOM) is gratefully acknowledged.

References

1. IEEE 802.11 standard,
   http://standards.ieee.org/about/get/802/802.11.html

2. IEEE Std 802. Part 15.1: Wireless Medium Access Control (MAC) and Physical Layer (PHY) Specifications for Wireless Personal Area Networks (WPANs). IEEE Standards Association (January 15, 2005) ISBN 0-7381-4707-9, doi:10.1109/IEEESTD.2005.96290
3. IEEE Std 802. IEEE Standard for Information technology - Telecommunications and information exchange between systems - Local and metropolitan area networks - Specific requirements - Part 15.4: Wireless Medium Access Control (MAC) and Physical Layer (PHY) Specifications for Low-Rate Wireless Personal Area Networks (WPANs) (April 15, 2006)
4. ZigBee specification, Zigbee alliance (2008), http://www.zigbee.org
5. Bluetooth, http://www.bluetooth.com
6. http://datatracker.ietf.org/wg/6lowpan/
7. IEC 62591 ed1.0 - Industrial communication networks - Wireless communication network and communication profiles - WirelessHART^{TM}
8. ISA-100.11a-2011 - Wireless systems for industrial automation: Process control and related applications
9. Scheible, G., Dzung, D., Endresen, J., Frey, J.-E.: Unplugged but connected – Design and Implementation of a Truly Wireless Real-Time Sensor/Actuator Interface. IEEE Ind. Electron. Mag. 1(2), 25–34 (Summer 2007)
10. Lee, J.-S., Su, Y.-W., Shen, C.-C.: A Comparative Study of Wireless Protocols: Bluetooth, UWB, ZigBee, and Wi-Fi. In: Proceedings of the Industrial Electronics Society (IECON 2007), November 5-8, pp. 46–51 (2007)
11. Valenti, M.C., Robert, M., Reed, J.H.: On the throughput of Bluetooth data transmissions. In: IEEE Wireless Communications and Networking Conference (WCNC 2002), March 17-21, vol. 1, pp. 119–123 (2002), doi:10.1109/WCNC.2002.993475
12. Sun, T., Chen, L.-J., Han, C.-C., Yang, G.: Measuring effective capacity of IEEE 802.15.4 beaconless mode. In: IEEE Wireless Communications and Networking Conference (WCNC 2006), April 3-6, vol. 1, pp. 493–498 (2006), doi:10.1109/WCNC.2006.1683513
13. Perkins, C.E., Royer, E.M.: Ad-hoc on-demand distance vector routing. In: Proceedings of the Second IEEE Workshop on Mobile Computing Systems and Applications, WMCSA 1999, February 25-26, pp. 90–100 (1999), doi:10.1109/MCSA.1999.749281

A Critical Evaluation of RFID in Manufacturing

Wei Zhou[1,3] and Selwyn Piramuthu[2,3]

[1] Information & Operations Management, ESCP Europe, Paris, France
[2] Information Systems and Operations Management, University of Florida
Gainesville, Florida 32611-7169, USA
[3] RFID European Lab, Paris, France
wzhou@escpeurope.eu, selwyn@ufl.edu

Abstract. The number and extent of supply chain-related RFID applications far exceed those in the general manufacturing domain. We discuss possible reasons for this state. We review existing applications of RFID in manufacturing and discuss possible applications and related advantages and challenges.

1 Introduction

Since the early 2000s, there has been a tremendous increase in applications involving RFID (Radio-Frequency IDentification) tags. A majority of these applications have been somehow associated with supply chains or pharmaceutical industry or both. Major reasons for this include the huge impetus from Wal-Mart and the U.S. Department of Defense (DoD) as well as various ePedigree and anti-counterfeit initiatives from large pharmaceutical firms. With the successful incorporation of RFID tags on pallets or even individual items that pass through supply chains, there has been increasing interest among stake-holders from other application areas (e.g., tickets used in public transportation, library books). While there is some spill-over effect, the general manufacturing domain has not received its fair share of attention for RFID implementations. The same is true for RFID-related research publications in the manufacturing domain.

RFID tags have several characteristics in a desirable form factor that allows for its dominance over other existing auto-identification technologies. These tags, with minimal memory and processing power, have unique identifiers and are capable of carrying on extended *conversation* with a reader. This capability facilitates unique identification of any given tag among a set of tags on a large scale as well as storing and retrieving essential information about the tagged object. Other beneficial characteristics of RFID tags include their readability without direct line-of-sight (unlike bar codes) whereby they can be embedded inside objects and still be read, their durability in harsh environments, and the ability to be (re-)programmed on-the-fly. These characteristics certainly render RFID tags their attractiveness in manufacturing environments where their presence can facilitate mass customization. Overall, the ability to identify and store/update information about an object at item-level and to communicate this information on demand enables its seamless integration in an automated system

C. Emmanouilidis, M. Taisch, D. Kiritsis (Eds.): APMS 2012, Part II, IFIP AICT 398, pp. 41–48, 2013.

(Zhou 2009). While progress in bar code technology allows for the possibility to store more information using two-dimensional bar codes, these can't be updated nor do they have the ability to carry on a two-way conversation.

For example, item-level information can readily be used to match the most appropriate set of components that go into the final product (e.g., Zhou and Piramuthu, 2012). This would reduce the amount of wastage due to final products that are beyond pre-specified tolerance levels, while also improving the quality of the final products resulting from reduced mismatch-related issues. Process mining of the paths taken by RFID-embedded pallets in a manufacturing shop floor can also be used to develop a map for appropriate placement of machines to improve the efficiency of the entire system (e.g., Hu et al. 2012). Sensor-enabled RFID tags mounted on the component or on the substrate carrying the component can be used to ensure that this component was processed properly, for example, in terms of appropriate temperature range and the amount of time spent at any given temperature (e.g., Zhou and Piramuthu 2011). The underlying thread among these applications is that item-level RFID tags greatly facilitate manufacturing with real-time information (e.g., Hua et al. 2008).

Increasingly, RFID tags are being introduced in more and more manufacturing environments. For example, in Ford's Essex Engine plant at Windsor Ontario, the entire work sequence for an engine is stored in its RFID tag when it starts down the line (Sharp 1999). As it reaches different stations, it is interrogated to determine the tasks that require completion. Moreover, results from (e.g., quality check) tests are stored locally in the tag. In Ford's Cuautitlan Mexico facility that produces 300-400 thousand cars and trucks per year, apparently they were previously using a manual paper-based identification system to keep track of production flows and vehicles. This manual system unfortunately was ineffective due to frequent errors and costs associated with production oversights. Moreover, identification sheets that were used to track the vehicles frequently suffered loss and were oftentimes switched or damaged, rendering it difficult to control manufacturing quality. The introduction of RFID-based system addressed several of these issues (Li et al. 2004). For building Passat cars at the Emden plant, Volkswagen tags 20,000 parts each day to efficiently utilize its press shop's two large 73,000KN presses that require a smooth material flow system and very high machine availability downstream. Sheets cut from coils are placed on pallets that are RFID-tagged. These tags contain quality and product data at an early stage in the process to ensure the traceability of each pressed part. This also enables transparency in the material flow and for the material flow to match production demand. Audi incorporated semi-passive tags that can withstand high temperatures and painting into the assembly process of its TT sports cars at its Ingolstadt manufacturing plant. Assembly instructions and other information such as the chassis' intended color and other process information are stored in these reusable tags for use by robots at about 80 manufacturing and assembly stations. These tags are designed to ensure that appropriate steps occur at the right time and to the right chassis and to help control the flow of the chassis through the production line. When a defect is discovered, the system allows for flexibility in changing the production sequence. As a part of the RFID-based Automotive Network (RAN) project, a consortium of about 20 automobile manufacturers, suppliers, logistics firms, research institutes and software companies is testing the use of RFID in production and logistics processes within Germany's automotive industry. Daimler uses RFID to track production containers between Stuttgart, Berlin and their plant in Tuscaloosa, Alabama. BMW monitors containers as they move between their facilities and suppliers along the production chain. Opel tests the continuous use of RFID from vehicle manufacturing and the entire supply chain until its use by the consumers.

Clearly, several initiatives with RFID in manufacturing as the focus have begun not only in automotive manufacturing but also in a wide variety of other manufacturing facilities. We briefly discuss related literature in the next section. In the following section, we critically evaluate the characteristics, advantages, as well as issues related to the incorporation of RFID tags in a manufacturing context. We conclude the paper with a brief discussion.

2 Literature Review

Given the structural similarities and natural synergy between item-level information and agent-based systems, several studies have combined these in developing their manufacturing system frameworks. For example, Wang et al. (2009) develop an agent-based agile manufacturing planning and control system (AMPCS) to respond to the dynamically changing manufacturing activities and exceptions. AMPCS comprises modules for controlling the manufacturing system, generating production and operations schedule through an agent-based advanced manufacturing planning, and for performance analysis. Using AMPCS, they show that the agile manufacturing planning and control system developed through the integration of RFID and multi-agent system enables visibility, accountability, track-ability, responsiveness, and flexibility in a distributed and dynamic manufacturing system. Zhang et al. (2011) develop a Smart Gateway technology that captures real-time production data through different types of RFID/Auto-ID devices. Each such tagged entity forms a smart object (SO). Using Web services, they develop and manage agents based on a service-oriented architecture (SOA). They illustrate their framework using an assembly workstation where a Smart Gateway is deployed in real-time for defining, configuring and executing assembly operations. Trappey et al. (2009) develop agent-based collaborative mold production (ACMP) that supports the collaborative and autonomous mold manufacturing out-sourcing processes. ACMP provides autonomous features to handle vendor selection, task selection, and track in real-time the progress of outsourced tasks. They use Analytic Hierarchy Process (AHP) to solve the vendor selection and task selection problems and use RFID to provide real-time tracking capability for remote collaboration, control and monitoring out-sourcing partners. Higuera et al. (2007) develop an RFID-enhanced information management system (RFID-IMS) and illustrate how a multi-agent system model can be used for controlling a machining system incorporating RFID-IMS technology.

Other studies consider RFID systems from different perspectives. We briefly discuss a select few. For example, Ivantysynova et al. (2009) observe the lack of dedicated models for determining the intangible and non-quantifiable costs and benefits of RFID adoption decisions in the manufacturing domain. They then suggest some guidelines to assess both the quantifiable and the non-quantifiable aspects of RFID in manufacturing. Using insights gained from case studies of production plants in different industries, they present a structured model that help guide decision makers understand the important trade-offs that need to be considered in the manufacturing domain.

Thiesse and Fleisch (2008) observe that the use of real-time location systems (RTLS) technology including RFID provides the opportunity for new levels of process visibility and control in comparison to conventional material-tracking systems. Specifically, they introduce dispatching heuristics that include the location information of each entity that waits to be processed in the manufacturing shop floor. They then illustrate the performance of their heuristics using an example scenario from a semiconductor manufacturing environment. Their results indicate that incorporating location information in dispatching heuristics helps accelerate existing processes and leads to efficiency gain.

Huang et al. (2008) show improvements in the effectiveness of managerial decisions and operational efficiency through real-time visibility provided by RFID tags. They argue that this level of visibility closes the loop of adaptive assembly planning and control. They propose and illustrate a high-level assembly line explorer facility that the line manager can use to oversee the status of the entire assembly line and a lower-level workstation explorer facility for operators to monitor the status of their operations at corresponding workstations. Through information generated at these different levels of granularity, they show that appropriate levels of control can be implemented at both local and global levels.

Zhou and Piramuthu (2011) study the process of remanufacturing through RFID-generated item-level information. Specifically, they consider the state of a component before it is remanufactured and attempt to match that component with its most appropriate complement.

Hozak and Collier (2008) use a simulation model to illustrate how RFID facilitates increased traceability and control in manufacturing, which in turn enables the use of more lot splitting and smaller lot sizes. They provide insights on operating policies (RFID vs. bar-code tracking mechanisms, extent of lot splitting, and dispatching rules) and an operating condition (setup to processing time ratio) that affect the mean flow time and proportion of jobs tardy in a job shop. Their results show that (i) performance worsens when bar code is used in the presence of extensive lot splitting, (ii) process changes such as extensive lot splitting may be necessary to justify RFID, (iii) the earliest operation due date dispatching heuristic is attractive under extensive lot splitting conditions, and (iv) the performance improvement with RFID under conditions of increased lot splitting is more when the setup to processing time ratio is small.

Brintrup et al. (2010) use the seven Toyota Production System wastes as a template and view RFID technology as a vehicle to achieve leaner manufacturing through automated data collection, assurance of data dependencies, and improvements in production and inventory visibility. They test their tool-set on two cases from push-based multi-national fast moving consumer goods manufacturing companies. Their results, developed through opportunity analysis, illustrate the identification of areas for improvement and other areas of value.

Hu et al. (2011) use RFID-generated path data in a manufacturing shop floor to develop their MP-Mine algorithm based on the Apriori association rule mining algorithm. Their goal is to develop a means to predict object movement patterns by mining frequent path information. Their results indicate the effectiveness of their algorithm, which can be used to predict the next location and arrival time of each entity in a manufacturing shop floor. In a similar vein, Arkan and Landeghem (2011) place RFID tags on the floor or on Automated Guided Vehicles (AGVs) in a manufacturing shop floor environment and study their movements, through readers placed on the ceiling, and then use this information to determine appropriate placement location for the processing machines.

While a majority of studies on RFID in manufacturing do not differentiate items that are tagged from those that are not, Li et al. (2004) argue otherwise. Sometimes, not all components that are manufactured need to be tagged. Li et al. (2004) argue that only a selected set of *smart* parts need to be tagged and that even these parts are not tagged during their entire stay in a manufacturing shop floor. The criticality of observing detailed conditions of a smart part at certain locations in a shop floor dictates what is tagged and for how long. They discuss a system that deals with smart parts as one that first identifies parts that need to be 'smart' (through RFID tags) at any point in time and a system that allows for seamless communication between such smart parts and equipment used in automated flexible manufacturing environment that also includes quality control, packing, storage and delivery.

3 RFID in Manufacturing

As discussed earlier, RFID's characteristic that is useful the most in a manufacturing context is its ability to store, modify, and communicate item-level information. As customers demand customized products, there is an increasing trend toward mass customization of manufactured products. A traditional manufacturing system does not easily lend itself to customization since its effectiveness derives from its ability to efficiently produce a large number of similar products. A majority of existing mass customization initiatives involve human(s) in the loop and this invariably results in slowing the process as well as introducing an appreciable amount of errors. It is difficult to automate a manufacturing system when mass customization is desired. However, the incorporation of RFID in manufacturing shop floors help alleviate this issue, as discussed earlier with examples from the automobile industry.

While RFID tags are rather flexible in their use, several issues still remain. The issues discussed in Kapoor et al. (2009) as related to supply chains are also relevant to RFID use in manufacturing environments. Moreover, a manufacturing environment has its own idiosyncratic characteristics that pose some additional challenges for RFID use. For example, when items pass through a supply chain, they are generally not *processed* along the way whereas this is not true in a manufacturing environment. When an RFID-tagged item goes through processing (e.g., milling, heat-treatment), at least two issues need to be addressed: (1) where (i.e., the physical location) to place the RFID tags on each item, and (2) the durability of these tags under extreme (e.g., temperature, pressure) conditions. For example, how and where does one place an RFID tag on a steel sheet that is pressed to form another shape in a high-pressure press and then heat-treated at high temperatures?

Several studies (e.g., Arkan and Landeghem 2011) consider the movement of entities as they are processed in a manufacturing shop floor environment. They generate a map of these movements either through placement of RFID tags on AGVs with readers on the ceiling or on (or slightly below the surface of) the floor with RFID readers on the AGVs and then mining the data thus generated for patterns. They then use these patterns to determine the most appropriate distribution of machines on the manufacturing shop floor. When RFID tags are placed on (or slightly under) the floor, two issues need to be considered: (1) use of physically stronger RFID tags (e.g., those that are embedded in a hard to break plastic or resin strip) and (2) readability of these tags, since it is difficult to read tags that are closer to steel reinforcements in the floor. This is another issue with the use of RFID tags in a manufacturing environment - the presence of materials (e.g., liquid, metal) that render it difficult to read RFID tags. Although progress is being made to alleviate this issue (e.g., through placement of a 'buffer' between the tag and the substrate metal or the use of an appropriate communication frequency).

In addition to process mining, it has been shown that traditional dispatching heuristics can be improved with the incorporation of part location information (e.g., Thiesse and Fleisch 2008). While this is a good first step, it is also possible to extend this further by learning the best (distance-based and otherwise) heuristic to use based on an instantaneous snapshot of the manufacturing shop floor (since any given dispatching heuristic is not dominant across different manufacturing shop floor conditions). Learning the best dispatching heuristic to use for any given set of instantaneous pattern exhibited by the shop floor and then instantiating them at appropriate time instances is readily accomplished using a knowledge-based system (e.g., Kriett et al. 2012).

In automobile manufacturing assembly lines, reusable RFID tags are generally placed on the side of a skid carrying the chassis down the production line via a conveyor system. The specific details (e.g., color, type of engine, other options) are stored in the RFID tag, which is then read and updated along the way as the process of manufacturing/assembly proceeds. Upon completion of work on a given chassis, the information stored in the RFID tag on the skid is refreshed with the specifications of the next chassis it carries. While this certainly facilitates the manufacturing/assembly process, RFID tag(s) attached to the automobile with necessary information would aid in maintenance and repair when it's with its owner (i.e., customer) in the long term.

Tolerance is important in manufacturing where consistencies in small levels of tolerance are difficult to achieve with limited resources. This results in discarded items when they fall even slightly outside the pre-specified tolerance limit. While this is an issue when only one item is considered, the extent of the problem explodes with the number of parts that are to be put together as a final product increases with each of these parts having their own tolerance limits (Zhou 2009, Zhou and Piramuthu 2012). For example, the best case scenario that illustrates the power of item-level information is a final product with two components - one that is at the positive extreme of its tolerance limit and the other at the negative extreme of its tolerance limit - that is close to a perfect match even though each of these are close to being discarded. Using item-level tolerance information stored in RFID tags, the different components can be matched appropriately resulting in a good (if not optimal) quality final product.

4   Discussion

RFID is a promising technology for manufacturing environments where automation is the norm. Through automation of storing, modifying, and retrieving critical information on parts that are processed in these environments, common errors due to mis-specification (when manual paper-based systems are used whereby the paper with the specifications/instructions gets damaged, misplaced, or switched) can be easily prevented.

To summarize, some of the benefits of using RFID-generated item-level information include (1) refined control of manufacturing systems which leads to quality improvement, (2) timely response in exception handling situations through use of real-time information, (3) the ability to track and trace and to monitor logistics and production operations. As a relatively new technology to wide-spread large-scale manufacturing applications, RFID implementations have potential issues that need to be considered, including (1) high adoption risk since there are only a scattered few ROI evaluations in existence and the complete benefits are somewhat unknown/unmeasurable, (2) the high expense since RFID implementations include the tags themselves in addition to readers, necessary back-end systems, specialized personnel, (3) issues related to security and privacy of the tagged object since it now has locally stored information (unlike bar codes, where information is stored externally in database(s)), and (4) sometimes the potential benefits may not warrant related issues (e.g., resistance) that arise with change.

References

1. Arkan, I., Landeghem, H.V.: Controlling in-plant Logistics by Deploying RFID System in the Item-level Manufacturing: A Case Study. In: Proceedings of the 13th International Conference on Modern Information Technology in the Innovation Processes of the Industrial Enterprise, MITIP (2011)

2. Brintrup, A., Ranasinghe, D., McFarlane, D.: RFID Opportunity Analysis for Leaner Manufacturing. International Journal of Production Research 48(9), 2745–2764 (2010)
3. Higuera, A.G., Montalvo, A.C.: RFID-enhanced Multi-agent Based Control for a Machining System. Int'l J. of Flexible Manufacturing Systems 19(1), 41–61 (2007)
4. Hozak, K., Collier, D.A.: RFID as an Enabler of Improved Manufacturing Performance. Decision Sciences 39(4), 859–881 (2008)
5. Hu, K.F., Zhao, L., Xu, Y.C., Chen, L.: Research on Mining Frequent Path and Prediction Algorithms of Object Movement Patterns in RFID Database. Journal Applied Mechanics and Materials 109, 715–719 (2012)
6. Hua, J., Liang, T., Lei, Z.: Study and Design Real-Time Manufacturing Execution System Based on RFID. In: Proceedings of the Second International Conference on Intelligent Information Technology Application, pp. 591–594 (2008)
7. Huang, G.Q., Zhang, Y.F., Chen, X., Newman, S.T.: RFID-enabled Real-time Wireless Manufacturing for Adaptive Assembly Planning and Control. Journal of Intelligent Manufacturing 19(6), 701–713 (2008)
8. Ivantysynova, L., Klafft, M., Ziekow, H., Günther, O., Kara, S.: RFID in Manufacturing: The Investment Decision. In: Proceedings of the pacific Asia Conference on Information Systems, PACIS (2009)
9. Kapoor, G., Zhou, W., Piramuthu, S.: Challenges Associated with RFID Implementations in Supply Chains. European Journal of Information Systems 18, 526–533 (2009)
10. Kriett, P., Grunow, M., Piramuthu, S.: Knowledge-based Dynamic Job Shop Scheduling with RFID-generated Item-level Information. Working paper (2012)
11. Li, Z., Gadh, R., Prabhu, B.S.: Applications of RFID Technology and Smart Parts in Manufacturing. In: Proceedings of DETC 2004: ASME 2004 Design Engineering Technical Conferences and Computers and Information in Engineering Conference, DETC 2004-57662, p. 7 (2004)
12. Sharp, K.R.: Lessons From The Front: Three Forward-thinking RFID Implementers are Paving the Way for Wide-scale, Real-world Applications. Supply Chain Systems 19(5) (1999), http://209.235.222.4/reader/1999_05/index.htm
13. Thiesse, F., Fleisch, E.: On the value of Location Information to Lot Scheduling in Complex Manufacturing Processes. International Journal of Production Economics 112(2), 532–547 (2008)
14. Trappey, A.J.C., Lu, T.-H., Fu, L.-D.: Development of an Intelligent Agent System for Collaborative Mold Production with RFID Technology. Robotics and Computer-integrated Manufacturing 25(1), 42–56 (2009)
15. Wang, L.-C., Lin, S.-K., Huang, L.-P.: A RFID Based Agile Manufacturing Planning and Control System. In: Wen, P., Li, Y., Polkowski, L., Yao, Y., Tsumoto, S., Wang, G. (eds.) RSKT 2009. LNCS, vol. 5589, pp. 441–451. Springer, Heidelberg (2009)
16. Zhang, Y., Qua, T., Hoa, O.K., Huang, G.Q.: Agent-based Smart Gateway for RFID-enabled Real-time Wireless Manufacturing. International Journal of Production Research 49(5), 1337–1352 (2011)
17. Zhou, W.: RFID and item-level information visibility. European Journal of Operational Research 198(1), 252–258 (2009)
18. Zhou, W., Piramuthu, S.: Manufacturing with Item-Level RFID Information: From Macro to Micro Quality Control. International Journal of Production Economics 135(2), 929–938 (2012)
19. Zhou, W., Piramuthu, S.: Remanufacturing/Refurbishing with RFID-generated Item-Level Information. In: Frick, J., Laugen, B.T. (eds.) APMS 2011. IFIP AICT, vol. 384, pp. 165–170. Springer, Heidelberg (2012)

Semantic Data Model for Operation and Maintenance of the Engineering Asset

Andreas Koukias, Dražen Nadoveza, and Dimitris Kiritsis

École Polytechnique Fédérale de Lausanne,
Laboratory for Computer-Aided Design and Production,
STI-IGM-LICP, Station 9, CH-1015, Lausanne, Switzerland
{andreas.koukias,drazen.nadoveza,dimitris.kiritsis}@epfl.ch

Abstract. The management of engineering assets within an organization is a challenging task that aims to optimize their performance through efficient decision making. However, the current asset data management systems suffer from poor system interoperability, data integration issues as well as an enormous amount of stored data, thus preventing a seamless flow of information. The aim of this work is to propose a semantic data model for engineering asset management, focusing on the operation and maintenance phase of its life cycle. Ontologies are proposed because they can capture the semantics of data, create a shared vocabulary to describe the knowledge for sharing in the domain and provide reasoning capabilities. This model will gather all the knowledge necessary to assist in the decision making process in order to improve the asset's availability, longevity and quality of operations.

Keywords: asset, asset management, maintenance, ontology model, semantics.

1 Introduction

Engineering assets within an organization can be the foundation for its success and future and are defined as "as any core, acquired elements of significant value to the organization, which provides and/or requires – according to a user or provider point of view – services for this organization" [1]. The management of physical assets, such as machining tools, can be a challenging task in order to optimize their performance through efficient decision making and reduce their maintenance costs, increase the revenue and guarantee their overall effectiveness [2]. Physical or engineering assets, such as machining tools and containers, are distinguished from intangible or virtual assets such as knowledge, software, or financial assets [3].

According to the definition of asset management proposed by the Cooperative Research Centre for Integrated Engineering Asset Management (CIEAM) [4], and adopted for this work, asset management is "the process of organizing, planning and controlling the acquisition, use, care, refurbishment, and/or disposal of physical assets to optimize their service delivery potential and to minimize the related risks and costs over their entire life through the use of intangible assets such as knowledge based decision making applications and business processes." Asset management is a holistic

C. Emmanouilidis, M. Taisch, D. Kiritsis (Eds.): APMS 2012, Part II, IFIP AICT 398, pp. 49–55, 2013.

and interdisciplinary approach that covers in the context of physical assets the whole life cycle of the asset, from the acquisition to the disposal of the asset. Its scope extends from the daily operations of assets trying to meet the targeted levels of service to supporting the organization's delivery strategies, satisfying the regulatory and legal requirements and minimizing related risks and costs [5-7]. Asset management is particularly important now with the ageing of the equipment, the fluctuating requirements in the strategy and operation levels and the emphasis on health and safety requirements [6].

We consider that the key concept to achieve optimization of asset management is the management of the asset's data. Information systems in asset management extend from collecting, storing and analyzing the asset information to supporting decision making and providing an integrated view [5]. Decision makers use a variety of tools on their day-to-day and long-term activities and their effectiveness depend greatly on the quality of data. The requirements for the asset data demand that it is always complete, accurate, timely, consistent and accessible [8]. It is important that organizations can efficiently track the current and historical information of the assets concerning their status and component configuration along their lifecycle [2]. However, asset data management systems currently suffer from system interoperability, data integration issues as well as the enormous amount of the stored data, thus preventing a seamless flow of information for monitoring and controlling the assets [8-10].

The vision of Semantic Web can be the key to the harmonization of the information models, since it suggests using software agents that are able to understand the meaning of data and create connections between data automatically, to gain new information. Based on this vision, ontologies can be used to capture the semantics of data, resolve semantic heterogeneities and optimize data quality and availability. Gruber [11] defines the ontologies as explicit formal specifications of the terms in a domain and relations among them whereas Noy and McGuiness [12] describes an ontology as a formal explicit description of concepts in a domain of discourse, with properties of each concept describing various features and attributes of the concepts and restrictions on slots. Ontologies offer a shared vocabulary to describe the knowledge for sharing in a certain domain or application area.

Among the main phases that consist the engineering asset lifecycle [2], the current work focuses on the operation and maintenance phase where the aim is to optimize the overall performance of the asset and guarantee its availability and longevity. The main obstacle is that available information concerning the asset's operation, configuration, maintenance and planning is currently disparate and thus not put to effective use in order to improve its quality of operations. The aim of this work is to propose a semantic data model that will integrate all this information for an engineering asset within an organization. Based on the Semantic Web vision, ontologies are proposed since they can capture the semantics of data, resolve semantic heterogeneities, create a shared domain vocabulary and optimize data quality and availability. We consider the various entities that are involved in the asset's usage and maintenance, as well as their relations, and try to develop a semantic data model that will assist in increasing the productivity of the asset and maintaining it, with minimum cost and high reliability.

2   Related Work

There are many research efforts using or recommending ontologies in the asset management domain, but to our knowledge none are focusing on the operation and maintenance phase of the asset's lifecycle. In [6] the authors develop an initial and fundamental asset management ontology and subsequent process architecture in order to support an organization's asset management initiatives, using a manual text mining approach. In [9], ontologies with Description Logic are used in a case study in asset lifecycle management in order to demonstrate the benefits of implementing ontology models in industry. An ontology-based implementation for exploiting the characteristics of time in asset lifecycle management systems is presented in [10], mainly in maintenance but also considering the entire lifecycle.

The development of a generic asset configuration ontology is recommended in [2], in combination with a prototype workflow management system, in order to provide a generic and active asset configuration management framework for a better visibility of through-life asset configurations. Furthermore, the authors in [13] propose a conceptual model for the adoption and implementation of ontologies in the area of Road Asset Management, in order to assist the automated information retrieval and exchange between heterogeneous asset management applications.

Moreover, in order to achieve an efficient asset management, the minimum functional requirements at the operational level are presented at [14], whereas in [8] the requirements are outlined and a model for improving the strategy by classifying the assets is proposed. Lastly, concerning the use of ontologies on the maintenance domain, an ontology to support semantic maintenance architecture is proposed in [15], a domain ontology for industrial maintenance is shown in [16] and an ontology in order to model the condition monitoring and maintenance domain knowledge is introduced in [17].

3   Asset Management Semantic Data Model

Based on the available literature in the defined scope of activities, we propose a semantic data model for the operation and maintenance of an engineering asset, which can be seen in Figure 1. The dotted line in the middle of the model separates the static asset data, e.g. asset function and specifications from the dynamic asset data e.g. operation data and maintenance schedule. The model consists of the main upper asset ontology and the related lower asset event domain ontology. In order to provide a better understanding, the top-level concepts of the proposed model are firstly defined below:

- Asset: the engineering asset, as previously defined. It may be possible to break down the asset in its technical components, which may be considered as assets themselves.

- Asset_Specification: static data originating from documentation and containing all asset specification data. This is developed during the design and building phases of the asset lifecycle and depicting the target asset operation and maintenance data in order to guarantee performance and availability.
- Asset_Function: the main functionality and possibly also secondary functionalities, performed by the asset.
- Actor: the person or group of persons in the plant who is responsible for operating and managing the asset and has a specific functional role
- Asset_State: the current physical state of the asset which can be either normal, degraded or in failure.
- Maintenance_Schedule: defines the sequence of asset maintenance activities, specifying the maintenance tasks and their frequency.
- Asset_Operation_Data: data stored during the operation of the asset, e.g. asset temperature. The instances over a period of time provide a historical view of the asset's operations. Depending on the values of the operation data, this can be separated into categories of operation status.
- Asset_Configuration_Data: record of the asset configuration status at any point of time. The instances can assist in tracking the current and historical changes of asset configurations.
- Asset_Maintenance_Data: data concerning the performed asset maintenance activities.

We consider that the events that take place during the asset's operation and maintenance phase can be modeled as a lower event domain ontology. Initially, we define an event as any transient occurrence of interest for the asset which can be distinguished between internal events as changes of state caused by an internal asset transformation and external events with direct effects on the asset. In this work the low-level events are considered, which declare every status update and are necessary for monitoring the state of the asset e.g. value update. The high-level events that exist on a higher abstraction level and concern the long term asset strategy are not in the scope. A special type of low-level event is the Alarm which represents an abnormal asset's state that requires the user's attention and has warning purposes.

The current approach recommends the use of the ontology reasoning capabilities on the proposed model. Reasoning can be applied in many different scenarios in the ontology, based on predefined rules, in order to provide the capability of answering queries e.g. if the asset fulfills the operational requirements, and thus generate new knowledge.

In order to provide a better understanding, a typical scenario is described using the proposed semantic model. Firstly, we define the different Operation_Data_Types for the asset according to its operation values and corresponding to different operation phases. These phases can be either normal, e.g. operating, warming up or belong to different types of abnormal operation mode. If a value from the operation data e.g. the asset temperature, exceeds its predefined thresholds according to the Asset_Operation_Specification, the Asset_Operation_Data is classified to its respective operation mode and the relevant Asset_Event is raised accordingly from the lower

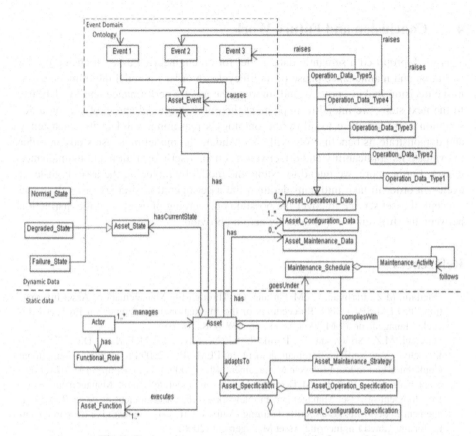

Fig. 1. Engineering asset management semantic data model

event ontology. When the specific Asset_Event is raised, the historical As-
set_Operation_Data, Asset_Configuration_Data and Asset_Maintenance_Data can be
examined, as well as other Asset_Event instances, in order to evaluate whether there
have been indications leading to this event e.g. temperature consistently rising towards and eventually surpassing the threshold or possibly skipping a maintenance
action or adapting a wrong configuration. Based on predefined rules and using the
reasoning capabilities, one possibility would be the classification of the asset in the
Degraded_State and the subsequent adjustment of the adapted Maintenance_Schedule
e.g. repair or replace a defective asset component before production begins. Another
possibility would be the need to modify the Configuration_Data, e.g. reduce the rpm,
in order to keep the Asset_Operation_Data within its specifications.

Overall, a set of rules and procedures can be defined to support the reasoning system to make knowledge which is implicit only to the experts, explicit, by using the
available events, operational data, configuration data and maintenance data in order to
adjust to an improved maintenance strategy as well as select an optimal operation
configuration, thus managing the evolution of asset configuration. Overall, the proposed model can use the ontology knowledge to improve the asset performance,
longevity and availability.

4   Conclusion and Future Work

This work proposed a semantic data model for an engineering asset, focusing on the operation and maintenance phase of its lifecycle, in order to model the domain, assist in the decision making process and improve the asset's performance and availability. In the next steps, we intend to implement the ontology model and evolve it on a description logic language to allow the ontology's reasoning, validate its consistency and demonstrate its benefits. We will also validate the model in a case study in order to evaluate its applicability and effectiveness on an asset's operation and maintenance phases. Furthermore, we intend to extend the model by including the asset high-level events in order to take into consideration the asset operation strategy, as well as the concept of asset service to cover the possible outsourcing of assets and the distinction between the different roles of asset owner and provider.

References

1. Ouertani, M.Z., Parlikad, A., McFarlane, D.: Through-life Management of Asset Information. In: PLM-SP4 - 2008 Proceedings of the International Conference on Product Lifecycle Management, PLM 2008, Seoul, pp. 438–448 (2008)
2. Ouertani, M.Z., Srinivasan, V., Parlikad, A.K.N., Luyer, E., McFarlane, D.C.: Through-life active asset configuration management. In: PLM-SP5 - 2009 Proceedings International Conference on Product Lifecycle Management, PLM 2009, Bath, UK, pp. 119–207 (2009)
3. Stapleberg, R.F.: Risk Based Decision Making in Integrated Asset Management: From Development of Asset Management Frameworks to the Development of Asset Risk Management Plan. Professional Skills Training Courses: CIEAM - Cooperative Research Centre for Integrated Engineering Asset Management (2006)
4. Cooperative Research Centre for Integrated Engineering Asset Management (CIEAM), http://www.cieam.com/
5. Koronios, A., Steenstrup, C., Haider, A.: Information and Operational Technologies Nexus for Asset Lifecycle Management. In: 4th World Congress on Engineering Asset Management, Athens, Greece (2009)
6. Frolov, V., Megel, D., Bandara, W., Sun, Y., Ma, L.: Building An Ontology And Process Architecture For Engineering Asset Management. In: 4th World Congress On Engineering Asset, Athens, Greece (2009)
7. Frolov, V., Ma, L., Sun, Y., Bandara, W.: Identifying core function of asset management. In: Amadi-Echendu, J. (ed.) Engineering Asset Management Review, vol. 1. Springer, London (2010)
8. de Leeuw, V., Snitkin, S.: ARC Advisory Group. Asset Information Management: From Strategy to Benefit. In: 7th International Conference on Product Lifecycle Management, PLM 2010, Bremen, Germany (2010)
9. Matsokis, A., Zamofing, S., Kiritsis, D.: Ontology-based Modeling for Complex Industrial Asset Lifecycle Management: a Case Study. In: 7th International Conference on Product Lifecycle Management, PLM 2010, Bremen, Germany (2010)
10. Matsokis, A., Kiritsis, D.: Ontology-Based Implementation of an Advanced Method for Time Treatment in Asset Lifecycle Management. In: 5th World Congress in Engineering Asset Management, WCEAM 2010, Brisbane, Australia (2010)

11. Gruber, T.R.: Towards principles for the design of ontologies used for knowledge sharing. International Journal of Human Computer Studies 43, 907–928 (1993)
12. Noy, N.F., McGuiness, D.L.: Ontology development 101: a guide to creating your first ontology, Stanford KSL Technical Report KSL (2009)
13. Nastasie, D.L., Koronios, A.: The Role of Standard Information Model. In: Road Asset Management. In: 4th World Congress on Engineering Asset Management, WCEAM 2009, Springer-Verlag London Ltd., Athens (2009)
14. Haider, A.: Information technologies implementation and organizational behavior: An asset management perspective. In: Technology Management in the Energy Smart World, PICMET, 2011 Proceedings of PICMET 2011, pp. 1–11 (2011)
15. Karray, M.H., Morello-Chebel, B., Zerhouni, N.: Towards a maintenance semantic architecture. In: 4th World Congress on Engineering Asset Management, WCEAM 2009, Athens, Greece (2009)
16. Karray, M.H., Morello-Chebel, B., Zerhouni, N.: A Formal Ontology for Industrial Maintenance. In: Terminology & Ontology: Theories and Applications, TOTh Conference 2011, Annecy, France (2011)
17. Jin, G., Xiang, Z., Lv, F.: Semantic integrated condition monitoring and maintenance of complex system. In: 16th International Conference on Industrial Engineering and Engineering Management, IE&EM 2009, pp. 670–674 (2009)

Towards Changeable Production Systems – Integration of the Internal and External Flow of Information as an Enabler for Real-Time Production Planning and Controlling

Volker Stich, Niklas Hering, Stefan Kompa, and Ulrich Brandenburg

Institute for Industrial Management at RWTH Aachen University,
Pontdriesch 14/16, 52062 Aachen, Germany
{Volker.Stich,Niklas.Hering,Stefan.Kompa,
Ulrich.Brandenburg}@fir.rwth-aachen.de

Abstract. In this paper, it will be shown how information and communication technologies (ICT) act as enablers to realize changeable production systems within the German machinery and equipment industry. A cybernetic structure is proposed to design and operate systems that have to cope with a high degree of complexity due to continuously changing environment conditions. The integration of IT-Systems along the order processing of small-and-medium-sized enterprises (SME) is shown to be one of the missing links of changeable production systems in practice. A demonstration case is presented in which standardized interfaces of IT-Systems enhance real-time data exchange between the relevant planning levels of producing companies, their suppliers and customers.

Keywords: Changeability, real-time capability, production planning and control, machinery and equipment industry.

1   Introduction

Nowadays, the German machinery and equipment industry faces many challenges. The increasing variety of products in combination with increasing market dynamics (e.g. shorter product life cycles) results in a growing complexity of the order management processes [1-4]. Additionally, the increasing and volatile demand of customers in combination with quantity and delivery time reduction has a direct impact on value creation processes of the order management [1]. On-time delivery of products has to be realized despite the volatile demand of customers[1] [5]. Today manufacturing companies cope with these turbulent market conditions by keeping extensive stock levels. High stock levels are treacherous. They hide problems within the production systems, are very cost intensive and do not increase flexibility. Additionally, the rapid spread of new technologies, aggressive competition, closer integration of

---

[1] Incoming orders may show an average monthly variation of 20-40 percent in the German machinery and equipment industry [5].

C. Emmanouilidis, M. Taisch, D. Kiritsis (Eds.): APMS 2012, Part II, IFIP AICT 398, pp. 56–63, 2013.

goods and capital flows as well as the fragmentation and dynamic reconfiguration of value chains pose unprecedented challenges for the German machinery and equipment industry [6]. These uncertainties directly affect the company's internal planning and control processes. The variety of these processes confronts organizations and information systems with a significant coordination effort [7]. According to a survey by the German association of the machinery and equipment industry (VDMA) the majority of companies considers the capability of order fulfillment processes as a key success factor for the future [5]. To this day, planning and execution of order processing – from offer processing to the final shipment of the product – is still a part of the production planning and control (PPC) [8]. Production planning and control is almost entirely integrated into information systems. In order to manage dynamic influences on processes within order processing, a deficiency in the processing of decision-relevant and real-time information can be observed [9], [10].

2   The Human Organism Acts as a Role Model for a Changeable Production System

One solution to these turbulent market conditions discussed by academia in recent years are flexible production systems. Flexibility may be described as the ability of a system to adapt quickly and cost efficient within a pre-defined time horizon [11]. However, flexible production systems are not sufficient enough to establish a sustainable, competitive position for the German machinery and equipment industry because of their limited long-term potential to react to rapidly changing external influences [12-14]. A systematic approach is quickly required for a suitable design and operation of changeable production systems. In this context changeability stands for the development of flexibility, which allows changing the system reactively or even proactively beyond known uncertainties [6], [12], [13] (cf. **Fig. 1**).

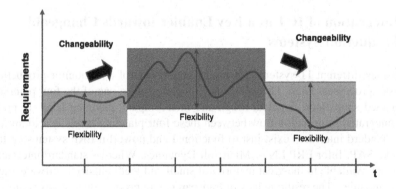

Fig. 1. Flexibility and Changeability [7]

The human organism has proven itself over millions of years as one of the most reliable and most flexible systems. Thus, it can be considered as a role-model of a functional, complex organization in management cybernetics [15-18].

A key success factor for the ideal control of the human organism is the existence of reflexive and conscious coordination mechanisms of the different organs, muscles and nerves. The reaction of human beings depends on the situation and the type of external influences[2]. Any relevant information on biomechanical or electrical pulses is available to the central nerve system for both types of responses to dynamic environmental conditions in real-time [16], [18]. Therefore human beings adapt to change or anticipate the need to adapt by having a varied repertoire of actions and activities at their disposal. Thus, the human is in the position to take the appropriate action or reaction consciously or unconsciously, based on real-time information.

Transferred to a production system, it means that only the transparency of information in real-time and subsequent real-time processes make changeability possible. Furthermore, decision-making mechanisms have to exist in order to select and evaluate the sum of the possible, appropriate alternatives regarding the situation requirements (cost effectiveness vs. operational effectiveness). Transferred to the machinery and equipment industry and thus transferred to concrete practical problems, it means in order to establish the ability to coordinate in real-time value networks, it needs:

1. to increase the ability of integration of various companies and business units. The use of biunique information throughout the supply chain and also a consistent definition of standardized interfaces between different IT-systems, that are being used for planning and control processes, form the technological enablers for the realization of a changeable production system [11].
2. to improve the ability to respond in planning and control processes significantly. This implies, that the static planning and control logic, which is based on the Manufacturing Resource Planning (MRP II) concept, must be replaced by a decentralized operating and real-time capable planning and control logic with closed-loops.

3   Integration of ICT as a Key Enabler towards Changeable Production Systems

In companies different IT-systems are used to plan, control and monitor production and logistic processes. These IT-systems may be assigned to one of the four planning levels, named shop floor, detailed, rough and intercompany planning level. In practice, an integrated information flow between these four planning levels is seldom (cf. **Fig. 2**). Standard interfaces exist just to functional and powerful ERP systems on the market like SAP, Infor ERP.LN or Microsoft Dynamics. Whereas standard interfaces are often not available to the great majority of small and medium-sized software engineering companies. The resulting lack of transparency in production systems is one of

---

[2] So e.g. they might react to heat on a reflex, but to cold they might react by making a conscious decision.

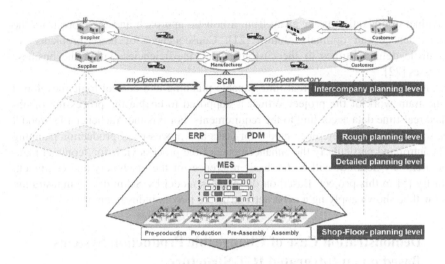

Fig. 2. Internal and external planning level

the biggest weaknesses of ERP, MES, PDM and Supply Chain Management (SCM) systems. Consequences of the problem are unrealistic delivery times to the customers and inefficiencies within the business processes [22].

Therefore the research project "WInD" aims at improving the integration ability of supply chains fundamentally. This aspect is the technological and informational enabler for the realization of a changeable production system. Thus, the crucial standardization gaps of the concrete use case for the machinery and equipment industry are being closed in the framework of the project. Standardized interfaces should not only connect the rough with the detailed planning level (ERP- to MES-systems), but also guarantee the accurate synchronization of master data between ERP- and PDM-systems. Additionally the transfer of the electronic product code (EPC) to the machinery and equipment industry should also improve the data quality by implementing an opportunity to identify the product data (standard and custom parts) biunique in the future.

The necessary data quality and information allocation in the machinery and equipment industry is currently not available due to heterogeneously constructed IT-environments (lack of standardized interfaces and subsystem diversity) [19]. Non-bidirectional data results in inconsistent master data for planning and control activities of the entire production network. Parallel manipulated master data (parts lists or material master data) in Enterprise Resource Planning- (ERP) and Product Data Management- (PDM) systems are not sufficiently (logically and in regard of content) synchronized. The concept of Manufacturing Resource Planning (MRP II) still represents the central logic of production planning and control. However, the centralized and push-oriented MRP II planning logic is not able to plan and measure dynamic processes adequately due to diverse disturbances, which often occur in production environments [20]. The traditional hierarchical planning method leads to an iterative planning process that dissects PPC-tasks into smaller work packages. Therefore, individual optimization is far away from a holistic approach and therefore from the achievement of an optimal solution [21]. Consequences of these problems are unrealistic delivery times to the customers and inefficiencies within the business processes [22].

A new decentralized and real-time capable planning and control logic, developed in the framework of the project WInD, is supposed to enable the processing of obtained real-time data according to the requirements. For this the Aachener-PPC-model as a science-accepted reference model for tasks and processes of production planning and control and particularly the enhancements of the process view for "contract manufacturers" by Schmidt will be the basic reference for the machinery and equipment industry [5] in this project. Based on the process model by Schmidt a demonstration case will be shown applying a cybernetic structure into an industry environment.

4   Demonstration Case of Changeable Production Systems Based on an Integrated ICT-Structure

One of the main issues of ICT research is that its results as presented by educational institutions are not directly accessible to industry. Therefore it is difficult for industry, especially SMEs, to comprehend and to adapt to the technological advances in a direct way. To overcome this gap numerous works have been conducted in the field of manufacturing education and industrial learning [23-25]. Demonstration is an established instructional method for manufacturing education. Within the research project WInD funded by the German Research Foundation DFG as part of the Cluster of Excellence "Integrative Production Technology for High-Wage Countries" the Institute for Industrial Management at RWTH Aachen University and participating SMEs develop a demonstration setting that visualizes the IT-integration as an enabler for changeability. Therefore, the academic solution to changeable production systems as described in chapters 2 and 3 is consequently transferred into a practical environment to be accessible for industry. **Fig. 3** illustrates the process and information flow model of the demonstration case. The process and information flow model visualizes the integration of five IT solutions: Enterprise Resource Planning (ERP), Product Data Management (PDM), Manufacturing Execution Systems (MES), an electronic market place (VDMA eMarket[3]), an Electronic Product Code Information Services (EPCIS)[4] framework and the myOpenFactory (myOF) platform[5]. The main goal of the

---

[3] The VDMA-E-Market (http://www.vdma-e-market.de/en/) is a platform for product search established the VDMA (Verband Deutscher Maschinen- und Anlagenbau - German Engineering Federation).

[4] EPCIS is a standard to capture EPCIS-events containing the information *What* (e.g. a certain product), *Where* (e.g. outgoing goods), *When* (e.g. 3.05 pm) and *Why* (e.g. product shipped).

[5] The myOpenFactory platform acts as a standardized interface between the different ERP-systems of participating SMEs. Their ERP-systems only have to be mapped once to the platform allowing automated exchange of order processing relevant data within the whole production network.

demonstration case is to show how the order processing with such a heterogeneous IT-structure can be automated through the integration of IT-Systems.

The demonstration case features the following highlights:

- Automation of the order processing of a customized product in a heterogeneous IT-landscape.
- Full integration and bidirectional information flows between ERP and MES (ERP-MES interface).
- Automated Engineering Change Requests (ECR) in PDM based on customer changes in ERP-system.
- Full integration and bidirectional information flows between ERP and PDM (ERP-PDM interface).
- Integration of a web shop for special demands and automated inquiry to potential suppliers.
- EPCIS communication framework to facilitate real-time information on changes of delivery dates.

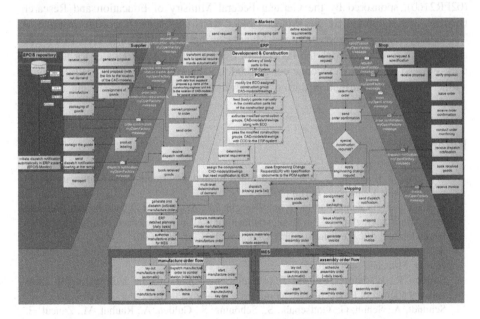

Fig. 3. Process and information flow model of the WInD demonstration case

5   Conclusion and Outlook

In this paper an approach for changeable production systems enabled by ICT-integration has been presented. It was shown how cybernetic principles have been transferred to a production network representative for the German machinery and equipment industry. A framework for the ICT-integration was introduced to facilitate changeable production systems in practice. To overcome the barriers between the research conducted by educational institutions and industry a demonstration case has been presented reflecting a typical setting within the SME-dominated industry. The main features of the demonstration case have been presented.

The demonstration case will be implemented at the Campus Cluster Logistic (CCL) which is currently under construction at RWTH Aachen University. Within the CCL a demonstration factory will be erected demonstrating the principles of changeability and IT-integration in the manufacturing industry. Further development stages of this demonstration case at the CCL will be the integration of a generator of transaction data. Therewith, it will be possible to simulate the effects of varying different setting within ERP-Systems in the whole supply chain. This research is part of the Cluster of Excellence "Integrative Production Technology for High-Wage Countries" at RWTH Aachen university were ontologies and design methodologies for cognition enhanced, self-optimizing Production Networks are being developed.

Acknowledgement. The research project "WInD - Changeable production systems through integrated IT-structures and decentralized production planning and control" (02PR2160), sponsored by the German Federal Ministry of Education and Research (BMBF) and supported by the Project Holder Karlsruhe at the Karlsruhe Institute of Technology (KIT) for Production and Manufacturing Technologies (PTKA-PFT). The authors wish to acknowledge the Federal Ministry and the Project Holder for their support. We also wish to acknowledge our gratitude and appreciation to all the WInD project partners for their contribution during the development of various ideas and concepts presented in this paper.

References

1. Westkämper, E., Zahn, E.: Wandlungsfähige Produktionssysteme – Das Stuttgarter Unternehmensmodell. Springer, Berlin (2009)
2. Westkämper, E., Zahn, E., Balve, P., Tilebein, M.: Ansätze zur Wandlungsfähigkeit von Produktionsunternehmen - Ein Bezugsrahmen für die Unternehmensentwicklung im turbulenten Umfeld. Wt Werkstattstechnik Online 90(1/2), 22–26 (2000)
3. Schuh, G.: Produktkomplexität managen: Strategien - Methoden - Tools. 2. Auflage. Hanser. München [u. a.] (2005)
4. Stratton, R., Warburton, R.D.H.: The strategic integration of agile and lean supply. International Journal of Production Economics 85, 183–198 (2003)
5. Schmidt, A., Schuh, G., Gottschalk, S., Schöning, S., Gulden, A., Rauhut, M., Zancul, E., Ring, T., Augustin, R. (2007) Effizient, schnell und erfolgreich - Strategien im Maschinen- und Anlagenbau. VDMA-Studie. VDMA. Frankfurt (2007)
6. Nyhuis, P.: High Resolution Production Management. In: Brecher, C., Klocke, F., Schmitt, R., Schuh, G. (hrsg.) AWK 2008 - Wettbewerbsfaktor Produktionstechnik. Aachener Perspektiven, vol. 2008, Shaker, Aachen (2008)
7. Scholz-Reiter, B., Philipp, T., de Beer, C., Windt, K., Freitag, M.: Steuerung von Logistiksystemen - auf dem Weg zur Selbststeuerung. Konferenzband zum 3. In: Pfohl, H.-C., Wimmer, T. (hrsg.) BVL-Wissenschaftssymposium Logistik, pp. 11–25. Deutscher Verkehrs-Verlag, Hamburg (2006)

8. Schuh, G., Roesgen, R.: Produktionsplanung und -steuerung. In: Schuh, G. (hrsg.) Grundlagen, Gestaltung und Konzepte (Hrsg.). völlig neu bearbeitete Auflage, vol. 3, pp. 28–80. Springer, Heidelberg (2006)
9. Swafford, P.M., Ghosh, S., Murthy, N.: Achieving supply chain agility through IT integration and flexibility. International Journal of Production Economics 116(2), 288–297 (2008)
10. Zhou, W.: RFID and item-level information visibility. European Journal of Operational Research 198(1), 252–258 (2009)
11. Nyhuis, P., Reinhart, G., Abele, E.: Wandlungsfähige Produktionssysteme – Heute die Industrie von morgen gestalten. PZH - Produktionstechnisches Zentrum, Garbsen (2008)
12. Spath, D., Hirsch-Kreinsen, H., Kinkel, S.: Organisatorische Wandlungsfähigkeit produzierender Unternehmen. Fraunhofer IRB, Stuttgart (2008)
13. Wiendahl, H.-P., Hernandez, R.: Wandlungsfähigkeit - neues Zielfeld in der Fabrikplanung. Industrie Management 16(5), 37–41 (2000)
14. Reinhart, G., Dürrschmidt, S., Hirschberg, A., Selke, C.: Reaktionsfähigkeit - Eine Antwort auf turbulente Märkte. ZWF (1-2), 21–24 (1999)
15. Strina, G.: Zur Messbarkeit nicht-quantitativer Größen im Rahmen unternehmenskybernetischer Prozesse. Aachen, Techn. Hochsch., Habil.-Schr. (2006)
16. Malik, F.: Strategie des Managements komplexer Systeme – Ein Beitrag zur Management-Kybernetik evolutionärer Systeme, Haupt, Bern (2006)
17. Espejo, R., Schuhmann, W., Schwaninger, M.: Organizational Transforming and Learning. A Cybernetic Approach to Management. John Wiley & Sons, Chichester (1996)
18. Beer, S.: Kybernetische Führungslehre. Herder & Herder, New York (1973)
19. Straube, F., Scholz-Reiter, B., ten Hompel, M.: BMBF-Voruntersuchung: Logistik im produzierenden Gewerbe. Abschlussbericht (2008)
20. Pfohl, H.: Logistiksysteme: betriebswirtschaftliche Grundlagen. Springer, Berlin (2004)
21. Hellmich, K.: Kundenorientierte Auftragsabwicklung - Engpassorientierte Planung und Steuerung des Ressourceneinsatzes. DUV, Wiesbaden (2003)
22. Schuh, G., Westkämper, E.: Liefertreue im Maschinen- und Anlagenbau: Stand – Potentiale – Trends. Studienergebnisse des FIR, IPA, WZL. Aachen u. Stuttgart (2006)
23. Chryssolouris, G., Mavrikios, D., Papakostas, N., Mourtzis, D.: Education in Manufacturing Technology & Science: A view on Future Challenges & Goals, Inaugural Keynote. In: International Conference on Manufacturing Science and Technology, ICMAST, Melaka, Malaysia (2006)
24. Chryssolouris, G., Mourtzis, D.: Challenges For Manufacturing Education. In: Proceedings of CIMEC 2008, CIRP International Manufacturing Engineering Education Conference, Nantes, France (October 2008)
25. Shen, J.Y., Dunn, D., Shen, Y.: Challenges Facing U.S. Manufacturing and Strategies. Journal of Industrial Technology 23(2), 1–10 (2007)

Integrated Model-Based Manufacturing for Rapid Product and Process Development

Vesna Mandic[1], Radomir Radisa[2], Vladan Lukovic[1], and Milan Curcic[1]

[1] Faculty of Engineering University of Kragujevac, Kragujevac, Serbia
{Mandic,vladan.lukovic,ctc}@kg.ac.rs
[2] Lola Institute, Belgrade, Serbia
radomir.radisa@li.rs

Abstract. The paper presents integrative model-based approach in application of virtual engineering technologies in rapid product and process design and manufacturing. This has resulted in integration of so called CA- technologies and Virtual Reality in product design and FE numerical simulations and optimization of production processes, as digital prototyping of product and processes, from one side, and rapid prototyping techniques as physical prototyping, on the other side. Reverse engineering and coordinate metrology have been also applied in re-engineering of sheet metal forming process of existing product, with aim at generation of initial digital information about product and final quality control on multi-sensor coordinate measurement machine.

Keywords: model-based manufacturing, virtual engineering, rapid prototyping, virtual manufacturing.

1 Introduction

Model-based manufacturing implies technological integration of CA technologies (CAD/CAM/CAE) in product development with VM technologies (Virtual Manufacturing) for modelling of manufacturing processes and application of rapid technologies (RP/RT/RM) for testing and validation purposes. It results in 3D digital model of a product/tool, but also in the virtual model of manufacturing processes in computer environment and physical prototypes of components and assemblies. VM is based on nonlinear finite element analysis and it enables optimisation of key factors of production for validation of different concepts of manufacturing processes and optimization of e relevant parameters for shop within the whole set of "what if" scenarios. In a word, a capability to "manufacture in the computer" is so powerful tool which reduces the errors, cuts the costs and shortens the time of design, because all modifications are made before the actual manufacturing process. Besides CAD modelling, 3D model of a product/tool can be also rapidly generated in digital form using reverse engineering, remodelled and exported to one of the systems for rapid prototyping (RP), rapid tooling (RT) or rapid manufacturing (RM). Virtual and rapid prototypes obtained in this way can be used for testing the functionality of product or assembly and different concepts in the early stage of design without expensive and long-term

C. Emmanouilidis, M. Taisch, D. Kiritsis (Eds.): APMS 2012, Part II, IFIP AICT 398, pp. 64–71, 2013.
© IFIP International Federation for Information Processing 2013

trial-and-error attempts in traditional design and production. Virtual manufacturing also uses virtual reality (VR) as advanced technology for 3D presentation of model's structure, composition and behaviour as if it were physically manufactured.

Large number of papers presents the most recent investigations and achievements in the area of virtual and rapid product and processes development, realized in the integrated model-based system, for modelling, simulation, optimization, control and verification of the real production systems and designed products [1-3]. This paper starts with description of the model-based manufacturing system components, i.e. technologies of virtual engineering, which are being applied in it. Through the case study is presented the proposed model-based manufacturing approach in the re-engineering of product and sheet metal multi-stage forming technology for its manufacturing. The proposed integrated system represents feasible and useful tool in engineering design, not only for researchers but for industrial engineers, too.

2   Components of Model-Based Manufacturing and Its Integration

Model-based manufacturing technologies are integrating engineering and manufacturing activities, using virtual models and simulations instead of real objects and operations. That is some kind of "digital tool" for simulation and optimization of production, through models of products and processes developed in the virtual environment, with advanced possibilities for rapid prototyping and rapid manufacturing, presentation in 3D environment, collaborative functions for efficient communication of teams, even the remote ones, with reliable storage of all the electronic data, which describe the product and processes for its manufacturing, servicing and sale. In Fig.1 are presented virtual engineering components and its interactions applied in model-based manufacturing approach, where the central position belongs to virtual model of product and manufacturing processes, namely their complete description and all the generated 3D digital data within the product life span, the so-called Digital mock up.

Virtual prototypes are the inevitable part of the new product development, which enable visualization of the product, investigation of its functionality and exploitation characteristics before the manufacturing itself, estimate of process parameters influence on the product characteristics in its conceptual design. Contemporary CAD/CAM/CAE systems are powerful tools that can simulate the complete life cycle of a product, from the conceptual to the parametric design, testing, assembling, maintenance and even sale. Possibilities of the automatic generating of the NC code and simulation of the tool motion, selection of strategies and tolerances checking, are especially important in the tool and parts manufacturing on the CNC machines within CAM technologies. Also, in the modern CA tools, the modules are available for automatic design of the tools' engraving based on the product model, in processes of the injecting moulding of plastics, forging, sheet metal forming and others.

Reverse engineering (RE) is a process of digitalization of the existing part, assembly or the whole product, by precise measuring or scanning. Application of this technology is especially useful when the electronic models of technical documentation are not available. The two phases are distinctive within the RE process: the first one which consists of the data digitalizing and the second one, within which the 3D modelling of the object is done, based on the acquired data. Output from the first phase of the RE process represents the digital description of the object in the three-dimensional space, which is called the point cloud.

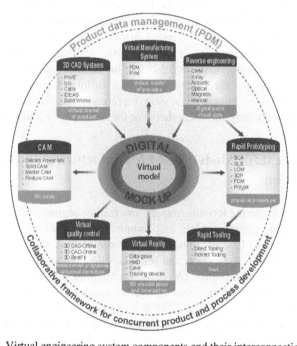

Fig. 1. Virtual engineering system components and their interconnections [4]

The Rapid prototyping (RP) technologies, through the physical model of a product/tool, enable an analysis of the product functionality within the assembly, checking of design, ergonomic analysis and other functional testing. The RP appeared as a key enabling technology, whose application exhibited reduction of the lead time for about 60 % with respect to the traditional way. The trend of reducing the product development time in RP caused appearance of the Rapid Tooling (RT). All together, they make the integrated rapid approach RPM (Rapid Prototyping/Manufacturing).

Natural continuation of the 3D computer graphics are the new Virtual Reality (VR) technologies with advanced input-output devices. Through the VR technology one generates synthetic, namely virtual environment in which is enabled the three-dimensional presentation of the product, tool, process in the real time, in the real conditions, with interaction with the user. Its application is especially significant in the product detailed design phase, virtual mounting of assemblies, or in checking characteristics of the complex products in the automobile and aerospace industries.

Application of Virtual manufacturing (VM), based on non-linear FE simulations, is a well verified and extremely useful tool for prediction of problems in manufacturing. Since the virtual models of processes are very flexible they enable investigation of design changes influences, both the tool layouts and the process parameters, on the product quality and manufacturing costs. Optimal choice of relevant production parameters has positive consequences on reducing the time-to-market, costs of manufacturing, material and tools, as well as increase of the final product quality.

It is known that metrology is the integral part of the production processes, and with development of the systems for digitalization of geometry and objects, which are also used in the RE technologies, it has a significant place in the early phases of the product design and verification of the design solutions alternatives. Possibilities of modern metrological systems are to the greatest extent supported by the powerful software which control data acquisition, its processing up to automatized estimate of the measurement uncertainty. Additionally, CAD on-line and CAD off-line functions enable preparation of programs for measurement based on its virtual model.

One of the basic problems in manufacturing is how to integrate engineering and production activities, considering that integration has to be based on interaction between designers, constructors, technologists, suppliers and buyers, throughout the product's life cycle. The integrated solution provides for unified environment for modelling, analysis and simulation of products and manufacturing processes and also prevents loss of information and electronic data, which often happens in their transfer. Moreover, virtual environment offers designers and researchers visualization of products and their better understanding, leading to improving of quality, reducing the lead time, securing the design solution which is the right one, without the need for later expensive redesign.

3   Case Study

The main objective of the presented case study is to present, on the arbitrary chosen product, i.e. product component, the integrated model-based approach in the re-engineering of manufacturing processes in sheet metal multi-stage forming and verification of the proposed tool design by application of the virtual and physical prototypes [5]. The handle made of the sheet, which is used in manufacturing different type of kitchenware, is obtained by processes of blanking, punching, deep drawing and bending. The last operation of bending and closing the handle could be unstable, depending on the shape of the blank and previous operation of deep drawing/bending and additionally caused by thin sheet anisotropy.

The applied re-engineering approach (Fig.2) comprises the following technologies:

- Reverse Engineering (CMM–optical&laser sensors) – for scanning of blank shape and free surfaces of handle
- CAD modelling – for 2D model of blank and 3D model of handle
- Virtual Manufacturing System (FE simulation) – for virtual verification of proposed technology layouts and tools design
- Rapid Prototyping (PolyJet) – for physical verification of simulation FE model
- Quality control (CMM) – for comparison between metal part and RP model
- Virtual Reality (Data glove, tracking system, 3D projector and stereoscopic glasses) – for 3D visualization and interaction with virtual models
- CAM modelling – for generating of NC code for CNC machining of tools

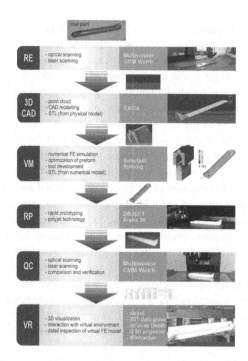

Fig. 2. Model-based engineering design and prototyping

Production processes for manufacturing the handle contains the following operations: 1) Blanking and punching 2) Two-angle bending and deep drawing 3) Bending – the final operation in which the final closure of top surface of the handle is obtained.

The finished part and the blank are scanned at the multi-sensor coordinate measurement machine WERTH VideoCheck IP 250, which is equipped with three sensors: optical, laser and fiber sensor. Since the blank is a planar figure the optical scanning of closed contour "2D" was done and as the output was obtained the ASCII file The option that was chosen there was backlighting when light that illuminates the workpiece comes from below, thus the contour edges are visible on the video screen as a shadow. In Fig.3 is shown the blank on the CMM table and corresponding display of the scanning results on the screen. The point cloud in the ASCII format was imported into the Digitzed shape editor. The contour line is used in the Part-design for obtaining the 3D model of a blank with defined sheet thickness.

Scanning of the finished part was done by use of the optical and laser sensors in the 3D scanning option. By optical scanning the contour shape was registered with the autofocus option, as presented in Fig.4, while the top surface of the handle was scanned by the laser sensor. On the portion of the handle with the variable cross-section and complex surface, the laser scan lines were registered at a distance of 0.75 mm from each other, while at the flat part of the handle 3D scanning of the object was done by lines separated from each other for 20 mm. As in the previous case, the results of both scans was exported as the ASCII file, later imported into CATIA through the Digitized shape editor.

In the Generative shape design are imported scan lines used for modelling the cross sectional surfaces, by what was generated the whole contact surface of the top part of

Fig. 3. Optical 2D scanning of blank contour on CMM

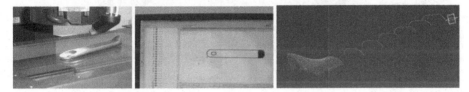

Fig. 4. Optical and laser 3D scanning of final part on CMM, and imported point cloud

the tool for the second operation. The generated surface was used for modelling the upper surface of the mandrel (Fig.5). The tool for the second forming operation consists of the upper die, mandrel and the supporting plate.

Finite element simulations of both operations were performed by using commercial software Simufact.forming, as a special purpose process simulation solution based on MSC.Marc technology. Non-linear finite element approach was used with 3D solid elements (HEX), optimized for sheet metal forming using a "2½ D sheet mesher - Sheetmesh". In Fig.6 is presented a blank on which was initially formed the FE mesh (element size 0.7 mm), virtual assembly for the first operation, the formed workpiece after the first operation with the FE mesh, virtual assembly for the second forming operation and the virtual model of a handle. The flow stress curve was determined by tensile test, defined by equation $\sigma = 180 + 350\varepsilon^{0.23}$, MPa. Interface conditions were described by the Coulomb friction law, with friction coefficient 0.1.

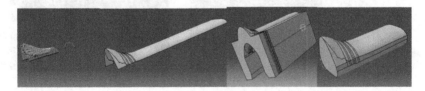

Fig. 5. Transforming scanned lines in CAD surfaces and 3D models (upper die and mandrel)

Fig. 6. Numerical models for FE analysis of virtual manufacturing

In Fig.7 are shown distributions of effective stress in the first forming operation, while in Fig.8 in the final forming operation. In this way, besides the estimate of the material flow and appearance of defects in forming, the quality of product, forming tolerances and residual stresses can be estimated.

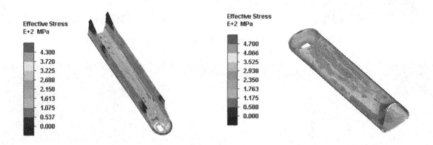

Fig. 7. Effective stress - 1st stage   **Fig. 8.** Effective stress - 2nd stage

No matter how the numerical models of processes and products, obtained by virtual manufacturing are complete, the need exists for such models to be transformed into RP models, in order to perform the final verification of dimensions and fitting. The virtual model of a handle, obtained by the FE simulation, was exported in the STL file (Figure 8 a) and it was used for the prototype made of plastics by application of the PolyJet technology. In Fig.9 is presented the RP model of a handle, which besides for the visual control of surfaces was used for precise measurement of the model on the CMM. The measuring strategy was identical as for measuring the real part. The positions of cross-sections for comparison of forms and dimensions of the real part and the RP model, indirectly the FE model, are shown in Fig.10. The graph in the same figure shows comparison of scanned lines for cross-section 4.

Fig. 9. Rapid prototyping from FE simulation result and control measurement on CMM

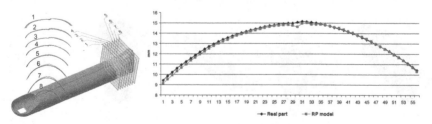

Fig. 10. Measurement results – comparison of RP-FE model and real part, cross-section 4

In the integrated environment the user can analyze processes, systems, products on relation virtual-physical-virtual, where the virtual model of the product is imported into the VR system for the 3D display and interaction with the user. The virtual model of a handle can be analyzed in more details in the VR environment. For those needs a VR application was developed by use of the following software and hardware components: 1)Wizard VR program, 2) 5DT Data Glove, 3) Wintracker, magnetic 6DOF tracking device. The screens form the VR application are shown in Figure 11. In such prepared application it is possible to import other 3D objects modelled in the CAD system or exported from the various VM systems in the form of VMRL files.

Fig. 11. Virtual reality application

4   Conclusion

In this paper are presented components of the model-based integrated system, which generates and/or uses the virtual/rapid prototypes of products and processes, whose analysis and verification are possible both in the physical and virtual sense. Each component of the system has its advantages and disadvantages, thus the integrated approach, which assumes their complementary application, became the powerful tool for designers and researchers. Through the presented case study at the example of process re-engineering of making the handle from the sheet metal, advantages and possibilities of the VE technologies integration were demonstrated, through application of the CAD/CAM/CAE, VM, RP/RM and VR techniques. It was shown that, due to development of the IT technologies, software and hardware components, engineering design and development, as well as the other phases of the product life cycle, can be very successfully realized, with respect to quality, costs and time, by application of the virtual/rapid prototyping/manufacturing technologies of virtual engineering.

References

1. Mandic, V.: Virtual Engineering, University of Kragujevac, Mechanical Engineering Faculty, Kragujevac (2007)
2. Ding, Y., Lan, H., Hong, J., Wu, D.: An integrated manufacturing system for rapid tooling based on rapid prototyping. Robotics and Computer-Integr. Manuf. 20, 281–288 (2004)
3. Yan, Y., Li, S., Zhang, R., Lin, F., Wu, R., Lu, Q., Xiong, Z., Wang, X.: Rapid Prototyping and Manufacturing Technology: Principle, Representative Technics, Applications, and Development Trends. Tsinghua Science & Techn. 14(S1), 1–12 (2009)
4. Mandic, V., Cosic, P.: Integrated product and process development in collaborative virtual engineering environment. Technical Gazette 18(3), 369–378 (2011)
5. Mandić, V.: Integrated virtual engineering approach for product and process development, Keynote paper. In: 3rd Management Technology - step to Sustainable Production, MOTSP 2011, Bol, Croatia, pp. 7–22 (2011)

Real-Time Production Monitoring in Large Heterogeneous Environments

Arne Schramm, Bernhard Wolf, Raik Hartung, and André Preußner

SAP AG, SAP Research Dresden, Chemnitzer Str. 48, 01187 Dresden

Abstract. Expensive production equipment requires continuous monitoring to gather data in real-time, e.g., to detect problems, to assess the quality of produced parts, to collect information about the machine states, and consequently to optimize production processes. However, the increasing amount of data – from sensors or systems – and its continuous processing are a big challenge for an IT infrastructure.

This paper presents a hybrid system, consisting of a distributed CEP (complex event processing) system to process data in real-time augmented with an in-memory database to extend the available memory as well as the processing capabilities of the overall system. Besides the description of the system architecture, details about the implementation of the concepts in a real production environment are given.

1   Introduction

Modern production facilities are being controlled and monitored by an IT back end consisting of various systems such as Enterprise Resource Planning (ERP), Manufacturing Execution Systems (MES), Supervisory Control and Data Acquisition (SCADA), and numerous analysis and decision support systems. The constant monitoring of production assets helps companies to save costs, predict downtimes, prevent the production of scrap, and dynamically adjust production processes. State-of-the-art production machinery often is equipped with numerous sensors, such as vibration, power or temperature sensors, giving information on the health and production state of the machine. In their effort to also optimize older equipments, manufacturers apply new sensors to existing machines to get more insight.

While more and more data is collected at the shop floor, analyzing this data has become a serious challenge. For instance, a mid size semi-conductor equipment can create up to 40.000 data values per second. Having an entire production line consisting of 500 to 1000 machines can easily generate more than one terabyte of data per day. This amount of data brings a number of challenges. The mere gathering of the data in a back end system can already be a problem for any network, given that it might not be used exclusively for this purpose. Analyzing this data in real-time is another non-trivial task that needs to be done in order to react in time to any event on the shop floor. In addition to scheduled analysis jobs like the extraction and continuous refinement of patterns found in historic data, system engineers need to query historical and real-time production

C. Emmanouilidis, M. Taisch, D. Kiritsis (Eds.): APMS 2012, Part II, IFIP AICT 398, pp. 72–79, 2013.
© IFIP International Federation for Information Processing 2013

data ad-hoc, to fully understand the systems in their responsibility, to react in time, and to find possibilities for improvements.

We present a hybrid system combining distributed complex event processing (CEP) [1] and in-memory database technologies to collect and analyze large amounts of data in typical heterogeneous production environments in real-time. The system enables users to dynamically query streams of data and subscribe to results. The combination of both technologies allows users to analyze live and historical data in real-time. Furthermore, analyses can be adapted dynamically to explore the behavior of the production system instantly.

2   Related Work

In our work we combine knowledge from two domains: stream processing and business intelligence (BI). Stream processing and CEP mechanisms are used for processing production data in real-time. The results can be analyzed like in typical BI scenarios using data warehouse applications. In this section earlier work from both areas is discussed.

Originally, the purpose of data warehouses (DW) was to support strategic decisions [2]. With the increasing dynamics of markets the demand for tactical or even operational decision support emerged and approaches for "active data warehousing" [3] were introduced. In [2] different scenarios for real-time data warehousing are discussed. An architecture is described which processes events in real-time and instantly stores the results to the DW. Analyses are executed based on the persisted DW data automatically or on a user's request, i.e., representing a snapshot at this time. However, updating the data in DW does not automatically update the results of analyses.

Over the last decade several stream processing and CEP systems were proposed and commercialized [4]. These systems enable real-time processing directly in the main memory of the system. Queries are continuously executed on the streaming data providing results updated in real-time. To increase performance and fault tolerance distributed stream processing systems were developed, that allow for early data processing close to the data sources. The disadvantages compared to a DW are that data in the main memory are volatile and limited to the much smaller size of the main memory (gigabytes vs. terabytes).

To leverage the advantages of both data processing paradigms, hybrid systems , such as the federated stream processing architecture MaxStream [5], were introduced. MaxStream extends the SAP MaxDB Database Federation Engine with data agents, that act as an access point to stream processing engines. Two new operations to support stream queries were implemented: Streaming Input and Monitoring Select. The first enables the system to pass data streams to the federator and to persist them. The latter returns results once as soon as new data sets are found in the output table. The benefit of this system is the possibility to deploy distributed queries over stream processing engines and databases. Thus, historical and current data can be considered in one query. Since continuous queries are not supported, results have to be polled from the federator by

using the monitoring select statement, which is a major drawback for real-time
processing.

3   The Hybrid Monitoring System

The systems architecture consists of four layers (Figure 1). Those layers are
clearly separated by concerns. Starting from the data sources (shop floor) to the
data sinks (users or systems) we defined the following layers:

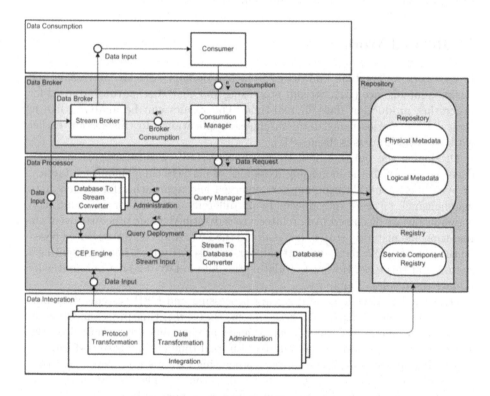

Fig. 1. Architecture Overview

The *Data Integration* layer guarantees the seamless integration of shop floor
data from arbitrary source systems into our solution. Its main tasks and components are described in Section 3.1.

The *Data Processor* layer receives and processes real-time as well as historical
data. Results are continuously forwarded to the next layer. A detailed description
of the layer is given in Section 3.2.

The *Data Broker* layer acts as a single point of entry to the system for various
data consumers. It takes care of distributing processing results, handling subscriptions and providing system information. Section 3.3 depicts details of this
layer.

All data of the system (raw data, processed data and metadata) can be accessed in the *Data Consumption* layer. Section 3.4 gives insight in tasks and requirements of this layer.

The management of the systems components as well as the provisioning of metadata is handled by a *Management* component (Section 3.5) spanning multiple layers.

3.1 Data Integration

Due to the fact that shop floor infrastructure is already defined in most application scenarios, our architecture needs to be integrated into it. This means it needs to connect to various systems, equipments and sensors that can have standardized or proprietary protocols and data format definitions. Data from the shop floor is sent to the *Data Processor* layer via the data input interface. Therefore, the *Data Integration* layer has to provide the following functionality:

- connectivity to sensors and systems,
- protocol and data transformation, and
- unified, push based data transfer to the *Data Processor* layer.

Since integration always needs to be tailored to the specific environment; there cannot be a generic solution to that. However, a common approach to minimize integration effort is the usage of standardized integration middleware. The integration solution in our architecture needs to fulfill the requirements listed above and support a distributed collection of all data. As stated in the introduction a single equipment can already produce thousands of values per second. Collecting all raw data of a whole production site centrally is not feasible. Therefore data has to be collected and integrated by a distributed integration solution.

3.2 Data Processor

The *Data Processor* layer contains the components needed to:

- query real-time data (e.g., calculate live performance indicators (PI)),
- query historical data (e.g., retrieve reference data),
- combine real-time and historical data (e.g., compare live and historical data),
- persist query results (e.g., for further reference), and
- manage running queries (create, deploy, start, stop, undeploy).

The *Data Integration* layer pushes all shop floor data to the CEP component in the *Data Processor* layer. There it can be processed, persisted, and forwarded to the next layer. The processing of data is done by CEP queries. These queries define logic that is executed on all or only selected data arriving. A typical CEP query could, e.g., collect all power consumption data of a machine for a given time and continuously calculate the moving average on it[1]. The results of queries

---

[1] Details of a reference model for performance indicators developed in the KAP project are described in [6].

can be input for further queries, persisted in the Database or forwarded to the Stream Broker (Section 3.3) for distribution.

Streams can also be persisted in the Database using the Stream To Database Converter. Previously persisted raw data or query results can be used for complex analyses like pattern detection or for combination with real-time data. The persisted data of a machine could, e.g., be used as a reference for the machine's currently collected data to detect changes in the machine behavior and predict failures or problems. To retrieve data from the Database, the Database To Stream Converter creates streams from database tables and passes them to the CEP Engine component.

The Query Manager component handles multiple CEP nodes which are located close to the integration nodes in the network. The management of these nodes comprises the starting and stopping of nodes as well as the deployment and distribution of queries.

3.3   Data Broker

The purpose of this layer is to provide a single point of access for data consumers. It consists basically of two components - the Stream Broker and the Consumption Manager. While the Stream Broker has the typical tasks of a broker in a Message-Oriented-Middleware (MOM) like JMS [7] or WS-Notification [8], the Consumption Manager provides the interface to the upper layer. By using the Consumption Manager, consumers can read all relevant data of the system, run queries and subscribe to results.

The benefit of this separation is increased scalability: Classical MOM approaches like JMS lack scalability because of the centralized broker. This limits the maximum number of messages the system can handle in a certain time frame. In our approach, this problem is solved by running multiple stream broker instances. Moreover, this is completely transparent for consumers, since they are only communicating with the Consumption Manager. The Consumption Manager stores, which result streams are registered at which broker instance, and forwards subscriptions accordingly.

3.4   Data Consumption

The *Data Consumption* layer at the top level groups all potential data consumers. A Consumer component can be a graphical dashboard or other IT systems like ERP, MES or SCADA. Dashboards can support engineers in various tasks such as monitoring production equipment or exploring the system and finding possibilities for improvements. IT systems can subscribe to streams to adapt production processes or trigger actions based on events in the shop floor.

Any Consumer in our architecture implements the Data Input interface to receive (processed) stream data from the Stream Broker. To retrieve metadata, to send subscriptions, and to deploy new queries, the Consumer uses the Consumption interface implemented by the Consumption Manager in the *Data Broker* layer.

3.5   Management

The Management component spans the *Data Processor* layer and the *Data Broker* layer. It contains two sub-components – the Registry and the Repository.

The Registry component is used by all other components for service discovery inside the system. Every component registers itself at the Registry when started. Other components can then find the registered components via the Registry, so that the system does not need to be configured manually when starting components on different nodes in the network. The Repository contains all metadata describing the system and the data available in it. We distinguish between physical metadata and logical metadata.

Physical Metadata Repository (PMR): The PMR provides data helping the user understanding the real-world system landscape and mapping it to data in the streaming system. It also contains data needed by the Query Manager and Consumption Manager to manage queries in the system. The PMR holds a hierarchy of physical components which is used to model the real-world environment. A physical component is meant to be any kind of shop floor device, e.g., a sensor. The hierarchy of physical components represents the structure at the shop floor.

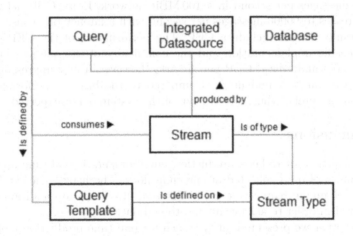

Fig. 2. Simplified Repository Structure

Logical Metadata Repository (LMR): The LMR contains information about streams and queries available in the system. A simplified structure of the LMR meta-model is depicted in Figure 2. The central entity is the stream. A stream can have different sources: it can either be produced from a database table, it can be retrieved directly from a physical component, be the result of a query, or a combination of these. A stream is an instance of a defined stream type. This classification allows to check, whether a stream can be processed in a certain query or not. We envision a query as the combination of a query template with concrete input streams and parameters. A query template defines the logic of a query that can be applied to streams of a certain stream type. The concept of streams, stream types, queries, and query templates allows the definition of complex logic by an expert, which can then be re-used by consumers of the system to analyze actual data from concrete streams.

4   Implementation

The concepts were implemented using SAP's CEP and in-memory solutions. However, other CEP or in-memory systems can be integrated in a simple way by utilizing the defined interfaces. The implementation is currently running in a real production facility processing PIs [6] in real-time.

A performance analysis showed the real-time capabilities of our system. For that, we distinguish between two message types: control and data messages. Control messages are used to manage the system and are not critical w.r.t. performance. In our architecture control messages are sent via web services usually taking less than 300ms. In contrast, data messages contain real-time stream data and are sent directly via UDP. The overall performance depends on the CEP, the Stream Broker, the networks bandwidth and the message size. With a typical message size of 250 Byte the Stream Broker can send and receive up to 40000 messages per second in a 100 MBit network. In a 1 GBit network the value increases to 90000 messages per second with a latency of 0.6 ms.

The results do not include a CEP. The performance of the CEP depends on the specific implementation and the complexity of the queries. There are currently no standardized CEP benchmarks, however, a first impression of the performance can be found in [9]. Compared to the broker's performance the throughput is similar, thus, a slowdown of the system is not expected.

5   Conclusions

A main challenge of today's production environments is real-time analysis of large volumes of data collected at the shop floor. The heterogeneous IT infrastructure, changing requirements and different standards are additional issues to be solved in order to achieve an end-to-end data integration.

In this paper we presented an approach for real-time production monitoring in large, heterogeneous environments. Our solution combines emerging data processing technologies, i.e., a distributed CEP system with in-memory databases. By this combination, we compensate the limitations of the CEP system in terms of available memory, and further integrate persisted data without having the update latency of a database. To further increase the performance of the data processing, stream brokers are utilized to separate the data processing from result distribution.

The application of this hybrid system to the manufacturing domain enables us to continuously (pre-)process data of the shop floor assets in real-time and close to its source. Consequently, network load is reduced whereas scalability is increased. Our system allows to create and deploy new queries dynamically so that running analyses can be adapted to changed requirements.

Acknowledgements. The paper presents results of the KAP project (260111), which is co-funded by the European Union under the Information and Communication Technologies (ICT) theme of the 7th Framework Programme for R&D (FP7).

References

1. Luckham, D.: The Power of Events: An Introduction to Complex Event Processing in Distributed Enterprise Systems. Addison-Wesley Professional (May 2002)
2. König, S.: Erfolgsfaktoren in Business Intelligence Projekten. Technical Report 03-2009, Fachhochschule Hannover, Fakultät IV – Wirtschaft und Informatik (2009)
3. Polyzotis, N., Skiadopoulos, S., Vassiliadis, P., Simitsis, A., Frantzell, N.E.: Supporting Streaming Updates in an Active Data Warehouse. In: Proceeding of the IEEE 23rd International Conference on Data Engineering 2007 (ICDE 2007), pp. 476–485. IEEE (2007)
4. Cugola, G., Margara, A.: Processing Flows of Information: From Data Stream to Complex Event Processing. ACM Computing Surveys 44(3), 15:1–15:62 (2012)
5. Botan, I., Cho, Y., Derakhshan, R., Dindar, N., Haas, L., Kim, K., Tatbul, N.: Federated Stream Processing Support for Real-Time Business Intelligence Applications. In: Castellanos, M., Dayal, U., Miller, R.J. (eds.) BIRTE 2009. LNBIP, vol. 41, pp. 14–31. Springer, Heidelberg (2010)
6. Hesse, S., Wolf, B., Rosjat, M., Nadoveza, D., Pintzos, G.: Reference model concept for structuring and representing performance indicators in manufacturing. In: Emmanouilidis, C., Taisch, M., Kiritsis, D. (eds.) APMS 2012, Part II. IFIP AICT, vol. 398, pp. 289–296. Springer, Heidelberg (2013)
7. Sun Microsystems Inc.: Java Message Service Specification – Version 1.1 (April 2002)
8. Graham, S., Niblett, P., Chappell, D., Lewis, A., Nagaratnam, N., Parikh, J., Patil, S., Samdarshi, S., Tuecke, S., Vambenepe, W., Weihl, B.: Web Services Notification (WS-Notification) – Version 1.0 (January 2004)
9. Sybase Inc.: Evaluating Sybase CEP Performance. Technical white paper, Sybase Inc. (October 2010)

Ontology-Based Flexible Multi Agent Systems Design and Deployment for Vertical Enterprise Integration

Christos Alexakos[1], Manos Georgoudakis[2], Athanasios P. Kalogeras[2], and Spiridon L. Likothanassis[1]

[1] Dept of Computer Engineering and Informatics, University of Patras, Greece
{alexakos,likothan}@ceid.upatras.gr
[2] Industrial System Institute, Greece
{kalogeras,georgoud}@isi.gr

Abstract. Empowering autonomic control in the enterprise environment highly contributes in the quest for a higher level of flexibility. Multi-Agent Systems (MAS) may be utilized to this end along with the enterprise environment model leading to a decentralization of the manufacturing production processes. The current work proposes a framework along with the necessary software tools for the modeling of MAS through ontologies, its design and deployment in the enterprise / manufacturing environment.

Keywords: ontologies, multi agent systems, vertical enterprise integration.

1 Introduction

The need to increase the competitiveness of enterprises, especially in the manufacturing sector, is profound. Intra-enterprise interoperability is a prerequisite to this end, making possible the vertical integration of systems / applications residing at different levels of the classical manufacturing environment hierarchy. This need is especially felt when modern enterprises have to support such advanced business models as mass customization that require a robust enough environment that may react effectively and adapt to unexpected events and uncertain timing. Distributing intelligence and providing autonomy to different levels in the manufacturing environment hierarchy may positively contribute to this end. MAS along with a model representation of the enterprise environment and the relevant semantics are fundamentals for such an approach.

The proposed framework is based on the concept of simple definition of the functionalities of an integration MAS that permits system semi-automatic implementation and deployment, with the following challenges:

- The description of MAS modules, their functionalities, processes and data exchange protocols must follow a human understandable way. Model-based design using UML is a good paradigm for design of systems behavior by engineers.
- The implementation phase of MAS must include the least possible code implementation, accelerating the deployment procedure and enforcing system re-usability. The use of modular system architecture, where the modules can be easily developed and re-used, in combination with code-generation of system main components can significantly decrease the need for code programming.

C. Emmanouilidis, M. Taisch, D. Kiritsis (Eds.): APMS 2012, Part II, IFIP AICT 398, pp. 80–87, 2013.
© IFIP International Federation for Information Processing 2013

- System definition must be computer-understandable, allowing computer software to read MAS description and proceed to the appropriate actions, such as code generation, agent creation and data mapping. XML and RDF are open standards that can easily define concepts, be delivered to systems and parsed by them.
- The information integration between heterogeneous systems is a major issue in enterprise system integration; without the "common understanding" of the data exchanged between systems the orchestration of the business processes is meaningless.

In order to face the aforementioned challenges, the proposed framework is accompanied by a concrete methodology for MAS definition, implementation and deployment phases based on GAIA [1] agent-oriented software engineering (AOSE) methodology. Furthermore, a set of tools support the three phases of the methodology establishing an integrated architecture for the framework.

The rest of the paper is organized as follows: In section 2 a brief presentation of the related works on ontology-driven design and deployment of MAS is provided. Section 3 presents the proposed framework methodology and its main components along with its supporting tools. Finally, some conclusion is given in chapter 4.

2   Related Work

MAS model development is supported by a number of AOSE methodologies and technologies [2], characterized by different levels of maturity. GAIA methodology is very popular [3] because it provides a strong design tool for engineers in order to describe the functionalities of a MAS along with the behavior of the agents acting in it. According to the GAIA-approach the behavior and interaction of an agent-based system is described by a set of roles with role related activities and a set of interactions among the roles. GAIA is used in various approaches for MAS design in enterprise / manufacturing integration [4].

During the recent years ontologies have been used as tools in model – driven architectures for defining the detailed functionality of a MAS. The semantic basis is the frame-based ontology ONTODM. ONTOMADEM [5] is a knowledge-based tool for designing MAS based on the MADEM MAS design methodology. ONTOMADEM is using a frame-based ontology constructed with Protégé tool. Bittencourt et al. [6] propose an ontological model for defining MAS functionalities and components driven for two ontologies, one describing GAIA methodology agents and one describing JADE agent implementation. The model uses SWRL rules for mapping GAIA agent roles and activities to JADE agents and behaviors. Nevertheless, a common denominator in most of these approaches is the lack of automatic creation of MAS.

In the runtime phase of MAS, ontologies in most approaches are used for supporting semantics common understanding of the integrated data exchanged between agents. Few proposals elaborate ontologies from the MAS design phase to deployment. O-PRS (Ontology driven Procedural Reasoning System like model) [7] utilizes OWL ontologies to express the concepts in Believe, Desire, Intention (BDI) agent architecture. The ontologies add the appropriate semantics to the exchanged messages in order for the agents to understand how to act. Nyulas et al. [8] proposed an ontology-driven framework for design and deployment of MAS on top of Java Agent DEvelopment Framework (JADE) framework (http://jade.tilab.com/). The framework is based on the definition of MAS functionality using three Ontology Web Language (OWL) ontologies (Data Source, Task-Method and Deployment). For MAS deployment, special purpose agents (Controller Agent and Configurator Agent) are used in order to create and monitor task agents according to the semantic configuration.

3   Proposed Integration Framework

3.1   Design to Deployment Methodology

The proposed methodology covers the three phases of system engineering: design, implementation and deployment. For simplicity, the testing phase is considered as part of the implementation phase. Figure 1 depicts the major and optional steps of the methodology in the three phases.

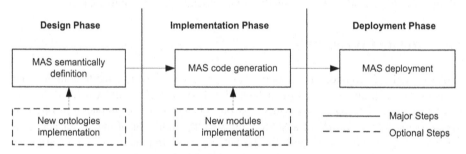

Fig. 1. Design to Deployment Methodology

The core aspect of the proposed methodology is the MAS semantic definition in terms of ontologies. Ontologies represent powerful tools for defining the knowledge of a domain. In the case of enterprise system integration knowledge includes the business processes, the exchanged information and business logic executed from the participating systems. Ontologies describe the concepts in terms of axioms that for the shake of simplicity can be considered as sentences such as "Agent A executes the Invoice Procedure". In modern ontology languages like OWL, a more object oriented approach is used where entities follow a hierarchical structure enforced by relationships between them. OWL is an ontology language generated on the concept of Semantic Web, thus its main representation format is based on XML and RDF, permitting both human and computer understandability. For this reason, it is used as the basis for MAS definition in the proposed framework.

OWL Ontologies follow the T-Box and A-Box distinction which is drawn in Description Logics. OWL ontologies are composed of two functional parts, the first part is the ontology scheme (T-Box) and the second is a set of instances of the ontology scheme containing the data related to the described domain (A-Box). The proposed methodology uses as core ontology scheme the OWL-GMO (Gaia MAS Ontology)

ontology that defines the core entities of MAS system following the widely accepted GAIA design methodology. Each agent role is depicted as an instance of OWL-GMO. Furthermore, OWL-GMO provides entities and relations for the definition of agent behaviors and messages exchanged. Other pre-existing ontologies or newly-composed ones can be integrated in the core ontology scheme in order to define the information semantics of the data used by the participating systems and agents.

The implementation phase includes the code generation of the components defined by OWL-GMO followed by the packaging of external modules that execute specific business logic functionalities. Agents and their functionalities (behaviors and message exchanged) are implemented following the specification of agent implementation of JADE. JADE supports the implementation of distributed software agent systems where software agents are running in different hosts. Moreover, the agent instances are managed according to globally accepted FIPA specifications. Finally, JADE agents follow Agent Communication Language (ACL), a well-structured schema for message exchange.

The specific business logic or functionalities that have to be executed by the agents must be implemented as modules providing specific APIs for invocation by the core agent implementation. In this case, the binaries or java code of these modules will be included in the core generated code. Finally, the code will be compiled and ready for deployment to the real enterprise environment.

3.2   Architecture Components

Each distinct step of the aforementioned methodology is supported by software tools either providing graphical user interface to the users or automatically executing tasks. Figure 2 depicts the system components of framework methodology software realization. The architectural components are:

- *Ontology Editor*. It is GUI for composing and instantiating the ontologies used in the concept of the framework. Protégé tool (http://protege.stanford.edu/) is used for this purpose.
- *Ontology Importer*. It is a module that manages the OWL ontology files composed by the Ontology Editor for a specific project (MAS definition). Furthermore, it keeps versions of the ontologies for potential use.
- *Code Generator* is the component responsible for the transformation of the MAS definition to code running on top of JADE MAS platform. The Code Generator uses an OWL Ontology Reasoner for the conceptualization –i.e. the identification of hierarchy and relations - of the imported ontologies. JENA semantic framework (http:// jena.apache.org) with Pellet (http://clarkparsia.com/pellet) reasoning support is used for this purpose.
- External Module Importer is a GUI responsible for collecting the external modules (binaries or code) needed for MAS implementation.
- Packaging Manager is responsible for managing the generated code and the imported modules and creating the final application package for compilation.

- Binary Builder is the tool that builds the final MAS system. Binary Builder can be directly connected to the deployment or testing environment in order to automatically deploy the binary code.

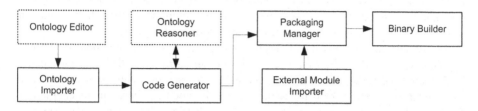

Fig. 2. Framework Methodology Software Realization Architectural Components

3.3   OWL-GMO

As aforementioned, OWL-GMO is the core ontology of the proposed framework used to define the agents and their behavior in MAS. OWL-GMO entities come from the terms defined in the GAIA methodology. The ontology is based on two super-classes:

- *AgentSystemEntity* which abstractly defines the entities used by GAIA methodology to define a MAS.
- *AbstractConcept* which defines supporting entities used to define concepts of the behavior and functionality of the MAS (data, processes, APIs, etc).

According to GAIA, each agent system comprises a set of agent roles. Each role is defined by four attributes: responsibilities, permissions, activities, and protocols. Responsibilities determine functionality and, as such, are perhaps the key attributes associated with a role. Responsibilities are divided into two types: liveliness properties and safety properties. In order to realize responsibilities, a role has a set of permissions. Permissions are the rights associated with a role. Therefore, the permissions of a role identify the resources that are available for that role in order to realize its responsibilities. In the kind of system that has been typically modeled in this work, permissions tend to be information resources. Activities are actions associated with the role and are carried out by the agent without interacting with other agents. Finally, a role is also identified with a number of protocols which define the way that it can interact with other roles. Each protocol is defined by its initiator role, the responder roles, input data, output data and the process executed.

Figure 3 depicts the OWL-GMO visualization. The classes *AgentRole, RoleResponsibility, RolePermission, RoleProtocol* and *RoleActivity* are the subclasses of the class *AgentSystemEntity* and define the main entities of GAIA methodology. For *RoleResponsibility* there are two subclasses, *LivenessProperty* and *SafetyProperty* following GAIA specifications. These classes following by relationships expressing specific concepts and restrictions (i.e. *AgentRole accessResourcesAccordingTo RolePermission*) are used for the definition of the MAS.

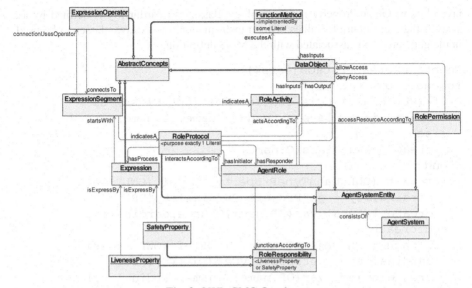

Fig. 3. OWL-GMO Ontology

Furthermore, OWL-GMO uses the subclasses *DataObject, FunctionMethod, Expression, ExpressionSegment* and *ExpressionOperator* to express additional concepts reading data, operations and processes. *DataObject* class is used to define the used data, usually enriched with external ontologies describing the information data used for a specific project. *Expression* denotes a concept that consists of *ExpressionSegments* which indicate either an activity or a protocol. *ExpressionSegments* are connected via *ExpressionOperator* in order to compose a flow of actions that define the activity. *FunctionMethod* is designed in order to be instantiated as a method from software libraries. It is mapped to the external modules API methods for executing specific business logic functionalities.

3.4   MAS Implementation

The outcome of the design phase is the instantiated OWL-GMO where individuals are depicted by the agents and their functionalities. At the next step, being MAS implementation, the relative code of the agents will be generated according to JADE agent framework guidelines. In order to generate code, sets of "transformation" scripts are executed, which logic follows the main principles presented by Spanoudakis and Moraitis [9].

In order to manage the data used by the agent system and depicted in the imported ontologies extending Data Object, the function *createDataObjects()* generates java classes based on the heredity feature which is supported by both OWL and Object oriented program languages. The *create_literal_var()* function creates a class public property of java common data type (String, int, etc) associated to DataProperty range type. The *create_object_var()* function creates a public property of the corresponding java class to ObjectProperty range ontology class. Java cardinality is defined by an array if there are multiple values. This transformation allows Java classes to be used in the generated code associated with the MAS definition.

```
Function createDataObjects():
foreach (OWL Class) C
  if (OWL Class) C is subclass of (OWL Class) C1
    create_java_class_extends(C.name,C1.name)
  else
    create_java_class(C.name)
  endif
  for each (OWL DataTypeProperty) DP of (OWL Class) C
    cardinality = getPropertyCardinality(DP)
    create_literal_var(DP.name,C.name,cardinality)
  endforeach
  for each (OWL ObjectProperty) OP of (OWL Class) C
    cardinality = getPropertyCardinality(OP)
    create_object_var(OP.name,C.name,cardinality)
  endforeach
endforeach
```

Having generated the Java data object classes, the next step is the creation of the agents. In JADE framework agents are realized as extensions of *jade.core.Agent and their* tasks (activities or protocols) are implemented as a JAVA classes extending the *jade.core.behaviours.Behaviour* class. The received / sent messages for each agent are implemented using the *jade.lang.acl.ACLMessage* class. Function *createAgents()* depicts the code generation script for agents and their behaviors.

```
Function createAgents():
foreach (AgentRole as Agent)
  create_Agent(Agent)
  foreach (AgentActivity(Agent actsAccordingto)as
    Activity)
    Behaviour = create_Behaviour(Activity)
    attach_Behaviour_to_Agent(Behaviour,Agent)
  endforeach
  foreach (RolePermission(Agent interactsAccordingTo)as
    Permission)
    DataObject = getDataObject_isAllowed(RolePermission)
    attach_Data_Object_to_Agent(DataObject,Agent)
  endforeach
  foreach (AgentProtocol(Agent hasInitiator ||
    interactsAccordingTo|| hasResponder)as Protocol)
    Expression = getExpression_hasProcess(Protocol)
    attach_protocol_behaviour(Expression,Agent)
  endforeach
endforeach
```

For the agent protocols that are released by *attach_protocol_behaviour( )* function, the corresponding behaviors and ACL messages are generated according to the process flow defined by the related Expression. In each transformation the input and output data of behaviors are mapped according to Java data objects created by the function *createDataObjects( )*.

The next step is the gathering of all the external modules/java classes and adding them to the project classpath. The final step comes with the compiling and building of agent executable code that will run on top of an installed JADE platform at the enterprise environment.

4   Conclusion

The paper presents a framework relevant to the modeling, design, implementation and deployment of a MAS for the enterprise environment allowing the increase of its flexibility and decision making autonomy. In this context production process may be easier and more effectively decentralized. The different software tools are presented that make it possible to model the MAS in terms of ontologies, implement it and deploy it to the enterprise environment through Java code generation.

References

1. Zambonelli, F., et al.: Developing Multiagent Systems: The Gaia Methodology. ACM Transactions on Software Engineering and Methodology 12(3), 317–370 (2003)
2. Akbari, O.Z.: A survey of agent-oriented software engineering paradigm: Towards its industrial acceptance. International Journal of Computer Engineering Research 1(2), 14–28 (2010)
3. Leitão, P., Vrba, P.: Recent Developments and Future Trends of Industrial Agents. In: Mařík, V., Vrba, P., Leitão, P. (eds.) HoloMAS 2011. LNCS, vol. 6867, pp. 15–28. Springer, Heidelberg (2011)
4. Girardi, R., Leite, A.: A knowledge-based tool for multi-agent domain engineering. Know.-Based Syst. 21(7), 604–661 (2008)
5. Bratukhin, A., Sauter, T.: Functional Analysis of Manufacturing Execution System Distribution. IEEE Transactions on Industrial Informatics 7(4), 740–749 (2011)
6. Bittencourt, I.I., Bispo, P., Costa, E., Pedro, J., Véras, D., Dermeval, D., Pacca, H.: Modeling JADE Agents from GAIA Methodology under the Perspective of Semantic Web. In: Filipe, J., Cordeiro, J. (eds.) ICEIS 2009. LNBIP, vol. 24, pp. 780–789. Springer, Heidelberg (2009)
7. Mousavi, A., Nordin, M., Othma, Z.A.: An Ontology Driven, Procedural Reasoning System-Like Agent Model, For Multi-Agent Based Mobile Workforce Brokering System. Journal of Computer Science 6, 557–565 (2010)
8. Nyulas, C., et al.: An Ontology-Driven Framework for Deploying JADE Agent Systems. In: IEEE/WIC/ACM International Conference on Web Intelligence and Intelligent Agent Technology, pp. 573–577. IEEE Press, New York (2008)
9. Spanoudakis, N., Moraitis, P.: Gaia Agents Implementation through Models Transformation. In: Yang, J.-J., Yokoo, M., Ito, T., Jin, Z., Scerri, P. (eds.) PRIMA 2009. LNCS, vol. 5925, pp. 127–142. Springer, Heidelberg (2009)

MANU Building – Bringing together Manufacturing Automation and Building Automation

Aleksey Bratukhin, Albert Treytl, and Thilo Sauter

Austrian Academy of Sciences, Institute for Integrated Sensor Systems
{Aleksey.Bratukhin,Albert.Treytl,Thilo.Sauter}@oeaw.ac.at

Abstract. Up to now, production systems only concern was to minimize production costs or optimize the utilization of production resources. But with the increasing energy prices and the growing concern over the environmental impact of production systems (industrial systems consume a quarter of all energy), efficient use of energy in manufacturing environment cannot be ignored any longer.

MANUbuilding concept brings together manufacturing systems requirements with building automaton concerns over the efficient energy use.

1   Introduction

Modern trends in automation require flexible production. While the current state of research shows a full range of solutions that satisfies mass customized dynamic production, it still assumes the constant level of energy consumption typical in centralized production with its long-time planning horizon.

However, existing production systems focus on production costs minimization, but ignore increasing energy prices and the growing concern over the environmental impact of production systems.

Therefore, the new automation paradigm would require not only flexible production but also adaptable energy management of a factory.

Energy efficiency is widely discussed these days. However, most of the research and most of the new solutions offered are aiming at smart grid systems [1,2] or energy savings in commercial and residential buildings [3]. In particular there is energy saving by including the industrial building is not investigated and there is a high potential for savings. The "building" (HVAC, lighting, water, alarms and security, occupancy) consume 40% of the industrial energy [3].

There are two main demands on industrial buildings: (a) providing a controlled stable environment for the production process challenged by the modern dynamic productions and (b) minimizing the energy required for this. The MANUbuilding concept joins together the manufacturing system with the building automation to optimize the overall energy consumption of a factory. The seamless interaction between building and production is crucial to overcome mutual negative effects existing today.

The MANUbuilding concept increases energy efficiency in the manufacturing environment (factory as a building) by developing distributed intelligent control system

C. Emmanouilidis, M. Taisch, D. Kiritsis (Eds.): APMS 2012, Part II, IFIP AICT 398, pp. 88–95, 2013.
© IFIP International Federation for Information Processing 2013

integrating knowledge from the building sensor and actuator network integrated with the available resources on the shop floor with the predictive analysis of the factory behavior based on the production plans and shop floor schedules. The resulting system provides:

1) a production driven building control concept that adapts building energy profile and behavior to the dynamically changing requirement of the production system represented by the Manufacturing Execution System (MES)

2) a control concept for building-aware production that would integrate the energy saving requirements of the building into production planning.

These goals serve a double purpose of optimization of both the energy use and production system performance. The concept is based on three pillars:

1) Cooperating objects – a sensor network concept combining sensor and actuators with intelligence represented by collectors that connect together and provide intelligence to different parts of the system (sensors, actuators, resources, MES, ERP, SCM) [4].

2) Function blocks – IEC 61499 is a modular, functionality based, event driven automation paradigm that is used as a platform for collectors implementation. It is the base for optimal integration in the production environment [5].

3) Distributed local decision making based on the dynamic expanding clusters where data fusion mechanisms are applied to find solutions in the most efficient way.

A solution providing substantial energy savings of 20 to 60%, while at the same time not restricting the flexibility of production and offering a convenient engineering will have a success on a 25 billion euro market (global building-automation market).

2   Integration of Production Planning and Manufacturing Environment

The main benefit of the MANUbuilding is in advanced concepts for efficient energy use in industrial environment based on function blocks with intelligent nodes and distributed algorithms that combine the production optimization requirements with the building energy saving goals. Taking into account physical parameters of the factory floor and ERP and MES production schedules MANUbuilding uses data fusion concepts to produce an efficient and safe yet cost efficient system for online energy monitoring of industrial buildings.

The two phase scenario of MANUbuilding allows making transition of existing system smoother: 1) In the first step the factory building adapts to the requirements of the manufacturing system, 2) And in the second step, the manufacturing system adapts its plans and behavior to consider energy needs of the factory.

Therefore, existing factories are able to use the system without changing their entire enterprise. The core of the MANUbuilding architecture is the concept of dynamically expanding clusters that calculate locally so-called Energy Health Status (EHS). The term EHM is inspired by the state of the art paradigm of Structural Health Monitoring (SHM) where a sensor network monitors the structural integrity of a building structure.

EHM applies the principles of SHM to the energy monitoring area in order to determine integrity of the energy usage. EHM combines the concept of Cooperating objects with software agents' platform and energy efficient communication mechanisms, and applies net-centric, clustered multi sensor data fusion and processing algorithms to create a platform for online energy status retrieval.

2.1   Distributed Decision-Making Based on Dynamic Clusters

The EHM approach focuses on recognizing and improving the Energy Health Status (EHS) of the system, where EHS is a resulting value of multiple calculations triggered by the events in the system that show the level of efficiency of energy use in a certain situation and location.

A simple example is when a user opens a window for full intermittent ventilation and temperature drops in a room. As a result a heater would start running. A simple solution to improve the EHS would be to stop the heater temporarily. In this way, the system can save the energy without interfering with user's intentions.

EHM system is based on expanding problem solving clusters to address the above mentioned drawbacks. Each cluster is a dynamically created community of intelligent components that cooperate with each to get enough information to solve a problem.

In case of the EHM, each member of a cluster has a set of algorithms that would allow recognizing an actual local EHS. In order to do so, it has to retrieve data from sensors and communicate with other members of the cluster to recognize and improve the EHS.

The initial creation of a cluster is trigged by an event that is predefined by the system developer or can be set by a user. In the case of the above given example, the cluster creation is initiated hen the window is open and the heater is on.

There is an endless number of scenarios possible from the very simple ones (as the above) to the very complex that involves regulation of the energy consumption on a scale of a complete building. The exact possible scenarios depend on the particular sensors related to an intelligent component as well as the location and designated tasks. The starting set of scenarios are assigned to a component during the initialization, but the new ones can be dynamically added during the system runtime when a new sensor or task is added to the system.

The key issue in developing such a system is flexibility and scalability of the solution. In EHM the problem solving approach is based on the expanding nature of the cluster formation and applied data fusion. Initially, there is only one member in the cluster that initiates and determines a problem. In the simplest case, its knowledge is sufficient to recognize the EHS and find an appropriate solution to improve it. But in the most cases it will require additional information and algorithms to improve the energy use efficiency.

Each intelligent component has a set of algorithms how to calculate and improve the EHS that has been assigned. And in order to do so, it needs to obtain information either from the sensors or from other intelligent units that also perform certain algorithms to calculate EHS. In EHM a brokering functionality is applied to find appropriate communication partners. Each system component publishes its algorithms and data points at the brokering component that manages the actual state of them via an event based update is triggered by the components themselves when a change in their algorithms occurs. The algorithm class description is encapsulated within a standard agent service description and can be understood by the collectors.

Hence, the system requires a very dynamic, flexible and scalable structure that includes both sensors and intelligent units to calculate the EHS.

2.2   System Behaviour

EHM uses an emerging concept of Cooperating objects and sets its focus on sensor networks and distributed control that fits perfectly to fulfill the above mentioned requirements. Each Cooperating object consists of one or several sensors or/and actuators that are controlled by a collector. A collector is an intelligent component that has certain functionalities and is used in EHM for calculating the (local) EHS and participating in the cluster based solution finding.

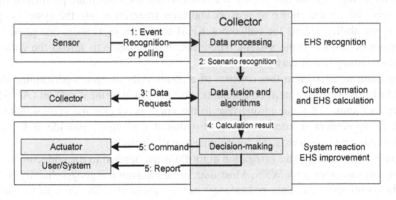

Fig. 1. Collector behavior

In the EHM architecture there are three main steps in a collector's behavior (Fig.1):

1. Raw sensor data retrieved by the collectors via polling or event-based mechanisms are processed locally. A single collector can be responsible for monitoring multiple sensors and has an ability to process and aggregate data.
2. A collector recognizes a scenario and if the processed data is not sufficient to calculate the EHS then a collector creates a cluster by contacting other collectors to retrieve required information. Each collector, depending on its functionality, has different data fusion algorithms to recognize and calculate the EHS.
3. If the collector cannot determine the EHS, then it expands the cluster to include collectors with more advanced algorithms that use the results of other collectors' calculations to recognize the EHS.
4. The final step is a decision making how to improve the EHS and the following (5) commands to the actuators and reporting to the upper level system control.

A flexible structure is one of the advantages of Cooperating objects concept that allow EHM to solve complex problems by including more collectors into the problem solving. Although, each collector in the EHM system is an independent acting entity, its position in the structure of the community is determined by the data management algorithms it can perform to calculate the EHS.

Some collectors in a cluster monitor one or few sensors and can only operate with the simple algorithms, on a higher level there are collectors that are not assigned to sensors but monitor other collectors and require the results of their calculations to perform more complex algorithms of their own. Due to the scalable structure of the Cooperating objects the number of collectors and resulting complexity is practically unlimited and hence allows the recognition of highly complex EHS.

However, it is important to mention that although the developed architecture allows dealing with complex algorithms requiring information from hundreds of sensors, in reality most of the situations can be dealt with a few collectors utilizing localized decisions.

All the computational and logical activities within the system are performed by the collectors making the choice of sensors and their integration into the system depend only on the ability to host the collectors. EHM uses sensors as hosts that provide the maximum flexibility to the system. Therefore, it is possible to spread the collectors over the existing sensor network.

The multi agent system that consists of a community of agents performing designated tasks as well as system components: an agent management system (AMS), directory facilitator (DF) and an interface to the upper level external system that allow EHM to implement a community of distributed collectors, provide a brokering functionality and use an existing communication platform [8].

Finally, data fusion and aggregation algorithms are applied to the collectors in context of software agents on WSN. Most data in monitoring are geographically or temporally correlated. And data redundancy can be avoided if the data were partially processed locally at the sensors by e.g., averaging it over time or space before forwarding [5]. There are several functions that can be used in data aggregation and fusion along its way to collectors. Examples of such functions include average, maximum, minimum, sum, or deviation that can be applied periodically or on-demand, such as delay-bounded and power-efficient data aggregation protocols. Most of the data fusion and aggregation protocols to be used in WSN net-centric environment are either centralized or do not consider power or delay efficiency. EHM applies data fusion and aggregation to the local problem solving hence minimizing power and delay concerns resulting in higher efficiency of sensor data usage.

2.3 Two Phase Scenario for Energy Efficient Industrial Environment

The proposed approach offers two possible implementation scenarios that allow a smooth transition from the existing systems to the energy aware productions.

In the **first phase**, MANUbuilding provides a production driven control of the building automation system, where the MES schedule will have a priority and the building will adapt its behavior to best fit the production needs.

The uniqueness of the MANUbuilding approach is the way production schedule is understood by the underlying building automation system. This direct control allows saving energy on the one hand by dynamic reaction to events of the shop floor and on the other hand by being able to pro-actively react to future events derived from the MES schedule. High savings by the latter are in particular expected for inert functions such as cooling.

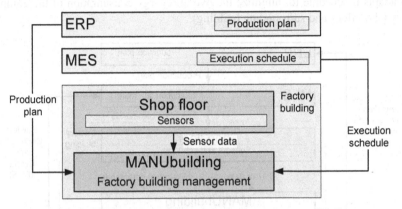

Fig. 2. Production driven control of the building automation system

As shown on Figure 2, MANUbuilding acquires three times of information:

- Production plans from the ERP; general, long-term planning on the enterprise level that allows planning factory maintenance depending on the shop floor project ted load. In this case MANUbuilding is able to more efficiently keep the required energy conditions and make transitions in the factory state smoothly.
- Execution schedule from the MES; short-term (minutes to hours, sometimes seconds) plan how certain operations are executed on the shop floor. In this case MANUbuilding behaves similar to the previous case with the different planning horizon and more local conditions up to a work cell or a robot. That allows a fine tuning of the shop floor, efficient energy use and longevity of the factory equipment.
- Sensor data from the shop floor as well as from the factory building in general. If the situations described above were proactive, then this case is a reactive behavior of MANUbuilding allowing to react on the events and critical situations on the shop floor that would usually require human supervision and a long command chain involved. Shorter reaction time (starting from the faster recognition to the actual reaction) save not only the energy of the factory but improves the production efficiency in general.

Within the first stage, there is no influence on neither production plan nor execution schedule from the MANUbuilding. All the improvements on the Energy Health Status is implemented by the MANUbuilding system. The advantage of such a solution is the fact that practically any ERP or MES system can be utilized. However, the level of energy efficiency that can be achieved with the phase two is much higher.

Phase two implements a building-aware production system where both a building and the production planning will have mutual influence on the integrated system behavior combining production and energy cost parameters as criteria for system optimization. In this case, not only the building adapts to the production system, but also MES adapts it schedule to minimize the overall energy consumption of the complete factory (shop floor and surrounding building).

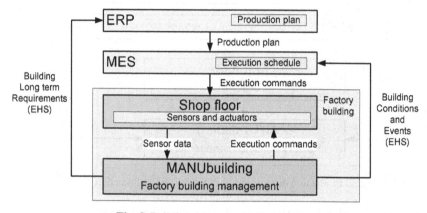

Fig. 3. Building-aware production system

Although not shown on Figure 3, phase two incorporates the activities of the phase one. Figure 4 only shows the extra communication that is performed during the phase two. The principal difference of phase two compare to phase one is that the production system considers energy requirements of the factory building in planning and operation execution. The mechanism is the following:

1. MANUbuilding sends long-term building energy requirements to the ERP system for the production plan decisions. Then it is a responsibility of the ERP system how to interpret this information: whether to include it into the planning or not. That requires the adjustment of the ERP system to be able not only to communicate with the MANUbuilding but also a set of rules and decision making procedures are required to implement MANUbuilding concept. Eventually, the energy requirements are passed down the MES system with the adapted production plan.

2. In addition to the long-term planning requirements, MANUbuilding sends events to the MES system to react on the changing energy profile of the factory during the runtime of the manufacturing system. These events are local and focused on particular sections or elements of the factory that change overtime. As with the ERP system it is up to the MES how to react to the events. And the MES system has to be adapted to be able to handle the communication and decision making procedures.

3. Finally, MANUbuilding itself may serve as management system on the same level as MES and issues commands to the shop floor to adapt to the energy requirements of the factory. Although, it might cause a conflict of interest in centralized MES solutions, recent developments towards distributed manufacturing systems are perfectly suited to handle such situations in a flexible, smooth and efficient way.

3   Outlook

The presented architecture bring together factory building management with the manufacturing system, but including factory energy requirements in the optimization decisions of the ERP and MES systems adjusting the formula of the total production costs that usually neglect energy costs of the production or count them as constant and therefore cannot be optimized.

The efficiency of the system lies in net-centric problem solution clusters that only extend themselves to larger aggregations if a problem cannot be solved on a local basis.

Two-phase solution offers flexible way of integrating MANUbuilding into existing systems without considerable changes to the already functioning environment.

However, the potential of MANUbuilding can be fully exploited in distributed manufacturing system, where MANUbuilding would be an integral part of planning and execution process, therefore, integrating energy costs and environmental concerns into the total production costs as a main criterion for optimization in manufacturing.

References

1. Singhal, A., Saxena, R.P.: Software models for Smart Grid. In: 2012 International Workshop on Software Engineering for the Smart Grid, SE4SG, June 3, pp. 42–45 (2012)
2. DongLi, J., XiaoLi, M., XiaoHui, S.: Study on technology system of self-healing control in smart distribution grid. In: 2011 International Advanced Power System Automation and Protection, APAP (2011)
3. Cf. The quest for the ideal office control system. Lighting Figures vol. 3(3), Lighting Research Center, Rensselaer Polytechinic Institute, Troy, NY (1998); Conference on, October 16-20, vol. 1, pp. 26–30 (2011)
4. Marron, P.J., Minder, D.: European Research on Cooperating Objects. In: 6th Annual IEEE Communications Society Conference on Sensor, Mesh and Ad Hoc Communications and Networks Workshops, SECON Workshops 2009, June 22-26, pp. 1–3 (2009)
5. Vyatkin, V.: The IEC 61499 standard and its semantics. IEEE Ind. Electron. Mag. 3(4), 40–48 (2009)
6. Treytl, A., Spenger, W., Riaz, B.: A secure agent platform for active RFID. In: IEEE International Conference on Emerging Technologies and Factory Automation, ETFA 2008, September 15-18, pp. 492–495 (2008)

Formal Specification of Batch Scheduling Problems: A Step toward Integration and Benchmarking

Gabriela Patricia Henning

INTEC (Universidad Nacional del Litoral, CONICET),
Güemes 3450, Santa Fe 3000, Argentina
ghenning@intec.unl.edu.ar

Abstract. This contribution presents a scheduling domain ontology, named SchedOnto, devised to tackle the formal specification of batch scheduling problems, as well as integration issues associated with the scheduling function. More specifically, this paper describes the ontological engineering approach that led to SchedOnto. The ontology characteristics along with its development process are presented, starting from the challenges that motivated the construction, the competency questions that defined the scope of the ontology, going afterwards through conceptualization and implementation stages, and finishing with some validation issues. SchedOnto relies on both, the ISA-88 and ISA-95 standards, which are well accepted in the industrial domain. After presenting SchedOnto, and its associated design process, this contribution addresses an example that shows the benefits of a formal representation of temporal aspects.

Keywords: Scheduling, Ontologies, Integration, Formal Specifications.

1 Introduction

Nowadays, the importance of effective tools for supporting scheduling and planning activities in the batch process industries is undeniable. Despite the inherent difficulties of the chemical production scheduling problem [1], the academic community has recently made tremendous advances, developing efficient solution methodologies for a wide collection of problem types and plant operation scenarios. The most accepted approaches rely on a diversity of mixed-integer linear programming (MILP) models and Constraint Programming (CP) formulations. Regardless of the research done in the field, advanced scheduling support systems are not very common in the chemical industry yet [2]. In addition, most commercial systems available nowadays are not based on the many solution methodologies that academia has developed. One of the reasons why these approaches are not being used in industry is related to tool usability. Nevertheless, perhaps the most important reason for not being adopted is the fact that scheduling tools do not integrate with the other applications that are regularly employed in industrial organizations. In fact, integration of scheduling support tools with other decision support systems and transactional applications is a true challenge.

C. Emmanouilidis, M. Taisch, D. Kiritsis (Eds.): APMS 2012, Part II, IFIP AICT 398, pp. 96–103, 2013.
© IFIP International Federation for Information Processing 2013

On the other hand, the ample variety of features that define a chemical production scheduling problem has led to a multiplicity of formulations that are generally oriented to better address very specific classes of problems. As a result, up to now there is no general approach that can effectively tackle the various problem classes that appear in the chemical industry [1]. Regarding evaluation, the testing of the many formulations has primarily focused on CPU requirements and is not extensive with respect to the different problem types. One key enabler for testing would be a library of case studies. However, not only such library is required, but also a way for specifying industrial-relevant case-studies in a formal, machine understandable way that can be used to automate data generation processes. Thus, there is a need for a more formal specification of scheduling problems that can help in testing and benchmarking.

This work addresses these challenges by proposing SchedOnto, a batch scheduling domain ontology. A similar approach, to tackle analogous dares that appear in the manufacturing domain, led to the PABADIS' PROMISE ontology [3]. SchedOnto has been devised to (i) tackle the formal specification of batch scheduling problems, and (ii) to serve as a foundation for the integration issues associated with the scheduling function. The contribution first describes the challenges to be faced and then presents the ontological engineering approach that led to SchedOnto. The development process is discussed in Section 3, starting from the motivation for its construction and the definition of its scope, going then through the conceptualization and implementation stages, and finishing with some future validation issues. Afterwards, a small example that shows the benefits of a scheduling domain formal specification is discussed in Section 4. It draws a distinction between the procedure function chart notation and the one proposed in SchedOnto. Finally, concluding remarks are offered.

2   Challenges to Be Addressed

The scheduling activity needs to be addressed within the context of the enterprise hierarchical planning pyramid. This pyramid, which includes activities performed at different time frames, and handles information having distinct granularities, involves scheduling interplaying with the Production Planning and Control (PPC) and Plant Control (PC) functions. The difficulties associated with these interactions were pointed out almost a decade ago [4] and this topic has recently gained renewed attention. To tackle the integration of PPC and scheduling, researchers have proposed various solution strategies [5]. In addition, a few authors have pointed out which are the requirements that apply to the data exchange to support such integration [6]. Alternatively, regarding scheduling and plant control integration, researchers have started to draw the attention to data exchange issues [7], [8]. However, a more comprehensive approach is required to address these integration problems, since this matter entails much more than data exchange. Thus, the integration of the scheduling activity within the hierarchical planning pyramid is one of the driving forces of this contribution.

A central component in the validation and verification process of any scheduling approach is the set of computational experiments employed to evaluate it from various points of view, like the ones of solution quality, computational requirements, robustness, scalability, extensibility, usability, flexibility, etc. Among the reasons for not making a comprehensive testing of the various scheduling formulations developed up to date, the lack of an appropriate problem library should be mentioned. However, not only a library of case studies is required, but also a way to specify industrial-relevant case-studies in a formal, machine understandable way. As shown is Section 4, current example descriptions combine textual and informal graphical representations (such as the STN or RTN graphs, precedence-based blocks, etc.), that may also have some textual annotations [1]. These descriptions might be vague, have a limited expressive power, and may lead to ambiguous interpretations. In some cases, supplementary material containing example data is provided [9], but the format varies from one contribution to the other and it is generally linked to both the notation and the mathematical programming software that has been adopted. Consequently, there is a need for a more formal specification of problems that can avoid these difficulties. Such a specification can then be employed to automate the generation of models and data required for the various approaches, thus improving the usability and spread of usage of the scheduling tools; in addition, comparisons can be promoted. Therefore, these new concerns constitute the second driving force of this contribution.

3   SchedOnto: Ontological Engineering Approach

Ontologies are semantic structures encoding concepts, relations and axioms, which provide a conceptual model of a given domain. Their aim is to capture consensual knowledge in a generic way that may be reused and shared across software applications and by groups of people [10-11]. Ontologies are widely employed for distinct purposes by different communities, but in the last decade they became popular when they turned into the backbone of the Semantic Web. In addition, ontologies are nowadays also setting the grounds for the integration of software applications.

An extensive state-of-the-art overview of methodologies for ontology engineering has been reported in [10]. This review points out different principles, design criteria and stages for ontology development. However, all of them involve at least the three stages proposed by the Enterprise ontology methodology [12] to build an ontology from scratch: (i) to identify the purpose and scope, (ii) to capture the concepts and relationships among these concepts, as well as the terms used to refer to concepts and relationships, and (iii) to codify the ontology.

3.1   Methodological Considerations

For the development of SchedOnto, and ad-hoc methodology based on well accepted principles has been proposed. It has the following four stages:

— Requirements specification; this stage identifies the scope and purpose of the ontology.
— Conceptualization stage, which organizes and converts an informally perceived view of the domain into a semi-formal specification using UML diagrams.

— Implementation stage, which implies the codification of the ontology using a formal language.
— Evaluation stage, which allows making a technical judgment of the ontology quality and usefulness with respect to the requirements specification, competency questions and/or the real world.

It should be noted that these stages are not truly sequential; indeed, any ontology development is an iterative and incremental process. If some need/weakness is detected during the execution of a stage, it is possible to return to any of the previous ones to make modifications and/or refinements. The two first stages have been completed and the last two are currently in progress. Some highlights of these methodological steps are given in the remaining of this section.

Requirements Specification. This first step involved an analysis of needs and demands for different types of batch processes, plant environments, and operations modes, when addressing a scheduling problem, along with a comprehensive bibliographical research. Based on the gathered knowledge it has been possible to recognize the following modeling requirements. The goal has been to provide a formal specification of the scheduling domain by identifying relevant objects and relationships that:

— Represent input information necessary for the scheduling activity: (i) products and their master recipes, which specify how to manufacture them in a given site, (ii) production environment characteristics (equipment features, plant topology, etc.), (iii) production requests (manufacturing orders/amounts to be produced/demands for various products, due dates, etc.), (iv) resource (personnel, utilities, raw materials, equipment, etc.) availability along the scheduling horizon, and any other pertinent data.
— Explicit capture of the outcomes of the scheduling function: (i) control recipes that reflect how each batch is going to be produced (instantiations of master recipes), (ii) schedule specific information, detailing the agenda of each resource, etc.
— Allow the representation of production execution information, including timely data of how things have progressed, as well as batch-specific history information that could be used for rescheduling activities and managerial purposes, like performance analysis.

Conceptualization Stage. The second main step in SchedOnto's development process required identifying and capturing the domain concepts and their relationships, trying to fulfill the previous requirements. To support this activity, UML (Unified Modelling Language) [13] was adopted. In addition to class diagrams, constraints about the objects in the model and invariants on classes have been added using OCL (Object Constraint Language) [14]. The results of this stage are not described due to lack of space. However, a partial model will be described in the next section.

Since ontologies are, by definition, based on consensual knowledge, both the ISA-88 [15-18] and ISA-95 [19-20] standards, which are well accepted in the industrial domain, have been taken into account during the conceptualization step. The mail goal of ISA-88 is the control of the batch process, whereas the final goal of the ISA-95 standard is the exchange of information between levels 4 and 3 of its hierarchical model. Though both have a close relationship with the scheduling activity, they differ in terms of their purpose and terminology. According to the ISA-95 standard, the scheduling functions that are of interest (i.e. determination of production schedule, raw material requirements identification, etc.) interface to the manufacturing operations and control system ones through product definition information, production capability information, production schedule, and production performance information. A detailed analysis of this standard shows some overlapping with the information and activities handled by the ISA-88 one (e.g. product definition vs. recipe specification, equipment capability vs. physical model, etc.), which reveals some possible collision points. These issues, which have already raised some concerns [21-22], have been taken into account in the conceptualization stage.

In fact, the different parts of both the ISA-88 and ISA-95 standards have been developed by different people and at distinct moments. This led to the presence of inconsistent and/or incomplete information. Thus, not only there are some consistency problems that still need to be addressed when using these two standards together, as the scheduling domain requires, but also there might be some incoherencies within each standard itself. For instance, Part I of the ISA-88 standard [15] was approved in 2010 and Part II [16] more than ten years ago. This brings about some lack of correspondence between the terms and definitions included in Section 3 of [15] and the data structures that are specified in Part 2 of the same standard [16]. These matters have also been carefully considered during the ontology development process.

Implementation Stage. The following planned activity in the methodology required the selection a formal language suitable for the codification of the concepts that were identified in the previous stage. Based on its ample acceptance, OWL 2 [23], developed by the W3C (World Wide Web Consortium), was chosen.

Evaluation Stage. The development of SchedOnto has been guided by the principles of coherence, conciseness, intelligibility, adaptability, minimal ontological commitment and efficiency. Some of these principles are conflicting among themselves. Due to such incompatibilities, a suitable balance between the clashing principles was sought. Nowadays it is widely accepted that there is a lack of a formal methodology that considers all these criteria, which could be applied to evaluate domain ontologies. According to some authors [10], the ontology evaluation phase comprises three aspects: (i) ontology validation, (ii) ontology verification, and (iii) ontology assessment. Validation and verification activities are associated with a technical judgment of the content of the ontology with respect to a frame of reference, which can be requirement specifications, competency questions, or the real world. In turn, assessment focuses on judging the ontology content from the user's point of view. To address this issue it is expected to employ SchedOnto in the development of different types of applications, in distinct contexts. As mentioned in Section 2, these applications will have as targets: (i) integration issues, (ii) scheduling problems specification, (iii) supporting a scheduling benchmarking framework. Up to now, SchedOnto has been successfully employed to develop a reactive scheduling framework based on a hybrid approach that relies on an explicit domain representation and a CP model [24].

With respect to the integration of heterogeneous information sources, a set of ontologies will be used to provide the semantics enabling the data mediation. For each application/data source to integrate a local ontology will be defined in order to make explicit the knowledge implicitly encoded in it. In addition, SchedOnto will serve as a reference ontology that unifies the terminology and conceptualization of the domain. The ontologies will be part of a platform having a three-layer architecture: a) the reference one, containing SchedOnto, b) the application/data sources to integrate, and c) the intermediate or connector layer, which contains a connector component for each application/data source (A/DS) to be integrated. These connectors, based on local ontologies, will be in charge of coping with the heterogeneity issues posed by each A/DS, which implies, among other things, translating the queries/information needs expressed in terms of local data sources into ontological instances stated in terms of the reference ontology, and vice versa. The connector mediation process will be carried out in two steps, one syntactic and one semantic. For instance, for lifting a case study represented in one of the popular formats (e.g., the State-Task-Network based representation used by an MILP model) it will be required to perform a syntactic transformation in which the XML representation of the example is translated into instances in terms of a local ontology; then, in the semantic step these local ontology instances are transformed into instances of the reference ontology. Likewise, in order to lower a SchedOnto compliant case study to the format employed by a given MILP solution approach, the same steps will be applied in the opposite order.

Another research line, regarding ontology quality evaluation, analyses the structural dimension and employs an estimation of the ontology complexity considering the depth of the class hierarchy, as well as the number of classes, relations and instances defined in the ontology. This structural evaluation is under way.

4   Formal versus Informal Temporal Representations

One of the weakest points of the ISA-88 standard is the representation of logical and temporal issues, which are generally dealt by means of textual annotations and graphs, like the Procedure Function Chart (PFC). These representations are not formal, can be ambiguous, and cannot be interpreted by a computer. For instance, let's consider the `Building Block`, which is one of the elements of a `Recipe`. In Table 5 of [16] it appears that one of its attributes is `UsageConstraint`, which has the following definition: "Defines other rules that determine the usage (e.g., "always succeeded by..." or "never runs in parallel with...")". Another illustrative example is the PFC, which depicts procedural logic to define the execution sequence of the procedural elements that comprise a recipe. It is described in detail in chapter 6 of [16]. It is easy to recognize that the logical aspects (alternative versus simultaneous sequences of recipe procedural elements) of this graphical representation, as well as its temporal and synchronization issues, are modeled by means of different types of vertical and horizontal lines, and by interpreting for the relative position of the procedural elements along the y-axis.

On the other hand, the temporal relations that SchedOnto requires, appearing in recipes, schedules, etc., have been explicitly modeled as shown in Fig. 1. It presents a partial view of the adopted temporal model, which is based on Allen's temporal relations [25]. This model is complemented by formal specifications of constraints.

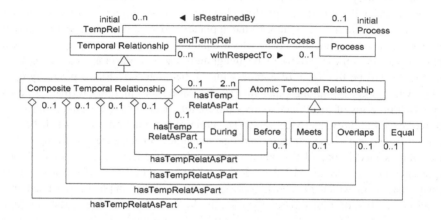

Fig. 1. Partial view of the temporal model adopted in SchedOnto

5   Conclusions

The paper described some features and the development process of SchedOnto, a domain ontology, which captures information of the scheduling field. Ontologies like SchedOnto play an essential role in describing and understanding complex fields. As a shared notation and a conceptual foundation, it might facilitate the communication, discussion, exchange of case studies, etc., among the members of scheduling community. In addition, since knowledge is explicitly and formally expressed, it supports inference processes and, therefore, the development of intelligent systems [24]. Last but not least, by providing a declarative, machine readable representation, SchedOnto can enable unambiguous communication between software agents that would otherwise be difficult or impossible. In this way, it can play a central role in solving nowadays integration problems that appear in the enterprise hierarchical planning pyramid. To illustrate the benefits of having a formal representation, the modeling of temporal aspects that are needed to represent recipe procedures was described and was contrasted with the graphical representation of PFCs proposed in [16].

Acknowledgments. The author acknowledges the financial support received from CONICET (PIP 2754), ANPCyT (PAE-PICT51) and UNL (CAI+D 2009, R4–N 12).

References

1. Maravelias, C.: General Framework and Modeling Approach Classification for Chemical Production Scheduling. AIChE Journal 58, 1812–1828 (2012)

2. Henning, G.P.: Production Scheduling in the Process Industries: Current trends, emerging challenges and opportunities. In: de Brito Alves, R.M., Oller do Nascimento, C.A., Chalbaud Biscaia Jr., E. (eds.) Computer-Aided Chemical Engineering, vol. 27, pp. 23–28. Elsevier Science Ltd., United Kingdom (2009)
3. PABADIS' PROMISE Ontology, http://www.uni-magdeburg.de/iaf/cvs/pabadispromise/dokumente/Del_3_1_Final.pdf
4. Shobrys, D.E., White, D.C.: Planning, scheduling and control systems: Why cannot they work together? Computers and Chemical Engineering 26(2), 149–160 (2002)
5. Maravelias, C., Sung, C.: Integration of production planning and scheduling: Overview, challenges and opportunities. Computers and Chemical Engineering 33, 1919–1930 (2009)
6. Kreipl, S., Dickersback, J.T., Pinedo, M.: Coordination Issues in Supply Chain Planning and Scheduling. In: Herrmann, J. (ed.) Handbook of Production Scheduling, pp. 177–212. Springer (2006)
7. Harjunkoski, I., Nyström, R., Horch, A.: Integration of Scheduling and Control – Theory or Practice? Computers and Chemical Engineering 33, 1909–1918 (2009)
8. Muñoz, E., Espuña, A., Puigjaner, L.: Towards an ontological infrastructure for chemical batch process management. Computers and Chemical Engineering 34, 668–682 (2010)
9. Castro, P., Harjunkoski, I., Grossmann, I.: Greedy Algorithm for Scheduling Batch Plants with Sequence-Dependent Changeovers. AIChE Journal 57, 373–387 (2011)
10. Gómez-Pérez, A., Fernández-López, M., Corcho, O.: Ontological Engineering: With Examples from the Areas of Knowledge Management, E-Commerce and the Semantic Web, 2nd edn. Springer (2004)
11. Studer, R., Benjamins, V.R., Fensel, D.: Knowledge Engineering: Principles and Methods. IEEE Transactions on Data and Knowledge Engineering 25, 161–197 (1998)
12. Uschold, M., King, M., Moralee, S., Zorgios, Y.: The Enterprise Ontology. Knowledge Engineering Review 13, 31–89 (1998)
13. Object Management Group. UML Unified Modeling Language Specification V2.1.1: Superstructure, OMG, http://www.omg.org
14. Object Management Group. UML 2.0 OCL Specification, http://www.omg.org
15. ANSI/ISA–88.00.01: Batch Control Part 1: Models and Terminology (2010)
16. ANSI/ISA-88.00.02: Batch Control Part 2: Data Structures and Guidelines for Languages (2001)
17. ANSI/ISA-88.00.03: Batch Control Part 3: General and Site Recipe Models and Representation (2003)
18. ANSI/ISA-88.00.04: Batch Control Part 4: Batch Production Records (2006)
19. ANSI/ISA-95.00.01-2000: Enterprise-Control System Integration. Part 1: Models and terminology (see also IEC 62264) (2000) ISBN/ID: 1-55617-727-5
20. ANSI/ISA-95.00.03-2005: Enterprise-Control System Integration. Part 3: Activity models of manufacturing operations management (2005) ISBN: 1-55617-955-3
21. Scholten, B.: Integrating ISA-88 and ISA-95. In: ISA EXPO 2007, Houston, TX (2007)
22. ISA-TR-88.95.0.: Using ISA-88 and ISA-95 Together (2008)
23. W3C OWL Working Group, OWL 2 Web Ontology Language Document Overview. Technical Report, http://www.w3.org/TR/owl2-overview/
24. Novas, J.M., Henning, G.P.: A Reactive Scheduling Framework Based-on Domain Knowledge and Constraint Programming. Computers and Chemical Engineering 34, 2129–2148 (2010)
25. Allen, J.: Maintaining Knowledge about Temporal Intervals. Communications of the ACM 26, 832–843 (1983)

Introducing "2.0" Functionalities in an ERP

Bernard Grabot[1], Raymond Houé[1], Fabien Lauroua[2], and Anne Mayère[3]

[1] Université de Toulouse, INPT, LGP-ENIT, Tarbes, France
{bernard.grabot,rhoue}@enit.fr
[2] SAP France S.A, La Défense, France
fabien.lauroua@sap.com
[3] Université de Toulouse, CERTOP, Toulouse, France
anne.mayere@iut-tlse3.fr

Abstract. Companies and ERP editors show an increasing interest for the Web 2.0 technologies, aiming at involving the user of a web site in the creation of content. We summarize in this communication what these tools are and give an overview of recent examples of their use in companies. We show on the example of the most recent ERP of SAP, Business By Design, that if "2.0 tools" are now available in some ERPs, their integration in the business processes is not yet fully done. We suggest in that purpose the first draft of a methodology aiming at developing "2.0 business processes" using an ERP 2.0.

Keywords: Web 2.0, ERP 2.0, business processes.

1 Introduction

The use of "Web 2.0" tools (including wikis, forums and social networks), which give an active role to Internet users, has dramatically increased during the last few years, creating a great interest from companies and organisations (including governments), all looking for new ways to better involve their stakeholders in their daily activities. Therefore, new paradigms like "Government 2.0" or "Enterprise 2.0" have been suggested for describing organisations re-structured in order to take full benefit of the "2.0" technologies. At the operational level, the idea of "ERP 2.0" (Enterprise Resource Planning 2.0) has been introduced, and several software editors have launched new version of their ERPs that include "2.0" functionalities.

In this quickly evolving context, the first objective of this communication is to make a panorama on recent applications of the 2.0 technologies in industry, illustrated on the example of the new version of the SAP ERP "Business By Design". We also show that existing applications only loosely integrate the 2.0 aspects to the existing business processes and we suggest guidelines for allowing to really design "2.0 processes" using an "ERP 2.0".

2 The "Web 2.0" Tools

The term "Web 2.0" refers to the new generation of Internet, characterised by innovative applications that break the barrier between creators and users of web sites.

C. Emmanouilidis, M. Taisch, D. Kiritsis (Eds.): APMS 2012, Part II, IFIP AICT 398, pp. 104–111, 2013.

The Web 2.0 mainly include wikis, blogs, tagging, syndication, mashups and social networks:

Wikis: A wiki is a web site which content can be edited by any user.

Blogs: A blog is a Web site containing inputs (posts) written on a specific subject by an individual or a group.

Social Bookmarking (tagging): A tag (or bookmark) is a key word added to a numerical object, which can be stored on a distant server and shared with other users.

RSS and Syndication: Syndication is the process that allows to make accessible information coming from a web site on another web site.

Social Networks: A social network is composed of people or organisations interacting in order to share mutual interests, contents, knowledge, etc.

Mashups: A "mashup" is a new applications, data or web page built on the base of multiple and heterogeneous sources.

These tools are of course of interest for companies, which permanently seek for new ways to more efficiently involve into their business processes their employees, but also their customers and suppliers. Especially, these new applications could address some of the problems linked to the use of ERP systems, often considered as creating social tensions within the companies by an increased centralized control and by imposing a standardised communication between employees, based on external "best practices" [1].

3   "2.0" Functionalities in Companies: Some Examples

Different uses of Web 2.0 tools can be noticed in companies:

The Web 2.0 as a Tool to Improve the Relationships with the Partners. An already classical use of the social networks in companies is to create links with potential customers [2], using the web site of the company, or existing social networks like Facebook, or blogs and topics in Twitter [3]. Web 2.0 tools can also be used for supplier support [4] and market places can be complemented with "chat" facilities [5], or by adding 2.0 functionalities to CRM tools [6]. In a context close to B2B (Business To Business), the Web 2.0 can also allow to gather partners for creating a "social" supply chain [7]. Adebanjo [8] underlines the interest of these tools for creating "e-clusters" of SMEs.

The Web 2.0 as a Mean to Create an Employees' Network. The goal is here a better interactivity between employees [9-10], like at Lockheed Martin for sharing purchase practices [11] or at EDF (Electricité de France) for allowing knowledge exchange [12]. At Dassault Systèmes, a platform of internal blogs has been implemented for facilitating the information transfer [9]. At HP, a "2.0" platform including bookmarking, tagging, RSS and social network allows employees to contact people with useful expertise. In [13] is presented an application in a company manufacturing flavours for the agro-food industry: the SocialText software, including microblogging, social networks and widgets, is used for creating networks allowing a fully decentralised management of tests of flavours by employees.

The Web 2.0 as a Tool for Knowledge Coproduction. Content management tools are of specific interest for knowledge coproduction [14-15]. A wiki dedicated to the creation of "trade encyclopaedia" has been implemented at Atos Origin [9] while Emerson Process Management and IFS North America use 2.0 tools for transferring knowledge from a generation of employees to another [14]. The improvement of an on-line support is mentioned in [15]. Carbone et al. [16] also describe results obtained in several Spanish companies on knowledge structuration through 2.0 tools, but Passant [12] emphasizes on the EDF case the problem of making exploitable the information recorded in a wiki.

The Web 2.0 as a Way to Open the Company on Its Environment. Some applications aim at creating a link between the company and external entities, outside formal working relations: at IFB, the access to "external users' wisdom" allows the employees to be aware of the practices promoted by other companies [15]. This need is also mentioned in [17].

The Web 2.0 as a Tool for Collaborative Work. Web sites can be turned into collaborative working platforms using Web 2.0 functionalities [18]. At Ford, the factory manager can publish the planning and may authorise on line improvements by other users [19]. In an operational way, social bookmarking tools like del.icio.us or "My Web 2.0" from Yahoo may allow users to share their bookmarks, and associated notes [20].

The Web 2.0 as a Mean to Increase Individual Productivity. In [21], an annotation system applied on the IBM Intranet is suggested for improving the performance of the search engines.

The Web 2.0 as a Social Experiment in the Company. 4000 employees of British Telecom were participating to a FaceBook group called "BT". The company decided to create internally a similar initiative, without any precise idea on its finality. A comprehensive set of tools including wiki/blog/social network was opened, and was massively adopted by the employees, with 1500 blogs opened in few days [22]. Nevertheless, no link seems to have been created with the existing information system of the company. A similar experience is described in [23], with the implementation of Taolin, a 2.0 platform, in the FBK research foundation in Italy.

In 2011, according to the ChessMedia survey [24], the 2.0 tools currently used in the organizations were Blogs (70%) and microblogs (58%), Full-feature collaboration platforms (60%), Videos (53%), Forums (51%), RSS feeds (34%) and Mashups (22%), in all the departments of the companies. In next section will be investigated more precisely how 2.0 functionalities could be introduced in companies, and more specifically in their main information systems: the ERP.

4   The "ERP 2.0"

4.1   From Enterprise 2.0 to ERP 2.0

The flexibility that could be given to an the ERP by the Web 2.0 is often discussed in blogs. For Andersson [25], the integration of tools like wikis and blogs to an ERP is firstly useful for "canalising" a tendency that may lead to a loss of productivity of the employees and to security breaches if not correctly addressed. For Botta-Genoulaz et al. [26], the "2.0" functionalities should participate to re-create the social links damaged by the standardisation of the exchanges between actors which may follow the ERP implementation, while Hawryszkiewycz [27] suggests an evolution of the corporate information systems towards a real "2.0" version for allowing "knowledge workers" to permanently update their social work connections. Kimberling [28] wonders whether these two technologies can really be aligned: on the one hand, 2.0 technologies (and especially social networks/wikis) group informal and unstructured social media tools allowing anyone to say anything without any real control or structure. On the other hand, ERPs are large, structured, enterprise systems with controls surrounding master data, security profiles, and standard workflows.

Few ERPs have at the moment publicized on the term "2.0". The example of "Business By Design", edited by SAP, is taken in next section for giving operational illustrations of what could be an "ERP 2.0".

4.2   The Example of "Business By Design"

Business By Design (ByD) has been launched by SAP in 2007 as a SaaS product (Software as a Service); it includes several functionalities of the Web 2.0:

RSS, allowing to have access to external information.

Mashups: Pre-configured mashups include communications with Google Map, Bing, Route planners (Google and Bing), search for a person (Tweeter, Facebook), and search for a company (Tweeter).

Tagging and Bookmarking: Tags can be associated to each object (customer, materials, customer order...). Other users will be able to access the tagged object via hyperlinks.

Web Services: ByD can create links with external Web services.

Collaboration Tools: a new tool, "Feed", allows group discussions and instant messaging.

Groupware Integration: a special add-on has been developed for Outlook for creating a direct link with ByD.

4.3   Examples of Use

Even if these functionalities have only been recently added, some real applications can already be listed:

Mashup Embedded Map: maps provided by Google Map have been used by several users in order to get information on their customer's environment.

Web Services: Web Services are often used for getting information on order delivery from other systems (Freight Forwarder). Such links have also been used for creating orders in a remote Online Sales service (an Internet based company linking retailers and consumers), the order being then automatically created in ByD.

Tags: some project managers have tagged their Projects with the technology that has been implemented. It is then easy to find people who have a comparable experience for other projects based on same technology.

RSS Feeds: users often select and filter feeds according to a customer name or product. Each time the user opens the "customer screen", RSS feeds are selected according to the on-line customer and sent to him. A SAP customer has also created two RSS feeds in order to inform his employees on IT maintenance and on company events.

In spite of several interesting applications, no clear methodology for developing 2.0 applications within Business by Design has yet emerged, and only "local" developments have been performed. The draft of a more systematic approach supporting the development of more comprehensive applications is suggested in next section.

5   Guidelines for Development of 2.0 Applications in an ERP

Some basic questions should be considered:

1. What is the main target of the project in the ERP context?
ERP systems can be considered according to (at least) two dimensions: the functions they address (broadly speaking: Customer Relationship Management, Logistics, Finances, Human Resource Management, Business Intelligence) and the steps of their life cycle (project organisation, training, process modelling, tests, go-live, optimisation). Additionally, an ERP has close connections with peripheral functions like Enterprise Modelling, Knowledge Management and Product LifeCycle Management. The goal is here the identification of a couple (step of implementation, function), called "Target" in what follows; for instance: CRM function in the Activity modelling phase.

2. What are the stakeholders involved in the Target?
The answer should be a list of roles for the people involved in the Target. For instance: customers and employees for the Marketing area, logisticians and suppliers in the "Logistic" function, key users and consultants in the "Optimisation phase" of the implementation, etc.

3. Inside the Target and between these Stakeholders, what are the objectives of the project?
The points listed in section 3.1 are examples of such objectives.

4. Which 2.0 tools should be relevant for meeting these objectives?
A decision tree has been developed for summarizing the criteria that should orientate on a given tool rather than on another, the objective of the introduction of the 2.0 tools being the root of this decision tree (see a part of the tree in Figure 1).

5. In reference to the pre-selected tools, what are the roles of the Stakeholders?
Example: in the "CRM" function, the goal is to disseminate news from the Marketing employees to the Customers. Marketing employees may so be the producers of one or several blogs, while the Customers will be the readers. If a formal group has to be built, a Social Network may encapsulate the process.
6. Develop the application inside the ERP, or choose external software.
In that purpose, it will be necessary to specify precisely what type of information or knowledge should be coproduced by each stakeholder according to his role.
7. Model the business processes based on the use of the "2.0" application.
The development of the "2.0" application should allow to reformulate the concerned business process and activities.

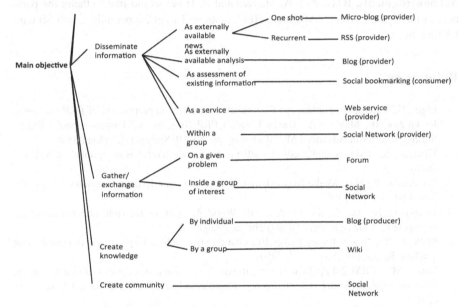

Fig. 1. Decision tree for the choice of a "2.0" tool (partial)

The validation of this step-by-step approach on real implementations of Business By Design is now in progress, promising initial results having already been obtained.

6   Conclusion

"2.0" tools, and especially Social Networks, pushed by their outstanding success in private uses, are nowadays "fashion" tools which utilisation gives a high-tech image to the companies. Many "minimal" implementations, often highly publicised, are a consequence of this "high-tech" image. Nevertheless, many interesting applications have also shown that these tools have a real potential for improving business processes, especially those related to coproduction of information or knowledge, which is a critical issue for the companies. In order to maximize the impact of these tools, it is therefore important to integrate them into the existing information system of the companies, the ERP. In that purpose, ERP editors begin to include "2.0" functionalities in their products, but a clear methodology for the definition of "2.0" business processes, supported by the ERP, is still missing. On the base of real applications using the new version of the ERP "Business by Design", edited by SAP, we suggest in this article to consider two dimensions in which the "2.0" tools could support ERP-based processes: the implementation project of the ERP, and the functions addressed by the ERP. This approach only provides some guidelines, and should be adapted to specific cases but we think that such methodology could allow to increase the use of these promising tools in industrial applications.

Acknowledgments. B. Grabot, A. Mayère and R. Houe would like to thank the partners of the SyGeo Project (MLState, HEC, Scan & Target), especially Layth Sliman, for their help.

References

1. Light, B., Papazafeiropoulou, A.: Contradictions and the appropriation of ERP packages. In: Grabot, B., Mayère, A., Bazet, I. (eds.) ERP Systems and Organisational Change. Springers Series in Advanced Manufacturing, pp. 85–99. Springer, London (2008)
2. Edwards, S.: Using social media to sell products, effectively! Blog (published July 14, 2010)
3. Goodbaum, B.: How Media Networking can help your manufacturing business. Blog (published January 18, 2010)
4. Doan-Huy, N., Xu, Y., Kondapaka, N.R., Wood, M.: Getting the right information to the right people at the right time. Blog (published August 2009)
5. Williams, P.: New software makes live chat an affordable reality for aviation component vendors. Blog (published July 7, 2010)
6. Sigala, M.: eCRM 2.0 applications and trends: The use and perceptions of Greek tourism firms of social networks and intelligence. Computers in Human Behavior 27(2), 655–661 (2011)
7. Hinchcliffe, D.: The Advent of the social Supply Chain. Blog (published April 22, 2010)
8. Adebanjo, D., Michaelides, R.: Analysis of web 2.0 enabled e-clusters: a case study. Technovation 30, 238–248 (2010)
9. Bourdier, S.: Enjeux et apports du Web 2.0 pour la circulation de l'information dans l'entre-prise: le cas du service de veille stratégique du groupe Yves Rocher. CNAM Thesis (2007)
10. Beverly, T.: Real-world intranets in 2010: SWOT analysis. Business Information Review 27(2), 85–93 (2010)
11. Rosen, A.: Lockheed Martin Sets up private social network. Blog (published July 14, 2009)
12. Passant, A.: Case Study: Enhancement and Integration of Corporate Social Software Using the Semantic Web (EDF). Blog (published June 2008)
13. Lynch, C.: FONA wins a CIO 100 award for use of Enterprise Social Networking software from Socialtext. Blog (published June 1, 2010)
14. Goodbaum, B.: Wikis in use in Manufacturing sector. Blog (published February 22, 2010)

15. Iversen, W.: Social Networking Tools Penetrate Manufacturing. Blog (published January, 2010)
16. Carbone, F., Contreras, J., Hernandez, J.Z., Gomez-Perez, J.M.: Open Innovation in an Enterprise 3.0 framework: Three case studies. Expert System with Applications 39(10), 8928–8939 (2012)
17. Williams, A.: Facebook in the factory: manufacturers want social software, too. Blog (published December 17, 2009)
18. Neil, S.: Teamwork 2.0. Blog (published July 17, 2009)
19. Neumann, G., Erol, S.: From a social wiki to a social workflow system. Blog (2008)
20. Millen, D.R., Feinberg, J., Kerr, B.: Dogear: social bookmarking in the Enterprise. In: CHI 2006, Montréal, Canada, April 22-27 (2006)
21. Dmitriev, P., Eiron, N., Fontoura, M., Shekita, E.: Using annotations in Enterprise Search. In: WWW 2006, Edimburgh, Scotland, May 23-26 (2006)
22. Dennison, R.: BT 2.0 Case study. Blog (published November 12, 2007)
23. Ferron, M., Massa, P., Odella, F.: Analyzing collaborative networks emerging in Enterprise 2.0: the Taolin platform. Procedia Social and Behavioral Sciences 10, 68–78 (2011)
24. ChessMedia: State of Enterprise 2.0 Collaboration, Q2. Blog (2011)
25. Andersson, D.: Enterprise 2.0 and social media coming to ERP. Blog (published December 22, 2010)
26. Botta-Genoulaz, V., Millet, P.A., Grabot, B.: A recent survey on the research literature on ERP systems. Computers in Industry 56(6), 510–523 (2005)
27. Hawryszkiewycz, I.T.: Perspectives for Integrating Knowledge and Business Processes through Collaboration. In: Bider, I., Halpin, T., Krogstie, J., Nurcan, S., Proper, E., Schmidt, R., Ukor, R. (eds.) BPMDS 2010 and EMMSAD 2010. LNBIP, vol. 50, pp. 82–93. Springer, Heidelberg (2010)
28. Kimberling, E.: ERP 2.0: Social Media and Enterprise Software. Blog (published November 19, 2011)

Designing and Implementing a Web Platform to Support SMEs in Collaborative Product Development

Marco Formentini, Michela Lolli, and Alberto Felice De Toni

Department of Electrical, Managerial and Mechanical Engineering
University of Udine Via delle Scienze, 208, 33100 Udine, Italy
{marco.formentini,michela.lolli,detoni}@uniud.it

Abstract. Research on the product development process lacks of investigation on the aspects related to its potential integration in a web-based collaborative environment, especially when considering the practical needs of Small Medium Enterprises (SMEs).Our study aims at investigating how is it possible to design and develop a web-based platform aimed at supporting SMEs in the product development process. On the basis of a thorough literature review and a mapping of the existing platform and tools available in the design domain, this paper describes in detail the development of a ICT platform, called iCommunity, which constitutes the backbone and the foundation upon which to build an ecosystem of innovation, that helps SMEs to: (1) manage the distributed collective intelligence in the new product development; (2) design and develop modular products in a collaborative way. The action research methodology has been chosen for its appropriateness to the characteristic of this study.

Keywords: Product development, Collaboration, Web platform, SMEs.

1   Research Context

Since the rise of the "open innovation" concept [1], much has been said about the benefits that companies may gain by opening up their innovation process. According to the open innovation paradigm, firms have the possibility to explore new sources for innovation, through an "inbound openness", with the aim of capturing technologies and ideas originated outside the organization's R&D facilities, and transfer them into the company. The underpinning concepts of the open innovation paradigm, which can be summarized in the exchange of ideas, interaction with external partners and new forms of collaboration among the actors involved, may be contextualized in another paradigm, that emerged in the digital domain in the same years of the spreading of the open innovation: the rise of Web 2.0.

With the "new" web applications able to facilitate collaboration, knowledge sharing and engagement among the users, the Web 2.0 has immediately represented an improvement in respect to the Web 1.0, characterized by a static use by the users without the possibility of interaction, and an opportunity "to harness collective intelligence" [2].

C. Emmanouilidis, M. Taisch, D. Kiritsis (Eds.): APMS 2012, Part II, IFIP AICT 398, pp. 112–119, 2013.

It appears clear how the web has straightway signified for firms a valid enabler to the open innovation practices. In the literature, we can find relevant contributions that depict the prominent role of the web as an intermediary for innovation: Sawhney et al. illustrate the communities of creation [3], and in particular the role of Internet as a platform for a valuable collaborative co-creation with customers. Pisano and Verganti propose four way to collaborate in the context of open innovation [4], two of which are made possible by the presence the web. Boudreau and Lakhani propose two ways to organize external innovators [5]: *collaborative communities* vs. *competitive markets*, putting in evidence how the former are driven by cooperative relationships, while the latter tend to have competitive relationships among one other.

In this context, virtually no company should innovate in an individualistic and independent way: "the new leaders in innovation will be those who figure out the best way to leverage a network of outsiders" [4].

2   Criticalities for SMEs in the Collaborative Innovation Environment

Specifically, the present research is focused on a significant gap that regards the context of Small and Medium Enterprises (SMEs): while Internet technologies are applied more widely by the large organizations to facilitate collaboration in the trading activities, in the learning, studying and managing of business processes, or in the services providing, there are significant barriers to the diffusion of e-business and advanced web applications in the context of SMEs. Companies, especially SMEs, that want to adopt a collaborative approach have not yet developed innovative application tools and well-established methodologies. More specifically, some of the SMEs key needs in the field of collaborative innovation may be summarized as follows:

- have a closer proximity and accessibility to cognitive diversity, and have the ability to connect directly with other industries or with the final users, in order to collaborate on innovation practices;
- be guided to realize the possibilities to access knowledge, for learning how to build an own innovation and social capital: "the collective capacity of a firm to innovate";
- be helped to identify future emerging trends and technological-economic discontinuities, structuring a network approach with others, that permits to capture the "weak signals";
- be supported in the managing of technical and creative approaches during the developing of ideas for new products and services;
- be helped to reduce market risks associated with investments in innovation and R&D, through the development of outside networks of intelligence which result in feedback from users and from the market;
- be driven to improve the design and product development process, in order to receive suggestions and co-develop a product or a service.

In particular, focusing on the latter aspect, there is limited research on how web communities can positively impact the product development process of SMEs. One interesting study in such context is offered by Pritchard et al. [6], who describe the effort of a group of Singapore SMEs to cooperate and set up a partnership to carry out product development in a design chain, through a set of tools which assists SMEs to quickly and profitably bid for and carry out early development of a major sub-section of a new product. This project is focused on collaboration during the early phases of product development, and people augmentation, not replacement, by enhancing natural communication and creativity.

Therefore, our research is directly linked to these recent areas of study, and aims to deal with them through an operative and functional approach in order to match the needs of SMEs.

3   The Product Development Process in the Context of Collaborative Innovation

The product development process lacks of investigation in the aspects related to its integration in a web-based collaborative environment [7] especially when considering the context of SMEs. Thanks to a literature review and a mapping of the existing solutions, we were able to shape a comprehensive "state of the art" of portals and tools, as described in Table 1.

Portals allow communities to interact through basic design environments. They provide different services, often in a crowdsourcing modality. Existing examples are several and heterogeneous, that we grouped into three main categories:

- *Innovation marketplaces* support companies in their R&D problems through innovation challenges. Even though the innovation seekers may be any type of companies, these challenges are mostly powered by large organizations, in spite of SMEs. The support given by these portals is limited to the initial phase of the R&D and innovation process, when seekers need to find proper solvers, but platforms usually do not sustain companies in the product development process.
- *Creativity hubs*, as the innovation marketplaces, use contests to match seeker and solvers, but in this case to support creativity instead of innovation. Their aim is to create ad-hoc and spot collaboration between organizations and creative designers. As before, they do not to sustain the entire product development, but the focus is instead on the resolution of specific design problems.
- *Distributed factories* are the place were advanced manufacturing technologies, such as 3D printers, match with the Web 2.0; they offer a world-wide prototyping and manufacturing service integrated with on-line CAD-CAM tools.

More than 50 standalone *design tools* were identified and analyzed. These tools range from simple open source web-based tools to commercially available desktop-based tools. The most popular tools regard established design and product development techniques such as QFD, FMEA and TRIZ methodologies. These tools help firms to manage specific issues throughout the phases of the product development project.

Table 1. Mapping of portals and tools

Typology	Category	Examples	Gaps
Portals	"Innovation marketplaces"	• Innocentive • Hypios • NineSigma • Idea Connection • Innovation Exchange	• Challenges are mostly powered by large organizations, in spite of SMEs. • Support limited to the initial phase of the R&D and innovation process.
	"Creativity hubs"	• Crowdspring • Idea Bounty • 99Design • Choosa • Zooppa • BootB • Threadless • Quirky • Logo Design Team • wooshii	• Ad-hoc and spot collaboration between organizations and creative designers. • The product development process is not entirely supported, since the focus is on specific design problems.
	"Distributed factories"	• Ponoko • eMachine Shop • Shapeways	• Focus on the last part of the product development process (i.e. prototyping and manufacturing phases).
Standalone tools	**"Online tools"**	• QFD Builder • Gliffy's SWOT Analysis • Sunglass.io	• Lack of connection with other tools or portals • Need of tutorials to support new users (especially SMEs) in the methodology implementation
	"Desktop-based tools"	• FMEA Facilitator • Autodesk Design Review • Acclaro DFSS	• Lack of connection with other tools or portals • Risk of creating "isolated" documents • Limited interaction

Considering the main gaps of the analyzed tools, they are mainly developed with an internal focus to the firm, in other words they typically allow only the interaction between designers of the same company, which are located in different production sites, through a web-based client-server.

Moreover, the main solutions integrate tools, such as Computer Aided Design and Manufacturing (CAD/CAM) and Virtual Reality, or key elements of a single stage of the product development process, focusing mainly on the prototyping phases, which are generally located at the end of the product development process [8]: the development of tools that facilitate collaborative interaction of various technical, planning and managerial skills and competences in product development must also take into account the upstream stages of the process, namely the concept generation, the functional analysis and the product improvement, allowing to analyze aspects related to cost reduction, functionalities improvement, thus enhancing the overall quality, safety and sustainability of the product.

Furthermore, a comprehensive tool requires an "external" perspective, in which not only internal designers, but also other skills may be involved in the process, embracing the paradigm of "open innovation" and following the evolution of the traditional web towards the perspective of Web 2.0.

In this context, companies should leverage on some key elements such as trust users as co-developers intended to link the various sources to connect [2].

Therefore, the evolution of the product development process in a web-based application for the development of Collective Intelligence must take account of the opportunity to integrate seamlessly some established methodologies used in the traditional product development process, although they have not been explored for possible implementation within a web platform.

4   Research Design

In order to address these research gaps, our research aims at investigating how is it possible to design and develop a web-based platform aimed at supporting SMEs in the product development process. The objectives of our study are twofold: to select the tools and methodologies that can effectively contribute to product development in a web-based environment for collective innovation on the basis of practical user needs within SMEs, and to adapt them seamlessly within a ICT platform.

The action research methodology [9] has been chosen for its appropriateness to the characteristic of this study, since the main research objective is investigating the development and the implementation of a collaborative web platform aimed at supporting SMEs in the product development process. The research leading to these results has received funding from the European Community's Seventh Framework Programme (FP7-SME 2008-2) under grant agreement no. 243593, project COLLECTIVE – "Emerging communities for collective innovation: ICT operational tool and supporting methodologies for SME Associations".

Action research may be defined as an emergent inquiry process to solve real organizational problems, simultaneously bringing about change in organizations and adding to scientific knowledge [10]. In fact, this methodology entails the active participation of researchers in a change process [9]. For this reason action research is appropriate when studying the development of a collaborative web platform, as actually happened in our study.

As usually happens in action research, the platform we developed emerged from iterative cycles of data gathering, feedback, analysis, action planning, implementation and evaluation in close interaction with SMEs and other research institutions involved in the research project.

5   Platform Development

The developed ICT platform, called iCommunity, which constitutes the backbone and the foundation upon which to build an ecosystem of innovation, especially tailored to fit SMEs needs, allows to:

- manage the distributed collective intelligence and creativity in the new product development process in order to find new product ideas and its business model;
- design and develop modular products in a collaborative way, reducing the market risk from the time when significant input and feedback from customers and users become an integrated component with the overall process design.

The focus of the research was also to include selected design methodologies (e.g. FMEA, FAST diagrams, Value Analysis, QFD, etc.) on the basis of practical SMEs user needs, and to adapt them seamlessly within the iCommunity platform. Based on the needed functionalities within each of the product development phases, supporting design methodologies were selected and included in the form of desktop or web-based tools to enable complex design performance. This was done by adding methodologies related tools to a specific functionality within selected design phase. The aim was to assist future users of the platform and propose a specific methodology when dealing with specific design domain functionalities in the platform. In this manner, the platform supports the users during the whole design process, thanks to the integration of methodologies and tools, thus filling the gaps detected in our mapping (Table 1).

Design methodologies may add complexity to the design process, especially when considering SMEs that could not have developed structured design and product development competences: in fact, during the action research process, less than five per cent of the SMEs involved in the research project answered to our questionnaires that they are familiar with any of the design methodologies. Therefore, it was crucial to include less complex tools or partial tools that do not support a specific methodology as a whole but only answer problems related to specific functionality of the design domain.

Moreover, tutorials for implementing methodologies and tools are available within the platform: users can choose interactive video based lectures (e.g. PPT slides) and PDF descriptions. To support SMEs users, an overall guidance is also provided to explain the navigation across the whole design workflow.

Users can choose the methodologies, tools and related tutorials as "blocks", in order to structure the workflow across the whole design process, modeled on Cooper's Stage-Gate model [8], as represented in Figure 1: among the main platform functionalities, when entering a new product development/product improvement project, users can configure the workflow on the basis of their needs.

The project initiator can also choose collaborators from the platform users' network to involve them in the project and review activities after each design stage. Thanks to a semantic engine, the platform also suggests to the users potential workflows, collaborators and resources, on the basis of the information given at the beginning of the design process in the inception phase.

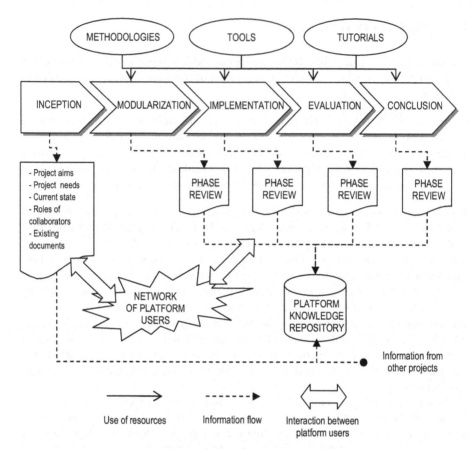

Fig. 1. Design process workflow

Moreover, data and information created in the whole design process can be stored and retrieved in the platform knowledge repository for future projects to allow knowledge transfer and reuse across different projects, which has been highlighted as a common pitfall in product development research [11].

6   Conclusions

From an academic perspective, our research contributes to the product development research stream with innovative insights in the context of collaborative innovation and web-based platforms, by offering:

- A classification of the "state of the art" of portals and tools that can support the product development process;
- A critical analysis of the methodologies and tools identified on the basis of SMEs target-users practical needs and of the identified trade-offs (i.e. usability, cost, time) for their subsequent introduction into the collective innovation platform iCommunity;

- The modeling and adaptation of the tools chosen for their inclusion in the design workflow within the iCommunity platform, in order to fill the previously described research gaps.

Focusing on managerial implications, the development of the iCommunity platform represents an important opportunity for SMEs to effectively support their product development process.

Future developments of the study will be focused on the complete validation of the platform in order to measure performance improvements in the product development process of the involved SMEs with a longitudinal perspective: the vision for the future is that the iCommunity platform will become a forum of research and development for innovation. The citizens of this *agorà*, fueled in particular by universities, software developers, experts, consultants, are associations and SMEs and their staff, but also visitors to the web, the "external" world.

References

1. Chesbrough, H.W.: Open Innovation: The New Imperative for Creating and Profiting from Technology. Harvard Business School Publishing, Cambridge (2003)
2. O'Reilly, T.: Web 2.0 Compact Definition: Trying Again, Radar (2006),
   http://radar.oreilly.com/archives/2006/12/web-20-compact.html
3. Sawhney, M., Verona, G., Prandelli, E.: Collaborating to create: The Internet as a platform for customer engagement in product innovation. Journal of Interactive Marketing 19(4), 4–17 (2005)
4. Pisano, G., Verganti, R.: Which kind of collaboration is right for you. Harvard Business Review 86(12), 78–87 (2008)
5. Boudreau, K.J., Lakhani, K.R.: How to Manage Outside Innovation. MIT Sloan Management Review 50(4), 68–76 (2009)
6. Pritchard, M., Wong, P.: Commercial Partnership for Collaborative Product Development (CPD). SIMTech Technical Report 5, 306—310 (2004)
7. Pappas, M., Karabatsou, V., Mavrikios, D., Chryssolouris, G.: Development of a web-based collaboration platform for manufacturing product and process design evaluation using virtual reality techniques. International Journal of Computer Integrated Manufacturing 19(8), 805–814 (2006)
8. Cooper, R.G.: Stage-gate systems: A new tool for managing new products. Business Horizons 33(3), 44–54 (1990)
9. Coughlan, P., Coghlan, D.: Action research for operations management. International Journal of Operations & Production Management 22(2), 220–240 (2002)
10. Shani, A.B., Pashmore, W.: Organisation inquiry: Towards a new model of the action research process. In: Warrick, D.D. (ed.) Contemporary Organisation Development: Current Thinking and Applications. Scott Foresman, Glenview (1985)
11. Formentini, M., Romano, P.: Using value analysis to support knowledge transfer in the multi-project setting. International Journal of Production Economics 131(2), 545–560 (2011)

Exploring the Impact of ICT in CPFR: A Case Study of an APS System in a Norwegian Pharmacy Supply Chain

Maria Kollberg Thomassen[1,*], Heidi Dreyer[2], and Patrik Jonsson[3]

[1] SINTEF Technology and Society, Industrial Management, Trondheim, Norway
maria.thomassen@sintef.no
[2] The Norwegian University of Science and Technology,
Dept. of Production and Quality Engineering, Trondheim, Norway
heidi.dreyer@ntnu.no
[3] Chalmers University, Dept. of Technology Management and Economics, Gothenburg, Sweden
patrik.jonsson@chalmers.se

Abstract. This study aims at exploring how ICT affects CPFR with focus on information flows in planning and control processes. A case study of a pharmacy supply chain in Norway is conducted to investigate process changes related to an APS system implemented to support a CPFR initiative. Process changes are investigated in view of enhanced information, automated processes and organizational transformation. This study shows that the main impact of ICT is associated with enhanced information flows and transformed processes that its contribution to reducing labour is more limited, and that large information volumes are critical. Adding to current CPFR literature this work provides insights to the contribution of ICT with focus on enhanced information and process transformation. The importance of automatic features of ICT in information processing and exchange and its contribution to improved planning and control information as well as to implementing a joint CPFR approach is especially highlighted.

Keywords: ICT, CPFR, supply chain collaboration, planning and control.

1 Introduction

Planning and control of demand and supply involves a wide range of decisions spanning from long term strategic to more short term operational perspectives, including for instance inventory location, production capacity scheduling, shop floor execution, demand planning, distribution planning and network planning (Vollmann et al., 2005). Along with the supply chain management concept, suggesting that business competition takes place between supply chains rather than individual companies (Mentzer et al., 2001), joint planning and control approaches for matching demand and supply in the supply chain, have emerged (Stadtler & Kilger, 2008). A wide range of concepts for collaboration between supply chain partners, on planning and control, have emerged during the last decades. These concepts can take different forms in

---

* Corresponding author.

C. Emmanouilidis, M. Taisch, D. Kiritsis (Eds.): APMS 2012, Part II, IFIP AICT 398, pp. 120–127, 2013.

practice and include for instance quick response (QR), efficient consumer response (ECR), vendor managed inventory (VMI) and collaborative planning, forecasting and replenishment (CPFR).

CPFR offers a general approach to collaboration between partners and may be adopted in a wide array of variants (Skjøtt-Larsen et al., 2003). CPFR emerged in the US in the mid 1990s and the Voluntary Interindustry Commerce Solutions (VICS) Association published its first CPFR voluntary guidelines in 1998, the consumer packaged goods industry being the primary target group (Seifert, 2003, Ireland & Crum, 2005). Despite a wide range of CPFR pilots implementations, several studies show that adoption has been slow in practice and large-scale implementations have been scarce (Barratt, 2004b, Olhager & Selldin, 2004, Seifert, 2003).

Recent developments in new technologies for storing, exchanging, processing and communicating information i.e. information and communications technology (ICT), have offered numerous opportunities to handle information within and between companies. Enterprise resource planning (ERP) systems have traditionally been adopted to support planning and control of operations within companies. However, CPFR may be supported also by other types of ICT applications including for instance automated replenishment systems, advanced planning and scheduling (APS) systems, collaborative software and electronic data interchange (EDI).

Considering the increasing interest for CPFR and that it is closely related to the use of technology, it is surprising that only a handful empirical studies have been identified that focus on ICT adoption. Moreover, CPFR initiatives may be realized without ICT, but ICT can also imply the realization of considerable potential benefits. Even though several successful CPFR pilots with ICT support have been reported on (ECR Europe, 2002), studies providing detailed insights to ICT benefits are scarce. Literature highlights for instance that ICT is important to increase efficiency (Smith, 2006, Cederlund et al., 2007), especially when dealing with large volumes of information (Barratt, 2004a) and that ICT may enhance scalability and level of detail in collaboration (Ireland & Crum, 2005).

Effects of adopting ICT in CPFR and other forms of collaboration are recognized in literature. Nevertheless, limited empirical evidence is presented to help draw strong conclusions about the consequences of technology. These need to be more systematically investigated in order to bring further structure to the wide range of effects that ICT may cause in CPFR settings, i.e. how ICT contributes to enriched information, automated processes and organizational transformation, for instance. Adopting a structured and comprehensive approach, several different dimensions of the impact of ICT may be taken into consideration in a systematic way.

The purpose of this paper is to explore how ICT affects CPFR with focus on information flows in planning and control processes. The empirical setting consists of a CPFR initiative established between a pharmacy retailer and a wholesaler in Norway. This work is expected to contribute to highlighting elements and aspects that are critical to how ICT affects CPFR.

2   Theoretical Background

2.1   Processes and Information Flows in CPFR

The CPFR framework by the VICS Association is used to define key processes and information flows (VICS Association 2004, 2002, ECR Europe, 2001, 2002). In brief, CPFR encompasses four main processes;

- Planning and strategy includes the collaboration agreement and joint business planning activities. It establishes the basic rules for the collaboration, develops event plans and defines product mix and placement.
- Demand and supply management includes the sales forecasting and order planning/forecasting activities, in order to projects consumer demand.
- Execution encompasses order generation and fulfilment and includes the administrative tasks related to placing orders and the physical order fulfilment tasks such as preparation and delivery of shipments, reception and stocking of products on retail shelves, record of sales transactions and payments.
- Analysis involves exception management and performance assessment, aggregating results of key performance metrics, sharing insights and adjusting plans for continuous improvements.

Because the responsibility of collaborative activities is often distributed between partners and activities depend upon input information from both customers and suppliers, information is often exchanged between partners. The exchange of information is considered to be necessary to establish joint plans and forecast to be used for generating replenishment orders. The key information types of CPFR are:

- Collaboration arrangement: defines overall guidelines, rules, goals and scope of collaboration, mission statement, roles and responsibilities and performance measurement.
- Business plan: defines overall strategies and tactics for replenishment items comprising promotions, inventory policy changes, store openings and closings, production introductions, category and promotional plans and item management profile.
- Sales forecast: a projection of future sales for a given time period and location.
- Order forecast: a forecast of anticipated orders.
- Order: defines quantities of items to be delivered to a specific location.
- Execution information: execution data of current events and results of order fulfilment.

Since the collaboration arrangement and business plan are established on a long-term basis and are primarily based upon joint discussions and negotiations, information exchange mainly takes place during meetings. Since more frequent activities including sales forecasting and order forecasting are often led by one partner but depend upon information input from both partners, the use of ICT for communicating information is especially relevant.

2.2   ICT and Process Changes

The framework by Mooney, et al. (1996) is used to structure identified process changes, **Table 1**. The framework is based upon three categories reflecting three different perspectives on the impact of ICT, including the automational, informational and transformational changes.

Table 1. Process changes categories

Category	Definition	Examples of performance metrics
Automational	Process changes related to the use of ICT as a means for directly substituting labour.	Employee productivity, information processing cost, cost of goods sold, utilization of resources, total supply chain management costs
Informational	Process changes related to the use of ICT for facilitating the use of information.	Delivery performance, product quality, information quality, inventory performance
Transformational	Process changes related to the use of ICT for facilitating and supporting process innovation and transformation.	Delivery flexibility and frequency, product flexibility, responsiveness to urgent deliveries, range of inventory and products, cycle times, response times and lead times

The automational category reflects the efficiency perspective of value deriving from ICT replacing labour. The use of ICT for eliminating human labour may be directly associated with mechanization of current ways of doing business, leaving existing processes intact.

The informational perspective reflects the use of ICT to collect, store, process and disseminate information to support decision making and enhance product quality. It also reflects the use of ICT to develop new intellectual skills and to enhance the use of information about process performance for purposes of understanding, closely monitoring of process status and objects, analysing information and decision-making.

The transformational view refers to the use of ICT to facilitate and support process innovation and transformation including re-engineering of processes and redesign of organizational structures.

3   Research Approach

A case study approach was adopted in this research. Empirical data was collected from a supply chain consisting of a wholesaler and a retailer in the Norwegian pharmacy industry. This industry has undergone major transformations since the new pharmacy law came into force in 2001. New competitive requirements with regard to sales and distribution have thus opened for new collaboration opportunities between wholesalers and retailers. The requirements on the logistics system in the pharmacy industry are similar to those of other retailing and FMCG industries, characterized by short lead times, high efficiency and high service levels

The investigation focused on the impact of ICT, especially an APS system that was implemented in 2006 to support a joint CPFR initiative between two companies that were part of the same company group.

This initiative was initiated to facilitate the replenishment of goods from the warehouse to 145 pharmacies in Norway. The empirical data were principally collected by semi-structured face-to-face interviews; a total of 18 interviews were conducted with employees representing the wholesaler, the retailer chain administration, the pharmacies, the joint management team and the joint replenishment team.

The analysis of empirical material is based on a comparison of CPFR processes before and after the APS system was implemented. This before-after comparison permitted the identification of process changes. In order to capture both before and after perspectives, interviewees were selected who had in-depth insights to how processes were carried out after the APS system implementation as well as before. Due to that the situation before the system implementation was investigated in a retrospective perspective, a larger amount of empirical data were related to after the system implementation compared to before.

4   Findings

Before the APS system was implemented, the retailer and the wholesaler collaborated primarily on long term planning. Planograms and other relevant market directives used to be transferred to the pharmacies from the pharmacy chain administration that was responsible for planning of market activities and sales forecasting. Pharmacies were responsible for deciding order quantities and timing, for generating orders locally and sending them to the wholesaler.

The new CPFR initiative implied that a joint planning and control approach was adopted and integrated in the APS system for replenishment of pharmacy inventories. A joint replenishment team was established with responsibility for the new APS system, ensuring centralized replenishment. The system enabled automatic demand forecasting and order generation with exception management. The control of planograms, campaigns, phasing in/out of items was also integrated in the new planning and control approach and the APS system supported daily and automatic update of assortment changes information in pharmacies. The information stored in the APS database was further used for detailed analysis and follow-up on performance.

Several major changes were identified by comparing processes before and after the APS system implementation, see **Table 2**. The majority of changes were concentrated to three principal activities; order planning/forecasting, order generation and performance assessment. The system helped to reduce the need for labour in pharmacies; time savings on ordering corresponded to 0.5 FTE per pharmacy. However, the main contribution of the system was related to its informational impact, by improving the accuracy in orders and order forecasts and the facilitation of the implementation of a common planning and control approach for pharmacy inventories. This led to major reductions in pharmacy inventory. Because the APS system was tightly integrated with the collaborative planning and control approach of the CPFR initiative, it facilitated the centralization of order planning/forecasting, order generation and performance assessment. Also, it improved the collaborative conditions in the CPFR initiative, by formalising, structuring and standardizing information flows and routines.

Table 2. Key process changes identified

Category	Key process changes	
Automational	Time savings in pharmacies	
Informational	New competence requirements Automatic update of assortment changes More standardized and varied assortment More formalized and standardized implementation of market plans Improved pharmacy inventory performance More planning flexibility and standardization Customized campaigns Higher forecast accuracy	Centralized and automatic order generation Automatic update of POS data and inventory levels Higher order accuracy Combined costs of pharmacies and warehouse in order calculations Reduced costs in warehouse Automatic exceptions management Centralized assessment and reporting of replenishment performance Availability of historical sales information Increased replenishment reporting
Transformational	Centralized responsibility of order planning/forecasting More integrated planning More planning flexibility and standardization	Centralized assessment and reporting of replenishment performance Centralized and automatic order generation

Findings of the pharmacy supply chain case show that:

- ICT primarily affected CPFR by enhancing information flows and by enabling process transformation. Compared to its informational and transformational impact, ICT had a less important impact in terms of automation i.e. the use of ICT for substituting labour.
- ICT enabled major enhancements of information flows that contributed to improved planning and control and especially major inventory reductions. Automatic processing and exchange of information was a key aspect for acheiving this outcome.
- ICT enabled major process transformations that were primarily related to the implementation of a common planning and control approach.

5   Discussion

This study revealed that the contribution of ICT in CPFR is primarily related to enhanced information used in planning and control and to the use of ICT in automatic
processing and exchange of information. The automatic features of ICT also seem
critical to ensure the execution of decisions that are agreed to and a high speed exchange and use of large amounts of information.

It also revealed that ICT contributes to organizational transformation related to the
establishment of the joint planning and control approach, especially in order plan-
ning/forecasting and order generation. ICT also seems to enable that agreed routines
and rules are formalized between partners, promoting collaborative actions. The dependency between ICT and process re-engineering points to that ICT is critical for
implementing the CPFR model and for framing a joint planning and control approach.

In view of current literature, this research shows that ICT has further implications
in CPFR besides increased efficiency. Findings suggest that ICT has major contributions related to enhancing information and transforming processes and organizations,
adding to current CPFR literature, which emphasizes the efficiency perspective of
ICT (e.g. Smith, 2006). This study confirms that ICT enhances information, including
for instance in terms of scalability and level of detail (Ireland & Crum, 2005), and that
large volumes of information is critical for realizing benefits of ICT (Barratt, 2004a).

A few new aspects, which are not discussed in literature, have also been identified
in this research. First, the automatic features of ICT for information processing and
exchange have major importance for achieving enhanced information flows. Second,
it points to that ICT also has considerable implications in a planning and control perspective, not only for improving information but also for implementing a joint
planning and control approach.

6   Conclusion

In this study we have explored how ICT affects planning and control processes in
CPFR. ICT, such as the APS system of the case study, is expected to improve the
performance and success of managing supply chain operations. As an instrument, ICT
will lead to benefits such as increased efficiency, supply chain integration and communication, service levels and enhanced speed of information flows. We have showed
how the impact of ICT in planning and control processes in CPFR can be related to
automational, informational and transformational effects. The main impact of ICT is
associated with enhanced information flows and transformed processes.

In an automational perspective, planning and control activities have become less
manual, more formalized and centralized. Resources have been allocated to a joint
and centralized planning and control team for replenishment decision making. Results
related to informational changes show that ICT has contributed to a more efficient
planning and control process regarding time and resources. The planning and control
instrument has become more precise and real time and demand oriented. ICT has also
led to significant transformational changes. The planning and control processes have

been integrated, redefined and restructured in line with a new and more demand driven joint planning and control approach. A vital element in the new planning and control approach is the real time information and processing capacity enabled by ICT.

This research adds to current CPFR literature by providing insights to the contribution of ICT with focus on enhanced information and process transformation. The importance of automatic features of ICT in information processing and exchange and its contribution to improved planning and control information as well as to implementing a joint CPFR approach, is especially highlighted.

References

1. Barratt, M.: Understanding the meaning of collaboration in the supply chain. Supply Chain Management 9, 30–42 (2004a)
2. Barratt, M.: Unveiling Enablers and Inhibitors of Collaborative Planning. International Journal of Logistics Management 15, 73–90 (2004b)
3. Cederlund, J.P., Kohli, R., Sherer, S.A., Yao, Y.: How Motorola put CPFR into action. Supply Chain Management Review 10, 28–35 (2007)
4. ECR Europe 2001. A guide to CPFR implementation (2001)
5. ECR Europe 2002. European CPFR: Insights (2002)
6. Ireland, R., Crum, C.: Supply chain collaboration. J. Ross, Boca Raton (2005)
7. Mentzer, J.T., Dewitt, W., Keebler, J.S., Min, S., Nix, N.W., Smith, C.D., Zacharia, Z.G.: Defining supply chain management. Journal of Business Logistics 22, 1–25 (2001)
8. Mooney, J.G., Gurbaxani, V., Kraemer, K.L.: A process oriented framework for assessing the business value of information technology. The DATA BASE for Advances in Information Systems 27, 68–81 (1996)
9. Olhager, J., Selldin, E.: Supply chain management survey of Swedish manufacturing firms. International Journal of Production Economics 89, 353–361 (2004)
10. Seifert, D.: Collaborative planning, forecasting, and replenishment: how to create a supply chain advantage. AMACOM, New York (2003)
11. Skjøtt-Larsen, T.K., Thernoe, C., Andresen, C.: Supply chain collaboration: Theoretical perspectives and empirical evidence. International Journal of Physical Distribution & Logistics Management 33, 531–549 (2003)
12. Smith, L.: West marine: a CPFR success story. Supply Chain Management Review 10(2), 29–36 (2006)
13. Stadtler, H., Kilger, C. (eds.): Supply Chain Management and Advanced Planning. Springer, Berlin (2008)
14. Vollmann, T.E., Berry, W.L., Whybark, D.C., Jacobs, F.R.: Manufacturing planning and control for supply chain management. McGrawHill, Singapore (2005)
15. Voluntary Interindustry Commerce Solutions Association (VICS), Global Commerce Initiative Recommended Guidelines: Collaborative planning, forecasting and replenishment, CPFR, version 2.0 (2002),
    http://www.vics.org/docs/committees/cpfr/
    CPFR_Tabs_061802.pdf (accessed January 20, 2009)
16. Voluntary Interindustry Commerce Solutions Association (VICS), Collaborative planning, forecasting and replenishment, CPFR (2004),
    http://www.vics.org/committees/cpfr/CPFR_Overview_US-A4.pdf
    (accessed January 29, 2009)

MES Support for Lean Production

Daryl Powell[1,2,*], Andreas Binder[3], and Emrah Arica[1,2]

[1] Department of Production and Quality Engineering,
Norwegian University of Science and Technology, Trondheim, Norway
{daryl.j.powell,emrah.arica}@ntnu.no
[2] SINTEF Technology and Society, Trondheim, Norway
{daryljohn.powell,emrah.arica}@sintef.no
[3] Department of Production Systems and Logistics,
Leibniz University, Hannover, Germany
andy_binder@web.de

Abstract. In the traditional sense, IT has often been viewed as a contributor to waste within lean production. However, as the business world changes and competition from low-cost countries increases, new models must be developed which deliver competitive advantage by combining contemporary technological advances with the lean paradigm. In order to make a contribution within this field of research, we evaluate the support functionality of Manufacturing Execution Systems (MES) for lean production. We address the fundamental principles of lean production and compare them to the functionality offered by MES, and by combining existing theoretical contributions with practical insights we develop a five-stage capability maturity model for MES support for lean production.

Keywords: Lean Production, Manufacturing Execution System, Production Control.

1 Introduction

Though the theory of lean production is nowadays well understood, the relationship between information technology (IT) and lean production remains a controversial and far less explored topic. While lean is often characterized by decentralized coordination and control, IT is typically best suited to support centralized production planning. However, more recently, IT is being used more and more as an enabler of decentralized decision making. For example, Powell and Strandhagen [1] explore the lean-ERP paradox, and suggest that there is a synergistic impact to be realized in combining ERP systems with the lean paradigm. For example, Powell et al. [2] introduce a capability maturity model for ERP support for pull production. Whilst Riezebos et al. [3] argue that modern IT can indeed be tailored to support lean; further research is required to investigate the combination of lean production principles and other modern applications of IT, such as manufacturing execution systems (MES). Therefore,

---

[*] Corresponding author.

C. Emmanouilidis, M. Taisch, D. Kiritsis (Eds.): APMS 2012, Part II, IFIP AICT 398, pp. 128–135, 2013.

the purpose of this paper is to evaluate the support functionality of MES for lean production by addressing the following research question: *How can MES be used to support lean production principles?*

2   Theoretical Background

The term lean production was popularized by Womack et al. [4] when they compared the mass production principles of the Western world to the very simple production principles of Toyota. As such, Lean production is based on the principles and working processes of the Toyota Production System, and has been defined as doing more with less [4]. In its simplest terms, lean production can be described as the elimination of waste [5]. Liker [5] suggests that the goals of lean production are highest quality, lowest cost, and shortest lead time. It was however Womack and Jones [6] who provided the world with a vision of what lean is about, and summarized lean thinking as five principles: precisely specify value by specific product; identify the value stream for each product; make value flow without interruptions; let the customer pull value from the producer; and pursue perfection.

However, the lean philosophy has so far been primarily directed at the organization and less on information technologies [7]. As such, IT has since been viewed as a contributor to the waste to be eliminated, rather than as a tool to help achieve and sustain positive change [8]. The increasing rate of development of IT today is constantly increasing manufacturing companies' ability to react quickly and reliably to demand through increased transparency, visualization and processing capabilities. Moody [9] suggests that, although profitability can be enhanced in any number of ways, one of the most rewarding and direct avenues is through the use of technology.

As an example of modern developments in IT, Arica and Powell [10] assert that Manufacturing Execution Systems (MES) are a highly plausible integration mechanism for linking the more traditional ERP systems to the production activity which occurs on the shop floor, which is where Lean efforts have traditionally been focused. As such, the application of MES has today become a very popular approach to the integration of manufacturing planning and control tasks, and has been applied in various types of industry. Though MES has emerged from the process industry, these types of execution system have more recently begun to be applied in discrete product manufacturing [11].

Though several authors attempt to analyze MES in terms of its complementarity for Lean efforts [e.g. 12, 13], so far an effort has not been made to establish a capability model for MES support for Lean Production. Therefore, by combining the approaches of Powell et al. [14] and Powell et al. [2], we use the five lean principles [6] in order to construct a capability model for MES support for lean production using both theoretical and practical insights.

3   Research Methodology

The primary research methodology is literature review. We analyze extant literature in the form of international journal publications, scientific textbooks, and white papers in order to explore the potential support functionality of MES for lean production. We systematically operationalize the five lean principles of Womack and Jones [6] in order to develop a framework and capability model for MES support for lean production. We also take insights from a practical, "illustrative" case study, which we have selected through convenience sampling. The case company is a Norwegian producer of jet engine components. The case study is conducted using data collected through semi-structured interviews of several informants in the company, including the production manager and production engineers. Direct observations and the analysis of secondary sources, such as company documentation and corporate website are used for triangulation, to check the internal consistency of data [15]. In this process a theory building approach is adopted to identify the potential support functionality of MES for lean production principles.

4   MES Support for Lean Production

In order to assess the depth of support provided by MES for lean production, we first conceptualize a capability maturity model (CMM) for the use of MES to support lean production principles. We consider existing capability maturity models [2, 16-18] in order to propose the various levels that should be contained within such a model. Then, by operationalizing the five lean principles with practical examples, we propose example criteria that a producer should fulfill in order to achieve each level of the capability model.

4.1   Capability Maturity Model

A maturity model gives a company the opportunity to compare the maturity of its operations relative to an industry best practice [19]. Furthermore, this tool supports the IT management in deriving and prioritizing improvement measures and subsequently controls the progress of their implementation [22]. All in all, a maturity model consists of a sequence of maturity levels for a class of objects that last from a bottom stage, which represents initial states e.g. characterized by an organization having little capabilities, up to the highest stage of total maturity [20]. Hence the developed capability maturity model (CMM) should provide the manufacturers with a framework to assess the support from their MES for the different levels of Lean Thinking. It delivers a five level scale for the maturity of the MES support within a company. Additionally, the manufacturers gain the opportunity to compare their maturity with each other and thus to identify the company's position compared to its best-in-class competitors, for example.

Several maturity models have been developed in the field of IT systems. The models listed in Table 1 have been considered during the development of our CMM. The IT balanced scorecard (BSC) maturity model deals with the use of the mentioned BSC regarding the measurement and improvement of present IT solutions. The CMM for Lean maturity and Lean sustainability provides a framework to distinguish the progress of the company regarding the maturity of the Lean implementation. It starts from the bottom stage of sporadic production optimizing to the top stage of a Lean execution beyond the own enterprise [17]. The capability maturity model integration (CMMI), developed by the Software Engineering Institute, focuses on improvements to the software process to ensure that they meet business needs more effectively. It can be considered as a framework to assist an organization in the implementation of best practice in software and systems engineering [18]. The last of the four considered capability maturity models deals with a topic closest to the present one. This model defines a scale for evaluating the maturity level and the extension of an organization's use of the ERP system to support Pull Production [2]. A summary of the models considered is given in Table 1.

Table 1. Summary of Capability Maturity Models considered

Author	Level 1	Level 2	Level 3	Level 4	Level 5
Powell et al. [2]	Initial	Planned	Validated	Controlled	Optimizing
Van Grembergen et al. [16]	Initial	Repeatable	Defined	Managed	Optimizing
Jørgensen et al. [17]	"Sporadic..."	"Basic..."	"Strategic..."	"Proactive..."	"Extended..."
O'Regan [18]	Initial	Managed	Defined	Quantitatively managed	Optimizing

Our CMM (Fig. 1) aims to classify the maturity of MES support for the five Lean principles [6]. Since it is recommended that the Lean principles be implemented in sequence, these principles directly represent the different stages of the maturity model. Though we place particular emphasis on the CMM for Lean maturity and Lean sustainability [17], we do however suggest that the extension of Lean practices beyond the enterprise can be achieved earlier then in level five, for example as early as level three (defined - flow). As it is the support functionality for MES for lean that we are most interested in, we take most insight from the CMM of Powell et al. [2]. A selection of examples of supported lean techniques for each of the five levels can be seen in Fig. 2.

5   Case Study: Volvo Aero Norge

This case study presents work from the research program SFI Norman. Part-funded by the Norwegian Research Council, SFI Norman aims at securing the future of Norwegian manufacturing through innovative working practices. The case itself draws on insight from Volvo Aero Norge (VAN) by comparing the company's current use of MES in light of our capability model.

VAN is an industrial partner organization within the SFI Norman program. Located in Kongsberg, Norway, VAN manufactures jet engine components for the world's largest aircraft engine manufacturers. The company is a technological competence center within advanced, mechanical production. This paper considers production operations at the Kongsberg plant, with a focus on production control.

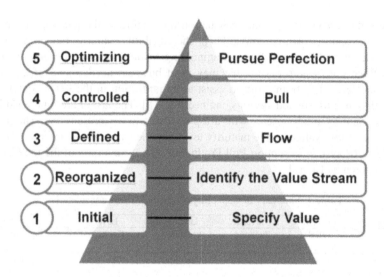

Fig. 1. CMM for MES support for lean production

5.1   Production Control at VAN

In this section we describe the production control activities at VAN. Firstly it should be duly noted that detailed scheduling of jobs to the resources is not carried out. Instead, dispatching of jobs is based on the First-In-First-Out (FIFO) principle. The dispatcher needs to consider and control all possible constraints in this highly complex manufacturing cell environment, which means traditional lean production control (with fixed schedules) is not ideal for VAN. A less myopic approach is therefore required. Also, as VAN have to meet the demands of the company's global objectives (e.g. reduction in WIP and lead-times), when work is released to the shop floor, information is needed to track the location and progress of the work during the entire production process. The status of the machines is automatically updated but some other activities require human intervention and paper work to update the information in the shop floor.

Information is collected from the shop floor in two ways. When the order is released to the resources its status is updated with the use of bar-code technology. This data is collected manually. The second way of data collection is carried out by tailor-made Manufacturing Execution System (MES), so called Machine/Cell Supervisor (MSUP/CSUP) that provides the control of the cell's operations and allows the visualization of all information needed to keep continuity in the production activities in terms of resources and equipment. The real time information is updated in a database and the resource status is displayed on screens on each of the machines on the shop floor.

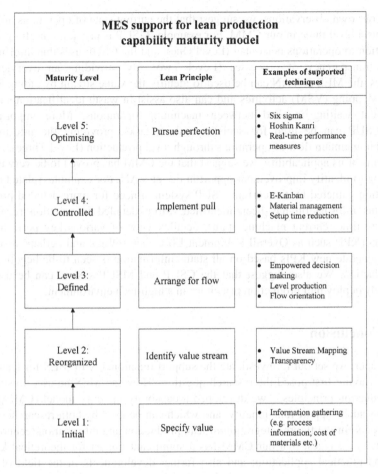

MES support for lean production capability maturity model		
Maturity Level	**Lean Principle**	**Examples of supported techniques**
Level 5: Optimising	Pursue perfection	• Six sigma • Hoshin Kanri • Real-time performance measures
Level 4: Controlled	Implement pull	• E-Kanban • Material management • Setup time reduction
Level 3: Defined	Arrange for flow	• Empowered decision making • Level production • Flow orientation
Level 2: Reorganized	Identify value stream	• Value Stream Mapping • Transparency
Level 1: Initial	Specify value	• Information gathering (e.g. process information; cost of materials etc.)

Fig. 2. Examples of supported techniques for each level of the CMM

The MSUP units that are installed on each machine provide a number of functions. Firstly, it forwards operational data from the ERP system (SAP) to each of the machining stations, and controls the machine start and internal transportation in the machines based on tooling status and availability, as well as the latest start date found within the ERP system. Additionally, it shows the status of the machine resources (e.g. machine, pallet, tools), and highlights any error messages that may occur. All MSUP units store status information in an MS SQL database, which is also accessed by the Cell Supervisor (CSUP). The CSUP then gives an overview of the entire production floor based on the status information from each individual MSUP.

5.2   MES Support for Lean Production at VAN

We applied our capability model to operations at VAN in order to gain practical insights into its applicability. From discussions with representatives at the company and through our own observations, we suggest that the current state of operations at VAN represents a level three in our CMM. For example, MSUP is providing useful process information to operations personnel (Level One); and the CSUP uses this information for the transparency of processes (Level Two). By providing an overview of processes, the MES at VAN can be used to identify the value stream by aiding Value Stream Mapping (VSM) activities and can also assist in waste identification such as time spent waiting in- and between machining operations. More importantly, MSUP/CSUP can be used for decision making tasks, providing the information required to maintain flow of operations through level production (Level Three).

In terms of its applicability, we suggest that the CMM has proved to be very useful in helping to identify improvement opportunities at VAN. For example, related to the information gathered by the current CSUP system, a need for more detailed production status information has been identified. More detailed information regarding machining time, current machine status, detailed view of various key performance indicators (KPI) such as Overall Equipment Efficiency (OEE), and perhaps a simple way to generate new KPIs based on all status information is seen to be beneficial in the production. We also suggest that the CSUP and MSUP system can be used to effectively deploy pull production principles in a high-tech environment.

6   Conclusion

In this paper, we set out to investigate the support functionality of MES for lean production. Having first posed the research question "How can MES be used to support lean production principles?" we developed a capability maturity model (CMM) that highlights such support functionality, and which can be used by both researchers and practitioners for the future integration of lean production and information technology. Therefore, we suggest that our CMM has a significant impact for theoretical knowledge and practical application; and also further developments in the field of lean and IT.

Further work should apply and test the CMM in other industrial settings, in order to test its generalizability. By applying our model to other cases, we suggest that a more generalized approach to improvement through the deployment of our CMM can be realized.

References

[1] Powell, D., Strandhagen, J.O.: Lean Production Vs. ERP Systems: An ICT Paradox? Operations Management 37, 31–36 (2011)
[2] Powell, D., Riezebos, J., Strandhagen, J.O.: Lean production and ERP systems in SMEs: ERP support for pull production. International Journal of Production Research (January 23, 2012)
[3] Riezebos, J., Klingenberg, W., Hicks, C.: Lean Production and information technology: Connection or contradiction? Computers in Industry 60, 237–247 (2009)

[4]   Womack, J.P., Jones, D.T., Roos, D.: The Machine that Changed the World. Harper Pe-
      rennial, New York (1990)
[5]   Liker, J.K.: The Toyota Way: 14 Management Principles From the World's Greatest
      Manufacturer. McGraw-Hill, New York (2004)
[6]   Womack, J.P., Jones, D.T.: Lean Thinking: Banish Waste and Create Wealth in Your
      Corporation. Simon and Schuster, New York (1996)
[7]   Zuehlke, D.: SmartFactory - Towards a factory-of-things. Annual Reviews in Control 34,
      129–138 (2010)
[8]   Bell, S.: Lean Enterprise Systems: Using IT for Continuous Improvement. Wiley and
      Sons, Hoboken (2006)
[9]   Moody, P.E.: With Supply Management, Technology Rules! Supply Chain Management
      Review (May/June 2006)
[10] Arica, E., Powell, D.: ICT Integration for Automatic Real-time Production Planning and
      Control: A Concept Note. In: Presented at the APMS 2010: International Conference on
      Advances in Production Management Systems, Cernobbio, Como, Italy, October 11-13
      (2010)
[11] Kletti, J.: Manufacturing Execution Systems-MES. Springer (2007)
[12] Cottyn, J., Landeghem, H.V.: The Complimentarity of Lean Thinking and the ISA 95
      Standard. In: Presented at the WBF 2008 European Conference, Barcelona, Spain (2008)
[13] Gerberich, T.: Lean und MES-Widerspruch oder Synergie? GABLER (2011)
[14] Powell, D., Alfnes, E., Strandhagen, J.O., Dreyer, H.: ERP support for lean production.
      In: Frick, J., Laugen, B.T. (eds.) APMS 2011. IFIP AICT, vol. 384, pp. 115–122. Sprin-
      ger, Heidelberg (2012)
[15] Scandura, T.A., Williams, E.A.: Research methodology in management: Current practic-
      es, trends, and implications for future research. Academy of Management Journal, 1248–
      1264 (2000)
[16] van Grembergen, W., Saull, R.: Aligning business and information technology through
      the balanced scorecard at a major Canadian financial Group: its Status Measured with an
      IT BSC Maturity Model. In: Presented at the Proceedings of the 34th Hawaii Internation-
      al Conference on System Sciences (2001)
[17] Jørgensen, F., Matthiesen, R., Nielsen, J., Johansen, J.: Lean maturity, lean sustainability.
      In: Olhager, J., Persson, F. (eds.) APMS 2007. IFIP, vol. 246, pp. 371–378. Springer,
      Boston (2007)
[18] O'Regan, G.: Introduction to Software Process Improvement. Springer, London (2011)
[19] Netland, T.H., Alfnes, E.: Proposing a quick best practice maturity test for supply chain
      operations. Measuring Business Excellence 15, 66–76 (2011)
[20] Becker, J., Knackstedt, R., Pöppelbuß, J.: Developing maturity models for IT manage-
      ment. Business & Information Systems Engineering 1, 213–222 (2009)

Handling Unexpected Events in Production Activity Control Systems

Emrah Arica[1], Jan Ola Strandhagen[1], and Hans-Henrik Hvolby[2]

[1] Norwegian University of Science and Technology, Trondheim, Norway
emrah.arica@ntnu.no, jan.strandhagen@sintef.no
[2] Aalborg University, Aalborg, Denmark
hhh@m-tech.aau.dk

Abstract. This paper highlights the important factors that influence the effectiveness of the event handling process in production control activity (PAC). Five key factors have been identified by the literature study. Production schedule generation and execution strategy under uncertainty, information and communication technology usage, coordination and feedback, human factor and interaction, and the performance measurement approach are the identified factors to be taken into account. Industrial interviews with three case companies, that are participating to the research program called The Norwegian Manufacturing Future (SFI NORMAN), have been carried out in order to gain practical insights as well as support and revise the findings by relevant empirical data.

Keywords: Production planning and control, Uncertainty, Event handling.

1 Introduction

The production control activity takes place in the context of production planning and control (PPC) which aims for matching customer demand with supply of products and materials in terms of timing, volume, and quality in a manufacturing company [1]. When the orders are released to the shop floor, the production control activity takes place in order to ensure that the plans are indeed executed on track. If any deviation is monitored, some corrective actions (e.g. rescheduling) are taken for tuning the schedules [2]. In this study, the production activity control system encompasses the handling of unexpected events and rescheduling activities. A dynamic manufacturing environment creates many unexpected events (e.g. machine breakdowns, material problems, tool status, defects, etc.) that must be captured and responded effectively, namely timely and appropriately [2]. However, the difficulty of addressing the issue of uncertainty in dynamic manufacturing environments is well recognized by researchers and practitioners for many decades [3-5].

Hence, this study questions: What important factors have been identified in literature to handle the unexpected events effectively and what insights can we get from companies, regarding the event handling process and identified factors? The study attempts to answer these questions and raises the issues that should be considered for

C. Emmanouilidis, M. Taisch, D. Kiritsis (Eds.): APMS 2012, Part II, IFIP AICT 398, pp. 136–143, 2013.
© IFIP International Federation for Information Processing 2013

successful development and implementation of the production control systems in practice. Clearly there are alternative interpretations of the system effectiveness and practicality. This is one perspective based on the related literature study, without aiming for a comprehensive review of each of the factors.

2   Methodology

This conceptual paper is mainly based on a literature study, supported with an iterative process involving three case studies to refine the findings. The literature review established the theoretical basis of the study and led to a framework that categorizes the literature and highlights the factors for effective handling of the unexpected events. Research lacks in such a holistic approach since the majority of research focuses on discussing a single factor. Hence, the purpose of the paper is to highlight and discuss some of the most critical factors that lead to gap between the theory and practice. Given the main purpose of the study with a focus on the practicality issue, multiple case studies were performed to gain insights into the industrial practice. Data was mainly gathered through interviews and observations.

3   Production Control Structures

Production Activity Control (PAC) includes the principles, methods, and techniques that are needed to schedule, control, measure, and evaluate the effectiveness of production operations [6]. The production control process assesses the situation during the production execution; identify the disturbances related to schedules, and takes corrective actions (e.g. immediate re-sequencing, task reallocation, or rescheduling) if needed. In order to achieve this, it utilizes shop-floor control data to maintain and communicate shop order and resource status information by functions such as WIP tracking, capacity feedback, quality control, status monitoring, etc. play critical role [1]. In general, there are two fundamental PPC approaches adopted to design the organisation, structure the information flow and perform the decision making functions: centralized/hierarchical and decentralized/distributed production control [4, 7, 8].

Hierarchical (Centralized) production control is the commonly applied approach in literature and practice. This paradigm decomposes the PPC problem into interdependent long term planning and short term scheduling levels to reduce the complexity and facilitate the solution [6]. The majority of the firms apply the Manufacturing Resource Planning (MRP II)/ Enterprise Resource Planning (ERP) system to create production schedules [9], with the core logic of Material Requirements Planning (MRP) to determine net material requirements. Output from the MRP run is a Planned Order Release (POR) schedule, which typically contains release dates and due dates of the orders. The production schedules further used to execute purchasing and manufacturing operations. Another alternative of scheduling the production orders on the shop floor is so called Advanced Planning System (APS), which outperforms the planning and control functionality of the ERP systems by simultaneously considering the finite capacity on the shop floor [10]. During the execution of schedules, any real time information can provide important input data for the production control. Over the last two decades, Manufacturing Execution Systems (MES) have been evolved to aid real-time production execution and control on the shop floor [11].

The hierarchical centralized approach coordinates the material flow and capacity for globally optimal outputs in the planning levels; however have drawbacks with handling unexpected events at the control level. One argument is that centralized systems are usually based on the aggregation logic in terms of time, material, location, and resources, which results in neglecting the level of detail in information flow and dynamics of decision making on the shop floor [2]. Another argument is that, in hierarchical control, the time and effort spent to react on changes by the right controller within the hierarchy (bottom-up), and then to make corrective decisions (top-down) generates ineffectiveness [8].

Heterarchical (Decentralized) production control is the other fundamental approach. Due to the complexity and difficulty of dealing with demand and capacity reconciliation, information processing, and unexpected events in a centralized system, distributing the decisional capabilities is receiving important attention recently [8]. There is therefore a rising trend of distributed MESs for real time production control [12]. Multi-agent scheduling systems are widely used to model the fully heterarchical systems [4]. These systems are composed of autonomous agents attached to physical and functional manufacturing entities, taking responsibility to carry out local scheduling and effectively responding local disturbances. They also try to achieve the required global performance by cooperating with each other. However, the difficulty of achieving a sufficient global performance is argued. This drawback led to the development of so called semi-heterarchical holonic production control systems, which enables localized decision making ensuring the global concerns of the factory [13]. However, there are many remaining issues (e.g. interoperability with existing information systems, complexity of interactions to understand and manage) that prevent the applicability of the distributed production control systems in industrial settings (see Trentesaux [8] for full review).

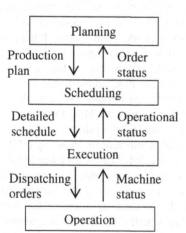

Fig. 1. Hierarchical production control (Adopted from Leitão, [7])

In summary, the modern production control literature, both in centralized and decentralized approaches, have been dominated by the modelling and analytical studies to improve the expected outcomes [14]. A great number of research papers published with regards to this topic, however, very few of them influenced the industrial practice [15]. These studies formulate the scheduling and rescheduling as a combinatorial optimization problem, neglecting many important aspects of reality [9, 16]. However, the event handling and rescheduling process involve equally important factors to be considered for the practicality of the production control systems. Hence next chapter attempts to outline the event handling process and the underlying factors. Furthermore, conducted interviews contributed to observe these factors and revise the findings of the literature study in an iterative process.

4   Event Handling Process and Underlying Factors

In literature, several terms are interchangeably used for the unexpected events, such as uncertainties, disruptions, disturbances, and rescheduling factors [9]. There have also been some studies to characterize and categorize the uncertainty in manufacturing systems (see for example Koh et al. [17]). Based on our discussions in the industrial cases, we think that it is also important to append the complexity aspect of the events into these categorizations. There are simple events that basically cause a time delay on the schedule, whereas complex events trigger further actions to be identified and evaluated due to significance of their impacts and interdependencies with lateral schedules and higher level plans. As discussed earlier, the effectiveness of handling unexpected events require timely and appropriate responsiveness. The majority of the studies focus on the "timely" requirement of the production control system [18], considering a simple discrete event with an impact on a single schedule [15, 16]. However, the "appropriateness" requirement is equally important for the practicality issue and requires a holistic view of the event handling process and involved factors.

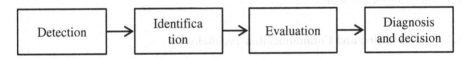

Fig. 2. Event handling process stages (Adapted from Cowling and Johansson, [3])

The event handling process typically consists of the following stages in practice: detection, identification, evaluation, diagnosis and decision making: When an unexpected event occurs it should be first detected by automated technologies or humans like operators [3]. The identification stage underlies the causes of the deviation, the context of the event for priority determination [15], and determines the relevant parties and information to handle the event. The evaluation stage identifies the required corrective actions based on the obtained information and evaluates the impacts of these actions on lateral schedules and plans. The final stage diagnoses if the required changes can be done with the current capacity and capabilities and leads to the decision making. The options are usually; to do nothing, repairing the schedule, or rescheduling [16]. On the basis of the literature study and industrial interviews, the following factors are identified to be important in the event handling process.

4.1   The Strategy for Production Schedule Generation and Execution

There are three main strategies applied for handling uncertainty in PPC [4, 15, 16]: predictive, reactive, and predictive-reactive strategies. In the predictive planning strategy, uncertainties are considered when the plans and schedules are developed, predicting the changes to be happened. In the reactive approach, no global schedule is generated in advance to the planning horizon and scheduling decisions are made locally in real time, applying simple priority dispatching rules. However, this approach still considers the information from higher level production plans. In the predictive-reactive approach, firstly, a global production schedule is developed over a future time horizon, and then modified in response to unexpected disturbances during the execution [15]. Regarding the insights from industry, the investigated companies have a typical hierarchical planning and control structure. In order to reduce the impact of potential disturbances, they apply the predictive techniques (e.g. safety lead time and safety stock) as well as react on changes with some *firefighting* methods. Their main challenge is that handling the unexpected events are not so straightforward, requiring further evaluation of the context that the event occurred and corrective actions, and the impacts of these actions on the schedules of shared resources and personal. As stated earlier, these strategies allow considering only a small number of uncertainties discretely. Uncertainty is unpredictable by nature and can generate unexpected conditions beyond what these techniques can foresee. Hence, we suggest extending these strategies with the proactive approach on the control level, diagnosing the likely disturbing impacts of the events on a real time basis and taking continuous corrective actions based on these early warning signs. This approach is especially important for *complex events* which may generate *side effects* of disturbances in complex manufacturing environments.

4.2   Information and Communication Technology

Lack of attention to the production control level can also be seen on the information systems widely used in practice. When it comes to adopt the plans and execution phases, they hardly provide any guidelines or mechanisms [19]. For instance, Ivert [20] reports the negative consequences of APSs used to handle disturbances on the lower shop floor level as extracting information from these kinds of systems is too complicated. Effective incorporation of real time information about the events into the manufacturing planning and control systems is critical to handle unexpected events. MESs are emerged to provide this functionality. However, there is still need for MES modules that will detect production exceptions and provide production personnel with online information and decision support [11]. These drawbacks are also notable in the case studies. All three companies use a standard ERP system on the planning level and a tailor-made or standard MES system for shop floor control. When a disturbance occurs, it is hard to obtain the detailed information (location, resource and material status, etc.) required from the ERP system. Moreover, the primary functionality of the employed MES systems is data collection and visualization, however, they fail to provide real time analysis and decision making support for the operators on the shop floor. While these requirements are not met, the monitoring and control task becomes difficult to be performed effectively and therefore still largely relies on manual interventions.

4.3   Coordination and Feedback

Handling an unexpected event in a production control system involves a substantial amount of coordination and feedback efforts between relevant parties. However, the majority of research studies consider uncertainties independently [17], which is not the case in reality. This factor has been recognized by some recent empirical studies (see for example de Snoo et al. [9]), showing the interdependencies, communication, and feedback process between planning and control levels during event handling process using an in-depth single case study. This factor especially grows in importance for the identification and evaluation stages in the event handling process described earlier. In these stages the environmental context of the event outlined and the actors to be involved are identified. Results of these stages significantly affect what actions to take and when. This issue has been recognised as a critical factor in the case studies. The context of an unexpected event (e.g. the exact time that the event occurred, the remaining time of the job in the plan, the status of the next operation) and joint evaluation meeting leads to different corrective actions with different urgencies, rather than mathematically better approvable solutions.

4.4   Performance Measurement

A great deal of performance measures guides the production control systems in scheduling and rescheduling actions. The majority of the manufacturing systems mainly focus on the classical measurement categories (cost and efficiency), however, especially in the dynamic and stochastic environments, stability, robustness, and instability (nervousness) are important measures to be defined and tracked [5]. Due to this fact, many research studies obtain conflicting results, regarding the benefits of frequent event driven rescheduling activity (see Hozak and Hill, [21]). The industrial practice is far from considering such advanced measures in the event handling and rescheduling process. The major concern of the investigated companies, which is quite understandable in the competitive market conditions, is the delivery due date adherence. It is even hard to notice any operational performance management practices for the PPC process. However through analysis and representation of the realistic instability and stability measures in the models can improve the rescheduling decision on specific work centres with relatively simple characteristics (e.g. stable process, continuous flow, and few machines).

4.5   Human Factors

Human interaction with the production control system is often underestimated, however, also plays an important role in practicality of the production control system [22]. Real life manufacturing planning and control systems to varying extents involve human judgment and decision making. Especially, production scheduling and rescheduling tasks, in many cases, are left to the supervisors or operators in practice. In order to support the cognitive strengths of humans in decision making process, visualization plays a significant role in practice. In the observed case companies, detailed dispatching decisions and the task of reacting on changes are often left to the shop floor personal, based on their experience and knowledge. The system-user interfaces are considered to be highly complicated, limiting the understanding of the plans for the personal. Furthermore, the usage of many ICT systems and tools create confusions. The interviewed employees expressed a clear need for an intuitive and easy-to-understand decision support tool that exploits and visualizes the required information, and guides them in the event handling process, taking human cognitive skills into consideration.

5   Implications and Future Research

The intent of this paper was to investigate and outline the requirements from a practical production control system in order to respond the unexpected events effectively. In summary, following maturity levels are proposed for each underlying factor.

Table 1. Proposed maturity level of each factor for effective event handling process

Strategy: Proactive control strategy besides the widely applied predictive-reactive strategy to handle the events
ICT: A semi-heterarchical information flow and decision making structure is needed to provide quick responsiveness to unexpected events in cooperation with the overall planning performance. Full interface with information systems and real time access to internal and external required data. MES module for real time decision support to handle unexpected events
Coordination and feedback: Events are sorted and categorized for each strategy at each planning and control level. Structured event handling process with clear roles and responsibilities for interdependent levels
Performance measurement: Adopted realistic stability and instability measures when making event-driven rescheduling decisions as well as diagnostic early warning measures for classified events for proactive control
Human factor: Responsible person adopts an event driven proactive approach. The system is developed with respect to the roles of human and computer component interactively, facilitating the diagnosis of disturbances. The system should be user-friendly, easy to interpret, and intuitive, reducing the cognitive workload

Further work will be related to the generalizability of the findings of this study, specifically for the proposed maturity level of each factor. In order to achieve this goal, a questionnaire survey will be sent to a sufficient number of companies from a range of manufacturing environments and the results will be analysed.

References

1. Slack, N., Chambers, S., Johnston, R.: Operations Management, 5th edn. FT Prentice Hall, Harlow (2007)

2. Meyer, G.G., Wortmann, J., Szirbik, N.B.: Production monitoring and control with intelligent products. International Journal of Production Research 49(5), 1303–1317 (2011)
3. Cowling, P., Johansson, M.: Using real time information for effective dynamic scheduling. European Journal of Operational Research 139(2), 230–244 (2002)
4. Ouelhadj, D., Petrovic, S.: A survey of dynamic scheduling in manufacturing systems. Journal of Scheduling 12(4), 417–431 (2009)
5. Sabuncuoglu, I., Goren, S.: Hedging production schedules against uncertainty in manufacturing environment with a review of robustness and stability research. International Journal of Computer Integrated Manufacturing 22(2), 138–157 (2009)
6. Jacobs, F.R., et al.: Manufacturing Planning and Control for Supply Chain Management: APICS/CPM Certification Edition. McGraw-Hill, USA (2011)
7. Leitão, P.: Agent-based distributed manufacturing control: A state-of-the-art survey. Engineering Applications of Artificial Intelligence 22(7), 979–991 (2009)
8. Trentesaux, D.: Distributed control of production systems. Engineering Applications of Artificial Intelligence 22(7), 971–978 (2009)
9. de Snoo, C., et al.: Coordination activities of human planners during rescheduling: Case analysis and event handling procedure. International Journal of Production Research 49(7), 2101–2122 (2011)
10. Steger-Jensen, K., et al.: Advanced planning and scheduling technology. Production Planning & Control 22(8), 800–808 (2011)
11. De Ugarte, B.S., Artiba, A., Pellerin, R.: Manufacturing execution system–a literature review. Production Planning and Control 20(6), 525–539 (2009)
12. Rolón, M., Martínez, E.: Agent-based modeling and simulation of an autonomic manufacturing execution system. Computers in Industry 63, 53–78 (2011)
13. McFarlane, D.C., Bussmann, S.: Developments in holonic production planning and control. Production Planning & Control 11(6), 522–536 (2000)
14. McKay, K.: Historical survey of manufacturing control practices from a production research perspective. International Journal of Production Research 41(3), 411–426 (2003)
15. Aytug, H., et al.: Executing production schedules in the face of uncertainties: A review and some future directions. European Journal of Operational Research 161(1), 86–110 (2005)
16. Vieira, G.E., Herrmann, J.W., Lin, E.: Rescheduling manufacturing systems: a framework of strategies, policies, and methods. Journal of Scheduling 6(1), 39–62 (2003)
17. Koh, S., Saad, S., Jones, M.: Uncertainty under MRP-planned manufacture: review and categorization. International Journal of Production Research 40(10), 2399–2421 (2002)
18. McKay, K.N., Wiers, V.C.S.: Practical production control: a survival guide for planners and schedulers. J. Ross Publishing (2004)
19. Kreipl, S., Pinedo, M.: Planning and Scheduling in Supply Chains: An Overview of Issues in Practice. Production and Operations Management 13(1), 77–92 (2004)
20. Ivert, L.K.: Use of Advanced Planning and Scheduling (APS) systems to support manufacturing planning and control processes. Doctoral Thesis. Chalmers University of Technology (2012)
21. Hozak, K., Hill, J.A.: Issues and opportunities regarding replanning and rescheduling frequencies. International Journal of Production Research 47(18), 4955–4970 (2009)
22. McKay, K.N., Wiers, V.C.S.: The human factor in planning and scheduling. Handbook of Production Scheduling, 23–57 (2006)

Analyzing IT Supported Production Control by Relating Petri Nets and UML Static Structure Diagrams

Henk Jan Pels

Technische Universiteit Eindhoven
h.j.pels@tue.nl

Abstract. A method to model the interaction between a production control process and an information system is presented. Colored Petri Nets are used to model the process and UML static structure. When the tokens in the internet are modeled as objects in the data model, the transitions in the process model can be specified as formal expressions over the data model. Thus the model verifies the consistency between the process and the information system and can be used as formal specification for e.g. an ERP implementation.

Keywords: process modeling, data modeling, ERP implementation.

1   Research Problem

Understanding the interaction between a business process and an information system has always been a difficult issue. When implementing ERP systems the users do not understand the logic of the Information System and the system integrators do not understand the business process. This problem calls for a formal technique to model, understand and discuss the interaction between the business process and the information system. Such a technique should enable to discuss the essential requirements for production control software to support the business strategy.

2   Approach

Petri Nets [Petri, 1962] provide a formal process modeling language. UML Static Structure diagrams [OMG, 2005] are a formal language to model the information that is relevant for a specific business process. In colored Petri Nets [Jensen, 1992] the tokens have attributes, which enables to consider them as objects. If a UML static structure model is used to specify the types of tokens and their state space, the transitions can be specified as pre- and post-conditions over this state space. Section 3 explains the modeling principles using the example of a simple assemble to order production situation with a one-level bill of material. In section 4 we demonstrate the suitability for more complex situations on a manufacture to order with a multi-level BOM. Then in section 5 we analyze the well-known MRP planning situation with multilevel BOM and stock of parts. In section 6 the results of the research will be discussed.

C. Emmanouilidis, M. Taisch, D. Kiritsis (Eds.): APMS 2012, Part II, IFIP AICT 398, pp. 144–151, 2013.

3   Assemble to Order Process

3.1   Petri Net

We introduce the modeling approach with a relatively simple situation: the Assemble to Order process. Figure 1 shows the AtO process modeled in a Petri Net, using the CPN notation [Jensen, 1992]. Places are denoted by ovals, labeled with a unique name. The label below a place is the class of the tokens in the place. Places essentially model delays in the process. Consequently their names correspond to states of tokens. Transitions are modeled as rectangles which correspond to decisions in the business process. The label on the arrow is used as identifier for the selected or created tokens in the pre and post conditions. Transitions model decisions to be taken in the process.

The basic principle of Petri Nets is that a transition fires if a token is present in each of its input places. This means that transitions with multiple input arrows model synchronization points. If more than one token is present in a place, the selection is arbitrary. In colored Petri Nets the firing of a transition also requires that the selected set of tokens satisfies the precondition. The post-condition specifies the change of state of the system. In particular it specifies which output arrow a token will follow. Every token is always in one and only one place.

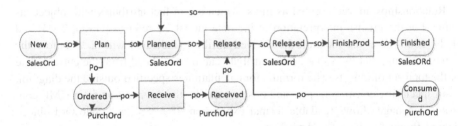

Fig. 1. Petri Net for Assemble to Order process

The process in figure 1 starts in the place New. Transition Plan moves the sales order to the Planned place. At the same time for each material as required for assembling the ordered product, a purchase order is created and moved to the Ordered place. The Release transition fires if it finds a Received purchase order that matches a Planned sales order. Release checks whether all required materials for the sales order have been received. If so it moves the sales order to place Released, else it places the sales order back in the Planned place. The purchase order is moved to place Consumed. Transition Produce takes orders from place Released and moves them to place Finished. Note that the transition Finished models the decision to accept an assembled product as finished. During actual production the sales order remains in state 'Released". The Petri Net models the process control decisions and the delays between them, not the process activities, like e.g. the assembly work.

3.2   The Data Model

The purpose of the model is to analyze the control decisions to be taken to create the desired behavior of the business process. The evolving state of the system is recorded as the arrival periods in the places. Figure 2 shows the UML static structure diagram (further referred to as data structure) for the AtO process.

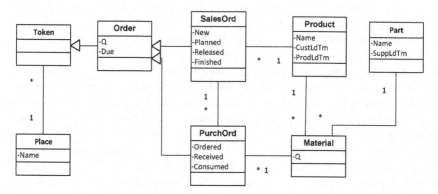

Fig. 2. Data structure for Assemble to Order process.

Relationships are represented as links, which are in fact attributes with objects as value. For the precise interpretation of the data model we refer to [OMG, 2005] and [Pels, 2006]. We just mention the derived attribute, indicated with a '/' before the name, meaning that the value of this attribute can be calculated from the current state of the total set of objects. The formula for calculation is specified outside the diagram.

In specifying constraints, pre- and post-conditions the dot notation from UML constraint language allows readable formal expression. If e.g. s1 is a SalesOrd object, then s1.Product is the ordered product.

In specifying constraints, pre- and post-conditions the dot notation from UML constraint language allows readable formal expressions. If e.g. s1 is a SalesOrd object, then s1.Product is the ordered product.

Object class Product models the products that can be ordered. Attribute ProdLdTm records the production lead time. Part models the parts used in the products. Each part has SuppLdTm for supplier lead-time. Material specifies the use of a specific part in a specific product. Attribute Q is the quantity used. The common properties of sales orders and purchase orders are modeled in class Order as generalization of SalesOrd and Purchord. Q is the quantity ordered, New the period of creation and Due the period due to be delivered. SalesOrd and PurchOrd have similar attributes for the period where phases start. Classes Token and Place connect the data structure to the Petri Net. Since they are common for this way of process-data modeling, they will be supposed to be implicitly specified in all further data structures.

3.3   The Transitions

Transitions are specified in terms of pre- and post-conditions. The precondition specifies which tokens are selected from the input places. The post-condition specifies the state changes caused by the transition. Since the post condition must reason over the old as well as over the new state, some special operators must be added to standard predicate logic:

- The <- operator is used to move tokens. The left operand specifies the output place, the right operand the token to be moved. If the right operand is not the label of one of the input arcs, a new token is created,
- The := operator is used to specify that in the new state the left operand has the value resulting from the right operand. All variables in the right operand refer to the new state, unless they are preceded by a   ~, in which case they refer to the old state,

Below we specify transitions Plan and Receive in terms of the data model.

```
Plan %for each material create a purchase order%
POST    Planned <- so ∧ ∀ m ∈ so.Product.Material [Ordered <- po ∧
po.SalesOrd := so ∧   po.Material := m ∧ po.Q := m.Q * po.SalesOrd.Q ∧
po.Ordered := so.New ∧ po.Due = so.New + m.Part.SupLdTime];
Receive %purchase orders are processed in order of delivery%
PRE po.Due = Min(n.Due: n ∈ Ordered.Token)%Ordered is a Place object,
so Ordered.Token is the set of tokens in this place%
POST Received <- po;
```

The formulas above show how the full behavior of the process can be specified in formal language. It verifies that process and data model are consistent. Note that the names of products and parts appear to be not relevant for the process. However, they are relevant in the user interface.

3.4   Discussion of the Modeling Approach

The colored Petri Net brings a process model that clearly shows the main characteristics of the process. It shows two parallel process lines for the sales order and the purchase order, that come together in the release transition. The data model enables an abstract, complete and unambiguous specification of control decisions in terms of information needed. So a consistent model verifies that the data model fits the process. If the systems integrator is ordered to implement the software system consistent with the data model, it is guaranteed that it will support the business process. Using this approach can reduce the risk and the cost for ERP implementation dramatically.

4   Manufacture to Order Process

4.1   MtO Process Model

The process model in Figure 3 shows that the MtO process has a third process line: the manufacturing process. A new sales order generates a manufacturing order for the product. The Plan transition not only creates purchase orders, it also creates manufacturing orders for non-purchased materials. A manufacturing order is released when all required materials, purchased and manufactured, are available. Production will start only when sufficient capacity is available. If not the InWork period is incremented and the manufacturing order is fed back to the Released place. Finished manufacturing orders are fed back to Received, unless their product is a customer ordered product. In that case it proceeds to Delivered. The sales order waits in Accepted until the end product has been manufactured and is then expedited to the customer.

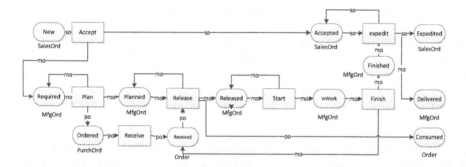

Fig. 3. MtO process

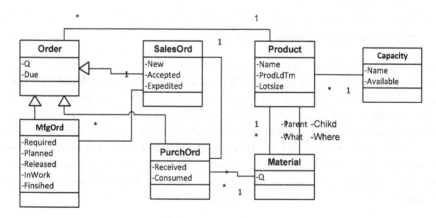

Fig. 4. MtO data structure

4.2   MtO Data Structure

In figure 4 object class MfgOrd represents the manufacturing orders with their specific states. Material now records the multi-level BOM by connecting the Child Product to the Parent Product. The set of Material objects linked to the same Parent is the What (used), while the set of material objects linked to the same Child   is the Where (used). New is the class Capacity, to specify capacity limits.

The MtO process as modeled above is perfectly just in time: materials are produced or purchased only when needed for a sales order and production and purchase orders are always uniquely linked to a sales order. The question now is what happens if the concept of stock is introduced is discussed in the next section.

5   MRP Process

5.1   MRP Process Model

Material Requirements Planning was introduced by APICS as a concept for computer aided production control. Manufacture to stock was still the most usual way of production, making stock control the central issue of production planning. APICS explained the MRP principles using the concepts of Net Requirements, Gross Requirements, Scheduled Receipts, Available Balance, Planned Orders Due and Planned Release [Bertrand, Wijngaard, Wortmann, 1990]. These concepts are rather abstract and difficult to understand, so let us try to achieve better understanding by extending the MtO model with stock. For simplicity we use unlimited capacity.

Figure 5 shows the process model. Sales planning transforms proposed sales plans into confirmed and generates a manufacturing order for the product. When MfgOrd's

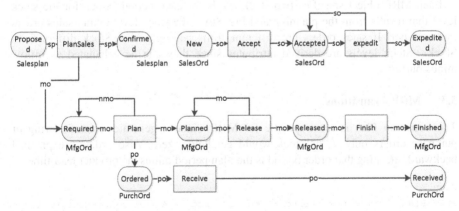

Fig. 5. MRP process

are planned the BOM is exploded, PurchOrd's are generated for purchased materials and new Required MfgOrd's are generated for other materials. Planned MfgOrd's are released for production when sufficient stock of materials is available. New SalesOrd's are accepted unconditionally and expedited if sufficient stock of the end product is found. If not the expedited period is incremented and the order is returned to accepted.

5.2   MRP Data Structure

The datamodel In figure 6 shows the MRP concept as class MRP.

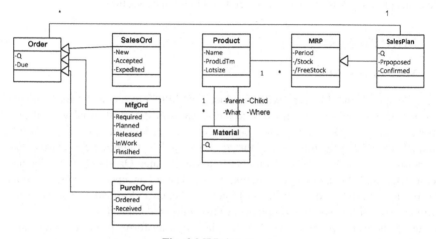

Fig. 6. MRP data structure

Each MRP object specifies two stock-levels for each period: Stock for the stock level that results from the planning and FreeStock the stock level taking sales orders into account. If sales orders are different from sales plan FreeStock differs from Stock. Stock levels are derived attributes since they can be calculated as inflow minus outflow.

5.3   MRP Transitions

The transition Plan is most specific for MRP, since it generates manufacturing or purchase orders only if the stock would get below zero. Also orders are planned backward, meaning that order period is the plan period minus the product lead-time.

```
Plan
POST Plan <- mo ∧ mo.Planned := mo.Required  ∧ ∀ m ∈ mo.Product.What:
IF ~mo.Stock < mo.Q THEN IF m.Child.What = {} %purchase part% Then po <-
Ordered ∧ po.Q = mo.Q * m.Q ∧ po.Due := mo.Due ∧ po.Ordered := mo.Due -
m.Child.ProdLdTm ELSE %mfg part% MfgOrd <- nmo ∧ nmo.Q := mo.Q * m.Q ∧
nmo.Due := mo.Due ∧ nmo.Ordered := mo.Due - m.Child.ProdLdTm ENDIF
ENDIF;
```

5.4   MRP Analysis

Now comparing the MRP process with the MtO process, the striking difference is that any synchronization between the three process lines has disappeared. This is because stock eliminates the direct links between the different order types, as can be seen in the data structure. As a result an expensive process is needed to control stock: the FreeStock levels must be monitored frequently in order to adapt plans to actual sales. However, stock causes longer lead-times and thus delay between a change in plan and the change of stock. From control theory it is known that such a delay may cause oscillations, increasing uncertainty and again increasing stock levels. This is a very strong argument to outsource the stock control problem to the suppliers and to apply MtO where possible.

Another surprise is that that original APICS concepts are not explicitly in the data structure, but boil down to just Stock and FreeStock. This means that they are not essential for understanding, indicating that our modeling approach leads to easier understanding of the problem. This does fear that MRP software designers, systems integrators and users may have very different and even conflicting understandings of the logic, without being able to discuss or detect these conflicts.

6   Results

The contribution of the modeling approach is demonstrated in that it enables us to explain and discuss production control processes in relation to the IT support. Even a complex process like MRP can be explained with a relatively simple process and data structure. A surprising result is that the analysis generates critics to a long established and extensively published mechanism like MRP. The method has been applied in ERP selection and implementation projects and appeared to contribute considerably to smooth and effective implementation.

References

1. [Aalst ea, 2002] van der Aalst, W.M.P., van Hee, K.M.: Workflow Management: Models, Methods,and Systems. MIT Press, Cambridge (2002)
2. [Bertrand, Wijngaard, Wortmann, 1990] Bertrand, J.W.M., Wijngaard, J., Wortmann, J.C.: Production control: A structural and design oriented approach. Elsevier (1990)
3. [Jensen, 1992] Jensen, K.: Coloured Petri Nets. Basic Concepts, Analysis Methods and Practical Use. EATCS, Monographs on Theoretical Comp. Science. Springer, Berlin (1992)
4. [OMG, 2005] Object Management Group (OMG), OCL 2.0 Specification. OMG document ptc/2005-06-06 (June 2005)
5. [Pels, 2006] Classification hierarchies for product data modelling. Production Planning and Control 17(4), 367–377 (2006)
6. [Pels ea, 2007] Pels, H.J., Goossenaerts, J.: A conceptual modeling technique for discrete event simulation of operational processes. In: Olhager, J., Persson, F. (eds.) APMS 2007. IFIP, vol. 246, pp. 305–312. Springer, Boston (2007)
7. [Petri, 1962] Petri, C.A.: Kommunikation mit Automaten. PhD thesis, Institut für instru-mentelle Mathematik, Bonn (1962)

Enabling Information Sharing in a Port

Peter Bjerg Olesen[*], Hans-Henrik Hvolby, and Iskra Dukovska-Popovska

Centre for Logistics, Department of Mechanical and Manufacturing Engineering,
Aalborg University, Denmark
pbo@m-tech.aau.dk

Abstract. Ports are integral parts of many supply chains and are as such a contributing factor to the overall efficiency of the supply chain. As the role of the
ports is increasingly changing towards being more integrated into the supply
chain, ports need to start focusing on optimising the activities and striving for
low-lead time. Ports are also complex entities comprising of different companies. The dynamic nature of ports is also a problem when trying to optimise the
utilisation of resources and ensure a low lead-time. Information sharing is crucial in the attempt to improve ports operations. This paper attempts to explain
how information sharing is enabled in such an environment, and which considerations are relevant, both in regards to the information and required technology. The paper highlights trust, availability of data, and complexity of solutions
and technology, as being the main hurdles.

Keywords: Information sharing, technology, ICT, information flow, port.

1 Introduction

Port systems are an important part of many supply chains, and an important contributor to the overall (in)efficiency of a supply chain. As the focus on supply chain efficiency has increased in previous years, the focus on the efficiency of ports is also
increasing. The activities in a port are directly dependant on the input from external
parties, both hinterland (the geographical inland area the port services) and foreland
(the customers sending and receiving goods through the port outside the hinterland).

The amount and time of transactions going to and from hinterland can be quite uncertain, which affects the planning and control of capacity and activities at a port.
The performance of a port terminal, can suffer greatly from this uncertainty in terms
of lead-time and bottle-necks i.e. the Forrester effect [1]. Therefore the uncertainty
needs to be minimised. In order to plan the capacity better, it is necessary to get
input from ships arriving, as well as information from transportation companies on
arrival of trucks.

The performance of a production unit, e.g. a port terminal, can suffer greatly from
this uncertainty in terms of lead-time and bottle-necks i.e. the Forrester effect [1].
Therefore the uncertainty needs to be minimised. To reduce these uncertainties there

---

[*] Corresponding author.

C. Emmanouilidis, M. Taisch, D. Kiritsis (Eds.): APMS 2012, Part II, IFIP AICT 398, pp. 152–159, 2013.

two general methods: First; reduce the uncertainty factors as seen in Lean production when levelling demand and supply. This is done by having more knowledge about your customers and suppliers activities. Second; be more responsive by communicating better between the partners in the supply chain so any changes are communicated as fast as possible, giving supply chain partners the chance to react to the changes [2]. This paper will explain how information sharing can be enabled in a port environment, and which considerations are relevant, both in regards to the information and required technology. Furthermore, the paper highlights the main obstacles for implementation.

To define information sharing as a possible solution to a problem, some of the benefits are introduced; hereafter the prerequisites for enabling information sharing are discussed. A case study is introduced to exemplify the problems identified towards implementing information sharing. As a first step to solve the lack of sharing, some of the general requirements are presented.

2   Information Sharing and Its Benefits

Bichou et al [3] describe the lack of close collaboration among supply chain members in the port and shipping industry and encourage ports to be more proactive in their role to increase collaboration. Further, Robinson [4] encourages ports to become active elements in the value driven supply chain.

The general level of supply chain integration and information sharing at small ports has not developed much, even though the benefits have been thoroughly described in the literature. Lee et al [5], Lee et al [6] and Flynn et al [7] show the positive effect of information sharing in the supply chain in general, but how to share the information is not thoroughly analysed. Even though technical solutions, for many years, have supported exchange of data, they have not been widely applied. According to Braziotis et al [8] one reason is that many companies focus on short term profit, which has kept them from building long term strategic partnerships in the supply chain. Also the fear for indirectly providing competitors with sensitive data has been main barrier. Further the complexity of some of the solutions has also been too high, as for small and medium sized companies to adapt them. This means there is a possibility in creating a form of data sharing that takes small/medium sized companies into account.

Zhou et al [9] shows how information sharing benefits supply chain practices in dynamic supply chain environments, by reducing the amount of unknown factors, increasing the ability of a company to plan their own operations in synchronisation with the rest of the supply chain. Based on the study done by Zhou et al [9], the effectiveness of information sharing as a means of performance enhancing, depends on the level of dynamism in the supply chain. This means that in supply chains where demand is very stable, extra information sharing has no performance enhancing effect. However, it is shown that when demand is unstable it can be essential to have an effective information sharing system, in order to receive important information as fast as possible, allowing companies to adjust capacity before it is committed.

One problem is the lack of information exchange in the dynamic port environment, in terms of having the most correct information when planning. The main causes leading to this problem have been identified as follows:

- Trust, [8]
- Availability of data, Quality of data [10]
- Complexity of system/technology

The trust issue is a major obstacle for information sharing as it is the basis of collaborating with anyone. In normal supply chain setups it is important to have trust, but in a port environment where there are a lot of shared resources it is even more important, as data can cross between users of the same resources. The information sharing solution should therefore focus on trying to circumvent the trust issue, by allowing companies to share according to their comfort level. Trust as a psychological phenomenon is outside the scope of this paper.

3   System Requirements for Enabling Information Sharing

According to a literature review by Perego et al [11], there is a lack of focus in the research on ICT solutions for transport companies, how they should operate and communicate with partners. However, in the literature, ICT is often named as a solution without providing information or analysis of how the ICT system should work in order to support certain functionality. This is a problem when trying to actually create an information sharing setup, as there no description of how to do this, and especially for smaller economic scale supply chain actors, such as a small/medium sized port, this is also confirmed by Robinson [4], especially in regards to implementing ICT solution.

For the small SC actors to involve in an exchange of information, it is important to find a way that is simple and not too expensive. Based on literature, three methods that comply with these criteria have been identified:

- Manual information sharing
    - Phone calls, meetings, email, spread sheets etc.
    - Kia et al [10] discuss reducing manual efforts in 2000, little has happened.
- Database access (ERP or similar ICT system)
    - Direct link to a partners ERP database, to read/write in real-time. Allow real-time transaction knowledge as well as the possibility to view order-lines etc.
    - Not useable due to the trust issues and security issues with remote access to central company systems.
- Dedicated ICT system for information sharing
    - Portal placed between partners allowing for easy database integration and permission configuration.
    - Keceli [12] presents an information model for a port, based on a centralistic system.

The third suggested method can provide new functionality, which has the possibility of innovating the information exchange climate, and does not pose trust and security issues directly. The two other methods have proven not to be the most effective solutions.

A system that enables information sharing should be easy to use and to add/extract information. Further it should handle the information exchange automatically, when signed up, and in real time. The updated information could help organisations adjust their plan to a more optimal order, e.g. before execution of an order line. Stefansson et al [13] have defined certain types of information that are essential to supply chain interactions, and therefor relevant for inclusion in such a system. These criteria should be used when deciding what to share.

The information sharing system should be trust neutral, so the information in the system is only there, because companies have decided to share the information and with whom to share it. This requires the system to provide easy data sharing configuration, with the option of managing each partner alone or as a group. The system will also have to support any ERP or other resource management systems. This would be obtained by configuring the integration in every installation. And as long as the data is available in the company's database it should be a question of pointing the sharing system to this location.

A voluntary system is not by any means a complete solution to the issue of uncertainty in demand and supply for a port. It is however an option for smaller supply chain partners as they will have the possibility to integrate information with others, without having to force a certain system to be used by all partners, as seen with large corporations e.g. Walmart. Therefore the system should not be dependent on every partner using it. It should be seen as an addition to traditional information sources.

With the description of what the system should be able to do, the next phase is to present a port context and the need for information sharing.

4   Case Study

The case port is a small to medium size port with around 1800 ship berths a year. The main traffic is oil, bulk, containers and specialised cargo.
In the port there are seven main actors:

- Port system
  - Port authority
  - Port Terminal
  - Stevedore
- Transporters
  - Shipping lines
  - Truck carriers
- Customer
  - Shipping brokers
  - Direct customers

The port authority handles docking permission and other things regarding pre docking activities as well as some services for the ships such as fresh water. The port terminal handles the goods and moves it from ship to truck or vice versa. The stevedore is the dockworkers handling some of the manual operation required in connection with loading and unloading. There are two types of transporters: one going to and from the hinterland, and another going to and from the foreland, here represented by trucks and ships. The final part of the port system is the customer making an order to have goods transported through the port, often represented by a shipping broker, who makes the transport bookings for the customer.

In this port, seven different actors are in possession of information that relates to the transport of e.g. a container. The terminal, which is the focus of the paper, does the physical movement of goods from one transport form to another. Currently, the terminal only receives information about when the goods arrive at the terminal. Ship arrivals is the only information the terminal has in advance, as the ship arrivals follow a calendar, but delays in ship arrival can cause problems as the arrival time is not monitored in real-time. All planning of capacity (docks, cranes, people) is done around the arrival of ships. When it comes to trucks delivering or picking up goods, there is no planning done at the terminal. It is known that trucks tend to arrive around the departure of the ship, but the order of trucks is unknown. The information exchange that does exist today between the operators (cranes, trucks, etc.) is done by phone and email, which results in the information sometimes is delayed, forgotten or simply not communicated.

The consequence of the missing information can be seen in trucks waiting at the gate and waiting to be serviced by the terminal operators. Every time there is a ship arrival, many truck carrier firms and customers tend to wait until latest possible time to deliver the goods to the terminal. The effect of this is that the terminal is overburdened at these peak periods, resulting with long lead time, and is equally unburdened in the remaining timeframe, i.e. low resource utilisation. These uncertainties also lead to frequent use of overtime for the workers, as well as lot of waiting time.

To remedy these issues for the case port, the concept of the information sharing setup is used to describe a future state scenario.

5   System Framework

Two things are considered when describe the model for the information sharing system: 1) information flow model and 2) technology considerations. To actually create and implement an information sharing system a lot of other aspects are also necessary, such as system interoperability, however this is not a scope of this paper.

5.1   Information Flow

This paper will focus on information that relates to capacity use, such as delivering a container or a ship docking and the processes that are tied to this activity, such as reach stackers picking and moving containers.

The information in a port system can be segmented into two types: first, order information that sets up the overall flow through the port, and secondly, real-time information that enables the capacity to be adjusted until a firming deadline. Because of the simplistic approach to real-time data the information needed for reducing dynamism is also reduced in complexity. According to Stefansson et al [13] it is value adding information that should be shared, and defining what information is value adding depends on the reference point. The terminal is the reference in this paper; therefore the information needed is arrival and departure time and dimensions of cargo. For a container the information needed is: size, weight, destination, departure and arrival time.

With this information the container terminal will be able to plan the containers route through the terminal. This can be seen in a simple general model of the information flow in a port, **Fig. 1**.

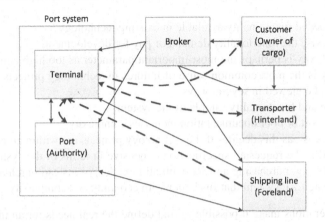

Fig. 1. Order flow and real-time information flow. Dotted line is the real-time information

The real-time information needed is related to the terminal as this is the focal point. The terminal communicates arrivals of goods to customers and transporters, and transporter and shipping line communicate to the terminal.

The point of Fig. 1 is to illustrate that the requirements for the information exchange system can be very simple, and only a limited subset of information needs to be shared with partners dynamically, decreasing the influence of the trust factor and the complexity. The dotted line represents the information that will benefit from being transmitted real-time, such as time and dimension information. The solid lines represent the existing flow of sales and purchase orders; this then needs to be supplemented with an information update scheme.

In terms of availability and quality of data, the reduced amount of real-time data exchange in this suggestion ensures that the resources needed for making and maintaining this information is kept at a minimum.

Lastly the complexity of the information flow is lower as opposed to a system that keeps track of all data, not just data that is changing. Further, the lower complexity of information ensures that the people working with the information can utilize it better and thus making improvements based on it. These assumptions are based on small companies without data specialists to understand and connect incoming data to their own system.

5.2   Technology Considerations

To enable the information sharing it is also necessary to have an IT system. This section will address technological considerations required for such a system. There are four aspects to technology in the scope of this paper: trust, availability, complexity and cost.

- The trust parameter is important to many companies, as they need to know and get comfortable with how the technology works. Further trust is also dependent on the security of the technology, and whether it can make the company vulnerable.
- The availability is the first parameter as a company evaluate its requirements specification.
  - Is the needed functionality available in existing technology?
  - If not revise the functionality demand or pay for development.
- The complexity is perhaps the most important parameter as too high complexity of technology is the most common cause of failures in technology projects. The complexity can be viewed in several ways.
  - The size and functionality sample of the system.
  - Bad support or poor documentation increases complexity.
- Last is the cost, as this decides if the technology projects are within an economical margin and is the requested specification expensive in terms of the systems possible benefits, e.g. purchasing an ERP with all modules, or instead purchase a smaller more basic ERP system that fits better with economy and complexity.

These considerations make it possible to find define the real needs for an information sharing system in small/medium sized port environment. The main focus is on trust, availability, complexity and cost of information and technology used to provide information to the port systems actors.

6   Results and Discussion

This paper highlights the benefits of information sharing, where dynamic environments have the largest benefits, as an increased information flow improves the responsiveness of the entire system. However, there where perhaps a lack in the literature on how this information sharing should be facilitated.

To enable information sharing there are a lot of considerations to be done, in this paper it is limited to information flow and technology considerations, as these are the first step in order to make a model of a complete information sharing system, including technical setup. The technology available today will support all required functions in some way, but in a complex and costly manner. So to find more optimal solutions, a sharing system has to adapt to the reality of the system it has to support.

The system should be easy to use and be a used on a voluntary basis, and not be dependent on every partner using the system, but an addition to traditional information sources.

The implications to research are an increased focus on the difficulties and possibilities of information sharing in small ports. Through further work the need for manual interfaces between supply chain partners should be reduced, and allow the possibilities of real-time information and adjustments.

The proposed approach does in itself not provide much in terms of performance improvement, but it builds a foundation that would allow for better coordination between supply chain partners. This would reduce waiting times, and improve resource utilisation by smoothing the demand.

References

1. Lee, H.L., Padmanabhan, V., Whang, S.: Information distortion in a supply chain: The bullwhip effect. Management Science 43, 546–558 (1997)
2. Christopher, M.: The Agile Supply Chain: Competing in Volatile Markets. Industrial Marketing Management 29, 37–44 (2000)
3. Bichou, K., Gray, R.: A logistics and supply chain management approach to port performance measurement. Maritime Policy & Management: The Flagship Journal of International Shipping and Port Research 31, 47 (2004)
4. Robinson, R.: Ports as elements in value-driven chain systems: the new paradigm. Maritime Policy & Management 29, 241–255 (2002)
5. Lee, H.L., So, K.C., Tang, C.S.: The Value of Information Sharing in a Two-Level Supply Chain. Management Science 46, 626–643 (2000)
6. Lee, H.L., Whang, S.: Information sharing in a supply chain. International Journal of Manufacturing Technology and Management 1, 79–93 (2000)
7. Flynn, B.B., Huo, B., Zhao, X.: The impact of supply chain integration on performance: A contingency and configuration approach. Journal of Operations Management 28, 58–71 (2010)
8. Braziotis, C., Tannock, J.D.T.: Building the Extended Enterprise: Key Collaboration Factors. The International Journal of Logistics Management 22, 4–4 (2011)
9. Zhou, H., Benton Jr., W.C.: Supply chain practice and information sharing. Journal of Operations Management 25, 1348–1365 (2007)
10. Kia, M., Shayan, E., Ghotb, F.: The importance of information technology in port terminal operations. International Journal of Physical Distribution & Logistics Management 30, 331–344 (2000)
11. Perego, A., Perotti, S., Mangiaracina, R.: ICT for logistics and freight trans-portation: a literature review and research agenda. International Journal of Physical Distribution & Logistics Management 41, 457–483 (2011)
12. Keceli, Y.: A proposed innovation strategy for Turkish port administration policy via information technology. Maritime Policy & Management 38, 151–167 (2011)
13. Stefansson, G., Lumsden, K., Mirzabeiki, V.: Smart Transportation Management Systems to Support Visibility of the Supply Chain Information Types. Presented at the 16th ITS World Congress and Exhibition on Intelligent Transport Systems and Services (2009)

Designing a Lifecycle Integrated Data Network for Remanufacturing Using RFID Technology

Young-woo Kim and Jinwoo Park

Department of Industrial Engineering/Automation System Research Institute (ASRI),
Seoul National University, Seoul, Republic of Korea
ywkim@mailab.snu.ac.kr, autofact@snu.ac.kr

Abstract. With the emergence of concerns regarding pollution and the exhaustion of resources, original equipment manufacturers have begun to take responsibility for environmentally sound manufacturing according to regulations that have been established. Manufacturers thus need to decide how much they will recycle and which options to pursue for minimizing operation costs and environmental impacts, while complying with regulations. They cannot, however, predict the quality of returned products, and as a result, the planning of recycling activities is not reliable. Moreover, the components of products all have different ages and lifetimes. Thus, there may be a number of components that can be recycled more than once. If the life history of these components is not available, though, recyclable components may be disposed of after being recycled once. In this paper, we propose an integrated data system that uses radio frequency identification technology to provide useful information that can make remanufacturing more efficient.

Keywords: Remanufacturing, Data System, RFID Technology, Closed-loop Supply Chain Management.

1   Introduction

In response to the threats of environmental pollution and the depletion of natural resources, several types of environmental legislation have come to be instituted worldwide. This legislation compels original equipment manufacturers (OEMs) to engage in environment-friendly manufacturing, based on the concept of extended producer responsibility (EPR). The term EPR, which is a preventive strategy for saving the environment, first appeared in a report of the Swedish government [1]. According to this concept, every OEM takes responsibility for the collection, recovery, and reuse of obsolete products, and performs its own disposal [2]. In addition, manufacturers must strive to implement this strategy in the design and manufacture of their products [3]. Once such environmental policies were established, a number of manufacturers invested in research on technologies that are related to recycling, such as design for disassembly [4-5].

According to Krikke (2010), the recycling of returned end-of-life (EOL) products can be classified in three ways: "product reuse," "component reuse," and "material

C. Emmanouilidis, M. Taisch, D. Kiritsis (Eds.): APMS 2012, Part II, IFIP AICT 398, pp. 160–167, 2013.
© IFIP International Federation for Information Processing 2013

recycling." under the level of disassembly [6]. It can be intuitively understood that from the standpoint of OEMs, the "product reuse" option is the most profitable approach because it requires much less additional treatment than the other options. However, the quality of returned EOL products may vary significantly according to their age and the environment in which they were used. For this reason, OEMs cannot accurately predict the quality of the returned EOL products, so their planning of recycling activities cannot be reliable.

With the development of mobile communication technologies, the use of personal electronic devices such as cellular phones has now become prevalent. The processors and components in these devices contain rare earth elements that have good stability and thermal conductivity to maximize their performance. These rare earth elements have a greater value than any other materials because they come from deposits that are smaller than the demand for them, and they are also hard to extract. In addition, about 90% of these rare earth elements are produced by the dominant producer. Hence, the recycling of personal electronic devices can be highly advantageous to OEMs from the perspective of resources and economics.

In this paper, we propose a lifecycle integrated data system for personal electronic devices that uses radio frequency identification (RFID) technology. The system assigns an exclusive identifier to every component and product to track and manage the data over the course of its entire lifecycle. This helps save natural resources by maximizing the recovery rate and save operational costs by eliminating unnecessary steps in the recovery process. It also enables manufacturers to obtain an obvious clue of recycling performance by gathering accurate information related to recycling.

2   Related Works

RFID technology facilitates faster and more efficient information flow and decision-making in supply chain management. For this reason, RFID technology has been applied in retail supply chains to streamline inventory management by providing statistical views of product shipments and inventory levels at unprecedented levels of detail [7]. It also promises to eliminate manual inventory counting, warehouse mispicking, and order numbering mistakes by providing precise data on product location, product characteristics, and product inventory levels [8]. The traceability afforded by RFID offers companies several advantages that enable them to effectively handle their daily operations with distribution transparency [9].

Based on the abovementioned advantages, the application of RFID technology to a closed-loop supply chain has also been discussed. Lee and Chan (2009) proposed an RFID-based reverse logistics framework and the optimization of the locations of collection points. These would help keep track of the quantity of returned products so as to determine the most economical transportation logistics and minimize the holding time as well as the depreciation of value [10]. Kulkarni et al. (2005) found that networked RFID systems can provide an automated and efficient approach for capturing and delivering comprehensive item-level product information in an accurate and timely manner, thereby improving both processes and decision-making during the stages of product recovery [11]. Nativi and Lee (2012) reported that RFID information-sharing strategies reduced inventory costs by coordinating the inventory policies of multiple decentralized players in a closed-loop supply chain [12].

The traceability afforded by RFID also facilitates lifecycle data management during the entire lifecycle of a product. Bajic and Chaxel (2002) addressed the use of automatic identification devices (Auto-ID tags) as permanent escort memories that would be associated with individual cars during their life cycle. This form of memory provides an integrated framework for vehicle lifecycle information, which is necessary to support the manufacturing, after-sales service, and recycling processes [13]. Jun et al. (2009) proposed an overall framework for RFID applications in product lifecycle management that makes use of a product-embedded information device [14]. In addition, Parlikad and McFarlane (2007) showed qualitatively that the availability of product information has a positive impact on product recovery decisions and discussed how RFID-based product identification technologies can be employed to provide the necessary information [15].

For launching RFID technology in a supply chain management system, it is essential for there to be consistent standards among the players who participate in the system. EPCglobal and GS1 are still working to develop the standards for launching RFID technology and identifying assets individually. In particular, the BRIDGE (Building Radio frequency IDentification solutions for the Global Environment) project has considered reusable assets and has defined seven identifier system keys with regard to the identifiers that are commonly employed in reusable asset management. However, they did not consider returned products, but only reusable assets such as pallets and containers [16]. Hence, alternatives for establishing standards continue to be studied because the existing standards cannot reflect the core features of recycling activities.

Luttropp and Johansson (2009) proposed the WEEE-RIM (Recycling Information Matrix) to support disassembly and recycling activities by improving the EPCglobal GID-96 standard [17]. They sought to incorporate instructions for recovery treatment into the RFID tags, which contain the following information: the company identifier, a statement as to who bears the responsibility as producer, and specific recycling information such as recycling targets, recycling actions, and hazardous materials. In this paper, we propose different ways of using external databases (DBs) based on the method proposed in their paper. We selected this approach because, in comparing these two methods, we found that the use of external DBs makes it possible to store much more detailed information than the WEEE-RIM, and that the use of the available space on the tags only for an identifier ensures that the system can identify a greater number of components.

3   System Design

3.1   Overall Framework

The information system proposed in this paper deals with data related to returned products and their components. Each piece of data will be entered in the product DB and the component DB when a component or a product is produced, repaired in its middle-of-life (MOL) phase, collected in its EOL phase, along with whatever other events are of interest during its entire lifecycle. These DBs would then consist of information about every product produced by the OEM, as well as every component that is included in every product family of the OEM. The details of these DBs will be presented in Section 3.3.

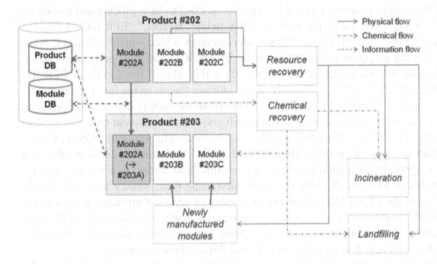

Fig. 1. Flows in remanufacturing system and recycling process

3.2   Design of RFID Tags

RFID technology is widely used to provide escort memory because an information system that uses RFID technology can perform the unambiguous labeling of objects by means of electronically stored data. The data identifying the object can also be read wirelessly through a radio frequency channel. A labeled object only transmits data when a matching reader initiates this process. Based on these features, RFID technology makes decision-making faster and more efficient by providing information that follows the product, by first sorting the main recycling target possibilities. We should note that in the design of tags and the corresponding DBs, the information must be coded in a systematic manner that can be understood by workers at the recycling plant. In this context, the importance of standards is an emerging issue. Fortunately, GS1, the international standards organization, has defined a standard for RFID tags called the electronic product code (EPC). EPC prescribes that a tag should contain exactly n-bits that are divided into a number of fields, where n is the capacity of the tag. The EPC standards set 8 bits of space on a tag for its header, which defines the overall length, identity type, and structure of the EPC tag encoding. For example, general identifier GID-96 is defined for a 96-bit EPC as follows: The header "00110101" indicates that the tag follows the GID-96 standard, and the general manager number, object class, and serial number occupy 28, 24, and 36 bits, respectively.

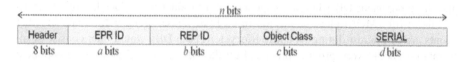

Fig. 2. Proposed design of RFID tags

In this study, we assume that n-bit tags are attached to each product and module to be identified. Thus, we divide n bits into five fields: "Header," "EPR ID," "REP ID," "Object Class," and "SERIAL." The header occupies 8 bits, which indicates that the tag is for the proposed information system. Every OEM and third-party reprocessing facility has its own exclusive ID, and this ID is the value of the 2nd field "EPR ID" and the 3rd field "REP ID." These ID fields indicate the exclusive ID of the manufacturer who is responsible for recycling and the ID of the facility that actually performs product recovery. When a manufacturer itself collects products and performs product recovery, the 2nd and 3rd fields will have same value. The 4th field, "Object Class," indicates the type of product. The last field, "SERIAL." stores a serial number that was assigned in the manufacturing stage, so this field serves as a primary key for products and modules. By identifying products using their primary keys, we can obtain useful data from DBs about the processing of returned products at each stage. "SERIAL" is assigned when a module or product is newly manufactured. At the same time, data for the module, such as time of birth, is entered in a module DB. A product DB, then, contains data regarding which modules compose the product.

The number of reprocessing facilities and OEMs depends on the size of the regulatory target. The total number of target OEMs and reprocessing facilities affects the total space of the RFID tags and the space that is occupied in each field, except for the header. The organization of the memory space of the tag can be flexible enough to accommodate any number of facilities and manufacturers.

As seen in Fig. 2, the proportions of storage available for "EPR ID," "REP ID," "Object Class" and "SERIAL" as well as the total capacity of the tag, can be flexibly adjusted according to a given situation in terms of the number of OEMs, facilities, and products and their modules. As a modification, we would propose that the space of the 2nd and 3rd fields be minimized as much as possible in order to assign a larger space to SERIAL. This would make the system more stable when new products and their components are introduced. It could then also deal with modules of a lower level in a bill of materials.

3.3   Design of External Databases and Transactions

In the beginning-of-life (BOL) phase, we assume that products contain components such as modules. The OEM starts with manufacturing subassemblies and manufacturing ends with assembly jobs. For component-level management, the OEM should record the birth history of every component as well as the information regarding which component is used for which product. The tag does not need to contain everything regarding this information, though, as it serves only as an identifier for efficient memory usage. All information should be stored in external DBs, and if more information about a product or component is needed, it can be accessed by sending a query with its identifier.

There are four external DBs: Product DB, Module DB, Instruction DB, and Result DB.

In the BOL phase, a product with components is manufactured. The tag to identify that product, which includes its exclusive serial number, is attached to it after the product's assembly is complete. The tag also includes information about the product and its components such as a timestamp of its birth, its object class, and its serial number, which are recorded in the product DB and module DB simultaneously. For the module DB in particular, there is a "Parent" field that indicates the component that it belongs to.

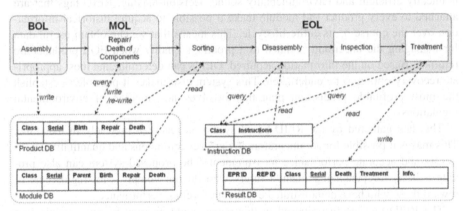

Fig. 3. Data interaction during product's entire lifecycle

In the MOL phase, component failure as well as product failure can take place. A failed component can be repaired or is considered dead if its condition renders it non-reusable. When a failed component of a product in the MOL phase is returned for repair and is replaced, the time of death should be entered in the module DB, and the product's record should be modified accordingly.

When these events take place, the timestamp of the repair or death is recorded in the product/module DB. The "Repair" field is thus an important sector in the recovery process.

In the sorting stage, the product's status that compares its expected life and its age is analyzed. If the timestamp of its repair has a null value, we can intuitively assume that the component is in good condition. If, on the other hand, the component has a repair history, the OEM should perform further inspection because the quality of the component is uncertain. This step makes the entire recovery process more efficient by omitting the additional inspection of returned products whose good quality is obvious.

Information that serves as a guide to the recycling process and as a warning to workers regarding hazardous materials can make the recycling process safer. Unlike the WEEE-RIM method, recycling information should be provided in the instruction DB, so that workers can access the information they need for any product they are working with. Loading recycling information by querying an instruction DB definitely saves a greater capacity of tags better than the WEEE-RIM method.

Once the recovery process is complete, the recycling results for the modules and products, such as which option has been pursued, are recorded in the DB. Administrative organizations that manage recycling can then find data logs of the recovery process in the results DB and can then accurately evaluate their recycling performance.

4   Conclusion

In this paper, we proposed an RFID-based integrated data system that facilitates economically efficient and environmentally sound decision-making. RFID tags that are attached to every product and module make it possible to acquire historical information over the course of its entire lifecycle. This means that we can obtain useful data for managing the uncertainty related to a product's quality when EOL products are returned. Based on the information acquired, OEMs can determine the most appropriate recovery option to be undertaken. This system also makes it possible to establish the most profitable production plan that involves no violation of environmental regulations.

The data gathered by the RFID-based system is recorded precisely in real time. This makes it possible for administrators to perform continuous and quantitative monitoring and accurate performance measurement. The proposed system can also provide a basis for penalizing manufacturers who do not comply with regulations or reward those who have demonstrated excellent recycling performance.

The RFID tag design proposed in this paper could be used by any organization with a flexible proportion of storage capacity because we have considered the existing standard. The individual identification of products and components is based on the Object Naming Service (ONS) of EPCglobal. In this context, we need to consider the existing concept of the Discovery Service to solve the security problem that information sharing will present in the future.

In this study, we did not analyze the economic aspects related to the cost of RFID integration and the possible advantages it could offer. One aspect we would mention here, though, is that RFID tags can be used semi-permanently until the tags are broken because they are used in a closed-loop system and are rewritable. This means that once the system launched, hardly any additional costs are incurred, except for maintenance costs.

To make the proposed system helpful to manufacturers, a decision-support system should be created that evaluates the economic value of returned products and their modules, and predicts how much additional value would be generated by the different options that are available.

References

1. Lindhqvist, T., Lidgren, K.: Model for Extended Producer Responsibility: In Ministry of the Environment, From the Cradle to the Grave – six studies of the environmental impacts of products, pp. 7–44. Ministry of Environment, Stockholm (1990)
2. Lindhqvist, T.: Extended Producer Responsibility in Cleaner Production. IIEEE Dissertatons, Lund University (2000)
3. Van Rossem, C., Tojo, N., Lindhqvist, T.: Extended producer responsibility: an examination of its impact on innovation and greening products. Greenpeace (2006), http://www.greenpeace.org/raw/content/international/press/reports/epr.pdf
4. Kuo, T.C.: Enhancing disassembly and recycling planning using life-cycle analysis. Robotics and Computer-Integrated Manufacturing 22, 420–428 (2006)
5. Das, K., Chowdhury, A.H.: Designing a reverse logistics network for optimal collection, recovery and quality-based product-mix planning. International Journal of Production Economics 135, 209–221 (2012)
6. Krikke, H.: Opportunistic versus life-cycle-oriented decision making in multi-loop recovery: an eco-eco study on disposed vehicles. International Journal of Life Cycle Assessment 15, 757–768 (2010)
7. Wailgum, T.: Tag, you're late: CIO Magazine, pp. 50–56 (November 15, 2004)
8. Niederman, F., Mathieu, R.G., Morley, R., Kwon, I.: Examining RFID Applications in Supply Chain Management. Communications of the ACM 50, 93–101 (2007)
9. Lee, D., Park, J.: RFID-based traceability in the supply chain. Industrial Management and Data Systems 108, 713–725 (2008)
10. Lee, C., Chan, T.: Development of RFID-based Reverse Logistics System. Expert Systems with Applications 36, 9299–9307 (2009)
11. Kulkarni, A., Parlikad, A., McFarlane, D., Harrison, M.: Networked RFID Systems in Product Recovery Management. In: IEEE International Symposium on Electronics and the Environment (2005)
12. Nativi, J., Lee, S.: Impact of RFID information-sharing strategies on a decentralized supply chain with reverse logistics operations. International Journal of Production Economics 136, 366–377 (2012)
13. Bajic, E., Chaxel, F.: Auto-ID Mobile Information System for Vehicle Life Cycle Data Management. In: IEEE Conference on Systems, Man and Cybernetics (2002)
14. Jun, H., Shin, J., Kim, Y., Kiritsis, D., Xirouchakis, P.: A Framework for RFID applications in product lifecycle management. International Journal of Computer Integrated Manufacturing 22, 595–615 (2009)
15. Parlikad, A., McFarlane, D.: RFID-based product information in end-of-life decision making. Control Engineering Practice 15, 1348–1363 (2007)
16. Bowman, P., Ng, J., Harrison, M., Illic, A.: Reusable Asset Management Model. BRIDGE Project WP3 (2009)
17. Luttropp, C., Johansson, J.: Improved Recycling with Life Cycle Information Tagged to the Product. Journal of Cleaner Production 18, 346–354 (2010)

Implementing Sustainable Supply Chain in PLM

Maria Bonvehí Rosich[1], Julien Le Duigou[2,*], and Magali Bosch-Mauchand[2]

[1] Universitat Politècnica de Catalunya – ETSEIB
ETSEIB – Av. Diagonal, 647 – 08028 Barcelona Spain
maria.bnvh@gmail.com
[2] Université de Technologie de Compiègne
UTC - Rue du Docteur Schweitzer – 60200 Compiègne France
{magali.bosch,julien.le-duigou}@utc.fr

Abstract. Sustainable supply chain has received growing attention in recent years. Due to the lack of relevant data to permit a credible analysis of sustainable supply chain, it is quite hard to propose an analytic method to guide sustainable supply chain strategies. Product Lifecycle Management (PLM) has provided companies with useful software to manage information using product as a central element. It consolidates all the information about product but also about production and distibution. For this reason it is interesting to integrate specific information in PLM systems necessary to manage sustainable supply chain and define a methodology to implement it. The proposal is a methodology based on a four steps process to guide companies which want to start a sustainable development using the information from their PLM tools such as Enterprise Resource Planning and/or Product Data Management.

Keywords: Sustainable Supply Chain, Product Lifecycle Management, Integration.

1 Introduction

Nowadays Supply Chain Management (SCM) is a crucial activity of a company to insure competitivity. In todays indsutrial context, suppliers, companies and customers are linked by numerous information and material flows (Seuring and Müller, 2008). For this reason SCM is an essential system for companies around the world. However due to the introduction of sustainability performance in companies SCM is evolving. In recent years supply chain has been extended and the complexity of networks has moved exponentially (Sekhari et al., 2010). All these changes and the globalization in demands have produced an impact on environmental, social and economic performance. Therefore sustainability is becoming one of companies' worries and they are trying to implement new systems in their process to achieve this objective. Among the multiple options which can be implemented one is the sustainable Supply Chain Management (sSCM).

---

* Corresponding author.

C. Emmanouilidis, M. Taisch, D. Kiritsis (Eds.): APMS 2012, Part II, IFIP AICT 398, pp. 168–175, 2013.

The sSCM is the integration of sustainable considerations into supply chain policies, programs and actions (Large and Gimenez Thomsen, 2011). One of the issues for sustainable supply chain analysis is the lack of relevant data available. Indeed the data available from the open database are not specific to the compagnies products and processes (Ketikidis *et al.*, 2008). A possible solution to assess and improve the sustainable performances of the supply chain is to integrate the Product Lifecycle Management data into the supply chain management analysis. PLM "is defined as a concept for the integrated management of product related information through the entire product lifecycle" (Schuh *et al.*, 2008). PLM gives necessary tools to a company in order to manage its products across their lifecycle, this management is essential to accomplish the company's aims.

This paper begins with a literature review to define an initial framework. Then the methodology is explained using four steps, and finally a conclusion provides lectors with a summary and future improvement for the methodology.

2   Literature Review

Sustainability has been defined as "the development that meets the needs of the present without compromising the ability of future generations to meet their needs" since the publication of the Brundtland Report in 1987 (Sekhari *et al.*, 2010). Sustainable development should ideally improve the quality of life without expending the earth's resources beyond its capacity. The achievement of sustainable development requires that companies, governments and individuals take actions, i.e., changing consumption habits, production behaviors, setting policies and changing practices (Remmen *et al.*, 2007).

Sustainability has three dimensions (Fig. 1) named "the triple bottom line" by Elkington in 1997. It implies that industries have to expand their economic objectives to include environmental and social dimensions, in order to achieve "sustainable business" (Remmen *et al.*, 2007).

To fully attempt sustainable development, companies could not work alone anymore. They have to integrate their customers and suppliers in their development, i.e. think at the supply chain's level. "SC encompasses all activities associated with the flow and transformation of goods from raw materials stage (extraction), through to the end user, as well as the associated information flows; material and information flow both up and down the supply chain" (Seuring and Müller, 2008). Mentzer *et al.* (2001) defined SCM as, "the systemic, strategic coordination of the traditional business functions and the tactics across these business functions within a particular company and across businesses within the supply chain, for the purposes of improving the long-term performance of the individual companies and the supply chain as a whole" (Ageron *et al.*, 2011).

Many articles have linked sustainability with SCM (Seuring and Müller, 2008; Sekhari *et al.*, 2010; Large and Gimenez Thomsen, 2011; Ageron *et al.*, 2011; Global Commerce initiative and Capgemini, 2008; MetroVancouvert, 2009; Azapagic, 2003; Perry *et al.*, 2011; Cuthbertson *et al.*, 2011; Linton, 2007). There are different terms to name that like sSCM or green supply chain, both terms have the same meaning which is to search more cooperation among partnering companies in order to make the SC operational and to reach sustainable performance (Ageron *et al.*, 2011).

There exist many guides talking about sustainable Supply Chain (sSC), for example "2016 future Supply Chain" (Global Commerce initiative and Capgemini, 2008) or "sustainable Supply Chain Logistics Guide" (MetroVancouvert, 2009) ; they furnish many proposals for greening your supply chain but there is a lack of specifications for their implementation.

Another difficulty in this research has been to find accurate indicators and data to evaluate the application of sSC. Indeed it can be found numerous information on sustainable indicators but a few of it is standardized.

One possible solution for sSCM implementation is to use data providing by PLM systems such as ERP and PDM. The advantage of PLM is to provide support for the integrated management of product related information through the entire product lifecycle and it stems from computer integrated manufacturing (CIM) and engineering data management (Schuh *et al.*, 2008). The aim of integrating management of product is to overcome the existing organizational barriers and to streamline the value creation chain (Schuh *et al.*, 2008).

In the next section a methodology of sSC using data contains in PLM systems is explained.

3   Proposed Methodology

The proposal resides in the definition of a methodology used to implement sSC by managing data in PLM software.

The methodology is based on lifecycle stage (Fig. 1): extraction of raw materials, design and production, packaging and distribution, use and maintenance, and disposal (Remmen *et al.*, 2007). The appropriate identification of all lifecycle stages is necessary for the establishment or optimization of environmental policies (Tsoulfas and Pappis, 2006). Each stage is going to have its own indicators and actions to achieve sSC depending on its needs.

The methodology process is divided in four main steps:

1. Select sustainable indicators.
2. Find causes and actions for improving indicators value.
3. List and define needed data from PLM software.
4. Implement action and evaluate indicators.

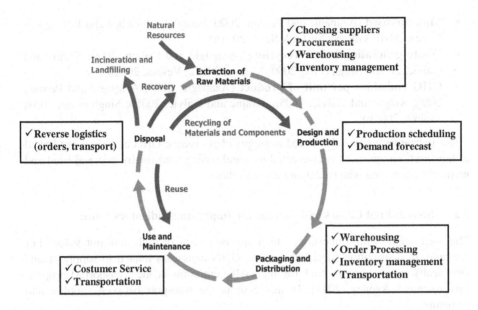

Fig. 1. Product lifecycle engineering vision (Remmen *et al.*, 2007) and SCM activities in LC stage based on (Larson and Rogers, 1998)

3.1   Step 1: Select Sustainable Indicators

At first, it is needed to select proper performance indicators covering different aspects of sustainability (Krajnc and Glavic, 2005a); indicators should be quantitative whenever it is possible (Azapagic, 2003). The selection of sustainable indicators begins with the understanding of which elements of sustainable development should be considered (Krajnc and Glavic, 2005a).

Indicators are needed for companies because there is an old saying that you can't manage what you don't measure. When it comes to measuring business performance, management has to know whether a company is accomplishing established goals and objectives and how to compare it to others in the sector (Veleva, 2001a).

Indicators are normally numerical measures that provide key information about a system. "They go beyond simple data to show tends or cause-and-effect relationship" (Veleva, 2001b).

The main objectives of indicators are to raise awareness and understanding, to inform decision-making and to measure progress toward established goals.

There are many indicators about sustainable development at different levels (Veleva, 2001b). For this reason this paper focuses only on environmental company indicators useful to measure achievements of implementing sSCM.

- **Energy used per unit of product** (Azapagic, 2003; Azapagic and Perdan, 2000; Veleva, 2001b; Fernández-Sánchez and Rodríguez-López, 2010; Krajnc and Galvic, 2005b).
- **Percent of raw materials from renewable resources** (Veleva, 2001b).

- **Material used** (Azapagic and Perdan, 2000; Fernández-Sánchez and Rodríguez-López, 2010; Veleva, 2001a; Veleva, 2001b).
- **Waste generation before recycling** (Azapagic and Perdan, 2000; Krajnc and Galvic, 2005b; Singh *et al.*, 2009; Veleva, 2001a; Veleva, 2001b).
- **GHG emissions per unit of product** (Azapagic, 2003; Azapagic and Perdan, 2000; Krajnc and Galvic, 2005a; Krajnc and Galvic, 2005b; Singh *et al.*, 2009; Veleva, 2001b).

These indicators are closely related to supply chain issues; GHG emissions are linked to transport, energy used is connected to warehousing, and finally material used and waste are connected with packaging among others.

3.2   Step 2: Find Causes and Actions for Improving Indicators Value

This step begins with a question; which are the causes of each indicator value? For example, in distribution stage; what cause GHG emissions related to supply chain? One really easy cause to find for the GHG emission is the transport (European Environement Agency, 2011). In this case is the transport between supplier and company.

This type of reflection is a essential step to move forward methodology; this step depends on company because each firm has its own process and its proper weak points in terms of sustainability.

After listing causes, it is the instant to propose actions to deal with these found causes. Actions will be based on cause-effect thinking and they will be various in each company because each firm owns its process and constraints. So it can find the most accurate form to enhance its sustainable indicators.

In the case of "Transport from suppliers" cause, possible actions are:

- **Giving more importance to suppliers' proximity:** local sourcing considers the trade-offs for remote sourcing between lower production cost and higher transport cost and CO_2 emissions. It quickly shows that CO_2 taxation needs to be quite severe to motivate more local sourcing (Global Commerce Initiative and Capgemini, 2008), but suppliers' proximity has to be bear in mind to find a balance between cost and CO_2 emissions.
- **Using eco-friendly transport:** It is necessary to explore freight transport alternatives that consume less fossil fuel (for example, vehicles fuelled by biodiesel or using hybrid technologies) (MetroVancouvert, 2009).
- **Improving accuracy in inventories and orders** (MetroVancouvert, 2009): Better interoperability between PLM software and suppliers' information systems avoids errors in orders and wrong deliveries because product can be taken directly from the suppliers' PLM system (Le Duigou *et al.*, 2011).

3.3   Step 3: List and Define Needed Data from PLM Software

In this section the solution applied is to link each action with the required data for monitoring the proposals and for integrating them in PLM software. PLM is related to a broad management concept which depends on the integration of multiple software components; the IT solution to support PLM results basically from the integration between Enterprise Resource Planning (ERP), Product Data Management (PDM) (Schuh *et al.*, 2008).

This step consists in the extraction and specification of all the needed data to introduce necessary information to execute the action proposed. This data can exist or not in the current PLM software. If it exists the implementation will be easier. If it doesn't exist it is required to create it.

In our example, if we select "Giving more importance to suppliers' proximity" as action, the data needed are:

- **Supplier code:** integrated in ERP.
- **Supplier location:** integrated in ERP. The distance between suppliers' factory and company's warehousing can be easely calculate from that data.

Finally the nature of data has to be defined in order to standardize information from suppliers to customers. It is essential to bear in mind that the implementation of new policies and development of new management practices require the cooperation of partners to achieve a more effective approach (Tsoulfas and Pappis, 2006).

In our example, the data needed to be implemented are:

- **Supplier code:** dimensionless number needed for the identification of the different suppliers. It is an attribute which exists in ERP.
- **Supplier location:** GPS coordinates of the supplier's factory will be a new data added for every supplier in ERP.

3.4   Step 4: Implement Action and Evaluate Indicators

The last step is the implementation of the chosen actions. The monitoring of the results can be precisely manage through a dashboard based on the PLM data. The methodology closes-loop on step 2 when new targeted values of indicators are selected. New actions are decided and possibly new data in the PLM software are selected or created to manage the new actions.

4   Conclusion

The Sustainable Supply Chain has a relevant importance to create a sustainable business, but manufactures share the responsibility of this process with suppliers, consumers and others in the life cycle chain (Tsoulfas and Pappis, 2006). There are many ways to work for sustainability like product definition, manufacturing possibilities, logistic strategies and end life alternatives (Perry *et al.*, 2011) but it is essential that main firms transfer across the whole supply chain the sustainability culture (Cuthbertson *et al.*, 2011).

This article proposes a method to help companies to accomplish their environmental objectives. Based on the specific data of the enterprise enclosed in their PLM software, this methodology helps to monitor sustainable supply chain strategies. There are some improvements that could be insert in this methodology, like for short-term research, adding economic parameters to help in the eco-efficient decisions and adding for deciding the most appealing actions, or for medium-term, adding the social evaluation of the actions based on the specific information of the company.

References

Ageron, B., Gunasekaran, A., Spalanzani, A.: Sustainable supply management: An empirical study. International Journal of Production Economics, 1–15 (2011)

Azapagic, A.: Systems approach to corporate sustainability: A General Management Framework. System 81, 303–316 (2003)

Azapagic, A., Perdan, S.: Indicators of Sustainable Development for Industry: A General Framework. Process Safety and Environmental Protection 78(4), 243–261 (2000)

Cuthbertson, R., Cetinkaya, B., Ewer, G., Klaas-Wissing, T., Piotrowicz, W., Tyssen, C.: Sustainable Supply Chain Management. Strategy. Springer, Heidelberg (2011)

European Environment Agency. Laying the foundations for greener transport (2011)

Fernández-Sánchez, G., Rodríguez-López, F.: A methodology to identify sustainability indicators in construction project management—Application to infrastructure projects in Spain. Ecological Indicators 10(6), 1193–1201 (2010)

Global Commerce Initiative, & Capgemini. 2016 Future Supply Chain (2008), http://www.futuresupplychain.com/

Ketikidis, P.H., Koh, S.C.L., Dimitriadis, N., Gunasekaran, A., Kehajova, M.: The use of information systems for logistics and supply chain management in South East Europe: Current status and future direction. Omega 36, 592–599 (2008)

Krajnc, D., Glavič, P.: How to compare companies on relevant dimensions of sustainability. Ecological Economics 55(4), 551–563 (2005)

Krajnc, D., Galvic, P.: A model for integrated assessment of sustainable development. Resources, Conservation and Recycling 43(2), 189–208 (2005)

Large, R.O., Gimenez Thomsen, C.: Drivers of green supply management performance: Evidence from Germany. Journal of Purchasing and Supply Management 17(3), 176–184 (2011)

Larson, P.D., Rogers, D.S.: Supply Chain Management: Definition, Growth and Approaches. Journal of Marketing Theory and Practice, Special Issue 6, 1–5 (1998)

Le Duigou, J., Bernard, A., Perry, N.: Framework for Product Lifecycle Management integration in Small and Medium Enterprises networks. Computer-Aided Design and Applications 8(4), 531–544 (2011)

Linton, J.D., Klassen, R., Jayaraman, V.: Sustainable supply chains: An introduction. Journal of Operations Management 25, 1075–1082 (2007)

MetroVancouvert. Sustainable Supply Chain Logistics Guide (2009), http://www.metrovancouver.org/smartsteps

Perry, N., Bernard, A., Bosch-Mauchand, M., Le Duigou, J., Xu, Y.: Eco Global Evaluation: Cross Benefits of Economic and Ecological Evaluation. In: Globalized Solutions for Sustainability in Manufacturing, pp. 681–686. Springer (2011)

Remmen, A., Jensen, A., Frydendal, J.: Life cycle management: a business guide to sustainability. United Nations Pubns. (2007)

Schuh, G., Rozenfeld, H., Assmus, D., Zancul, E.: Process oriented framework to support PLM implementation. Computers in Industry 59(2-3), 210–218 (2008)

Seuring, S., Müller, M.: From a literature review to a conceptual framework for sustainable supply chain management. Journal of Cleaner Production 16(15), 1699–1710 (2008)

Sekhari, A.S., Hossain, S.A., Bouras, A., Santiteerakul, S.: Sustainable Supply Chain Management from the Perspectives of Risk Management. In: Proceedings of the APMS Conference, Italie (2010)

Singh, R., Murty, H., Gupta, S., Dikshit, A.: An overview of sustainability assessment methodologies. Ecological Indicators 9(2), 189–212 (2009)

Tsoulfas, G., Pappis, C.: Environmental principles applicable to supply chains design and operation. Journal of Cleaner Production 14(18), 1593–1602 (2006)

Veleva, V.: Using Sustainable Production Indicators to Measure Progress in ISO 14001, EHS System and EPA Achievement Track. Corporate Environmental Strategy 8(4), 326–338 (2001)

Veleva, V.: Indicators of sustainable production. Journal of Cleaner Production 9(5), 447–452 (2001)

Full Exploitation of Product Lifecycle Management by Integrating Static and Dynamic Viewpoints

Dario Antonelli[1], Giulia Bruno[1], Antonia Schwichtenberg[2], and Agostino Villa[1]

[1] Politecnico di Torino, Corso Duca degli Abruzzi 24, 10129 Torino, Italy
[2] Ontoprise GmbH, An der RaumFabrik 33a, 76227 Karlsruhe, Germany

Abstract. Even if PLM offers a wide range of functionalities, they are currently not fully exploited by most of the companies, which use it mainly as a file manager. In this paper we aim at helping the full exploitation of PLM systems. To this aim, we propose a model of the product lifecycle management in the form of an ontology integrating both the static structure of product's data and the dynamic description of the related processes.

Keywords: PLM modeling, information integration, ontology, UML, IDEF0.

1   Introduction

Initially, to control data proliferation in design activities, Product Data Management (PDM) systems were created, which allowed data integration and secured files exchange. Within PDM the focus was on managing and tracking the creation, updating and storage of all information related to a product (e.g., CAD models, FE simulations and administrative documents). Product Lifecycle Management (PLM) is the logical evolution of PDM systems. PLM integrates people, data, software, processes and business systems to provide a complete product information backbone [16]. However, the concept of PLM is not completely received by companies, which do not exploit the full potentiality of PLM systems but use them only for data management functionalities. Especially for small and medium enterprise the exploitation of PLM is a problem due both to the lack of business process models and strict roles separation.

The paper provides an approach to allow a better exploitation of PLM systems by integrating static and dynamic viewpoints of product lifecycle. Particularly, we propose a model to contemporarily represent the data structure of PLM, thus allowing interoperability and data exchange among different systems, and the dynamic processes of product lifecycle. The model is presented in the form of an ontology, due to the ontology capability of including both the static representation (in its structure) and the dynamic view (in its instances).

Ontologies support several useful features, such as to share common understanding of the structure of information among human or software agents, to enable reuse of domain knowledge, to separate domain knowledge from operational knowledge and to provide formal analysis of terms [15]. Ontologies have already been proposed for knowledge management in product design processes [1]. Ontologies have been

C. Emmanouilidis, M. Taisch, D. Kiritsis (Eds.): APMS 2012, Part II, IFIP AICT 398, pp. 176–183, 2013.

developed for closed-loop PLM [12], for the Open Assembly Model [6], and for STEP (Standard for the Exchange of Product Model) [18]. A product design ontology that formalizes the functionality of shape processing methods in the design workflow is defined in [2], while an ontology to manage both the product and the PLM is proposed in [15]. A method for semantic integration of PLM objects based on an integrated ontology is described in [14] and the work in [17] uses ontologies for interoperability and present a model for using data of the entire life of the products as an input for the design and production of new products. Differently from the previous works, in which the ontologies were developed starting from general concepts of the product processes or from general models of PLM, we generated an ontology from the integration of the static structure of PLM and the dynamic description of the product lifecycle processes.

The rest of the paper is organized as follows. Section 2 describes the dynamic model of product lifecycle, while Section 3 provides the static structure of PLM. In Section 4 the derived ontology is presented. Finally, Section 5 draws conclusions and states future works.

2 Dynamic Model of Product Lifecycle

The dynamic (or behavioral) model makes explicit the processes and the interactions among entities involved in the product lifecycle. IDEF0 [4] is selected in the present study as a formalism for the dynamic representation due to two reasons: (i) it is a well-established methodology in the industrial environment, thus companies had less problems representing their processes with this formalism, and (ii) it is suitable to our scope because it allows the separate identification of resources, files and tools inside activities. Furthermore it was demonstrated that IDEF0 models can effectively complement UML models when the objective is the system design instead of the software development [3].

Product lifecycle is a complex process and it is composed by several phases. We focused on the Beginning of Product Life (BPL), trying to generalize the very detailed process of the car body and chassis design employed by an automotive industry. Since this process is among the most long and complex, it represents a good starting point to build a general model. BPL has been divided in Concept Design, Preliminary Design, Detailed Design, and Development. For sake of shortness we report in Fig.1 the overall activity diagram (A0) and in Fig.2 the details of the first activity, i.e., the Concept Design (A1). The concept design is composed of activities oriented to the definition of the schematic design of product and process and to the set-up of general project guidelines. Care should be paid to the fact that the position of blocks in the diagram does not represent the temporal sequence of activities. As an example, in the investigated companies the economic feasibility study follows the engineering feasibility study (see Fig.2).

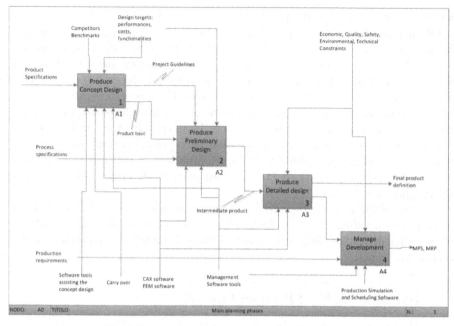

Fig. 1. IDEF0 diagram of product Beginning of Life

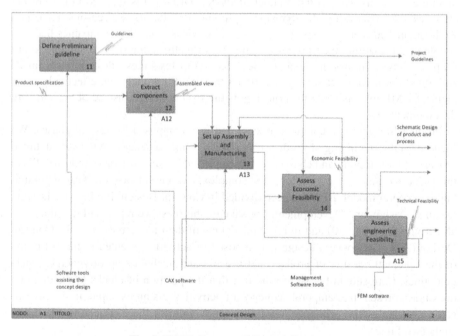

Fig. 2. IDEF0 diagram of Concept Design

3   Static Model of PLM

The static (or structural) model aims at representing the structure of the system by using entities, attributes, relationships and operations. The most used formalism for structural models is the Unified Modeling Language (UML) class diagram [8], which has been already used to model PDM systems [5].

The UML class diagram of PLM is reported in Fig.3. The upper part of the diagram contains information about the product and its characteristics, while the most consistent part is focused on the product lifecycle management.

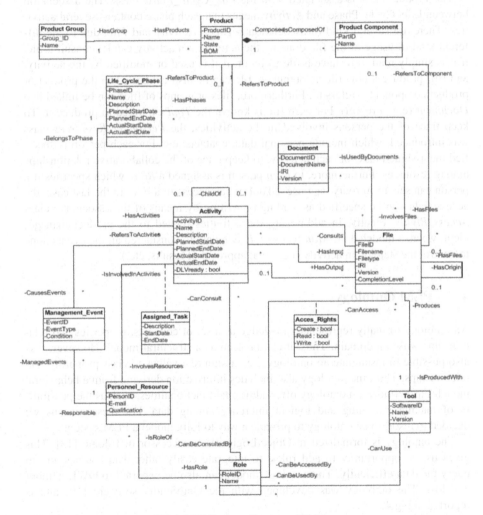

Fig. 3. UML class diagram of PLM

Since we are not interested in providing a detailed description of the product (for a more complete UML diagram of a product, the Core Product Model developed in [7] can be taken as a reference), we modeled the most important concepts of product in three classes. The class *Product* contains the information about products. It is associated to the *Product_Group* class, which contains information about the product group it belongs to. The composition association between the Product class and the *Product_Component* class represents the fact that each product can be made of several components, and each of them can have associated files that describe their state in the PLM.

The Product class is associated with the *Life_Cycle_Phase* class. The association between Life_Cycle_Phase and *Activity* means that each phase contains several activities. There are several kind of association between Activity and *File*, due to the different kind of usage of the file done by the activity. An activity can (i) consult a file, if it is simply read,   (ii) have a file as input, if it is used or modified by the activity, and (iii) produce a new file as output. A file can be also connected to the product or product component it refers to. Furthermore, files or groups of files can be linked in a *Document* (e.g. a report). For each file is known the *Tool* exploited to produce it. To keep trace of the persons involved in the activities, the *Personnel_Resources* class was introduced, which include personal data, contacts, etc. For each person is specified the assigned task for each activity, to keep trace of the collaborative relationships among resources. Furthermore, to each person is assigned a *Role*, which specifies if a person can see an Activity, can use a Tool or can access to a File. In the last case, the access right can be specified as reading or writing by means of the associative class *Access_Rights*. Finally, in addition to the activities related to the product management, we also modeled the *Management_Event* class to considered all the events done to control the state of an activity (i.e., final approval of results, etc.).

4   PLM Ontology

An ontology formally represents knowledge as a set of concepts, properties and relationships within a domain. Thus, it can be seen as a structural model. However, it is also possible to instantiate an ontology, i.e., assign real values to class properties and relationships. Thus, the ontology also includes information deriving from a behavioral model. Furthermore, an ontology offer additional functionalities, such as the possibility of making reasoning and logical inference among data. For these reasons we decided to resort to an ontology to provide a way to fully model a PLM system.

The ontology is formalized in ObjectLogic [9], a successor of F-logic [13]. This gives us the opportunity to add rules, to integrate easily other data sources and to query the data efficiently. The ontology model can also be exported to OWL without any lost. The ontology was developed with the OntoStudio software [10] and is reported in Fig.4.

The schema of the ontology is a direct representation of the structural model for PLM described in the UML diagram. The classes in the UML are concepts in the ontology with named relations between them having the cardinality restrictions and the names as defined in the UML. For the attributes, it is possible to define ranges according to the XML Schema Definition [11]. So our model can be used together with any repository offering URIs for the documents stored there (e.g. by providing a REST interface).

Once the model has been developed, it is possible to fit it with the data providing from the behavioral models, i.e., to give real values to products, activities, files, resources, etc.. This forms the workflow within a concrete product lifecycle. Fig. 5 shows an example of an instantiation of our ontology for a Production Planning activity of a small industry.

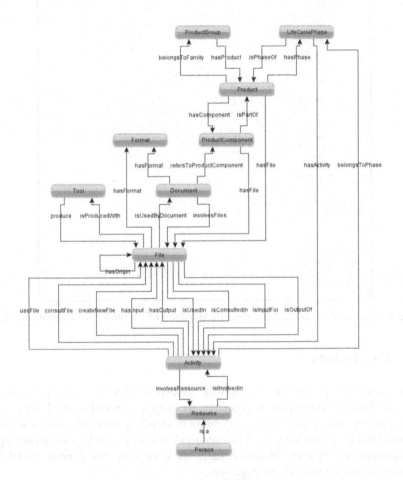

Fig. 4. Ontology of PLM

We would like to clarify that the proposed ontology aims at helping companies that would like to adopt a PLM system, and thus need to first produce a behavioral model of their process, and then to organize the information about product lifecycle among the entities and relations specified by the static UML class diagram of PLM. To have a more complete ontology of the system, additional information arising from the specific PLM software chosen by the company should be also considered.

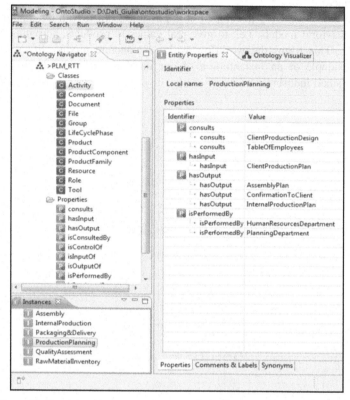

Fig. 5. Example of an instantiation of the PLM ontology for a Production Planning activity

5   Conclusions

In this paper we describe an approach to full exploit PLM systems by integrating static and dynamic viewpoints. Particularly, we propose a model of PLM in the form of an ontology, due to the ontology capability of including both the static view (in its structure) and the dynamic view (in its instances). We are currently working on applying our approach to some industrial cases to show how this general model can improve the product lifecycle management.

Acknowledgments. The research presented in this paper is supported by the EU-FP7 research project on Advanced Platform for Manufacturing Engineering and Product Lifecycle Management (amePLM).

References

1. Brandt, S.C., Morbach, J., Miatidis, M., Theißen, M., Jarke, M., Marquardt, W.: An ontology-based approach to knowledge management in design processes. Computers and Chemical Engineering 32, 320–342 (2007)
2. Catalano, C.E., Camossi, E., Ferrandes, R., Cheutet, V., Sevilmis, N.: A product design ontology for enhancing shape processing in design workflows. J. Intell. Manuf. 20, 553–567 (2009)
3. Kima, C.-H., Westonb, R.H., Hodgsonb, A., Leea, K.-H.: The complementary use of IDEF and UML modelling approaches. Computers in Industry 50, 35–56 (2003)
4. Chen, Y.-Q., Hu, J., Mo, P.: The Development of The Lifecycle Function Model By IDEF0 For Construction Projects. In: International Conference on Wireless Communications, Networking and Mobile Computing, pp. 1–4 (2008)
5. Eynard, B., Gallet, T., Nowak, P., Roucoules, L.: UML based specifications of PDM product structure and workflow. Computers in Industry 55, 301–316 (2004)
6. Fiorentini, X., Gambino, I., Liang, V.-C., Foufou, S., Rachuri, S., Bock, C., Mani, M.: Towards an Ontology for Open Assembly model. In: Proceeding of the International Conference on Product Lifecycle Management, pp. 445–456 (2007)
7. Foufou, S., Fenves, S.J., Bock, C., Rachuri, S., Sriram, R.D.: A Core Product Model for PLM with an illustrative XML implementation. In: International Conference on Product Lifecycle Management (2005)
8. Fowler, M., Scott, K.: UML distilled. Addison-Wesley (2000)
9. http://www.ontoprise.de/fileadmin/user_upload/Publications_EN/ObjectLogic_Tutorial.pdf
10. http://www.ontoprise.de/de/produkte/ontostudio/
11. http://www.w3.org/2001/XMLSchema#
12. Jun, H.-B., Kiritsis, D., Xirouchakis, P.: A primitive ontology model for product lifecycle meta data in the closed-loop PLM. In: Enterprise Interoperability II: New Challenges and Approaches, pp. 729–740. Springer, London (2007)
13. Kifer, M., Lausen, G., Wu, J.: Logical foundations of objectoriented and frame-based languages. J. ACM 42(4), 741–843 (1995)
14. Kwak, J.-A., Yong, H.-S.: An Approach to Ontology-Based Semantic Integration for PLM Object. In: IEEE International Workshop on Semantic Computing and Applications, pp. 19–26 (2008)
15. Matsokis, A., Kiritsis, D.: An ontology-based approach for Product Lifecycle Management. Computers in Industry 61, 787–797 (2010)
16. Stark, J.: Product lifecycle management: 21st century paradigm for product realization. Springer, London (2005)
17. Suh, S.-H., Shin, S.-J., Yoon, J.-S., Um, J.-M.: UbiDM: a new paradigm for product design and manufacturing via ubiquitous computing technology. International Journal of Computer Integrated Manufacturing 21(5), 540–549 (2008)
18. Wang, Q., Peng, W., Yu, X.: Ontology based geometry recognition for STEP. In: IEEE International Symposium on Industrial Electronics, pp. 1686–1691 (2010)

Enterprise Information Systems' Interoperability: Focus on PLM Challenges

Dorsaf Elheni-Daldoul[1,2], Julien Le Duigou[1,*], Benoit Eynard[1],
and Sonia Hajri-Gabouj[2]

[1] UTC, Université de Technologie de Compiègne, Département Génie des Systèmes
Mécaniques, UMR CNRS 7337 Roberval, BP 60319 - 60203 Compiègne Cedex, France
julien.le-duigou@utc.fr, benoit.eynard@utc.fr
[2] INSAT, Institut National des Sciences Appliquées et de Technologie, URAII
Centre Urbain Nord BP 676 - 1080 Tunis Cedex, Tunisie
daldouldorsaf@yahoo.fr, Sonia.Gabouj@insat.rnu.tn

Abstract. Nowadays, in industry, the interoperability of Information Systems throughout the product's life cycle is primordial for a successful Product Life-cycle Management approach. However, there are still scientific and technological locks that prevent the integration of information between enterprise Information Systems. Especially, the lack of interoperability between Product Data Management systems, Manufacturing Process Management and Enterprise Resource Planning to be able to ensure a continuous and bidirectional information flow from the design to the manufacturing and the assembling of a product. This paper presents firstly a literature review of research works developed to define and solve the problems of interoperability in general terms. Then, it exposes most of the recent works on interoperability on the product development linking the different Product Lifecycle Management tools. Finally we proposed an approach to guarantee the interoperability of Product Data Management, Manufacturing Process Management and Enterprise Resource Planning systems.

Keywords: Interoperability, PDM, ERP, MPM, Integration.

1 Introduction

The PLM strategy can be defined as a solution addressing many components for managing product data (Porter, 1987; Amann, 2002). In industrial companies, PLM has become a paradigm for several decades. It is the process of managing all phases of a product's life cycle (design, manufacturing, sale, recycling) which effectively provides a method to integrate and share product information from department to department within a company, and also externally. It also increases business productivity in terms of cost, quality and time (Terzy et al., 2010).

---

* Corresponding author.

C. Emmanouilidis, M. Taisch, D. Kiritsis (Eds.): APMS 2012, Part II, IFIP AICT 398, pp. 184–191, 2013.

To preserve the overall coherence of the company information system, the interoperability of Information Systems (IS) must be guaranteed throughout a product's life (Noel and Roucoules, 2010). Among these, we mention PDM software (essential in design), that drive virtual product development, also ERP (used in manufacturing) which manages real product.

This paper presents firstly a state of the art of interoperability: definition and levels of interoperability. Then, it exposes specific works on interoperability on the product development linking the different Product Lifecycle Management tools. Finally it concludes on a framework integrating PDM, MPM and ERP.

2   Definition of Interoperability

Interoperability still means many things to many people and is often interpreted in many different ways with different expectations (Chen and Doumeingts, 2003). So, in the literature, we find different definitions of the interoperability. IEEE defined the interoperability as "The ability of two or more systems or elements to exchange information and to use the information that has been exchanged" (IEEE, 1990). Also, projects (ATHENA, 2003) and (INTEROP, 2003) define it as the ability of interaction between enterprises (or part of it). So, the enterprise interoperability is achieved if the interaction can, at least, take place at the three levels: data, application and business process. In summary enterprise interoperability is the ability to (a) communicate and exchange information; (b) use the information exchanged; (c) access to functionality of a third system (Chen and Doumeingts, 2003).

Here, interoperability is defined as "The ability of two systems (or more) to communicate, cooperate and exchange services and data, thus despite the differences in languages, implementations, executive environments and abstraction models" (Wegner, 1996).

2.1   Levels of Interoperability

According to (EIF, 2004), there are three levels of interoperability: the technical, semantic and organizational levels. The technical level ensures the continuity of the semantic flow (e.g. technology solutions, standards and tools for the exchange of data between IS). The semantic level ensures the sharing of information and service for preserving the semantic flow. And the organizational level concerns the business unit, process and people interactions across organization borders (Paviot et al., 2011). Most articles in the literature tend to satisfy the technical and semantic levels (Paviot et al., 2011; Assouroko et al., 2010). In fact, organizational barriers are additional barriers. Compared with technical barriers (concerned with machine problems) and semantic barriers (centered on information problems), organizational barriers originate from the problem of humans (Chen, 2009). In this research we will focus on the technical and semantic levels.

2.2   Semantic Level

From (ISO, 1999; Kosanke, 2006), there are three manners of achieving semantic interoperability: *integration* (there exists a common format for all models), *unification* (there is a common format but it only exists at meta-level) and *federation* (it is a more recent approach, based on the use of ontologies and Semantic Web standards for automation in the transfer and mapping of data between heterogeneous applications (Assouroko et al., 2010)).

Most of the works in the literature use unification approaches (Paviot et al., 2011; Tursi et al., 2009), because it is more flexible and dynamic than the integration approach. According to (Paviot et al., 2011; Benaben et al., 2008), the use of the STEP standard has the potential to save up to one billion dollars per year by reducing interoperability coasts in the automotive, aerospace and shipbuilding industries. So, the STEP standard is a possible way for the product driven interoperability. On the other hand, the federation approach requires modifying the ontology according to ontology of higher level. As there it may be several top-level ontologies, which implies that the ontology which is chosen must be regularly updated and the mappings are built manually (Hoffman, 2008). However, the federation approach seems to be appropriate and interesting for the interoperability of IS of PLM, despite the disappointing results on methods and tools for ontology alignment (Pratt, 2005).

2.3   Technical Level

According to (Booth et al., 2004), Web services provide a standard means of interoperating between different software applications, running on a variety of platforms and/or frameworks. The trend, today, of major PLM commercial products becoming Service Oriented Architecture (SOA) (e.g. TeamCenter, Windchill, SAP, etc.) invites us to explore this direction to ensure the technical interoperability of IS.

The mediator architecture is also a promising solution for treat the problems of interoperability (Benaben et al., 2008; Wiederhold, 1992). In fact, the mediator architecture is more efficient in terms of agility of IS and the total cost of ownership of interfaces, compared with a point-to-point architecture (Guyot et al., 2007).

3   Interoperability in PLM

This section will study literature concerning the links between the different steps of the development of a product. We will focus on the interoperability view of those works to understand which level of interoperability is realized and with which methods. In the development phase, we distinguish three links that need to be analyzed:

- The design/ simulation information flow
- The design/manufacturing information flow
- The design/assembling information flow

In the same way, the three levels of interoperability see before are used to classify the works:

- Technic level
- Semantic level
- Organizational level

From those criteria of analysis, we can construct a table to classify the works on this topic. The result of the analysis is synthetized in table 1.

Table 1. Synthesis of bibliographical analysis

	Semantic level	Technical level	Organizational level
Design/simulation	(Nguyen Van, 2006; Assouroko et al., 2010; Charles, 2005)	(Troussier, 1999)	
Design/manufacturing	(Le Duigou et al., 2012; Paviot et al., 2011; Ou-Yang and Chen, 2003 ; Guyot et al., 2007)	(Martin, 2006; Paviot et al., 2011)	(Laureillard, 2000)
Design/assembling	(Demoly, 2010; Le Duigou et al., 2012)	(Rejneri, 2000)	(Demoly, 2010)

A. Design / simulation information flow

The link between design and simulation is essential to the designers that based their technological choices on simulation analysis. Indeed the bidirectional flow of design and simulation can decrease the number of modifications between CAD and FEM models, decreasing the development time of the validated product model.

(Nguyen Van, 2006) defines architecture to facilitate the collaboration loops between design and simulation. He uses standard format to share information between those phases, ensuring the semantic flow conservation.

(Assouroko et al., 2010) proposes an approach for managing interoperability software CAD/CAE. To do so, he defines a model based on ontologies. To link the different ontologies, he defines a relations management method and tool.

(Charles, 2005) defines a simulation data management system to ensure the semantic flow between software. His model is based on STEP format.

(Troussier, 1999) uses the information contain in the calculation notes to determine the dependencies between the design and the simulation data. Her tool is based on a database that links the attributes of each simulation models to allow the designer to take into account the simulation data in his design model.

B. Design/manufacturing information flow

The design/manufacturing link from the CAD to the CNC allows an optimized design for manufacturing. Moreover the interoperability between design and manufacturing allows propagating the information, avoiding costly backtracking.

(Ou-Yang and Chen, 2003) develops a high-level PDM/MRP integration framework. (Martin, 2006) proposes a Visual Basic tool to develop a mediator for the useful API in the link between design and casting.

(Guyot et al., 2007) or (Paviot et al., 2008) are interested in the problems of interoperability of CAD/PDM systems. Similarly (Paviot et al. 2011) proposes an unified approach for the interoperability of PDM/ERP systems. With the notion of mediator linking ontologies, he discusses the technical level. However, beyond the technical process, based on a model based on "semantic tags", he develops the semantic level of interoperability.

(Le Duigou al., 2012) deals with interoperability between design and manufacturing by defining a generic data model. He first uses a unified approach to model business specific models then he proposes a generic model integrating the specific models ensuring the semantic flow.

(Laureillard, 2000) deals with the link between design and manufacturing at organization level: "integration appears in the effective action of design through the combination of several factors, including the tool but also the organization or knowledge." The reconciliation between the different business actors promotes the exchange of information to increase knowledge for the conception of new systems.

C. Design/assembling information flow

The link between design and assembling essentially helps the designers in its approach of technical choices.

(Rejneri, 2000) develops an "offer of professional tools for designers of mechanical systems and are particularly interested in the assembly business." The tools developed are then able to help the designer in his choice allowing him to see a semi-automatic scenarios assembly and disassembly of the system. Through this tool it addresses the technical level of interoperability.

(Demoly, 2010) defines an assembly model Multi-Views Oriented (MUVOA) which aims to ensure the link between design and assembly. Semantic flow is thus ensured through the involvement of business actors, treating the problems of organizations.

Therefore, research to be explored in the short and medium term relate to the transition to a strategy and an essential component of PLM, which is the Manufacturing Process Management (MPM), which eliminates this challenge by integrating information on a single system. In fact, According to the Frost and Sullivan research firm (Keith Robinson, 2002), *"Manufacturing Process Management (MPM) software is its own unique category and provides links between upstream PLM software, such as computer-aided design (CAD) and Product Data Management (PDM), and downstream applications, such as Enterprise Resource Planning (ERP)"*.

In addition, the MPM responds to several challenges faced by business-critical today, including the need to shorten the time-volume, optimize production execution, ensure integration of information, allowing engineers, designers, and corporate staff to work interactively, etc.

4   Conclusion

This paper has presented technical and semantic barriers of interoperability, and the different approaches to solve the semantic level (integration, unification and federation). In addition, we presented our framework which focuses on interoperability between PDM-MPM-ERP systems.

In this article, we have not discussed how the different axes will be defined and specified, as well as technologies that will be used to implement them. This will be done in detail in the next stages of our work. However, due to our state of the art, very interesting and promising approaches such as Web technologies and ontologies approach of data exchange and interoperability software have been identified. They will certainly technology watches, see potential solutions to explore and use in the implementation of our approach.

References

Amann, K.: Product Lifecycle Management: Empowering the Future of Business. CIM Data Inc. (2002)

Assouroko, I., Boutinaud, P., Troussier, N., Eynard, B., Ducellier, G.: Survey on standards for product data exchange and sharing: application in CAD/CAE interoperability. International Journal of Design and Innovation Research 5(1) (2010)

ATHENA, Advanced Technologies for Interoperability of Heterogeneous Enterprise Networks and their Applications. FP6-2002-IST-1, Integrated Project (2003)

Benaben, F., Touzi, J., Rajsiri, V., Truptil, S., Lorré, J.P., Pingaud, H.: Mediation Information System Design in a Collaborative SOA Context through a MDD Approach. In: Proceedings of MDISIS 2008, pp. 89–103 (2008)

Booth, D., Haas, H., McCabe, F., Newcomer, E., Champion, M., Ferris, C., Orhcard, D.: Web Services Architecture. W3C Working Group. Note 11/2/2004 (2004)

Charles, S.: Gestion Intégrée des données CAO et EF - Contribution à la liaison entre conception mécanique et calcul de structures. PhD thesis, Université de Technologie de Troyes (2005)

Chen, D.: Framework for Enterprise Interoperability (2009)

Chen, D., Doumeingts, G.: European Initiatives to develop interoperability of enterprise applications - basic concepts, framework and roadmap. Journal of Annual Reviews in Control 27(2), 151–160 (2003)

Demoly, F.: Conception intégrée et gestion d'informations techniques: application à l'ingénierie du produit et de sa séquence d'assemblage. PhD thesis, Université de Technologie de Belfort-Montbéliard (2010)

EIF, European Interoperability Framework, White paper, pp. 1–40 (2004)

Guyot, E., Ducellier, G., Eynard, B., Girard, P., Gallet, T.: Product data and digital mock-up exchange based on PLM. In: Proceedings of PLM 2007 Conference (2007)

Hoffman, P.: Similarité sémantique inter-ontologies basée sur le contexte. PhD thesis, Université Claude-Bernard Lyon 1 (2008)

IEEE. «Standard Computer Dictionary - A Compilation of IEEE Standard Computer Glossaries.» Standard Computer Dictionary - A Compilation of IEEE Standard Computer Glossaries, New York (1990)

INTEROP, Interoperability Research for Networked Enterprises Applications and Software, Network of Excellence, Proposal Part B (2003)

ISO 14258, Industrial Automation Systems- Concepts and Rules for Enterprise Models, ISO TC184/SC5/WG1, 1999-April-14 version (1999)

Kosanke, K.: ISO standards for interoperability: a comparison. In: Konstantas, et al. (eds.) Interoperability of Enterprise Software and Applications. Springer, London (2006)

Laureillard, P.: Conception intégrée dans l'usage Mise en œuvre d'un dispositif d'intégration produit-process dans une filière de conception de pièces forgées. PhD thesis, INPG (2000)

Le Duigou, J., Bernard, A., Perry, N., Delplace, J.C.: Generic PLM system for SMEs: Application to an equipment manufacturer. Int. J. Product Lifecycle Management 6(1), 51–64 (2012)

Martin, L.: Intégration du métier de la fonderie dans les processus de conception - méthodologies et outils associés. PhD thesis, Ecole Nationale Supérieure d'Arts Et Métiers (2006)

Nguyen Van, T.: Ingénierie système appliquée à la gestion des données techniques en entreprise étendue: Application aux boucle de conception / simulation. PhD thesis, Ecole Centrale Paris (2006)

Noel, F., Roucoules, L.: The PPO design model with respect to digital enterprise technologies among product life cycle. International Journal of Computer Integrated Manufacturing 21(2), 139–145 (2008)

Ou-Yang, C., Cheng, M.C.: Developing a PDM/MRP integration framework to evaluate the influence of engineering change on inventory scrap cost. Int. J. Adv. Manuf. Technol. (22), 161–174 (2003)

Paviot, T., Cheutet, V., Lamouri, S.: A PLCS framework for PDM/ERP interoperability. International Journal of Product Lifecycle Management 5(2-3-4), 295–313 (2011)

Paviot, T., Morenton, P., Cheutet, V., Lamouri, S.: MultiCAD/MultiPDM integration framework. In: 5th International Conference on Product Lifecycle Management, Seoul, Korea (2008)

Porter, M.: From competitive advantage to corporate strategy. Harvard Business Review, 43–59 (May/June 1987)

Pratt, M.J.: ISO 10303 : the STEP Standard for Product data Exchange and its capabilities. Int. J. Product Lifecycle Management 1(1), 86–94 (2005)

Rejneri, N.: Détermination et simulation des opérations d'assemblage lors de la conception de systèmes mécaniques. PhD thesis, Institut National Polytechnique de Grenoble (2000)

Robinson, K.: MPM Market Primed for Robust Growth (2002), http://www.promantechnology.com/mpm-plm.asp

Terzi, S., Bouras, A., Dutta, D., Garetti, M., Kiritsis, D.: Product lifecycle management – from its history to its new role. International Journal of Product Lifecycle Management 4(4), 360–389 (2010)

Troussier, N.: Contribution à l'intégration du calcul mécanique dans la conception de produits techniques: proposition méthodologique pour l'utilisation et la réutilisation. Thèse de doctorat de l'Université de Grenoble 1 (1999)

Tursi, A., Panetto, H., Morel, G., Dassisti, M.: Ontological approach for product-centrics information system interoperability in networked manufacturing enterprises. Annual Reviews in Control 33(1), 238–245 (2009)

Wegner, P.: Interoperability. ACM Computing Survey 28(1), 285–287 (1996)

Wiederhold, G.: Mediators in the architecture of future information system. IEEE Computer 25(3), 38–49 (1992)

Closed-Loop Life Cycle Management Concept for Lightweight Solutions

Fatih Karakoyun and Dimitris Kiritsis

Laboratory for Computer-Aided Design and Production,
School of Engineering, Swiss Federal Institute of Technology, Switzerland
{fatih.karakoyun,dimitris.kiritsis}@epfl.ch

Abstract. Lightweighting is the point of interest especially for automotive and aerospace industries. Wrought aluminum alloys have great potential in lightweighting. There is a need to increase post-consumer recycling and use of recycled aluminum in high-end structural components to exploit the full potential of wrought aluminum alloys. Closed-loop product life cycle management (PLM) may enable to increase the recycling of wrought aluminum alloys by providing essential information about the individual parts. Considering separate life cycle phases, products and processes may seem environmentally friendly, but it is not possible to be sure unless the entire life cycle is taken into account. LCA and LCC are scientific investigative processes which take into account entire life cycle of the products and help decision makers to evaluate between alternatives in product development. The work

Keywords: Wrought aluminum alloys, Closed-Loop PLM, LCA, LCC.

1 Introduction

Lightweighting is essential for automotive and aerospace industries for a number of reasons. First of all lightweighting directly reduces the fuel consumption because the energy required to move a vehicle is, except for aerodynamic resistance, directly proportional to its mass [1]. Due to the reduction of the fuel consumption GHG emissions are also reduced. There are metal (high strength steel, aluminum, magnesium) and composite (SMC, glass fiber and carbon fiber) alternatives for lightweighting. Among all other alternatives aluminum is the most feasible choice in both environmental and economic sense. Aluminum, especially wrought aluminum alloys, have large potentials for dramatic weight reduction of structural parts. Recycling is a major aspect of continued aluminum use, as more than a third of all the aluminum currently produced globally originates from old, traded and new scrap [2].

Global recycling rate of aluminum in transport is ~90% [3], which is driven by the high material value of aluminum scrap. However the recycling rate of aluminum in transport is high, most of the aluminum scrap is recycled into cast products due to number of reasons. One of the most important reasons is lack of sufficient information about the parts produced from wrought aluminum alloys. It is not possible to

C. Emmanouilidis, M. Taisch, D. Kiritsis (Eds.): APMS 2012, Part II, IFIP AICT 398, pp. 192–199, 2013.

track and gather information about individual parts after delivery of the vehicle to the customer. The closed-loop product life cycle management (Closed-loop PLM) system focuses on tracking and managing the information of whole product life cycle, with possible feedback of information to product life cycle phases [4]. Closed-loop PLM may enable to increase the recycling rate of wrought aluminum alloys by providing essential information about the individual parts. The work reported in this paper is a funded by EU FP7 project called SuPLight, which aims to increase use of recycled material in production of high-end structural components.

2   Background

Weight savings in the overall car mass is considered to be a major research focus [5]. Weight reduction is particularly important because average vehicle weight is expected to increase since the automobile industry will continue to market new models with increased luxury, convenience, performance, and safety as demanded by their customers [6]. Aluminum is proven to be among the potential materials capable of achieving weight reduction without sacrificing the vehicle safety and performance [5]. Wrought aluminum alloys have great potential in weight reduction. Tests have shown 75% reduction of the weight with sustained performance using wrought aluminum when compared to a conventional steel based solution, and 50% reduction when compared with aluminum castings [6].

Recycling aluminum saves 95% of the energy and 95% of emissions associated with production of metal from the ore, as well as reduces the amount of waste consigned to landfill [7]. Green stated that on life cycle basis all the energy required to produce primary aluminum is recovered in vehicle fuel savings within 3 years, and in less than 3 months when recycled metal is used [7].

The European Union is structurally dependent on aluminum recycling for its domestic metal supply, because of limited ore mining and lack of sufficient domestic primary aluminum production, growing end-use demand and energy constraints in Europe [3,8]. More than half of all the aluminum currently produced in the European Union (EU-27) originates from recycled raw materials and that trend is on the increase, however it should be noted that Europe is a net importer of aluminum and aluminum ore. In 2010, 79% of the bauxite, 41% of alumina for production of primary aluminum and 30% of total aluminum supply was net-imported by European aluminum industry. From a total metal supply of 12.5 million tons in 2010, 35 % is produced by European primary smelters, 30% is net-imported and 34% is recycled by European refiners and remelters [9]. Efficient aluminum recycling will be more important in the future because of the import dependence and rising energy constraints in Europe.

However recycling is the key issue to increase the use of aluminum, wrought aluminum recycling is difficult due to their low impurity and alloy content. Kevorkijan stated that the main difficulty in production of wrought aluminum alloys from scrap is to achieve the proper chemical composition of the melt with minimal addition of primary aluminum and alloying elements [10]. Whether wrought alloys completely made from wrought alloy aluminum scrap can assume the same quality as the primary aluminum alloy is frequently questioned. Over time, it has become clear that such concerns are largely unwarranted; with very few exceptions, quality requirements can be met by remelted material [11].

Das studied on recycling aerospace alloys in which cost effective recycling is difficult because aircraft alloys are typically high in alloying elements and contain low levels of impurities to optimize toughness and other performance characteristics [12, 13]. He emphasized that the most overlooked aspect of maximizing recycled metal appeared to be the development of new alloys tailored to meet composition and performance criteria when produced directly from recycled metal [14].

Scrap for the production of wrought alloys should be sorted with strict control of the concentration of alloying elements in order to achieve the prescribed compositional tolerances [10]. The efficiency of collection and sorting of aluminum scrap could be maximized by accurate life cycle information of the product. Jun et al. have provided system architecture and framework for closed-loop PLM. Closed-loop PLM allows all actors of the whole lifecycle to access, manage, and control product related information, especially, the information after a product delivery to the customer and up to its final destiny, without temporal and spatial constraints [15]. In the closed-loop PLM, it is possible to know the product location and usage history and to predict the degradation status and remaining lifetime of parts or components. Recyclers/reusers may be able to obtain accurate information about value materials arriving via EOL routes by closing the product life cycle information loop [4]. Material recycling can be significantly improved because recyclers and re-users can obtain accurate information about "value parts and materials" arriving via EOL routes: what materials they contain, who manufactured them, and other knowledge that facilitates material reuse [4].

Closed loop PLM allows to gather information but it is also necessary to evaluate economic and environmental performance of the products and processes. Life cycle analysis (LCA) is one such tool that can help companies to understand the environmental impacts associated with their products, processes, and activities [16]. Life cycle costing is a methodology directed at the evaluation of all the costs associated with an activity or a product over its entire life cycle, thus assuming the dual role of a Life Cycle Assessment in economic terms [17]. LCA and LCC help decision makers chose the most environmentally friendly or less costly alternative among alternatives.

3   Closed Loop PLM

Capability of tracking their products and components is an important issue for car manufacturers and their suppliers, OEMs. They need to have seamless information flow about the location, situation and working conditions of their products through in all phases of their life cycle because they are strategically important, valuable, dangerous etc. In general, the product lifecycle consists of three main phases: beginning of life (BOL), including design and production; middle of life (MOL), including logistics (distribution), use, service, and maintenance; and end of life (EOL), including reverse logistics (collecting), remanufacturing (disassembly, refurbishment, reassembly, etc.), reuse, recycle, and disposal [15]. Holistic lifecycle approach, depicted in Fig.1, takes into account material and data/information flows, and provides a broader perspective to all activities of the product or process through all phases of the lifecycle.

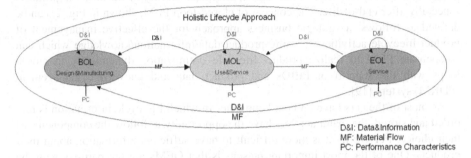

Fig. 1. Holistic life cycle approach

All of the car manufacturers and most of their suppliers use PLM systems to manage their business activities. Although the vision of the PLM is to gather information through the life cycle of the product and produce knowledge for all the actor of the life cycle, lack of efficient tools, in efficient use of existing tools makes it impossible to enable this. On the other hand, closed-loop PLM that is equipped with product identification and communication technologies may enable to meet the expectations from PLM. The closed-loop PLM system focuses on tracking and managing the information of the whole product lifecycle, with possible feedback of information to product lifecycle phases. It provides opportunities to reduce the inefficiency of lifecycle operations and gain competitiveness [18].

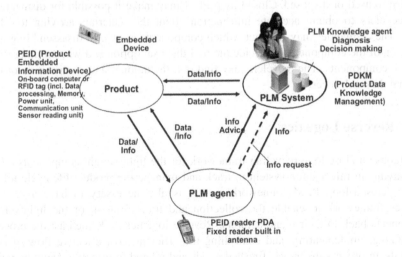

Fig. 2. Framework for closed-loop PLM

Closed-loop PLM may enable to establish a close loop recycling framework for lightweight components. The technology needed for close loop recycling of lightweight components is simpler, economical and more environmentally friendly than, recycling the high end components to cast aluminum and produce the components from virgin material. One of the most important limitations for close loop recycling is the lack of sufficient information, and impossibility of tracking the products especially after end-of-life. The concept of closed-loop PLM, shown in Fig. 2, can be defined as follows: a strategic business approach for the effective management of product lifecycle activities by using product data/information/knowledge which can compensate PLM to realize product lifecycle optimization dynamically in closed loops with the support of PEIDs and product data and knowledge management (PDKM) system [19].

As most of the cars have on board computer in which life cycle information is recorded and stored, the manufacturers have the opportunity to follow the components of their choice. For OEMs it is more difficult to have sufficient information about their products. One of the most important reasons is that OEMs are not partners with the car manufacturers but suppliers for them. The manufacturers do not have any responsibility, need or urge to share information about the components. OEMs are given dimensional and mechanical requirements that their part should provide but they do not get any feedback unless there is a problem about their products. With the current trends and legislations like, extended product responsibility and End-of-Life vehicles directive, car manufacturers have the responsibility to take care of their products after the end-of-life. They should also share the responsibility with their OEMs in order to do this properly and economically.

In closed-loop PLM, all life cycle actors should ensure secure and accurate flow of information related with the material flow. To establish a closed loop recycling framework, information flow through the EOL phase should be ensured. EOL is the phase where EOL products are collected, disassembled, refurbished, recycled, reassembled, reused or disposed. Closed-loop PLM may make it possible for dismantlers and recyclers to obtain accurate information about the materials arriving to EOL phase. The dismantler may find out, which components are worth disassembling, the condition of the components to decide the best disposal option and who are interested in these components. The recyclers may find out, the amount and composition of the material they will receive.

4   Reverse Logistics

To establish a close loop recycling framework for the light weight components other than having an information system to track and manage the product life cycle information (closed-loop PLM framework) and it is also necessary to have a reverse logistics framework to enable the collection and transportation of the lightweight components back to their manufacturers. Reverse logistics is defined as; the process of planning, implementing, and controlling the efficient, cost effective flow of raw materials, in-process inventory, finished goods and related information from the point of consumption to the point of origin for the purpose of recapturing value or proper disposal. More precisely, reverse logistics is the process of moving goods from their typical final destination for the purpose of capturing value, or proper disposal [20].

In the last decades, economic, legislative and social engaging incentives have driven industrial sectors and governments to become active in reverse logistics. The engagement of companies with society and environmental issues also can generate incentives to manage return flows in a supply chain. Moreover, marketing, competitiveness and strategic issues are other incentives for companies to become active in reverse logistics [21].

In case of lightweight components which are made of materials that are economically valuable and tailored to meet the requirements of the car manufacturers and assure their function, reverse logistics of the components. In practice, ~90%of an automobile is recycled; however precious lightweight components made of aluminum and magnesium need special afford to retrieve the effort spent for them. Otherwise high end automotive and aeronautic parts turn into door handles and coat hangers. With the help of closed-loop PLM, accurate information may be fed into reverse logistics framework and the EOL actors will be aware of the amount and the condition about the components. By the help of this information, the EOL actors may take action and arrange their business activities with their stakeholders.

5   LCA & LCC of Automotive Components

The footprint of a product is the environmental impacts caused directly and indirectly during the life cycle of a product from raw material acquisition through production use and disposal. LCA is an internationally recognized approach that evaluates the potential environmental and human health impact associated with products and services throughout their life cycle. Among other uses, LCA can identify opportunities to improve the environmental performance of products at various points in their life cycle, inform decision-making, and support marketing and communication efforts. The unique feature of LCA is the focus on products in a life-cycle perspective, which is useful in order to avoid problem shifting [22]. Automotive industry supports holistic life cycle approach and promotes using LCA to evaluate the life cycle environmental impacts of new designs and technologies and the effect of decisions made through the life cycle of their products.

Furthermore, it is also necessary to evaluate the economic performance of the components, which is more interesting for the manufacturers. Life cycle cost (LCC) analysis is a tool that produces important metrics for choosing the most cost-effective approach from a series of alternatives. LCC generally refers all the costs associated with a product throughout the product's life. [23] A major portion of the projected life-cycle cost (LCC) for a specific product, system, or structure is traceable to decisions made during conceptual and preliminary design. These decisions pertain to operational requirements, performance and effectiveness factors, the design configuration, production methods and quantity, utilization factors, logistic support, phase-out planning, and disposal [24].

6   Case Study: Front Lower Control Arm (FLCA)

The FLCA is one of the case studies of SuPLight project. FLCA is used to connect suspension members to the vehicle's chassis and to control both the lateral and longitudinal location of the wheel. Lightweighting the control arm improve the ride quality and handling, additional to fuel consumption and emissions reduction. The analysis showed that the hot spot in the life cycle of the FLCA is end-of-life processes. Material flows based on different production routes and different amount of recycled material in production have been defined. These models are further used in formation of LCA&LCC models. The proposed holistic life cycle approach might enable evaluation of not only the performance of the product and processes product producer, but also the performance of processes of other related life cycle actors. Closed loop PLM system is necessary to combine the life cycle actors and enable necessary information flow between life cycle actors. LCA&LCC are the decision support systems needed in the concept and closed loop PLM is capable of obtaining and processing the huge amount of data needed for LCA&LCC and distribute the performance characteristics to related parties for self-evaluation. Establishment of a reverse logistics framework is also necessary, and it should also be evaluated in economic and environmental senses.

7   Conclusion

Lightweighting is an important issue for automotive industry in order to reduce fuel consumption and emissions of vehicles. Wrought aluminum alloys have high potential in weight reduction of structural components. However, a close-loop recycling framework for these alloys is necessary to retrieve their full potential. Closed-loop PLM and reverse logistics framework are the two important elements of close loop recycling framework. Although, aluminum is thought to be environmentally friendly, it is necessary to evaluate the environmental performance of these components. LCA is such a tool that enables the estimation of the total environmental impacts resulting from all stages in the product life cycle. Other than environmental performance, economic performance of the lightweight components is important, that could be evaluated by LCC.

Acknowledgements. The authors would like to express our deep gratitude to all SuPLight partners and European Comission.

References

1. European Aluminum Association: Aluminum in Cars (2008)
2. International Aluminum Institute: Global Aluminium Recycling: A Cornerstone of Sustainable Development (2009)
3. Gesing, A.J., Wolanski, R.: Recycling Light Metals from End-of-Life Vehicles. Journal of Materials 53(11), 21–23 (2001)

4. Jun, H.B., Shin, J.H., Kiritsis, D., Xirouchakis, P.: System Architecture for Closed-loop PLM. International Journal of Computer Integrated Manufacturing 20(7), 684–698 (2009)
5. Ungureanu, C.A., Das, S.K., Jawahir, I.S.: Life-cycle Cost Analysis: Aluminum versus Steel in Passenger Cars. Aluminum Alloys for transportation, packaging, aerospace and other Applications, TMS, pp. 11–27 (2007)
6. International Aluminum Institute: Improving Sustainability in the Transport Sector through Weight Reduction and the Application of Aluminum (2008)
7. Green, J., Skillingberg, M.: Recyclable Aluminum Rolled Products. Light Metal Age (2006)
8. Boin, U.M.J., Bertram, M.: Melting Standardizing Aluminum Scrap: A Mass Balance Model for Europe. JOM 57(8), 26–33 (2005)
9. European Aluminum Association (EAA), http://www.alueurope.eu
10. Kevorkijan, V.: Advances In Recycling Of Wrought Aluminum Alloys For Added Value Maximization. MJoM 16(2), 103–114 (2010)
11. Kevorkijan, V.: The Recycle of Wrought Aluminum Alloys in Europe. JOM 54(2), 38–41 (2007)
12. Das, S.K., Kaufman, J.G.: Recycling Aluminum Aerospace Alloys. Light Metals 1161-1165 (2007)
13. Das, S.K.: Recycling Aluminum Aerospace Alloys. Advanced Materials & Processes 166(3), 34 (2008)
14. Das, S.K.: Emerging Trends in Aluminum Recycling: Reasons and Responses. Light Metals (2006)
15. Jun, H.B., Kiritsis, D., Xirouchakis, P.: Research issues on closed –loop PLM. Computers in Industry 58(8-9), 855–868 (2007)
16. Note on Life Cycle Analysis, National Pollution Prevention Center For Higher Education (1995), http://www.umich.edu/~nppcpub
17. Giudice, F., La Rosa, G., Risitano, A.: Life Cycle Cost Analysis. In: Product Design for the Environment: A Life Cycle Approach, pp. 111–134. CRC Press (2006)
18. Kiritsis, D.: Product lifecycle Management and Embedded Information Devices. In: Springer Handbook of Automation, pp. 749–765. Springer (2009)
19. Jun, H.B., Kiritsis, D., Xirouchakis, P.: Closed-loop PLM. Advanced Manufacturing: An ICT and Systems Perspective, pp. 90–101. Taylor & Francis, UK (2007)
20. Rogers, D.S., Tibben-Lembke, R.S.: Going Backwards: Reverse Logistics Trends and Practices. Reverse Logistics Executive Council (1998)
21. Cruz-Rivera, R., Ertel, J.: Reverse logistics network design for the collection of End-of-Life Vehicles in Mexico. European Journal of Operational Research 196(3), 930–939 (2009)
22. Finnveden, G., Hauschild, M.Z., Ekvall, T., Guinée, J., Heijungs, R., Hellweg, S., Koehler, A., Pennington, D., Suh, S.: Recent developments in Life Cycle Assessment. Journal of Environmental Management 91(1), 1–21 (2009)
23. Kleyner, A., Sandborn, P.: Minimizing life cycle cost by managing product reliability via validation plan and warranty return cost. International Journal of Production Economics 112(2), 796–807 (2008)
24. Fabrycky, W.J., Blanchard, B.S.: Life-Cycle Cost and Economic Analysis. Prentice Hall (1991)

Design Support Based onto Knowledge to Increase Product Reliability and Allow Optimized Abacus Development

Jérémy Boxberger[1,2], Daniel Schlegel[2], Nahdir Lebaal[2], and Samuel Gomes[2]

[1] Zurfluh-Feller, 45 Grande Rue, 25150 Autechaux-Roide
[2] Laboratoire M3M, UTBM, 90010 Belfort Cedex

Abstract. High competition and low manufacturing costs in emerging countries, force European firms to improve quality, cost and delivery. Research and development departments have to look towards high production design methods and tools in order to stay competitive. Our research allow to reduce routine design process and thereby increase time for added value design tasks, particularly innovative design activities. We have applied our methodology onto a roller shutter tube. Existing abacuses are used to define tube deformation, but these abacuses are too restrictive. Our case determine the input information and create a model using our method to create new abacuses more relevant. Our contribution uses the explicit knowledge embedded in a KBE application to co-create or update parametric 3D models with its assembly environment. By implementing this method in an industrial company, we have reduced routine design tasks and improved the robustness of the product design and the product assembly.

Keywords: Abacus, Robust design, Design for X, Knowledge Based Engineering, Product lifecycle management, Product data management, Optimization.

1 Introduction

The current industrial context forces companies to develop new concepts at ever increasing speed. Quality, cost and lead time are the relevant performance indicators for firms [1][2]. However, after having shifted manufacturing to low cost countries, to prevent the relocation of work dedicated to routine design, we must reduce the length of the non value-added tasks to free up time for innovative projects. Engineering design is a source of competitive advantage for manufacturing companies. Reducing the development time is a key factor in the successful completion of the product development process. During the last decades, the design process is subject to new methodologies and tools to make it more and more efficient. Like what was done in manufacturing, lean engineering techniques were introduced into the design process. The objective is to reduce the non-added value tasks of the design process. Design is an information intensive activity. Because of the complex information dependencies that exist between design tasks, we cannot perform the design process as a once-through procedure. Therefore, iterations are necessary to resolve design

C. Emmanouilidis, M. Taisch, D. Kiritsis (Eds.): APMS 2012, Part II, IFIP AICT 398, pp. 200–207, 2013.
© IFIP International Federation for Information Processing 2013

problems. These iterations are often seen as non-added value tasks. Understanding and controlling iterations can improve the design process, and reducing them would have positive effects for the product development cycle time [3]. The purpose of lean engineering is to introduce new methodologies helping the designer approach the ideal design solution as rapidly as possible. This paper is organized as follows: first, we relate our current research on reducing routine design time, especially Design for X, knowledge capitalization, top down design and optimization. The second section deals with our methodology, including the parametric model, finite element and optimization loops. The main goals of our contribution will be explained in this part. The next section presents an industrial applied case, where we have applied our methodology to a shutter assembly. Today, in order to minimise loss of information, different departments in a firm work together around the product lifecycle (product lifecycle management: PLM) from the customer's needs, to the end of life [4][5] Thus, different approaches, called integrated design, parallel design or collaborative design have already been developed [6]. These methods have allowed us to deal with the knowledge domain earlier in the design process. In this context, the Design for X approach [7] (design for manufacture, design for assembly, design for quality, design for recycling etc...) has been introduced in order to reduce product lifecycle and also increase engineering productivity by reducing non value-added tasks. A large number of papers have been delivered over the last forty years about product design [8], with the resounding view that routine design occupies a large place in firms. Innovative design could be increased by reducing routine design and this could also release time for other tasks. Within Design for X, design for manufacturing and design for assembly have been the most discussed topics in the last thirty years. The knowledge available in the manufacturing process has to be known by the designers in order to speed up product design and find the best quality product faster. Swift describes some standard rules about DFM [9]. Using these rules as a base for KBE application, parametric models can be created and coupled with an optimization algorithm for problem resolution [10]. In addition to this, thanks to the development of CAD tools, different types of product design approach have appeared. The most used, called 'bottom-up design', consists in parts creation before assembly. At the opposite end, 'top down design' is a methodology that starts at the highest level of a design concept and proceeds towards the lowest level, starting with the broad project specification in mind and putting that information in a centralized location. The design progresses from this information to the individual parts. This makes it easy to design and manage large product assemblies. Changes made in a central location will propagate to all levels of the design. As a result, multiple designers can work on a project in parallel and communicate design data easily and quickly, with full confidence that all components will fit seamlessly into the final product. The same idea was applied with the integration of knowledge. On one hand, some studies have been done with bottom-up knowledge extraction [11][12] whilst others have focused on top-down knowledge extraction or knowledge lead by models. Some works show this kind of methodology, such as MKSM (Methodology for Knowledge System Management)[13], MASK (Méthode d'Acquisition et de Structuration des Connaissances) [14], CYGMA (CYcle de vie et Gestion des Métiers et Applications) [15], etc. Our objective is articulated around decision support and assembly configuration validation. A non-experienced user can lose time selecting the correct reference among a large number of references for the first time. In addition, he may choose the wrong reference or not the best one. Obtaining the optimum settings is often the result of tiresome trial and error corrections, during which time the various solutions are tested and modified. As a result, the settings are often non optimal and are just acceptable. Achieving the optimal design is time consuming and one of the highest material and manpower costs. However, in many processes and structural designs, in order to improve quality and reduce time, the combination of numerical simulation using the finite element method with numerical optimisation techniques cannot be avoided [16][17]. Our contribution will deal on a multi-objective optimization procedure, used to improve performance of an assembly design based on expert knowledge, simulation and optimized abacuses. Reducing non value-added tasks in this project domain improves productivity and quality of the product and the design process activities. The first issue is to keep the information usable for all users, and not only for experts. Another issue consists in defining how to preserve various knowledge typologies embedded in Project, Product and Process data and information management systems (PDM, PLM, MPM, etc.). The other relevant issue is to validate a new geometry definition for the product or a new combination of components. We have applied our methodology onto a roller shutter tube assembly in order to define a less restrictive abacus for the customer. Existing abacuses are used to define tube deformation according to the weight and the length, but these abacuses are too restrictive. Tests reveal, in some cases, that the abacus security level has a coefficient of 10. The objective of our case was to determine the input information and create a model using our methodology in order to create new abacuses more representative of the reality. Our contribution uses the explicit knowledge embedded in a KBE application in order to co-create (or update) a parametric 3D model with its assembly environment. Then the application allows a new combination to be validated by the use of optimisation loops with a finite element tool. Decision support applications lead by knowledge will reduce routine design and will help a customer to check his system reliably using a parametric abacus. These parametric abacuses are created using optimization loops. They will replace existing standard abacuses which are too restrictive and in some cases obsolete. A last loop explained in our use case allows the parametric abacuses to be tested on extreme and worth value cases in real.

2   Methodology

The purpose of the following methodology is to facilitate routine design reduction. Routine design is present in all domains: from the project domain, to the product domain; our contribution will also deal with the process domain. Obviously, all are linked together. The first project domain is relative to the whole methodology used in the firm: from the customer needs to the final product and marketing. A standard methodology has been built taking into account the firm's history and modus operandi. [18] This methodology contains two different types of standard methods. According to the length and the complexity of the project, a short or long project-types is chosen by the direction. However, this method contains a large number of tasks, some are more relevant than others and some contain non-value added actions. We can also perform a microscopic analysis in a task to reveal routine subtasks which can be considered as value added. Many parts are often available in a large range of sizes within a family of parts. If a new assembly is modified, e.g. new geometry or new size of one or several features, the user has to select a new component, compatible with the new assembly, from within the same family. This method is based on the Design for manufacturing method and on knowledge-based engineering models that contain help for decision making while choosing the correct reference. Besides, the tool features automatic 3D model generation, including the part and the manufacturing tool together. The goal of the whole methodology is to allow extraction and knowledge re-use from the new models created. At the beginning, the experts input the rules related to their particular domain (equations, interactions, manufacturing tool settings, etc...) into a PLM tool. This information collection leads to the creation of the KBE application. The creation process of the KBE application depends on the particular case and on the manufacturing.

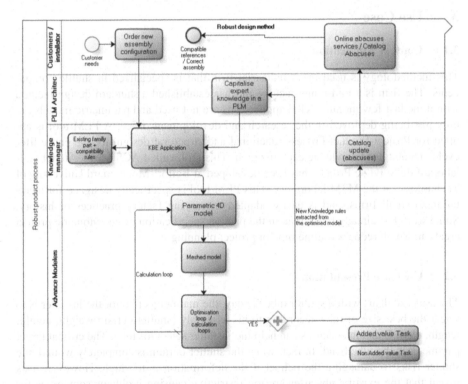

Fig. 1. Methodology represent by a BPMN Diagram

Our methodology is represented Fig.1 by a BPMN graph. It shows the methodology used and also the works currently tested and the results that we are expecting. The green tasks are added value tasks. There is added value when the actions performed can be used by the customers, for example, the CAD model can be used by the customer to visualise his assembly. On the other hand, the KBE model is only usable by the designer - it only allows time reduction for the designer. That's why the non value-added tasks must be performed in the minimum of time in order to meet the needs of customers faster. Then, by the connections established between the parametric model, the meshing tool and the optimization tool, loops can be performed in order to generate a large number of simulations to build precise curves. A last loop is performed between the optimized model and the PLM tool. This last loop contains information and knowledge according to the value stream defined and optimized in the first loops. This methodology allows a knowledge loop between the model, the PLM tool, the expert and the customer / installer to be created. This will lead to an increase of productivity and a knowledge record without any loss of information. The experts must validate the new knowledge implemented in the PLM knowledge base, but we can envisage experts not having to include this in the loop when the models are stabilized and reliable. In the next section, we will see that an additional real-time test was performed to check the reliability of the simulation model and the real model.

3   Use Case

3.1   Context Application

This methodology is used in an industrial firm that is specialized in shuttle components. The firm is a mid-range factory and has established a standard design method within the last few months. KBE applications are not used and parametric models are only just being deployed in the research and development office. A PLM tool is applied for Project-Product-Process functional and structural design, for the entire lifecycle and also for knowledge capitalization. This tool, called ACSP for « Atelier Collaboratif de Suivi de Projet » has been developed at Belfort-Montbéliard University of Technology, at the M3M laboratory. This PLM tool is specifically designed for adaptation to small firms, and is easily adapted to varying factory practices or history. Some work has already been done in the past on specification or on automatic project creation, which reduces routine time of project planning.

3.2   Use Case Presentation

The use case deals with a shutter tube. Today, the main objective for the installer is to select the best size of tube according to his assembly (shutter curtain weight, height, length, etc.). Existing abacuses can help the installer select his tube. The critical target parameter is the tube bend. In fact, when the shutter curtain is completely wound, the shutter risks to damaging the pelmet if the deformation is too high. However, tests reveal that the existing abacuses are too restrictive causing problems sometimes for the installer. These existing abacuses do not take account of the slat rigidity when the shutter is wound. However, the finite element calculations for the whole assembly (Fig. 2) take more than 10 hours. To address this, a simplified model was built with slats represented by squares which replicate the same quadratic movement as the slats. Using this geometry, the calculation was reduced to 10 minutes for 1 loop.

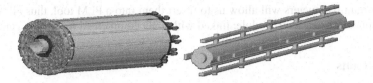

Fig. 2. Full assembly compared to simplified assembly

Our model uses as parameters, the length, the weight and the height of the shutter, the quadratic moment of the slat, the plug end length and the tube's dimension. The first parameter is the type of tube and its length. The type of fixation is selected according to the tube - only the size and the type can be changed. In addition the slat shape will modify the quadratic modulus, so this parameter is also needed. For the abacus the standard shape was used which represents 80 % of the market. However, the KBE application allows this modulus to be changed.

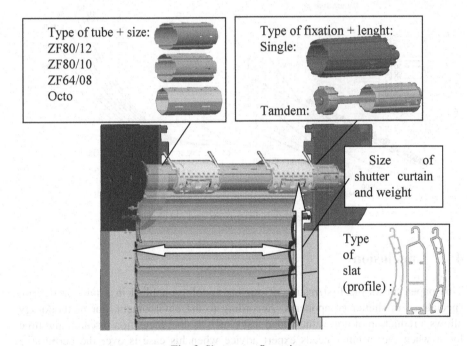

Fig. 3. Shutter configuration

The target is the deformation. The model is linked with a finite element tool and an optimisation tool which allows us to make loops between both modules.

3.3 A KBE Modelling Method for Shutter Tube Components

In order to create a KBE application we have to consider all of the parameters involved in the process and also all the knowledge embedded in the product. Knowing the important parameters will allow us to insert them into a PLM tool, thus allowing a KBE application extractor module, linked with a 3D commercial tool, to be generated.

3.4   Results

Six new abacuses were built, and validated with real testing on ten different sizes: 3 sizes for the 80/10 and the 64/08 and 4 for the 80/12 with different weights and tube lengths. In each case the difference in results between real and computer simulated has been a maximum of 1 mm. Figure 4 compares the new abacuses with the shutter fully rolled and the old Abacuses. As these values were tested in real and validated by the expert, the new abacuses will be implemented in the next catalogue.

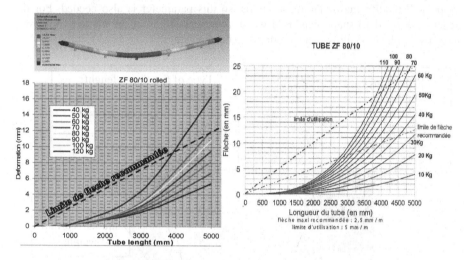

Fig. 4. Difference between new and old abacuses

4   Conclusion

This paper shows the first results of our methodology applied in a mid-sized firm, specialized in shutter components. According to the environment, our methodology allows a reduction of non value-added tasks such as documentation research and time loose when the installer needs expert advice when his case is over the permissive curves of the abacuses. This time saving allows the user and experts to devote more time to innovative design and saves time for the installer. In the short term perspective, the new abacuses will be implemented in the firm's standard catalogue for all installers. Additionally, an on line decision support system will be integrated on ZURFLUH-FELLER website, available to every installer along with the abacuses. As mid-term perspectives, other applications using the same method will be built in order to check their reliability and reassure the installer in his choice of component for his shutter assembly.

References

1. Miles, B.L., Swift, K.G.: Working together. Manufacturing Breakthrough 4, 69–73 (1992)
2. Yeh, R.T.: Notes on concurrent engineering. IEEE Transation on Knowledge Data Engineering 4(5), 407–414 (1992)
3. Boudouh, T., Anghel, D.C., Garro, O.: Design iterations in a geographically distributed design process. In: ElMaraghy, H., ElMaraghy, W. (eds.) Advances in Design, vol. 4, pp. 377–386. Springer (January 2006) ISBN: 1-84628-004-4
4. Stark, J.: Product Lifecycle Management: 21st Century Paradigm for Product Realisation. Springer London Ltd., London (2004) ISBN: 978-1852338107
5. CIMdata Incorporated. PLM Market Growth in 2008 A Mid-Year Look in 2009-Weathering the Storm'. White Paper (August 2009)
6. Lu, S.C.Y., Elmaraghy, W., Schuh, G., Wilhelm, R.: A scientific foundation of collaborative engineering. CIRP Annals - Manufacturing Technology 56(2), 605–634 (2007)
7. Baxter, D., Gao, J., Case, K., Harding, J., Young, B., Cochrane, S., Dani, S.: A framework to integrate design knowledge reuse and requirements management in engineering design. Robotics and Computer-Integrated Manufacturing 24(4), 585–593 (2008)
8. Hauschild, M., Jeswiet, J., Alting, L.: From LifeCycle Assessment to Sustainable Production: Status and Perspectives. CIRP Annals - Manufacturing Technology 54(2), 1–21 (2005)
9. Swift, K.G.: Process Selection: From Design to Manufacture, Butterworth Heinemann (2003)
10. Toussaint, L., Lebaal, N., Schlegel, D., Gomes, S.: Automatic Optimization of Air Conduct Design Using Experimental Data and Numerical Results. Int. J. Simul. Multidisci. Des. Optim. 4, 77–83 (2011)
11. Djiaz, C., Monticolo, D., Matta, N.: Capitalization of Knowledge from Projects. In: International Conference of Concurrent Engineering (CE), Antibes, France (2006)
12. Matta, N., Ribiere, M., Corby, O., Lewkowicz, M., Zaclad, M.: Project Memory in Design. In: Rajkumar, R. (ed.) Industrial Knowledge Management - A Micro Level Approach. Springer (2000)
13. Ermine, J.-L.: La Gestion des Connaissances, un levier stratégique pour les entreprises. IC'2000 Ingénierie des connaissances, Toulouse (2000)
14. Ermine, J.: La gestion de connaissances. Hermès Sciences publications (2002)
15. Serrafero, P.: Vers la mesure de la quantité de connaissance et de compétence industrielle: le modèle KnoVA. 1er colloque du Groupe de Gestion des Compétences et des Connaissances en Génie Industriel. Nantes, France (2002)
16. Ou, H., Wang, P., Lu, B., Long, H.: Finite element modelling and optimisation of net-shape metal forming processes with uncertainties. Computers and Structures, 90–91, 13–27 (2012)
17. Grundstein, M.: gameth®: un cadre directeur pour repérer les connaissances cruciales pour l'entreprise. Nogent-sur-Marne, MG Conseil: 29 (2007)
18. Boxberger, J., Lebouteiller, M., Schlegel, D., Lebaal, N., Gomes, S.: Vers une démarche d'ingénierie "hautement productive" des domaines projet-produit-process en contexte PME-PMI. 20ème Congrès Français de Mécanique, Besançon (2011)

Towards an Harmonious and Integrated Management Approach for Lifecycle Planning

Frédéric Demoly*, Samuel Deniaud, and Samuel Gomes

IRTES-M3M,
Université de Technologie de Belfort-Montbéliard (UTBM),
90010 Belfort Cedex, France
{frederic.demoly,samuel.deniaud,samuel.gomes}@utbm.fr

Abstract. The paper presents an initiative towards the harmonious and integrated management of lifecycle planning, such as assembly planning, disassembly planning, maintenance planning and so on. This stake currently meets industrial requirements and research issues, mainly in product lifecycle management, integrated design, and lifecycle engineering fields. The fact of managing X planning during product design requires therefore a complete understanding of the product lifecycle processes and various abstraction layers of data-information-knowledge. In such a way, the critical outcome is to ensure the development of well-balanced product by considering the rationale of lifecycle planning and managing its related data, information and knowledge.

Keywords: Product Lifecycle Management, Integrated Design, Lifecycle Planning, Closed-Loop PLM, Concurrent Engineering.

1   Introduction: Current Stakes

The current ultra-competitive context, in the manufacturing and energy industries, has raised challenging issues for improving the elicitation and use of intellectual heritage (i.e. knowledge, know-how, intents, competencies ...) and business actors involved in the company. Here several phases of the product lifecycle need to be identified as strategic and critical to ensure the development and the delivery of well-balanced products. In other words, a well-balanced product can be considered as a product taking into account, consistently, all the constraints of its life cycle with an optimum cost (i.e. assembly-friendly products, green products, service-oriented products ...). At this stage, the proposed research project focuses on the following product lifecycle processes: product design and X planning definition where X stands for manufacturing, assembly, disassembly, maintenance, transport ...

At a critical place, the design phase requires the consideration and integration of all constraints and knowledge (business processes, business terms, expert rules, job experience ...) of product lifecycle phases. However, the consideration of a large amount of rules increases the work complexity of product architects and designers. An emerging way allows to overcome this issue differently: over the

---

* Corresponding author.

C. Emmanouilidis, M. Taisch, D. Kiritsis (Eds.): APMS 2012, Part II, IFIP AICT 398, pp. 208–215, 2013.
© IFIP International Federation for Information Processing 2013

past two decades, engineering paradigm has shift from sequential engineering to concurrent engineering, therefore facilitating the integration of specific concerns into product design stages [1]. It seems that this shift has generated potential gains by using heuristics rules in addition to qualitative information (such as described in Fig. 1) [2]. Today, the concurrent engineering philosophy has reached its limit. Indeed, current approaches, in the field of concurrent engineering, do not provide enough information layer for a full understanding of product architects and designers. In such a way, it is important to address a proactive vision of the product development by considering downstream processes as early as possible in product design (Fig. 1) [3]. Thus awareness and understanding will be promoted to product/process architects and designers. This can be done with relevant data input and some specific layers which may introduce qualitative context based on formal description (Fig. 1). Here qualitative context may include formal description of engineering intents and knowledge such as explained in [2].

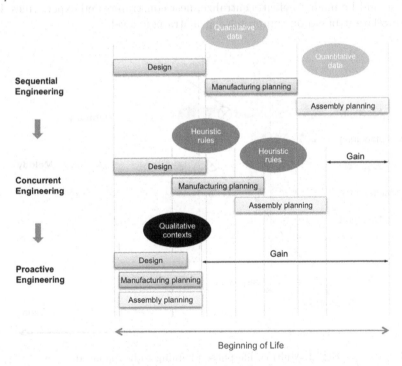

Fig. 1. Current stakes: From sequential to proactive engineering

2   Description of the Research Project

2.1   Computational Intelligence

The definition of lifecycle planning (i.e. manufacturing planning, assembly planning, maintenance planning, disassembly planning ...) by taking into account the appropriate knowledge, at the earlier stage of product design, enables the introduction of a context layer for architects and designers, as described with "The design context knowledge can be defined as the related surrounding knowledge of a design problem at a moment in time for given consideration" [6]. Recent research results have shown that it is possible to generate and define an assembly sequence before defining any product geometry of mechanical products, such as in the domains of automotive and aerospace industries [3,4]. This early-defined assembly sequence has influenced the product design by structuring the product with various assembly levels and introducing skeleton entities related to product relationships [5].

The today's challenge of R&D focuses not only on the definition of a single assembly plan but also requires now the incorporation of a wider range of lifecycle phases such as manufacturing planning, maintenance planning, transport planning, selective disassembly planning to name a few, and this needs to be considered in a harmonious and coherent manner (Fig. 2). To do this, a major effort should be made to elicit, centralize, nest constraints and expert rules, but also to relate it based on compromise at a strategic level.

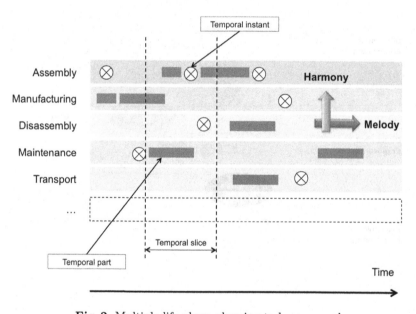

Fig. 2. Multiple life phase planning to be managed

On a more technical level, and regarding the data model, the research project will highlight a product-process ontology, in order to connect formally and semantically objects in space (parts, sub-assemblies, resources ...) and objects time (assembly, maintenance, disassembly and transport operations ...). Based on this formal ontology, different approaches may be proposed.

The first effort consists in generating all the admissible lifecycle plans from a minimal product model, the product-process ontology, expert rules and strategic constraints as quick as possible. This will require the development of mathematical algorithms based on patterns recognition matrix previously developed in collaboration with automotive industry [3]. The generation of feasible solutions can be achieved automatically or semi-automatically, so that lifecycle planners will be able to control the definition of their sequences.

In order to control the combinational complexity, due to the number of operations generated in all lifecycle plans, a multi-level approach will be implemented to generate and break down these plans. Therefore the aim is to get high levels plans or sequences, also called – macro plans/sequences – almost invariant thus facilitating reuse and low levels plans/sequences, called – micro plans/sequences. Once all admissible plans have been generated, it will be necessary to identify the plans which meet the best engineering compromise. An additional effort will be added to allow the reconfiguration of lifecycle plans if an unpredictable event that may occurs to different phases of the life cycle (e.g. the reconfiguration of a selective disassembly sequence for maintenance in use). Consequently, the selection of the sequence/plan during product design and definition will have to take into account specific criteria aiming at selecting a sequence/plan while minimizing, on one hand the reconfiguration cases, and on the other hand giving multiple reconfigurations solutions if appropriate. The search of reconfigurations cases will be applied in a special way at micro sequences/plans level.

2.2   Systems Engineering Applied to Multiple Sequence Planning

In parallel to the generation of these lifecycle plans, a specific allocation of customer and lifecycle-oriented technical requirements will be addressed at various abstraction levels of the life phase plan. In order to address this requirement allocation activity, a framework is proposed as illustrated in Fig. 3. First an ontological level is done in order to define the different concepts and their relations. Second, these concepts and relations are expressed into specific diagrams that give different viewpoints about the lifecycle plans to the planners. Third, specific diagrams are built following a specific process to formalize the lifecycle plans of the system-of-interest. This process needs to investigate the necessary objects to realize the solution. They are characterized by various attributes captured at the data level. Language such System Modeling Language (SysML) [7] is a good candidate to express the needed concepts and relations in specific diagrams. It provides profile mechanism in order to specialize and extend the elements of the language.

A specific allocation of customer and lifecycle-oriented technical requirements will be addressed at various abstraction levels of the life phase plan (Fig. 4). At each decomposition level, activity diagram (act), internal bloc diagram (ibd) and requirement diagram (req) are modeled based on each operation and its attached requirements. The first one expresses the behaviour of the operation

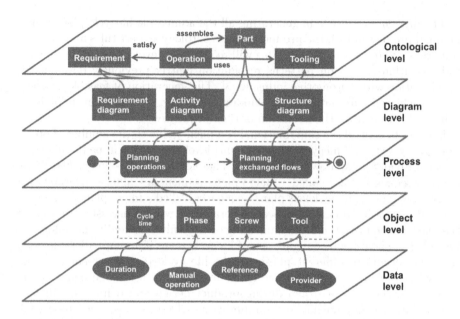

Fig. 3. Proposed framework

i_{n+1} by decomposing it into several operations. The second one depicts the various flows of matters, energy and information exchanged by the operations and the environment of the operation i_{n+1}. Finally, the third one explains the decomposition of the requirements of the operation i_{n+1} and their allocation links. Recursively, these three diagrams are modeled at the level i_{n-1} respectively for the operations $1n$, $2n$ and $3n$.

In such a way the system engineering principles can be applied the generation of the lifecycle plans in order to master the complexity of such sequence planning. For instance, these allocation links will allow to perform impact analysis when requirements change. Needless to say, these links will also ensure traceability of decisions.

2.3   Systems/Tools Implementation

The set of all lifecycle sequences/plans (including operations) will highlight the need to be managed by data management system. This novel system will enable the access to all lifecycle planners in order to define constraints, operations, temporal logic ... A solution consists in proposing an approach for managing compromises between lifecycle plans and decisions made during the definition lifecycle plans. In addition and in order to ensure the digital chain covering the product lifecycle, the proposed platform will have to be integrated and connected to existing systems and tools of the company, such as PDM (Product Data Management), ERP (Enterprise Resource Planning), and CAD tools (Computer Aided Design).

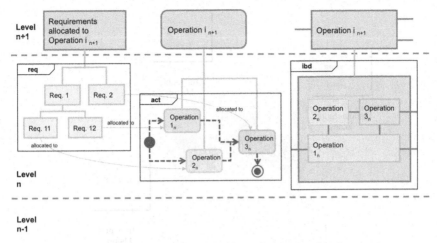

Fig. 4. Diagrams defined at abstraction level

Currently, some commercial tools and systems close to the envisioned platform have been identified of which MPM (Manufacturing Process Management), but are only limited to the definition of manufacturing and assembly planning (welding, final assembly ...) for the manufacturing phase of the product. It therefore becomes critical to expand the capability of these systems to the definition of all lifecycle planning such as required all along the product lifecycle, and the integration of expert knowledge and logical reasoning.

2.4   Project Objectives

As a consequence, the proposed research project mainly aims at:

- Developing a knowledge model called ontology, integrating formal descriptions of the product-process, applied to the domains of automotive and energy industries;
- Developing methods to define lifecycle plans (manufacturing, assembly, maintenance, disassembly, transportation ...);
- Proposing methods for managing lifecycle plans in a real-time manner by integrating the management of consents and compromises, in order to promote a smart, harmonious, dynamic and symphonic orchestration;
- Representing the lifecycle plans in the form of causal knowledge in order to create decision making supports for the design and geometric modeling phases;
- Specifying and developing a Web-based platform by considering initial efforts towards the development of PEGASUS tool which works at the interface of PDM, MPM and CAD systems [4].

Fig. 5. Harmonious management of lifecycle process planning

3   Synthesis

This research initiative has been proposed by following an original analogy: the harmonious and integrated management of lifecycle plans can be considered as the management of symphonic orchestra. A symphony is an intelligent instrumental composition, with generally large proportions, and including several joints or disjointed movements, and using the resources of the symphony orchestra. Indeed, it is easy to compare between a sequence/plan and a musical partition. The originality here is to manage the sequence/plan of the melody (which means operations concatenation by respecting time as shown in Fig. 2) as well as harmony between the sequences/plans (which means operations superposition during a period of time as shown in Fig. 2) to ensure the symphony engineering (Fig. 5).

References

1. Huang, G.Q., Lee, S.W., Mak, K.L.: Web-based product and process data modeling in concurrent design for X. Robotics and Computer-Integrated Manufacturing 15, 53–63 (1999)
2. Demoly, F., Matsokis, A., Kiritsis, D.: A mereotopological product relationship description approach for assembly oriented design. Robotics and Computer-Integrated Manufacturing 28(1), 681–693 (2012)

3. Demoly, F., Yan, X.-T., Eynard, B., Rivest, L., Gomes, S.: An Assembly oriented design framework for product structure engineering and assembly sequence planning. Robotics and Computer-Integrated Manufacturing 27(1), 33–46 (2011)
4. Demoly, F., Yan, X.-T., Eynard, B., Kiritsis, D., Gomes, S.: Integrated product relationships management: a model to enable concurrent product design and assembly sequence planning. Journal of Engineering Design 23(7), 544–561 (2012)
5. Demoly, F., Toussaint, L., Eynard, B., Kiritsis, D., Gomes, S.: Geometric skeleton computation enabling concurrent product engineering and assembly sequence planning. Computer-Aided Design 43(12), 1654–1673 (2011)
6. Rehman, F.U., Yan, X.T.: Supporting early design decision making using design context knowledge. Journal of Design Research 6(1-2), 169–189 (2007)
7. Object Management Group: OMG Systems Modeling Language (OMG SysML) specification, version 1.3 (2012), http://www.omg.org/spec/SysML/1.3/PDF

An MDA Approach for PLM System Design

Onur Yildiz[1,2], Lilia Gzara[2], Philippe Pernelle[3], and Michel Tollenaere[2]

[1] Audros Technology
F-69003 Lyon, France, 41 rue de la cité
oyildiz@audros.fr
[2] INP Grenoble, Laboratory G-SCOP
F-38000 Grenoble, France
lilia.gzara@grenoble-inp.fr,
Michel.Tollenaere@inpg.fr
[3] University of Lyon 1, Laboratory DISP
F-69621 Villeurbanne Cedex, France
philippe.pernelle@univ-lyon1.fr

Abstract. Design and reconfiguration of industrial information systems is an important issue for SME/SMI. In this context, these small enterprises need tools and methods that allow them to adapt their system to their business while ensuring its consistency. The aim of this paper is to provide an approach for both the design method and the control method. This approach for PLM (Product lifecycle management) system is based on MDE (Model Driving Engineering). First, we will present a metamodel for PLM and the model transformation concepts. Then, we will present an application with the Audros PLM system.

Keywords: PLM system, MDE, MDA, metamodel.

1 Introduction

In recent years, many SME/SMI have structured their information system on PLM systems. Their initial goal was to optimize the development process. Thanks to customization capabilities of PLM systems, these SME/SMI have configured their own product models based on their business activity. In addition to these changes, they have mostly added automation tasks, in order to optimize their business processes. All these configurations should not be an obstacle to the flexibility which is nevertheless one of their major assets.

In this context the main problem for its businesses, is to have a simple means to manage adaptations. In this way, the necessary system reconfiguration is constrained by a double consistency. The first is structural consistency. This is to keep consistency between the rules for structuring models (Product and Organization). For example, the business views trades use attributes of the data model, users rights depend on the attributes of the classess trades. This structural correlation implies dependence in case of modification of the company's customer model. Thus, the suppression of a class object's attribute should generate its own suppression in all the business views.

C. Emmanouilidis, M. Taisch, D. Kiritsis (Eds.): APMS 2012, Part II, IFIP AICT 398, pp. 216–223, 2013.

The second relates to the process consistency. To this end, it is necessary to verify impacts of process changes on structural models (and vice versa). In some cases, the management of trades processes is distributed between the Audros PLM and other tools. In other cases, a process managed in the PLM can call upon points in external processes managed in tools. For example, business management in the PLM may require a call to points in external processes managed in some other tools like ERP (Enterprise Resource Planning), to start the order process of some components identified during the study of the business or to start the invoicing process of the business. These interactions imply the transmission between the PLM and ERP of certain data (business data, components data, customers data).

In this paper, we present a design or reconfiguration approach of PLM systems around MDE (Model Driving Engineering). Indeed, the main advantage of PLM systems is to adjust to business needs. These needs (data customization) exist in all cases and whatever the company size, but it increases the implementation time. In fact, many objects are handled from the same concepts. This has motivated our approach. In section 2, we reiterate the fundamental principles of the MDE approach (more particularly MDA) by proposing a metamodel. Then in the next section we illustrate model design from metamodel and instantiated in the PLM system Audros

2 Design His PLM by MDE/MDA Approch

2.1 Model Driving Engineering

Model Driving Engineering (MDE) [1] was at the origin of improvements in complex system development. It consists in a form of generative engineering or all of a part of an application is generated starting from models. There are two key stages in the engineering directed by models: the definition of the DSM (Domain Specific Modelling) and the transformation of these models. Contrary to the object approach, which is based on instantiation and inheritance relations, engineering directed by models uses different relations concept : "RepresentedBy" and "ConformAt".

The second key phase of the IDM is the transformation of model. It allows to make models operational, to transform a source model into another target model of the same system but on a different level [2]. We can identify two types of transformations:

- Endogenous transformation from the same meta-model, the source model and the target are in conformity with the same meta-model
- Exogenic transformation starting from different meta-models, the source model and the target are not in conformity with the same meta-model.

It is on these general principles that the OMG (The Object Management Group) is based to define its standards. With OMG's vision, the abstraction level to a meta level is limited. OMG set up a language of definition of meta-models which has the form of a model, the MOF (Meta-Object-Facility) [3]. So to avoid a too great number of abstraction levels, the MOF has the capacity to describe itself. The MOF is at the top of architecture on four abstraction levels for modeling systems presented in the following diagram :

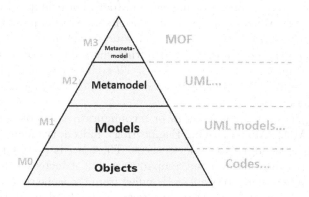

Fig. 1. modeling pyramid by OMG

MDA (Model Driven Architecture) [4] [5] is an approach to system development provided by the OMG and using models, metamodels, and meta-metamodels. MDA proposes three perspectives (CIM : Computation Independent Model, PIM : Platform-independent Models, PSM : Platform-Specific Models) to design models.

The CIM is independent of any information system. It allows the system vision and helps to represent what the system will do exactly. It is useful to understand a problem as a source of vocabulary shared with other models. The technical independence of this model allows it to keep all its interest over time and is changed only if the knowledge or business model needs change.

The PIM is independent of any technical platform (EJB,. NET ...) and does not contain information on technologies that will be used to deploy the application. This is a model that represents a partial view of an CIM. It shows the operation of entities and services. It describes the system, but does not show the details of its use on the platform.

The PSM is dependent of the platform used. It is used for code generation. The PSM describes how the system will use these platforms. There are several levels of PSM. The first, derived from the transformation of a PIM. The others are obtained by successive transformations. They allow to obtain the code in a specific language. In our context, the PSM level stops at an execution level within a PLM system.

The idea is to be able to manage heterogeneous models independently from any platform (PIM) and to pass by transformations to specific models depending on selected platform (PSM) and to finish with specific elements (table structure, scripts,...) executed in a PLM system.

Our work is on levels M2 (metamodel), M1 (business model), M0 (PLM implementation model)

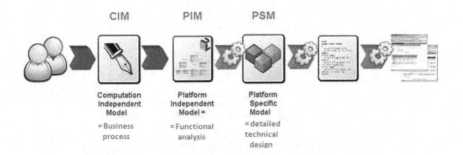

Fig. 2. OMG's workflow

2.2 A Meta-Model for PLM

There is no one standard metamodel for PLM. There are several proposals which are related to the structural dimension of the product [6] [7]. In this paper, the first approach is an approach to design and reconfiguration. The metamodel is one element that allows to develop consistent models.

Our proposal is leaning on an MDA approach. In this approach, we propose a generic meta-model (M2) that describes the CIM viewpoint (Computation Independent Model). The meta-model is the result of a abstraction process of different models/frameworks proposed [8] [9] [10]

These are the concepts for industrial products development (application domain).

- the actor is a person or an organizational element who has expertise in business or in information system.
- the business object is the main type of concepts that is readily understandable by all business stakeholders. A business object is a bearer of product information and must be unambiguous.
- the IS resource is a concept that is used by the information system designer
- the business properties characterize a business object. These properties are defined on quantifiable domains.
- the IS property is a design element that is necessary to any PLM (eg in a PLM system any object has an unique ID)
- the functional link is a dependency between business objects

These concepts are represented in the following class diagram 3

2.3 PIM and PSM Viewpoint in PLM Systems

A PIM must have a sufficient degree of independence in order to enable its mapping to more platforms. In our context, it relates to be independent of the various PLM systems. The business model is based on stereotypes characterization from the CIM metamodel. Thus, the resulting model will be in accordance

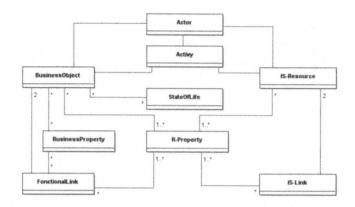

Fig. 3. Metamodel from CIM viewpoint

with previous metamodel. It represents the business concept that will be handled in the enterprise. The compliance control is ensured by a set of constraints (eg all business object should possess at least a system property and a business property).

For example, enterprises working with CAD documents, a PIM model is given by the following diagram (Fig. 4)

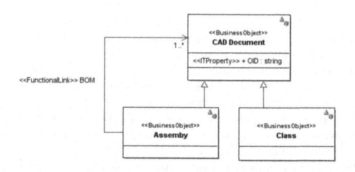

Fig. 4. Example 1 of PIM model

Another example is the viewpoint notion that is present in all PLM systems and that allows to characterize the access rights on the business objects (Fig. 5)

PSM level is the level of implementation models. In our case, the PIM concepts transformation does not produce executable code. Indeed, our approach is intended to be used in a PLM context (or reconfiguration definition). The execution platform is implicitly a PLM system and generated elements are in fact elements that will be instantiated in the PLM by the application server.

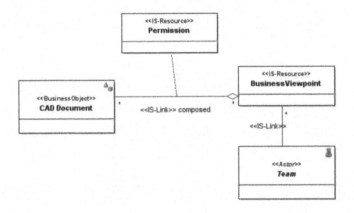

Fig. 5. Example 2 of PIM model

The purpose of PDM (platform definition model) is precisely to describe the templates for the models transformation (from PIM to PSM).

In the next section, we illustrate a business model (PIM) within a PLM platform (Audros) which is very used in SME/SMI.

3 Application with an Industrial PLM Context

3.1 Use Case with Audros PLM System

Audros is a PLM system which is deployed mostly in SME/SMI. His architecture model breaks up into various elements allowing data management, business views and users rights management. These elements are in strong correlation.

From these constraints and the metamodel, we built the Audros model Audros (the 'Standard Edition'). This model is designed for small business who want to quickly deploy a PLM system

3.2 Modeling Example: Audros's Standard Edition (SE)

The SE model is proposed by Audros for its PLM system. The objective of SE is to propose a minimalist model that works for an SME . it must contain :

- useful objects (Part, Product, Document, CAD doc, BOM, ...)
- standard viewpoints (design, engineering , manufacturing, ...)
- standard change management (ECR, ECO, ...)

The following diagram (fig. 6) shows an extract from the SE's PIM model. In this model, the metamodel concepts are represented by stereotypes (UML2.0)

At this level the model is not dependent on the Audros platform, compliance is checked by the metamodel and constraints.

In the next step, the creation of the elements in PSM viewpoint is using templates and transformation rules. The PSM elements have to be executed

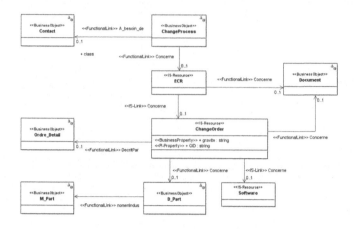

Fig. 6. Extract from PIM model

in Audros either under structural shape (Database) or under dynamic shape (ScriptAUPL). About structural aspects, the transformations of a *BusinessObject* or an *ISRessource* is realized from transformation relations (BusinessOjbect-ToAudrosCTable, BusinessPropertyToAudrosCColumn, ISPropertyToAudrosC-Column, ComplexAttributeToColumn, ...)

For example, in Audros's SE, the transformation of part and BOM is given by

$$
M\_PART, D\_PART, BOM \rightarrow \begin{pmatrix} 2 \ tuples \ in & ClassAudrosTable \\ 1 \ tuple \ in & RelationAudrosTable \\ 3 \ tables & M\_PART\_Table \\ & D\_PART\_Table \\ & BOM\_Table \\ 1 \ tuple \ in & BOM\_Table \end{pmatrix}
$$

Changing needs is carried on the PIM level. Such changes, modifications, additions or deletions must meet the metamodel.

4 Conclusion

The goal of this paper is to verify the pertinence of an MDE approach in design and reconfiguration of a PLM system. With the metamodel proposed, we define a set of minimalist concepts for the control of conformity. With templates and transformation rules, we validated the feasability of a generation in an industrial system for SME/SMI. Currently constraints and transformation rules are not exhaustive especially for dynamic aspects of the model.

Moreover, in the case of Audros, automated jobs can modify data depending on users events (for example: BOM creation following an event Project creation). These tasks are carried out by AUPL scripts (AUdros Programming Language).These can modify the data model or interact with it. To manage these various dependences and to maintain coherence a total of the system, Audros would need mechanisms to control the dependences (for creation and modification) between the various elements of its structure, as well as mechanisms of synchronization of scripts respecting the modifications of the model. The ideal would be to lay out a tool which detects modifications and propagates their impacts within the model and scripts.

References

[1] Favre, J.: Concepts fondamentaux de l IDM (2005)
[2] Combemale, B.: Approche de meta-modelisation pour la simulation et la verification de modele. Application a l ingenierie des procedes. PhD thesis, Institut Polytechnique de Toulouse (2008)
[3] OMG: Meta object facility (mof) (2011) http://www.omg.org/spec/MOF/2.4.1/
[4] OMG: Omg model driven architecture (2001), http://www.omg.org/mda/
[5] Bezivin, J., Gerbe, O.: Towards a precise definition of the omg/mda framework. In: 16th IEEE International Conference on Automated Software Engineering, San Diego, USA (November 2001)
[6] Srinivasan, V.: STEP in the context of Product Data Management. In: Advanced Design and Manufacturing Based on STEP. Springer (2009)
[7] Abid, H., Pernelle, P., Noterman, D., Guillmot, M., Ben Ama, C.: Integration of mechatronic products within a plm system. In: INCOM (2012)
[8] Sudarsan, R., Fenves, S., Sriram, R.: A product information modeling framework for product lifecycle managemen. Computer Aided Design 37(13) (2005)
[9] Chettaoui, H.: Interoperabilite entre modeles heterogenes en conception cooperative par des approches d'Ingenierie dirige par les modeles. PhD thesis, Institut polytechnique de Grenoble (2008)
[10] Eynard, B., Gallet, T., Roucoules, L., Ducellier, G.: Pdm system implementation based on uml. Mathematics and Computers in Simulation 70(5-6), 330–342 (2006)

Dynamic Alarm Management in Next Generation Process Control Systems

Eva Jerhotova, Marek Sikora, and Petr Stluka

Honeywell Prague Laboratory
V Parku 18, 148 00 Prague, Czech Republic
{Eva.Jerhotova,Marek.Sikora,Petr.Stluka}@Honeywell.com

Abstract. Current process control systems are composed of a large number of components and subsystems operating at different layers of the control system architecture model (i.e. measurement and control devices, Distributed Control Systems, Advanced Process Control systems, and Manufacturing Execution Systems). The IMC-AESOP project aims at designing the next generation architecture of process automation systems. In order to ensure system scalability and modularity, the new architectural design follows the SOA (Service-Oriented Architecture) design principles. Moreover, the design assumes adoption of various technologies with the aim to enable the control systems to meet all functional and performance requirements. The CEP (Complex Event Processing) technology has been selected for being able to provide efficient asynchronous communication (within and across architecture layers) and the capability of temporal reasoning over large amounts of system-generated events. This paper describes the intermediate results of the IMC-AESOP project, outlining the architectural concepts related to the use of the SOA and CEP technologies in the context of advanced alarm management applications - alarm load shedding and state-based alarming.

Keywords: next generation DCS/SCADA, system of systems, process monitoring and control, alarm management, dynamic alarming, state-based alarming, alarm load shedding, software-oriented architecture, SOA, complex event processing, CEP, IMC-AESOP project.

1 Introduction

Current industrial process control and monitoring systems – DCS/SCADA – are becoming increasingly complex and heterogeneous [1]. Communication among their components is evolving from synchronous to asynchronous. In the system architecture design, multiple key challenges need to be appropriately addressed, such as interoperability, real-time performance, security or availability. The European R&D-project IMC-AESOP (ArchitecturE for Service-Oriented Process - Monitoring and Control, http://www.imc-aesop.eu) proposes consistent use of Service-Oriented Architecture (SOA). This architectural approach assumes that all autonomous and intelligent devices, applications and systems that are deployed nowadays or in near future will

C. Emmanouilidis, M. Taisch, D. Kiritsis (Eds.): APMS 2012, Part II, IFIP AICT 398, pp. 224–231, 2013.

expose their capabilities, functions and structural characteristics as services. Under such paradigm, the industrial process environment will be mapped into a "Cloud of Services" where devices and applications distributed across different layers of the enterprise-control system hierarchy expose the services that they provide and at the same time they are able to access and use other services located in the cloud.

The SOA approach [12] has been widely adopted by enterprise architects for a number of reasons, which include increased flexibility in application design, providing opportunity of functionality reuse at the macro level (or the service level) rather than at the micro level (or the class level), and making the relevant businesses more agile and capable to respond more quickly to changing market conditions. The IMC-AESOP project aims at bringing the SOA architectural approach into the industrial automation world. A considerable part of the project efforts has been invested into describing the service-based architecture of a DCS/SCADA system and identification of services which could be exploited in multiple environments or applications. Some of the services are rather specialized, such as configuration services, data acquisition services, or alarm processing services, while other services may be more generic, such as discovery (e.g. service registry) or event broker services.

In the recent years, Complex Event Processing (CEP) [2] has gained considerable importance as a means to extract information from distributed event-based (or message-based) systems. It became popular in the domain of business process management but is now being applied in the industrial monitoring and control domains. This method enables efficient asynchronous communication (both within and across architecture layers) and a temporal reasoning functionality capable of processing large amounts of system-generated events in real time. CEP allows control systems to evolve from scan-based systems to event-based systems, which significantly increases the system performance and data throughput. In the IMC-AESOP project, Microsoft StreamInsight is used as a CEP engine. This engine is wrapped in an alarm processing service, which is being reused in different applications or use cases.

The remainder of the paper is organized as follows. Section 2 describes the advanced alarm handling techniques, whose specific implementations using SOA and CEP are being explored in the project. Section 3 summarizes the underlying architectural principles. And finally, section 4 discusses implementation challenges and plans for validation.

2   Advanced Alarm Handling Techniques

Alarms used in industrial manufacturing facilities are sound and/or visual announcements of abnormal process situations addressed to operators. These announcements are typically triggered when a given process variable (measured by a dedicated sensor) exceeds a predefined limit. Alarms require operator assessment and action in order to avoid (or at least mitigate) plant upsets, which may otherwise cause injuries, loss of production or equipment damage [6, 7, 8].

The alarming capability is ensured by the alarm system within the plant control system. As a consequence of process or equipment changes over time (e.g. equipment addition or replacement) the alarm system requires maintenance to sustain its best performance and full functionality. Alarm rationalization and continuous alarm system improvement [6, 7, 8, 11] are the processes for achieving the goal of keeping the alarm system performance at an appropriate performance level during its life-cycle. During alarm system maintenance, certain alarms may be configured or de-configured and alarm parameters, such as limits, priority, deadband, or delay timer, may be changed.

Despite considerable investments into alarm system improvement efforts which have been made by operating companies, the performance of the alarm system in plant upsets remains a challenge and operators still experience alarm floods[1]. Occurrence of alarm floods can be mitigated by the use of advanced alarm handling techniques [6, 7, 8, 11], such as

- **alarm grouping** (i.e. presenting related alarms as a group),
- **state-based alarming** (i.e. using different alarm settings or suppressing alarms for different process or equipment states). This technique is sometimes called mode-based alarming, dynamic alarm masking, alarm suppression, or automatic alarm shelving
- or **alarm load shedding** (i.e. displaying only the most critical alarms during alarm floods and delaying presentation of alarms of less critical).

The phenomenon of alarm flooding is one of the pain points in the process industry and it was one of the main driving forces for establishing dedicated professional consortia, such as the Abnormal Situation Management Consortium (ASMC). Within the IMC-AESOP project, the capabilities of SOA and CEP are demonstrated on the state-based alarming and alarm load shedding methods that have a great potential for alarm flood reduction.

2.1   State-Based Alarming

In certain process states, static alarms can be inadvertently triggered due to normal process changes (e.g. different operating mode or equipment shutdown). In such situations, certain alarms become meaningless or their limits must be set too wide to accommodate the different states. State-based alarming is a dynamic alarm handling method based on switching the alarm system configuration to the settings which correspond to the identified process states. For the different states, new alarms may be enabled, certain alarms may be disabled or their parameters may be altered (such as the alarm priority or the alarm limit).

---

[1] An alarm flood is a situation in which the operator is presented with too many alarms than he/she can effectively respond to [7]. Such situations are potentially dangerous, since the operator may overlook important alarms or assess the situation wrongly because of stress and information overload.

The process states may be grouped into the following categories:

- **Unit or equipment shutdown,** such as stopping or shutdown of a redundant piece of equipment (e.g. when a redundant pump is turned off, all pump low-flow alarms are disabled), shutdown of a unit (e.g. for maintenance), or equipment out-of-service. Fig. 1 displays an example of alarm settings for shutdown of a tank. For the shutdown state, the low-energy alarms (e.g. low level in the tank) should be de-configured, while the high-energy alarms (e.g. high pressure) should not be de-configured, but only reconfigured to much lower values in order to be able to detect isolation failures and unexpected reactions from contamination [11].
- **Different operation modes,** such as start-up, steady operation, different feed, de-coking (e.g. higher temperatures for heater decoking).
- **Major event suppression** [8], such as suppression of a suction pressure alarm when the compressor trips off.

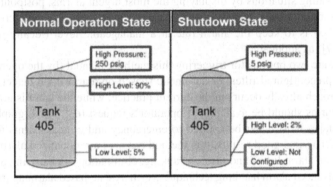

Fig. 1. State-based alarming for a shutdown state [11]

State-based alarming is becoming increasingly used in practice. This is true mainly for the shutdown-state alarming, for which the setup is relatively easy and many implementations already exist. In contrast, the other two groups of techniques are not currently much used because of requiring deeper analysis, such as the cause and effect analysis for consequential alarm suppression.

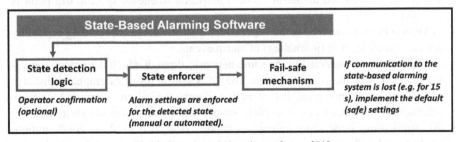

Fig. 2. State-based alarming software [11]

Regarding state-based alarming implementation, switching between states may be done manually (by the operator), semi-automatically (when the operator either identifies or confirms the automatically identified state and initiates the configuration change), or automatically (when no input is required from the operator). For the automatic approaches, the state detection logic must be reliable and must not chatter. As depicted in Fig. 2, the state-based alarming implementation must include reliable alarm settings enforcement and a fail-safe mechanism. Under any circumstances, the operator must be kept informed about which alarms have been disabled or reconfigured and why and also should be able to override the state change.

2.2   Alarm Load Shedding

Alarm load shedding is a technique which supports operators in prioritizing actions in alarm flooding situations by displaying the most urgent alarms, postponing displaying of less important ones, and filtering out alarms of log priority and alerts. The aim of this method is to keep the alarm rate at a manageable level (ideally one alarm per minute [7]) as applicable.

There are two options for triggering this method: manual (by the operator who may select a preconfigured filter) or automatic (based on alarm flood detection). The former approach already occurs in the current practice, while the latter is not yet used.

All alarms should be available at operator's request (e.g. in the graphical display) and no delay must never be applied to emergency and critical alarms for safety reasons [7]. To yield good results, this method requires a rationalized alarm system with appropriate alarm limits and priority ranking, elimination of chattering alarms, eclipsing, or advanced alarm handling techniques, such as state-based alarming [6, 7, 8, 9, 11].

3   Advanced Alarm Management Using SOA and CEP

Alarm management functionality of a DCS/SCADA system is usually distributed among several system components including:

- **Automation devices** (or controllers) generating alarm events via systematic comparison of the actual values of all monitored points with the pre-configured alarm trip points (limits) and an alarm event is activated whenever specific trip point is reached
- A **DCS server** (connected to the supervisory control network) providing capability for automated logging (journaling) of alarm events.
- A **DCS station** (connected to the same network) through which the process operator interacts with the control system. The DCS station provides graphical displays visualizing a chronological list of active alarms (i.e. alarm summary), process schematics, and other types of displays supporting operator situation awareness.
- An **application node** representing a computer dedicated to alarm configuration, analysis and maintenance applications, which are usually designed for off-line use during alarm system improvement activities

The advanced alarm management techniques (described in section 2) are usually residing in the supervisory control network with individual functions shared between the server and stations. Several functional blocks (alarm configuration, alarm processing, event detection and others) are needed for successful implementation. Within the IMC-AESOP project, the advanced alarm management functions are realized through specific services or their combinations, as illustrated in Fig. 3.

- The **Sensory Data Acquisition** service delivers data from the process exploiting either the scan-based method (sending values regularly) or the event-based method (delivering values only when there has been any change)
- The **System Configuration** service provides information of the current process state (such as startup, normal operation, shutdown, maintenance, fault, off)
- The **Alarm Configuration** service lists all available alarms with their description, properties, and relation to process units and equipment

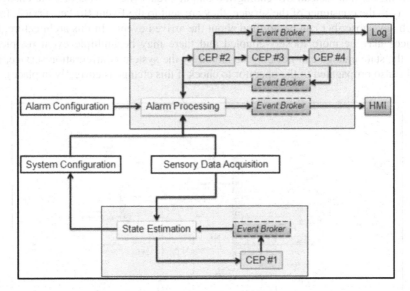

Fig. 3. Alarm processing architecture

There are also several instances of the CEP service that are being directly used by the alarm processing services. Each of them has the same StreamInsight service running in the background. The difference lies in the input and/or output events and the definition of the query (as described below). The following two services are the core of the SOA/CEP-based alarm processing application:

- Referring to Fig. 3, the **State Estimation** service uses the CEP#1 service, which evaluates predefined rules on the values of relevant process variables. For example, when a certain set of variables turns zero, it may be assumed that the associated unit has been turned off, or variables oscillation outside the predefined bounds may indicate that a corresponding unit is in a startup mode. The information about the identified state change of the unit is then stored.

- The **Alarm Processing** service represents an implementation of the alarm handling techniques described above. The CEP#2 service generates alarm events via comparing given process variables with their limits, while taking into account the process state identified by the State Estimation service. The CEP #3 service reduces alarm chatter by concatenating multiple closely-spaced alarms into a single alarm event. Finally, the CEP#4 service provides the alarm load shedding functionality. As illustrated in Fig. 3, the alarms identified by the CEP#2 block can be stored in the alarm log for possible further investigation, while the operator is presented only with the alarms output by the CEP#4 block. The SOA nature of this application also allows dynamic combining of the individual CEP alarm processing blocks. For instance, when only the state-based alarming functionality is implemented, the alarm load shedding block can be omitted.

Additionally, the **Event Broker** service can be used in the application architecture, which means that instead of sending the output events (i.e. alarms or state changes) directly to the consumer of the service, they are sent to the Event Broker service, from which any subscriber can be notified about the arrived events. In this architecture, the services may be more loosely-coupled and there may be multiple event recipients (e.g. the state change can not only be stored by the system configuration service, but can be also propagated to the operator to check if this change is correctly in place).

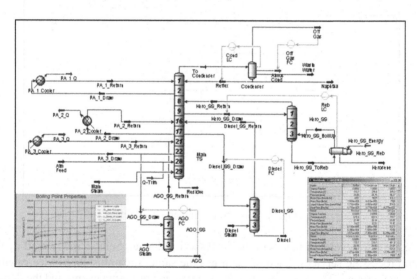

Fig. 4. Dynamic Unisim model of an atmospheric distillation column with three side strippers

4   Future Work and Conclusion

As the next step in the project, state-based alarming and alarm load shedding [8] will be implemented to the process data generated by a Unisim model of an atmospheric distillation column shown in Fig. 4. This facility produces naphtha, kerosene, diesel, atmospheric gas oil, and atmospheric residue products from a heavy crude feed.

The model is dynamic – i.e. comprising controllers and process specifications, such as the size of the distillation column trays and the side stripper tray sections, and the pressure flow. The incorporated dynamics allow for more realistic modelling of the facility behavior. Using this model, the process data will be generated by making changes to key process variables and also by simulating disturbances (e.g. failure of the reflux pump). The considered states for state-based alarming are shutdown, start-up, and different feed rate.

Based on the demonstration, we shall be able to assess the advantages and disadvantages of the SOA/CEP-based implementation for this type of applications. The main advantage of SOA lies in the loose-coupling of services which enables dynamic composition and orchestration. For CEP, it is the event-based functionality which yields improved performance and scalability. However, there are still a few open questions that need to be answered, such as how flexible the used CEP services really are, or if there will be any performance loss due to SOA or the Event Broker.

Acknowledgement. The research efforts described in this paper are co-funded by the European Union within the IMC-AESOP project (www.imc-aesop.eu). The authors would like to express thanks to the consortium partners for the fruitful discussions and cooperation.

References

1. Karnouskos, S., Colombo, A.W.: Architecting the next generation of service-based SCADA/DCS system of systems. In: Proc. 37th IEEE Annual Conf. IECON, Melbourne (November 2011)
2. Karnouskos, S., et al.: A SOA-based architecture for empowering future collaborative cloud-based industrial automation. In: 38th IEEE Conf. IECON, Montreal (October 2012)
3. Jammes, F., et al.: Technologies for SOA-based Distributed Large Scale Process Monitoring and Control Systems. In: Proc. 38th Conf. of the IEEE Industrial Electronics Society, IECON 2012, Montreal (October 2012)
4. Duca, A., Freeman, N., Drews, S.: SOA What? Demystifying SOA for the Process Industry. Honeywell International Inc. Tech. Rep. (2008)
5. Etzion, O., Niblett, P.: Event Processing in Action. Manning Publications, USA (2011)
6. Rothenberg, D.: Alarm Management for Process Control, A Best-Practice Guide for Design, Implementation, and Use of Industrial Alarm Systems. Momentum Press (2009)
7. EEMUA, Alarm Systems, A Guide to Design, Management, and Procurement, EEMUA Publication No. 191, London (1999)
8. Errington, J., Reising, D.V., Burns, C.: Effective Alarm Management Practices. In: ASM Consortium Guidelines, ASM (May 2007)
9. Andow, P., Cade, J., Clark, R., Foslien, W.: Alarm Flood Analysis Report, Honeywell HPS, ASM Consortium (2007)
10. Speight, J.G.: The Chemistry and Technology of Petroleum, 3rd edn. Marcel Dekker, Inc., USA (1999)
11. Hollifield, B.R., Habibi, E.: Alarm Management: Seven Effective Methods for Optimum Performance. ISA (2008)
12. Erl, T.: Principles of service design. Prentice Hall (2007)

Sustainable Layout Planning Requirements by Integration of Discrete Event Simulation Analysis (DES) with Life Cycle Assessment (LCA)

Victor Emmanuel de Oliveira Gomes[1,2], Durval Joao De Barba Jr.[1],
Jefferson de Oliveira Gomes[1], Karl-Heinrich Grote[2], and Christiane Beyer[3]

[1] Institute of Aeronautical Technology, Brazil
{victor,debarbajr,gomes}@ita.br
[2] OvG University Magdeburg, Germany
{victor.gomes,karl.grote}@ovgu.de
[3] California State University Long Beach, USA
chris.beyer@csulb.edu

Abstract. Discrete Event Simulation (DES) provides computational models with different scenarios in which it is possible to check waste and capacity-constrained resources to generate comparative results. However, these analyses are guided by questions such as cost and production time without regard for wastes that impact on the environment. This paper examines how a tool of Life Cycle Assessment (LCA) can supplement DES in performing analyses of production systems taking into account environmental impacts, such as energy consumption and greenhouse emission. These ideas are demonstrated by a case study developed in an automotive company. The results ratify the importance of global projects with local solutions, even for layout planning.

Keywords: Discrete Event Simulation, Life Cycle Assessment, layout planning.

1 Introduction

A proper evaluation of manufacturing is a fundamental step to decision making in planning layouts. In these cases the support of mathematical tools, such as Discrete Event Simulation (DES), have been used for identifying waste on the shop floor and cost analyses for manufacturing optimization [1].

One of the advantages resulting from the application of DES in a corporate environment is its capability to include the impact of randomness in a system. All the dynamics and the non-deterministic nature of the parameters eliminate the use of static tools such as spreadsheets for solving many line design problems. Furthermore, all commercial simulation software provides detailed animation capabilities. The animation of the manufacturing process and flow can help engineers to visually detect problems or bottlenecks and also to test out alternate line designs. For these reasons DES may be applied to generate requirements and sustainable systems specifications

C. Emmanouilidis, M. Taisch, D. Kiritsis (Eds.): APMS 2012, Part II, IFIP AICT 398, pp. 232–239, 2013.
© IFIP International Federation for Information Processing 2013

for manufacturing. However, the analyses results realized by using DES are not sufficient for the joint assessment of impacts on the three dimensions of sustainability [2].

There are distinct tools and techniques to analyze and provide environmentally sustainable manufacturing systems. In most cases they consist of cost analyses integrated with pollutant emissions and energy efficiency analyses [3]. One of the biggest challenges for new production systems projects is obtaining data incorporated into the typical analyses of production (production capacity, material flow, transport, occupation rate of posts etc.)for the environmental impacts analysis. The Life Cycle Assessment (LCA) is a tool widely used in the academic environment and by corporations to calculate pollutant emissions rates. Through an LCA study it is possible to develop a systematic analysis of the environmental consequences associated with products during their life cycle, which improves the decision-making in areas such as innovation, regulations (industrial, environmental), strategies and policies.

This work discusses the combined use of DES with LCA to analyze production resource utilization in manufacturing systems. The combination of DES with LCA produces a powerful tool for analyzing the cause and effect of various scenarios where time, resources, place and randomness of input variables affect the outcome in sustainable manufacturing design. This joint application establishes the dynamic environment for sustainable production systems assessments and is an unexplored area addressed by few research publications. A case study was conducted, as a contribution towards this discussion, to analyze this joint use in decision-making for purchasing forklifts according to sustainable premises.

2   Materials and Methods – Case Study

The chosen problem for the proposed discussion was a sequencing process layout involving automotive door panels and it included situations concerning two important criteria contained in an industrial layout plan, which were transport performance and space. Transports cost can improve the efficiency of the product flow. It concerns the design of layout, the accommodation of people, and the machines and activities of a system or an enterprise within a physical spatial environment. Inefficient space utilization may cause cost increase and lead to competitive disadvantage in the market. As the result of less space demand in the planning phase, the company can either save rent cost or use the saved space for further development.

The system was a supermarket where automotive door panels, sequenced by the operators according to the customer's orders, were transported by forklift trucks until the dispatch sector. Each cell-sequencing had twelve containers overlapping with panels out of sequence from the assembly line, arranged in six sequenced pairs, and two containers with already sequenced panels, also overlapping. The production system goal was to provide a minimum amount of 380 containers daily in the dispatch area, with the minimum amount of operators and forklifts and reduced space utilization. From these premises, models with a pre-established configuration were simulated through DES software Plant Simulation-Tecnomatix™. A type of model is illustrated in Figure 1.

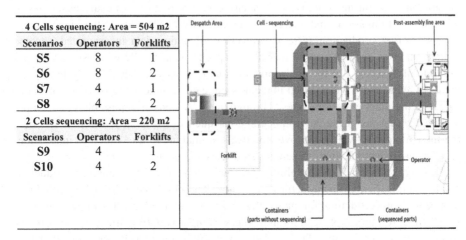

4 Cells sequencing: Area = 504 m2		
Scenarios	**Operators**	**Forklifts**
S5	8	1
S6	8	2
S7	4	1
S8	4	2
2 Cells sequencing: Area = 220 m2		
Scenarios	**Operators**	**Forklifts**
S9	4	1
S10	4	2

Fig. 1. - Computational model and proposed scenarios

For each proposed scenario the cost of forklift acquisition and personnel (labor/salary cost + incidental wage/salary cost – e.g. sickness, insurance fund, pension insurance fund etc.) was considered.

It is known that the usage phase of forklifts is of greatest environmental impact factors within its life cycle [4]. This high rate is directly related to the fuel consumption. In this way, the main factor to materially influence the choice of layout in forklift used must be the type of fuel used in addition to forklift performance. For this reason an LCA study was conducted in parallel with results supplied by the simulation analyses to verify the use of forklifts with different energy sources. Data from fuel utilization were acquired in different research sources.

This is a problem in which there are several objectives to be achieved simultaneously. Among the methods developed for evaluation in a multi-criteria decision environment the method PROMETHEE (Preference Ranking Organization Method for Enrichment Evaluation) was employed to support the decision-making process. It is appropriate in situations where decision-makers previously identified criteria and alternatives, by-passing structuring phase, and emphasizing the evaluation phase.

3   Results and Discussion

By the DES analysis, the scenario S9 was chosen due to better fulfillment of production requirements and the relation between cost and production with a lower shop-floor area (Figure 2).

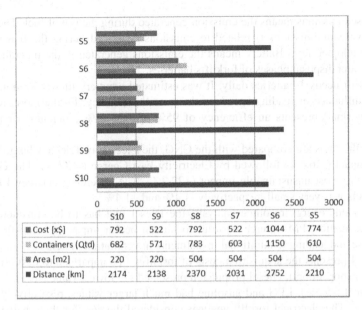

	S10	S9	S8	S7	S6	S5
▦ Cost [x$]	792	522	792	522	1044	774
▨ Containers (Qtd)	682	571	783	603	1150	610
▩ Area [m2]	220	220	504	504	504	504
■ Distance [km]	2174	2138	2370	2031	2752	2210

Fig. 2. – Proposed scenarios analyses

However, the scenario choices depends on the decision-making approach that can be done according to the area, the fuel consumption analysis, the forecast of future demands and other considerations which can form a decision-making matrix.

Based on [6-9] by the Lifecycle assessment, a comparison of five types of fuels used by forklifts was performed listing their environmental impacts due GWP (Global Warming Potential), displayed in metric tons CO_2 equivalent per unit per year (ETC-Electricity Trickle Charge; EFC-Electricity Fast Charge; LPG- Liquefied Propane Gas; CNG-Compressed Natural Gas; Diesel and Gasoline) (Figure 3).

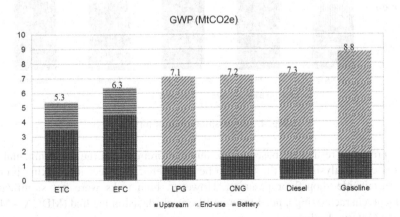

Fig. 3. - Comparison of fuels used by forklifts according GWP (Global Warming Potential): ETC-Electricity Trickle Charge; EFC-Electricity Fast Charge; LPG- Liquefied Propane Gas; CNG-Compressed Natural Gas; Diesel and Gasoline

End-use emissions means the emission generated during the use of fuel. The meaning of upstream-emissions is related to emissions generated during the fuel production. The adopted term Battery means the emissions generated in the manufacturing, recycling and disposal phases of forklifts batteries.

A forklift needs 3 batteries daily. It was estimated a battery life of 50 months and also the influence of loading speed on the overall efficiency. Furthermore, a trickle charge (normal) presents an efficiency of 95% against 72% efficiency for a quick charge [5].

When the fuels are compared with the CNG, the Electricity Trickle Charge had the lowest impact (-26.4%) followed by Electricity Fast Charge (-12.5%). The Gasoline fuel had the most unsustainable impact (+22.2%). The difference between LPG and Diesel fuels was very small, respectively -1.4% and +1.4%.

Beyond this energy resource analysis, the Diesel fuel has to be considered as a particulate matter (PM) source harmful to human health impacting shop-floor area forklift use and leading to additional investments in ventilation systems.

Figure 4 presents the acquisition costs of forklifts. In comparison to CNG (normally used on shop-floors), Diesel propulsion presented the lowest value (-6%), followed by electrical (-5.6%). LPG and gasoline had much larger values, respectively 29.6% and 30.4%. The electrical forklift analysis considered the cost for three batteries, including acquisition and maintenance for 50 months use.

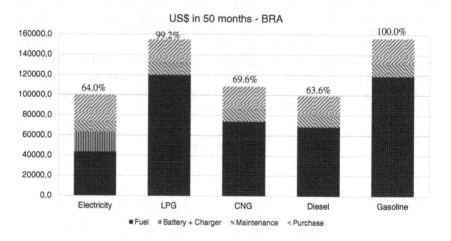

Fig. 4. - Acquisition costs of forklift

The presented results are based on the authors' premise that the environmental impact and cost analysis were the tasks to be considered in a decision making process for a sustainable shop-floor planning. However, both tasks were not significantly dependent, characterizing a need for a multi-criteria decision method (MDCA – Multi Decision Criteria Analysis).

In the application of PROMETHEE method, a MDCA tool, the authors considered weighted environmental impact and cost analysis 35% and 65% respectively.

Using this method it presented a ranking of alternatives from the best to worst. Table 1 shows the sort of decision in accordance to the standards proposed by the decision maker.

Table 1. – PROMETHEE II Ranking

Alternatives	ETC	EFC	LPG	CNG	Diesel	Gasoline
PROMETHEE II Ranking	0.0724	0.0304	-0.0060	-0.0079	-0.0115	-0.0774
Score	100	91.92	85.47	85.13	84.52	74.06

In accordance to the results, both electricity batteries were considered first choice. There were no significantly difference between LPG, CNG and Diesel. Gasoline fuel was the worst alternative. This analysis was considered for a land with high percentage of hydraulic generation, like Brazil and Norway.

However, considering a multinational company, which has global projects (there are differences in the amount of product demand and also areas occupied by production resources, different kinds of energy generation), the main idea is the consideration for applying local decisions.

In that case, considering the application of the MDCA method for a scenario in a land with high percentage of thermal generation, like USA, UK and Germany, the final results will be different than those for lands with a high percentage of hydraulic generation (Figure 5).

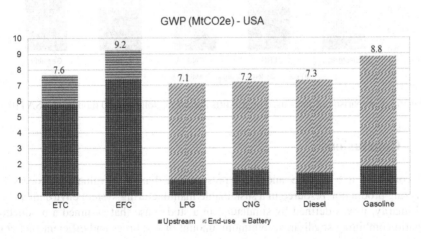

Fig. 5. - Comparison of fuels used by forklifts according GWP in lands with high percentage of thermal generation

For example, if the analysis had been conducted in the USA (percentage of hydraulic generation of 7.4%), the results would be different than in Brazil (percentage of hydraulic generation of 83.2%).

Similarly, the fuel costs are very different in those lands, being more expensive in Brazil. Electricity in Brazil is approximately three times greater than in USA [10].

For a MDCA analysis with the same alternatives, criteria and weights, a different ordering can be obtained. In this way the choice of the type of forklift in the USA would be preferably by LPG followed by CNG (Table 2).

Table 2. – PROMETHEE II Ranking for a new analysis considering lands with high percentage of thermal energy generation

Alternatives	LPG	CNG	Diesel	ETC	Gasoline	EFC
PROMETHEE II Ranking	0.0318	0.0301	0.0236	0.0113	-0.0408	-0.0559
Score	100	99.67	98.37	95.98	86.48	83.90

It is observed that in this case there is a big difference between the forms of batteries, because the Fast Charge would be the worst choice (Figure 6).

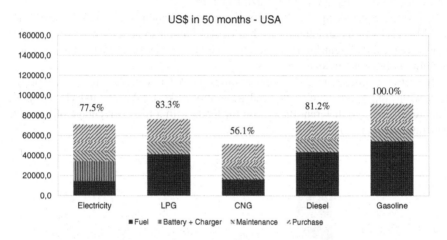

Fig. 6. - Comparison of fuels used by forklifts according dollars in 50 months in USA [10]

4   Conclusions

The combined use of DES and LCA presented a dynamic evaluation process for analyzing production resource in a sustainable manufacturing system environment.

Primarily, it was defined by simulation in a study case that assumed a production scenario combining small area, minimum amount of resources and efficient fuel consuming.

Supported by a Multi Criteria Decision Analysis Tool (PROMETHEE II), the use of forklifts was rationalized for distinct applications in shop-floors located in lands with high percentage of hydraulic and thermal energy generation.

The results ratify the importance of global projects with local solutions, even for layout planning.

References

1. Standridge, C.R., Marvel, J.H.: Why Lean Needs Simulation. In: Winter Simulation Conference, pp. 1907–1913. Institute of Electrical and Electronics Engineers, Piscataway (2006)
2. Joschko, P., Page, B., Volker, W.: Combination of Job Oriented Simulation with Ecological Material Flow Analysis as Integrated Analysis Tool for Business Production Processes. In: Winter Simulation Conference (2009)
3. Helu, M., Rühl, J., Donfeld, D.: Evaluating Trade-Offs Between Sustainability, Performance, and Cost of Green Machining Technologies. In: Proceedings of the 18th CIRP International Conference on Life Cycle Engineering (2012)
4. Suzuki, N.: LCA Activities of Toyota Industries Corporation: Case Study. JLCA News Letter (2) (2006)
5. LPG AUSTRALIA. GHG life cycle assessment of LPG in the Australian stationary energy market. Report (49p) (August 2011)
6. Gaines, L.L., Elgowainy, A., Wang, M.Q.: Full Fuel-Cycle Comparison of Forklift Propulsion Systems (2008), http://greet.es.anl.gov/files/oh77n5k5
7. Antes, M., Brindle, R., McGevey, J., Pack, L., Zotter, B.: Propane's Greenhouse Gas Emissions: A Comparative Analysis. Propane Education & Research Council (PERC). Report (39p) (2007)
8. Sullivan, J.L., Gaines, L.: A Review of Battery Life-Cycle Analysis: State of Knowledge and Critical Needs. Center for Transportation Research, Energy Systems Division, Argonne National Laboratory. Report (45p) (October 2010)
9. Wang, M.: Fuel Cycle Analysis of Conventional and Alternative Fuel Vehicles. Argonne National Laboratory. Encyclopedia of Energy, vol. 2.r, pp. 771–789. Elsevier Inc. (2004)
10. U.S. International Energy Agency (IEA): Key World Energy Statistics (2008)

Equipment's Prognostics Using Logical Analysis of Data

Alireza Ghasemi[1], Sasan Esmaeili[1], and Soumaya Yacout[2]

[1] Dalhousie University, Halifax, Canada
{alireza.ghasemi,sasan.esmaeili}@dal.ca
[2] École Polytechnique de Montréal, Montréal, Canada
soumaya.yacout@polymtl.ca

Abstract. This paper demonstrates the implementation of Logical Analysis of Data (LAD) methodology in the field of prognostics in Condition Based Maintenance (CBM). In this paper the LAD classification methodology, based on Sensitive Discriminating and Equipartitioning methods for data binarization, Mixed Integer Linear Programming (MILP) and Hybrid Greedy methods for pattern generation, is used. Using the generated patterns, two methods of calculating the survival function are introduced. The methodology is applied on Prognostics and Health Management Challenge dataset, which is a condition monitoring dataset provided by NASA Ames Prognostics Data Repository. The results obtained by using LAD methodology, are compared with that obtained by using the Proportional Hazards Model (PHM).

Keywords: Condition Based Maintenance (CBM), Logical Analysis of Data (LAD), Prognostics, Condition Monitoring.

1 Introduction

Widely applied in maintenance, *Condition Based Maintenance* (*CBM*) [1] was introduced in order to use the equipment's health condition in optimizing or improving the maintenance activities. In recent years, many statistical methodologies have been introduced to model the relation between equipment's age and its health condition and its failure. Since the statistical assumptions are not always met, new methodologies which aim at presenting structural relations between the equipment's conditional survival probability and its age and/or health condition are required.

Logical Analysis of Data (*LAD*) [2], is a combinatorial optimization and Boolean logic based methodology for the analysis of datasets. The aim of LAD is to extract knowledge hidden in observations of a dataset in order to detect patterns that lead to different classes of observations. A pattern is defined as a conjunction of features or indicators' (*Attributes'*) values which are found in one class and never in another class. A class is a distinct state of equipment. In CBM, an attribute can be the monitored equipment's age or a health condition of the equipment. Observations are classified into two classes: observations of failure during the coming period, referred to as the *Positive Class*, and observations of survival at least until the end of the coming period, referred to as the *Negative Class*. A *Positive (Negative) Pattern* is a

C. Emmanouilidis, M. Taisch, D. Kiritsis (Eds.): APMS 2012, Part II, IFIP AICT 398, pp. 240–247, 2013.

conjunction of literals that is reflected in one or more of the observations of the positive (negative) class while not reflected in any of the observations of the negative (positive) class. A *literal* is either a binary attribute or its *Negation*. The historical data base is divided into two sets; the training set and the testing set. LAD constructs the classification model based on the given historical dataset, which is called *Training Set*. Then, by using the classification model, it tests the quality or accuracy of this model by classifying the other part of the historical dataset, which is called *Testing Set*. The former process is *Training Phase*, and the latter one is the Testing *Phase*.

LAD has been widely applied to the analysis of datasets in different fields. Recently, it has been used in equipment's failure diagnostic [3-6], and has proved to be a promising technique that gives practical and interpretable results. Herein, our focus is on calculation of the probability of failure at a certain future moment, which is the prognostic objective of CBM, which has been comparatively untested when using LAD. We have extended the LAD methodology to predict the equipment's chance of survival at each observation's moment, when new observation of the equipment's attributes is available. Unlike the earlier applications of LAD in failure diagnostic, we consider both age and the equipment's condition as LAD's attributes.

The paper is structured as follows: Section 2 describes two data binarization methods and two pattern generation methods. Section 3 introduces two prognostic methods. Section 4 provides the experimental prognostic results obtained by using LAD methodology along with a comparison with those obtained when using PHM. Conclusions are presented in the section 5.

2   Data Binarization and Pattern Generation

LAD deals with Boolean attributes, whereas the monitored attributes may appear in numerical form (e.g. temperature), nominal form (e.g. color), or ordered form (e.g. temperature which can be high, medium or low). Therefore, all the attributes have to be converted to a binary format. Binarization transforms each non-binary attribute into several binary ones, by comparing attribute's values to certain thresholds, called *Cut-Points*. In the literature, there are several approaches to define cut-points [7-9], among which, we will use *Sensitive Discriminating* method and *Equipartitioning* method. In the sensitive discriminating method, a cut-point is defined as the average of two consecutive attribute's values, each belonging to a different class. The outcome cut-point represents a threshold that differentiates between positive and negative classes. In the equipartitioning method, the cut-points are defined in such a way that all the attribute's values are approximately equally divided into a pre-defined number of intervals.

A pattern discriminates between one or more of the observations of a class from all or many of the observations of the opposite class. The basic pattern generation algorithms are mainly based on generating all combinations of literals, and examining whether each of the combinations can be considered as a pattern. Recently, some heuristic methods have been introduced that require less computational effort while providing equivalent performance [10-12]. Among all the proposed pattern generation algorithms, we will use the *Mixed Integer Linear Programming (MILP)* method and *Hybrid Greedy* method in order to solve the MILP.

Reference [12] introduced a Mixed Integer Linear Programming to generate optimal *Strong Pure* patterns. A pattern is strong if the set of observations covered by the pattern is not a subset of that covered by any other patterns. A pattern is pure if it does not cover any observation from the opposite class. An observation will be considered *Covered* only if all the attributes forming the pattern are reflected in the observation. Since the optimality of a strong pattern is measured with respect to its coverage, the MILP's objective is to generate a pattern with the maximum number of covered observations. By solving the MILP model, a generated pattern doesn't necessarily cover all the observations of its class. So, the model is reconstructed to generate more patterns, up to a point that all the observations are covered by at least one of the generated patterns. Although each generated pattern differs from previously generated ones, yet it might cover some or all of the previously covered observations. In order to avoid generating redundant patterns, all the observations that were previously covered by the generated patterns will be removed from the training set before reconstructing the model.

Reference [13] introduced two heuristic algorithms, called *Bottom-Up* and *Top-Down*, to obtain optimal *Prime* pure patterns. A pattern is prime if removal of any of its literals results in coverage of observations from the opposite class. If the restriction of obtaining pure patterns is relaxed, a pattern becomes a combination of literals covering at least a minimum number of observations of the pattern's class, and at most a maximum number of observations of the opposite class. These two parameters are defined by the user, and are called *Coverage* and *Fuzziness* parameters, respectively, where fuzziness means the maximum number of observation from the opposite class that is covered by the pattern. Obviously, a pure pattern is a better indication of a certain class than a pattern that has certain fuzziness. However, this relaxation is frequently used when the separation between classes is difficult. In order to solve the MILP, we use a hybrid greedy method, which is composed of two phases: the bottom-up phase and the top down phase. If any observation is left uncovered by the end of the first phase, the second phase is performed.

3   Failure Prognostic

In the following section, we introduce two methods to calculate the conditional survival probability of the equipment, based on the estimated survival functions using *Kaplan-Meier (KM) estimation* [14].

Assume a training set includes 5, 3 and 4 observations corresponding to three pieces of equipment of the same type. The observations of equipment one are indicated by 1-0, 1-1, 1-2, 1-3, 1-4, where the first number means equipment number 1, and the second number is the equipment age. This means that equipment one has failed sometime during the fifth period. Each observation has a health condition attribute corresponding to each observation that is not shown in this example. 1-0, 1-1, 1-2, and 1-3 are considered negative observations, and 1-4 is considered positive observation. Using MILP positive and

Table 1. List of the generated patterns and covered observations

+ Pattern	Covered Observations	- Pattern	Covered Observations
P1	1-3 , 1-4 , 3-3	N1	1-0 , 1-1 , 1-2 , 2-0 , 2-1 , 2-2 , 3-0 , 3-1 , 3-2
P2	2-2 , 3-3	N2	1-0 , 1-1 , 1-3 , 2-0 , 2-1 , 3-0 , 3-1

negative patterns are generated. For each generated positive or negative pattern, the list of its covered observations is presented in Table 1.

We associated to each pattern P, Pattern Conditional Survival Probabilities $SP_P(i)$ for $\forall i \in \{1,2,...,T\}$, which represent the pattern's survival estimation of a piece of equipment for at least i periods, when the equipment's observation is covered by the pattern. T is the maximum available survival period within training set. T is 5 in the example.

KM estimation of pattern conditional survival probability is defined as the proportion of the number of observations covered by pattern P whose corresponding pieces of equipment survived at least i periods after being covered by the pattern, to the total number of observations covered by pattern P.

$$SP_P(i) = \#(P \cap S; \tau > \tau_0 + i\Delta)/\#(P \cap S; \tau > \tau_0) \qquad (1)$$

Where S is the set of observations in the training set, and $P \cap S$ represents the subset of observations in the training set S that are covered by the pattern P. Function $\#(N)$ counts the number of members of a set N. τ is the failure time of the corresponding equipment, and τ_0 is the current age of the corresponding equipment at observation moment at which it is covered by pattern P. Δ is the observation period length.

Table 2 shows KM estimation of the conditional survival probability of the generated patterns, based on their corresponding covered observations in the Table 1. For example, $SP_{P1}(1)$ is equal to 0.333 because $P1$ covers observations 1-3, 1-4, 3-3 in the Table 1, but only observation 1-3 has corresponding equipment (i.e. equipment 1) that survives more than one period after being covered by $P1$. Both corresponding equipment of observation 1-4 and 3-3 have failed during next period, as soon as they were covered by $P1$.

Table 2. KM estimation of patterns conditional survival probability for the problem

$i\Delta$	1	2	3	4
$SP_{P1}(i)$	0.333	0	0	0
$SP_{P2}(i)$	0	0	0	0
$SP_{N1}(i)$	0.889	0.667	0.333	0.111
$SP_{N2}(i)$	1	0.714	0.428	0.143

We also defined the Baseline Conditional Survival Probability to indicate time-based survival function, regardless of the equipment's condition. KM estimation of the baseline conditional survival probability is calculated as the proportion of the number of pieces of equipment that survived at least i periods, to the number of all the pieces of equipment in training set.

$$SP_b(i) = \#(E; \tau > i\Delta)/\#(E) \qquad (2)$$

where E is the set of all pieces of equipment in the training set. Table 3 shows the KM estimation of baseline conditional survival probabilities. $SP_b(3)$ equal to 0.667 means that two out of three pieces of equipment in training set have survived more than 3 periods.

Table 3. KM estimation of baseline conditional survival probability for the problem

$i\Delta$	1	2	3	4
$SP_b(i)$	1	1	0.667	0.333

By combining both, $SP_p(i)$ and $SP_b(i)$ for each observation at period i, we introduce two methods to calculate the conditional survival probability of the equipment from which a new observation is collected. The first method favors the Pattern Conditional Survival Probability (SP_P), while takes into account the Conditional Survival Probabilities that were calculated for the equipment previously (SP_{former}), less weightily. It also contains the Baseline Conditional Survival Probability (SP_b). Defining n as the number of patterns that cover an observation, the conditional survival probability of the equipment for period i is calculated as follows:

$$SP_{obs}(i) = \begin{cases} \left[\sum_{P=1}^{n} SP_P(i) + SP_b(i)\right]/n+1 & , if \ t=0 \\ \left[\sum_{P=1}^{n} SP_P(i) + SP_{former}(i+1)\right]/n+1 & , if \ t>0 \end{cases} \quad (3)$$

As an example, we assume four consecutive testing observation record for a piece of equipment covered by the patterns shown in Table 4. As introduced in *eq.* (3), the conditional survival probabilities of the equipment at different observation moments are shown in the Table 4. $SP_{obs}(2)$ for 1-0 is equal to 0.794 because the observation 1-0 is covered by patterns $N1$ and $N2$ for which $SP_{N1}(2)$ and $SP_{N2}(2)$ are equal to 0.667 and 0.714 respectively (see Table 2), and $SP_b(2)$ is equal to 1 (see Table 3). As a result $SP_{obs}(2)$ for 1-0 is equal to (0.667+0.714+1) / 3 = 0.794. $SP_{former}(1)$ for 1-1 is also equal to 0.794 because its corresponding equipment was formerly predicted to survive for at least 2 periods with the probability of 0.794 ($SP_{obs}(2)$ for 1-0 is 0.794).

Table 4. Conditional survival probabilities of hypothetical equipment at different observation moments–the 1st calculation method

Obs	Covering Patterns	$\Sigma SP_p(t)$				$SP_b(t)$				$SP_{former}(t)$				$SP_{obs}(t)$			
		1	2	3	4	1	2	3	4	1	2	3	4	1	2	3	4
1-0	-N1,-N2	1.89	1.38	0.76	0.25	1	1	0.67	0.33	-	-	-	-	0.96	0.79	0.48	0.19
1-1	-N1,-N2	1.89	1.38	0.76	0.25	-	-	-	-	0.79	0.48	0.19	0	0.89	0.62	0.32	0.08
1-2	-N1	0.89	0.67	0.33	0.11	-	-	-	-	0.62	0.32	0.08	0	0.76	0.5	0.21	0.06
1-3	+P1,+P2	0.33	0	0	0	-	-	-	-	0.5	0.21	0.06	0	0.28	0.07	0.02	0

The second method also favours the latest observation to older ones, but, it attributes equal weight for Pattern and Baseline Conditional Survival Probabilities. The conditional survival probability of the equipment is calculated as follows:

$$SP_{obs}(i) = \begin{cases} \left[\left[\sum_{P=1}^{n} SP_P(i)\right]/n + SP_b(i)\right]/2 & , if \ t=0 \\ \left[\left[\sum_{P=1}^{n} SP_P(i) + SP_{former}(i+1)\right]/n+1 + SP_b(i)\right]/2 & , if \ t>0 \end{cases} \quad (4)$$

The conditional survival probabilities of the same testing equipment at different observation moments using the latter method are shown in Table 5. $SP_b(1)$ for 1-3 is equal to 0.5 because one out of two pieces of equipment that have survived more than 3 periods, has survived more than 4 periods.

Table 5. Conditional Survival probabilities of hypothetical equipment at different observation moments–the 2nd calculation method

Obs	Covering Patterns	$\Sigma SP_p(t)$				$SP_p(t)$				$SP_{former}(t)$				$SP_{obs}(t)$			
		1	2	3	4	1	2	3	4	1	2	3	4	1	2	3	4
1-0	-N1 , -N2	1.89	1.38	0.76	0.25	1	1	0.67	0.33	-	-	-	-	0.97	0.85	0.53	0.23
1-1	-N1 , -N2	1.89	1.38	0.76	0.25	1	0.67	0.33	0	0.85	0.53	0.23	0	0.96	0.65	0.33	0.04
1-2	-N1	0.89	0.67	0.33	0.11	0.67	0.33	0	0	0.65	0.33	0.04	0	0.72	0.42	0.09	0.03
1-3	+P1 , +P2	0.33	0	0	0	0.5	0	0	0	0.42	0.09	0.03	0	0.38	0.02	0	0

4 Experiments

We applied the LAD methodology on Prognostics and Health Management Challenge dataset, a condition monitoring dataset provided by NASA Ames Prognostics Data Repository, which we randomly divided to one testing set and 10 training sets. The performances of the equipartitioning method and the hybrid greedy method are examined for 4 and 12 different settings, respectively. We also used the PHM [1] to calculate a survival function in order to compare the different LAD settings' performances with that of the PHM.

For each observation in the testing set, we calculate the set of conditional probability of survival for the future predictable periods. However, this set is not meaningfully comparable to its matched pair set provided by other experiments. Therefore, we transform the information of the set into a single comparable value, the *Mean Residual Life (MRL)*, so that we can compare performance of different experiments. *MRL* represents the expected value of equipment residual life. The MRL is formulated as following [15]:

$$MRL = \sum_{i=1}^{\infty} i\Delta \times P(\tau > \tau_0 + i\Delta | \tau > \tau_0) \tag{5}$$

Where $P(\tau > \tau_0 + i\Delta | \tau > \tau_0)$ shows the probability of survival for at least i periods, knowing that the equipment has not failed until τ_0. This conditional probability is the conditional survival probability $SP_{obs}(i)$, introduced in this work. So the *MRL* is formulated in terms of $SP_{obs}(i)$ as follows:

$$MRL = \sum_{i=1}^{\infty} i\Delta \times SP_{obs}(i) \tag{6}$$

The measurement compared between different experiments is the absolute value of differences between the MRL and the actual *Residual Life (RL)*. *Friedman matched-pair test* [16] is used to compare the performance of all Hybrid Greedy methods. The best Hybrid Greedy method (*coverage*>10% and *fuzziness*=0), then was compared with the MILP and PHM methods. Comparison shows that the PHM slightly outperforms both LAD methods, while the Hybrid Greedy and MILP methods are not statistically different (see Table 6). However, LAD methods profit from interpretable patterns, and no statistical assumptions.

Table 6. |MRL - RL|: Hybrid Greedy vs. MILP vs. PHM

	Hybrid Greedy	MILP	PHM
Sensitive Discriminating	3.751	3.811	3.507 [+]
Equipartitioning 20	3.748	3.867	3.51 [+]
Equipartitioning 30	3.731	3.826	3.509 [+]
Equipartitioning 40	3.723	3.801	3.51 [+]
Equipartitioning 50	3.728	3.801	3.51 [+]

[+] *Minimum mean value*

Figure 1 shows the difference between the MRL and the actual RL of one of the 15 pieces of equipment, in testing set, using the Hybrid Greedy, the MILP, and the PHM methods. It shows that the LAD methods underestimate the MRL at the early observation moments. As time passes, the estimations get closer to the actual RL, and they correctly estimate the MRL around the mid-age observation moments. Later, when getting closer to the actual failure moment, they overestimate the MRL. The PHM method overestimates the MRL by about one period or more. Overestimation grows as the equipment approaches to its failure.

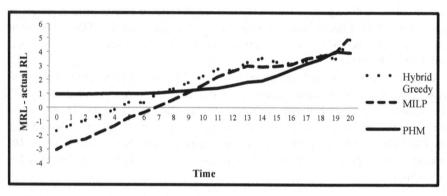

Fig. 1. Difference between MRL and actual RL using the best Hybrid Greedy, MILP, and PHM methods

5   Conclusions

In this research, we extended the LAD methodology to predict equipment's conditional probability of survival. Prognostics using LAD methodology were compared with that using PHM. Comparison with respect to the accuracy of estimated MRL showed that: A conditional survival probability calculation method that equally favors the Baseline and Pattern conditional Survival Probability, statistically outperformed the one that favours the Pattern conditional Survival Probability. The Hybrid Greedy method with the parameters *coverage*>10% and *fuzziness*=0, statistically outperformed the Hybrid Greedy methods with other parameter settings. The PHM statistically slightly outperformed both LAD methods, while the LAD methods were not significantly different.

Our results also showed that the PHM method had an optimistic outlook about the equipment's survival. The LAD methods' outlooks change gradually from pessimistic to optimistic, as the equipment health deteriorates over its lifetime.

However, the LAD has the added advantage of generating meaningful patterns that can be used as indicators of probable failure. It also has the advantage of being free of any statistical assumptions such as the correlation between the attributes, or independance of variables. It has no statistical parameters that need to be estimated, and it has also been proven [3, 18] that LAD is a robust method that reacts very well to incorrect or missing data, which is the case of most real databases. This last property t has not been tested with other methods.

References

1. Jardine, A.K.S., Lin, D., Banjevic, D.: A review on machinery diagnostics and prognostics implementing condition-based maintenance. Mechanical Systems and Signal Processing 20(7), 1483–1510 (2006)
2. Crama, Y., Hammer, P.L., Ibaraki, T.: Cause-effect relationships and partially defined boolean functions. Annals of Operations Research, 16(1) 16(1), 299–326 (1988)
3. Bennane, A., Yacout, S.: LAD-CBM; new data processing tool for diagnosis and prognosis in condition-based maintenance. Journal of Intelligent Manufacturing 23(2), 265–275 (2012)
4. Mortada, M., Carroll, T., Yacout, S., Lakis, A.: Rogue components: Their effect and control using logical analysis of data. Journal of Intelligent Manufacturing 23(2), 289–302 (2012)
5. Mortada, M., Yacout, S., Lakis, A.: Diagnosis of rotor bearings using logical analysis of data. Journal of Quality in Maintenance Engineering 17(4), 371–397 (2011)
6. Yacout, S.: Fault detection and diagnosis for condition based maintenance using the logical analysis of data. In: 2010 40th International Conference on Presented at Computers and Industrial Engineering (CIE) (2010)
7. Boros, E., Hammer, P.L., Ibaraki, T., Kogan, A.: Logical analysis of numerical data. Mathematical Programming 79(1), 163–190 (1997)
8. Kotsiantis, S., Kanellopoulos, D.: Discretization techniques: a recent survey. GESTS Int. Transact. Comput. Sci. Eng. 32, 47–58 (2006)
9. Liu, H., Hussain, F., Tan, C.L., Dash, M.: Discretization: An enabling technique. Data Mining and Knowledge Discovery 6(4), 393–423 (2002)
10. Alexe, S., Hammer, P.L.: Accelerated algorithm for pattern detection in logical analysis of data. Discrete Applied Mathematics 154(7), 1050–1063 (2006)
11. Hammer, P.L., Kogan, A., Simeone, B., Szedmak, S.: Pareto-optimal patterns in logical analysis of data. Discrete Applied Mathematics 144(1-2), 79–102 (2004)
12. Ryoo, H.S.: MILP approach to pattern generation in logical analysis of data. Discrete Applied Mathematics 157(4), 749–761 (2009)
13. Boros, E., Hammer, P.L., Ibaraki, T., Kogan, A., Mayoraz, E., Muchnik, I.: An implementation of logical analysis of data. IEEE Transactions on Knowledge and Data Engineering 12(2), 292–306 (2000)
14. Kaplan, E.L., Meier, P.: Nonparametric estimation from incomplete observations. Journal of the American Statistical Association 53(282), 457–481 (1958)
15. Banjevic, D., Jardine, A.K.S.: Remaining useful life in condition based maintenance: Is it useful? In: Proceedings of MIMAR 2007, the 6th IMA International Conference, pp. 7–12 (2007)
16. Friedman, M.: A comparison of alternative tests of significance for the problem of m rankings. The Annals of Mathematical Statistics 11(1), 86–92 (1940)
17. Boros, E., Crama, Y., Hammer, P., Ibaraki, T., Kogan, A., Makino, K.: Logical analysis of Data: Classification with justification. Rutcor Research Report, RRR 5-2009 (2009)

Designing an Optimal Shape Warehouse

Lucio Compagno, Diego D'Urso, and Natalia Trapani

Dipartimento di Ingegneria Industriale
Università degli Studi di Catania
{lcompagno,ddurso,ntrapani}@dii.unict.it

Abstract. The paper addresses the topic of designing the shape of a warehouse and shows a comparison between a standard storage-handling system, which is designed taking into account the minimization of the handling planar path, and the one which is designed trying to minimizing the overall handling energy consumption. This comparison leads to a discussion on the opportunities which result from the construction of a shallow warehouse in term of building construction costs, layout management and storage surface efficiency. This paper is the first step in the analysis of a more comprehensive research about the life cycle assessment of a warehouse, the manpower utilization and the balanced equilibrium between handling energy requirement and performances of most used handling systems.

Keywords: warehouse design, storage-handling system, sustainability.

1   Introduction

Contemporary literature reviews about research on warehouse design show that a perfect solution of the problem is yet missing [1].

A literature breakdown on warehouse design shows five main focus areas:

- conceptual design;
- sizing & dimensioning;
- internal layout;
- equipment selection;
- operations management optimization.

Sizing & dimensioning and internal layout are the most frequent research issues. Warehouse sizing defines the storage capacity and throughput requirements of a warehouse, while dimensioning translates the capacity requirements into a detailed floor space in order to assess construction and operating costs. Internal layout and equipment have to be assessed in order to achieve the best performances about:

- construction and maintenance costs;
- material handling costs;
- effective storage and throughput capacity;
- space and equipment utilization.

Usually the phases of a warehouse design are developed sequentially and entail an iterative analysis; this recursive procedure becomes as necessary as difficult if the

C. Emmanouilidis, M. Taisch, D. Kiritsis (Eds.): APMS 2012, Part II, IFIP AICT 398, pp. 248–255, 2013.

contribution of operations management strategies to the warehouse capacities is to be considered (e.g. the class based storage strategy reduces storage requirement but increases the throughput time).

Relatively little has been written about the conceptual design; some authors try to define the high level warehouse structure as the type and number of areas (i.e. receiving, storing, order picking, shipping), the equipment and technologies that will be used and the operations strategies that would be implemented: usually the goal is to meet storage and throughput requirements minimizing only the overall discounted cost without an integrated life cycle analysis according to the sustainability methodology.

The state-of-the-art in warehouse designing entails a lot of simplifying hypotheses based on the uncertain knowledge about future operating conditions. On the other hand, there is a significant gap between the literature about warehouse design and operations research and practice, probably due to difficulty of dealing with complex systems design: a principle-based assessment of appropriate decision aiding for these high level design decisions is primarily requested [2], [3], [4, [5].

This paper evaluates the optimal shape of a warehouse and tries to suggest a different way to approach the conceptual design problem, based on the minimum action principle. This paper, principally, tries to move the attention on the human role and its "re-thinking" under a sustainable and not only economic plant scenario [6], [7].

2   Methodology

In order to evaluate the optimal warehouse shape a leading principle was chosen: the principle of minimum action. According to this law, everything happens in order to minimize some kind of mathematical functional. In designing an optimal shape warehouse, the material handling energy consumption was evaluated as such functional.

At this stage we considered only the energy consumption due to material-handling, neglecting the energy balance of the whole warehouse life cycle, as the energy sustainability assessment (e.g. the annual heat transfer, the initial construction energy, the energy requested by the end-of-life management).

Moreover, we didn't take in to account other environmental variables, for instance, the (agricultural) soil consumption.

We imposed also the following hypotheses [8], [9]:

h1. the warehouse geometry belongs to a continuous space;
h2. each point of the warehouse is visited with constant probability;
h3. the start/end point of material handling or picking is placed on a single point and it belongs to a vertex of the warehouse operative area (i/o in Figure 1);
h4. handling/picking requires single command cycles;
h5. the rolling friction coefficient is known and doesn't change with the mass of the unit load.

So the average expected path (P) is (see Figure 1):

$$P = H + W + D \tag{1}$$

where H, W and D are height, width and depth respectively of the operative warehouse volume.

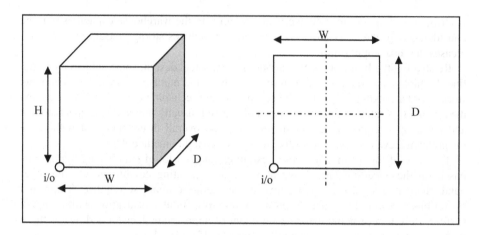

Fig. 1. The warehouse operating volume

The average expected energy consumption (*EC*) can be written as a sum of horizontal and vertical contributions:

$$EC = mg\,[H + r(W + D)]$$ (2)

where, *r* is the rolling friction coefficient.

It can be shown that the minimum expected path and energy consumption on the ground, according to hypothesis h3, happens when:

$$W = D$$ (3)

So the equation (2) can be rewritten in the following form taking into account the constant value of the required warehouse volume V_R:

$$EC = mg(\frac{V_R}{W^2} + 2rW)$$ (4)

The EC function of a single variable can be minimized according to the following differential process:

$$\frac{dEC}{dW} = -2\frac{V_R}{W^3} + 2r = 0 \qquad (5); \; W_{opt} = \sqrt[3]{\frac{V_R}{r}}$$ (6)

We can now arrange again equation (6) in order to derive the optimal warehouse shape: it has a square base and a height that depends on the rolling friction coefficient:

$$W_{opt}W_{opt}^2 = \frac{V_R}{r}$$ (7)

where $V_R = HWD = HW^2 W_{opt} = \sqrt[3]{\frac{V_R}{r}}$; $H_{opt} = rW_{opt}$; $D_{opt} = W_{opt}$.

3   A Case Study

The above mentioned procedure was applied in order to evaluate the optimal shape of a case study warehouse; we called it *optimal shape warehouse* (OSW); this optimal shape warehouse is then compared with a solution (SSW) - that we consider "standard"- of the same logistics problem considering the maximum number of warehouse levels (NL_{SSW}) enabled by the building height.

With regard to the storage system, we assume the two warehouse scenarios are provided with a standard pallet racking solution; with regard to the handling system, we assume the SSW warehouse is also provided by an electric forklift (front loader) whereas the OSW one is provided by a hand pallet truck.

Table 1 shows the performances required to the handling-storage systems; packaging features are also showed.

Table 1. Case study designed performances and packaging features

Variable	Symbol	Value	Units
Designed warehouse performances			
Designed storage capacity	DSC	2.000	ul
Designed handling capacity	DHC	30,0	ul/h
Unit load measures			
Average mass	m	500,0	kg
Width	w	0,80	m
Depth	d	1,20	m
Height	h	0,15	m

Table 2 shows the measure of the unitary module measures of the storage system; those measures take into account the ergonomic handling distances between the unit load and the shelf or among one unit load and the others. To the unitary modules doesn't belong the pillars of the building.

Table 2. Unitary module features

Unit module measures	Symbol	OSW	SSW	Units
Width	UMW	4,30	5,30	m
Depth	UMD	2,90	2,9	m
Height	UMH	1,65	1,65	m
Aisle width	AW	1,80	2,80	m
Horizontal tolerance between unit loads	a	0,10	0,10	m
Horizontal tolerance between unit load and the shelf pillar centre	b	0,15	0,15	m
Vertical tolerance between unit load and the shelf beam centre	c	0,15	0,15	m
Horizontal tolerance between unit loads	e	0,05	0,05	m
Number of unit load per unitary module	NUL	6,0	6,0	-

Two different procedures were followed in order to design the optimal shape and the standard warehouse. Table 3 shows the main steps of calculations.

Table 3. Relevant features and outcomes of the proposed case study (ul = unit load)

Variable	Symbol	Formula OSW	Formula SSW	Value OSW	Value	U.M.
Volume utilization efficiency	VUE	NUL/(UMW UMD UMH)	-	0,28	-	ul/m^3
Requested storage volume	V_R	SC/VUE	-	7.177,5	-	m^3
Net building height/ Uplift height	H_b, H_{up}	-	-	4,0/1,80	117,0	m
Number of warehouse levels	NL	Min(Round down [H_{opt}/UMH]; Round down (H_{up}/UMH])	Min(Round down (H_{up}/UMH]; Round down [H_b/UMH])	2,0	4,0	-
Effective warehouse height	He	NL UMH		3,30	6,60	m
Surface utilization efficiency	CUE	NL(UMW UMD)		0,46	0,39	ul/m^2
Requested operative area	ROA	SC/NL/CUE		2.175,0	1.280,80	m^2
Optimal warehouse width	W_{opt}	$(V_R r)^{1/3}$	$(ROA)^{0,5}$	46,64	35,80	m
Rolling friction coefficient	r			0,02	0,02	-
Optimal warehouse height	H_{opt}	r W_{opt}		1,4	-	m
Number of aisles	NA	Round[ROA^{0,5}/UMW]	Round[W_{opt}/UMW]	10,0	7,0	-
Effective warehouse width	We	NA UMW	NA UMW	45,0	37,10	m
Number of modules	NM	Round[SC''/(NA NUL)]		17,0	12,0	
Effective warehouse depth	De	UMD NM		49,30	34,80	m
Effective storage capacity	ESC	NUL NL NA NM		2.040,0	2.016,0	ul
Expected horizontal /vertical path	EHP/EVP	NA UMW + NM UMD/2 (NL-1) UMH		94,3/1,8	71,9/6,6	m
Average human mass	AHM	-	-	70,0	70,0	kg
Expected handling energy	EHE	½ (M + m) g EHP r + ½ EVP m g + ½ Mg EHP r + MHC	½(M + m + AHM)g EHP r + ½ EVP m g + ½ (M + AHM) g EHP r + MHC	38,10	57,80	kJ/cycle
Forklift mass	M	-		545	2.560	kg
Shift	T			6,0	6,0	h/d
Daily energy consumption	Cd	T EHE		5.482	8.321	kJ/d
Horizontal/uplift forklift speed	Vh/Vv	-		1,16/0,10	2,0/0,5	m/s
Startup handling period	Ts			20	20	s
Single command period	SCP	EHP/Vh + EVP/Vv		89,1	41,1	s

4   Findings

Table 4 shows a comparison among performances of the two above mentioned warehouses; both storage and handling systems fulfill the requested features and have comparable construction costs.

Table 4. OSW and SSW performances comparison

Description	Value		Units	Δ(OSW-SSW)/SSW
	OSW	SSW		
Requested Storage capacity	2.000	2.000	ul	-
Effective Storage capacity	2.040	2.016	ul	+1,19%
Requested handling capacity	24,0	24,0	h^{-1}	-
Effective handling capacity	33,2	59,1	h^{-1}	-43,98%
Daily energy consumption	5.482,45	8.321,38	kJ/d	-34,12%
Requested operative volume	7.321,1	8.521,1	m^3	-14,08%
Requested operative area	2.175,00	1.280,80	m^2	69,81%
Estimated cost of warehouse construction	150.000	140.000	€	7,14%

In order to model the building construction cost (Cc) an additive and parametric cost function was assumed, [10], [11]:

$$C_c = C_s(S, h) + C_f(S, h) + C_p(S', h) + C_g(S, h)$$

where:

C_s is the cost of elevated structure which can be considered as an assemble of precast concrete pillars and beams; C_f is the cost of foundation; C_p is the cost of side walls which are again constituted by precast concrete panels; C_g is the cost of ground surface manufacturing.

The height of the building (h), the covered surface (S) and the building side surface (S') are the main cost drivers; Table 5 shows the analytic correlations which were taken in to account and how the scale factors influence the unitary cost evaluation; at the state of study the building height influences only the cost of the elevated structure; a further analysis is requested in order to better assess the cost reduction which a broader building entails in term of concrete foundation and ground surface arrangement.

At the state of study, material transportation and excavation costs were considered as not differential between the two scenarios. As regards to storage and handling systems we can again consider the procurement and assemble costs as no differential.

Table 5. Drivers of main industrial building construction costs

Cost description	Symbol	Driver	SSW	OSW	Units	Equation
building elevated structure	C_s	S, h	41,47	33,42	€/m²	$C_s = (-8,495 \ln(S) + 98,2)(1+k(h))$
building perimeter walls	C_p	S'	51,00	47,08	€/m²	$C_p = 0,0014\ S' + 36,91$
building foundation	C_f	S, h	5,28	5,01	€/m²	$C_f = -0,568\ln(S) + 9,3438$
building ground surface	C_g	S, h	20,00	15,00	€/m²	$C_g = -11,28\ \ln(S) + 102,28$

The optimal shape warehouse (OSW), which is provided by a simpler material handling system, shows quite the same start up cost of the standard shape one (SSW) but enables a great reduction of the handling energy consumption.

The developed case study points out the following issues.

First of all, the optimal shape of a warehouse is broader than we would expect; that's because we take into account the energy consumption in a three dimensional handling problem with slip factors that change enormously moving from a horizontal path to a vertical one.

This broader geometric solution enables the manual material handling by using manual hand trucks.

Under the same boundary conditions, the requested manual material handling activity is comparable with the one of a slow walker (3,0 MET, Metabolic Equivalent of Task, [12]).

On the other side a broader warehouse can be structurally constituted by the same shelves which are used as a storage system; the focus can be now moved on the following opportunities:

1. a further cost reduction can be accomplished as a consequence of a more distributed mass load on foundation;
2. a more efficient surface utilization can be achieved if building pillar are inside the storage system;
3. a more sustainable building can be realised by using recycled material or innovative material with regard to the heat transfer;
4. a flexible layout management due to the disassembling capability allowed by this construction method.

Finally we want to point out another feature of the discussed optimal shape warehouse: the requested handling power is comparable with the power of the handling system implemented; the same requested handling power is comparable with the one provided by human activity; so a further analysis could verify if human material handling can be introduced, for example when a unit load has to be pushed during a horizontal path, in order to optimize the operations energy consumption.

5   Conclusions and Future Works

The optimal warehouse shape is square base, according to the position of the single input/output point, and has a height that depends on the rolling friction coefficient. Due to the rolling friction coefficient value, $r \approx 0,02$, a minimum energy consumption warehouse should be shallow ($H = rW$). A shallow warehouse enables the manual material handling and requires resources that belong to a natural life style (daily energy requirement), as shown in the above mentioned case study.

This study doesn't consider any discounted cash flow rate of return about the warehouse-plant but it wants to consider the warehouse design process from another points of view: the human, the natural and the sustainable one.

A further analysis is to be performed in order to quantify the contribution of energy and material balance during the phases of warehouse construction, operating life and end of life.

The above mentioned case study can be considered as a preliminary analysis of a whole life cycle assessment. The study points out on a better tradeoff between the effective handling-system energy requirement and the potential which is usually implemented.

References

1. Gu, J., Goetschalckx, M., McGinnis, L.F.: Research on warehouse design and performance evaluation: A comprehensive review. European Journal of Operational Research 203, 539–549 (2010)
2. Baker, P., Canessa, M.: Warehouse design: A structured approach. European Journal of Operational Research 193, 425–436 (2009)
3. Ashayeri, J., Gelders, L.F.: Warehouse design optimization. European Journal of Operational Research 21, 285–294 (1985)
4. Apple, J.: Plant Layout and Material Handling, 3rd edn. John Wiley, New York (1977)
5. Rouwenhorst, B., Reuter, B., Stockrahm, V., Van Houtum, G.J., Mantel, R.J., Zijm, W.H.M.: Warehouse design and control: Framework and literature review. European Journal of Operational Research 122(3), 515–533 (2000)
6. Cormier, G., Kersey, D.F.: Conceptual design of a warehouse for just-in-time operations in a bakery. Computers and Industrial Engineering 29(1-4), 361 (1995)
7. Hung, M.S., Fisk, C.J.: Economic sizing of warehouses – A linear programming approach. Computers and Operations Research 11(1), 13–18 (1984)
8. Caron, F., Marchet, G., Perego, A.: Routing policies and COI-based storage policies in picker-to-part systems. International Journal of Production Research 36(3), 713–732 (1998)
9. Caron, F., Marchet, G., Perego, A.: Optimal layout in low-level picker-to-part systems. International Journal of Production Research 38(1), 101–117 (2000)
10. Cosenza, E., Fabbrocino, G., Iervolino, I., Lando, M.: Preventivazione sintetica del costo degli edifici industriali prefabbricati. Impiantistica Italiana, Anno XV (1), 43–50 (2002)
11. PCI Design Habdbook, Precast and Prestressed Concrete, 5th edn., PCI Institute, Chicago (1999)
12. Ainsworth, B.E., Haskell, W.L., Herrmann, S.D., Meckes, N., Bassett, D.R., Tudor-Locke, C., Greer, J.L., Vezina, J., et al.: 2011 Compendium of Physical Activities. Medicine & Science in Sports & Exercise 43(8), 1575–1581 (2011)

A Fourth Party Energy Provider for the Construction Value Chain: Identifying Needs and Establishing Requirements

Sergio Cavalieri, Stefano Ierace, Nicola Pedrali, and Roberto Pinto

CELS – Research Center on Logistics and After Sales Services
Department of Engineering, University of Bergamo
Viale Marconi, 5 - I - 24044 Dalmine, Italy
{sergio.cavalieri,stefano.ierace,nicola.pedrali,
roberto.pinto}@unibg.it

Abstract. Today's building and energy management market is heterogeneous and complex. Most of the players in the construction market are not in possession of the managerial capability to fully control the dynamics that affect their energy costs in terms of energy sourcing and energy management. Moreover, construction industry needs to rely on a stronger technical and commercial expertise. On one hand, there is a need of an in-depth and extensive level of technical know-how that most of facility managers, property developers and building owners at private and public level scarcely hold. On the other hand, this industry is characterized by a fragmentation within the single tiers of the value chain. In this context, the paper aims at proposing a new vision of the building value chain towards a collaborative network led by a new player, namely the Fourth Party Energy Provider, acting as the "one-stop contracting and managing" operator, integrating resources, capabilities, best available technologies and practices for providing energy-efficient building solutions.

Keywords: Sustainable manufacturing, Construction Industry, Energy efficiency, 4PEP (Fourth Party Energy Provider).

1 Introduction

The construction industry today plays a relevant role in the European context in which it is responsible for more than 11% of the European GDP and with 32 million people employed [1]. Also from the environmental point of view, this industry plays a critical role since the buildings are the major actors in terms of energy consumption (more than 40%) and emissions (about 33%) at European level [2]. In addition, the average age of buildings, which is very high, has a negative impact on the building energy performance.

A more in-depth analysis needs to take into account also the rules provided by standardization organizations. On March 2007, the European Council underlined the need to increase energy efficiency within the European Union to achieve the goal of reducing by 20% the power consumption in 2020. This action plan has identified the

C. Emmanouilidis, M. Taisch, D. Kiritsis (Eds.): APMS 2012, Part II, IFIP AICT 398, pp. 256–264, 2013.

significant potential for energy savings effective in terms of costs in construction. To achieve the goal of 20% reduction in energy consumption, the European Union has adopted directive 2010 31/CE [3] through which are set guidelines for improving building energy performance: (i) methodology for the calculation of energy performance, (ii) establishment of minimum requirements in terms of energy efficiency, (iii) nearly zero energy buildings, (iv) certification system of energy performance, (v) system control and independent experts.

Despite the regulatory and standardization efforts, in the construction market most of the players are not in possession of the managerial capability to fully control the dynamics that affect their energy costs, in terms of energy sourcing and energy management. There is the evident risk for them to sustain high financial costs, not neglecting the indirect strong environmental and social impact. This complexity is further challenged by the need to have a building lifecycle management perspective, which stretches over a temporal dimension the structure of a construction value chain.

In addition, this specific value chain is characterized by a high fragmentation and heterogeneity of actors. As depicted in Figure 1, involved roles in this value chain are local authorities, capital providers, developers, agents, materials and equipment suppliers, contractors, engineers, designers, owners and users. Most of the operating companies are SMEs or even micro-companies normally specialized in the provision of a specific technology with often a short-sighted vision of their role within the value chain.

The complexity of interaction among these participants is one of the greatest barriers to energy efficient buildings. All the above mentioned players do have their specific impact on the energy consumption of a building throughout its life cycle.

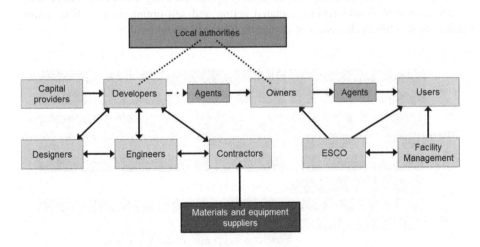

Fig. 1. The actors involved in the construction value chain (adapted from [4])

In this context, the paper aims at tackling some peculiar issues of the construction industry, considering in particular:

- which are the current models for the evaluation of the building energy performance during its whole lifecycle (thus not only considering the usage phase);
- the potential role of a new actor, namely the 4PEP (Fourth Party Energy Provider), who would act as the mediator between the constellation of companies operating in a construction network and a generic client, in order to manage the whole construction lifecycle processes and master the enabling technologies required.

2   Nature of the Construction Value Chain

In the construction value chain, a client has to interact with a multitude of suppliers, each providing a specific competence and accounting for a narrow slice of the overall energy bill. In some cases, the customer selects the manufacturer (contractor), the suppliers of specialist parts and the material suppliers. This raises up several issues since: (i) more independent organizations are involved, often with reciprocal conflicting interests; (ii) there are evident diseconomies in terms of transactional costs, having to relate with a multitude of players; (iii) single decisions are made in different phases of the building lifecycle with different counterparts, thus creating evident inconsistencies; (iv) it is not possible to define a fully comprehensive performance-based contract, but rather local service level agreements with the single service providers [5], [6], [7].

A collaborative value chain approach is needed where the client could be involved from the early moments in co-creating the value of such a relation. Information and material flows relevant to energy efficiency and a comprehensive environmental assessment would be established between the players, and integrated collaboration with a common goal would replace isolated acting and self-optimization. These actors should have a life cycle vision of a building, very often neglected.

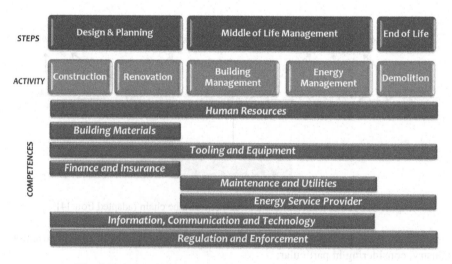

Fig. 2. Building lifecycle: main phases and competences required

Two different models are identified in literature in order to perform a lifecycle energetic and environmental assessment:

a) Multi-criteria Indicators models which take into account several dimensions affecting an environmental assessment such as: material and energy consumption, people "energy behavior", material recycling and re-use, pollutant emission reductions, water consumption. Hereafter the most relevant multi criteria models are reported:

- *BREEAM (Building Research Establishment Environmental Assessment Method)* developed by the Building Research Establishment, which takes into account seven criteria to perform building life cycle assessment: (i) energy; (ii) transport, (iii) pollution, (iv) materials (v) water, (vi) region features and (vii) health; for each criterion a specific evaluation is provided [8]

- *LEED (Leadership in Energy and Environmental Design)* which takes into account seven criteria: (i) site sustainability, (ii) water management, (iii) energy, (iv) materials, (v) internal environmental quality, (vi) innovation in design and (vii) regional priorities [9].

- *GBtool (Green Building Tool)* which classifies a building using four hierarchical levels: (i) performance classes, (ii) performance categories, (iii) performance criteria and (iv) sub-criteria [10].

- *CASBEE (Comprehensive Assessment System for Built Environment Efficiency)* which evaluates the building energy performance in different building phases: (i) pre-design, (ii) design and (iii) post-design [11].

b) Synthetic Indicators models, which take into account quantitative analyses rather than qualitative ones. The most relevant model in this category is represented by the life cycle assessment (LCA) methodology which provides a quantitative assessment of the "consumption" of a building in its lifecycle considering also the design and the end of life phases, traditionally neglected in the construction field [12].

In table 1 a review of multi-criteria indicators and synthetic indicators is provided, underlying the main benefits and weaknesses of each model.

Table 1. A comparison between Multi Criteria and Synthetic models

Model	Main weaknesses	Main strenghts	Threaths
Multi criteria	• Procedural simplifications • Scoring systems • Using quantitative and qualitative indicators • Unreliable and misleading results • Using a prescriptive legislation	• Results clear and easily understandable • Possibility to carry out self-certification • Very popular model	• Diversification of the results according to the used model • Economic and political difficulties for its application
Synthetic	• Need of a high number of information • Analysis performed by specialists • Lack of data from literature	• Detailed and reliable analysis • Focus on the entire building life cycle • Using quantitative indices • Use of performance norms	• Economic and political difficulties for its application

From the extensive literature review conducted by [13], although LCA is recognized as an innovative methodology which could improve sustainability in the construction industry, it emerges that there has been a large number of LCA studies which merely deal with a specific part of the building life cycle. Only few of them really encompass the whole life span. In their concluding remarks, the same authors strongly maintain how entities involved in the construction industry must be proactive in creating environmental, social and economic indicators, which bring about building sector sustainability and promote the use of consistent construction practices.

What is missing is a common platform where all the different actors operating in a construction consortium could have a mutual understanding of their role and their contribution in terms of real added value and impact on the overall lifecycle of a building, not neglecting the involvement of the customer. Without this platform there is the evident risk that any environmental and energetic assessment would be quite myopic to the specific lifecycle phase (i.e. either on its construction or on its use) or peculiar to the instances and objectives of the single operator. In addition, it would be too generic, since it needs to consider also the habits and requirements of the users that will be living in the building during its existence.

What could fill this gap is the definition of a building value framework based on the concept of a business model. In the most basic sense, a business model is the method of doing business by which a company can generate profit. It spells out how a company makes money or gets paid [14], by specifying how it intends to create value to all the stakeholders [15].

Literature definitions about the concept underlying a business model are various and heterogeneous. Quite acknowledged in literature is the Business Model Canvas by Osterwalder and Pigneur [16] which has been tested in various organizations. The model is composed by nine building blocks: (a) *Customer segments*, defines the different groups of people or organizations an enterprise aims to reach and serve; (b) *Value propositions*, describes the bundle of products and services that create value for a specific Customer Segment; (c) *Channels*, describes how a company communicates with and reaches its Customer Segments to deliver a Value Proposition; (d) *Customer Relationships*, describes the types of relationships a company establishes with specific Customer Segments; (e) *Revenue Streams*, represents the cash a company generates from each Customer Segment (costs must be subtracted from revenues to create earnings); (f) *Key Resources*, describes the most important assets required to make a business model work; (g) *Key Activities*, describes the most important things a company must do to make its business model work; (h) *Key Partnerships*, describes the network of suppliers and partners that make the business model work; (i) *Cost Structure*, describes all costs incurred to operate a business model.

Many authors argue that business models are not able to deliver long term goals due to their focus on short-term, internal and financial performance. This is particularly true for the current business models in the energy management and construction area, which are characterized by self-optimization and a strong focus of the individual companies instead of focusing the attention on the value provided to the customer [17]. The idea of the 4PEP Business Model - that will be described in the next section - is to overcome this issue in order to provide a comprehensive business model for the whole construction chain.

3   The Proposed Model: The 4PEP Energy Provider

This section is devoted to the description of a new acting role in the building value chain: the Fourth Party Energy Provider (4PEP). It represents an integrator that assembles the resources, capabilities, and technology of more organizations to design, build and manage a solution for fulfilling the specific needs and composite requests related to the energy aspects drawn from the construction market, by:

- actively involving the customer in the creation of a value added solution;
- acting on the levers that impact on energy costs (mainly in terms of price and quantity);
- selecting the best available technologies and practices for the specific situation;
- qualifying and selecting the key actors, according to their competences, assigning them a specific role in the emerging construction value chain;
- mastering all the dynamics that affect the building lifecycle;
- being the main responsible in the elaboration, monitoring and accomplishment of PBEE (Performance Based Energy Efficient) contracts, and relative KPIs towards the customer.

The term 4PEP finds its root in the homologous player in the manufacturing logistic context, namely the Fourth-Party Logistics (4PL) provider. The 4PL concept was put forward by the consulting group Accenture. The essence and core superiority of this concept lies in its ability to integrate the supply chain resources, through integrating the most high-quality resources (individuals) of the supply chain. A 4PL offers services considering a 360 degree view, which is not focused only on its ability to implement the recommendations it gives, but on all the technological and managerial options available in the market [18]. In a sum, a 4PL provider manage and direct the activities of multiple 3PLs, serving as an integrator. In this way, a 4PL can leverage the whole supply chain network from an integrated perspective rather than from a specific, narrow perspective related to a single service category.

The main tasks performed by the 4PEP are not fully and consistently achievable if they are not supported by a specific toolbox of processes, methodologies and tools. The 4PEP would fill the current gap by adopting a Business Model Framework for the construction industry with a corresponding subset of tools and methods which empowers it to develop specific business models in order to evolve from offering standalone standard services to integrated solutions.

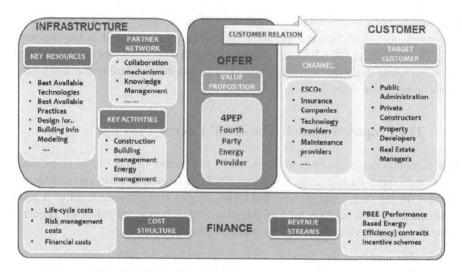

Fig. 3. The 4PEP Business Model Framework

As highlighted in Figure 3, the 4PEP Business Model Framework would rely on a specifically designed business model ontology, based on the Osterwalder and Pigneur's canvas, in order to share a common and standardised terminology and with an explicit definition of the relations between the constructs (i.e. from a technological, organizational, managerial, financial perspective) identified as a source of value for fulfilling the specific needs and requests from the market.

The implementation of a 4PEP Business Model Software Platform would be crucial for gaining concrete results of this vision. It would provide the collaborative environment involving the 4PEP focal actor and the different stakeholders in the emerging creation of a customised business model and in simulating its affordability, robustness and durability throughout the whole building lifecycle.

In particular, it would support a stage–gate process, where "gates" or decision points are placed at specific phases of the 4PEP business model development process, and embed in its functionality a dashboard for monitoring throughout a contract lifecycle the main technical and financial KPIs in order to enable a prompt understanding of any deviations from expected targets SLAs (Service Level Agreements) and highlight eventual counter-measures.

4   Conclusions

This papers stems from the consideration that in the construction industry there is a need of an actor integrating competences and companies in this fragmented market. The presence of the 4PEP would quite relevant since it could act as the "one-stop contracting and managing" operator providing a direct and durable relation with the customer. The potential behind this concept is quite evident if we refer to public administrations where the low managerial capability, the multitude of contracts to deal with, as well as the need to maintain a continuous monitoring of their performance can become quite compelling and affect the overall quality of a public-private partnership.

Some issues are also open: (i) which are the main competences and capabilities required for such an actor? (ii) is there a need of new professionals or are these skills already available in some companies (i.e. Energy Service Companies or within the same construction companies)?

Moreover, for this research it is fundamental to focus also on the technology and tools for enabling the business models, in particular:

- Building Technology Solutions: technologies related to building both in design, construction and usage phase (HVAC, advanced material, ...);
- energy performance models in order to monitor and improve the performance of the building;
- coordination and collaboration mechanism among the whole building value chain in order to involve the different partners towards the same main objective.

The next steps of this research will be mainly devoted to design the main constructs at the basis of the 4PEP business model and to apply this vision to a pilot study on the renovation of a building stock related to social housing.

References

[1] IEA (2001), International Energy Agency: World Energy Outlook,
http://www.iea.org/weo/

[2] Buildings Performance Institute Europe (BPIE), Cost optimality - Discussing methodology and challenges within the recast Energy Performance of Buildings Directive (2010) ISBN: 9789491143021

[3] Directive 2010/31/EU of the European Parliament and of the Council of 19 May 2010 on the energy performance of buildings (2010),
http://eur-lex.europa.eu/LexUriServ/
LexUriServ.do?uri=CELEX:32010L0031:EN:NOT

[4] WBCSD (World Business Council for Sustainable Development) Energy Efficiency in Buildings: Facts and Trends—Full Report (2008),
http://www.wbcsd.org/DocRoot/qUjY7w54vY1KncL32OVQ/
EEB-Facts-and-trends.pdf

[5] Akintoye, A., McIntosh, G., Fitzgerald, E.: A survey of supply chain collaboration and management in the UK construction industry. European Journal of Purchasing & Supply Management 6, 159–168 (2000)

[6] Vrijhoef, R., Koskela, L.: The four roles of supply chain management in construction. European Journal of Purchasing & Supply Management 6(3-4), 169–178 (2000)

[7] Saad, M., Jones, M., James, P.: A review of the progress towards the adoption of supply chain management (SCM) relationships in construction. European Journal of Purchasing & Supply Management 8(3), 173–183 (2002)

[8] Building Research Establishment Environmental Assessment Method,
http://www.bream.org

[9] United States Green Building Council, Foundations of the Leadership in Energy and Environmental Design, Environmental Rating System, A Tool for Market Transformation (2006)

[10] Green Building Challenge, GBtool User Manual (2002)

[11] Comprehensive Assessment System for Built Environment Efficiency, http://www.ibec.or.jp/CASBEE/english

[12] Erlandsson, M., Borg, M.: Generic LCA-methodology applicable for buildings, constructions and operation services—today practice and development needs. Building and Environment 38(7), 919–938 (2003)

[13] Ortiz, O., Castells, F., Sonnemann, G.: Sustainability in the construction industry: A review of recent developments based on LCA. Construction and Building Materials 23(1), 28–39 (2009)

[14] Chesbrough, H., Rosenbloom, R.: The role of the business model in capturing value from innovation: evidence from Xerox Corporation's technology spin-off companies. Industrial and Corporate Change 11(3), 529–555 (2002)

[15] Linder, J., Cantrell, S.: Changing Business Models: Surveying the Landscape. Accenture Institute for Strategic Change (2000)

[16] Osterwalder, A., Pigneur, Y.: Business Model Generation – A Handbook for Visionaries, Game Changers and Challengers. John Wiley and Sons, Inc., Hoboken (2010)

[17] Kouloura, C., Genikomsakis, K.N., Protopapas, A.L.: Energy management in buildings: A systems approach. Systems Engineering Journal 3, 263–275 (2008)

[18] Yao, J.: Decision optimization analysis on supply chain resource integration in fourth party logistics. Journal of Manufacturing Systems 29(4), 121–129 (2010)

Performance Measurement Systems for Craft-Oriented Small Enterprises

Inger Gamme[1], Eva Amdahl Seim[2], and Eirin Lodgaard[3]

[1] Gjøvik University College, Gjøvik, Norway
inger.gamme@hig.no
[2] Norwegian University of Science and Technology, Trondheim, Norway
eva.amdahl.seim@sintef.no
[3] SINTEF Raufoss Manufacturing, Raufoss, Norway
eirin.lodgaard@sintef.no

Abstract. Many leisure boat manufacturers have thrived on designing and building highly customized boats based on longstanding traditions of craftsmanship. The industry is to some extent moving towards the paradigm of "Mass Customization" in which the low cost of mass production is combined with customization.

Existing research on performance measurement systems (PMS), covers in little extent the implementation process and use of PMS in SMEs (small and medium sized enterprises). In this article, important elements for implementing a PMS and how it relates to creating a learning environment have been identified.

Keywords: SMEs, Performance Measurement System, Crafts man, Continuous Improvement.

1 Introduction

Craft oriented small enterprises make up the vast majority of SMEs in Europe, and contributes the main share of job creation in the European Union [1]. Furthermore, SMEs are shown to be important to the maintenance of a sustainable industrial economy, as they are assumed to be the main driving force in future economic growth in industrialized world economics. They often belong to the craft and artisan sector, and employ around one third of the total European workforce [2].

In an ever-changing environment, work conditions are becoming more complex, and what was considered good or core competence yesterday might not be so today. Competition in modern craft industries require craft manufacturers and their supply chains to innovate, improve, and increase their efficiency to meet the challenges from globalization and other forces for change [3]. The leisure boat industry is one example of an industry in which manufacturers are facing increased competition. In particular, the advance of industrialized leisure boat manufacturers is putting even high quality craft based "high end" manufacturers under strong competitive pressure. These manufacturers and their supply chains are now grappling with the challenge of how to meet

C. Emmanouilidis, M. Taisch, D. Kiritsis (Eds.): APMS 2012, Part II, IFIP AICT 398, pp. 265–272, 2013.

this competitive pressure while preserving their unique quality of craft production [4]. A way for companies to deal with these dynamic and changing conditions could be to link strategies to overall objectives, to ensure a level of standardization. Although the importance of performance measurement is emphasized in the literature, it is rarely used in SMEs. Existing literature on performance measurement in SMEs does to a small extent capture the differences between using PMS in larger organizations versus using them in SMEs. However, after the realization that SMEs are not smaller versions of larger firms, but rather differed from larger firms in fundamental ways, the focus on management and performance measurement emerged [5]. The purpose of this paper is to contribute to a better understanding of the challenges in implementing a PMS in a craft-oriented small enterprise.

2   Theory

2.1   Craft-Oriented SMEs

Craft manufacturing still plays an important role in the economy. Principles and skills related to craft manufacturing has shown to be important for e.g. European economies to compete with new evolving economies. However, also craft manufacturing has to adapt to new manufacturing principles to be competitive. The focus on quality and time are critical to minimize waste, and obtain a high productivity performance level. As they deal with increased complexity in manufacturing, and some adoption of formalized managerial practice, PMS is especially important to support the required managerial development in order to meet market needs [6]. Moving from a craft oriented production to a more streamlined production with higher production volumes, requires more standardized processes and trained workers. The "knowledge stair" illustrates what is called an evolution of a "built to order" craft company into an industrialization process, where it is possible to lift the production step by step [7].

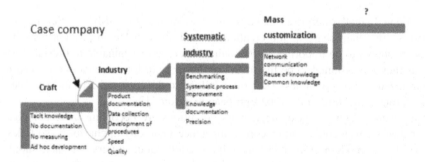

Fig. 1. Our company is currently in between the craft and industry level in the knowledge stairs presented by Svensson [7]

'SMEs tend to have different needs and decision making process than larger firms [8]. Hence, operational processes seems to be more acknowledged than managerial processes, the organizational knowledge is mainly tacit, decision-making processes are poorly formalized and there is little understanding of the benefits of implementing a PMS. Craft oriented small enterprises are typically less formal organized with an ad hoc decision making structure [6]. Essential knowledge is often kept by few vital employees, which could be critical, especially in periods with high turnover of skilled workers [9]. To achieve organizational learning it is important to share tacit knowledge[10], and even though the SMEs may have a competitive advantage in being less bureaucratic and use of more informal communication than larger companies, it is also a need for more formal communication in the SMEs [11]. A study by Lovett [9] confirms that the information flow in SMEs mainly is informal, which could make it difficult for the management to get a complete overview of the use of knowledge and information within the organization. A way to improve the communication process, could be to use visual tools (like team boards), which means that every person involved must be able to see and understand different aspects of the process and its status at any time [12]. This will make the process more transparent and enabling feedback of current status [13]. Six basic mechanisms to integrate, or coordinate work in organizations are suggested: mutual adjustment, direct supervision, standardization of work, outputs, skills and norms. Mutual awareness enables individual workers to coordinate themselves by adjusting their own work to the work of others during the unfolding of activities and requires understanding of ongoing activities [14].

Larger companies often have more financial flexibility than small companies; and therefor easier could adjust to short time variations. Furthermore, SMEs tend to have a flat organization structure with few resources, which means that the same employees often have several job roles [15]. This shows the importance of using PMS to assure elements such as customer satisfaction, minimizing waste etc. even though the company has limited resources.

2.2   Performance Measurement

A PMS can be defined as *"a system which is based on multi-dimensional performance measures that are derived from organization strategy with the purpose to implement the strategy, evaluate business performance, provide feedback and ensure communication, help in creating a learning environment and continuously improving the organization"* [16]. Further, it can be illustrated as an instrument panel, which provides necessary information to enable employees at all levels of the organization to make the right decisions [17]. Most PMS's in use in SMEs today are of typical informal character, unstructured and mainly focusing on financial figures [15]. Additional research on *"what can (not) be done in small organizations?"* is required [18].

A resource effective PMS process is recommended, with short term benefits from the performance measures and also flexibility enough to cope with changes in strategy. This process focuses on establishing only one objective at a time with short term benefits, hence there will always be some measures fully implemented even though the implementation process stops after some iterations [15]. It is also important to put existing systems into an overall framework, and develop it together with additional new modules, when implementing new PMS. Occasionally generation of new systems without foundation and inter-linkage to overall system, should not be allowed [19]. Two drivers and four blockers can influence the success or failure of the implementation. The two driving factors are top management commitment and apprehended benefits from the process, while the four main obstacles are defined as: Lack of time and resources, insufficient access to necessary data, resistance to the PMS process and change of focus from parent company [20].

Many PMS implementation processes fail to succeed because the psychological effects of the PMS have not been taken into consideration. One of the most typical pitfalls is using measures on a personal level, where characters being measured can be tracked to one person. Finding excuses for poor performance figures, and therefore not striving to continuous improve them, could be other obstacles in achieving good performance system. There is also seen that the targets become the limit for continuous improvements; Organizations are satisfied when targets are reached, without aiming for further improvement [17]. To better cover the complete challenge that the companies face, there is a need for a more holistic system-based approach [5] [19].

3   Method and Material

3.1   Introduction Case Company

The case is a part of a larger research project where the main objective was to develop an effective, competitive and profitable production within leisure boat and craft oriented industry in Norway. The company is a craft oriented leisure boat producer with approximately 20 employees. The production line consists of three departments; molding, pre-assembly and assembly. The overall project period was from 2008 until 2012, focusing on modularization and standardization of work processes. The challenge of the project has been to keep or improve the high quality level and customization that has characterized the craft manufacturing, but at the same time be more cost efficient. Furthermore, preservation of the craft tradition in addition to industrialization was emphasized to improve the competitive ability of the industry.

Even though the organization has made steps towards integration of its internal supply chain, it has a quite functional oriented structure, with several potentially built-in delays and inventories. There are very few formal reporting structures and systems, and those that exists are to a little extent process-oriented. However, there are a lot of contact and communication between the people in the manufacturing process and also between the technical resources in planning, problem solving etc. The manufacturing processes are mainly manually and adjustments are made all along the production process. There are few figures which are being measured today, and the main measure is "number boats produced per week". The quality of the manufactured boats is perceived by the market to be very high. Summarized, the company has several of the characteristics from the previously described craft manufacturing.

3.2   Data Collection

We have used mixed methods with field and interview based studies among operators in the production line in a single craft oriented small enterprise. The researchers participated in project meetings at the leisure boat manufacturer in a research project aimed at improving their competitiveness. This included project board meetings, task meetings and workshops related to the projects. The interview session consisted of 12 in-depth interviews with operators from different process steps of the production line. A document analysis was carried out focusing on strategic documents. There were also performed a study of the measurement-, quality-, and planning systems. However, most of the time was spent at the shop floor together with the workers in action research. Action research is a valuable method where both researchers and professionals at a company collaborate to develop theory in the field. The action research cycle – diagnosing, planning, action, reflection, and evaluation of the results – was followed during the research [21].

4   Findings and Discussion

Current layout in the production line gives challenges in achieving transparency in the value chain. The production area is divided into sections where the operators are working in separate compartments which affect the information flow. The operators are not familiar with working in teams. Moving towards industrialization (knowledge stairs), it is necessary to formalize the information flow. To improve the transparency in the production area and create a learning environment with common arenas for information sharing and collaboration, team boards were introduced as the first step in a PMS implementation process. However, interviews and field studies revealed some resistance to this process.

Fig. 2. Obtaining organizational learning through team boards

Three main issues have affected the PMS implementation process; (1) Lack of confidence in and compliance with established systems among the operators, (2) The operators do not see the need for any new system, and focus only upon their own process step and (3) Mainly single sourced information flow, and mostly linked through the foreman.

Lack of confidence in and compliance with established systems among operators:
Through several expressions, an apparent overall lack of confidence in and compliance with established systems (production plans, process descriptions etc.) was revealed. As a part of the research project, several new systems were established, and one of these systems was a visual inventory control. The operators were responsible for the implementation process, and participated actively and apparently eagerly in this process, and seemed to be satisfied with the new system. However, the researchers became aware of incomplete or inconsistent compliance with the system and some operators even indicated that someone was sabotaging the new system.

Each operation had a satellite storage containing some of the smaller components, In addition to this; some operators also had their own additional safety stock, since they did not trust the storage system to secure supplies at all time. Some also indicated that the reliability of the system was dependent on which operator was responsible for the ordering process. The production plan was occasionally referred to as "not always correct". As compensation for the mistrust, the operators communicated the data orally. Some operators questioned if the reports produced at deviations were used for improvements at all, and could be seen as a tool for controlling and justifying, and to find out who is responsible when something goes wrong, instead of finding out what went wrong. Additionally some claimed that if deviations were too large, it would be hushed up, and no action would be taken.

The operators do not see a need for any new system, and focus only upon their own process step: Although the standardization process had been going on for a while, a lack of ownership to the system was noticed. Several of the operators said they were satisfied with the current situation, and that any further improvements would only be experienced as superfluous workload, which fits in with Garengo's [6] observation, that one of the main obstacles when introducing PMS in SMEs, is the perception of PMSs as a bureaucratic an rigid system. The production people, with facilitation of the researchers, were given the authority to run the PMS process. However, some operators seemed to perceive the implementation process to be minor important, since the management did not directly participate, and therefore seemed to have focus on other issues.

The work load per operator is more difficult to identify when the production line is unorganized. Thus, an understanding of the inter-relationship between their process-step and other process steps could be lacking. In order to facilitate coordination among the workers, expedient approaches to information sharing and transparency seem necessary. The information was mainly informal, and to some extent occasionally who got the information. This shows the importance of information coordination in order to create a learning environment[16]. The operators trust the foremen to give them the needed information, and they feel that further information was not necessary.

Mainly single sourced information flow, and often linked through the foreman:
The foremen are the main sources for both the horizontal and the vertical information flow. Information sharing through meetings or arenas for information sharing such as team boards etc. was among some operators considered as superfluous. Some of them commented: "It is not necessary; we just go and talk to each other".

Between the operators it seemed to be a mutual adjustment mechanism, whereby two or more people equally adapt to each other, usually by informal communication, in order to flexible handle unexpected happenings [14]. Coordination between the foreman and the operators consist of direct supervision, where the foreman is the responsible for coordinating the work. There is also a risk that the foreman becomes a bottleneck in coordination and information sharing, when verbatim work coordination is the only solution.

5   Conclusion

Based on the case study, it has been shown that there exist different challenges when implementing a PMS. The experiences from this case study indicate the importance of finding the correct degree of implementation of a PMS which fits this type of organization. When an organization establishes a new system such as PM, it must be considered how to proceed for the implementation phase to achieve successful integration. First, we recommend putting management commitment to PMS as the base or foundation. Once the foundation is in place, attention should be given to the implementation process and how to proceed. Without the management commitment and direct involvement in the implementation process the usefulness of the PMS is expected to be limited. Resistance towards implementation of new systems among the operators must also be taken into consideration. One way to reduce this resistance could be to ensure that the employees actively participate in the implementation process, which further could contribute to a better confidence and compliance with new systems. Although operators themselves are highly skilled, collaboration with the management function is important to develop a common understanding of the impact and the need of a PMS, and also ensure the linkage towards the overall strategy.

Literature indicates that use of team boards may be valuable to formalize information flows and collaboration between management and workers. Based on the findings from our research, we find this type of tool helpful to strengthen both the horizontal and vertical communication and information flow. Furthermore it can contribute to reveal tacit knowledge and increase organizational transparency, and through visual follow-up ensure the success of the PMS implementation process.

References

1. Buschfeld, D., Dilger, B., Hess, L., Schmid, K., Voss, E.: Identification of Future Skills Needs in Micro and Craft (-type) Enterprises up to 2020. Final report, Cologne, Hamburg, Vienna (January 2011)
2. de Vries, H., Margaret, J.: The Development of a Model to Assess the Strategic Management Capability of Small- and Medium-Size Businesses. Journal of American Academy of Business 3, 85–85 (2003)

3. O'Sullivan, D., Rolstadås, A., Filos, E.: Global Education in Manufacturing Strategy. Journal of Intelligent Manufacturing 22, 663–674 (2011)
4. Økland, A., Lillebo, B., Amdahl, E., Seim, A.: A Framework for Transparency. In: POMS 21st Annual Conference, Vancouver, Canada (2010)
5. Bititci, U., et al.: Performance Measurement: Challenges for Tomorrow. International Journal of Management Reviews (2011)
6. Garengo, P., Biazzo, S., Bititci, U.S.: Performance Measurement Systems in SMEs: A review for a Research Agenda. International Journal of Management Reviews 7, 25–47 (2005)
7. Svensson, C., Barfod, A.: Limits and Opportunities in Mass Customization for "Build to Order" SMEs. Computers in Industry 49, 77–89 (2002)
8. Shrader, C.B., Mulford, C.L., Blackburn, V.L.: Strategic and Operational Planning, Uncertainty, and Performance in Small Firms. Journal of Small Business Management 27, 45–45 (1989)
9. Lovett, P.J., Ingram, A., Bancroft, C.N.: Knowledge-Based Engineering for SMEs - a Methodology. Journal of Materials Processing Technology 107, 384–389 (2000)
10. Nonaka, I., Takeuchi, H.: The Knowledge-Creating Company. Oxford University Press, New York (1995)
11. Vinten, G.: Corporate Communications In Small- and Medium-Sized Enterprises. Industrial and Commercial Training 31, 112–119 (1999)
12. Parry, G.C., Turner, C.E.: Application of Lean Visual Process Management Tools. Production Planning & Control 17, 77–86 (2006)
13. Womack, J.P., Jones, D.T.: Lean Thinking: Banish Waste and Create Wealth for Your Corporation. Simon & Schuster, New York (1996)
14. Glouberman, S., Mintzberg, H.: Managing the Care of Health and the Cure of Disease– Part II: Integration. Health Care Management Review 26, 56–69 (2001)
15. Hudson, M., Lean, J., Smart, P.A.: Improving Control through Effective Performance Measurement in SMEs. Production Planning & Control 12, 804–813 (2001)
16. Khan, K., Shah, A.: Understanding Performance Measurement Through the Literature. African Journal of Business Management 5, 13410–13418 (2011)
17. Andersen, B., Fagerhaug, T.: Performance Measurement Explained - Designing and Implementing Your State-of-the-Art System. American Society for Quality, Milwaukee (2001)
18. Van Dooren, W.: What Makes Organisations Measure? Hypotheses on the Causes and Conditions for Performance Measurement. Financial Accountability & Management 21, 363–383 (2005)
19. Andersen, B., Henriksen, B., Aarseth, W.: Holistic Performance Management: an Integrated Framework. International Journal of Productivity and Performance Management 55, 61–78 (2006)
20. Mike Bourne, J., et al.: Designing, Implementing and Updating Performance Measurement systems. Emerald Group Publishing 20, 754–771 (2000)
21. Karlsson, C.: Researching Operations Management. Routledge, New York (2009)

State-of-the-Art Review on Operational Resilience: Concept, Scope and Gaps

Seyoum Eshetu Birkie[1,2,*], Paolo Trucco[1], and Matti Kaulio[2]

[1] Management, Economics and Industrial Engineering Department, Politecnico di Milano, Italy
Seyoum.birkie@mail.polimi.it, paolo.trucco@polimi.it
[2] Department of Industrial Economics and Management,
Royal Institute of Technology, Sweden
mkaulio@ug.kth.se

Abstract. This state-of-the-art review analyses literature on resilience paradigm perspectives and conceptualizations in business and management. Attempts have been made to produce a definition that reflects on and attempts to resolve inconsistencies and pursue with the conception of operational resilience. Future research directions are indicated by arguing on the possible relationships among operational resilience and modern operations management paradigms like lean thinking in view of operational performance.

Keywords: resilience, operational resilience, operational risk, operational performance, state-of-the-art.

1   Introduction

The uncertainty of business environments and complexity of risks has increased much more than ever before. Literatures present attempts to understand and utilize the resilience paradigm for improving decisions for business success departing from antecedent paradigms and practices in the face of uncertainties and turbulences [1], [2].

To mention an incident, in 2002, the 29 West Coast ports in USA were closed for around ten days due to longshoremen's strike. Firms in different sectors were left with delayed incoming supplies and outgoing deliveries for the Christmas sales. Dell, being one of the firms faced with the situation, was able to outperform competition using its internal capabilities to re-arrange product configurations and make early deals with airfreight service providers to re-secure deliveries [3]. Resilience has to do with features in business firms to be ready for such unforeseen (mis-)fortunes and respond fast in the intent of reducing unwanted influences. There are several similar examples in publications mentioned in this paper and elsewhere (e.g. [2], [4]).

The resilience concept has been in use in different knowledge domains (e.g. psychology, ecology, engineering) for decades [5–7]. Its use in business and management studies (dominantly in supply chain management) boosted post 9/11 [2], and the

---

[*] Corresponding author.

C. Emmanouilidis, M. Taisch, D. Kiritsis (Eds.): APMS 2012, Part II, IFIP AICT 398, pp. 273–280, 2013.
© IFIP International Federation for Information Processing 2013

global financial crisis in 2008 as evidenced by large number of articles published, and still growing, in the field. Resilience has been conceptualized differently in different disciplines [5], [8]. It could be argued that the differences in the definitions of the concept are partly influenced by the research knowledge area and applicability specifics; but there are concerns that the term is in danger of becoming "vacuous buzzword" due to usage without consensus in meaning and concept [9].

Accordingly, one of our objectives in this review is to understand what has been done to-date and propose a conceptual definition in an attempt to reduce prevailing inconsistencies by identifying relevant core elements that operational resilience constitutes. By pursuing with this, we also intend to reflect on reviewed literature and pinpoint some gaps for future research about operational resilience.

2   Methodology

The approach we followed is as follows. First some general literature bearing the topic of resilience (in domains of ecological studies, engineering, psychology sociology, risk management and other business related areas) is studied to identify the important reference publications, resilience definitions and descriptive explanations. To aid our focus in operational resilience in business firms, we performed a keyword search of publications (books, chapters, journal articles, chapters, proceedings, reports) using the logical combination of relevant keywords (see appendix for detail). The search has been limited to publication sources related to management, business, risk and decision science related studies. Web of Knowledge, Scopus, and Google Scholar served as primary search aids.

Abstracts (and when necessary full paper) of publications have been scanned to shortlist relevant papers in line with our objectives and scope. Some interesting publications are also identified from the reference list of shortlisted papers and included in the review. For publications which are extended forms of previously published literature by the same author(s) and when they do not appear to bear significantly different contributions for our objectives and scope, only the version that appeared more comprehensive is considered.

The findings and brief discussion are presented in succeeding sections. First we start with synthesizing core aspects of resilience from literature from which we propose an operational resilience definition. We jointly discuss how different perspectives of resilience in business contribute to operational resilience. We finally discuss issues that extend beyond definitions to pinpoint gaps for future research.

3   Discussion: The Review

In business environments, uncertainties are not only unavoidable but also getting more and more complicated [2], [10]. Such dynamism made business decisions more difficult than ever before. An important challenge in dealing with risks and uncertainties through resilience is the inconsistency of conceptual understanding of resilience in publications, which may also affect how business practitioners perceive it. Some scholars also argue that resilience concepts related to it (vulnerability, risk and robustness) also lack formal conception apart from verbal definition (e.g. [11]). We therefore assumed reviewing different definitions as well as perspectives or lines of descent for operational resilience would be helpful.

A recent literature review on resilience by Bhamra and others [12] summarizes findings from literature on resilience studies considering three main aspects: perspectives, concepts, and research methodologies used. Accordingly, resilience perspectives were viewed as ecological, individual, socio-ecological/community, organizational, and supply chain. They classified concepts into aspects like strategy, performance and capabilities. They also present list of resilience definitions and brief descriptions. We take this a step further to plot such definitions in several resilience papers to extract relevant aspects to construct a definition for operational resilience.

3.1 Definitions: The Synthesis

In the field of ecological studies, a typical resilience definition given by Holling in 1973 is referred by many articles including those outside the ecological domain (e.g. [5], [6], [13], [14]). It states resilience as "a measure of the persistence of systems and of their ability to absorb change and disturbance and still maintain the same relationships between populations or state variables" ([15], p. 14).

In engineering, resilience is defined as the physical property of a material that can return to its original shape (state or position) after deformation that does not exceed its elastic limits (e.g. [6]).

In a broader sense, definitions and conceptions of resilience in different domains seem to agree that: unanticipated changes (disorders) occur following some triggering event ([2], [4], [13]) which influence entities (individuals, physical or ecological systems, business enterprises or organizations) to go through some state change. Entity could mean. The entities may possess internal capabilities of coping (with limit) shaped by interaction with the environments. Resilience papers in ecosystem studies regard change (disorder) solely from causes "external" to entities whereas "internal" causes of disruptive events appear equally important in operational resilience. Some papers in business related resilience (e.g. [5], [9], [16]) capture multiple response modes when faced with (disruptive) uncertainties. A few of them (especially those on operational resilience) additionally recognize the opportunity (upside) of risk as well as the threats (downside) that are possible consequences of unanticipated pressures and changes (e. g. [8], [17–19]).

We argue that the definitions (category I of table 1) and descriptive discussions for papers providing no verbal definitions (category II of table 1) of resilience in business firms can be seen in view of five broad aspects or phases: sense, build, adapt/reconfigure, sustain, and recover/enhance.

Sense. Because the focus of resilience is mainly to deal with unanticipated changes and pressures in the business environments, this aspect is related to how firms try to improve visibility of indicators and proxies for detecting influential changes and/or their potential influences yet to come [7]. A common term used in several papers is "situation awareness" (e. g. [8]).

Build. Different literature in resilience discuss about resisting influence of (for example disruptive) changes ([13]) and coping mechanisms or mitigations ([20]). Building proper capabilities inherently or acquiring them from somewhere depending on vulnerability levels is essential for both of these.

Table 1. Literature sources of resilience concept, definition and relevant aspects

Year	Sources of resilience concept (author(s), [citation])	Core aspects					Breadth		Perspectives
		Sense	Build	Adapt/Re-configure	Sustain	Recover/Enhance	threats	opportunities	
Category I: Definition based									
1973	Holling [15]	X	X	X			X		-
2000	Frost et al. * [18]		X	X		X	X		GC
2003	Hamel & Välikangas [19]	X	X				X	X	SO
2004	Christopher & Peck [2]	X	X			X	X		SC
2004	Walker et al [6]	X	X	X	X		X		-
2006	Caralli * [21]	X	X	X	X		X	X	BC, GC
2006	Oh & Teo * [7]	X	X	X	X		X		SO
2007	Rose [9]		X	X		X	X		-
2007	Sheffi [4]		X	X		X	X		SC
2008	Falasca et al. [22]	X	X	X		X	X		SC
2008	Stolker et al. * [23]	X	X	X	X	X	X		SC
2009	Ponomarov & Holcomb [5]	X	X	X	X	X	X		SC
2010	Välikangas [17]	X	X	X	X	X	X	X	SO
2012	Scholz et al. [11]	X	X	X		X	X		-
Category II: Description based									
2005	Sheffi & Rice [1]	X	X	X	X	X	X		SC, SO
2006	Allen et al.* [18]		X	X	X	X	X		SC
2007	Craighead et al. [20]	X	X	X		X	X		BC, SC
2007	McManus et al. [8]	X	X	X	X		X	X	SO
2007	Waters [10]	X	X	X		X	X		SC
2010	Melnyk et al. [24]	X	X	X	X	X	X		SC
2010	Colicchia et al [25]		X	X		X	X		SC
2010	Pettit et al. [26]	X	X	X		X	X		BC, SC
2011	Carvalho & Cruz-Machado [16]		X	X		X	X		SC
2011	Jüttner & Maklan [27]	X	X	X		X	X		SC
2011	Ismail et al. * [28]	X	X	X	X	X	X	X	SO

* indicates papers that dealt with operational resilience in significant details

Key: OP=Operational, GC=Governance/control,
SO=strategic/organizational, SC =supply chain, BC=business continuity

Adapt/reconfigure. This aspect marks the beginning of feeling some real pressure and initial effects. Depending on decision preferences and available capabilities built, the firm attempts to respond. Firms may need different (multiple) forms of agility features to reconfigure the what, how and when they do in responding to unanticipated changes. While adaptive capabilities do not exclude responses to enhance opportunities, majority of the literature reviewed considers threats and disruptions only (conf. table 1).

Sustain. The essence of adapting/reconfiguring is sustaining the meeting of business objectives (i.e. delivery function). Continuing to perform one way or another is an important feature that reduces unwanted long term consequences which may happen if the firm discontinues functioning and recover back after sometime (e.g. [8]).

Recover/enhance. This aspect is about re-attaining competitive performance levels once the effects of shocks or pressures are felt. Recover is mainly concerned with disruptive events (conf. disruption profile in [1]). For operational resilience it is important that firms try to enhance and realize potential gains from opportunity events which otherwise may become threats (e.g. [19]).

Another way of looking at these features is from time horizon viewpoint. *Sense* and *build* focus on firms' capabilities of utilizing and rearranging strategic assets before an unwanted change event happens. They are also referred to as preparedness. *Adapt/reconfigure* and *sustain* reflect on capabilities and actions during the course of the unwanted change prevalence. Readers may refer to details of the Dell example mentioned before [3] to see how the company performed in these phases. *Recover/enhance*, as the name implies, has to do with efforts to bring a performance level that is better from long term perspective in relation to some reference. It is not guaranteed that the reference performance measure and level remain the same as they were before the encounter. The operational resilience towards pressure/change circumstances can also be viewed based on nature of the circumstances with regard to continuity and intensity of happenings (i.e. typologies like transient, cyclic, long-lasting, etc) which needs further investigation in itself.

To meet our objective of consistent and comprehensive operational resilience definition, we have tried to concentrate on the core aspects identified from extant literature while trying to avoid dependence on indicative mechanisms since specific capabilities depend on prevailing circumstances, industry and other firm related variables in addition to selective arrangement of capabilities being what makes resilience a source of competitive advantage. We, therefore, state that *operational resilience is the inherent (integrative) capability of an enterprise at different management levels and business units to defy unanticipated pressure (threats and opportunities) coming from internal and external causes, to persist on guaranteeing the efficient achievement of objectives and targets before, during, and after encounter of the pressure.*

3.2   Further Insight on Operational Resilience Features

In essence, operational resilience integrates the different resilience perspectives in business firms. Supply chain operations of plan, source, make, deliver (and return) can be less prone to unwanted influences of pressures from within (internal focus) or from outside (customers, suppliers, competitors, or other stakeholders) to operationally perform better for improved and consistent achievement of objectives.

Our understanding from literature is that conceptual contributions on operationally resilience in business firms can be outlined as follows (conf. Table 1 last column).

1. From supply chain risk and resilience management perspective;
2. From emergent strategic management organizational perspective;
3. From business functioning, continuity and crisis management view; and
4. As a way to fulfil governance and control requirements.

The number of publications corresponding to these resilience perspectives shown in table 1, in respective order as the above list, are: 14, 6, 3 and 2.

The literature on supply chain resilience concentrate on resilience aspects that are related to velocity, flexibility, visibility, and collaboration [7], [27]. Organizational resilience literature mainly is concerned with learning and dynamism in humans as collective decision makers (cognitive and behavioural aspects). When resilience is viewed from strategic perspectives reconfigurations and enforcing changes before changes force a firm unwillingly change something at higher expenses [19], [17]. Governance related resilience literature dealt mainly with issues of compliance, control, mandate and commitment (e. g. [18]). When managed in an integrative manner with the other perspectives, it contributes to building leverages. Sustaining continuous fulfilment of objectives mainly emanates from business continuity viewpoint [21]. These perspectives in integration provide a broader view of operational resilience.

3.3   Operationalization of the Resilience Concept

Even though some inconsistencies in conceptualization exist, several conceptual models and frameworks have been developed. Scholars have also tried to devise ways on how resilience is practically implemented and measured. Attempts include creating a balance between capability building efforts and vulnerability levels [26]. Regardless of the attempts on measuring business value of building operational resilience capabilities, quantifying the gains of resilience capability building investment against other alternative or opportunity costs still remains challenging. Some scholars (e.g. [16]) tried to compare resilience with other paradigms qualitatively, others (e.g. [22]) tried to measure resilience based on supply chain network features but only considering the downside o risk.

In a very structured form of risk management a typical procedure would be to identify risk events as exhaustively as possible, analyzing their likelihood of occurrence, and potential selective response mechanisms (e.g. [2], [29]). A limitation to this widely used approach is revealed as and when uncertainties and risk event counts dramatically increase, impairing soundness of managerial decisions. Argued benefit of pursuing operational resilience conception with dynamic capabilities is that building higher order capabilities that entail agility in terms multifaceted [7] applications helps to generate lower level capabilities suited to run operations under the prevailing circumstances. So, the need to make extensive analysis of every possible risk factors and consequences can be reduced. We also recall that the operational resilience definition adopted here implies cost conscious thinking because whatever investment we make and however we do it has implications to stakeholders, including customers.

4   Conclusion

The state-of-the-art review of literature reveals that the inconsistencies in conceptualizing and defining resilience can be narrowed down by identifying relevant aspects and reconstructing a definition. In addition to concepts the review has also tried to indicate interesting gaps that could lead to possible future research. In resilience literature maintaining redundancy of strategic assets is dominant which in lean thinking paradigm were needed to be minimized to reduce non-value adding costs (*wastes*), and boosting efficiencies. Does this imply that operational resilience is essentially against the principles and implementation practices of lean thinking? Several scholars claim that lean thinking is suitable for stable (not turbulent) business environment. On the other hand, some global companies following lean strategy showed better performance than their competitors amid a common dynamic unfavourable circumstance. Could there be scientific explanation? Could there be some 'better capability' of the companies in utilizing some principles and tools that enable them to practice lean and resilience features together? How do operational resilience features improve competitive advantages? Such questions need a detailed study for justified answers with future research.

Acknowledgement. This paper has been produced as part of the EDIM Joint Doctoral Programme between POLIMI, KTH, and UPM funded by EACEA (EC) under the EMJD Programme.

References

1. Sheffi, Y., Rice, J.B.: A supply chain view of the resilient enterprise. MIT Sloan Management Review 47, 41–48 (2005)
2. Christopher, M., Peck, H.: Building the resilient supply chain. International Journal of Logistics Management 15, 1–13 (2004)
3. Breen, B.: Living in Dell time, Fastcompany, New York (November 2004)
4. Sheffi, Y.: The resilient enterprise: overcoming vulnerability for competitive advantage. MIT Press, London (2007)
5. Ponomarov, S.Y., Holcomb, M.C.: Understanding the concept of supply chain resilience. The International Journal of Logistics Management 20, 124–143 (2009)
6. Walker, B.H., Holling, C.S., Carpenter, S.R., Kinzig, A.: Resilience, adaptability and transformability in social – ecological systems. Ecology and Society 9, 5 (2004)
7. Oh, L.-B., Teo, H.-H.: The impacts of information technology and managerial proactiveness in building net-enabled organizational resilience. In: Donnellan, T.J., Larsen, L., Levine, J.I. (eds.) The Transfer and Diffusion of Information Technology for Organizational Resilience. IFIP, vol. 206, pp. 33–50. Springer, Boston (2006)
8. McManus, S.T., Seville, E., Brunsdon, D., Vargo, J.: Resilience management: A framework for assessing and improving the resilience of organisations (2007)
9. Rose, A.: Economic resilience to natural and man-made disasters: Multidisciplinary origins and contextual dimensions. Environmental Hazards 7, 383–398 (2007)
10. Waters, D.: Supply chain risk management: vulnerability and resilience for logistics. Kogan-Page, London (2007)
11. Scholz, R.W., Blumer, Y.B., Brand, F.S.: Risk, vulnerability, robustness, and resilience from a decision-theoretic perspective. Journal of Risk Research 15, 3133–3330 (2012)
12. Bhamra, R., Dani, S., Burnard, K.: Resilience: the concept, a literature review and future directions. International Journal of Production Research 49, 5375–5393 (2011)

13. Vugrin, E.D., Warren, D.E., Ehlen, M.A., Camphouse, R.C.: A framework for assessing the resilience of infrastructure and economic systems. In: Gopalakrishnan, K., Peeta, S. (eds.) Sustainable and Resilient Critical Infrastructure, pp. 77–116. Springer-Verlag B-H (2010)
14. Fiksel, J.: Designing resilient, sustainable systems. Environmental Science & Technology 37, 5330–5339 (2003)
15. Holling, C.S.: Resilience and sustainability of ecological systems. Annual Review of Ecology and Systematics 4, 1–23 (1973)
16. Carvalho, H., Cruz-Machado, V.: Integrating lean, agile, resilience and green paradigms in supply chain management (LARG_SCM). In: Li, P. (ed.) Supply Chain Management, pp. 27–48. InTech, New Delhi (2011)
17. Välikangas, L.: The resilient organization: how adaptive cultures thrive even when strategy fails. McGraw-Hill (2010)
18. Frost, C., Allen, D., Porter, J., Bloodworth, P.: Operational risk and resilience: understanding and minimizing operational risk to secure shareholder value. Elsevier (2000)
19. Hamel, G., Välikangas, L.: The quest for resilience (2003)
20. Craighead, C.W., Blackhurst, J., Rungtusanatham, M.J., Handfield, R.B.: The severity of supply chain disruptions: design characteristics and mitigation capabilities. Decision Sciences 38, 131–156 (2007)
21. Caralli, R.A.: Sustaining operational resiliency: A process improvement approach to security management (2006)
22. Falasca, M., Zobel, C.W., Cook, D.: A decision support framework to assess supply chain resilience. In: Fiedrich, F., de Walle, B.V. (eds.) Proceedings of the 5th International ISCRAM Conference, Washington DC, USA, pp. 596–605 (2008)
23. Stolker, R.J.M., Karydas, D.M., Rouvroye, J.L.: A comprehensive approach to assess operational resilience. In: Hollnagel, E., Pieri, F. (eds.) Proceedings of the 3rd Resilience Engineering Symposium, Antibes-Juan-les-Pins, France, pp. 247–253 (2008)
24. Melnyk, S.A., Davis, E.W., Spekman, R.E., Sandor, J.: Outcome-driven supply chains. MIT Sloan Management Review 51, 33–38 (2010)
25. Colicchia, C., Dallari, F., Melacini, M.: Increasing supply chain resilience in a global sourcing context. Production Planning & Control 21, 680–694 (2010)
26. Pettit, T.J., Fiksel, J., Croxton, K.L.: Ensuring Supply Chain Resilience: Development of a Conceptual Framework. Journal of Business Logistics 31, 1–22 (2010)
27. Jüttner, U., Maklan, S.: Supply chain resilience in the global financial crisis: an empirical study. Supply Chain Management: An International Journal 16, 246–259 (2011)
28. Ismail, H.S., Poolton, J., Sharifi, H.: The role of agile strategic capabilities in achieving resilience in manufacturing-based small companies. International Journal of Production Research 49, 5469–5487 (2011)
29. ISO: ISO 31000 Risk management — Principles and guidelines (2009)

Appendix: Literature Search Keywords

These are the list of keywords used in literature search: *risk* AND *resilience*; (*enterprise* OR *organization* OR *operation* OR *"supply chain"*) AND *resilience*; (*vulnerability* OR *disruption* OR *uncertainty* OR *adaptability* OR *recovery* OR *agility* OR *flexibility* OR *mitigation* OR *crisis* OR *disaster*) AND *resilience*; (*resilience* OR *risk* OR *"business continuity"*) AND (*management* OR *analysis* OR *assessment*).

Modeling and Presentation of Interdependencies between Key Performance Indicators for Visual Analysis Support

Stefan Hesse, Volodymyr Vasyutynskyy, Martin Rosjat, and Christian Hengstler

SAP Next Business and Technology Dresden, SAP AG
Chemnitzer Str. 48, D-01187 Dresden, Germany
{s.hesse,volodymyr.vasyutynskyy,martin.rosjat,
christian.hengstler}@sap.com

Abstract. In this paper we propose the modeling and visual presentation of dependencies between key performance indicators. By doing this, explicit presentation and analysis of expert knowledge about dependencies between manufacturing processes can be achieved. This enables route-cause analysis and decision support. Further, using multiple techniques for the visual support we provide the user a high user experience, resulting in a quicker analysis and better user acceptance.

Keywords: decision support, visual analysis, key performance indicators, user experience.

1   Introduction

Nowadays, key performance indicators (KPIs) are an important instrument to analyze manufacturing systems. They allow the responsible experts or assigned staff e.g. at the production line to get quickly an overview and status of the production processes, detect possible issues, set targets and trigger actions. Accordingly, a lot of software tools support the analysis of KPIs by providing dashboards indicating the status of KPIs etc. Typical dashboards are shown in [1] [2] and [3].

However, these tools are currently limited to a mere visualization of the KPI values. Dashboards lack in scalability for displaying all data. At the same time the processes in modern manufacturing are getting more complex and are tightly connected with each other, so that the processes and their KPIs cannot be considered separately. The analysis of the internal interdependencies between KPIs, which is necessary to assess the causes of possible issues and to make the correct decisions, is still not supported enough by the tools and depends a lot on the experience of human experts. This exposes a lot of potential risks to companies, which include making false decisions due to disregarding of important interdependencies, possible loss of expert knowledge due to human factors etc. Accordingly, this gap should be closed by providing the means for explicit modeling, visualization and analysis of interdependencies between KPIs.

C. Emmanouilidis, M. Taisch, D. Kiritsis (Eds.): APMS 2012, Part II, IFIP AICT 398, pp. 281–288, 2013.

This paper describes the approach for visual support to analyze KPIs by providing a graph of KPIs showing their status and interdependencies, extended by several features to facilitate the visual perception of the users. The approach is a result of a joint project of several partners towards creating the production logistics and sustainability cockpit (PLANTCockpit, [4]). The approach has been prototypically implemented and tested on a use case from the automotive industry.

2   Motivation

In recent years the gathering, interpretation and analysis of business data has become an important key success factor. Single interpreted and calculated values over multiple information items are called key performance indicator (KPI). These indicators describe the state or value of a dedicated object in the business hierarchy. Examples for such indicators are the efficiency of a supplier, duration of the creation of a dedicated product, an error of a machine or the stop of a production line. The key challenges for managers are to have a consolidated and visual fast way of getting an overview about their responsible factory areas as well as potential problems and their causes. Nowadays, KPIs are analyzed using different business intelligence tools like SAP's Business Objects [1] [2]. BI tools can create reports based on data cubes e.g. from data warehouses. Typical reports of these multidimensional items are provided as two dimensional tables, charts or gauges and value based dashboards. Dashboards for KPIs show mostly single values and independent KPIs. As long as more values are stored in a KPI analysis table, these tables may become very complex and need a lot of explanations or background knowledge to be interpreted. This means that after a critical amount of KPIs is reached, those visualizations as tables and dashboards lose their comprehensibility and the semantics of KPIs are not further recognizable anymore. Also interdependencies between different KPIs (in this case cells of tables) are not visual recognizable by the expert within these tables. In most cases these interdependencies are not explicit maintained or even do not exist in common analysis tools, so that the relations between the KPIs (i.e. how they influence each other) are only known from human expert experience or generated by multivariate statistics methods. Since the KPI queries are being created during long periods of time and by different experts, the background knowledge about the interdependencies can get lost over time. If no relations between KPIs explicitly exist, no visual links between the KPIs can be provided automatically.

A typical scenario of KPI analysis is when the cause of the state change of a KPI has to be investigated. For example if the change of a KPI (e.g. KPI A) is influencing another KPI (e.g. KPI B), the cause for changing KPI B can now only be found by background knowledge of the users, but not by direct visibility. This lacking of explicit visualization of logical and visual dependencies makes especially the route cause analysis very hard or impossible. As result, quick and profound decisions cannot be made. Our approach is intended to close this gap.

3   Related Work

Different key performance indicators have been defined in literature and applied in the practice, acquiring quantitative, measurable information and representing them as result of relations and facts [5] [6]. The further development of KPIs and KPI systems into a performance indicator reference model can be found in [7]. The application areas of KPIs include visibility of changes, measurement of current state, comparison of targets and actual business results, decision support, support for coordination and adequate presentation of the information [8] [9]and [10]. Dedicated recommendations for visualization of KPIs can be found in [11].

An investigation of different kinds of data visualization for expert support started in 1960s with the work of Jacques Bertin und Edward Tufte [12] [13]. Also approaches of graph theory for presentation of large data sets appeared [14] [15] [16] [17]. As for now, graphs are a part of different analysis tools as well as visualization libraries. Graphs are also used for different purposes and analysis tools like decision trees, data structures, semantics (RDF), concepts etc. However, till now no approaches are known that support the analysis of KPIs from manufacturing processes using graph-based presentations. Moreover, the approach presented here also includes the method for creation of such KPI dependency graphs. Additionally different interaction features supporting the analysis are introduced.

4   Graph Model

4.1   Graph-Based Presentation of KPIs

We propose to introduce the graph-based presentation for KPIs to allow the explicit modeling and display of interdependencies. The interdependencies represent the mutual influences between KPIs, and a graph is an intuitive form for representation of such dependencies. Unexpected or undesired KPI state changes can be easily detected. In this way different kinds of analysis will be supported, including root-cause analysis of issues, what-if analysis of future KPI values as well as detecting of possible risks. The elements of the graph-based presentation are shown in Fig. 1.

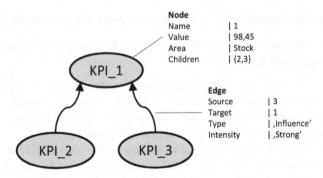

Fig. 1. Elements of the graph-based KPI presentation

The nodes of the graph represent the KPIs itself. The edges between nodes present the dependencies. Both nodes and edges can have further attributes to represent additional KPI properties, e.g., values, status, etc.

4.2   Lifecycle of the Graph-Based Presentation

The realization of the proposed graph-based presentation consists of 2 main phases, a design and a runtime phase. Both phases include further steps which are described in the following.

Design-phase
In the design phase the configuration of the tool and modeling of dependencies is done. This includes the definition of an overall dependency graph as well as the definition of different user views on the graph created before. First of all abstract KPIs acting as templates for concrete KPI instances are created. Following the dependencies between those abstract KPI templates are modeled. These templates represent generic KPIs without concrete instance relevant properties, e.g., connections to data sources in the business data warehouse. In this state, the design phase can use KPI hierarchies, reference models or results of multivariate statistics methods as input for the creation of the model.

The next step covers the definition of user views. User views contain KPI instances derived from abstract KPIs, e.g., throughput of machine A, which are of interest for the user analysis. This step includes the refinement of the generic KPI properties with concrete values, e.g., the assignment of a query string to a data source. Using the dependencies modeled earlier between abstract KPIs eases the configuration in terms of modeling the dependencies twice or more times on instance level. Detailed information about the different abstraction levels to implement KPIs can be found in [7].

Runtime-phase
This phase covers the presentation of user views with KPI instances and their values, states, etc. to the user. Depending on the type of analysis (status check, problem cause analysis, what-if analysis etc.), the user interacts with the dependency graph and visually inspects the KPI properties and their status.

4.3   Features for Support of Visual Perception and User Experience

To support the visual perception and the user experience, the graph is enhanced with the following interaction features:

- Drill-down possibilities. By clicking on a node, an analysis on its further properties can be made. Folding and expanding of nodes allow the display of a large set of nodes at the same time as well as root cause analysis by expanding and inspecting the relations between single nodes.
- Definition of different user views on top of the overall KPI dependency graph showing different sets of nodes and edges depending on the analysis task and user roles (like manager or dispatcher). For example, the manager is

interested only in high-level KPIs like overall efficiency or quality ratio. For a dispatcher, the status of the production line (e.g. throughput of the production line) and single machines (working/not working) is important. By choosing the corresponding view, the user can immediately see only the KPIs and dependencies he is interested in and authorized for.

- Definition of sub-graphs and groups of nodes representing specific areas of interest. The sub-graphs or groups can be again folded to limit the visual overload for the user when viewing large graphs.
- Drag-and-drop of single nodes, node groups or sub-graphs to support easy creation of the KPI dependency graph as well as user views.
- Highlighting of nodes or edges, e.g., based on values. For example, the color of a node may represent if the KPI values is within acceptable limits defined by matching targets (e.g., green) or exceeds these limits, (e.g., yellow or red).
- Filtering (e.g. hiding or increasing opacity) of nodes according to different criteria. During the interactive analysis, the user may be interested only in a subset of KPI instances, which is supported by filtering. For example by setting the criteria "area=Painting", the user will see only KPIs from this area.
- Graph layout algorithms like Sugiyama or energy-based [18] [19] can be used to adjust the presentation to the users' expectations. For example, for hierarchical KPIs should be intuitively presented by hierarchical trees.

5   Implementation

The proposed concepts are implemented in a prototype shown in Fig. 2 and developed in .Net. The prototype retrieves the KPI data and values from a connected business warehouse system out of test OLAP cube. The prototype has been applied on sample data of a use case from automotive industry and presents an exemplified user view.

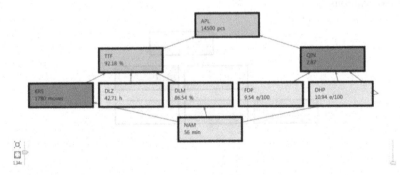

Fig. 2. Sample user view of a KPI dependency graph of the prototype. States of KPIs are represented by different colors of nodes.

The implementation is based on the PLANTCockpit architecture described in [20]. This component based architecture is designed for gathering, interpreting and analyzing data from heterogeneous data sources such as ERP, MES, Files, databases and data warehouses or other external systems.

The prototype implements the user experience features of graph visualization described in Section 4.3. Using the paradigm of Zoomable User Interfaces (ZUI), the expert can dive into large graphs with up to thousands of KPIs (see Fig. 3), still seeing most relevant parts.

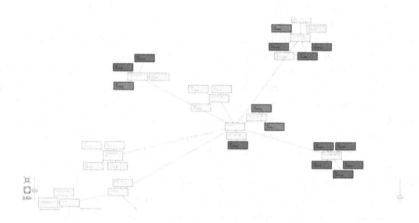

Fig. 3. Filtering support on different KPI states, names or tags

According to user's preferences large graphs, sub-graphs or groups of KPIs can be folded, expanded or repositioned by the user. Furthermore, the prototype allows the filtering of nodes using content, tags or states of the single KPI. In our prototype, the result of the filtering is shown in a decrease of the opacity of non-relevant KPIs. The filtering on the status of KPIs is depicted in Fig. 4. The automatic use of different graph layout algorithm allows the creation of KPI representations according to the user's expectations.

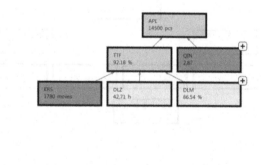

Fig. 4. User support by folding of sub graphs

The prototype was tested on the use cases of KPI analysis of manufacturing KPIs of a large automotive company. The prototype was connected to the data warehouse of the company, allowing presentation of the status of the real KPIs. The data warehouse contains thousands of KPI types as well as their current and historical values, which are usually accessed by data cube queries, based on which the table- and chart-based reports are created.

The KPI graphs have been created together with the experts of the company. Using our approach, the analysis of the huge amounts of KPIs could be managed in an easier way, facilitating and accelerating the work of human experts.

6   Conclusion and Future Work

The proposed approach will enhance the decision support by a higher visibility of respective influences and dependencies. It allows root-cause and what-if analysis for KPIs by utilizing links between dependent KPIs. With this capability the approach can be used for analysis of any complex business process, among others in the production or logistic management, and for production performance measurement.

With the presented method, the implicit logical connections between KPIs are turned into visual dependencies. This allows the user to explore KPIs and their dependencies in a visual way. Using a graph for visualization and interpreting KPI data allows a much more interactive presentation than tables and reports. This interactive presentation is enhanced with visual support like filtering, drag and drop or zoom.

One of our future works will cover further enhancements in interactivity and a user test with KPI experts from the automotive industry to refine the assumed models and to enhance the user experience. This test will lead to new insights into the interpretation and realization of KPI results using our visual approach. An additional study will provide information about the effects of the approach for our use case partner.

Acknowledgment. The authors would like to thank the European Commission for co-funding of the research project PLANTCockpit (under the project number 260018).

References

1. SAP AG: Simple, Affordable, and Open BI Tools for Everyday Use. In: SAP Crystal Solutions, http://www.sap.com/solutions/sap-crystal-solutions/index.epx
2. SAP AG: See Your Business Clearly. In: SAP BusinessObjects Dashboards, http://www.sap.com/uk/solutions/sapbusinessobjects/large/business-intelligence/dashboards/sapbusinessobjects-dashboards/index.epx
3. Siemens AG: SPPA-M3000 Plant Management. In: Siemens, http://www.energy.siemens.com/co/en/automation/power-generation/sppa-m3000/sppa-m3000-plant-management.htm#content=Description
4. The PLANTCockpit Consortium: PLANTCockpit EU-funded Project, http://www.plantcockpit.eu

5. International Organization for Standardization (ISO): ISO/CD 22400-2: Automation systems and integration - Key performance indicators (KPIs) for manufacturing operations management - Part 2: Definitions and descriptions (May 2012)

6. Reichmann, T.: Controlling mit Kennzahlen und Management-Tools: Die systemgestützte Controlling-Konzeption, 7th edn. Vahlen, München (2006)

7. Hesse, S., Wolf, B., Nadoveza, D., Pintzos, G., Rosjat, M.: Reference model concept for structuring and representing performance indicators in manufacturing. In: Emmanouilidis, C., Taisch, M., Kiritsis, D. (eds.) APMS 2012, Part II. IFIP AICT, vol. 398, pp. 289–296. Springer, Heidelberg (2013)

8. Gladen, W.: Kennzahlen- und Berichtssysteme.: Grundlagen zum Performance Measurement. Gabler (2001)

9. SAP AG: SAP Developers Network - KPIs,
   http://wiki.sdn.sap.com/wiki/display/KPI

10. Chryssolouris, G.: Manufacturing Systems: Theory and Practice, 2nd edn. Springer (2006)

11. Wenzel, S., Bernhard, J., Jessen, U.: Visualization for modeling and simulation: a taxonomy of visualization techniques for simulation in production and logistics. In: Proceedings of the 35th Conference on Winter Simulation: Driving Innovation, pp. 729–736 (2003)

12. Bertin, J.: Semiology of graphics. University of Wisconsin Press (1983)

13. Tufte, E.: The visual display of quantitative information. Graphics Press (1986)

14. Lamping, J., Rao, R., Pirolli, P.: A focus+context technique based on hyperbolic geometry for visualizing large hierarchies, pp. 401–408 (1995)

15. Wattenberg, M.: Visual exploration of multivariate graphs, pp. 811–819 (2006)

16. Horsfall, F., Tanev, S., Bontchev, B., Gigilev, T., Gruev, A.: Visualization of complex data relationships and maps: using the BLOOM platform to provide business insights, pp. 266–272 (2011)

17. Doganata, Y., Topkara, M.: Visualizing meetings as a graph for more accessible meeting artifacts, pp. 1939–1944 (2011)

18. Eiglsperger, S.: An Efficient Implementation of Sugiyama's Algorithm for Layered Graph Drawing (2005)

19. Noack, A.: An Energy Model for Visual Graph Clustering (2006)

20. Vasyutynskyy, H.C., Nadoveza, D., McCarthy, J., Brennan, K.G., Dennert, A.: Layered Architecture for Production and Logistics Cockpits. In: 17th IEEE International Conference on Emerging Techonologies and Factory Automation (ETFA), Krakow, Poland (2012)

Reference Model Concept for Structuring and Representing Performance Indicators in Manufacturing

Stefan Hesse[1], Bernhard Wolf[1], Martin Rosjat[1], Dražen Nadoveza[2], and George Pintzos[3]

[1] SAP AG, SAP Research Dresden, Chemnitzer Str. 48, 01187 Dresden, Germany
s.hesse@sap.com, b.wolf@sap.com, martin.rosjat@sap.com
[2] École polytechnique fédérale de Lausanne EPFL, 1015 Lausanne, Switzerland
drazen.nadoveza@epfl.ch
[3] University of Patras, Rio, Patras 26500, Greece
pintzos@lms.mech.upatras.gr

Abstract. Performance indicators (PIs) are used to monitor and assess production systems. There are thousands of PIs described in standards or in commercial PI collections; however, the PIs implemented in the factories may differ enormously due to use-case-specific requirements. In this work a reference model is proposed to support the process from a generic description to a use case specific PI implementation. There are two exemplary implementations described utilizing data stream processing and database technologies.

Keywords: performance indicators, KPI modeling, manufacturing.

1 Introduction

In modern manufacturing, performance indicators (PIs) are used to express certain conditions in the production, e.g., efficiency of machines and processes, quality of products, probability of failures, or resource consumption of certain machines or production facilities. There are PIs that are common to particular industry domains or to the whole manufacturing industry, such as OEE (Overall Equipment Effectiveness), but also very specialized PIs that are used by only one manufacturer.

An analysis of available PIs – including standards, public PI collections, and industrial use cases – showed that there are performance indicators, which share the same name and descriptive information but have a different semantic, even in the same factory. Furthermore, the implementation of PIs often distinguishes from the common description since PIs are adapted to use cases and individual requirements. This situation makes it difficult to compare performance indicators in industry domains or even between departments inside one enterprise.

To solve this problem a reference model is proposed, which consists of five layers to describe performance indicators and their application in a structured manner, beginning with a very generic PI description and adding more use case specific details

C. Emmanouilidis, M. Taisch, D. Kiritsis (Eds.): APMS 2012, Part II, IFIP AICT 398, pp. 289–296, 2013.

in the following layers. The model also supports references to hierarchical plant or product descriptions, as well as relations to other performance indicators.

2   Motivation

Monitoring and analyzing production processes is usually done from different perspectives. PIs can be related to different physical or logical entities, e.g., energy consumption can be relevant for a machine or a whole plant, but also for single products or a product series. While these use cases are different on the first view, both formulate same requirements to performance indicators:

- *Extensibility*: Attributes are used to describe PIs. There are common attributes that are shared by all PIs, e.g., name, but also attributes that are specific to domains, companies etc. To describe PIs appropriately, standard attributes as well as a possibility to add further attributes are needed.
- *Flexibility*: Common PI descriptions sometimes include alternative attribute values, e.g., for units. However in a certain scenario only a subset of the units is relevant. PIs should support refinements of attributes.
- *Dependencies*: PIs can depend on other PIs, i.e., one PI is calculated from other PIs. However, PI dependencies do not necessarily have to be modeled bi-directional. For simple models it is sufficient to list only input PIs.
- *Relations*: PIs can be related to different physical or logical entities, even at the same time. For instance, a performance indicator may be calculated for machines or product instances as well as for work centers or product series.
- *Aggregation*: PIs are sometimes aggregations of other PIs, e.g., when particular plant levels are considered.
- *Comparability*: PIs are used to compare for instance machines, resources, departments, or products inside and across enterprises.

3   Related Work

Currently there is an increasing usage and importance of PIs across several industries and there are attempts to collect and even standardize PIs and their descriptions, e.g., ISO 22400 [1] and VDMA 66412 [2]. The ISO 22400 contains the definitions and descriptions of 35 manufacturing PIs, including two PIs related to energy, while the VDMA 66412 is an industrial standard that includes 21 PIs related to manufacturing provided by the German association for engineers (VDMA). Furthermore, a number of (commercial) collections of PIs exist in the internet such as KPI Library [3], SAP Community Network [4] and SmartKPIs.com [5].

Although these PI standards and collections use a number of characteristics to describe a PI they are lacking in three areas: specific descriptions of the relations between the different indicators, descriptions of the use of indicators in specific systems or use cases, and a detailed description of how the indicators are calculated. In current literature, specific architectures have been proposed for all manufacturing systems together with specific hierarchy levels, which can be used to describe in which type of system or on which hierarchy level an indicator is applied. In [6] [7] [8] [9] similar hierarchy levels have been proposed that can lead to a more specific description of an indicators application.

Furthermore, the indicators can be described through their relevance to a process or a product part and therefore additional product compositions can be used such as final product, subassembly, raw materials etc.

4   Reference Model

Based on the requirements described in Section 2 we built a five-layer reference model for the definition of performance indicators, depicted in Fig. 1. Beginning at the top layer, every layer can be seen as a refinement of PIs towards a use-case-specific implementation. This means that every layer inherits the attribute values from the layer above and defines more specific information by additional attributes and by substantiating the inherited attribute values. The details of the layers are described below.

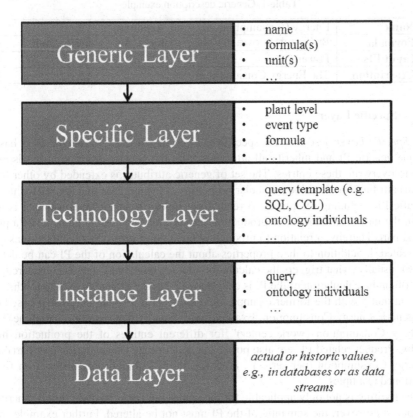

Fig. 1. Performance indicator reference model

4.1   Generic Layer

The *Generic Layer* describes PIs in the most common way, i.e., *generic PIs*. It is comparable to known standards; however, the number of attributes used to describe generic PIs might be less compared to PIs in the standards. The attributes to describe generic PIs are name, acronym, formula(s), unit(s), description, as well as relations to other performance indicators. To build a dependency model for PIs, for each PI a list of PI inputs is sufficient. For the exemplary performance indicator Energy Consumption, the formula would contain `EnergyConsumption=sum(Power)`, where Power is another PI summarized over a specified time. Therefore, Power is also listed in the relations (see Table 1).

The formula and unit attributes can contain none, one or more entries. There are cases where semantically equal PIs are specified with various calculation formulas, e.g., Mean Time Between Failures (MTBF). Especially for units usually a set of potential units is defined, e.g., sec, min, hours, etc. for time-based PIs such as Cycle Time.

Table 1. Generic description example

Name	Energy Consumption	Acronym	EnC
Formula	`EnC=sum(Power)`	Unit	Wh, kWh, J
Input PIs	Power		
Description	The Energy Consumption ...		

4.2   Specific Layer

The *Specific Layer* describes PIs specific to a certain use case. A *specific PI* is based on one generic PI and inherits all attributes from the generic description but is also able to overwrite these entries. The set of generic attributes is extended by other (optional) attributes to describe particular properties of the use case that are related to the specific PI, including references to related machines, the plant level where it is applied, the industrial domain, or production information such as components of a produced part. Thereby, a relation to production hierarchies or product compositions can be created. In addition to that, properties about the calculation of the PI can be determined, usually, what triggers the calculation of a PI, how many data is considered, or how often the calculation of the PI is executed, e.g., every minute or every month.

Continuing with the former example; several specific PIs can be created based on the generic Energy Consumption. Examples are "Energy Consumption (machine)" or "Energy Consumption (work center)" for different entities of the production hierarchy. Product-related PIs are also possible, e.g., "Energy Consumption (per part)" or "Energy Consumption (per series)", however, the calculation may differ from first-mentioned examples.

Overwriting is not only applicable for the names but could be done for all inherited attributes; however, the semantic of the PI must not be altered. Further examples are the extension of a description with additional information or the restriction to use-case-relevant relations or units, basically subsets of the generic definitions. The most varying changes are probably assigned to the formula field. In simple cases the formula is not modified or one of the generic formulas is selected. Apart from that, we observed cases in real-world scenarios, where formulas were only defined on the specific layer; i.e., the formula attribute of the generic PI is empty. In the concrete example, formulas were specific for product series and depending on certain features of a product a quality PI is calculated. The results are semantically equal and can be used to compare certain product series.

Another way to calculate PIs is aggregation. Where the Energy Consumption for a machine might be calculated from the Power that is measured at the machine, the Energy Consumption of a work center is the sum of the consumed energy of all machines in the work center over a specified time. In that case, the formula is not relevant, but a definition of an aggregation. To decide which machines belong to the work center, relations to the production hierarchy can be used.

Table 2 extends the generic Energy Consumption example used above. The specific PI refers to a machine in the production facility. The calculation is triggered every hour and done considering power data over the last day, i.e., the last 24 hours. Therewith, a hopping window is realized. The set of potential units is reduced to kWh only.

Table 2. Specific description example

Name	Energy Consumption (machine)	Acronym	EnC
Formula	EnC=sum(Power)	Unit	kWh
Input PIs	Power (machine)		
Plant level	machine	Event type	hourly
Window Size	1 day	Window type	hopping
...	...		
Description	The Energy Consumption ...		

The specific descriptions can be used to create calculation templates for PIs or models of the overall PI structure in a factory.

4.3 Technology Layer

The Technology Layer refers to abstract and technology-specific artifacts or expressions, which describe the specific PIs. Examples are individuals of an ontology and query templates for databases (e.g. SQL, MDX) or for data stream systems (e.g. CCL, Linq) respectively. Introducing technology-specific templates saves time and cost during the configuration and maintenance of the PI processing system. So, query instances can be created quickly without too much repetitive efforts. Query templates contain placeholders for inputs and parameters to be replaced during the runtime by concrete values. An exemplary query template for the CEP (complex event processing) query language CCL [10] for the energy consumption PI above may look like follows. Placeholders for parameters, input streams, and output streams are represented by #par:...#, #in:...#, and #out:...#, respectively.

```
CREATE OUTPUT WINDOW #out:EnCStream# PRIMARY KEY DEDUCED
KEEP #par:windowSize# #par:windowSizeUnit# AS SELECT
sum(inStream.Power) EnC, inStream.ID   ID
FROM #in:PowerStream# AS inStream GROUP BY inStream.ID
OUTPUT EVERY #par:stepSize# #par:stepSizeUnit# ;
```

4.4   Instance Layer

The Instance Layer relates to entities of the PI processing system. Based on the PI templates concrete instances of PIs are created. Such queries are instantiated replacing the placeholders in a query template with proper data sources and parameters.

So, one PI query template can be used to create several PI instances. In the Energy Consumption example, the template for "Energy Consumption (machine)" can be instantiated for each machine that has a power measurement, assigning the appropriate input (the power signal of that machine) and setting the parameter for the duration, e.g., one hour. The same can be done for work centers utilizing an "Energy Consumption (work center)" template. Based on the template example and the parameters of the specific description above a query for "machine 1" could be:

```
CREATE OUTPUT WINDOW EnergyConsumption_Machine1 PRIMARY
KEY DEDUCED KEEP 1 DAY AS SELECT sum(inStream.Power) EnC,
inStream.ID ID FROM Power_Machine1 AS inStream
GROUP BY inStream.ID OUTPUT EVERY 1 HOUR ;
```

4.5   Data Layer

The *Data Layer* symbolizes all data that is created by or associated to PI instances. There is a wide range of potential data consumers. In the following, just a few cases from the research projects are mentioned. The PI data can be visualized to monitor and analyze the processes by the plant personnel. In other cases, PIs are calculated to identify critical situations and trigger further activities. PI data can be fed back into the production process to control or improve it or used as input for other systems, e.g., optimization tools, for scheduling, or reporting. Moreover, data can be stored for later analyses or as a reference.

5   Implementation

The reference model was implemented in two industrial use cases utilizing different technologies.

The first implementation is a hybrid system consisting of a CEP engine and an in-memory database where PIs are calculated in real-time using continuous data stream queries. Further details of the architecture are described in [11]. For monitoring of a production facility, performance indicators were selected and described as specific PIs. Based on that, data stream query templates for two different CEP engines were created using the CEP-specific query languages. Depending on the CEP that executes the calculation, the proper query template is selected to create PIs instances in the system. In addition to that, the generic and specific PI descriptions were used to create an ontology. The ontology can be used for root cause analysis, i.e., supporting the user to find out which PIs influence other ones or are influenced by others. Sophisticated scenarios for the ontology usage are planned, e.g., (semi-) automatic query generation or production optimization based on PI data.

The second implementation used the reference model for a PI monitoring application in the automotive industry [12] on top of a database and a data warehouse. Like in other industries various PIs exist with the same or similar semantics. The proposed model was used to find similarities. Thus, a better overview and the ability to compare PIs in a consistent way could be provided to end users. The application provides user-configured views on relevant PIs instances. Besides the monitoring of PI values the application offers a possibility to express dependencies between single PIs. Using the new approach simplifies the configuration of views and dependencies. Traditionally, users define relevant PIs (instances) out of a set of available and authorized PIs. Dependencies between the selected PI instances are individually modeled afterwards. In most of the cases, same or similar dependencies are modeled multiple times and by different users. The introduction of the generic and specific models allowed for a description of PI dependencies already at a higher level of abstraction. Once available, this information can be used during the creation and analysis of single PI instances. Out of the general descriptions the dependencies on instance level can be retrieved automatically. The dependency model is used for root cause analyses, as well.

6   Conclusion and Future Work

The application of performance indicators in manufacturing shows the necessity of a consistent model to define and re-use PI descriptions with different granularities. In this paper a reference model for performance indicators is presented. It can be used as a generic approach to describe PIs for specific use cases. Starting with an abstract description, use-case-specific details are added resulting in a PI description ready for implementation. Future work will include a semantic PI model implementing the reference model to allow for a detailed description of the inheritance attributes as well as the extern relationships. As a further aspect, time dependent properties will be included into the reference model, such as absolute and relative time relations (e.g. yesterday, last quarter).

Acknowledgments. The projects PLANTCockpit (260018) and KAP (260111) are co-funded by the European Union under the Information and Communication Technologies (ICT) theme of the 7th Framework Programme for R&D (FP7).

References

1. International Organization for Standardization (ISO): ISO/CD 22400-2: Automation systems and integration - Key performance indicators (KPIs) for manufacturing operations management - Part 2: Definitions and descriptions (May 2012)
2. Verband Deutscher Maschinen- und Anlagenbau e.V (VDMA): VDMA-Einheitsblatt 66412-1 – Manufacturing Execution Systems (MES) – Kennzahlen (October 2009)
3. KPI Library B.V.: KPI Library, http://kpilibrary.com/
4. SAP AG: SAP Developers Network - KPIs, http://wiki.sdn.sap.com/wiki/display/KPI
5. The KPI Institute Pty. Ltd.: SmartKPIs.com, http://www.smartkpis.com
6. Chryssolouris, G.: Manufacturing Systems: Theory and Practice, 2nd edn. Springer (2006)
7. Jones, A., McLean, C.: A proposed hierarchical control model for automated manufacturing systems. Journal of Manufacturing Systems 5(1), 15–25 (1986)
8. Westkämper, E., Hummel, V.: The Stuttgart Enterprise Model - Integrated Engineering of Strategic & Operational Functions. CIRP Seminars on Manufacturing Systems 35(1), 89–93 (2006)
9. Catron, B.A.: A Framework for Semiconductor Manufacturing. In: 3rd DARPASCR CIM-CI Workshop, Stanford, CA (1988)
10. Sybase Inc.: CCL Reference Guide - Sybase CEP Option R4 (2011), http://infocenter.sybase.com/help/topic/com.sybase.infocenter.dc01031.0400/doc/pdf/CEP_CCLReference.pdf
11. Schramm, A., Wolf, B., Hartung, R., Preußner, A.: Real-time production monitoring in large heterogeneous environments. In: Emmanouilidis, C., Taisch, M., Kiritsis, D. (eds.) APMS 2012, Part II. IFIP AICT, vol. 398, pp. 72–79. Springer, Heidelberg (2013)
12. Hesse, S., Vasyutynskyy, V., Rosjat, M., Hengstler, C.: Modeling and Presentation of Interdependencies between Key Performance Indicators for Visual Analysis Support. In: Emmanouilidis, C., Taisch, M., Kiritsis, D. (eds.) APMS 2012, Part II. IFIP AICT, vol. 398, pp. 281–288. Springer, Heidelberg (2013)

Productivity Measurement and Improvements: A Theoretical Model and Applications from the Manufacturing Industry

Peter Almström

Chalmers University of Technology, Sweden
peter.almstrom@chalmers.se

Abstract. At many companies, workers associate productivity or efficiency increase with something negative, it is interpreted as an increase in speed and the "sweat factor". Productivity is not only made up of the speed factor, but these misconceptions and lack of knowledge tend to put "a wet blanket" on all attempts to increase productivity. It is therefore important to clarify what productivity is and especially how it can be improved.

In general, the productivity at shop-floor level can be improved through improving the method, increasing the performance, and increasing the utilization. The design of the products and the amount of scraped products also affects the productivity in both manual tasks as well as work performed by machines. These aspects of productivity will be elaborated in the theoretical model and the industrial applications presented in this article.

Keywords: Productivity, Performance measurement, OEE, KPI.

1 Introduction

Productivity is an important factor to create wealth and well-being at national level as well as creating competitiveness at corporate level. But productivity itself is only a mean to create high standard of living for nations or high profitability for companies [1, 2]. Productivity can in general be defined as output over input. The choice of outputs and inputs are dependent upon the intended application. For example is the standard definition[1] for productivity at national level gross domestic product (GDP) over total amount of work hours for the total population. On a factory level the productivity may be defined as added value per employee and on cell or station level a typical productivity measure is the number of products produced per hour planned production time. Vora [3] has made a study of the industrial use of different productivity definitions at three separate levels in manufacturing companies. The conclusion was that at first and middle manager level the most common productivity measure used was physical output per labor. Labor can be interpreted as number of people or planned working time.

---

[1] See e.g. Eurostat (http://ec.europa.eu/eurostat)

C. Emmanouilidis, M. Taisch, D. Kiritsis (Eds.): APMS 2012, Part II, IFIP AICT 398, pp. 297–304, 2013.

This article concerns productivity improvement at factory floor level, i.e. at station, cell, or line level. There are many ways to achieve these improvements and people associate different feelings and have corresponding attitudes towards productivity improvements. At many companies, workers associate productivity or efficiency increase with something negative. It is interpreted as an increase in speed and the "sweat factor". However, the sweat factor is only one way of increasing the productivity, and probably the least desirable one in most situations. Managers at different levels have often a low level of knowledge about productivity measurement and therefore also about its improvement. These misconceptions and lack of knowledge tend to put "a wet blanket" on all attempts to increase productivity in good times and productivity improvements are only discussed in bad times when the company is bleeding and at that time it's often too late. For these reasons it's important to clarify what productivity is and how it can be improved. In general, the productivity at shopfloor level can be improved through improving the method, increasing the performance ("the sweat factor"), increasing the utilization, improving the product design, and reducing the scrap. These aspects of productivity will be elaborated in the theoretical model presented in this article.

In order to measure the real productivity potential in Swedish manufacturing companies an assessment method was developed: Productivity Potential Assessment (PPA) [4]. Since 2005, close to one hundred PPA studies have been carried out in the manufacturing industry. The productivity improvement potentials have thus been assessed and measured for a wide variety of companies: large and small companies from different industries. The majority of the studies have been performed at suppliers to the automotive industry. The focus of PPA is on the utilization aspect of productivity, however it is not given that utilization has the greatest impact on the productivity. In most cases it is the method factor, i.e. the selected machines or the manual work method that represent the greatest potential. The potential for improvement in manual work methods is especially interesting, since substantial improvements often can be achieved without or with very limited investments. The manual work methods are often an effect of the production system design (or lack of intended design) or the management of the system. For example, it is common that the manual work is the bottleneck for machine operations; the machines must be loaded and un-loaded by operators, the operators perform the set-up work, and so on. Thus, the machine utilization is heavily affected by the manual work. However, very few companies in the Swedish manufacturing industry acknowledge this fact and actually design and measure manual work tasks in a systematic way. According to the PPA studies merely around 25% of the manufacturing companies are able to carry out work studies and set standard times in reasonably accurate way by using either time studies or a predetermined time system. The vast majority are either using operation times for similar products, set the times based on pre-production runs, or are simply guessing based on experience. The reason for this misconduct is a mix of the work organizations' and the salary systems' historical development and the managers' lack of insight and competence [5].

2   Theoretical Productivity Increase Model

There are many ways to increase productivity. Taylor [6] was the most famous pioneer in the beginning of last century. He emphasized the productivity potentials in improving the methods used by introducing better tools and, more importantly, how the speed of people working could be enhanced greatly by proper motivation. Later were the socio-technical factors for motivation and productivity increase discovered in the famous Hawthorne studies [7]. In the last decades has the productivity been raised through increased automation and by outsourcing labor intensive work to locations with low salary level. The competence to carry out time- and motion studies vanished in the Swedish industry when new salary models and work organizations were introduced in the 1970-80ies. These days when Lean Production is the norm, the lost competence is needed again. Every company that tries to implement a Lean Production system will need standard work procedures and stable operation times at the lowest shop-floor level, as a base for continuous improvement and steady flows. The methods that were invented by Taylor and his followers (e.g. The Gilbreths, Gantt, Segur, and Maynard [8]) are still valid today even though the purpose of using them (to set the salary in piece rate systems) is not the same today.

Regardless of method, improvement program, or production philosophy applied to increase productivity, it is important to know what factors that actually affect the productivity. In the following text will a model be presented that has the potential to pedagogically explain what productivity is and at the same time provide a concrete way to calculate a potential productivity increase.

2.1   Productivity Model

Productivity can be improved through better methods (M), increased performance (P), and increased utilization (U). This can be expressed in the following equation:

$$Productivity = M \times P \times U \tag{1}$$

Consultants ([9], [10], and [11]) have used this formula or parts of the formula at least since the 1960ies[2]. However, it has not been described or analyzed in an academic context. The model has been developed and previously used for manual work only, but it is actually applicable for all kind of work, even if it's carried out by a machine.

The method factor (M) is defined as the ideal or intended productivity rate. It is the inverse of the ideal cycle time for the specific work task. In order to determine the ideal cycle time for manual work tasks it is necessary to use a predetermined time system. There are a number of available systems and most of them are based on MTM [8]. The MTM systems were in wide use in the Swedish manufacturing industry after WWII until mid-1980ies. At that time, the use was for setting times in piece-rate salary systems. These salary systems have almost vanished now, and with them the

---

[2] According to Bengt Isaksson who was employed at Maynard's in Sweden in the 1960ies and Shigeyasu Sakamoto who has been employed at JMAC in Japan for a long time.

competence of using the predetermined time systems. This has resulted in a situation where companies are unable to calculate an ideal cycle time before the work station is up and running. The time for the work task can then be timed with stop watch, but the resulting time will not be the ideal cycle time; it will be affected by the P and the U factor in equation 1.

The performance factor (P) corresponds to the speed the work is carried out at in relation to the ideal cycle time. For manual work the performance factor can be both below and above 100%. The normal speed in MTM is set to be valid for a "normal" person working at this speed for 8 h a day and for the whole working life without getting exhausted or injured. The performance rate is lower for not fully trained workers and for people with disabilities. For machine work can performance by definition never go beyond the ideal cycle time, i.e. 100%.

The utilization factor (U) represents the time that is spent on performing the intended work in relation the total planned time. Utilization can never go beyond 100%. The planned production time is usually defined as the paid working time minus planned stops, like weekly meetings or planned maintenance stops.

2.2   Expanded Model

Apart from the three base factors in Equation 1, other factors that affect the productivity are perceivable. The quality rate (Q) or yield affects the productivity if the productivity is defined as the number of quality approved products produced per time unit. All production engineers (and obviously not all product designers) are aware that the product design has a very important impact on the productivity. This can be expressed with a design efficiency rate (D). These two extra factors together with Equation 1 give the expanded model in Equation 2.

$$Productivity = M \times P \times U \times Q \times D \tag{2}$$

The quality factor (Q) is the yield or 100% minus the scrap rate. Yield is common in the electronics industry while scrap rate is normally used in the mechanical products industry. The quality loss is usually very small in comparison to the other productivity losses. However, the scrap rate has other implications as well; such that the errors need to be detected by a quality control system and that the scrap also is a waste of material and energy.

The final factor in equation 1 is the design (D) factor. The factor for improving the design to decrease the cost of manufacturing and assembly is treated in the DFMA (design for manufacturing and assembly) literature. Specifically for assembly, Boothroyd et al [12] have suggested a design efficiency factor. That factor is 100% if the design is ideal from an assembly point of view. The design factor is clearly outside the limitation to the factory floor, and in practice it is very hard for a manufacturing company to affect in many cases. In fact, contract manufacturers have normally little to gain and possibly a lot to lose by suggesting design changes to the customer company. The contract manufacturer will lose their value adding work since the customer most likely will decrease the price paid because of the design change.

3   Applications

The focus of the applications has been to find and demonstrate how simple, low cost changes, in the production will affect the productivity factors and because of the multiplying effect will provide substantial increase in productivity. The special application to machine work will also be discussed.

3.1   A Fictive Case Based on Today's Average and Best Practice

The first application example is fictive in order to demonstrate the three factors in equation 1 and their multiplicative effect. The example is based on an assumed situation with facts based on the average figures in today's industrial practice compared to best practice. The figures are based on previous studies using the PPA method and subsequent improvement studies carried out in Swedish industry [13].

Consider an assembly work station. A specific work task takes 3 minutes or 180 s to carry out according to a well-defined standard work description. However, the worker does not work at standard speed (100%) but rather a bit lower; at 90%. The utilization is 65%, 15% of the time is spent on supporting activities like moving the material to and from the work area, planning and reporting, and cleaning. The remaining 20% of the paid working time is personal time and breaks.

The method can be improved 30% with small means, mainly by putting material closer and minimizing the number of steps. The cycle time decreases to 180 s – 30% = 120 s. The performance shall always be on 100% if not special conditions apply, e.g. work performed by a not fully trained employee. The utilization can increase to 81% assuming that the personal time and breaks can be lowered to 9% which is a normal agreed level and the supporting tasks can be reduced to 10% using a better method for those tasks as well. The resulting productivity increase can be calculated step by step assuming one hour production of the particular product (table 1).

Table 1. Calculation of productivity increase step by step for 1 h = 3600 s production (p/h = products per hour)

Factor	Productivity before	Productivity after
Method improvement	3600/180 = 20 p/h	3600/120 = 30 p/h
Performance improvement	20×0,9 = 18 p/h	30×1 = 30 p/h
Utilization improvement	18×0,65 = 11,7 p/h	30×0,81 = 24,3 p/h
Actual productivity	11,7 p/h	24,3 p/h
		Total improvement = (24,3 – 11,7)/11,7 = 108%

The total productivity improvement by going from the average level to the best practice level identified in the PPA studies is over 100%. This example, based on realistic improvement levels, clearly demonstrates the importance of the multiplicative effect of the small improvements in each factor.

3.2   Improvement of Manual Assembly

This application is from a manufacturer of heat, ventilation, and air condition (HVAC) units for vehicles like buses and trucks. The production is highly customized and the products are manufactured and assembled in relatively small batches, typically around 10 units in each batch. The study was a part of a government supported program to suppliers to the automotive industry and it was carried out by professional consultants.

The study commenced with a PPA study of the factory's general productivity potentials. The final assembly area was selected for the work sampling study and that revealed that the utilization rate (U) for carrying out the actual assembly work was 60%. The remaining time was split equally on supporting (necessary) activities, e.g. fetching material from the warehouse and reporting, and personal time. To formally measure the method improvement potential is not a part of the PPA study. However, while the work sampling is conducted it usually becomes obvious to the experienced analyst if the method potential is large. After the initial PPA study a total of 10 consultancy days were spent on analyzing the method in detail and involving the operators in the work to improve the assembly area's productivity.

The analysis was delimited to the assembly of the factory's volume products; two varieties of ventilation units. The performance factor (P) was measured to be close to 100%. The productivity was 0,27 units/h and 0,44 units/h for the two products before the improvements. The present assembly was conducted at stations and in batches, where the worker assembled several units in parallel. A lot of time was wasted on walking to and from the material storage areas. The improvement was to transform the station assembly into a simple flow, where the work was divided into three parts and corresponding workstations were designed. The workers were involved in the design and they constructed some simple material racks out of scrap material from the production. The new work method was documented in work instructions and the assemblers started to work according to the new standard. Virtually no investment apart from workers' time was needed.

The productivity for the two products was improved to 0,37 units/h and 0,68 units/h respectively. This corresponds to a productivity increase of 37% and 54%. The improvement was verified in running production. The performance rate was most likely 100% afterwards as well. The utilization was not measured afterwards, but it is likely that it improved slightly due to less external material handling. The personal time and break time was probably not changed at all since that was a matter of culture and old habits. In other words; almost all of the productivity increase was thanks to the method improvement. That confirms what has been concluded from similar studies [13]: It is much easier to improve the M factor than trying to improve the U factor, even though the potential is considerable in that factor. The U factor is affected by the company culture and the management of the production. That takes a lot of time to change compared to involving the operators in method improvements.

3.3   Improving Machine Work Productivity

The theoretical model can be applied to machine work as well, but the definitions are a bit different to that of manual work activities. The M factor is defined as the inverse of the ideal cycle time. Ideal cycle time is the fastest time either recorded or simulated for a particular job in the machine. In practice it is hard to determine the ideal cycle time for a running production, especially if manual tasks are a part of the work cycle. The prepared times (e.g. from a CAM simulation) can be used in many cases, but it is not certain that used machine programs are optimal and "ideal".

The ideal cycle time is important for calculating OEE (Overall Equipment Effectiveness) [14]. The OEE ratio is commonly used in the Swedish manufacturing industry and it is included as one parameter in PPA. The basic definition of OEE is the ratio between the time that was spent on producing a certain amount of quality approved products and the planned production time. OEE can be calculated by multiplying the availability (A) which is the planned production time minus larger stoppages and break-downs, the operation efficiency (O) (including both small stops and speed reductions), and the yield (Q):

$$OEE = A \times O \times Q \tag{3}$$

The OEE figure is not a productivity measure, there is no M factor. The A factor plus the small stops of the O are the same thing as U losses and the speed reduction part of O is the same as P losses. That gives the following relations:

$$M \times OEE = M \times P \times U \times Q \tag{4}$$

$$OEE = P \times U \times Q \tag{5}$$

Equation 4 and 5 explains the applicability of Equation 1 (and 2) to machine work.

4   Conclusions

The presented productivity model has great practical importance for industry. There is a need in industry too understand what productivity is and how it is defined and measured. The equation is simple, yet it pedagogically describes the important factors that can be improved in order to increase the productivity. The model is well founded on the experiences from the PPA studies and it has been validated through applications by academics and consultants.

Acknowledgment. This research is carried out within the Sustainable Production Initiative and the Production Area of Advance at Chalmers University of Technology. The support is gratefully acknowledged by the authors.

References

1. Sink, D.S., et al.: Productivity Measurement and Evaluation: What is Available? National Productivity Review (3) (Summer 1984)
2. Tangen, S.: Demystifying productivity and performance. International Journal of Productivity and Performance Management 54, 34–46 (2005)
3. Vora, J.A.: Productivity and Performance Measures: Who Uses Them? Production and Inventory Management Journal 33(1) (First Quarter 1992)
4. Almström, P., Kinnander, A.: Assessing and benchmarking the improvement potential in manufacturing systems at shop-floor level. International Journal of Productivity and Performance Management 60(7), 758–770 (2011)
5. Almström, P., Winroth, M.: Why is there a mismatch between operation times in the planning systems and the times in reality? In: Proceedings of APMS 2010, Como (2010)
6. Taylor, F.W.: Principles of Scientific Management. Harper & brothers, New York (1911)
7. Dipboye, R.L., Smith, C.S., Howell, W.C.: Understanding industrial and organizational psychology: An integrated approach. Harcourt Brace, Fort Worth (1994)
8. Freivalds, A.: Niebel's Methods, Standards, and Work Design, 12th edn. McGraw-Hill, New York (2008)
9. Saito, S.: Reducing labor costs using industrial engineering techniques. In: Zandin, K.B. (ed.) Maynard's Industrial Engineering Handbook, pp. 151–200. McGraw-Hill, New York (2001)
10. Helmrich, C.: Productivity Processes - Methods and experiences of measuring and improving. InformgruppenFörlag, Stockholm (2001)
11. Sakamoto, S.: Beyond world-class productivity – Industrial engineering practice and theory. Springer, London (2010)
12. Boothroyd, G., Dewhurst, P., Knight, W.A.: Product Design for Manufacture and Assembly. CRC Press Inc. (2010)
13. Almström, P., Kinnander, A., Sundkvist, R., Hedman, R.: How to realize the productivity potentials in the manufacturing industry. Accepted for publication in the Proceedings of the Swedish Production Symposium 2012, Linköping (2012)
14. Nakajima, S.: Introduction to TPM - Total productive maintenance. Productivity Press, Cambridge (1988)

Manufacturing Service Ecosystems

Towards a New Model to Support Service Innovation Based on Extended Products

Stefan Wiesner[1], Ingo Westphal[1], Manuel Hirsch[2], and Klaus-Dieter Thoben[1]

[1] Bremer Institut für Produktion und Logistik, Hochschulring 20, 28359 Bremen, Germany
{wie,win,tho}@biba.uni-bremen.de
[2] DITF-MR , Koerschtalstrasse 26, 73770 Denkendorf, Germany
manuel.hirsch@ditf-mr-denkendorf.de

Abstract. The trend for servitization is increasingly affecting manufacturing enterprises. Products are bundled with associated services to so called "Extended Products" (EP). However, the share of services becomes more and more important. This requires on the one hand an evolution of the EP concept towards greater interoperability of the physical product and on the other hand additional competencies in service innovation. Traditional manufacturing enterprises are not able to handle the related challenges by themselves. The paper presents a more open and service-oriented "EP 2.0" concept and introduces the Manufacturing Service Ecosystem as a model to support service innovation by facilitating collaboration.

Keywords: Servitization, Service Innovation, Extended Product, Manufacturing Service Ecosystem, MSEE Integrated Project.

1   Introduction

A trend for servitization of products is affecting manufacturing enterprises. By looking for benefits, the customers force the manufacturer to give increasing attention to understand and solve their problems. The key success factor is the provision of additional value to the customer [1]. Thus, physical products are combined with associated services to so called "Extended Products" (EP) [2].

Take for instance a traditional manufacturing SME, which has evolved from the production of parts for machine tools, over the offering of standard drilling machines, towards customization of high precision machining centres. While in the past it has been sufficient to provide standard maintenance services like replacing expendables and spare parts, the customers now expect permanent availability of the machines. However, the complexity of the machining centres sometimes requires very difficult maintenance tasks. Although the distance between the manufacturer and the customer can be many thousand kilometres, immediate technical assistance is expected to minimize breakdown times. However, as a traditional manufacturer the SME has neither the competencies nor the resources to provide individual maintenance

C. Emmanouilidis, M. Taisch, D. Kiritsis (Eds.): APMS 2012, Part II, IFIP AICT 398, pp. 305–312, 2013.

services, which leads to high costs for preventive and corrective actions. The need is clearly to support the SME to innovate some kind of "smart maintenance service" and make their products interoperable accordingly (e.g. with sensors and remote control), which could produce additional revenues and profit.

Innovation of such Extended Products, from idea generation to realization and commercialization, requires on the one hand a better understanding of the customer requirements [3] and on the other hand additional competencies for the integrated design and provision of the product and services. Thus, the involvement of the customers as partners (e.g. to identify maintenance needs) and collaborative arrangements with other enterprises (e.g. local maintenance service providers) become more and more important [4]. Manufacturing enterprises do not only have to support service innovation and provide the required physical resources, organizational structures, as well as IT tools. Furthermore, they have to ensure the interoperability of their products to existing and newly developed services.

2   State of the Art for Service Innovation in the Context of Extended Products

2.1   The Extended Product Concept and a Step beyond to Service Innovation

The concept of an Extended Product (EP) describes a complex combination of tangible and intangible assets as a "utility package" to satisfy the customers' needs [2], [5]. In this concept, the core of the EP is the physical product and the services are aligned in circles around it. However, the share of services becomes more and more important even for the manufacturers of physical products. In some cases they are making more profit with the services than with the physical products [6]. In addition, development and production processes become more and more "open", this means that the manufacturers have to involve partners with specific competences and that they exchange information with the "outside world" like customers or even competitors. The concept of open innovation [7] is one example that represents this trend. Therefore, the initial concept of the EP has to be evolved in the direction of interoperability of the physical product with different services to avoid unnecessary restrictions.

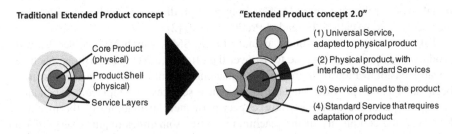

Fig. 1. Towards a more open and service-oriented Extended Product concept

According to **Fig. 1**, one of the main extensions in comparison to the initial EP concept is that in "EP 2.0" there are not just services that are developed specifically for the physical product (3). Rather, the EP can make use of services that already exist independently from the particular physical product. However, some of these services need adaptations to work with the physical product (1). There are for example existing service centres that monitor data from sensors and take defined actions in case of alerts or if the received sensor data show critical values. If the machining centre mentioned above should be monitored by such a service provider, it is necessary to establish the data connection and to define threshold and corresponding actions.

Another category of services that extend the initial EP concept are available standard services that are applied without further adaptations (4). However, it may be necessary to prepare the physical product with interfaces according to the correct standards to make the service work (2). In the machining centre example, such a standard service could be express spare part logistics that enable the exchange of components and modules within 24 hours, 365 days per year. To apply the service, it could be necessary to align the size and weight of machine components to the standards of the specialized logistics provider that offers the service.

According to this widened view on the EP concept, there are different options for service innovation. Usually, it is assumed that service innovation leads to new services. E.g. Toivonen and Tuominen define service innovation as "a new service or such a renewal of an existing service which is put into practice and which provides benefit to the organization that has developed it" [8]. However, in the context of EP this does not cover all options of service innovation: Additional possibilities are new combinations of existing services with a certain physical product. Innovation also includes new adaptations of universal services or of the physical product to enable the application of standard services. This leads to certain challenges for manufacturing enterprises, if they are aiming at innovative EP:

- They need competencies in service development if they want to develop new services for their product or new products with related services.
- For new combinations of existing services with their products, they need to get to know potential service candidates. This means that they have to "look beyond their own backyard" into branches that are not yet related to their product.
- In both cases it could be necessary to have competencies in equipping the already existing product with standard interfaces to services. Therefore they need some "service thinking" that they can obtain from cooperation with services providers.

2.2 Existing Approaches to Support Service Innovation

In the past, approaches towards innovation in manufacturing enterprises have been focusing on the physical product, as their outcome has been rare in services [9]. Manufacturing and distribution as well as maintenance, repairs and recycling (in case such services are offered) were organized in linear deterministic Supply Chains. A new approach to support service innovation in manufacturing enterprises will have to overcome these rigid structures and address the challenges identified in the previous section. Two possible options to deal with this situation are described below: A top-level perspective on the reconfiguration of Supply Chains and the approach to apply a Virtual organization Breeding Environment in the context of service innovation.

Reconfiguration of the Supply Chain Using the Open Universe of Organizations. The traditional way to initiate the innovation of a new Extended Product is the reconfiguration of the Supply Chain by selecting new partners from the "open universe" of organizations (suppliers, service providers etc.). This is usually done by first identifying the needs of the customer and then selecting the EP components from more or less standard parts and services available on the market (see **Fig. 2**).

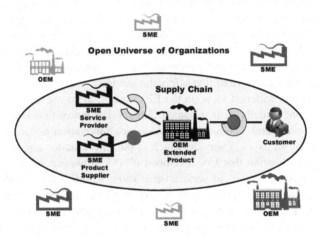

Fig. 2. Open Universe of Organizations

However, in this approach the innovation process (ideation, research, most of the development) is mainly conducted by the OEM. No guidelines or tools support this enterprise in service innovation. The interoperability of products and services is restrained by missing ICT support, thus mainly standard components are combined to a traditional EP. As there are also no "yellow pages" available to identify and acquire third party expertise and potential service candidates, reconfiguration of the Supply Chain is time consuming.

Virtual Organization Breeding Environment for Service Innovation. A suggested approach to overcome the drawbacks of dealing with an open universe of organizations is the Virtual organization Breeding Environment (VBE) [10]. It provides common operating principles and infrastructures based on long term cooperation agreements. The involved organizations and supporting institutions are in that way prepared for ad-hoc short-term collaborations. According to the needs of the customer, partners with the required competencies are selected from the pool of the VBE and form a Virtual Organization (VO) to innovate the required EP (see **Fig. 3**)

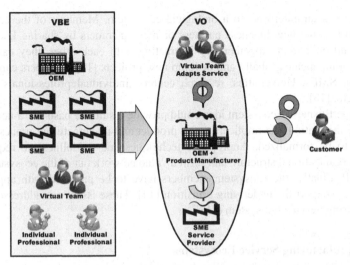

Fig. 3. Virtual organization Breeding Environment

While partner search and selection are supported by common rules and ICT platforms, this is not true for the innovation process itself. Although the reduced time required for the VO configuration allows for limited adaptations of services, the selection of components and competencies is still restricted to the partners of the VBE. Once configured, the VO cannot easily react to changing requirements by adding other standard services to the EP. Therefore, a new approach is required to fully support the full potential of the more open and service-oriented Extended Product 2.0 concept.

3   Manufacturing Service Ecosystems

3.1   Requirements towards a New Model to Support Service Innovation

As stated above, Extended Products need integrated development of physical product, services, and the manufacturing processes. Service requirements can have implications on the whole product life-cycle. Consequently, the product structure and additional components may have to be redesigned. Therefore, on the one hand a special development environment is needed to design and implement Extended Products. On the other hand, a set of models, methods, and tools to manage and align the product life-cycle with the service life-cycle is required. Besides, the governance of innovation processes needs "freedom" for new ideas and has to regard the common and complementary objectives of different stakeholders.

3.2   The Business Ecosystem Concept

A promising concept to tackle the challenges identified for service innovation is the Business Ecosystem. Introduced originally by Moore [11], it compares the business environment of an enterprise to a biological ecosystem. Members of the ecosystem are able to become new business partners or new customers by sharing knowledge, innovate and collaborate together. By interacting with each other, they can design new EP, communicate globally and develop new projects [12]. Members can involve big OEMs, SMEs, Universities, research centers, individual professionals and the customer etc. [13].

While the Business Ecosystem idea could provide a suitable basis for a new model for service innovation, the implications on product and manufacturing process design have still to be formalized. Appropriate techniques and guidelines are required to adapt the organizational structure and form a value network out of the ecosystem for a specific EP. Finally, the ecosystem members have to be provided with appropriate ICT tools to support the underlying transition [14]. These issues are addressed in the Manufacturing Service Ecosystem (MSE).

3.3   Manufacturing Service Ecosystems

The MSE is a non-hierarchical form of collaboration where various different organizations and individuals work together with common or complementary objectives on new value added combinations of manufactured products and product-related services. This includes the promotion, the development and the provision of new ideas, new products, new processes or new markets. Future Internet architectures and platforms enable the active participation of all stakeholders in all the phases of the product and service life cycle (see **Fig. 4**).

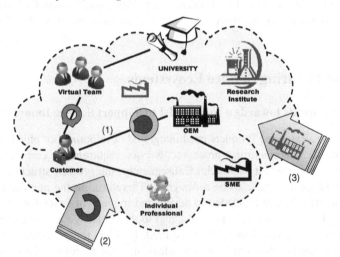

Fig. 4. The Manufacturing Service Ecosystem

The customer is part of the MSE, allowing for collaborative ideation and research in the ecosystem, based on the customer's requirements. The later steps of service innovation, like development, manufacturing and provision of the EP, are supported through the formation of a Virtual Manufacturing Enterprise (VME) structure (1). The VME flexibly adapts to changing requirements and can incorporate new partners from the MSE. Should a required service (2) or competency (3) not be available in the MSE, its permeable border allows for extension of the ecosystem. In addition, the broad variety of the ecosystem support the "look beyond the own backyard". Thus, an EP 2.0 of interoperable products and services can be configured through the MSE members.

Service innovation within the MSE is enabled via ICT through a Service Oriented Architecture (SOA) and the Digital Business Ecosystem (DBE) concept. SOA supports the processes and workflows in a Business Ecosystem through dynamic, on-the-fly compositions of the available ICT services. DBE amends the Business Ecosystems with a pervasive Internet-based environment, showing an evolutionary and self-organizing behavior [15].

4   Conclusion

This paper has shown that the trend for more and more individualized products requires bundling of tangible and intangible assets to Extended Products. The provision of services becomes more and more important for manufacturing enterprises, causing a shift of the original EP concept towards more openness for service innovation. The analysis of existing approaches towards service innovation has revealed that simple reconfiguration of Supply Chains or the application of the VBE concept is not sufficient for the EP 2.0 concept.

The Business Ecosystem has been identified as an environment that provides the necessary "freedom" to service innovation processes. Enhanced by techniques and guidelines and supported with Future Internet architectures and platforms, it can form a Manufacturing Service Ecosystem as the new model to support service innovation for EP 2.0 in temporary collaborative VME initiatives. The MSE allows new value added combinations of manufactured products and product-related services.

While the basic concepts of EP 2.0 and the MSE have been defined and presented, the required models, tools and ICT support have still to be described in detail. Further elaboration of the EP 2.0 concept and the design of a service innovation framework for MSE will be addressed in subsequent works.

Acknowledgements. This work has been partly funded by the European Commission through the FoF-ICT Project MSEE: Manufacturing SErvice Ecosystem (No. 284860), which is fostering the research in this area and will develop the final MSE concept and several practical implementations in the manufacturing industry until 2014. The authors wish to acknowledge the Commission and all the MSEE project partners for their contribution.

References

1. Baines, T., Lightfoot, H., Evans, S., Neely, A., Greenough, R., Peppard, J., Roy, R., Shehab, E., Braganza, A., Tiwari, A., Alcock, J., Angus, J., Bastl, M., Cousens, A., Irving, P., Johnson, M., Kingston, J., Lockett, H., Martinez, V., Michele, P., Tranfield, D., Walton, I., Wilson, H.: State-of-the-art in product-service systems. In: IMechE Proc., J. Engineering Manufacture, vol. 221, Pt. B (2007)

2. Thoben, K.-D., Eschenbächer, J., Jagdev, H.: Extended Products: Evolving traditional Product Concepts. In: 7th International Conference on Concurrent Enterprising, Bremen (2001)
3. Miller, D., Hope, Q., Eisenstat, R., Foote, N., Galbraith, J.: The problem of solutions: balancing clients and capabilities. Business Horizons, 3–12 (March/April 2002)
4. Windahl, C., Andersson, P., Berggren, C., Nehler, C.: Manufacturing firms and integrated solutions: characteristics and implications. European Journal of Innovation Management 7(3), 218–228 (2004)
5. Tukker, A., Tischner, U.: New Business for Old Europe: Product-Service Development, Competitiveness and Sustainability. Greenleaf Publishing, Sheffield (2006)
6. Johnston, R., Clark, G.: Service operations management: improving service delivery. Financial Times, Prentice Hall (2008)
7. Chesbrough, H.W.: Open Innovation: The new imperative for creating and profiting from technology. Harvard Business School Press, Boston (2003)
8. Toivonen, M., Tuominen, T.: Emergence of innovations in services. The Service Industries Journal 29(7), 887–902 (2009)
9. Djellal, F., Gallouj, F.: Innovation in services: Patterns of innovation organisation in service firms: postal survey results and theoretical models. Science and Public Policy 28(1), 57–67 (2001)
10. Afsarmanesh, H., Camarinha-Matos, L.M.: A framework for management of virtual organization breeding environments. In: Camarinha-Matos, L.M., Afsarmanesh, H., Ortiz, A. (eds.) Collaborative Networks and their Breeding Environments. IFIP, vol. 186, pp. 35–49. Springer, Boston (2003)
11. Moore, J.: Predators and Prey: The New Ecology of Competition. Harvard Business Review 71(3), 75–83 (1993)
12. Tapscott, D., Williams, A.: Wikinomics: How Mass Collaboration Changes Everything. Penguin Books, New York (2006)
13. Peltoniemi, M., Vuori, E.: Business Ecosystem as the New Approach to Complex Adaptive Business Environments. In: Proc. 4th Annu. Conference eBRF (eBusiness Research Forum), Tampere (2004)
14. Sitek, P., Sesana, M., Hong-Linh, T.: On Baseline IT-Services to Support Enterprise Collaboration. In: Proceedings of the 15th International Conference on Concurrent Enterprising (ICE 2009), Leiden (2009)
15. Nachira, F., digital-ecosystems.org, http://www.digital-ecosystems.org/events/2006.06-sardegna/nachira-sardegna-ict.pdf (accessed April 25, 2012)

Multiagent System-Based Simulation Method of Service Diffusion in Consumer Networks – Application to Repeatedly Purchased Plural Services –

Nobutada Fujii, Toshiya Kaihara, and Tomoya Yoshikawa

Graduate School of System Informatics, Kobe University
Rokkodai 1-1, Nada, Kobe 657-8501, Japan
nfujii@phoenix.kobe-u.ac.jp, kaihara@kobe-u.ac.jp,
yosikawa@kaede.cs.kobe-u.ac.jp
http://www21.cs.kobe-u.ac.jp/

Abstract. This paper presents a simulation based analysis method for service diffusion in consumer networks. Services with good qualities do not always diffuse because service quality is often unstable because of the nature of service delivery systems involving human. Consumers cannot also confirm the quality of service before purchase because service has no shape. Therefore, it is necessary to study diffusion process of service by computer simulations to clarify the process of acceptance among consumers in consideration with heterogeneity of consumer utility due to the unstable service quality. This paper proposes a multiagent-based model for diffusion of plural competing services repeated purchased in consumer networks including heterogeneity of consumer utility. It is verified that the heterogeneity of consumer utility and network structure affect service diffusion process in the results of computer simulations. Finally, the diffusion process of services is concluded in terms both of the number of service and repetition of service purchase.

Keywords: Service, Diffusion, Simulation.

1 Introduction

Current vigorous research activities on the fields of Service Science [1], Product-Service System (PSS) [2] and Service Engineering [3] mainly focuses on the design methodologies of services. However, services with good qualities do not always penetrated in the market; not only services design method but also services diffusion analysis method is important to realize services innovation. This paper describes a multiagent system-based simulation method for analysis of service diffusion mechanism in consumer networks.

Because of characteristics of services such as intangibility, inseparability, heterogeneity or perishability, the following influences can be identified in the purchase decisions of consumers; presumably, the utility of a service is more heterogeneous among consumers than utility of a product. Expectations before

C. Emmanouilidis, M. Taisch, D. Kiritsis (Eds.): APMS 2012, Part II, IFIP AICT 398, pp. 313–320, 2013.

purchase become heterogeneous because consumers can not check the quality of the service a priori. The utility from service use also becomes heterogeneous because of the heterogeneity of service quality. This study employs the heterogeneity of consumer utilities.

Externality is also an important factor affecting service diffusion. Externality is definable as a situation by which a certain economic subject affects other subjects without a market, perhaps by word of mouth or through fashion. Because the influence of the externality occurs as a result of interaction among consumers, it is also necessary to consider connections of consumers to study service diffusion. Kawamura created the multiagent-system-based model of the market in which the connection network of consumers is expressed as complex networks [4] based on the early study of network externality [5]. Although those earlier studies investigate consumer connections as well as the externality, they do not consider the heterogeneity of consumer utilities due to the services characteristics.

Previous works [6][7] focused on the service purchased only once such as an Internet connection provider, then, the proposed method was applied to the diffusion of one kind of the service purchased repeatedly [8]. The proposed method is extended and applied to service diffusion process of plural competing services repeatedly purchased in this study. Finally, the diffusion process of services is concluded in terms both of the number of service and repetition of service purchase.

2   Service Diffusion Model

2.1   Consumer Agent Model

A consumer agent is modeled as following; each consumer agent i has a utility $U_{im}(t)$ about service m and a threshold T_{im} at the simulation step t. The consumer agent i purchases a service m when $U_{im}(t)$ exceeds T_{im}:

$$U_{im}(t) \geq T_{im} \tag{1}$$

Consumer agent i's utility $U_{im}(t)$ is defined as

$$U_{im}(t) = R_{im}^{exp}(t) + \sum_{j \in N \backslash \{i\}} g_{jm}(t) y_{im}^{j}(t) + L_{im}(t) \tag{2}$$

where $R_{im}^{exp}(t)$ represents the expected utility before purchasing the service m; $g_{jm}(t) y_{im}^{j}(t)$ signifies the utility acquired through interaction with other consumers. N is the set of consumers. $L_{im}(t)$ represents influence from the experience of the previously purchased service m.

It is assumed that the consumer utilities become heterogeneous among consumer agents according to the characteristics of service; the expected utility becomes heterogeneous because the service quality cannot be confirmed before purchase by consumers. The actual utility also includes heterogeneity since the service quality is also heterogeneous due to the service provider's ability. To model such heterogeneity of the consumer utilities, normal distribution is introduced as following:

$$\begin{cases} R_{im}^{exp}(t) = N(\alpha, \beta_e), & \text{before the first purchase} \\ R_{im}^{act}(t) = N(\alpha, \beta_a), & \text{after purchase} \end{cases} \tag{3}$$

Furthermore, $R_{im}^{act}(t)$ affects the expected utility at the next purchase decisions:

$$R_{im}^{exp}(t+1) = \begin{cases} R_{im}^{act}(t), & \text{if } i \text{ purchases service } m \text{ at time step } t \\ R_{im}^{exp}(t), & \text{otherwise} \end{cases} \tag{4}$$

It is also assumed that each consumer evaluates a service based on the difference between expectation of and results from the service: consumer i's degree of satisfaction is represented as $S_{im}(t)$. Referring to the earlier research [9], $S_{im}(t)$ is formulated based on prospect theory. The formula of $S_{im}(t)$ is divided into plus-number and minus-number sides around the point that R_{im}^{exp} and R_{im}^{act} coincides. The influence of dissatisfaction is greater than the influence of satisfaction. The value of $S_{im}(t)$ is represented as follows:

$$S_{im}(t) = \begin{cases} f(R_{im}^{exp}, R_{im}^{act}), & \text{if } i \text{ use service } m \\ 0, & \text{otherwise} \end{cases} \tag{5}$$

$$f(R_{im}^{exp}, R_{im}^{act}) = \begin{cases} a^+\{1 - e^{-\frac{b^+}{a^+}(R_{im}^{act} - R_{im}^{exp})}\}, \\ \quad (R_{im}^{act} \geq R_{im}^{exp}) \\ a^-\{1 - e^{-\frac{b^-}{a^-}(-R_{im}^{act} + R_{im}^{exp})}\}, \\ \quad (R_{im}^{act} < R_{im}^{exp}) \end{cases} \tag{6}$$

Therein, a^+ and a^- represent the values at which equation (6) converges; b^+ and b^- represent the values of inclination around origin of equation (6). $|a^-|$ $(a^- < 0)$ is set to the larger value than $|a^+|$ $(a^+ > 0)$, so that the influence of dissatisfaction is greater than the influence of satisfaction.

The consumer agent purchasing the service notifies other connected consumers about the effect of the externality. The utility obtained by the externality $y_{im}^j(t)$ is represented as

$$\begin{aligned} y_{im}^j(t) = &(R_{jm}^{act}(t) + S_{jm}(t))w_{ij} \\ &+ (R_{jm}^{act}(t) + S_{jm}(t)) \sum_{x \in N \backslash \{i,j\}} w_{ix}w_{xj} \\ &+ (R_{jm}^{act}(t) + S_{jm}(t)) \sum_{x,y \in N \backslash \{i,j\}, x \neq y} w_{ix}w_{xy}w_{yj} \end{aligned} \tag{7}$$

where w_{ij} represents the degree of closeness between connected consumers, defined as

$$\begin{cases} w_{ij} > 0, & \text{if } i \text{ and } j \text{ are friends} \\ w_{ij} = 0, & \text{otherwise} \end{cases} \tag{8}$$

$$\text{subject to} \sum_{j \in N_i} w_{ij} = 1 \tag{9}$$

where N_i represents the set of consumers connected to the consumer agent i.

The effect of the externality is considered until the third term of $y_{im}^j(t)$ because the value after the fourth term of $y_{im}^j(t)$ is neglected according to eqs. (8) and (9). Furthermore, $g_{jm}(t)$ is defined as the following because a consumer who does not purchase the service can not note the effects of the externality:

$$g_{jm}(t) = \begin{cases} 1, \text{if } j \text{ is using service } m \\ 0, \text{otherwise} \end{cases} \tag{10}$$

Referring to Guadagni's report about brand choice [10], the influence from the experience of the previously purchased service m, $L_{im}(t)$, can defined as

$$L_{im}(t) = \begin{cases} S_{im}(t), & \text{if } i \text{ purchases service } m \text{ first} \\ \lambda L_i(t-1) + (1-\lambda)S_{im}(t), \text{otherwise} \end{cases} \tag{11}$$

where λ represents a weight value between the loyalty at step $t-1$ and the satisfaction at step t.

2.2   Consumer Networks Models

This study adopts complex networks [11] to express connections among consumers. The complex networks can model networks in the real world including the networks of the information and communication technology, the biological network, the social network, and so on.

Networks comprise nodes and links: nodes represent consumers and links express acquaintance relations between consumers. In the study of complex networks, three major indices express network features: average distance L, clustering coefficient C, and degree distribution. Node i's average distance L_i is the average of distances from node i to all other nodes; the distance $d_{i,j}$ is defined as the minimum number of links that an agent passed from node i to node j. The clustering coefficient C is an index to express the group degree of the network. The number of links connected to agent i is called agent i's degree k_i. The degree distribution is the distribution of degrees of all nodes.

To model connections of consumers, six network models proposed in the research area of complex networks are adopted: a Regular model, Random model [12], WS model [13], BA model [14], KE-1 model [15], and KE-2 model [16]. In this study, the six models are introduced to express the connection of consumers under the condition; the number of nodes is set to 1000 and the number of links is set to 3000.

3   Experimental Results and Discussion

3.1   Experimental Conditions

The computer simulations are conducted using above mentioned consumer agent and networks models. The number of service purchased by consumers is set to two where $m = 2$; simulations reveal how two kinds of competing services penetrate among consumers. The market model is constructed where the number of consumer agent and the average degree are set to 1000 and six, respectively. The threshold values of consumer agents, T_{im}, are set by uniform random $U(3,6)$. Values a^+, a^-, b^+ and b^- in the equation (6) are determined to make S_{im} set to -3.0 and 1.5 when the difference between R_{im}^{act} and R_{im}^{exp} is -3.0 and 3.0. The rate of the innovator consumers that have purchased the service at the initial state is set to 2.5% based on Rogers's theory [17]. The simulation is terminated at time step 50 ($t_{end} = 50$).

Simulations are executed under three conditions that each expected utility and actual utility is set to the value shown in Table 1 due to the difference of heterogeneity using normal distribution.

Table 1. Experimental Condition

	Service 1		Service 2	
	R_{i1}^{exp}	R_{i1}^{act}	R_{i2}^{exp}	R_{i2}^{act}
Condition 1	3	3	$N(3, 0.5^2)$	$N(3, 0.5^2)$
Condition 2	3	3	$N(3, 1^2)$	$N(3, 1^2)$
Condition 3	$N(3, 0.5^2)$	$N(3, 0.5^2)$	$N(3, 1^2)$	$N(3, 1^2)$

3.2 Results and Discussion

The results of the experiments are shown in Table 2. Values in the table represent resultant average diffusion rate in 100 trials obtained by dividing the number of purchased consumers by the total number of consumers at the end of the experiments. In the point of average diffusion rate, every results in the three experimental conditions shows that service with lower heterogeneity (service 1) can obtain higher diffusion rate than the service with higher heterogeneity (service 2) although the service with higher heterogeneity can obtain higher diffusion rate in some trials. These results are in contrast with the previous experimental results in the case of diffusion process of one kind of service; more heterogeneous service could obtain higher diffusion rate.

Fig. 1 represents transition of the consumer utilities who changes the purchased service from Service 2 to Service 1 during a simulation under the condition 2 and Regular network model. In the early stage of the simulation, the consumer purchases Service 2 with higher heterogeneity of consumer utility. In turn, as the simulation progresses, because of the effect of dissatisfaction with the service and the influence of the externality from the connected other consumers, the consumer stops buying Service 2 and starts purchasing Service 1 with homogeneous consumer utility. The experimental results reveal that services with more homogeneous utility tends to penetrate in the market with plural services purchased repeatedly.

As a summary of simulation results in the proposals, Table 3 concludes service diffusion from the viewpoints both of the number of services diffused and the

Table 2. Experimental Result

Network model		Regular	Random	WS	BA	KE-1	KE-2
Condition 1	Service 1	51.43	70	68.78	67	46.31	58.61
	Service 2	40.72	30.00	29.77	33.00	40.62	36.25
	Total	92.15	100	98.55	100	86.93	94.86
Condition 2	Service 1	81.47	100	98.10	85.00	68.11	88.72
	Service 2	8.30	0	0.63	14.76	15.34	5.69
	Total	89.77	100	98.73	99.76	83.44	94.41
Condition 3	Service 1	66.61	68.00	95.72	63.00	51.07	76.02
	Service 2	13.62	31.50	1.99	36.39	19.61	12.53
	Total	80.23	99.49	97.71	99.34	70.68	88.55

Table 3. Summary of service diffusion

	Single service	Plural services
Service purchased only once	Service diffuses with properly heterogeneous consumer utility	Service diffuses with heterogeneous consumer utility
Service purchased repeatedly		Service diffuses with homogeneous consumer utility

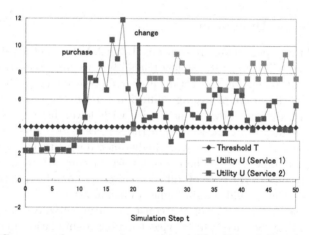

Fig. 1. Consumer changes service purchased (Condition 2, Regular model)

repetition of purchase. In the single service market, service with heterogeneous consumer utility diffuses among consumers regardless of frequency of purchase. However, too much heterogeneity of consumer utility ends in no diffusion. In the case of plural competing services, service with heterogeneous consumer utility penetrates among consumers, which is purchased only once. In turn, service with homogeneous consumer utility diffuses in the case of repeated purchased services.

These results reveal that service provider needs to develop the new services with taking into account the characteristics of the services from the viewpoints of the existence of the plural services and the frequency of purchase.

4 Conclusion

In this study, a multiagent-based simulation method of service diffusion was proposed, which was modeled by using multiagent system and consumer's communication networks based on complex networks. Heterogeneity of consumer utilities composed by expected and actual utilities of service were also introduced. The proposed method was applied to the repeatedly purchased plural service market. Computer simulation results revealed that diffused services are difference from the viewpoint of the service market; the number of the services and the frequency of purchase.

References

1. Spohrer, J., Maglio, P.P., Bailey, J., Gruhl, D.: Steps toward a science of service system. Computer 40(1), 71–77 (2007)
2. Mont, O.K.: Clarifying the Concept of Product-Service System. Journal of Cleaner Production 10(3), 237–245 (2002)
3. Shimomura, Y., Tomiyama, T.: Service Modeling for Service Engineering. In: Arai, E., Kimura, F., Goossenaerts, J., Shirase, K. (eds.) Knowledge and Skill Chains in Engineering and Manufacturing. IFIP, vol. 168, pp. 31–38. Springer, Boston (2005)
4. Kawamura, H., Ohuchi, A.: Evaluation of present strategies in multiagent product market model with network externality. Transactions of the Operations Research Society of Japan 48, 48–65 (2005) (in Japanese)
5. Katz, M.L., Shapiro, C.: Network externalities, competition, and compatibility, American Economic Reviews. American Economic Reviews 75(3), 424–440 (1985)
6. Fujii, N., Kaihara, T., Yoshikawa, T.: Multiagent system-based simulation of service diffusion in consumer networks - Introducing heterogeneity into consumer utility. International Journal of Organizational and Collective Intelligence 2(1), 49–62 (2011)
7. Fujii, N., Kaihara, T., Yoshikawa, T.: Simulation based diffusion analysis of plural competing services in consumer networks - Introducing heterogeneity into consumer utility. In: Proc. of International Symposium on Scheduling 2011 (ISS 2011) (2011)
8. Fujii, N., Kaihara, T., Yoshikawa, T.: Simulation based Service Diffusion Analysis in Consumer Networks Introducing Heterogeneity of Consumer Utility - Application to repeatedly purchased service. In: Advances in Production Management Systems, cd-rom (2011)
9. Yoshimitsu, Y., Kimita, K., Arai, T., Shimomura, Y.: Analysis of Service Using an Evaluation Model of Customer Satisfaction. In: Proc. of the 15th CIRP Life Cycle Engineering Seminar 2008, CD-ROM (2008)
10. Guadagni, P.M., Little, J.D.C.: A Logit Model of Brand Choise Calibrated on Scanner Data. Marketing Science 2(3), 203–238 (1983)
11. Newman, M., Barabási, A.L., Watts, D.J.: The Structure and Dynamics of Networks. Princeton University Press (2006)

12. Erdös, P., Rényi, A.: On random graph. Publicationes Mathematicae 6, 290–297 (1959)
13. Watts, D.J., Strogatz, S.H.: Collective dynamics of 'small-world' networks. Nature 393, 440–442 (1998)
14. Barabási, A.L., Albert, R.: Emergence of scaling in random networks. Science 286, 509–512 (1999)
15. Klemm, K., Eguíluz, V.M.: Highly Clustered Scale-free Networks. Physical Review E, 65(3), 036123 (2002)
16. Klemm, K., Eguíluz, V.M.: Growing Scale-free Networks with Small World Behavior. Physical Review E 65(5), 057102 (2002)
17. Rogers, E.M.: Diffusion of Innovations. Free Press (1982)

Manufacturing Service Innovation Ecosystem

Marco Taisch, Mohammadreza Heydari Alamdari, and Christiano Zanetti

Politecnico di Milano, Piazza Leonardo Da Vinci 32, 20133, Milan, Italy
{marco.taisch,mohammadreza.heydari,cristiano.zanetti}@polimi.it

Abstract. Due to the increasing global commercial competition, the current economic crisis and globalization, enterprises would like to shift from a pure product sales structure towards after-sales services and related activities. It is noteworthy that "profit generated by after-sale service is often higher than the one obtained with sales; the service market can be four or five times larger than the market for products" [1].

The purpose of this paper is to lay down the foundations for a governance framework, by using the models and methods which can support various levels of performance indicators in service, servitization, governance and innovation. The basic idea behind of a governance framework is to create a trust relationship between seller and buyer for covering the customer requirements.

Keywords: Key Performance Indicator, Servitization and ecosystem governance.

1 Introduction

Manufacturing companies which want to support the service life cycle need to improve the service structure by using complementary pillars like collaborative innovation, IT interaction and internet business infrastructure to characterize new service ecosystem. "Most important aim of this ecosystem is enabling companies to self-organize in distributed, autonomous, interoperable, non-hierarchical innovation ecosystem in tangible and intangible manufacturing assets" [2].

This paper introduces two main classes of scenarios, which are useful to reach the above-mentioned ecosystem features:

1- The Product2Service scenario, based on manufacturing of goods and selling of service, emphasize on selling long-life service instead of one-shot physical goods sale. This model helps to beat the low-wages countries competition by using intangible values like reliability, accuracy, innovation and social responsibility.

2- The product+service scenario is less radical, in principle, as manufacturers foresee the simultaneous offering of physical products and extended tailored service. In this case, both physical products and services contribute to the revenues; their balance needs to be adaptively determined and continuous innovation of service is key competitive advantages [2].

The new service ecosystem needs a governance framework to evaluate and defining performance measurements and service level, so to create a trust relationship among

C. Emmanouilidis, M. Taisch, D. Kiritsis (Eds.): APMS 2012, Part II, IFIP AICT 398, pp. 321–328, 2013.
© IFIP International Federation for Information Processing 2013

seller and buyer, and support customer requirements and priorities. This paper stressed out on creating a set of Key Performance Indicators (KPI) and Service Level Agreement (SLA) for monitoring and controlling the procedures.

A Performance Indicator (PI) is a quantified data which measured the efficiency of decision variables in the achievement of objectives defined at a considered decision level and in coherence with the defined business strategy [3]. Meanwhile, a Service Level Agreement (SLA) is a technical contract between seller and buyer which is clarified service provider's duties and roles by setting boundaries, conditions, penalties and expectations. SLA sets a clear customer relationship and bridge a gap between user and service provider [4]. Service performance assessment and governance specifically addressed the KPIs and SLAs to the below mentioned levels:

1. Service as such;
2. Servitization process;
3. Ecosystem governance;
4. Innovation in ecosystem.

Refer to above mentioned levels, KPIs will be evaluated in Model Driven Service Engineering Architecture (MDSEA) method and its decomposition levels (BSM-TIM-TSM) which will be later explained, to assure that performance indicators have been properly identified through the organization [5]. In order to accomplish Servitization process, InnoScore model will be preferred to using for servitization assessment. InnoScore model is on the basis of the innovation capability.

Likewise, the term of Unified Governance Framework (UGF) will be intended to support Ecosystem governance, with a focus on how IT-related components can help the governance. It can be stated that ECOGRAI method [6] has been selected after evaluating some of the popular methods and tools to govern frameworks through performance indicators, essentially because ECOGRAI is based on recursive decision making process. This model is designed to aim at business control and development. And finally related KPIs classified by VRM (Value Reference Model) which provides pre-defined measurable indicators for value chain goals in several dimensions.

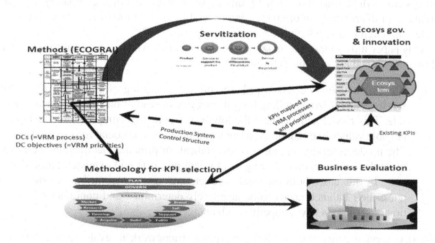

Fig. 1. KPI management method

Consistent with our results classified KPIs will be tested in real condition for evaluating effectiveness at end-users pilot. As shown in the figure below, the relevant interaction among different modules have been highlighted for KPIs generation and management.

The highlighted process in the above figure is started by designing and implementing the performance indicators by ECOGRAI model, this model generates performance indicator system (PIS) for industrial and service organizations. The basic idea behind ECOGRAI selection is that this model is based on decision making, furthermore this model is established by two main steps: design and implementation, in order to a coherent set of specification sheets explaining each Performance Indicators by design step then implementation step operating the PIS by business intelligence tools. The Whole of the mentioned process is done in six phases.

Once the KPIs have been defined by ECOGRAI, VRM model is used to classify specific KPIs to define, to prioritize and assess the PIs which are needed to govern every process. In addition, keeping in mind that servitization process specifically addressed the product shift to service by monitoring this transition. Furthermore classified KPIs should be used to monitor the service ecosystem both at design and run time; consequently, specific type of KPIs must be designed to cover the various stages of ecosystem.

Finally, the KPIs which are designed by ECOGRAI method and listed by VRM model should be tested in a real situation by End users for monitoring and evaluating the effectiveness. As shown on the figure 1, and refer to above mentioned illustration relevant stream of this literature mainly rooted on definition of sets and methods to manage the KPIs related to the service ecosystem.

2   Definition of PIs and KPIs and Existing Situation in Companies

This paper stressed out on creating a set of Key Performance Indicators (KPI) for monitoring and controlling the procedures. Refer to the performance indicator definition which was mentioned in previous pages, there are several kinds of PIs that can be defined. The first kind is the PIs for results. These measure directly the achievement of objectives. Let's consider for an instance a total amount of turn over raised by service against overall organization revenue. The second kind is the progress PIs. These are measuring a progress in the achievement of the objective. For example: total number of service occurrences per month and average service value vs. organization monthly objectives. So, these two types of PI's are complementary [7].

The second typology of PIs concerns the three steps of monitoring: (1) measuring the performance of a part of the system at the daily routine works which is called operational PIs, (2) tactical PIs used for measuring the middle term of current system operations (3) finally, strategic PIs used for measuring the performance of the whole controlled system.

3   KPIs and SLAs for Service Oriented Production System

By defining the framework for service ecosystem modeling around three abstraction level which will be defined in later paragraphs, and in order to accomplish this framework a description of KPIs for service presented: Business Service Modeling (BSM), Technology Independent Modeling (TIM), Technology Specific Modeling (TSM) level is important thus giving the foundations to governance of the performance indicators within the ecosystem. In here below, brief definition of mentioned levels are considerable:

-   Business Service Modeling (BSM), which specifies the models, at the global level, describing the running of the enterprise or set of enterprises as well as the links between these enterprises.
-   Technology Independent Modeling (TIM), which is the model at a second level of abstraction independent from the technology used to implement the system.
-   Technology Specific Modeling (TSM) that combines the specification in the TIM model with details that specify how the system uses a particular type of technology (such as, for example, IT platform, Machine technology organization structure or human profile).

So, based on the previous decomposition (BSM, TIM & TSM) it is necessary to ensure that at each level of decomposition, performance evaluation is possible. In order to verify the achievement of objectives and the use of action means or interoperable solutions. The framework of the performance indicators is shown in figure 2.

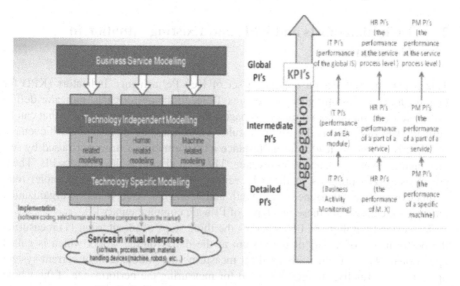

Fig. 2. Performance Indicator in the frame of MDSEA

The proposed MDSEA framework defines KPIs for the service ecosystem governance then is analyzed in terms of implementation and monitoring. So, by focusing on KPIs definition in detail, it is defined related to the three kinds of components: IT, Organization and human resources. The criteria of these performance indicators will be related to traditional performances such as cost, quality, lead time, efficiency or other kinds of performances such as interoperability, flexibility, environment, etc.

4   KPIs and SLAs for Servitization

"There is clear evidence that manufacturing firms are servitizing–either adding services to or integrating services in their core products" [8]. This concept clearly shown in figure 3, where servitiziation level goes from "tangible product" as lowest level to "product as a service" as highest level. In particularly:

- First level: the servitization process starts by adding a simple service to the product and the evolution shift from pure product toward Product+Service.
- Second level: it is an evolution of the previous one. The service is more elaborated and increases the differentiation.
- Third level: physical goods remain the property of the manufacturer and are considered as investment, while revenues come uniquely from the services.

Manufacturing companies need to evaluate their current level of servitization and then, recognize the requirements for moving to the upper level. Change management practices are needed to implement promoting the process.

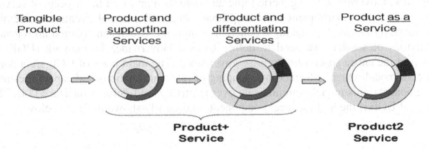

Fig. 3. Different level of servitization [9]

Servitization Assessment

Several methods and frameworks were developed for evaluating the innovation capability in service. All selected methods like: IMP^{3}rove, DIUS and InnoScore have their own pros and cons, and it is quite difficult to say which one is the best; nevertheless, in this paper we choose InnoScore-model which is oriented on the frequently used and accepted EFQM model [10]. With linking the consulting methods of the "InnoAudits" [11] and the innovation model of the Fraunhofer – Institute for Industrial Engineering and Organization it is developed a self-assessment tool.

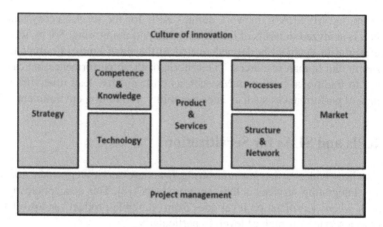

Fig. 4. The nine areas of InnoScore [12]

InnoScore method is implemented as a web based benchmarking platform [13], and made by nine different area where create the Meta-Model to measure and assess the innovation capability. These areas are shown on the above figure.

5   KPIs and SLAs for Service Governance

A good starting point for elaborating service governance can be borrowed from monitoring efficiency and effectiveness of each service activities like customer service satisfaction, flexibility, service performance and customer satisfaction toward the network. Governance is a generic topic and able to support all the aspects of service activities from environment level as primary stage till external events as extremity stage; nevertheless, for making a coherent monitoring which can covered all relevant activities of service, we need to define Unified Governance Framework (UGF) to support the entire space of enterprise governance. The main parts of UGF are a component model which is formed by grouping of relevant functions and capabilities into components, this model communicate over relatively well-defined interface [14]. The core of UGF is the highest-level components and clearly shown in figure below.

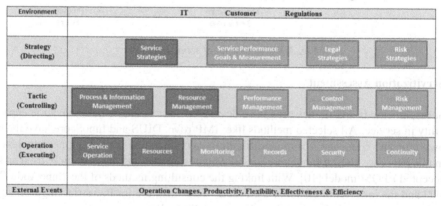

Fig. 5. UGF component model

The basic idea behind UGF is focusing on enterprise governance, like clarifying and describing governance components more deeply than the rest of the enterprise. In the figure 5, the normal enterprise capabilities are summarized in strategy layer. On the contrary in the tactical layer, the normal enterprise capabilities are defined in terms of process and information management and resource management. Finally the normal enterprise capabilities are evaluated in a similar way at operation layer.

As a summary, if we focus on dynamic UGF view, a combination of a top-down measuring model and bottom-up KPIs analysis will be necessary to manage service within the ecosystem.

6   KPIs and SLAs for Innovation Ecosystem

In the previous chapters different perspective on KPIs and SLAs in Service ecosystem were described. But in this chapter we focused on specific performance indicators that can be used to describe and assess innovation process in service ecosystem. Indeed at first step innovative PIs should follow the criteria which are generated by ECOGRAI method for designing and implementing the PIs and then VRM model classify and list the PIs to use them in real situation for testing by end users. There is broad range of approaches to classify indicators which are related to innovation; on the other hand, the common elements of these approaches can be presented like: PIs based on condition, output, input and interaction.

Meanwhile, in the VRM model innovation is only process beside various other processes and there is only a very limited set of indicators that are more related to the output than to the process.

7   Conclusion

Finally, this paper tries to provide assessment for creating comprehensive KPIs and SLAs to measure actors' performances in various stages by following the mentioned methods. These methods including (1) ECOGRAI model which is established to design and implement KPIs (2) VRM method defined to classify the KPIs refer to service ecosystem (3) the InnoScore method used for servitization assessment (4) UGF framework for monitoring service activities. This evaluation creates conditions to have disclosure and sharing resource within an enterprise network, creating trust among actors and exchanges based on the value added into the different processes and enterprises.

References

1. Bundschuh, R., Dezvane, T.: How to make after sale services pay off. The McKinsey Quarterly 4, 116–127 (2003)
2. Manufacturing SErvice Ecosystem (2011)
3. Fitz-Gibbon, C.T.: Performance indicators (1990)

4. Wustenhoff, E.: Service Level Agreement in the data center. Sun Microsystem (April 2002)
5. Marr, B.: How to design Key Performance Indicators Neely, A. I. V. The servitization of Manufacturing Further Evidence (October 2006)
6. Ducq, Y.: Contribution à une méthode d'analyse de la cohérence des systèmes deProduction dans le cadre du modèle GRAI.Thèse de doctorat de l'université deBordeaux I (1999) (in French)
7. Ducq, Y.: Definition and aggregation of a performance measurement system in threeAeronautical work shop using the ECOGARI Method. Production Planning and Control, 163–177 (2005)
8. Neely, A., Bourne, M., Kennerley, M.: Performance measurement system design: Developing and testing a process-based approach (1995)
9. Thoben, K.D.: Extended Products: Evolving Traditional Product concepts. Engineering the knowledge Economy through Co-operation, Bremen, pp. 429–439 (2001)
10. Lay, G.S.: Analyse von Verbreitung und Wirkung der Anwendung des EFQM-Modells in deutschen Betrieben. EFQM-Nutzung in Deutschland, ZWF, S. 884–S. 888 (2009) (in German)
11. Rogowski, T.H.: Methods and tools to support the innovation framework: Tools of the VIVA toolbox, Open innovation for small und medium sized enterprises (2007)
12. Wagner, K.S.: Fit für Innovationen: Untersuchung von Erfolgsfaktoren und Indikatoren zur Steigerung der Innovationsfähigkeit anhand von sechs innovativenFallbeispielen produzierender KMU. Fraunhofer, Stuttgart (2007) (in German)
13. Rogowski, T.: Internetgestütztes Benchmarking zur Bestimmung der Innovations fähigkeit. In: Henning, K. (ed.) Präventiver Arbeits- und Gesundheitsschutz 2020, pp. S. 100–S. 104. Tagungsband zur Jahrestagung 2007 des BMBF-Förderschwerpunkts, Aachen (2008) (in German)
14. Pfitzmann, B.: Unified Governance framework (UGF) initiative. IBM (December 2007)

Improvement Method of Service Productivity for Taxi Company

Takashi Tanizaki

Department of Information and Systems Enginnering,
Faculty of Engineering, Kinki University, Hiroshima, Japan
tanizaki@hiro.kindai.ac.jp

Abstract. We propose improvement method of service productivity for Taxi Company of rearranging taxi drivers working hours. There are two ways a taxi company gets customers. One is to deliver taxi for a telephone request, and the other is to get customers on street. In Japan, there are many taxi companies where the ratio of the former method is higher. Therefore we research rearrangement method of the taxi drivers working hours so as to operate many taxis with many telephone requests. We find it effective strategy to increase taxi drivers in midnight and early morning with many customers per taxi instead of decreasing taxi drivers in daytime with few customers per taxi.

Keywords: service productivity, taxi company, rearrangement working time, simulation, staff scheduling.

1 Introduction

In recent years, it became very severe to get customer between taxi companies in Japan. The number of taxis is increased, because it was easy to start Taxi Company from 2002 by regal revision, but customers decreased. As a result, income of a taxi per day was decreased (see Fig.1). Then taxi companies introduce various method to gain customers, for example, customer membership, information system for efficient

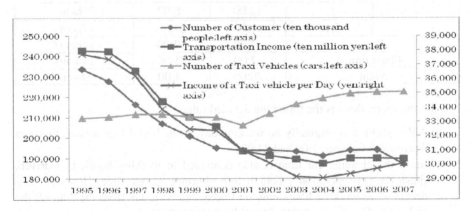

Fig. 1. Income of taxi per day

C. Emmanouilidis, M. Taisch, D. Kiritsis (Eds.): APMS 2012, Part II, IFIP AICT 398, pp. 329–336, 2013.
© IFIP International Federation for Information Processing 2013

taxi operation [1][2]. There are many taxi companies which introduce a taxi operation system using GPS and radio system to shorten taxi waiting time. But taxi waiting time couldn't be shortened, if the operation demands of a taxi exceed the number of taxis which can be worked. Furthermore, there is a problem that suitable service arrangement method is not established to the operation demands of a taxi. From above reason, we analyze telephone requests data and taxi operation data from the Taxi Company, and research taxi driver arrangement method to improve service productivity.

In this paper, we analyze present situation of the Taxi Company which we research (we call Company A in this paper), research improvement method of rearranging taxi drivers working hours using computer simulation, and verify validity of our method.

2   Subjects of Company A

2.1   Taxi Driver's Working Hours for Company A

Leaving and returning garage time according to taxi driver's service pattern of Company A are shown in Table 1. Taxi driver's service pattern consists of four groups, such as Shift, Day, Fixed time, and Night.

In Shift, taxi drivers change service pattern I, II, III, IV, and Free by every other day. In Day, taxi drivers work from Monday to Saturday. In Fixed time, taxi drivers change working group A and B in each week. They work on Monday, Wednesday, and Friday in group A, Tuesday, Thursday, and Saturday in group B. In Night, taxi drivers work on "Monday, Wednesday, Friday" and "Tuesday, Thursday, Saturday" in each week or work on Friday and Saturday every week.

Table 1. Leaving and returning garage time

Service pattern		Leaving	Returning	Total working hours
Shift	I	7:00	1:00	18hours
	II	8:00	2:00	18hours
	III	8:00	3:00	19hours
	IV	12:00	8:00	20hours
	Free	7:00	24:00	17hours
Day		7:00	19:00	12hours
Fixed time		7:00	21:00	14hours
Night		20:00	4:00	8hours

Furthermore, there is the following detailed rule.

(a) Although Free is originally no working day, if the taxi driver wishes, they can freely work between 7:00 and 24:00.

(b) Since the cleaning car time is also contained in working hours, taxi drivers finish the taxi operation 1 hour before returning garage time. However, they drive taxi as working hours only on Friday and Saturday from the 20th till the end of the month, because there will be many customers.

2.2   Subjects of Company A

There are two customer acquisition methods for Taxi Companies in Japan. One is to deliver a taxi for a telephone request, and the other is to get customers on street. For the former method, it is required to deliver a taxi immediately by telephone a request. For the latter method, it is required to allocate taxis for a place with many customers who need a taxi. In Japan, there are many taxi companies whose customer acquisition ratio of former method is higher than latter one. We research a service system with which many taxis work in time zone with many telephone requests.

In order to extract present subjects, we analyze the number of telephone requests per taxi in every hour (we call it load) shown in (1).If load is high, taxis for telephone requests are short, and if low, taxis are enough.

$$L_{ijk} = \frac{R_{ijk}}{T_{ijk}} \qquad (1)$$

L_{ijk} : Load per taxi on i-month j-day k-time
R_{ijk} : The number of telephone requests on i-month j-day k-time
T_{ijk} : The number of taxis which can be worked on i-month j-day k-time

We get telephone request data from Company A, and calculate the number of telephone requests per hour, day of the week, and load based on (1), respectively. From Fig.2 and Fig.3, we find out subjects of Company A as follows.

  (a) The peak hours of the number telephone requests and load differ (See Fig.2).
  (b) The distribution according to day of the week of telephone requests and load is
     almost the same. They are high on Friday and Saturday (See Fig.3).

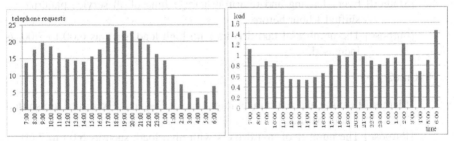

Fig. 2. The number of telephone requests (left Fig.) and load (right Fig.) per hour

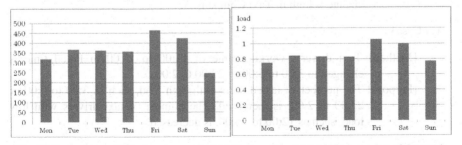

Fig. 3. The number of telephone requests (left Fig.) and load (right Fig.) per day of the week

3   Improvement Method of Customer Acquisition

From present data analysis, if the number of taxis which can be worked on high load time zone or day of the week is increased, "delivering a taxi immediately for a telephone request" will become possible, and service productivity will increase. Increasing the number of taxi drivers increases labor cost, and it may become rising income and falling profits. Therefore, we decide to rearrange the taxi driver's working hours without increasing the number of taxi drivers.

This problem is formulated as staff scheduling problem. There are several research results for nurse scheduling problem which is one of the staff scheduling problems. In previous research, optimum solution method to minimize the number of constraints violation was researched [3][4]. In this research we research method to minimize the summation of load described in (1). Therefore we choose computer simulation analysis to work many taxis in the time zone with many telephone requests. In addition, we research the methodology which can be applied to the other taxi companies.

3.1   Computer Simulation Cases

It turns out that the peak hours of the number of taxi which can be worked and telephone requests differ. We research service system so as to increase taxi drivers with high load and decrease taxi drivers with low load according to five simulation cases on condition that the service pattern is not so much different from the present one.

(a) Case1

> [Method] Every leaving and returning garage time of all service patterns are shifted 1 hour before.
> [Purpose] The number of taxi drivers with high load, such as 6:00 to 7:00, is increased.

(b) Case2

> [Method] Leaving and returning garage time of Day and Fixed time are shifted 1 hour before.
> [Purpose] The number of taxi drivers with high load, such as 6:00 to 7:00, is increased, only on Day and Fixed time because those flexibility of change is high in Taxi Company A.

(c) Case3

> [Method] Taxi driver's working time of 12:00 to 16:00 in Fixed time is changed to 3:00 to 6:00 or 22:00 to 2:00.
> [Purpose] The number of taxi drivers with high load, such as 3:00 to 6:00 or 22:00 to 2:00, is increased. The number of taxi drivers with low load, such as 12:00 to 16:00, is decreased.

Table 2. Considerable patterns for each case

Case	Considerable Patterns
1	(a)1 hour before[*1]
2	(a)1 hour before(Service pattern: Day), (b)1 hour before(Service pattern: Fixed time), (c)both (a) and (b)
3	(a)1 hour before, (b)1 hour after, (c)2 hours before, (d)2 hours after, (e)1hours before and 1hour after, (f)3 hours before (g)3 hours after, (h)2 hours before and 1 hour after, (i)1 hour before and 2 hours after, (j)4hours before (k)4 hours after
4	(a)A[*2]:Mon,Wed,Fri B:Tue,Fri,Sat or Thu,Fri,Sat, (b)A:Mon,Fri,Sat or Wed,Fri,Sat B:Tue,Thu,Sat, (c)A:Mon,Fri,Sat B:Tue,Fri,Sat, (d)A:Wed,Fri,Sat B:Tue,Fri,Sat, (e)A:Mon,Fri,Sat B:Thu,Fri,Sat, (f)A:Wed,Fri,Sat B:Thu,Fri,Sat
5	(a)One taxi driver is changed, (b)Two taxi drivers are changed, (c)Three taxi drivers are changed

*1) Leaving and returning garage time are shifted 1 hour before.
*2) "A" means Group A.

Table 3. Example (1 hour before)

Non-working hours	Working hours
From 12:00 to 13:00	From 6:00 to 12:00, From 13:00 to 21:00
From 13:00 to 14:00	From 6:00 to 13:00, From 14:00 to 21:00
From 14:00 to 15:00	From 6:00 to 14:00, From 15:00 to 21:00
From 15:00 to 16:00	From 6:00 to 15:00, From 16:00 to 21:00

(d) Case4

[Method] Taxi driver's working day of Monday to Thursday in Fixed time is changed to Friday or Saturday.

[Purpose] The number of taxi drivers with high load day, such as Friday or Saturday, is increased.

(e) Case5

[Method] According to the Taxi Company A's know-how, taxi driver's working pattern is changed as follows.
   • Taxi driver's working pattern Free on Friday or Saturday is changed to working pattern I on Sunday or Monday.
   • Taxi driver's working pattern III on Friday or Saturday is changed to working pattern IV on Sunday or Monday.

[Purpose] The number of taxi drivers with high load day, Friday or Saturday, is increased.

We verify all considerable patterns about change of time, day of the week, or the number in each simulation cases (see Table 2). Furthermore, in case3, considerable pattern is subdivided by non-working hours between 13:00 and 16:00 (See Table3). We find out the best taxi drivers working hours which minimizes the summation of load described in (1) from 42 simulation patterns.

3.2   Simulation Results

Top 5 patterns in 42 simulation patterns using telephone request data in 2010/1 to 2010/10 from the Company A are shown in Table4. All of them belong to Case3.

Load average and load variance of top 5 patterns are improved compared with the present situation. Load per hour of the best pattern, such as 4 hours before, is shown in Fig.4. We find the following results compared with the present situation shown in Fig.2. The load between 4:00 to 5:00 and 6:00 to 7:00, which is high in the present situation, decreases. Especially, the load between 6:00 to 7:00 decreases to less than 1.0 from 1.4. It causes a little enough time in taxi operation. Taxi driver must drive a round trip under 40 minutes to achieve 1.4 taxi operations per 1 hour. On the other hand, taxi driver drives a round trip in 60 minutes to achieve 1.0 taxi operation per 1 hour. The load between 12:00 to 16:00 remains 0.6 times per hour. Namely, load doesn't increase in daytime steeply.

It turns out that it is effective strategy to increase taxi drivers in midnight and early morning with high load instead of decreasing taxi drivers in daytime with low load so as to gain customers who reserves taxi by telephone requests.

Table 4. Top 5 patterns

Rank	Pattern	Working hours	Load average	Load variance
1	4 hours before	3 – 12, 16 – 21	0.820796	0.227361
2	3 hours before, 1 hour after	4 – 12, 16 – 22	0.828395	0.233268
3	3hours before	4 – 12, 15 – 21	0.831021	0.237765
4	3hours before	4 – 13, 16 – 21	0.831176	0.237569
5	2hours before, 2hours after	5 – 12, 16 – 23	0.832495	0.230137
–	present situation	–	0.868584	0.283285

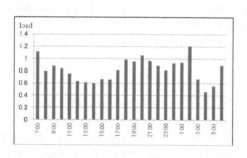

Fig. 4. Load per hour (4 hours before)

3.3   Verification of the Validity of Simulation Results

We verify the validity of simulation results using the other data from the Taxi Company A. We use all of the taxi operation data (e.g. telephone requests and getting customers on street) in 2010/2 to 2011/1. The reason for using all of the taxi operation data is for checking whether a problem appears for in customers who get a taxi on street in daytime, when the number of taxi which can be worked in daytime is decreased.

Top 5 patterns of 42 simulation patterns which are same case as 3.2 are shown in Table5. Load average and load variance of top 5 patterns are improved compared with the present situation. Although the 3rd place and the 4th place of ranking are changed, top 5 patterns are same patterns as results in 3.2. Load per hour of the best pattern, such as 4 hours before, is shown in left Fig. of Fig.5. We find the following results compared with the present situation shown in right Fig. of Fig5. The load between 6:00 to 7:00, when load is high in the present situation, decreases to 1.2 from 2.0. It causes a little enough time in taxi operation. Taxi driver must drive a round trip under 30 minutes to achieve 2.0 taxi operations per 1 hour. On the other hand, taxi driver drives a round trip in 50 minutes to achieve 1.2 taxi operations per 1 hour. The load between 12:00 to 15:00 remains 1.0 times per hour. Namely, load doesn't increase in daytime steeply.

Table 5. Top 5 patterns of all the taxi operation data

Rank	Pattern	Working hours	Load average	Load variance
1	4 hours before	3 – 12, 16 – 21	1.207361	0.365542
2	3 hours before, 1 hour after	4 – 12, 16 – 22	1.216663	0.367898
3	3hours before	4 – 13, 16 – 21	1.218303	0.371616
4		4 – 12, 15 – 21	1.219509	0.373924
5	2hours before, 2hours after	5 – 12, 16 – 23	1.219803	0.356295
–	present situation	–	1.262712	0.394881

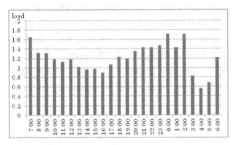 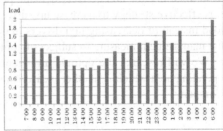

Fig. 5. Load per hour (4 hours before (left Fig.) and present situation (right Fig))

3.4   Subjects of Applying New Strategy to Taxi Drivers

From above discussion, it is effective strategy to increase taxi drivers in midnight and early morning with high load instead of decreasing taxi drivers in daytime with low load. Applying this strategy, load descried in (1) decreases and service productivity is improved. There are non-working hours in working hours of Fixed time. For example, taxi drivers work from 3:00 to 12:00, don't work from 12:00 to 16:00, work from 16:00 to 21:00 in the best pattern. We suppose that it is difficult for taxi drivers to receive this service pattern. Therefore, we design new service pattern for Fixed time. We divide one working hours of Fixed time into two working hours, such as "a.m. working hours" and "p.m. working hours", rotate working groups of Fixed time across Sunday (See Fig.6). This service pattern enables taxi drivers to secure the same working hours per one month as the present service pattern, without non-working hours between working hours.

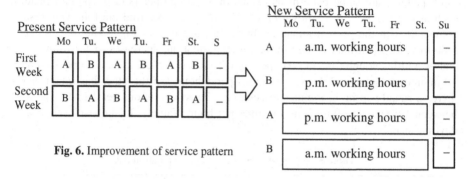

Fig. 6. Improvement of service pattern

4   Conclusions

We research service methodology so as to improve service productivity in Taxi Company. For the above mentioned purpose, we research improvement method of rearranging taxi driver's working hours so as to work many taxis with many taxi delivery demands by telephone requests. Using telephone request data from Taxi Company A, we analyze present situation of Taxi Company A, and perform simulation analysis so as to minimize the taxi delivery demand per taxi and hour. As a result, it turns out that it is effective strategy to increase taxi drivers in midnight and early morning with high load instead of decreasing taxi drivers in daytime with low load. Finally, we consider the management measure to subject of applying this strategy to taxi drivers.

We will research the optimal arrangement of the taxi waiting position in the taxi operating area which is another measure so as to improve service productivity of Taxi Company.

References

1. Ministry of Land, Infrastructure, Transport, and Tourism, White Paper on Land, Infrastructure, Transport, and Tourism in Japan (2008) (in Japanese)
2. Sugiyama, M., Yamauchi, H., Yamamoto, Y.: Bus & Taxi in Deregulation Age, The Institute of Regional Studies (2002) (in Japanese)
3. Ikegami, A.: Nurse Scheduling – Site Research, Modeling and Algorithms. Proceedings of the Institute of Statistical Mathematics, 53(2), 231–259 (2005) (in Japanese)
4. Ikegami, A., Shigeno, M.: Staff Scheduling for Providing Quality Service. The Journal of the Institute of Electronics, Information and Communication Engineers 94(9), 760–766 (2011) (in Japanese)

The Servitization of Manufacturing: A Methodology for the Development of After-Sales Services

Ottar Bakås[1,*], Daryl Powell[2], Barbara Resta[3], and Paolo Gaiardelli[3]

[1] SINTEF Technology and Society, Trondheim, Norway
ottar.bakas@sintef.no
[2] Department of Production and Quality Engineering,
Norwegian University of Science and Technology, Trondheim, Norway
daryl.j.powell@ntnu.no
[3] University of Bergamo, Bergamo, Italy
{barbara.resta,paolo.gaiardelli}@unibg.it

Abstract. It has been suggested that though many companies realize the importance of providing after-sales services, most do not fully understand the maximum benefit from such offerings. Though several research papers document an approach for the implementation of a service operations strategy, a practical guide for the development of after-sales services is lacking in the current literature. Therefore, in this paper, we apply existing theory and use practical insights in order to propose a nine-step methodology for the development of after-sales services. The methodology links customer value from services to portfolio management theory. Two case studies describe application of the methodology. It can be used by practitioners in order to exploit the untapped potential of providing product-service offerings, with the aim to generate greater profits and a higher level of customer service.

Keywords: After-sales service, Product-Service System (PSS), action research, portfolio management.

1 Introduction

A widespread decrease of margins on product sales coupled with changing customer expectations is driving manufacturing companies to find addtitional profit centres, moving beyond the traditional manufacturing realm towards the service domain [1, 2]. This phenomenon, usually termed as servitization of manufacturing, represents the evolution of companies' business models from a "pure-product" orientation towards integrated Product-Service Systems (PSSs), based on the provision of integrated bundles consisting of both physical goods and services [3].

In general, adopting a servitization strategy entails several advantages for a company, in terms of higher profit margins, more stable source of profits and a lower cash flow vulnerability, providing at the same time a powerful competitive weapon, as summarised by Mathieu [4].

---

[*] Corresponding author.

C. Emmanouilidis, M. Taisch, D. Kiritsis (Eds.): APMS 2012, Part II, IFIP AICT 398, pp. 337–344, 2013.
© IFIP International Federation for Information Processing 2013

As a consequence, the old dichotomy between product and service has been replaced by a product-service continuum [5], where three categories of PSS can be placed, with an increasing level of servitization [6]: i) Product-oriented, where the business model is still mainly based on product sales with some additional services; ii) Use-oriented, where the traditional product still plays a central role, but it stays in ownership of the provider and is made available in a different form; and iii) Result-oriented, where the client and provider agree on a result, and there is no pre-determined product involved. Among these three categories, product-oriented PSSs, still represent the most common type of services provided by manufacturing companies to ensure the functional capability for the period in which the customer uses the product [7], and constitute the focus of this paper.

Even if it is argued by Cohen *et al.* [8] that we are now in *"the golden age of services"*, and that to survive and prosper, *"every company must transform into a service business"*, most companies either don't know how or don't care to provide after-sales services, and PSSs in general, effectively and fall into the so called "service paradox" [9]. The latter describes situations in which companies investing heavily in extending their service business increase their service offerings and incur higher costs, without any expected corresponding returns. Indeed, current corporate structures and processes of many manufacturing companies are not designed to efficiently develop and launch services on the market. Among others, difficulties arise because the new services introduced in the portfolio by firms are not clearly defined, and there are no unequivocal descriptions of the service contents, the relevant processes and the necessary resources [10].

To overcome this gap, the first aspect to consider is the creation of a suitable portfolio of service products [8]. By addressing the following research question, we propose a methodology for the development of after-sales services: *Which steps should a producer take in order to develop a competitive after-sales service portfolio?*

In order to address our research question, the paper is structured as follows: firstly, we explain our choice of action research as the selected research methodology; then we give an overview of the relevant existing theory within the field. We then use this theory to propose a methodology for the development of after-sales services before describing the application of parts of the methodology in two companies that are currently developing their portfolio of aftersales services. To end the paper, we summarize the work that has been carried out so far, and identify directions for further work.

2   Research Methodology

The primary research methodology is action research [11]. We made some empirical observations related to the current state-of-the-art of after-sales services, from work carried out in Norwegian companies operating within the maritime and subsea industry. The action research methodology has been chosen due to the practical nature of the problem, and the companies were selected through convenience sampling.

Action research can be defined as a participatory, democratic process concerned with developing practical knowing in the pursuit of worthwhile human purposes, grounded in a participatory worldview [12]. Essentially, it focuses on bringing about change (action) and contributing to knowledge (research). Reason and Bradbury [12] go on to say that action without reflection and understanding is blind, just as theory without action is meaningless.

In this paper we present a methodology for the development of after-sales services, which we have formulated from a short analysis of the portfolio management literature combined with the theory surrounding PSSs and after-sales services. The methodology has been developed concurrently as the action research process unfolded, and represents a true account of the various implementation cycles inherent to the action research methodology [11]. In this process a theory building approach is adopted to identify the relevant steps involved in the development of a manufacturer's after-sales service portfolio.

3   Theoretical Background

In general, portfolio management can be described as a dynamic decision process about investment mix and policy [13], aiming at matching investments to strategic objectives, maximising value, and balancing risk against performance [14].

As argued by Kendall and Rollins [15], portfolio management has six major objectives:

1. Determining a viable investment mix, capable of meeting the goals of the firm;
2. Balancing the portfolio to ensure a mix of investments that balances short term vs. long term, risk vs. reward, research vs. development, etc.;
3. Monitoring the planning and execution of chosen investments;
4. Analysing portfolio performance and ways to improve it;
5. Evaluating new products and services against the current portfolio and comparatively against each other;
6. Providing information and recommendations to decision-makers at all levels.

In the literature, models for portfolio management are usually built around four general phases: 1) strategic considerations, 2) individual project/investment evaluation, 3) portfolio selection, and 4) stage/gate evaluation [16][17][18][19].

Even if portfolio management is typically associated with financial assets (financial portfolio management - FPM), projects (project portfolio management - PPM) and information technology (IT portfolio management), we believe that its implementation can be very useful also in the PSS domain to develop new product-service offerings. As argued by Hanski et al. [20], a product-service portfolio should be managed in a similar way to a financial portfolio: riskier strategic investments should be balanced with more conservative investments and the mix should be constantly monitored. Consequently, besides product-service characterised by low or medium uncertainty and aiming at maximising economic value, high-uncertainty solutions should be introduced in the portfolio in order to strengthen the company's competitive position. To this end, companies should look not only at products and services in areas close to their business, but also explore new landscape and create new strategic opportunities

[21]. Interdependencies among product-service offerings should also be considered to avoid cannibalisation and the utilisation of the same resources.

Despite the great importance covered by this subject, literature lacks of portfolio management models and methodologies specifically tailored for product-service offerings. Thus, the empirical part of this paper describes a research initiative undertaken to develop a methodology for the development of product-oriented PSS, also referred to as after-sales services.

4   A Methodology for the Development of After-Sales Services

Based on portfolio management and the associated four phases identified previously, we suggest that a methodology for the development of after-sales services should begin with a mapping of existing service offerings (Step 1); followed by a SWOT analysis of strengths, weaknesses, opportunities and threats.

Step 3 is a key to the methodology, where the team begin to define value from the point-of-view of the customer (Step 3). This steps starts with a cross-departmental workshop where customer value is defined in three phases: before purchase, during delivery, and in the after-sales phase. Then a small set of representative customers are selected and interviewed in order to check if the defined value propositions match the expectations and perceptions of their current customers. This helps the organisation to evaluate the value propositions of their current product-service offerings [20].

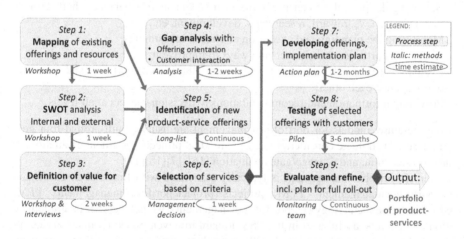

Fig. 1. A methodology for the development of after-sales services

Step 4 involves a gap analysis between internal resources, capabilities and the value for customer. These four steps represent the necessary considerations in terms of strategy formulation. For example, we suggest that a company must first map the current state of operations before it can possibly identify future directions. Also, by gaining an overview of existing service offerings, the organisation is able to conduct a

SWOT analysis in order to identify external opportunities and threats. This subsequently enables the organisation to conduct a thorough gap analysis, taking into consideration the orientation of the offering, its product- or process focus, and the type of interaction with the customer [22].

When combined, the result of Steps 1-4 will allow the organisation to identify any new potential product-service offerings (Step 5). Having identified new offerings, it is then time to select potential opportunities based on the following criteria (Step 6):

- *Market attractiveness* (profit potential in a given market)
- *Feasibility of the offering* (technical complexity, reliability, availability, maintainability)
- *Sustainability of the offering (profitability, environmental effects, social effects)*
- *Internal resource requirements* *(physical, human and financial resources)*

Having surpassed the decision point, the organisation is encouraged to develop the selected offering/s with an action plan to implement (Step 7). The action plan should involve a test period with selected customers (Step 8), before eventual evaluation and refinement, which will also include a plan for full roll-out (Step 9).

5   Practical Insights

Our methodology has been developed through systematic combination of existing theory with practical insights gained from two companies in Trondheim, Norway as part of an action research project that is still currently live. The project started in 2011, and is due to finish in 2014. Therefore, the findings reported in this paper represent the work carried out so far in the project, where we have only reached Step 4 of the methodology. It is the intention to refine the model and report its development as further work.

5.1   Case 1: Oil and Gas

Case company 1 is a leading technology provider to the oil and gas industry. At its site in Norway, it produces corrosion and erosion equipment for oil and gas pipelines, with applications for both top-side and subsea installations. The company has 72 employees and an annual turnover of approx. 20 Mill Euro.

Step 1 Mapping: The company conducted an assessment of their current service offerings and found that they are currently offering 6 main types of after sales services (see table 1). After-market activities are supported by a team of 5, in addition to a software team and a larger group of skilled on-site service engineers. *Step 2* highlighted the lack of time and tradition for development of new after sales services.

The company spent much effort on *Step 3* to identify what represents *value* for their customer. They classified their value offerings in 3 phases: the purchase situation (order winners vs. qualifiers), at time of delivery and in the after-sales phase.

The Gap analysis in step 4 revealed that most services (# 1, 2, 3, 4) are delivered to ensure product availability and functionality, and few (# 5, 6) aim at supporting customer's activities. Moreover, only service # 3 is based on a long-term relationship with the customer.

A list of ideas of new product-service offerings have been updated along each step in the process, and the company is now planning to go deeper in dialogue with a set of representative customers to check if their view on value propositions is in line with what customers really want. Their next step is to select a pilot service offering for further development and testing.

Table 1. Current after-sales services offered by case companies

Type of service	Case 1: Oil and gas	Case 2: Ocean
Installation and implementation	1. Upgrade of installations 2. Service for new installations	1. Rebuilding and reparation
Maintenance and support services	3. Fixed service agreements 4. Spare part offerings	2. Service agreements 3. Spare parts offerings 4. Technical support
Consulting services	5. Training of local agents and operators	5. Training and courses for end users
Systems and solutions	6. Data analysis and presentation	6. Retrieve data, analyse and present

5.2   Case 2: Ocean

Case company 2 is a high technology company specialising in delivering environmental monitoring, ocean observing and forecasting systems. Based in Norway, the company develops, manufactures and supplies measuring, measurement buoys, instruments, monitoring stations all across the world supported by mathematical models and presentation software. The company has 30 employees and an annual turnover of approx. 13 Mill Euro.

Step 1 Mapping: The company conducted an assessment of their current service offerings and found that they are currently offering 6 main types of after sales services (see table 1). After-market activities are supported by a team of 4, in addition to experienced on-site service engineers. *Step 2 SWOT:* identified a current weakness in the lack of systematic follow-up of customers after time of purchase.

The company also spent much effort on *Step 3* to identify what represents *value* for their customer. They benefited from making thorough customer segmentation, and selected the National Marine Institutes as a case for further study. Credibility, customer dialogue, market presence and financial arrangements were identified as important order winners.

The Gap analysis in step 3 revealed that most services (# 1, 2, 3, 4) are delivered to ensure product availability and functionality, and few (# 5, 6) aim at supporting customer's activities. Moreover, only service # 2 is based on a long-term relationship with the customer. Multiple ideas have occurred at each step in the methodology, resulting in a list of 17 potential product-service offerings. They are now subject for revision and selection of a pilot for further development.

6   Discussion and Conclusion

By systematically combining existing theory on after-sales services and portfolio management with practical insights form an action research project, we have developed a nine-step methodology for the development of after-sales services (Figure 1). We suggest that this makes a valid contribution within the field of product-service systems and the growing arena of servitization.

In this *"golden age of services"*, the findings expressed in this paper suggest that such a methodology shows signs of promise in the development of customer-focused, value-adding after-sales services. Companies need to continuously ask whether expansion into new service arenas will take them outside the logical scope of their capabilities and organizational culture [21]. Therefore, our methodology maintains a focus on a company's current practices and competences, in order to evaluate whether the development of new competence is required before greater service offerings can be provided. For example, the mapping of existing offerings, SWOT analysis and Gap analysis that are conducted in steps one to three of our methodology help to identify the scope of the organizations current setup, and then the definition of customer value in step four allows the company to identify the directions in which its service offerings should be progressing. The testing of new service offerings in step eight also allows the service provider to make reflections as to whether or not the new offering will be a success, or whether refinements are needed.

In terms of the limitations of this research and possible further work, we suggest that the remainder of the methodology be tested and refined in the two case companies currently involved in the development process, before further case studies can be carried out in order to test the applicability and generalizability of our methodology.

References

1. Vandermerwe, S., Rada, J.: Servitization of business: adding value by adding services. European Management Journal 6(4), 314–324 (1988)
2. Wise, R., Baumgartner, P.: Go downstream. Harvard Business Review 77(5), 133–141 (1999)
3. Resta, B.: Designing and configuring the value creation network for servitization: a product-service provider's perspective. Unpublished Doctoral Thesis, University of Bergamo, Italy (2012)
4. Mathieu, V.: Service strategies within the manufacturing sector: benefits, costs and partnership. International Journal of Service Industry Management 12(5), 451–475 (2001)
5. Oliva, R., Kallenberg, R.: Managing the transition from products to services. International Journal of Service Industry Management 14(2), 160–172 (2003)
6. Tukker, A.: Eight types of product–service system: eight ways to sustainability? Experiences from SusProNet. Business Strategy and the Environment 13(4), 246–260 (2004)
7. Gebauer, H., Krempl, R., Fleisch, E., Friedli, T.: Innovation of product-related services. Managing Service Quality 18(4), 387–404 (2008)
8. Cohen, M.A., Agrawal, N., Agrawal, V.: Winning in the Aftermarket. Harvard Business Review 84(5), 129–138 (2006)

9. Gebauer, H., Fleisch, E., Friedli, T.: Overcoming the service paradox in manufacturing companies. European Management Journal 23(1), 14–26 (2005)
10. Bullinger, H.J., Fähnrich, K.P., Meiren, T.: Service engineering—methodical development of new service products. International Journal of Production Economics 85(3), 275–287 (2003)
11. Coughlan, P., Coghlan, D.: Action Research for Operations Management. In: Karlsson, C. (ed.) Researching Operations Management. Taylor & Francis, New York (2009)
12. Reason, P., Bradbury, H.: Handbook of Action Research. Sage Publications, London (2006)
13. Dayananda, D., Irons, R., Harrison, S., Herbohn, J., Rowland, P.: Capital budgeting: financial appraisal of investment projects. Cambridge University Press (2002)
14. Cooper, R.G., Edgett, S.J., Kleinschmidt, E.J.: Portfolio management for new products. Perseus (2001)
15. Kendall, G.I., Rollins, S.C.: Advanced project portfolio management and the PMO: multiplying ROI at warp speed. J. Ross Publishing, Florida (2003)
16. Archer, N.P., Ghasemzadeh, F.: An integrated framework for project portfolio selection. International Journal of Project Management 17(4), 207–216 (1999)
17. Bridges, D.N.: Project portfolio management: ideas and practices. In: Dye, L.D., Pennypacker, J.S. (eds.) Project Portfolio Management. Selecting and Prioritizing Projects for Competitive Advantage Center for Business Practices, USA (1999)
18. Nelson, B., Gill, B., Spring, S.: Building on the stage/gate: An enterprise-wide architecture for new product development. In: Proceedings of the 28th Annual Project Management Institute Seminars & Symposium, Chicago, Illinois (1997)
19. Sanwal, A.K.: Optimizing corporate portfolio management: aligning investment proposals with organizational strategy. Wiley, New Jersey (2007)
20. Hanski, J., Kunttu, S., Räikkönen, M., Reunanen, M.: Development of knowledge-intensive product-service systems. VTT Technical Research Centre of Finland, Espoo (2012)
21. Sawhney, M., Balasubramanian, S., Krishnan, V.V.: Creating growth with services. MIT Sloan Management Review 45(2), 34–44 (2003)
22. Gaiardelli, P., Martinez, V., Turner, T.: Toward a Product-Service Business Model Configuration. In: Proceedings of the 10th Euram Conference (2003)

Do Consumers Select Food Products Based on Carbon Dioxide Emissions?

Keiko Aoki[1] and Kenju Akai[2]

[1] Institute of Social and Economic Research, Osaka University, Osaka, Japan
k_aoki@iser.osaka-u.ac.jp
[2] Graduate School of Engineering, The University of Tokyo, Tokyo, Japan
akai@css.t.u-tokyo.ac.jp

Abstract. This study investigates whether consumers select foods based on the levels of carbon dioxide emissions by a real choice experiment. Respondents are asked to purchase one orange based on price and level of CO_2 emissions under no monetary incentives. The willingness to pay estimate for the reduction of 1g of CO_2 emissions per orange is significantly lower for the low environmentally conscious group than it is for the high environmentally conscious group.

Keywords: carbon dioxide emissions, choice experiment, consumer preference for foods, survey, random parameter logit model.

1 Introduction

Recently, the problem of greenhouse gases also has given rise to a new type of eco-label for a product's carbon footprint (hereafter referred to as CFP) as well as previous eco-labels as Green Seal (United States), Eco-Mark (Japan), Blue Angel (Germany), and Nordic Swan (Scandinavia). The CFP may provide more information to consumers than previous eco-labels as it indicates the amount of CO_2 emitted through the process from production to disposal. Indicating this quantity may benefit consumers in that they will be able to select goods with a higher environmentally quality than other eco-labels provide, enabling more environmental consciousness consumption. In previous studies on the effects of previous eco-labels, an emphasis has been placed on testing the effectiveness of eco-labeling on consumers choices, i.e. selection of products having such a label versus those without one as well as the weight consumers give to public certification. The effectiveness of eco-labeling has been shown to have a positive result, according to several previous studies which have analyzed such effectiveness using empirical analysis (Wessells et al., 1999; Johnston et al., 2001; Teisl et al., 2002; Bjørner et al., 2004; OECD, 2005; Teisl et al., 2008; Brécard et al., 2009)[1], theoretical models (Kirchhoff, 2000; Amacher et al., 2004; Hamilton and

---

[1] Seafood products were used in Wessells et al. (1999), Johnston et al. (2001), Teisl et al. (2002) and Brécard et al. (2009). Toilet paper, paper towels and detergents were used in Bjørner et al. (2004), and "greener" vehicles in Teisl et al. (2008).

C. Emmanouilidis, M. Taisch, D. Kiritsis (Eds.): APMS 2012, Part II, IFIP AICT 398, pp. 345–352, 2013.

Zilberman, 2006; Ibanez and Grolleau, 2008), and an experimental method (Cason and Gangadharan, 2002). Therefore, one may be able to extrapolate that attaching a label indicating the CFP also has a positive effect from the results of these previous studies. However, a question still remains: Do consumers prefer a lower amount of CO_2 emissions among the food products also which do not have merits as decreasing a running cost?

The present study reports on how consumers value indications of CO_2 emissions for Satsuma mandarin oranges (*Citrus unshiu* Marc.) as compared to price. A choice experiment (CE) was conducted in which respondents actually bought the oranges. The respondents were provided with the price and CO_2 emission based on the life cycle inventory of the orange and asked to purchase them in 12 rounds. After each round, they also selected the reason for their choice from among three factors: price, CO_2 emission, and appearance. After the CE, the respondents were also asked to answer general questionnaires related to ecologically conscious consumer behavior (hereafter referred to as ECCB) (Roberts, 1996), environmental knowledge about several eco-labels in Japan, environmental behavior of respondents in daily life, and their socioeconomic characteristics.

As for the rest of the paper, Section 2 explains the survey designs. Section 3 presents the results, and Section 4 proffers the conclusion.

2   Survey Design

We conducted a survey based on the CE method. The design of the survey was as follows. As shown in Table 1, the three alternatives in the designated choice sets were Satsuma mandarin orange A, Satsuma mandarin orange B, and Satsuma mandarin orange C.[2] The attributes being tested were price and the CO_2 emission levels in each round of this study. Each price attribute was at the following levels: 25 JPY, 35 JPY and 45 JPY. The CO_2 attribute was at the levels of 20 g, 30 g, and 40 g per a Satsuma mandarin orange. The total number of rounds in one session was 12.

2.1   Products

We used Satsuma mandarin oranges[3] for the following reasons. First, along with apples, it is Japan's leading fruit in terms of production and consumption. Therefore, the respondents ought to be familiar with these products. Second, unlike vegetables and

---

[2] In the study, there is not an alternative "no purchase" because our purpose is to test whether consumers choose foods based on the amount of the CO2 emissions. The results of using this alternative were found by Lusk and Schroeder (2004) which the frequency of individual choosing it was greater in real condition.

[3] We used the goku-wase, a type of Satsuma mandarin orange, in this study. Its color was of a bluish-orange tinge. The taste was sour as compared to other types of Satsuma mandarin oranges. The sugar content in it was approximately from 9 to 11 brix. For more details on Satsuma mandarin oranges, see Morton (1987).

other fruits, the Satsuma mandarin orange is eaten directly without cooking or using any other tools. Most vegetables require the use of fire and kitchen utensils (e.g., a knife) when they have to be consumed, which influences the amount of the CO_2 emissions. Each Satsuma mandarin orange was approximately 7 cm in diameter, and its weight was approximately 100 g. We bought the Satsuma mandarin oranges from three different prefectures (i.e., Wakayama, Ehime, and Kumamoto) where the largest quantity is available[4] at supermarkets and stores in the area.

Table 1. An example of choice sets

	Satsuma mandarin orange A	Satsuma mandarin orange B	Satsuma mandarin orange C
Price (JPY)			
Carbon dioxide emissions (grams)			
I would choose...	ϓ	ϓ	ϓ
The most important reason affecting my choice	ϓPrice ϓCarbon ϓOthers[the reason:]	dioxide emissions	ϓAppearance

The price attribute was based on the prices of Satsuma mandarin oranges in the three largest supermarkets in the area and on the data obtained from the Statistical Bureau in the Ministry of Internal Affairs and Communications.[5] The CO_2 emissions attribute was based on the life cycle assessment (LCA) because it was found that the amounts of the CO_2 emitted in the LCA process differed for different food products. Our use of the LCA comprised four stages: production, fruit sorting and box packing, transportation, and packaging.[6] Table 2 displays the CO_2 emissions calculated in each process, which is referred to by Nemoto (2007).

---

[4] In the case of the 2007 data obtained from the Ministry of Agriculture, Forestry and Fisheries in Japan, the largest amount of goku-wase Satsuma mandarin oranges is available in Saga prefecture; the second largest, in Kumamoto prefecture; the third largest, in Ehime prefecture; and the fourth largest, in Wakayama prefecture. In our study, we did not use the goku-wase variety of Satsuma mandarin oranges from Saga prefecture because their appearance is more bluish than those in the other prefectures and they are less common in Osaka prefecture.

[5] This data shows the prices of the Satsuma mandarin oranges that were sold at all the supermarkets and shops in Japan. We selected the prices from the price data available in Osaka prefecture.

[6] In our study, we do not add the amount of the CO_2 emitted during selling products in a supermarket and a store.

2.2   Questionnaire

The environmental factors used in this study consist of three factors.[7] First factor is environmental consciousness (hereafter EC). This factor consist of 10 questions that

Table 2. The CO_2 emissions based on life cycle inventory

Prefecture	Total CO_2 emissions (g/ a Satsuma mandarin orange)	Products[a]	Fruit sorting and box Packing[b]	Transportation[c]	Packaging[d]
Wakayama	23.192	16.295		1.587	
Ehime	32.268	20.391	0.402	6.570	4.716
Kumamoto	34.304	16.591		12.402	

Note: [a] quotes from the data in National Institute of Agro-Environmental Sciences (see:)(i.e., 360–370 g-CO_2/10 a) and Ministry of Agriculture, Forestry and Fisheries (see: In our study, the CO_2 emissions level is approximately 365 g-CO_2/10 a and the annual yield in Satsuma mandarin oranges in Wakayama, Ehime, and Kumamoto are, 2,240,000, 1,790,000; and 2,260,000 g per 10 a, respectively. We calculate the CO_2 emissions per a Satsuma mandarin orange.

[b] quotes from data in Nemoto (2007).

[c] is based on data obtained from the Ministry of Land, Infrastructure and Transport. We calculate the CO_2 emissions from each prefecture from where the oranges are obtained to the supermarket in the area via Osaka prefecture central wholesale market by track. A lot of food products are collected in this market and sent to supermarkets and stores. The running distance is calculated using a searching route by car on the Nippon Oil Corporation site

[d] is based on the Ajinomoto Group LC-CO_2 emissions factor database for food related materials (1990, 1995, and 2000 editions; 3 EID compliant (Ajinomoto Co., Inc.). We calculate the CO_2 emissions when 12 pieces of goku-wase Satsuma mandarin oranges are packed in a plastic bag and sealed with tape. The plastic bag is made from polyethylene (PE) and weighs an average of 4.1 g. In the Ajinomoto Group LC-CO_2 emissions factor database for food related materials (1990, 1995, and 2000 editions; 3 EID compliant (Ajinomoto Co., Inc.), the CO_2 emissions in goods made from PE is 10.302 g-CO_2/g. A tape made of polyethylene terephthalate (PET) weighs 0.1 g on average. In the Ajinomoto Group LC-CO_2 emissions factor database, the CO_2 emissions in goods made from PET (excluding fabric goods) is 2.333 g-CO_2/g.

---

[7] They are as follows: 1) I have purchased a household appliance because it uses less electricity than other brands;2) I have purchased light bulbs that are more expensive but that save energy; 3)I will not buy products that have excessive packaging; 4) If I understand the potential damage to the environment that some products can cause, I do not purchase these products; 5) I have switched products for ecological reasons; 6) I have convinced members of my family or friends not to buy some products that are harmful to the environment;7) Whenever possible, I buy products packaged in reusable containers; 8) When I have a choice between two equal products, I always purchase the one that is less harmful to other people and the environment; 9) I will not buy a product if the company that sells it is ecologically irresponsible; 10) I do not buy household products that harm the environment.

are selected from the consumers' ecological purchase behaviors scale (Roberts, 1996), which is designed to characterize the extent to which environmental concerns influenced respondents' purchasing behavior. The scale is five-point likert-type scales such that they run from 1, which denotes that I "never agree", to 5, which denotes that I "always agree".

Second factor is the environmental knowledge of eco-labels (hereafter EK), the effect of which is estimated by asking respondents to identify 24 eco-labels that aid the purchase of environmentally friendly goods and 11 eco-labels that serve as identifying marks in Japan.[8] The respondents are asked to answer the number of the labels as possible as they know.

Third factor is environmental behavior in daily life (hereafter EB), the effect of which is estimated using seven questions. Of these, six questions evaluate consumer's behaviors in daily life and the seventh one is alternative "others". The respondents are asked to answer the number of the behavior as possible as they do in daily life.

2.3   Samples

The respondents were recruited from among the neighborhood residents from 10,000 households around the university.[9] We gathered 212 participants and conducted survey in March 2012. The participation fee of the survey was 1000 JPY.

3   Results

Here, we divide each environmental factor into two groups by the median. The two groups under EC are defined as the high group, which consists of respondents whose responses are more than the median synthesis scale of 30 (Sd. = 7.349) in pooled, and the low group, which comprises the other respondents. The median number of total scales per respondent is 35 (Sd. = 3.771) and 26 (Sd. = 5.262) in high and low groups, respectively. In the EK, the high group includes respondents whose responses are more than the median number of twelve (Sd.=3.533) in pooled, 15 (Sd.= 1.891) in high group, and 10 (Sd.=2.230) in low one. In the EB, the high group includes respondents whose responses are more than the average number of 4 (Sd.=1.289) in pooled, 5 (Sd.= 0.483) in high group, and 3 (Sd.=0.840), which excludes question 7 as others.

In order to investigate which environmental factors consumers are influenced when they select the oranges based on the levels of CO_2 emissions, we will employ the results of the three environmental factors, i.e., EC, EK, and EB. Subsequently, we consider the hypothesis of equal utility parameters among the high group, low group, and pooled data for each environmental factor. We apply the likelihood ratio (LR) test suggested by Swait and Louviere (1993) in order to test these hypotheses by using the

---

[8] They are selected from the database of the Ministry of the Environment
(http://www.env.go.jp/policy/hozen/green/ecolabel/f01.html)
[9] Residents only were recruited through leaflets inserted in some famous Japanese newspapers (i.e., Mainichi, Asahi, Yomiuri, and Sankei).

log likelihood values obtained by estimating main effect results in the Random Parameter logit model. The LR test shows that the hypothesis that the vector of common utility parameters is equal across groups for each factor can be rejected only for the EC factor.[10] The results for these two groups will only be analyzed for the EC factor.

Table 3. The random parameter logit regression results for high and low environmentally conscious groups

Variables	Definition	RPL model High Coefficient	RPL model High Standard deviation	RPL model Low Coefficient	RPL model Low Standard deviation	RPL model interactions High Coefficient	RPL model interactions High Standard deviation	RPL model interactions Low Coefficient	RPL model interactions Low Standard deviation
Fixed parameter									
Price	Price of Satsuma mandarin oranges:25, 35, and 45 JPY per orange	-0.09*** (0.00)	-	-0.11*** (0.00)	-	-0.09*** (0.00)	-	-0.11*** (0.00)	-
Random parameter									
CDE	The amount of carbon dioxide emissions: 20, 30, and 40 gram per orange	-0.06** (0.00)	0.00 (0.02)	-0.03*** (0.00)	0.00 (0.02)	-0.07*** (0.01)	0.00 (0.02)	-0.03*** (0.00)	0.00 (0.03)
An interaction terms of CO₂ with socioeconomics chacteristics									
CDE × Female	An interaction term of CO_2 with a dummy variable that is equal to 1 if the respondent is female.					-0.02* (0.01)	-	-0.01 (0.01)	-
CDE×Old	An interaction term of CO_2 with a dummy variable that is equal to 1 if the respondent's age is over 30 years.					0.03*** (0.01)	-	0.02* (0.01)	-
CDE × High Income	An interaction term of CO_2 with a dummy variable that is equal to 1 if the respondent's income is over 5,500,000 JPY					0.01 (0.01)	-	-0.02* (0.01)	-
CDE × University	An interaction term of CO_2 with a dummy variable that is equal to 1 if the respondent holds a university or a higher degree					0.00 (0.01)	-	0.02* (0.01)	-
Marginal willingness to pay (JPY)		0.64 [0.63;0.64]		0.28 [0.27;0.29]	-		-		
Log likelihood		-1228.26		-1046.81		-1100.43		-900.18	
McFadden's R^2		0.17		0.19		0.18		0.19	
Observations		1356		1188		1356		1188	

Notes: Standard errors are in parentheses. ***, **, and * denote that the parameters are different from zero at the 1%, 5%, 10% significance levels, respectively.

---

[10] In RPL model also, the results by the LR test were as follows: LREC = -2(-1107.619 - (-545.345 - 550.968)) = 22.612; LREK = -2(-1107.619 - (-553.594 - 552.000)) = 4.050; LREB = -2(-1107.619 - (-639.083 - 467.007)) = 3.058. Therefore, Only LREC statistics in both models were larger than 5.911 (i.e., the critical value of the distribution at the 5% significance level on 2 degrees of freedom).

With respect to the Random Parameter logit regression results in main effect as shown in Table 3, two variables, *PRICE* and *CDE*, were estimated to be statistically significant and negative signs, implying that all the respondents prefer Satsuma mandarin oranges at a cheaper price and at lower levels of CO_2 emissions. The cheaper price result supports the results of Prescott et al. (2002), which found that Japanese consumers particularly valued price. The marginal WTP estimate for the reduction of 1 g of CO_2 emissions per orange was 0.642 JPY in high environmental consciousness group and 0.286 JPY in low group, respectively.

Next, with respect to the choice reason in main effect with interact, the variables CDE×Female and CDE×Old in high group were estimated to be statistically significant as well as negative and positive signs, respectively. They imply that female prefer to less the CO_2 emissions as compared to male and that above 40 years olds do not prefer to do them as compared to others. Meanwhile, the variables CDE×Old and CDE×High Income in low group were estimated to be statistically significant as well as positive and negative signs, respectively. They imply that above 40 years olds do not prefer to less the CO_2 emissions as compared to others and that people with high income prefer to do them as compared to them with low income.

4   Conclusions

The present study researches estimated WTP for CO_2 emissions regarding oranges before the CFP starts in Japan and the socioeconomics characteristics of those people who show an environmental consciousness for foods displaying the amount of CO_2 emitted over the product's lifecycle. The results imply that Japanese consumers prefer reducing CO_2 emissions through food purchases also, though they may not select fresh foods based on CO_2 emissions. This conclusion supports Bougherara and Combris (2009) such that consumers preferred food characteristics such as taste or appearance to environmental protection.

References

Amacher, G., Koskela, E., Ollikainen, M.: Environmental quality competition and eco-labeling. J. Environ. Econ. Manage 47, 284–306 (2004)

Bjørner, T.B., Hansen, L.G., Russell, C.S.: Environmental labeling and consumers' choice-an empirical analysis of the effect of the Nordic Swan. J. Environ. Econ. Manage. 47, 411–424 (2004)

Bougherara, D., Combris, P.: Eco-labelled food products: what are consumers paying for? Eur. Rev. Agric. Econ. 36(3), 321–341 (2009)

Brécard, D., Hlaimi, B., Lucas, S., Perraudeau, Y., Salladarré, F.: Determinants of demand for green products: An application to eco-label demand for fish in Europe. Ecological Econ. 69, 115–125 (2009)

Cason, T., Gangadharan, L.: Environmental labeling and incomplete con-sumer information in laboratory markets. J. Environ. Econ. Manage. 43, 113–134 (2002)

Hamilton, S.F., Zilberman, D.: Green markets, eco-certification and equilibrium fraud, J. Environ. Econ. Manage. 52, 627–644 (2006)

Ibanez, L., Grolleau, G.: Can ecolabeling schemes preserve the environment? Environ. Res. Econ. 40, 233–249 (2008)

Johnston, R.J., Wessells, C.R., Donath, H., Asche, F.: Measuring consumer preferences for ecolabeled seafood: an international comparison. J. Agric. Res. Econ. 26(1), 20–39 (2001)

Kirchhoff, S.: Green business and Blue Angels: a model of voluntary over-compliance with asymmetric information. Environm. Res. Econom. 15(4), 403–420 (2000)

Lusk, J.L., Schroeder, T.C.: Are choice experiments incentive compatible? A test with quality differentiated beefsteaks. Amer. J. Agr. Econ. 86, 467–482 (2004)

Morton, J.: Home page, Satsuma Mandarin Orange, Fruits of Warm Climates, Julia F. Morton, Miami, Florida, pp. 142–145 (1987),
http://www.hort.purdue.edu/newcrop/morton/
mandarin_orange.html

Nemoto, S.: Change in quality of consumption and environmental burden—All-year consumption of fresh-tomatoes and LCI analysis—. The Japanese Society of Household Econ. 26, 55–67 (2007) (in Japanese)

OECD, Effects of eco-labelling schemes: compilation of recent studies. Joint Working Party on Trade and Environment, COM/ENV/TD(2004) 34/FINAL (2005)

Prescott, J., Young, O., O'Neill, L., Yau, N.J.N., Stevens, R.: Motives for food choice: a comparison of consumers from Japan, Taiwan, Malaysia and New Zealand. Food Qual. Prefer. 13, 489–495 (2002)

Roberts, J.A.: Green Consumers in the 1990s: Profile and Implications for Advertising. Journal of Business Research 36, 217–231 (1996)

Teisl, M.F., Roe, B., Hicks, R.L.: Can eco-labels tune a market? Evidence from dolphin-safe labeling. J. Environ. Econ. Manage. 43(3), 339–359 (2002)

Teisl, M.F., Rubin, J., Noblet, C.L.: Non-dirty dancing? Interactions between eco-labels and consumers. J. Econ. Psychology 29, 140–159 (2008)

Wessels, C.R., Johnston, R.J., Donath, H.: Assessing consumer preferences for ecolabeled seafood: the influence of species, certifier, and household attributes. Am. J. Agric. Econ. 81(5), 1084–1089 (1999)

A Choice Experiment for Air Travel Services

Kenju Akai[1], Keiko Aoki[2], and Nariaki Nishino[1]

[1] Graduate School of Engineering, The University of Tokyo, Tokyo, Japan
akai@css.t.u-tokyo.ac.jp,
nishino@tmi.t.u-tokyo.ac.jp
[2] Institute of Social and Economic Research, Osaka University, Osaka, Japan
k_aoki@iser.osaka-u.ac.jp

Abstract. Our purpose of this study is evaluating preferences for air travel services connected between the east and west central cities in Japan, Tokyo and Osaka, to consider the appropriate re-allocation design of airports in Japan. We employ a choice experiment and recruit more than 500 respondents in east and west areas in Japan and investigate their preferences. Our results are as follows. The existing airline connected west hub airport, Itami, in Osaka and east hub airport, Haneda, in Tokyo is much preferred to the other lines connected cities surrounding Osaka and Tokyo. Kobe and Kansai international airports are preferable to Itami airport, while Haneda is the much preferable to Ibaraki and Narita international airports. Increasing the mileage program and the availability of web check-in have positive significant effects but these impacts are small. These results imply that the most important factor for using air travel services is convenience for traveling by using the nearest airports. In this meaning, if the new airlines can be connected to Haneda, the government's re-allocation plan from Itami airport to Kobe and Kansai international airports has a chance to succeed to minimize the economic efficiency loss for the people traveling between east and west areas in Japan.

Keywords: Air travel service, choice experiment, internet survey.

1 Introduction

Relaxation of regulation in an entrance of airplanes becomes attractive for people who want to select cheap airplanes over the world. Entrancing of low cost carriers (LCC) enhances competitions in air travel market, which makes air travel much more familiar and convenient not only for sightseeing for abroad but for daily business scenes in domestic areas.

Now LCC market is rapidly increasing in Japan because of relaxation of regulation. In the past five decade, domestic airplane market in Japan was restricted and allowed to remain duopolies or oligopoly. Especially, in Japan, the railways are developed very well and the technology for the rapid express is highly qualified, which is often compared with TGV in France and imported to Taiwan and Vietnam. In this situation, the government allows to oligopoly in the airplane market in order to protect airplane market from hard competition with railways.

C. Emmanouilidis, M. Taisch, D. Kiritsis (Eds.): APMS 2012, Part II, IFIP AICT 398, pp. 353–360, 2013.
© IFIP International Federation for Information Processing 2013

This protective policy has, however, imposed incurring high cost for people who use the airplanes and block the entrance of newcomers and disturbed competitions between incumbents and newcomers. In this situation, LCC is expected as useful newcomers because of much cheaper tickets than existing airplanes. The price of ticket in LCC is often less than two thirds of that in existing airplanes and sometimes a half of its price. That price facilitates people who want to travel in the long distance because the air travel saves time for travel relative to the railway travel.

Although LCC became a newcomer to introduce attractive price for air traveling, it is concerned to hold an issue of safety and security commitment and that of comfort for people taking the in-flight services as well as ground services at the airport. In the safety issue, it is criticized that cost saving induces cut-off appropriate human and technological resources they need to spend. In the in-flight services, LCC save the space and reduce the seat-pitch in order to increase the number of seats. Additionally, almost all the beverages are not free. In the ground services, a web check-in is not available so that people need to wait for long line to obtain a boarding-pass. Additionally, the airports for LCC are located in the countryside far from the hub port and facilities in those airports tend to be poor. People need to walk from the getting on/off the airplane because buses are not employed in order to save cost for running.

Considering these issues allows us to explore what kinds of people prefer LCC to existing airplanes and which factors are important to choose airplanes and airports in their air travels. In this study, we focus on Japanese domestic air travel services. Our target regions are Tokyo, the principle of Japan, and Osaka, the west central Prefecture. They are located in east area and west areas in Japan, respectively, and it takes about 300 miles between these areas. There are the most many airlines and rapid express railways between these prefectures. There is the most competitive traveling area in Japan. Although the rapid express takes at least two hour and half, airplanes take within one hour.

Additional interesting viewpoint for considering air travel market in Japan, both Osaka and Tokyo have three airports surrounding these areas. Haneda airport, Ibaraki airport, and Narita international airport are candidates to go to Tokyo from Osaka. Haneda is the domestic hub airport and Narita international airport is the international hub airport. Ibaraki is a local area and it takes two hour and half from Tokyo but it spends only 500 JPY by bus and the airplane is LCC so that a ticket price from Osaka to Tokyo is the cheapest among these airports.

On the other hand, Itami airport, Kobe airport, and Kansai international airport are candidates to go to Osaka from Tokyo. Itami airport is the domestic hub in the west area and Kansai international airport is the hub for international airlines in the west area. Kobe airport is the newest airport that has only domestic airlines and only Kobe has a LCC to go to Ibaraki airport.

Now Japanese government tries the re-allocation of airlines in those airports and re-constructs strategy for airport services, but it is hard journey because re-constructing allocation of airlines changes the people moving, traveling and business, which leads economic loss or benefits. This makes stakeholders not reach a consensus.

Our purpose of this study is evaluating preferences for air travels between these two areas in order to consider the appropriate allocation design of air travel services in Japan market. Solving this issue leads economic benefits not only to the other domestic areas but also to the world. Since Japanese are one of the biggest travelers in the world, appropriate re-allocation in the domestic market enhances the efficient moving and traveling, which leads saving cost and time for leaving abroad.

In this end, we employ a choice experimental method to evaluate preferences for air travel services. We use the internet survey system and recruit 500 recipients living in the east area (called Kanto district) near to the three east airports and west area (called Kansai district) near to the three west airports in Japan. We found that the airline connected between east and west domestic hub airports, Itami and Haneda, is the most preferred for air traveling. Kobe and Kansai international airports are preferable to Itami airport, while Haneda is the much preferable to Ibaraki and Narita international airports. On the other hand, in the in-flight and ground services, only the availability of web check-in and increasing mileage programs are preferred but these impacts are small. Based on the results above, the government's re-allocation plan from Itami to Koabe and Kasai international airports has a chance to succeed to minimize the economic efficiency loss if they are connected to Haneda airport.

Air travel services have been studied by lots of survey analysis by using multinominal logit analysis. For instance, Hess and Polak (2005) consider the multi-airport regions and evaluate preference for these airports. Balcombe et al. (2009) evaluate consumer willingness to pay for in-flight service. Hough and Hassanien (2010) investigate preference of transport choice behavior of Chinese and Australian tourists in Scotland. Bliemer and Rose (2011) surveyed previous all studies on preferences for air travel services. Especially, in Japan, Furuichi and Koppelman (1994) investigate multi airports choice and discover that access time, accest cost and flight frequency has significant effects. Additionally, Keumi and Murakami (2012) consider the utility of connection between local airports and international hub airports. Based on these studies, we focus on the combination of airport locations and in-flight and ground services as the air travel services and compare these preferences.

The remainder of the paper is organized as follows. Section 2 presents the design of a choice experiment. Section 3 shows the model structure. Section 4 analyzes the result and Section 5 summarizes the conclusions.

2   Design of a Choice Experiment

We conducted an internet survey based on the choice experimental method. Recipients are recruited from Kanto and Kansai districts. Kanto district is the group of Prefectures located in the east side of Japan including the principle of Tokyo. Kansai district, on the other hand, is the group of Prefectures located in the west Japan including Osaka, the second biggest Prefecture and central city in the west side of Japan. Kanto district has Haneda, Narita and Ibaraki airports. Kansai district has Itami, Kansai and Kobe airports.

In the choice experiment, the three alternatives of departure airports in the designated choice sets were Itami airport, Kansai International airport, and Kobe airport as shown in Figure 1. These airports are departure airports for people living in Kansai district, while those are arrival airports for people living in Kanto district.

Airports in Kansai district	Itami	Kansai	Kobe
Airports in Kanto district	Narita	Haneda	Ibaraki
Airfare (JPY)	14000	5000	9000
Number of frights	14	10	2
Web check-in	Available	Available	Non-available
Seat-pitch (cm)	78	68	78
Mileage program (%)	100	50	0
Your Choice			

Fig. 1. An example of choice sets

The attributes and the levels being tested were show in Table1. We also inform how long it takes from each airport to Tokyo by bus and its cost. Therefore, a full factorial design with three airports in Kanto district, three values of airfares, four numbers of flights, two types of web check-in, two types of seat-pitch and three levels of mileage programs resulted in 432 (=2^2*3^3*4) alternative management combinations. Since these combinations constituted an unreasonably large design in practice, a D-optimal fractional factorial design with 42 alternatives was developed and separated into three blocks of 14 choice sets by using Design Expert (version 7).

Table 1. Attributes and levels used in the choice experiment

Attributes	Levels
Airports in Kanto district	Haneda airport, Narita International airport, Ibaraki airport
Airfare	4000 JPY, 9000 JPY, 14000 JPY
Number of flights	2, 6, 10, 14
Web check-in	Available, Non-available
Seat-pitch	68 cm, 78 cm
Mileage programs	0 %, 50%, 100%

3   Model Structure

Random utility theory is central to the concept of choice modeling. The basic assumption embodied in the random utility approach to choice modeling is that decision makers are utility maximizers, which implies that decision makers choose the alternative that maximizes their utility, given a set of alternatives. The utility of an alternative for an individual (U) cannot be observed; however, it can be assumed to consist of a deterministic (observable) component (V) and a random error (unobservable) component (ε). Formally, an individual q's utility of alternative i can be expressed as follows:

$$U_{iq} = V_{iq} + \varepsilon_{iq} . \tag{1}$$

Hence, the probability that individual q chooses alternative i from a particular set J, which comprises j alternatives, can be written as the following:

$$
\begin{aligned}
P_{iq} &= P(U_{iq} > U_{jq}; \text{ for all } j(\neq i) \in J) \\
&= P(\varepsilon_{jq} < \varepsilon_{iq} + V_{iq} - V_{jq}; \text{ for all } j(\neq i) \in J)
\end{aligned} \tag{2}
$$

To transform the random utility model into a choice model, certain assumptions regarding the joint distribution of the vector of random error components is required. If random error components are assumed to follow the type I extreme value (EV1) distribution and to be independently and identically distributed (IID) across alternatives and cases (or observations), a conditional logit model (McFadden, 1974) can be obtained. In the conditional logit model, the choice probability in Equation 2 is expressed as

$$P_{iq} = \frac{\exp(\mu V_{iq})}{\sum_{j=1}^{J} \exp(\mu V_{jq})} . \tag{3}$$

Further, assuming that the deterministic component of utility is linear and additive in parameters $V_{iq} = \beta' X_{iq}$, the probability in Equation 3 can be rewritten as

$$P_{iq} = \frac{\exp(\mu \beta' X_{iq})}{\sum_{j=1}^{J} \exp(\mu \beta' X_{jq})} , \tag{4}$$

where μ represents a scale parameter that determines the scale of the utility, which is proportional to the inverse of the distribution of the error components. It is typically normalized to 1.0 in the conditional model. X_{iq} are the explanatory variables of V_{iq}, normally including alternative-specific constants (ASCs) , the attributes of alternative i and socio-economic characteristics of individual q, and β' is the parameter vector associated with matrix X_{iq}.

Based on the above discussions, this study estimates two indirect utility functions.

Model 1: $V_{iq} = ASC_{kansai} + ASC_{kobe} + \beta_1 Airport_k + \beta_2 Airfare_i$
$\qquad + \beta_3 Flights_i + \beta_4 WebCheck - in_i + \beta_5 Seat - pitch_i + \beta_6 Mileage_i$

Model 2: $V_{iq} = \beta'_1 ASC_{kansai} * Airport_k + \beta''_1 ASC_{kobe} * Airport_k + \beta_2 Airfare_i$
$\qquad + \beta_3 Flights_i + \beta_4 WebCheck - in_i + \beta_5 Seat - pitch_i + \beta_6 Mileage_i$

where ASC_{Kansai} and ASC_{Kobe} are dummy variables indicating the selecting of alternative Kansai or alternative Kobe with respect to alternative Itami such as reference alternative. k represents Haneda, Narita, and Ibaraki airports. $Airport_k$ is a dummy variable indicating k airport. $Airfare_i$ is the price of airline ticket for alternative i. $Flighst_i$ is the number of the flight per day for alternative i. $WebCheck-in_i$ is a dummy variable taken the value 1 if a web cheak-in is available. $Seat-pitch_i$ is the seat pitch size by shown in cm for alternative *i*. *Mileage$_i$* is the percentage of mileage program where one can earn mileages for alternative *i*. ASC_{Kansai}*$Airport_k$ and ASC_{Kobe}*$Airport_k$ are interaction term of ASC_{Kansai} and ASC_{Kobe} with dummy variable indicating *k* airport, respectively. Finally, β_1, β_2, β_3, β_4, β_5, β_6, β_7, β_1', and β_1'' are the parameters to be estimated.

4   Results

The internet survey was conducted in June 2012. The respondents were recruited from among residents from 10,000 households in the Kanto and Kansai districts by the internet survey system. 505 participants answered the survey. Their socio-economic backgrounds are summarized in Table 2.

Table 2. Socio-economic background

Variable	Mean	Definition
Age	51.00	Year in age
Gender	1.39	1: Male; 2: Female
Income	3.54	1: less than 3 million yen; 2: 3-5 million yen; 3: 5-7 million yen; 4: 7-10 million yen; 5: 10-15 million yen; more than 15 million yen
Marriage	1.80	1: No; 2: Yes
Children	1.30	1: Yes; 2: No

Here we show conditional logit estimation results by LIMDEP 9.0 and NLOGIT 4.0. Table 3 shows the results of conditional logit model in Models 1 and 2. In Model 1 as show in main effect, two alternative specific constants, ASC_{Kansai} and ASC_{Kobe} are significantly and positive signs, which imply that people will get higher utility from alternative Kansai or Kobe than from alternative Itami. Two variables *Narita* and *Ibaraki* are significantly and negative sings, which imply that people prefer Haneda airport to others. The variable *Airfare* is significantly and negative sign, which imply that people prefer cheaper price. The variables *WebCheck-in*, *Seat-pitch* and *Mileage* are significantly and positive signs, which imply that people prefer to be able to check-in the website, to be longer size in the seat and to earn more mileages. We further consider estimation results by the marginal willingness to pay (WTP), which means how much people want to pay for each attribution, estimates for each variable. People have a willingness to pay 8,478 JPY to use Haneda airport as compared to Narita one, or 16,375 JPY to Ibaraki one, respectively. They imply that Haneda airport is very important among airports in Kanto district for both people in Kansai and Kanto districts. People have a willingness to pay 1362 JPY to be able to check-in in the website.

In order to consider the preference between airports in Kansai and Kanto districts, we use interaction terms such as ASC_{Kansai} *$Airport_k$ and ASC_{Kobe}*$Airport_k$ in the Model 2. The reference alternative is alternative Itami for both interaction terms.

The variables $ASC_{Kansai}*Haneda$ and $ASC_{Kobe}*Haneda$ are significantly and positive signs, which imply that people prefer Kansai and Kobe airport to Itami if they use the Haneda airport. They are as same as the results of two alternative specific constants in Model 1. Since other interaction terms are significantly and negative sings, which imply that people prefer Itami airport to others if they use Narita or Ibaraki airports. The results in the variables *Airfare*, *WebCheck-in*, and *Mileage* are the same as the Model 1. However, the variable *Flights* is significantly and negative sign, which imply that people prefer the less number of the flights between two areas. In the marginal WTP estimates, people value between Kansai and Haneda airports at 4305 JPY and between Kobe and Haneda at 1758 JPY as compared to using between Itami and Haneda. They imply that people prefer Kansai and Kobe airports as same as the results in Model 1. Moreover, people prefer Itami airport when they use Narita and Ibaraki airports because the WTP estimates in other interaction terms with Narita and Ibaraki are more than 3596 JPY and 8832 JPY, respectively.

Table 3. The conditional logit regression results in the Models 1 and 2

Variables	Model 1 Coefficient (S.E.)	Model 1 Marginal WTP (JPY)	Model 2 Coefficient (S.E.)	Model 2 Marginal WTP (JPY)
ASC_{Kansai}	0.78*** (0.03)	-	-	-
ASC_{Kobe}	0.49*** (0.03)	-	-	-
Narita	-0.84*** (0.04)	8478	-	-
Ibaraki	-1.63*** (0.04)	16375	-	-
$ASC_{Kansai}*$Haneda	-	-	0.43*** (0.04)	4305
$ASC_{Kansai}*$Narita	-	-	-0.35*** (0.04)	3596
$ASC_{Kansai}*$Ibaraki	-	-	-0.88*** (0.05)	8832
$ASC_{Kobe}*$Haneda	-	-	0.17*** (0.05)	1758
$ASC_{Kobe}*$Narita	-	-	-0.83*** (0.04)	8398
$ASC_{Kobe}*$Ibaraki	-	-	-1.81*** (0.07)	18165
Airfare	-0.00*** (0.00)	-	-0.00*** (0.00)	-
Flights	0.00 (0.00)	-	-0.00** (0.00)	78
WebCheck-in	0.13*** (0.03)	1362	0.16*** (0.03)	1605
Seat-pitch	0.01*** (0.00)	104	0.00 (0.00)	-
Mileage	0.00*** (0.00)	12	0.00*** (0.00)	13
Log likelihood	-6321.4		-6587.1	
McFadden's R^2	0.15		0.11	
Observations	7070		7070	

Notes: ***, **, and * denote that the parameters are different from zero at the 1%, 5%, 10% significance levels, respectively. WTP is calculated by using the estimated price parameter.

5   Conclusions

In this study, we evaluate the preference for air travel services constituted of airport locations and in-flight and ground services by using conditional logit model in the internet survey. Our results are as follows.

- Among all line alternatives, the existing line connected west and east hub airports, that is, Itami and Haneda, obtains the highest marginal WTP.
- Kobe and Kansai international airports are preferable to Itami airport.
- Ibaraki and Narita international airports are less preferable to Haneda airport.
- Haneda airport obtains the highest marginal WTP for people living in east and west areas in Japan.
- Increasing the mileage program and the availability of web check-in have the small marginal WTP.

These results imply that the most important factor for using air travel services is convenience for using the nearest airport. Based on Haneda as the east domestic hub airport, Kobe and Kansai international airports have a possibility to become an alternative to Itami as the west domestic hub airport. However, Haneda does not have alternative airports because Ibaraki and Narita international airports have less values than Haneda airport. Therefore, the most important airport is Haneda. If the new airlines can be connected to Haneda, the government's re-allocation plan from Itami airport to Kobe and Kansai international airports has a chance to succeed to minimize the economic efficiency loss for the people traveling between east and west areas in Japan.

In this study, we combine the survey answered by people living in east and west areas. In the future research, we need to divide them into two groups and compare their preferences. We also consider the difference in preferences between sightseeing travelers and business travelers. In our models, the frequency of flights does not have big impact to their choice. When we focus on the business scenes, it is likelihood to be important factor as the measure of convenience for air travel services. To obtain the robust results, we further need much more recipients.

References

1. Hough, G., Hassanien, A.: Transport Choice Behaviour of Chinese and Australian Tourists in Scotland. Research in Transportation Economics 26, 54–65 (2010)
2. Balcombe, K., Fraser, I., Harris, L.: Consumer Willingness to Pay for In-flight Service and Comfort Levels: A Choice Experiment. Journal of Air Transport Management 15, 221–226 (2009)
3. Furuichi, M., Koppelman, F.S.: An analysis of air traveler's departure airport and destination choice behavior. Transportation Research 28A, 187–195 (1994)
4. Keumi, C., Murakami, H.: The Role of Schedule Delays on Passengers' Choice of Access Modes: A Case Study of Japan's International Hub Airports. Transportation Research Part E 48, 1023–1031 (2012)
5. McFadden, D.: Conditional LogitAnalysis of Qualitative Choice Behavior. In: Zarembka, P. (ed.) Frontiers in Econometrics, pp. 105–142. Academic Press, New York (1974)
6. Michiel, C.J., Bliemer, J., Rose, M.: Experimental Design Influences on Stated Choice Outputs: An Empirical Study in Air Travel Choice. Transportation Research Part A 45, 63–79 (2011)
7. John, H.S., Polak, W.: Mixed Logit Modelling of Airport Choice in Multi-airport Regions. Journal of Air Transport Management 11, 59–68 (2005)

Product-Service Systems Modelling and Simulation as a Strategic Diagnosis Tool

Thècle Alix and Gregory Zacharewicz

Univ. Bordeaux, IMS, UMR 5218, F-33400 Talence, France,
CNRS, IMS, UMR 5218, F-33400 Talence, France
firstname.name@ims-bordeaux.fr

Abstract. Manufacturers have developed Product/Service-Systems (PSS) strategies to increase their competitiveness and reach objectives of profitability, satisfying customer's specific and evolving needs as well as environmental needs in term of grasp reduction and pollution decrease. Despite, the announced success of such a strategy, industrialists fears that the strategy will not give the expected results. To avoid unsustainable developments and reach product-service systems features, manufacturers are looking forward methods and tools that can help them predicting an a priori level of performance of the whole system they intend to design in terms of sustainability, use, profit, etc. Precisely, we aim at proposing a demonstrator able to support decision in the design of new sustainable and eco-efficient product-service system.

Keywords: Product/Service-System, PSS modelling, PSS simulation, diagnosis tool.

1 Introduction

The individual and collective awareness of the huge importance of environmental issues led politics, researchers, and citizens to focus on sustainable production and consumption. Some of the most indicative incentives are focusing on green economy, circular economy, function-oriented business model, industrial ecology, functional service economy, etc. A common call is the need for a new strategy to stimulate the change in current production and consumption patterns. According to some statements, rising levels of consumption by the rich and doubling of the world population over the next 50 years would require a factor 4 increase in food production and a factor 6 increase in energy use. An estimate mentions that by the middle of the century, global consumption of natural resources could triple if the coupling between economic growth and the rate of natural resource consumption remains as it is. Theories are developed about the factor by which the environmental performance can be improved. Solutions are devised to support the change around reducing the population, lowering the level of consumption or changing technology.

The first option is not feasible in the short term. The second one: decreasing consumption levels does not appear to be a simple option either because, on the one hand, people from industrialised countries do not show any obvious willingness to

C. Emmanouilidis, M. Taisch, D. Kiritsis (Eds.): APMS 2012, Part II, IFIP AICT 398, pp. 361–368, 2013.
© IFIP International Federation for Information Processing 2013

minimise consumption and, on the other hand, there is a need to increase consumption levels in developing countries just to provide basic amenities. The third option: changing technology is a matter of considerable study as it concerns the branch of knowledge that deals with the creation and use of technical means and their interrelation with life, society, and the environment, drawing upon such subjects as industrial arts, engineering, applied science, and pure science. In pragmatic way, technology gather knowledge and practises used to provide customers with products and services.

The service growing need driven by the market gradually led the service sector to dominate the economy and to be the lifeblood of job creation. Partly unsatisfied, service demand, perceived by the society as a way to have access to basic or complex amenities, is of prime importance while the product demand becomes secondary. This prompted the secondary industry to consider service activities as a potential source of benefits [1]. At the same time the increasingly aggressive competition in the service sector challenged service industrialization and more and more service providers attempted to include a product in their offer.

As a result, the boundary between products and services get blurred [2]. Mixing product and service demand, socio-economic, technologic and environmental constraints and statements combinations of product (physical artefact) and service (functionality from the product or added expected by the customer regarding his needs and product usage) under different denomination have been developed [3]. Variants come from the focus: economic (variety of business model [4], technological (functional engineering), commercial (new ownership pattern [5]), environmental, etc. The System resulting from the combination Product(s) and Service(s) (PSS) extends the traditional functionality of a product by integrating additional services giving emphasis on the 'sale of use' rather than the 'sale of product'. PSS are also supposed to have positive impacts in terms of sustainability, by the reduction of resource and/or energy consumption.

PSS design and development, result in a matter of huge importance. To avoid unsustainable developments, manufacturers are looking forward for methods and tools that can help them in predicting the level of performance the whole system they intend to design would reach. We propose to use simulation to calculate that level of performance and assume that as simulation is based on modelling, the first step is to propose a PSS modelling to have a complete description of the components of a PSS, the links between them and with performance criteria associated to the design of new sustainable and eco-efficient services system. The main focus of the article is on modelling. After a prompt recall of PSS concepts, an overview of the status of modelling and simulation research is presented. The fourth part presents our vision for PSS modelling and simulation before concluding.

2   PSS Complexity as a Response to the Society, Customers and Manufacturers Awareness

A PSS is "Product(s) and service(s) combined in a system to deliver required user functionality in a way that reduces the impact on the environment" [7]. The definition extended through the years acknowledges that the concept of PSS also embraces value in use and sustainability [8], [9]). PSS appear to be a possible and promising business strategy which can achieve the leap that is needed to move to sustainable society. PSS development is therefore concerned with satisfying customer, society and company in providing the latter with a closer contact to the user and a possibility to get new market opportunities by exploiting the knowledge from the contact. Despite an undeniable interest, the willingness of manufacturers to move to that business strategy is challenged by their ability to create value added [6], and to make direct and indirect profit. The literature mentions many flops to this end. Furthermore, as there exists lot of variants, it is not clear which variant is to develop and if it is really sustainable and profitable.

In addition, even if advices were given to manufacturers to simultaneously consider products and services, industrial developments are mainly product-centric. Services and their performances (value in-use) and characteristics (customer-centric) are developed in a second phase according to options offered by products. The system pushed at the customer is not properly appreciated. Innovation aimed at increasing customer satisfaction does not find an echo and company return on investment is negligible. In addition, each system is unique and does not benefit from the experience of previous systems. Moreover new resources are each time consumed. To achieve the goal of sustainability, the strategy requires considering simultaneously industrial and service developments.

Furthermore, economically the return on investment of the different systems proposed by the firms is mostly calculated a posteriori, i.e. once the system is set up and delivered to the customers rather than being identified and anticipated a priori. This sometimes leads to wrong system specifications and practices that penalize the enterprise such as misleading coupling between products and services.

PSS developments face many challenges: sustainability, value, economy of use, profitability, etc. A first step towards sustainability is to use virtual testing to determine the ability of different product and service components having common features to interoperate to create value. Virtual testing enables to modify product and service configurations and give results without any physical resource intensive realization. Then, our contribution does not concern PSS design for which a wide range of tools and methodologies are proposed. The action is upstream in PSS life cycle innovation and concerns the ideation phase. Objective is to help project managers to determine among potential innovations the most relevant one.

3   Status of PSS Modelling and Simulation Research

PSS Simulation is an emerging field suffering from a lack of background and unanimous knowledge in its essential: the service and the service modelling [10]. Many authors describe modelling and simulation as one process, assessing that modelling is a sort of prerequisite for simulation and not an activity by itself.

3.1   Service and PSS Modelling

Due to the varying definitions and characteristics of the term service, service modelling has not yet adopted a unique common standard for developing frameworks to manage services processes. Even if simulation has been used to model manufacturing systems and specific service systems (banking, healthcare hospitality, etc.) and sometimes in modelling business operations of both systems, characteristics of each system need to be taken into account [11].

Furthermore, the specification of Service Modelling can involve different process, application and actor components, which are essential to the service execution, but heterogeneous. The specification standards are numerous. Becker reports more than 15 main reference models [12]. Some authors transpose to service the administrative or production workflow process sequence description [13]. Others use the graphical definition of a Service-Oriented Modelling Framework (SOMF) [14]. An essential breach concerns the model correctness checking. The W3C proposed an XML representation of Service Modelling Language (SML) accepted as a standard in the Service modelling community. Service Modelling Language (SML) and Service Modelling Language Interchange Format (SML-IF) [15] are a pair of XML-based specifications created by leading information technology companies that define a set of XML instance document extensions for expressing links between elements, a set of XML Schema extensions for constraining those links, and a way to associate Schematron rules with global element declarations, global complex type definitions, and/or model documents. It is to note that the proposed description is more Computer Science Service Modelling oriented than PSS oriented.

3.2   PSS Simulation

Only few contributions to simulation of PSS have emerged since 2000. Most of the projects performed over the past decade focused the dynamic behaviour of the PSS process and were mainly driven by the goal to provide feedbacks to designers to support the design of a relevant model of the system and to verify some desired properties.

In the literature, Bianchi has chosen the system dynamic methodology for PSS simulation [16]. The methodology allows analysing the dynamic of a PSS strategy managing interrelated factors features by non-linear complex dynamics and negative/positive reinforcement loops. The approach is serious game to support a hypothetical organization to invest or not in a PSS strategy depending it will be generating welfares or not. The model takes into account four possible stakeholders (government, Product-Oriented Manufacturers, PSS providers and consumers), some market parameters, strategic policies, capacity of PSS transition for PO, etc. [17]. The main advantage of the method lies in the easy combination with others (i.e. multi criteria approach) to provide decision support systems.

Bulk simulation is another simulation method that allows considering simultaneously many parameters and characteristics that are simulated in batch [18]. Van der Vegte proposes in [19] to simulate at the level of interaction sequences, in a non-interactive fashion and with consideration of multiplicity the use of information-intensive products and PSS in design. Designers can investigate the use of a product over a long time or massive batches of smaller intervals of use and then predict outcomes of use during design. Bulk simulation proposes to model stakeholders (users and service providers) as well as products as individual agents.

Agent based simulation is a wide used simulation technique to model a system as a pool of autonomous decision-maker agents. The simulation results are produces by and their interactions [20]. The assumption is that the global system behaviour can be studied based on the M&S of individual behaviour and their interactions.

Others studies focus on Discrete-Event System simulation [21]. The structural components of a PSS discrete-event simulation typically include: model entities, model activities, model resources and model layout. Simulators based on that technic can be used to increase the added value of the system companies might design. The different researches identify the variables to be followed during simulation including the price, process costs lifetime, sales frequency, lifetime, etc. In [22] the simulation was running customer behaviour in term of buying habits. The results were giving feedbacks on the comparison between buying goods and using PSS. But none of the current research works specifically focus on customer use, sustainability and synergies between products and services in the PSS context.

3.3   Few Findings to Focus on

The literature review leads to the following conclusions:

- There is no unanimous reference model of a PSS and a fortiori no modelling language dedicated to PSS. Objective is to propose a generic PSS model based on constructs that can be instantiated according to particular cases.

- Modelling and simulation are most of the time integrated in one thought leading to underestimate the difficulties inherent to service modelling and to position upstream problematic specific to the time dependency of the system to model. We propose to distinguish the two steps and consequently to first model a PSS and then simulate the model.

- A PSS is a sequence of multiple, interrelated life phases and activities throughout the product's service time [23]. Both static and dynamic models are mandatory to have a complete representation of a PSS.

- Two main kinds of studies are supported by simulation: the identification of the added value of systems manufacturers intent to develop, the determination of the profit a design can lead to. Added value is the main consumer concern while profit is the manufacturer concern. As these two elements are of huge importance and dependent, the simulation must support value and profit analysis i.e. a customer perspective and a manufacturer one.

- Stakeholders are taken into account in all models and PSS life cycle needs to be considered carefully.

- Product usage is important and is not taken into account in all models. Usage can give information on the sustainability of the product as a behavioural performance indicator enabling to get knowledge to design lean PSS and to increase the system added value.

- Adaptability to the customer environment is to be analysed and the product might be integrated in the value added process of the customer. The PSS reference modelling based on UML modelling is depicted in next section.

4   Methodology for Service Modelling

4.1   Modelling Principles

The PSS modelling is based on the following assumptions.

- Three stakeholders are interested in the "success" of new PSS design and development: the provider of the system, the customer and the society (eco-system).
- PSS are designed to respond to customers' usage requirements defined a priori (i.e. before the system is delivered to customer) and combine products and services. Each product can be described through functions designed to fit service requirements. Each PSS designed and delivered can then be seen as a unique complex set composed of products subsets (tangible component) and services subsets (intangible components). Components are structured in modules having functionalities. These functionalities allow some usages that can be challenged to customers' specific usage needs (identified a priori or a posteriori). The gap between both influences the PSS value perceived by the customer. Modules can be combined differently according to specific usage needs and lead to PSS variants. Variants objective is to increase the value perceived by customers.
- PSS providers design PSS processes supported by resources, with the aim of generating profit. Profit is maximized when PSS value is high and resource consumption of the PSS process low. Obviously variants modify processes and decrease profitability. Furthermore, variants impact resource consumption.
- Finally, society put pressure on the environmental impact of new development. Accordingly, functionality and resource consumption have to respect ecosystem requirements in terms of sustainability.

The resulting PSS modelling is depicted in figure 1. Each functionality can be described through its components and characterized by attributes: cost, environmental impact, associated usage, or else resource needs to deliver the functionality. Attributes are described from a qualitative and quantitative point of view. Once the description is complete, the functionality can integrate a library and potential coupling with other functionality can be virtually tested.

4.2   Simulation Principles

New PSS design and development is based on a strategic analysis whose objective is to define lines of innovation. Most of the time, innovations are incremental - series of small steps - as enterprises find ways to update their products and processes or to integrate basic services. Simulation principle is to analyse the possibility that new functionalities supplement a PSS existing ones while receiving benefits, if any, of components already used to fill these existing functionalities. Specifically, the assembly of components can be simulated in order to measure their capacity to easily interact and to cope with the customers' need and use, with the manufacturers' profit expectations and with the environmental incentive. The simulation of scenario tests can give clue to manufacturers to develop and set up a win-win strategy for them, their customers and the environment.

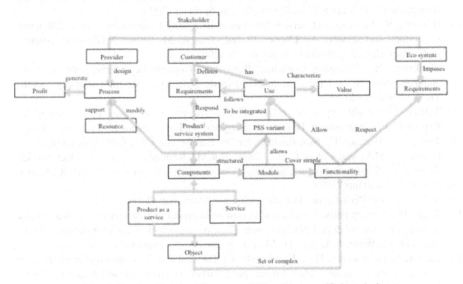

Fig. 1. Product Service System modelling for eco-efficient design

5 Conclusion

The design and development of product-service systems is a hot topic regarding its economic and societal impact. Although successful designs are mentioned in the literature, many flops exist and disrupt the willingness of manufacturers to innovate in that sense. Objective of our works is to use simulation as a decision aid tool in the design of new sustainable and eco-efficient product-service system. A first step to reach that objective consists in modelling a PSS. This modelling represents the main contribution of this article. The following step is to quantify attributes of functionalities and components; investigations on best compromise or optimization strategies for building services in awareness of both enterprises and customer needs, and environmental impact and societal value have to be conducted. A simulator is then to be developed.

The authors trust that defining key performance indicators to follow regarding dynamic of the PSS delivery process the simulation is a promising technic that can help to PSS designer to anticipate problems and to dimension properly the offer regarding client's requirements. It will anticipate claims and increase client loyalty.

References

1. Oliva, R., Kallenberg, R.: Managing the transition from products to services. International Journal Service Industrial Management 14(2), 160–171 (2003)
2. Mont, O.: Product-service systems: Panacea or myth? PhD thesis, The International Institute for Industrial Environmental Economics. Lund University, Sweden (2004)
3. Sundin, E.: Life-Cycle Perspectives of Product/Service- Systems: in Design Theory. In: Introduction to Product/Service-System Design. Springer (2009)
4. Hockerts, K.: Eco-Efficient Service Innovation: Increasing Business-Ecological Efficiency of Products and Services. In: Charter, M. (ed.) Greener Marketing: A Global Perspective on Greener Marketing Practice, Sheffield, UK (2007)
5. Meijkamp, R.: Changing Consumer Behaviour Through Eco-efficient Services: an empirical study on car sharing in the Netherlands. Delft University of Technology, Delft, The Netherlands (2000)
6. Tukker, A.: Eight types of productservice system: eight ways to sustainability? Experiences from suspronet. Business Strategy and the Environment 13, 246–260 (2004)
7. Tukker, A., Tischner, U.: New Business for Old Europe. Greenleaf Publishing (2006)
8. Goedkoop, M.J., van Halen, C.J.G., Riele, H.R.M., Rommens, P.J.M.: Product Service Systems, Ecological and Economic Basis. Pricewaterhouse Coopers N.V. / Pi!MC, Storrm C.S., Pre consultants (1999)
9. Stahel, W.: The Performance Economy. Palgrave Macmillan (2006)
10. Touzi, W.: Conceptualisation et modélisation de la production de service: application aux domaines de la santé et de l'enseignement. Thèse de doctorat, Université Bordeau 1 (2001)
11. Lovelock, C., Wirtz, J., Lapert, D.: Marketing des services. Pearson Education (2004)
12. Becker, J., Beverungen, D.F., Knackstedt, R.: The challenge of conceptual modelling for product-service systems: status quo and perspectives for reference models and modelling languages. Information Systems and E-Business Management Journal 8(1), 33–66 (2010)
13. Meier, H., Roy, R., Seliger, G.: Industrial Product-Service Systems-IPS2. CIRP Annals - Manufacturing Technology 59(2), 607–627 (2010)
14. Bell, M.: Service-Oriented Modelling: Service Analysis, Design, and Architecture. John Wiley & Sons, Inc., Hoboken (2008)
15. http://www.w3.org/TR/sml/
16. Bianchi, N.P.: Influencing factors of successful Transitions towards product-Service Systems: a simulation approach. International Journal of Mathematics and Computers in Simulation 3(1) (2009)
17. Sterman, J.D.: Business dynamics: systems thinking and modelling for a complex world. Irwin McGraw Hill (2000)
18. Wile, B., Goss, J.C., Roesner, W.: Comprehensive functional verification the complete industry cycle. Morgan Kaufmann (2005)
19. Van der Vegte, W.F., Horvath, I.: Bulk simulation of using information intensive products and product-service systems: formal underpinnings. In: Proceeding of TMCE 2012 (2012)
20. Bonabeau, E.: Agent-based modelling: Methods and techniques for simulating human systems. Proceedings Natl. Acad. Sci. USA, 280–7287 (2002)
21. Phumbua, S., Tjahjono, B.: Simulation Modelling of Availability Contracts. In: Simulation Modelling of Product-Services Systems: The missing Link, MATADOR Conference (2010)
22. Alix, T., Zacharewicz, G.: Product-service systems scenarios simulation based on G-DEVS/HLA: Generalized discrete event specification/high level architecture. Computers In Industry 63(4), 370–378 (2012)

Contribution to the Development of a Conceptual Model of Service and Service Delivery

Wael Touzi, Thècle Alix, and Bruno Vallespir

Univ. Bordeaux, IMS, UMR 5218, F-33400 Talence, France,
CNRS, IMS, UMR 5218, F-33400 Talence, France
firstname.name@ims-bordeaux.fr

Abstract. For a long time, it was highlighted that services have specific characteristics mainly used to differentiate themselves from goods. Proposed definitions and characteristics led to debates between specialists in economics, marketing and management for several years and result in different points of view and approaches. There is still no consensus in these disciplines. More recently, new ones have contributed to define the concept of service. The goal of this paper is to present, on the one hand, the existing literature proposed by economists and managers about services (definitions and specificities) and, on the other, perspectives proposed by other disciplines such as computer science, engineering science or the SSME that challenge them. The bibliographical analysis results in a conceptual modeling of service and service delivery.

Keywords: service modeling, service production, service delivery.

1 Introduction

The tertiary sector is particularly important in the current economy and drove the recent job creation contributing to more than 4 million of "full-time equivalents" between 1990 and 2009 in France while other business sectors lost 1,4 millions over the same period[1]. In 2009, the tertiary sector represented about three quarters of the value-added and employed 89 % of the working population. The main reason of the shift to the service sector is linked to the high level of productivity gains in the primary and secondary sectors, to the automation of the processes in these sectors as well as to a growing need for services to individuals (health, leisure, culture, etc.) and to enterprises (transport, maintenance, accounting, commercial service, etc.).

Today, the share of unsatisfied service demands still lead to the creation of companies in the tertiary sector. As a result is an increase of the competition in the market and non-market-services that rise many questions such as the management of service production processes, service productivity measure, the quality measure of the services supplied and of the activities contributing to provide them, as well as the measure of the real service value-added for customers. Accordingly, rationalization and industrialization are of huge importance for those companies producing services as well as the positioning of their value-added in the competition.

---

[1] http://www.insee.fr/fr/themes/tableau.asp?ref_id=natnon03146

C. Emmanouilidis, M. Taisch, D. Kiritsis (Eds.): APMS 2012, Part II, IFIP AICT 398, pp. 369–376, 2013.
© IFIP International Federation for Information Processing 2013

The increasing use of information and communication technologies for service delivery strengthens this need as it allows to increase the number of service delivery over a given period by the automation of all or any of the service delivery process. Thus, the length of the interaction between the customer and the contact personnel is even decreased as the role and place of the customer is changed as he takes a position upstream and downstream to the production, as is in the industrial production. The resulting phenomenon may be assimilated to industrialization of the service sector.

To prepare this shift, it seems obvious to reuse approaches from the secondary sector. Unfortunately, optimization models stemming from industry do not really allow to analyse the value chains of the tertiary sector because of its specific characteristics: a fuzzy border between production and distribution, a value dependent on the context and not fixed a priori, a contribution of the customer to the production even to the design of the service, only few physical movement of material and finally the impossibility to reduce the hand of work.

Thus, before focusing on the rationalisation of service production activities, it is of vital importance to define the production ins and outs and to clarify upstream what is a service. On the later point, it must be noted there are as many definitions and characterizations of the concept of "service" as domains which are interested in it. Accordingly, with the objective of proposing a conceptual model of services and of their production, the paper presents a multidisciplinary literature review on the service concept and on the service production as well as some approaches that directly or indirectly address the service production.

2   The Service Concept through a Multidisciplinary State of the Art

Some disciplines such as the Management Science are interested since a long time in services. Others, such as the computer science approach the service concept in a different way and address the service-oriented architectures (SOA), the cloud computing and XaaS, the web services, etc. The functional analysis or value engineering method used in engineering and more specifically in product design does not evoke directly the concept of service but focuses on the concept of function that is similar to a certain extent to the concept of service. Finally, the service science, management and engineering (SSME), aiming to be a new discipline, addresses several concepts relative to services. The definitions and concepts relative to services on which these various disciplines lean are presented hereafter. The presentation is restricted to the relevant concepts with regard to our objective of modelling.

The contribution of the **management science** is multiple and concerns at the same time service definition, service specific characteristics as well as the characteristics of the system used to deliver the service. Regarding its definition, a service is defined at the same time by opposition to goods [1], [2], as an activity [3], [4], or as a result [5], [6]. Each point of view lead to introduce specific notions: i.e. some works aims at characterizing the system producing the service often called service delivery system [7]; others propose specific service characteristics called IHIP characteristics standing for immateriality, heterogeneity, inseparability, and perishability [8], [9], [10], [11].

The **service-oriented architecture** developed in the frame of **the computer science** aim to insure a company with the realization of technological advances and business progress [12]. This is done by combining process innovation with an effective-governance, a technological strategy centred on the definition and on the re-use of services. Here, a functionality is decomposed in a set of functions or of services supplied by components. A business service is a company functionality that seems to be atomic from the service consumer point of view. In this frame, a service is a connection to an application offering an access to some of its functionalities [13]. It appoints an action executed by a component "service provider" to the attention of a "service consumer" component, possibly based on another system. A service can propose different functions such as: data processing, information research, etc. A customer relationship management application can give access to a customer data processing service for example (address, telephone, etc.). As the service is available somewhere, a process is required to get it [14], [15]. Then, among the available services, it is necessary to choose the one that fits the best the requirements. A **service Broker** can be used to convey the information among the servers.

The **functional analysis** part of the **value engineering (VE) method** was firstly used to identify the needs within the frame of new products design (NPD) [16]. **VE** is characterized by a functional approach proposing to formulate NPD in terms of objectives rather than in terms of solutions. For that concern, VE method rests on several fundamental concepts: the value [17], the need [18], and the function [19]. The value is the assessment of the product based on the product user expectations and motivations expressed by a quantity that grows when, ceteris paribus, the user satisfaction increases and/or the expense concerned to the product decreases. The need is defined as a necessity or a desire felt by a user. Finally, a function is an action of a product or of one of its constituents expressed exclusively in terms of objective. The functions of a product define what the product/product subset is doing or what it is going to do. That perspective is very close to the service concept.

The **service science, management and engineering** (SSME) works on the principle that the world has became a system of huge service composed of six billion persons, million companies, and million high-technology products, linked to service networks. It has thus became necessary to develop a " service science, management and engineering" to better understand the design, the evolution and the emergent properties of the service systems and also to understand how the innovation leads to productivity gains in this sector [20]. The SSME consider the services as processes, performances or else results that a person (company, organization) realizes for the profit of another company/organization. It is thus the nature of the relation with the customer that characterizes at best the service sector. Several approaches such as " the triptych of technical criteria " [21], or the " triangle of services " are proposed [22].

3   A Conceptual Model of Service and Service Delivery

In this section is presented a conceptual model of service based on the above-presented contributions. Objective is to embrace the main part of these contributions to be as generic as possible. The model details are developed in [23].

3.1   Basic Principles

The first principle of the proposed approach is that a service is an interaction within a couple service provider/consumer; oriented from the provider to the consumer. The intensity of the service delivered grows in the same way than a parameter that characterises the coupling provider/consumer. A provider is identified with regard to his function and is noted F. A consumer is characterized by his need and is noted B (figure 1, left part). This classification obliges to position an object as provider or consumer and excludes the possibility for an object to be both at the same time. To avoid the limitation, a third possibility is added to the typology: the hybrid object able to behave simultaneously as both.

The initial principle presents an object as a one service provider or consumer. Obviously, a complex object is able to return several services and/or to consume several ones. Accordingly, an object can be a provider/consumer of several services and becomes a cross service (figure 1, right part). Service delivery relations become then more complex i.e. each relation is defined for a given service. A hybrid object is then part of a service delivery series, linked to another upstream object as service consumer and a downstream object as service provider.

Fig. 1. Basic principle and hybrid object generic representation

3.2   Service Delivery Process

A service is not immediately returned as a coupling between both objects is to be established at first. The process leading the service to be returned might then be defined. According to the existing terminology, we call service delivery a service production and service delivery process, the process of service production.

The coupling between both objects enables a service delivery. This service is returned as long as the coupling exists. The coupling is momentary, when it is interrupted, the service stops and each object finds back its freedom. A first change around this principle concerns the case where the coupling persists. In that case, it is not necessary to insure the sustainability of the service. A second change corresponds to the case where the service is not only associated to a coupling existence but also by the check to an exogenous functioning conditions. The service delivery is then synchronous with a condition or similarly is framed by a start up event and a closing event. The service delivery process is here non-autonomous.

The abovementioned situations suppose that the service delivery process can only be led during the coupling. Obviously, the interaction between the service supplier/consumer is the main part of the service delivery process. However, in more complex cases both actors can require to be prepared in an upstream phase (some sort of pre-process) and to get free in a downstream phase (some sort of post-process) (figure 2). The corresponding phases are the following ones:

Initialization: this phase does not require the coupling to be established but requires to know that the service must be returned. Information on the service needs is necessary to activate the phase.

Customization and Contextualisation: in case the service is not standard, a phase of customization based on information coming from consumers is to be envisaged. The contextualisation focuses on the adaptation to the context (consumer, surrounding conditions, etc.) of the service to be returned and of the service delivery process.

Closing and De-contextualisation phases exist when both actors require a process to close the activity. This process is similar to the one of the initialization phase but occurs after the service delivery.

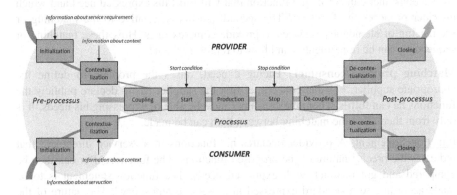

Fig. 2. Cartography of the whole service delivery process

3.3   Function Capacity and Need Load

An object may use its function in different ways: possibility to implement a function one or several times, in a successive or simultaneous way. These operational situations differ according to the object capacity to implement a function. Conversely, when an object possesses a need, the need can lead to different load levels.

Valuation of Capacity and Load: the capacity is a variable belonging to an interval $[0, Max_c]$. It can be boolean or expressed on a continuous or discrete scale. When the capacity is lower than Max_c, the object is able to implement the function but not with its maximum potential. Similarly, the load need can be boolean, continuous or discrete. As function and load are intrinsic characteristics of an object, as function capacity and need load are time variables. In particular, the provider capacity can be low or non-existent at a given moment because, at this moment, the object is occupied or not operational for example.

Capacity Variability: Several phenomena can lead to a temporary or long-lasting capacity variation of an object to return a service. When an object returns a service, its capacity is decreased. Once the service is returned and the service delivery process ended, two situations can occur: either the capacity returns to its initial value (the function is long-lasting), or the capacity maintains its new value (the function is consumable). The first case corresponds to non-perishable objects while the second one corresponds to the consumption of not renewable resources.

In the case of long-lasting functions, several phenomena can appear: wear (capacity decreases each time the process is launched), learning (capacity increases each time the process is launched) and unlearning phenomenon (capacity decreases because the process is not launched as often as it should).

3.4   Global Dynamics of Complex Services

The above-presented model focuses on an elementary service. Indeed, even if the provider (resp. consumer) proposes several functions (resp. need), the result is systematically a set of coupling function/need (i.e. a set of elementary services).

The first arising question concerns the matching between a function and a need. How a consumer can define the function that will fulfil his expressed need and which provider proposes the function? The second question is relative to the matching or sequencing of elementary services to provide complex ones. How these matching or sequencing can be implemented and how to represent them?

Matching provider/consumer: Facing a need, raises the problem to define the appropriate supplier. For that concern, at first the supplier has to declare publicly the functions he can fulfils. Then, the consumer must be able of expressing his needs. It is only from there, that the matching between both can be made.

Function Statement. A provider declares his functions in a "service directory" that indicates the precise nature of the proposed functions. The function offer can then be compared and got in touch with expressed needs. The function statement is to be made according to a standard expressed in a "service repository". The nature of the function is the static part of the statement while the capacity that can be used at a moment corresponds to the dynamic part (figure 3, left part).

Expression of Needs. A consumer expresses his needs at first in term of nature and then in term of load. From a nature point of view, the expression will be done according to the service repository and then completed by the requirement in term of associated load (figure 3, central part).

Matching. The two previous steps allow the matching provider/consumer. Once the service statement, the dynamic is the following (figure 3, right part): (1). expression of needs by the consumer, (2) comparison to functions reported in the service repository, (request), (3) choice among providers able to fulfil the need, (4) provider selection.

Service Composition: In the practice, technico-economic transactions lean on composite services that are "compositions of several existing services to obtain a

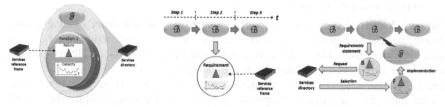

Fig. 3. Service statement, expression of needs and matching sequence

more complex service which can meet the needs of the user". These composite services are generated thanks to complex dynamics of elementary service implementation. In this frame, the service description above-presented corresponds to these elementary services. Objective is now to represent the dynamics of the system.

We assume that the studied system can be modelled based on a set of states. A set of active services corresponds to a state implying that the service delivery process runs within the framework of this state. A change of state means that at least a service delivery process starts or stops. It is possible that a service delivery process takes place during several successive states. A change of state is conditioned by a logical function consisted of conditions and events relative to the starting up or to the stop of a service. The logical function corresponding to the stop of a service will be similar to that of the starting up of another service when both are linked without intermediate state (figure 4). It is to note that, even if the approach seems to focus on a sequential composition of services, it also supports parallel compositions as when several elementary services are attached to one state, they might be activated simultaneously.

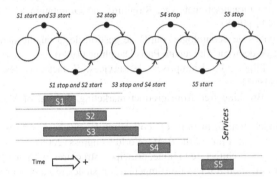

Fig. 4. Global dynamics of complex services

4   Conclusion

The conceptual service and service delivery modeling presented here is built upon concepts stemming from disciplines initially remote but which become integrated rather naturally to get a first level of modeling of service activities. The modeling is to be tested in the short term, to achieve its robustness to any kind of service. Till now, only personal services were considered: higher education or health services [23]. Others are to be tested as well as market services (B to B or B to C). At the same time, other concepts need to be explored (around service quality, web services, etc.) and specific issues should be duly addressed (how to select a provider when the function capacity is similar from one to another? or else, in the case of service composition, how to compose? and how to ensure composition effectiveness? etc.)

Considering middle term perspectives, three aspects need to be explored: At first, as there is a difference between buying a service and buying a product returning a service, all which concern service provider ownership and transactional aspect of the object or of its functions is to be integrated into the modelling. Second: provider or consumer lifecycle was not considered. Knowing in which phase of its lifecycle a provider is able to implement its functions, or knowing what it becomes in the other phases or, the phases over which it can consume a service, are so many questions which have to find answers within the framework of a lifecycle modelling. Third, service measurement is a problem of huge importance. In case of similar function, is a provider service delivery better than another one? Even if the problem of measurement is difficult to be settled, it would enable to clear up some other aspects presented here.

References

1. Rathmell, J.M.: What is meant by Services? Journal of Marketing 30, 32–36 (1966)
2. Judd, V.C.: The case for redefining Services. Journal of Marketing 28, 58–59 (1964)
3. Berry, L.L.: Services Marketing is different. Business Journal 30, 24–29 (1980)
4. Lovelock, C., Wirtz, J., Lapert, D.: Marketing des services. Pearson Education (2004)
5. Hill, T.P.: On goods and services. Review of Income and Wealth 23(4), 315–338 (1977)
6. Zarifian, P.: Valeur de service et compétence. In: La relation de service: regards croisés, vol. (28), L'Harmattan (2001)
7. Eiglier, P., Langeard, E.: Servuction, le marketing des services. Mc Graw Hill (1987)
8. Rosengren, W.R.: Organisational Age, Structure and Orientation toward Clients. Social Forces 47(1), 1–11 (1968)
9. Issac, J.: Les codes de déontologie: outils de gestion de la qualité dans les activités de services, Thèse de doctorat, Université Paris Dauphine (1996)
10. Dumoulin, C., Flipo, J.P.: Entreprises de services: 7 facteurs clés de réussite. Ed. d'organisation (1991)
11. Shostack, G.L.: Breaking free from product marketing. Journal of Marketing 41, 73–80 (1977)
12. Touzi, J.: Model transformation of collaborative business process into mediation information system. In: Proc. of the IFAC World Congress (2008)
13. Raymond, G.: SOA: architecture logique, principes, structures et bonnes pratiques (2007)
14. Zaidat, A.: Spécification d'un cadre d'ingénierie pour les réseaux d'organisations. Thèse de doctorat de l'Ecole des Mines de Saint-Etienne (2005)
15. Izza, S.: Intégration des systèmes d'information industriels, une approche flexible basée sur les services sémantiques. Thèse de doctorat, Ecole des Mines de Saint-Etienne (2006)
16. Miles, L.D.: Definitions: Lawrence D. Miles value Engineering Reference Center: Wendt Library (1963)
17. Grandhaye, J.P., Soltan, E.: Value management project: processing Unforeseen events in Design and production activities; a methodology and a case study. In: Proc. of the 5th European Project Management Conference (2002)
18. Perrin, J.: Valeurs et développement durable: questionnement sur la valeur économique. L'harmattan (2004)
19. Grandhaye, J.P., Poisson, P.: Le Management par Valeur pour Concevoir et Rédiger un Projet d'Etablissement. In: Proc. of the Congrès International AFAV (2001)
20. Zhao, G., Perros, H.G., Xin, Z.: How service science management and engineering (SSME) can evolve to an academic discipline? Int. Journal of Web Engineering and Technology 5(4) (2009)
21. Spohrer, J., Maglio, P., Bailey, J., Gruhl, D.: Steps Toward a Science of Service Systems. IEEE Computer 40(1), 71–77 (2007)
22. Tabas, L.: Designing for Service Systems.ISD Symposium, UCB I School Report (2007)
23. Touzi, W.: Conceptualisation et modélisation de la production de service: application aux domaines de la santé et de l'enseignement. Thèse de doctorat, Université Bordeaux 1 (2001)

PSS Production Systems: A Simulation Approach for Change Management

Guillaume Marquès, Malik Chalal, and Xavier Boucher

Ecole Nationale Supérieure des Mines, FAYOL-EMSE, CNRS-UMR5600,
EVS, F-42023 Saint-Etienne – France
{gmarques,chalal,boucher}@emse.fr

Abstract. The research presented in this paper is oriented on the transition of the manufacturing industry towards the delivery of product-service system. The paper presents the first results in the development of a decision support system dedicated to help in configuring service-oriented production systems, notably with an objective of capacity management. An illustrative case study is presented, linked to the production of washing machines.

Keywords: Servicization, Product Service Systems, Production System, Modelling, Simulation.

1   Introduction

In an increasing business competition world, industrial companies are faced to the necessity to develop strong innovations on their business models. The development of service based added-value is one of these innovations inducing progressive integration of services along the whole life-cycle of industrial offers. The transition of the manufacturing industry towards the integration of services is known in the literature as servicization [1]. It is not only a new business model, but requires strong organizational changes. Anticipating this transition is becoming crucial for decision makers (DM). The overall orientation of the research work presented, consists in developing a relevant decision support system to help managing the organizational transition. First, we present a background on PSS systems. Then, we present our proposition to model behavior of a manufacturing system faced with servitization. Section 4 proposes an industrial case study to illustrate the use of this model. The last part presents conclusions and future research works related to this approach.

2   Background on PSS Systems

PSS is a new concept that has emerged in the research world after the work of [2]. Here, we are interested in modeling 2 main subsystems associated to PSS literature: the user-oriented subsystem (2.1) and the production subsystem (2.2).

C. Emmanouilidis, M. Taisch, D. Kiritsis (Eds.): APMS 2012, Part II, IFIP AICT 398, pp. 377–384, 2013.

2.1   User-Oriented System

Use is large research issue addressed through different point of view and mainly by ergonomics and marketing. Both deal with the analysis of the asset in use in order to design product with a maximum of value in use. Two main families of analysis of the user system may be identified: (i) the user's behaviour faced with the commercial offer, and (ii) the user's behaviour with the asset in use. The first one is linked to the set of PSS for which is ready to pay in order to satisfy a need. The second one is related to the need in service providing induced by the usage of the product.

A lot of studies have a macroscopic view of the user behaviour faced with commercial offer and only model a global market volume, often timely constant. However, these simulations require a high level of description of the service offer: kind of customer product segmentation, contract term [3], service providing lead time [4]... Different kind of services, called industrial services [5] main be implicated.

Life Cycle Simulation is a current approach to evaluate performance (eco. and env.) of life cycles of products in use [3]. Discreet event simulation is mainly used in this case. These kind of models are supported by a detailed description of the product and its characteristics [3, 6]: lifespan, maximum of operations per period, break-down rate, wear-out propensity, reparability, reusability... The user is described through: a functionality need per period or usage intensity. Modeling the appearance of customer needs most often implies stochastic processes in order to characterize this uncertainty.

2.2   PSS Oriented Production System

To implement PSS, a manufacturing company has to develop new production capabilities, covering both new structural characteristics of the system as well as new managerial abilities. Academic and industrial contributions underline the necessity for the company to manage 2 new production areas: product remanufacturing processes on one side, and service design, production and delivery on the other side. So, the full PSS Production System has to be considered as composed of 3 sub-systems: the manufacturing (1), the remanufacturing (2) and service production (3) sub-systems.

Remanufacturing is a process in which worn-out products are restored to like-new condition [7]. A discarded product is partially or completely disassembled. Among disassembled parts, usable ones are cleaned, refurbished, and put into inventory. Then, the new product is reassembled from both old and sometimes new parts to produce a unit equivalent or superior in performance and expected lifetime to the original new product [8]. In comparison to manufacturing, it is difficult to assess the number and the timing of the returns and to preview the quality of the used products [9].

To configure a service production system, a first difficulty consists in identifying service offers which could be consistent with the strategy of the firm. The service opportunities in the context of PSS are distributed along the PSS life-cycle. In [5, 10] authors propose a typology of "industrial services". This framework emphasizes the combination of service life cycle and product life cycle.

Capacity planning is a key strategic component in designing goods/services production system in achieving a match between the long term supply capabilities of an organization and the predicted level of long term demand. The service production area is submitted to variations of capacity needs much more notable and unpredictable than for traditional manufacturing. The classical a product stock policy optimization approach has to evolve towards the possibility to manage stocks of "capacity to deliver service". "The management of capacity is not trivial in PSS context" [11]: How should capacity level be managed to support new goods manufacturing as well as after-sales service if they share the same resources.

3   A Modelling Approach for PSS Production Systems

We intend to build decision aid method and tool, to support the dimensioning and evaluation of alternative configurations of a PSS production system. To study this transition of production system, this paper proposes a modelling approach dedicated to PSS Production Systems. This approach aims at implementing event driven simulation of various sub-systems of the full PSS Production System. Simulation is used as a decision support to build comparative analyses of alternative transition scenarios.

We propose, at first, a general conceptual model which considers two subsystems: the user-oriented and the production subsystems. The user-oriented subsystem represents the usage environment which generates the various demands of products and services. It is dedicated to model and simulate user behaviours which impact the production system. The production-oriented subsystem represents a set of services providing, manufacturing and remanufacturing processes. This second subsystem is dedicated to model and analyse the internal organisation, planning mechanisms, interactions and performances of both manufacturing-oriented and service-oriented processes. Decoupling two subsystems allows a twofold objective. On the one hand, both production and user oriented systems can be modelled individually with a lot of details. On the other hand, a particular interest may be taken in their interactions. The two subsystems are in constant interaction through several business events. This coupling makes possible investigating different transition scenarios and analyse their impacts on the sustainable performance of production subsystem, decomposed in economic, environmental and societal externalities. Performance analysis has to emphasize the existence (or not) of balancing mechanisms between decision levers associated to each subsystem (capacity management and PSS offer engineering).

3.1   User-Oriented Subsystem

This subsystem represents behavioural aspects of the customers. Two main types of behaviours are modelled: the commercial behaviours leading to PSS purchase decisions; and utilization behaviours which notably generate strong variations in needs of services triggered along the product lifecycle.

We adopt stochastic representation to model market and utilization behaviours. The commercial behaviours is characterized by different kinds/families of markets and/or customers (professional or not, exigent or not, intense use or not...). Thus, this subsystem represents the global behaviour of the market, and the commercial behaviour of the customer with regards to the PSS market offer. The variables represent the decision levers associated to the PSS offer engineering: price, contract term, service-mix, service quality… Then, the utilization behaviours depend on different characteristics, also represented by variables: characteristics of the product, of the user and of the use processes. During the PSS lifecycle, all these variables influence the level of product solicitations and so the needs of service providing.

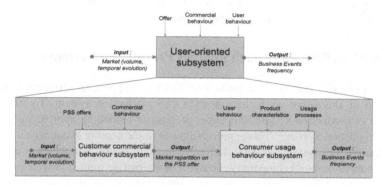

Fig. 1. Global view of the user-oriented subsystem model

3.2   Production Subsystem

The production-oriented subsystem represents a set of services providing, manufacturing and remanufacturing processes. It is dedicated to model both manufacturing-oriented and service-oriented processes. It is built on a discreet-event simulation approach distinguishing two classical horizons: strategic and operational decisions.

From a strategic point of view, the model is focused on the DM's behavior with regards to the capacity balance strategy. Different DM's planning strategies have been identified: (i) Chasing strategy (the capacity is adapted to the demand), (ii) Stable strategy (the capacity level is kept constant and proportional to the average demand), and (iii) Smoothing strategy (demand variation may be anticipated). The 3 strategies may be added to stock-out acceptation or subcontracting strategies.

From an operational perspective, the objective is to represent the daily decision-makers's behavior towards the resources balancing. In a context where the global capacity level is fixed (by strategic decision), managers have to establish resources – jobs affectations. Resources are defined by a set of competencies. A first level of strategy concerns the priority between production and services providing operations. Then, different behaviors may be modeled in term of resources affectation (% of utilization, competency level, cost per hour…).

4   Case Study

ENVIE is a French enterprise in the Waste Electrical and Electronic Equipment (WEEE) sector. ENVIE is committed to conducting every aspect of its business in a responsible and sustainable manner. This includes being a work-integration social enterprise. ENVIE covers whole French territory through a local Small and Medium Enterprises (SME) network. This study particularly focuses on a regional dimension of the enterprise (17 persons). Choosing this company to support this feasibility study presents a twofold interest: (i) a strategic question relative to PSS adoption by ENVIE, and (ii) the sustainable orientation of the enterprise. The target is to emphasize the interest (or not) for the PSS transition, through a simulation and analysis of the performance of the production system.This case study will be used to demonstrate: (i) the feasibility and the relevance of the modelling approach, and (ii) the kind of results, analyses and decision support provided by the model.

4.1   User-Oriented Sub-system

We model the market through the evolution of a specified product family (VPF,t). "washing machines". The market will be decomposed into two segments, classical selling (VC,t) and PSS (VPSS,t), that represent the temporal evolution of the PSS or classic customer volumes. Different PSS customers' commercial profiles are distinguished. The distribution of all PSS customers on different commercial profiles is represented by a discrete probability distribution αi and associated with each commercial profile Pcomi as $\Sigma \ \alpha i = 1$. Each contract offer (OC)i is defined by: (i) a type of product TPi,(ii) a bundle of services {Sk} k=1,p and (iii) a service quality SQ. The company brings to market a portfolio of contracts offers, denoted: {(OC)j} j=1,n / (OC)j=(TPi, {Sk} k=1,p, SQ). Commercial profiles ({Pcomi}j=1,q) describe users' behavior when selecting a specific contract offer among {(OC)j}. The purchasing decision process is represented stochastically where each commercial profile is associated to a discrete random variable denoted Disc(μq,n). This last one traduces the attraction of a commercial profile (q) to a type of offer (n).

To simulate user behaviors, this study focuses on the washing machine utilization process which affects the demand for maintenance services. A set of variables is used to represent stochastically various user utilization profiles.

The simulation of this user-oriented sub-system provides a set of demand signals, which can be utilized afterwards as input to simulate the production sub-system. By simulating commercial as well as usage behaviors, we finally generate stochastically various demand signals for service operations: 'delivery and installation', 'maintenance and repair' and 'take back' services.

4.2   Production Subsystem

In this feasibility study we focus on analyzing internal logistic regulation parameters to manage the variability generated by service demands: the impact of affectations rules and resources competencies on the industrial performance.

We consider two types of product called Pf1 and Pf2 respectively characterized by high and medium quality levels. Pf2 is a remanufactured product. Product was assembled with three parts (A, B and C). For Pf1, only new parts are used. For Pf2, reused parts called A', B', C' are used. In case of inventory stock out, new parts (A or B or C) can be used to assembly Pf2. The manufacturing system is composed by 3 workstations (Fig. 2). The 3 operations have to be made in sequence.

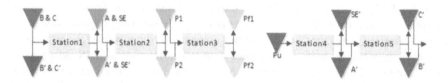

Fig. 2. Production routing sequence   **Fig. 3.** Remanufacturing routing sequence

Products are remanufactured through disassembly, test, repair, refreshing, reassembly, and packing operations. We consider that the remanufacturing can be decomposed on the two sub-processes (Fig. 3). The disassembly line is composed by two stations. The disassembly sequence is the reverse of the assembly routing sequence.

We consider in this paper a list of potential services: Selling, Product Delivery (including installation), Maintenance (including repairing) and product Take-Back. All the processes necessary to deliver these services are represented through a simulation model. Each service is modeled as an operational process which uses resources (during a given time). Each resource is characterized by a flexibility level which authorize or not the resource to be used to provide a service.

5   Simulation

The results presented are the average results of 20 replications and the Simulation duration is 4 years. In our simulation, we consider that company provide four different contract offers (OC) j=1..4. For this paper, we consider 3 performance indicators: (i) Service Level (SL), assessed by the average time of response maintenance and average time of service delivery, (ii) Inventory Level, and (iii) Rate of use of resources. We consider three commercial profiles ({Pcomi}j=1,2,3) with two scenario of the distribution of PSS customers on different commercial profiles α1i and α2i .

2 contract durations, 2 affectation rules (priority to Production "P-R-S" or to Service "S-R-P") and 2 situations of resources skills (Flexibility "F", Specialization "Sp") have been defined. So, we have 6 scenarios, which are analyzed in the 2 situations (distribution of commercial profiles), which gives us a total of 12 scenarios (table 1):

Table 1. Scenarios simulated

Scenarios	α_i	Contractduration	Resources Comp.	Affectation
Sce 1.1 (α^1_i) / Sce 2.1 (α^2_i)	α^1_i= (0.2,	1 year	F	P-R-S
Sce 2.1 (α^1_i) / Sce 2.2 (α^2_i)	.4, 0.4)	2 years	F	P-R-S
Sce 3.1 (α^1_i) / Sce 2.3 (α^2_i)		1 year	F	S-R-P
Sce 4.1 (α^1_i) / Sce 2.4 (α^2_i)		2 years	F	S-R-P
Sce 5.1 (α^1_i) / Sce 2.5 (α^2_i)	α^2_i=(0.4,	1 year	Sp	----
Sce 6.1 (α^1_i) / Sce 2.6 (α^2_i)	0.4, 0.2	2 years	Sp	----

6 Results and Interpretations

The following Fig. 4, 5 and 6 give the influence of commercial profile distribution and contract duration on service performance using the indicators described in Table 2. We note that the distribution of commercial profiles affects the services performance (Fig. 4) for all scenarios, we note that in the case of a specialization of resources, service performance are better in the case of α2 (we have 13% of gain for maintenance reaction times and25% for the delivery time). For the influence of contract duration on service performance, we note that the duration contract of 2 years allow the company to reduce the response time for delivery and maintenance reaction (Fig. 5). The Fig. 7 gives the influence of resources skills on service performance using the indicator. We note that in both cases (α2, α1), giving the priority to service, allows company to reduce the delivery time and maintenance reaction time. The Fig. 8 gives the average resource utilization rate. We note that in both cases, the average rate is substantially identical. In scenario 3 and 4, resources are less utilized, because priority is given to the services, and therefore the resources are allocated to services, the execution time and demand are less important than the production process and remanufacturing. To overcome this problem of unavailability of certain resources for the production process and remanufacturing when priority is given to service, the system draws the finished product stock as shown in Fig. 9. The stock is used to allow some resources to support service activities.

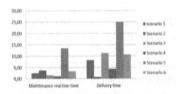

Table 2. Formula of calculation of indicators

	Indicator
Fig 5	$\forall i \in (1;3;5), \dfrac{(SL(scenario_i)) - (SL(scenario_i))}{(SL(scenario_i))} \times 100$
Fig 6	$\forall i \in (1;3;5), \dfrac{(SL(scenario_i(\alpha^1))) - (SL(scenario_i(\alpha^2)))}{(SL(scenario_i(\alpha^1)))} \times 100$
Fig 7	$\forall k \in (1;2), \forall (i,j) \in \{(5,1);(5,2);(6,2);(6,3)\},$ $\dfrac{(SL(scenario_i(\alpha^k))) - (SL(scenario_j(\alpha^k)))}{(SL(scenario_j(\alpha^k)))} \times 100$

Fig. 4. Influence of commercial profile repartition (Pcom repartition)

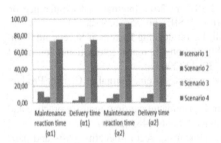

Fig. 5. Influence of Pcom repartition

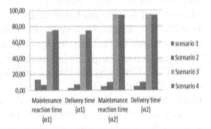

Fig. 6. Influence of resources skills

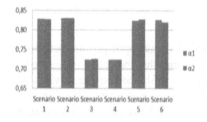

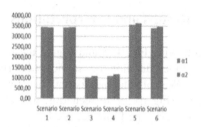

Fig. 7. Average Utilization rate of resources   **Fig. 8.** Average Stock (Pf1+Pf2)

7   Conclusion and Perspectives

The study conducted in this paper shows the impact of the commercial offer of the company on the one hand, and on the other hand the impact of the competence based rules for task assignation on business performance. We have to extending further the coupling between the User-oriented subsystem and the productions subsystem to find rules of resource management for a given commercial offer situation.

References

1. Baines, T.S., Lightfoot, H.W., Evans, S., Neely, A., Greenough, R., Peppard, J., Roy, R., Shehab, E., Braganza, A., Tiwari, A., et al.: State-of-the-art in product-service systems. Proceedings of the Institution of Mechanical Engineers, Part B: Journal of Engineering Manufacture 221, 1543–1552 (2007)
2. Hockerts, K.: Eco-Efficient Service Innovation: Increasing Business-Ecological efficiency of Products and Services. In: Charter, M. (ed.) A global Perspective on Greener Marketing Practice. Gereenleaf, Pub., Sheffield (1999)
3. Komoto, H., Tomiyama, T., Nagel, M., Silvester, S., Brezet, H.: Life Cycle Simulation for Analyzing Product Service Systems. In: Fourth International Symposium on Environmentally Conscious Design and Inverse Manufacturing, Eco Design 2005, pp. 386–393 (2005)
4. Phumbua, S., Tjahjono, B.: Towards product-service systems modelling: a quest for dynamic behav-iour and model parameters. International Journal of Production Research 50, 425–442 (2012)
5. Kowalkowski, C.: Managing the industrial service function (2008)
6. Wangphanich, P.: Simulation model for quantifying the environmental impact and demand amplification of a Product-Service System (PSS). In: 2011 International Conference on Management Science and Industrial Engineering (MSIE), pp. 554–559 (2011)
7. Bianchi, N.P., Evans, S., Revetria, R., Tonelli, F.: Influencing Factors of Successful Transitions towards Product-Service Systems: a Simulation Approach. International Journal of Mathematics and Computers in Simulation 3, 30–43 (2009)
8. Mont, O.K.: Clarifying the concept of product–service system. Journal of Cleaner Production 10, 237–245 (2002)
9. Guide, V.D.R.: Production planning and control for remanufacturing: industry practice and research needs. Journal of Operations Management 18, 467–483 (2000)
10. Mathieu, V.: Service strategies within the manufacturing sector: benefits, costs and partnership. International Journal of Service Industry Management 12, 451–475 (2001)
11. Olhager, J., Rudberg, M., Wikner, J.: Long-term capacity management: Linking the perspectives from manufacturing strategy and sales and operations planning. International Journal of Production Economics 69, 215–225 (2001)

Improving Customer's Subjective Waiting Time Introducing Digital Signage

Takeshi Shimamura[1,2], Toshiya Kaihara[3], Nobutada Fujii[3], and Takeshi Takenaka[1]

[1] Center for Service Research, National Institute of Advanced
Industrial Science and Technology, Tokyo, Japan
[2] Ganko Food Service Co. Ltd., Osaka, Japan
[3] Graduate School of System Informatics,
Kobe University, Kobe, Japan
t-shimmura@aist.go.jp

1   Introduction

In the 1970s, the Japanese restaurant industry introduced the chain store system, which was later introduced into the retail industry in the USA to enhance productivity [1] [2]. The chain store system was designed to realize "low-cost operations". For instance, chain store restaurants simplify and automate service operations to reduce the number of service staff. Moreover, they standardize service operations by introducing service manuals for use in training part-time staff. Prices of dining decreased throughout chain store systems, and Japanese consumers came to enjoy restaurants casually. Consequently, the market scale of the Japanese restaurant industry expanded from 8 trillion yen to 250 trillion yen during the 1970s to 1990s. Restaurants in Japan numbered approximately 737,000 in 2006 [3].

In the mid-1990s, the Japanese restaurant market ceased its expansion, and gradually shrank. One reason is diversification of customer's preferences. As customers have come to enjoy dining at restaurants, their preferences have become diversified [4]. Moreover, customers' criteria used in selecting restaurants have become extremely well defined. The chain store system can not adapt easily to today's customer requirements for restaurants. A second reason is tough competition among restaurant stores. As restaurant stores have become more numerous, the Japanese restaurant market has become extremely competitive. Therefore, restaurants must add distinguishing and appealing features to their restaurants. Restaurant companies should therefore strive for a "sophisticated and diversified" restaurant store model [5].

In recent years, Service Engineering has been introduced to service industries to enhance service quality and productivity by streamlining service operations, by improving employee skills, and by enhancing customer satisfaction. The Japanese Ministry of Economy, Trade and Industry started a national project promoting service engineering to improve service sector productivity [6] [7]. The Japanese restaurant industry has introduced service engineering to improve service quality and productivity. For example, in the IT field, Process Management Systems based on POS systems have been developed to enhance customer satisfaction and productivity [8]. In the marketing field, new CS examination methods using questionnaires and

C. Emmanouilidis, M. Taisch, D. Kiritsis (Eds.): APMS 2012, Part II, IFIP AICT 398, pp. 385–391, 2013.

measurements of leftovers were incorporated into menu planning [9]. In the IE field, the new worker's operation estimation system is created by measuring flow lines of staff by RFID devices and is replayed using 3D computer graphic technology [10]. Although these methodologies are effective to improve productivity, they mainly address reduction of labor input. The restaurant industry should also create a "customer value based" restaurant management system.

As described in this paper, we present results of recent studies which suggest effective means of enhancing customer satisfaction based on service engineering.

2   Improving Customers' Subjective Waiting Times Using Information Indication System

2.1   Research Objectives

Food preparation speed is an important parameter for both revenue management of restaurants and customer satisfaction [11]. Traditionally, kitchen staffs prepare dishes manually. Consequently, preparation speed depends deeply on skills of the kitchen staff. The revenue capacity of a restaurant is limited by its food preparation capacity. Moreover, food preparation speed is important for customer satisfaction. If dishes are delayed, customers will become angry. Restaurants must therefore improve food preparation speed to enhance both revenue management and customer satisfaction.

In the middle 20th century, restaurants introduced central kitchens, and limited the variety of menus to improve food preparation speed. Restaurants thereby improved revenue and productivity [1]. Moreover, fast food restaurants introduced POS systems to reduce waiting times and to increase accountability [12]. In fast food restaurants, capabilities of ordering and accounting deeply depend on waiting times. In fact, POS is an effective means to reduce waiting times. Furthermore, industrial engineering methodology is introduced to improve food preparation operations. For instance, simulation systems of restaurant operations are developed to improve food preparation speed and capacity of restaurants [13]. Menu planning methods for fast food service were developed to reduce customer waiting times. Customers who choose a normal menu wait at a cashier queue, and customers who choose an express menu stand in line at another cashier queue. By reducing the total menu items at a cashier queue, staff can minimize food preparation times and customers can reduce waiting times [14].

Although many related technologies have been developed, conventional studies have not addressed problems of customers' subjective sense of time. Conventional methods can improve the waiting times of customer using these methods. However, these methods are intended to improve actual food preparation speed. Customers do not look at a clock to grasp food preparation speeds because they are talking to each other, reading a book, sending email on a mobile phone, and so on while they wait. Restaurants must address the issue of subjective sense of time.

Many studies of subjective passage of time have been done in the cognitive psychology field. Conventional studies have shown that people feel the passage of time less if they do something, than if they do nothing. As our study described in chapter 2 indicates, customers regard information related to food is important and interesting. A chance exists that the restaurant can improve a customer's subjective waiting time through information presentation.

For this study, we developed an information presentation system to present information related to dishes. The device is displayed at a restaurant to show them to a customer. We measured whether a digital display can reduce a customer's subjective sense of time or not.

2.2   Methodology

This study was conducted at a Japanese restaurant operated by Ganko Food Service Co. Ltd. (Osaka, Japan). The restaurant chain offers Japanese cuisine such as tofu, sushi, and sashimi. Especially, tofu is a popular Japanese food, and the company produces tofu independently of suppliers. Ganko's tofu contains 15% soy milk, which is one of the highest densities in all of Japan.

Conventionally, information related to tofu is shown in a photograph, captions on menus, and item descriptions by service staff members. However, those methods apparently offer insufficient information about the volume of food, compared to video images. It is not easy for customers to understand information related to foods solely through reference to the folding menu.

An information presentation system was created to present tofu-related information. The system equipment consists of a digital display, a small computer server, and a memory chip. The program has four contents. The first content shows a tofu symbol, the method used to make tofu, and health-related tofu information. The second is a questionnaire and game. Three questions are shown: whether customers know Ganko tofu or not, whether they order tofu or not, and whether tofu tastes good or not. Users can try games to receive prizes if customers give correct answers. The third content is a quiz about tofu. Customers learn about tofu in an enjoyable format.

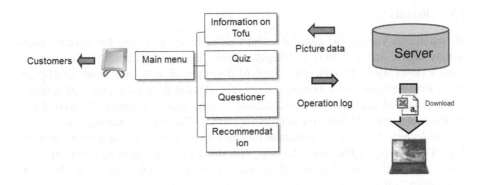

Fig. 1. System structure

The last contents are combinations of tofu dishes and drinks recommended by a sake sommelier. It recommends interesting combinations for customers for example, ice cream made of tofu and plums. Customers can choose combinations by referring to it. Figure 3 portrays the system structure.

The system was installed at a Japanese restaurant: Coms-Kyobashi (Osaka, Japan). For this study, 10 tables were selected. 5 digital displays are placed on 5 tables to show the contents (*display tables*); the other 5 tables had none (*non-display tables*). Tables divided by a wall were selected to prevent non-display table customers from seeing display tables.

Measurements were conducted from 12 Jan. 2011 to 28 Feb. 2011. Waiting times were measured at lunch time because customers typically ordered one dish, and because it is easy to measure the waiting time. In contrast, dinner time data might be difficult to measure because customers ordered several dishes and drank alcohol when dining. Both actual and subjective waiting times were recorded to the minute.

Actual waiting times were measured using the following method. The dish-ordered times were recorded using a clock function display on the POS system. The dish-served times were recorded by service staff members. Staff members wrote dish-served times on paper when referring to a wristwatch. POS and staff watches were synchronized to measure waiting times accurately. The order-received time and dish-served times were merged by a reference ID number assigned by the POS system.

Subjective waiting times were elicited by questionnaire to customers of each table. When a dish was served, the staff member handed a question sheet to the customer. The questionnaire asked "How long do you feel you waited?" and "Do you feel that the waiting time was long or short?"

To grasp a customer's interest and knowledge related to tofu, answers to questions were recorded to a memory chip when customers replied.

Two databases were produced based on the data. One contained actual waiting times and the display / non-display table parameter. The other contained subjective waiting times, the display / non-display table parameter, and a customer's statement of "long or short", in addition to answers for questions. The two databases were used to confirm the efficacy of digital displays.

2.3   Results

Measurements yielded 491 data for actual waiting times, of which 304 were for non-display tables, and 187 were for display tables. The average waiting time of non-display tables was 9.11 min, with standard deviation of 3.38 min. Those of display tables were 8.94 min and 3.37 min, respectively. Results show no marked difference.

We collected 226 answers for subjective waiting times, of which 105 were for a display tables and 121 were for non-display tables. The average waiting time of display tables was 6.72 min, with standard deviation of 12.30 min. The average waiting time of non-display tables was 5.83 min, with standard deviation of 9.04 min. Subjective waiting times of display tables were shorter by 0.88 min than those of non-display tables.

The result of the customers' estimated waiting times were the following: 82.7% replied that the waiting time was short, 7.3% replied that it was long, and 10.0% did not reply at display tables. Additionally, 79.4% replied that the waiting time was short, 13.0% replied that it was long, and 17.6% did not reply at non-display tables. Table 1 presents results of analyses.

In all, 100 answers of respondents were recorded by the system: 53% of customers knew information related to Ganko tofu and 47% did not; 25% of customers ordered tofu by recommendation, and 75% did not; 96% of customers who ordered tofu felt that the tofu tasted nice, and 4% did not.

Table 1. Average and SD of waiting times

Classification	Display	Average	SD
Actual waiting time	Display	5.83	9.04
	No display	6.72	12.31
Subjective waiting time	Display	9.11	3.38
	No display	8.94	3.37

2.4   Discussion

Results show that the system reduces customers' subjective waiting time. As Table 1 shows, the average subjective waiting time of customer of display tables was shorter by about 1 min than that of non-display tables. Moreover, as answers for the "Do you feel that the time was long or short?" question show, those at display tables felt that the waiting time was shorter than customers at non-display tables did. We infer that the presentation of interesting information improves customers' subjective waiting times.

Some reasons seem readily apparent. First, 95% of customers answered the questions, which indicates that almost all customers use the system to get tofu-related information. Why do so many customers use it even though tofu is already shown on the menu and although staff members have recommended tofu for many years? Tofu has been produced for over a quarter century and the company advertises it. Moreover, the restaurant has many regular customers because it has been managed for over a decade: it is one of the oldest restaurants in the area. Tofu is apparently well known by customers.

However, approximately half of customers replied that they did not know that Ganko produces tofu. Put simply, conventional information presentation methods do not provide information to customers adequately. Naturally, incentives such as presents promote customers' use of the system. In addition, customers use the system ardently to obtain information related to tofu. Actually, 25% of customers ordered tofu, which is a very high ratio of the order number because even the most popular food sold at Ganko was ordered by only 4.6% of customers.

Second, the system provides a reciprocal information loop between the system and customer. Customers only receive information if the restaurant provides it by menu or POP. Communication can occur if staff members offer information. However, if a restaurant is rushed or crowded, staff can not communicate well with customers because they become extremely busy. Consequently, customers can not communicate with them, and customers should refer to the POP system and the menu to get information related to food. Recently, restaurants have introduced digital POP systems to resolve such problems. The system can play video images and sound, not only still images and flash frames. Customers can get the latest information using the system. However, digital POP systems show information unilaterally, and customers only receive information. No cross-interaction occurs between digital POP and customers. Under such circumstances, there is little to distinguish digital POP systems from menus.

However, information presentation systems create a cross-interaction between the device and a customer. Initially, the system shows contents to the customer. Customers must operate it by themselves if they would like to get information. Moreover, information is offered as a quiz, and customers can get information related to food in an amusing and enjoyable format. Furthermore, the system provides incentives such as presents. Therefore, customers are motivated to use the system. Customers positively use the system, and customers feel that the waiting time is short.

2.5   Conclusions

This study shows that restaurants can improve customer's subjective passage of time using an information presentation system. Customers are interested in information about food or dishes, and customers feel that the waiting time is short if they are offered information presentation systems. Moreover, they are more effective for information presentation than folding menus, POP, or oral presentations. Cross-interaction between customers and the information presentation systems is an important factor to achieve improved efficiency and effectiveness in restaurant service.

Acknowledgements. This study was partially supported by the project of promotion of Service Research Center from Japanese Ministry of Economy, Trade and Industry (METI) in 2010, and the project of service science from RISTEX in 2010.

References

1. Mariani, J.F.: America eats out: an Illustrated history of Restaurants, Taverns, Coffee shops, Speakeasies, and other Establishments that have Fed us for 350 Years, William Morrow and Go. (1991)
2. Chase, R.B., Apte, U.M.: History of research of service operations: What's the big idea? Journal of Operations Management 25, 375–386 (2007)
3. Japanese Ministry of General Affairs, and Communications,
   http://www.stat.go.jp/data/jigyou/2004/kakuhou/gaiyou/gaiyou (retrieved November 22, 2001)
4. Jensen, Ø., Hansen, K.V.: Consumer values among restaurant customers. International Journal of Hospitality Management 26(3), 603–622 (2007)

5. Muller, C.C.: The business ofrestaurants: 2001 and beyond. Hospitality Management 18, 401–413 (1999)
6. Japanese Ministry of Economy, Trade and Industry, http://www.meti.go.jp/english/report/downloadfiles/ 0707ServiceIndustries (retrieved November 22, 2001)
7. Shimamura, T., Takenaka, T., Akamatsu, M.: Improvement of Restaurant Operation by sharing Order and Customer Information. International Journalof Organization and Collecting Intelligence 1(3), 54–70 (2010)
8. Shimamura, T., Takenaka, T., Akamatsu, M.: Real-time Process management system in a Restaurant by Sharing Food Order Information. In: Proc. International Conference on Soft Computing and Pattern Recognition, pp. 703–706 (2009)
9. Shimamura, T., Takenaka, T.: Analysis of Eating Behavior in Restaurants Based on Leftover Food. In: Proc. International Conference on Industrial Informatics, pp. 956–960 (2010)
10. Kurata, T., Kourogi, M., Ishikawa, T., Hyun, J., Park, A.: Service Cooperation and Co-creative Intelligence Cycles Based on Mixed-Reality Technology. In: Proc. INDIN 2010, pp. 967–972 (2010)
11. Davis, M.M., Maggard, M.J.: An analysis of customer satisfaction with waiting times in a two-stage service process. Journal of Operations Management 9(3), 324–334 (1990)
12. Swart, W.: A Microcomputer Network to Enhance Restaurant Productivity. Computers & Industrial Engineering 11(1-4), 430–433 (1986)
13. Brann, D.M., Kulick, B.C.: Simulation of restaurant operations using the restaurant modeling studio. IEEE, New York (2002)
14. Luo, W.J., Liberatore, M.L., Nydick, R.B., Chung, Q., Sloane, E.: Impact of process change on customer perception of waiting time: a field study. Omega 32(1), 77–83 (2004)

Framework for Lean Management in Industrial Services

Günther Schuh and Philipp Stüer

Philipp.Stueer@fir.rwth-aachen.de

Abstract. Industrial Service providers face the challenge of generating maximum customer value on the one hand and the efficient utilization of internal resources on the other hand. This challenge is further intensified by a worldwide growing market of industrial service providers. This paper presents a holistic approach for lean service management facing the named challenges. The framework is derived from various optimization projects in industrial service operations and supports companies to achieve excellent productivity within their service delivery.

Keywords: Key words: service management, lean services, service operations, customer value, service delivery processes.

1 Introduction

Within the next years industrial services will gain relevance not only in Germany [1]. The constantly growing number of jobs in Germanys' service sector is one indicator of this development (see Figure 1).

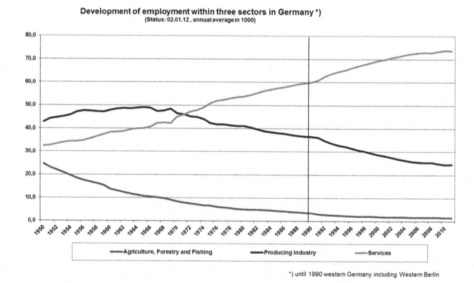

Fig. 1. Development of employment within three sectors in Germany [2]

C. Emmanouilidis, M. Taisch, D. Kiritsis (Eds.): APMS 2012, Part II, IFIP AICT 398, pp. 392–398, 2013.
© IFIP International Federation for Information Processing 2013

Growth of industrial services and increasing competition lead the focus of the scientific community towards service operations and approaches to increase productivity in this field. Industrial service companies suffer from a lack of procedures for increasing productivity and ensuring profitability. The question is how to efficiently and effectively design and operate service delivery processes. Adaptation of manufacturing proven management approaches would be one obvious way, which is intensively discussed within the scientific community. This paper describes a lean management framework for industrial services rooted in three significant service specific characteristics being described within the next chapter.

2   Relevance and State of the Art

As one of the most widespread techniques Lean Management has already been successfully transferred from manufacturing to adjacent fields like administration [3] and innovation [4], [5]. That Lean Management in its original form cannot directly be applied in the service context has already been stated by several publications [6], [7], [8]. Existing management approaches for industrial services either do not or only partly address service specific characteristics or they do not regard lean principles for industrial services until now [9].

Focusing industrial services three constitutive characteristics have to be regarded. First characteristic is the immateriality of services. Even if service delivery is often combined with a material good into an incentive system, the service part of the incentive system is immaterial. One exemplary process from industrial services is a repair process, in which spare parts are installed for ensuring technical availability of a machine or component. Experience and professionalism of the service staff together with high quality spare parts build an incentive system for the owner of the manufacturing plant as the customer.

Second constitutive characteristic is the integration of the external factor. As direct interaction between service provider and service customer or service object is required in industrial services [10]. Machines, components or a material good are also examples for the external factor.

The third characteristic refers to value as an original lean management principle. It says, that lean service delivery ether increases the customer value related to a material good, or the value contribution in a core value creation process (or value stream) of the customer.

3   Objectives and Research Approach

Regarding the named three characteristics a lean management approach for industrial services has to scope and analyze the customers' core processes before designing the service delivery processes with the purpose of adding customer value. Scope of lean service management also includes controlling, assessment and continuous improvement of running service delivery processes. Existing approaches for the description of a service lifecycle such as Raverdy 2008 [11] (see Figure 2) have also been influencing the creation of the core result of this paper.

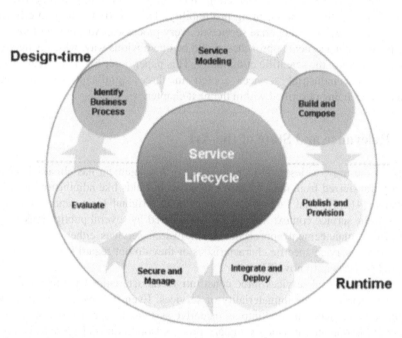

Fig. 2. Service lifecycle designed for mobile service platforms [11]

Within the following subchapters phases and principles of the framework for lean management in industrial services will be described. The following aspects have been extracted from several case study analyses. Keynote for this approach is the waste-free realization of customer value.

4   Results: Framework for Lean Service Management

The Lean Services Framework is divided in five phases. Each phase contains three principles for orientation towards excellence in lean service management. The phases and principles of the framework are positioned in a consecutive order. The framework begins with the phase defining strategic benefit and then leads to definition of service delivery processes and breadth of service offering. The last part of the framework focusses operational aspects of service management.

4.1   Defining Strategic Benefit

Before focusing service operations constraints for a waste-free realization of customer value have to be considered. Added value for the service customer can only be generated, when the service provider is capable to handle core processes of his customer complete or partly and with a higher productivity. Therefore *Identification of Core Processes* at the customer with potential for being delivered "as a service" has to be conducted.

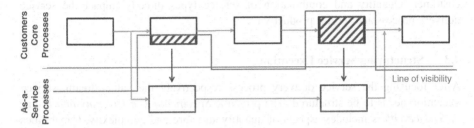

Fig. 3. Core processes at the customer and "as a service" processes delivered by the service provider

When core processes of the customer have been identified, the *Strategic Positioning of Core Processes* is the next principle within the framework. Core processes with high strategic importance for the customer bear lower chances for being offered to an external service provider. Strategic benefit for the customer is obvious, when service delivery strengthens him to achieve his goals with lower effort. For ensuring the realization of synergies within service delivery from the providers perspective *Locating Priorities of Customers Goals* is necessary. The phase Definition of Strategic Benefit is the root for high productive service delivery within the customers' core processes.

4.2   Creating Service Value Stream

Interaction between service customer and service provider significantly improves overall productivity of the core processes. Therefore the service provider has to describe a *Definition of the Ideal Core Process* including his contribution to value creation, meaning the added value for the customer. Result is transparency through Identification of *Options for Added Value and Wastes* within the customers' core processes.

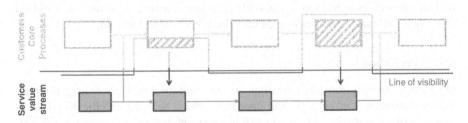

Fig. 4. Service value stream

The service provider can identify options for added value and transparent wastes from comparing the ideal core process with the actual customers' core process. Building on the ideal core process the next principle of the framework is *Definition of Service Types* to be offered to the customer. Depending on quantity and possible combinations of options for added value, different types of services can be defined for the customer. Quantity and combination of service types directly impact the service delivery process and service productivity.

4.3   Structuring Service Execution

After focusing the service delivery process respectively the value stream, service execution needs to be structured. The principle *Specification of Diversity and Range of Service Offers* includes aspects of quantity structure and complexity. Capabilities of the service provider in terms of resources predominantly influence this phase of the lean service management framework. *Service Configuration* is the subsequent principle when structuring the service execution. Before considering characteristics of service operations, added value for the customer and the service provider has to be ensured through the subsequent principle *Service Calculation*. Objective is to quantify and validate the productivity advantage of the service-provider-performance towards the customers'.

4.4   Simple Synchronization

The phase Simple Synchronization is introduced by one of the core lean management principles rooted in the manufacturing context. To assure minimum waste through unnecessary resource disposition or wrong service configuration, decentralized control instruments through *Implementing Pull Mechanisms* are necessary. Synchronization of the customers' core processes with service delivery processes requires the *Introduction of Tact*. For synchronization with the customer the processes as well as resources have to be taken into account. The principle Introduction of Tact needs to receive further enhanced attention in terms of planning and scheduling, if several service providers are involved in one core customer process. After implementing pull mechanisms and introducing tact, *Leveling Demand* helps service providers to further increase resource efficiency. Decoupling point of service demand and point of service delivery as well as utilization of stackable activities supports balancing the workload of service staff under consideration of the principle Leveling Demand.

4.5   Perfection

Progress in striving towards perfection in lean industrial services management requires transparency of strategic and operative values. Selected specific Key Performance Indicators display the impact of improvement actions and customer satisfaction. Service Controlling allows an insight into the performance of service delivery which is related to the Simple Synchronization phase as well as the validation of Service Calculation aspects. The principle *Service Controlling and KPI´s* is also closely related to the Structuring Service Performance phase of the framework. Steps on the path towards perfection can be described by a capability maturity model which is displayed in the principle *Lean Performance Levels*. Completing the framework for lean management in industrial services a *Release Management* describes milestones for service updates and detachment of obsolete service types and offers.

5   Conclusion

The framework for Lean Management in Industrial Services, which is described in this paper, sets apart from existing management approaches in this field. Industrial services underlie three main distinguishing characteristics towards manufacturing as the root of the classic five lean principles. These characteristics require a specific management approach for industrial services. Based on state of the art literature analysis, project work with leading providers of industrial services in Germany and the analysis of several case studies, this approach for Lean Management in Industrial Services was created. Customer value, the core processes of the customer and the lasting pursuit for productivity improvement have led the authors' research to the Framework for Lean Management in Industrial Services (see Figure 5). Together with the five phases "Defining Strategic Benefit", "Creating the Service Value Stream", "Structuring Service Execution", "Simple Synchronization" and "Perfection" 15 Principles help service companies to identify chances and implement Lean Management in their operational business.

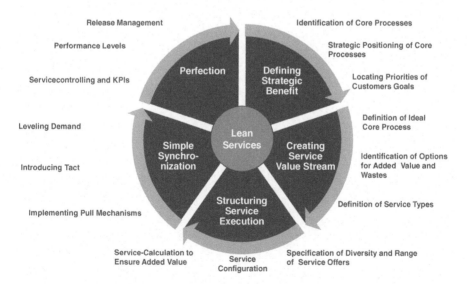

Fig. 5. Framework for Lean Management in Industrial Services

References

1. Berger, R.: Studie Industrieservices Deutschland (2010)
2. Statistisches Bundesamt, B3-Presse- und Informationsservice (2012), https://www.destatis.de
3. Wiegand: Lean Administration (2007)
4. Lenders: Lean Innovation - Prinzipien und Methoden für Innovation ohne Verschwendung; Siemens Plm Connection 2010 (2010)
5. Schuh: Mit Lean Innovation zu mehr Erfolg (2007)
6. Bicheno: The Lean Toolbox for Service Systems (2008)
7. Womack/Jones: Lean Thinking (2004)
8. Åhlstrom: Lean Service Operation: translating lean production principles to service operations (2004)
9. Portioli-Staudacher: Lean Implementation in Service Companies (2010)
10. Corsten/Gössinger: Dienstleistungsmanagement (2007)
11. Raverdy: Whitepaper Service Lifecycle Management (2008)

The Role of IT for Extended Products' Evolution into Product Service Ecosystems

Klaus-Dieter Thoben[1] and J.C. (Hans) Wortmann[2]

[1] Bremer Institut für Produktion und Logistik GmbH (BIBA),
Hochschulring 20, 28359 Bremen, Germany
tho@biba.uni-bremen.de
[2] University of Groningen, Nettelbosje 2, 9747 AE Groningen, The Netherlands
j.c.wortmann@rug.nl

Abstract. This paper elaborates on the notions of extended products and product service systems. It argues that product service systems evolve rapidly into offerings which cross traditional domains of competition, and move into service ecosystems.

The paper investigates the role of ICT in the development of product services systems, and relates the concepts of software-as-a-service and cloud computing to product service systems. It shows that it is almost unavoidable to connect product service ecosystems to larger service ecosystems in other domains. This development has many consequences, opening many areas of future research.

Keywords: Product Service Systems, Cloud Computing, Service Ecosystems, SaaS.

1 Introduction

It is well known, that manufacturing industries are increasingly engaged in adding services to their products. Early papers on the subject (e.g. [1]) coined the term *extended products* in relation the notion of *extended enterprise* (see [2]). Later publications (e.g. [3]) emphasized the role of services even further and used the term *product service systems* (PSS), in which products and services are complementary components of an offering. The servitization of industry can be observed abundantly in practice. It is well documented, in e.g. Meier et al. [3]. Regarding the responsibility of the PSS provider of production means, according to Meier et al. three PSS related types of business models can be distinguished. A *function-oriented* business model includes e.g. a maintenance contract in order to guarantee the functionality of the production means for an agreed period of time. In an *availability-oriented* business model the usability of the means of production is also guaranteed. Accordingly, the PSS provider takes over some business processes of the customer at his own responsibility and thus bears a part of the production risk. With the third type of business model, the *result-oriented* business model, the complete responsibility of the production process is transferred to the provider, as the customer pays for the faultlessly produced parts respectively products.

C. Emmanouilidis, M. Taisch, D. Kiritsis (Eds.): APMS 2012, Part II, IFIP AICT 398, pp. 399–406, 2013.
© IFIP International Federation for Information Processing 2013

However, although the role of ICT is acknowledged in ongoing research work, it is not elaborated. Moreover, the nature of services (i.e. ICT based services vs. human based services, the role of ICT in the evolution of services, etc.) is not fully explored. Accordingly, it is generally not precisely understood which role is played by different types of services and what role is exactly played by ICT. Therefore, it is not easy to interpret the ongoing developments and anticipate future developments. In particular, the possibilities for service re-engineering in order to obtain remote delivery of services, the possibilities for service automation and the interconnectivity of service networks are not well understood.

This paper will elaborate on the role of ICT in the development of product service ecosystems, and relates the concepts of software-as-a-service and cloud computing to product service systems. It discusses two conjectures, which follow partly from a literature survey and partly from empirical investigations. These conjectures are:

1. Physical products will take the role of an information hub, which creates an extended relationship of value producers with the product. Avatars of physical products may even engage in interactions similar to social networks [14].
2. Services in whatever domain are rapidly connected to services in other domains, creating a service ecosystem which transcends traditional boundaries between domains of life.

The remainder of the paper is structured as follows. After a discussion of the methodology in Section 2, a literature review discusses related work in Section 3 and 4. Section 3 presents an analysis of PSS literature, from which various trends are derived. Section 4 provides an analysis of IT technologies (incl. SaaS and Cloud technology) enabling future developments of PSS. A corroboration of this vision, presented in section 5, is based on likely scenarios of services in the area of mobility. Following these scenarios we will show the role of cloud computing and the necessity of the SaaS developments sketched in Section 4. Section 6 concludes the paper.

2   Methodology

This paper is focussed on application areas where the servitization of physical products becomes manifest. The methodology followed can be described as follows:

1. Based on empirical observations, the two conjectures formulated above were formulated.
2. These conjectures are transformed into more precise research questions, viz.:
    a. Are extended products move to service ecosystems?
    b. What is the role of ICT in realizing this vision?
3. Literature research, both on PSS and on relevant ICT developments
4. Analysis, from two perspectives (PSS and ICT)
5. Corroboration via scenario development in the mobility domain.

3   Literature Survey of Related Work in PSS

As ever more physical products become servitized, new service components are developed and existing service components get re-engineered in order to increase efficiency, profitability, etc. Accordingly services will be decomposed into customized vs. standard services (service modules), remote vs. location-based ("on-site") services, human resources involved vs. automated services, etc. The servitization of industry can be observed abundantly in practice. In a recent publication Meier et al. [9] propose to use cloud computing as a backbone for the integrated control of PSS.

Boyer et al. [11] propose a product–process–proximity matrix (P3 service matrix) as a framework for guiding research and practice for e-service design. The additionally proposed models of e-service customer retention and e-operations profiling provide ways to examine the impact of the ICT on three levels of the supply chain. Blau et al. [12] propose means to enable a transformation from hard-wired value chains to adaptive service value networks. An approach based on cloud-computing and advanced collaboration spaces is proposed by Camarinha-Matos, et al. [7] for the manufacturing and life cycle support of solar parks. Other authors emphasize developments in relation to Product Lifecycle Management (PLM) including all phases of the value chain and multi product life management [5].

To summarize, the main findings of the ongoing literature analysis have lead to the identification of trends relevant for the evolution of PSS:

- Services in PSS are getting reengineered, customized, automated
- Services in PSS, including human services, become more remote
- Services by electronic delivery are preferred in PSS (except if these services are intrinsically location-bound *and* if human resources are needed)
- Services between different PSS (i.e. different areas of life / business) become rapidly intertwined

4   Survey of Relevant IT Technologies Enabling the Evolution of Service Ecosystems

In the following, concepts like cloud computing, Software-as-a-Service etc. will be discussed. Cloud Computing enables the provision of computing services as a commodity (service). There are often three cloud computing service levels distinguished (Marston et al. [13]):

- IaaS: Infrastructure (computer hardware/networking equipment) as a service
- PaaS: Platform (hardware, networking, operating system and runtime environment) as a service
- SaaS: Software (applications) as a service

The economic basis for IaaS stems from the low utilization of many hardware facilities at data centers [6]. When ICT companies became aware of the huge storage and server capacity standing idle as back-up or redundant facility, they invented *grid* technology to share hardware amongst many users. This shared usage results in lower costs of hardware and energy.

The economic basis for PaaS stems from *virtualization*. This is technology to create one or more runtime environments on top of a variety of hardware. Accordingly, a runtime platform for applications can be offered to customers which meets their needs and can be very scalable.

The economic basis for SaaS stems from the fact that installation of many versions of application software is one of the main cost drivers. The SaaS technology allows software to be installed only once and be used as a service, which can be called whenever needed. This *single install* technology provides in general substantial coat benefits. In enterprise software, the SaaS principle is more difficult than elsewhere because data must be stored and secured for each enterprise using the service. This requires so-called *multi-tenacy* technology in addition to the earlier technologies.

In general, Cloud computing refers to an all-embracing virtual software (computing) service environment. The essence is to build / move the main parts of the service generation and delivery from the user sites (devices) to the server sites.

The overall benefits of cloud computing are decreased maintenance issues, decreased labor costs, increased computing power, increased performance, increased information security, increased software updates and increased storage capacity. However from the perspective of the provider the "single install" principle is a key advantage for cost reduction, whereas the "pay-per-use" principle provides cost advantages for the user.

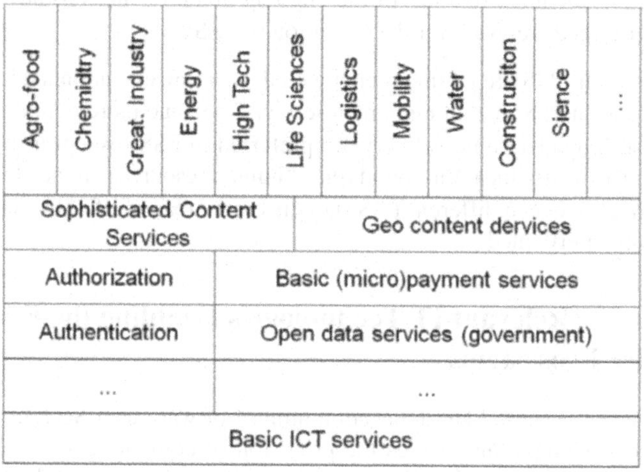

Agro-food	Chemidtry	Creat. Industry	Energy	High Tech	Life Sciences	Logistics	Mobility	Water	Construciton	Sience	...
Sophisticated Content Services				Geo content dervices							
Authorization				Basic (micro)payment services							
Authentication				Open data services (government)							
...				...							
Basic ICT services											

Fig. 1. SaaS Service stack

The extended relationship of the producer with the product triggers continued information exchange. The product will become an information service hub from the producer's point of view. Accordingly in future software and data services will be architected (configured) with the product and embedded in a SaaS ecosystem. It is expected that IT service stacks will emerge and boost the previously described developments of PSS. A first draft of such a service stack is shown in figure 1.

It is to be expected, that the horizontal layers in the above picture will become available as generic SaaS services across various branches and companies. However, it is also to be expected that vendors of capital goods and industrial equipment will engage in developing new services which increase the value proposition of their offering. These services will initially center around the physical product, which becomes an information hub for all parties with a legitimate interest in the physical product. Such a hub exists on the internet and provides access to related data that also resides on the web.

5   Discussion

To illustrate the role of ICT as well as the findings from chapter 3 for the future developments of PSSs the evolution of a core product into a product service ecosystem
is described in figure 2. From the physical perspective the key functionality of a
transport device (e.g. a car) is to transport an object from a location A to a location B.
From that perspective the first cars had very limited functionalities and provided
transportation as the core functionality only. Over the years additional functionalities
were added and the car was nicely packaged (designed). Nowadays, where cars have
turned into commodities, many people take the transport functionality for being
granted. Instead, features such an unlimited availability, the comfort and the safety
during the transportation are very much in the foreground of the users / customers and
get more attention than before. Whereas the pure transport functionality has to be
realized and implemented by physical means i.e. within the physical domain, functionalities like an unlimited availability, the comfort and/or the safety of the customer
can be achieved by physical means, human services, IT services or a combination of
these assets. For example: extreme expressions of a comfortable transport (taking a
car as the physical transport asset) could be a human, acting as a driver (chauffeur), or
a fully automated routing of a car from A to B where no involvement of the user is
required. By adding services the former core product has been transformed into a so
called extended product (see [1]), as shown in fig. 2.

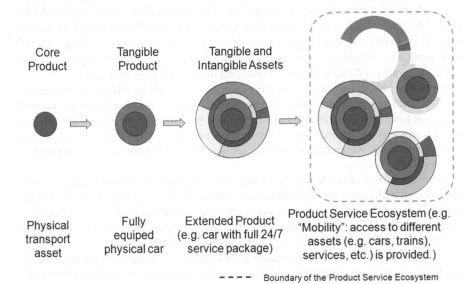

Core Product	Tangible Product	Tangible and Intangible Assets	
Physical transport asset	Fully equiped physical car	Extended Product (e.g. car with full 24/7 service package)	Product Service Ecosystem (e.g. "Mobility": access to different assets (e.g. cars, trains), services, etc.) is provided.)

– – – –   Boundary of the Product Service Ecosystem

Fig. 2. Evolution from a core product into a product service ecosystem: The case of mobility
(inspired by Mejer et al. [3])

However, when moving the focus from a single transportation process to a *mobility*
service, we may sketch new and interesting scenarios, which are likely to be offered
in the foreseeable nearby future. Consider for example a traveler in a car which is

informed about a traffic jam, due to an accident. The traveler's vehicle may be packaged with a service which calculates the arrival time, and concludes that the traveler will miss his/her appointment. Accordingly, the service may check alternative means of transportation (bikes, public transportation), or may advise the traveler to propose a video conference. The services may direct the traveler to convenient nearby location. If the traffic jam causes the traveler to miss e.g. a plane, the services may automatically inform the airliner and reschedule the air journey.

By integrating and embedding a product into an overall network of products and services a product service ecosystem evolves. Within these environments physical products (take the car as an example) will take the role of an information hub, which creates an extended relationship of value producers with the product. In analogy to the definition of Web-Service ecosystems [15] a product service ecosystem can be seen as a rich, integrated collection of physical products as well as various types of services independent from the nature of the service (human, IT), the art of provision, etc. Product service ecosystems have in common that physical elements are a central part of the system and access these products is provided.

Even this simple mobility scenario can serve to explain why the developments discussed in Section 4 are needed. First of all, an accident and the resulting mobile communication require a very scaleable ICT infrastructure: it is well known, that mobile phones fail to get connectivity in case of a crises. Assuming that there is a sophisticated way to share bandwidth, the ICT facilities need huge scalability, for which *cloud computing* (lowest level of figure 1) is the enabling technology. Calculation of the traffic delay requires *open data* services (for example to know if the road is blocked or open). Access to services such as cancelling and rescheduling appointments requires *authentication*: our wellness would be jeopardized if anyone else can hack our identity. (These services are specified on the next layer in fig.1)

Moreover, the above scenarios require calendars to be accessible for authorized users in a SaaS mode. Accordingly, (sophisticated) *authorization* services are needed. On top of that, services will in general have to be paid for (the current misunderstanding that services are for free holds only if consumers are willing to sell their attention to advertisement), which requires billing services for small amounts of money (micro payments).

Authorization is also needed for sharing other information. For example, the traveler may be willing to share special diet information with an airline company, but not with business partners. Emerging services around personal digital vaults (sometimes called *gems*) allow support of sophisticated sharing of information in a SaaS mode. If the traveler needs health care support, this could be arranged as well.

To summarize, this mobility scenario shows the development of a car as extended product to mobility as a product service ecosystem. This ecosystem comprises a complex, integrated transportation process, different transportation means (bikes, trains, etc.), human services as well as IT services integrated in order to provide a mobility service as an end-to-end process to the customer. By integrating and embedding an extended product into an overall network of products and services a product service ecosystem evolves. This illustrates the transition form the extended product to the *mobility services ecosystem.* The car as physical product becomes an information hub for mobility services.

This development is enabled by the growth of Software-as-a-Service offerings. When the car-related services expand to public transportation, it means that the services of the car service ecosystem link to a different domain, in this case the public transportation ecosystem.

However, there is no reason why expansion of service offerings should stop at the boundary of the public transportation. On the contrary, these service offerings will easily expand to domains such as entertainment, tourism, payment, telecom, health care and other domains.

6   Conclusions and Outlook

This paper has argued that the notion of *extended products* is proceeding towards product service ecosystems. The original ideas related to extended products focused on servitization of the physical product, but without giving due recognition to the delivery of such services.

Meanwhile it is clear that services which *can* be delivered remotely *will* be delivered remotely, at least if the quality of the service is equal in the eyes of the customer. This remote delivery requires scalability and security of IT delivery, which is enabled by *cloud computing* as introduced in Section 4.

Moreover, remote delivery of services is enabled by the SaaS technology. This technology will be boosted by the adoption of generic services in several layers as depicted in Figure 1.

Remote service delivery is greatly enhanced, if services can be re-used across domains. Accordingly, a mobility service which is centered around a traveler's wish for comfortable transportation may lead to services which go far beyond the extended product 'car'. The mobility product service ecosystem quickly links into other domains such as financial services, authentication, health care, etc. This was illustrated in Section 5.

Of course, the vision developed in this paper needs further corroboration. Moreover, it leads to challenging research questions such as related to the strategy of product vendors, the risks involved for vendors and customers, the role of ICT companies, the nature of competition and many other research challenges.

References

1. Thoben, K.-D., Eschenbächer, J., Jagdev, H.S.: Extended Products: Evolving Traditional Product Concepts. In: Proceedings of the 7th International Conference on Concurrent Enterprising, Bremen, Germany, pp. 429–440 (2001)
2. Browne, J., Sackett, P.J., Wortmann, J.C.: Future Manufacturing Systems – Towards the extended enterprise. Computers in Industry 25, 235–254 (1995)
3. Meier, H., Roy, R., Seliger, G.: Industrial Product-Service Systems—IPS². CIRP Annals – Manufacturing Technology 59, 607–627 (2010)

4. Heinrichs, M., Hoffmann, R., Reuter, F.: Mobiles Internet - Auswirkung auf Geschäftsmodelle und Wertkette der Automobilindustrie, am Beispiel MINI Connected. In: Proff, H., Schönharting, J., Schramm, D., Ziegler, J. (eds.) Zukünftige Entwicklungen in der Mobilität - Betriebswirtschaftliche und technische Aspekte, pp. 611–628. Springer Gabler - Research, Gabler Verlag (2012)

5. Seifert, M., Thoben, K.-D., Eschenbaecher, J.: Mechanisms to conduct Life Cycles of Extended Products. In: Hesselbach, J., Herrmann, C. (eds.) Functional Thinking for Value Creation, Proceedings of the 3rd CIRP International Conference on Industrial Product Service Systems, pp. 39–43. Springer, Heidelberg (2011)

6. Kettunen, P.: Rethinking Software-Intensive New Product Development: From Product Push to Value Evolution, University of Helsinki, Department of Computer Science, Helsinki, Finland, http://www.cloudsoftwareprogram.org (accessed June 03, 2012)

7. Camarinha-Matos, L.M., Afsarmanesh, H., Koelmel, B.: Collaborative Networks in Support of Service-Enhanced Products. In: Camarinha-Matos, L.M., Pereira-Klen, A., Afsarmanesh, H. (eds.) PRO-VE 2011. IFIP AICT, vol. 362, pp. 95–104. Springer, Heidelberg (2011)

8. Khajeh-Hosseini, A., Sommerville, I., Sriram, I.: Research Challenges for Enterprise Cloud Computing. In: Proceedings of 1st ACM Symposium on Cloud Computing, SOCC 2010 (2012), http://arxiv.org/ftp/arxiv/papers/1001/1001.3257.pdf (accessed June 03, 2012)

9. Meier, H., Funke, B., Dorka, T.: Cloud Computing für eine integrierte Leistungssteuerung. Industriemanagement 28(1), S.49–S.52 (2012)

10. Yassine, A., Kim, K.-C., Roemer, T., Holweg, M.: Investigating the role of IT in customized product design. Production Planning & Control 15(4), 422–434 (2004)

11. Boyer, K.K., Hallowell, R., Roth, A.V.: E-services: operating strategy—a case study and a method for analyzing operational benefits. Journal of Operations Management 20, 175–188 (2002)

12. Blau, B., Conte, T., van Dinther, C.: A Multidimensional Procurement Auction for Trading Composite Services. Electronic Commerce Research and Applications, 9(5), 460–472 (2010)

13. Marston, S., Li, Z., Bandyopadhyay, S., Zhang, J., Ghalsasi, A.: Cloud computing — The business perspective. Decision Support Systems 51, 176–189 (2011)

14. Wuest, T., Hribernik, K., Thoben, K.-D.: Can a Product Have a Facebook? A New Perspective on Product Avatars in Product Lifecycle Management. In: Rivest, L., Bouraz, A., Louhichi, B. (eds.) Product Lifecycle Management: Towards Knowledge-Rich Enterprises. IFIP AICT, vol. 388, pp. 400–410. Springer, Heidelberg (2012)

15. Barros, A.P., Dumas, M.: The Rise of Web Service Ecosystems. IT Professional 8(5), 31–37 (2006)

Demand Control Loops for a Global Spare Parts Management

Uwe Dombrowski[1], Sebastian Weckenborg[1], and Michael Mederer[2]

[1] Technische Universität Braunschweig,
Institute for Advanced Industrial Management,
Langer Kamp 19, 38106 Braunschweig, Germany
[2] m²hycon, 55270 Ober-Olm, Germany

Abstract. Timely, reliable supply of customers with spare parts is a key factor for business success in many branches. In the field of aviation the competition and cost pressures in the MRO sector (Maintenance, Repair and Overhaul) increased strongly in recent decades. Large maintenance organizations offer component pooling services for aircraft operators. A main challenge in the processes of MRO service providers is the calculation of the optimal stock level for pool components. The basis of an optimal inventory planning for the supply of spare parts is the quality of the demand input parameters used for the calculation. This paper describes the processes and the challenges of the MRO spare parts management as well as the approaches of a research project to face these challenges.

Keywords: Spare Parts Management, MRO, Maintenance, Repair, Overhaul.

1 Introduction

The efficient delivery of spare parts during the entire life cycle of the product is a differentiating quality characteristic in competition that leads to improved customer loyalty and, therefore, strengthens the company in the market. Changing conditions, such as the increasing number of product variants with rapidly shortened innovation cycles and increased competition in many sectors, are new challenges in the spare parts business, which the companies have to meet. In the field of electronics the situation is more complicated. Electronic components are generally built for the entire life cycle of the primary product (e.g. cars or aircrafts). Nevertheless, a failure may occur during the life cycle of the component. This can be the result of internal influences, e.g. production failures, or external influences like an accident. [1]

In the field of aviation the competition and cost pressures in the MRO sector (Maintenance, Repair and Overhaul) increased strongly in recent decades. The main goal of a MRO service provider is to ensure on-time supply of spare parts. In addition, the spare parts inventory and thus the capital costs and process costs have to be minimized. Spare parts logistics and inventory planning therefore are a major challenge in globally networked structures.

C. Emmanouilidis, M. Taisch, D. Kiritsis (Eds.): APMS 2012, Part II, IFIP AICT 398, pp. 407–414, 2013.

Four main characteristics of the spare parts supply in the field of aviation are the global need for parts, the demand unpredictability, the traceability of parts for safety reasons and especially the high cost of not having a part. The latter situation is called AOG (Aircraft on Ground). [2] In order to avoid long-term ground time of an aircraft and an AOG situation, so-called Line Replaceable Units (LRU) are used in aircrafts when possible. A change of these LRUs is carried out quickly and the aircraft is therefore immediately ready for use again. Meanwhile, the exchanged part is repaired or overhauled and preserved for the next installation.

2   Inventory Pooling

2.1   Description of the Processes of Inventory Pooling

In addition to the standard maintenance services, large maintenance organizations sometimes offer a component pooling service for aircraft operators. According to the individual user agreements the pool participants get access to the pooled aircraft components. If a defect of a component occurs and a pool contract is closed through the customer and the MRO service provider, a new component is provided by the pool provider. The pool provider can also be the MRO service provider at the same time. In this case the component will be replaced by a new or repaired pool component directly by the MRO service provider. Meanwhile, the removed part will be analyzed in a service center of the pool provider and depending on technical and economic aspects the decision is made whether the component will be repaired or replaced. [3], [4]

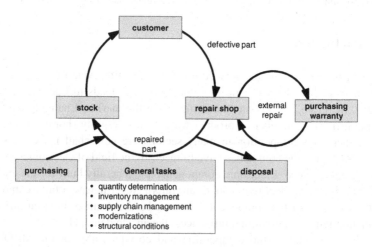

Fig. 1. Tasks of the MRO service provider [3]

The task of the MRO service provider is to ensure the availability of the spare parts. The general process of the inventory pooling service is shown in Fig. 1. The process starts with the delivery of the defective part by the customer. The MRO service provider analyzes the part in the repair shop and decides whether it can be repaired in the own repair shop or it could be done by an external repair shop. The disposal of parts and the purchase of new parts are options as well. In the meantime the customer is supported with another part from the stock of the service provider. General tasks of the service provider are the determination of the repair float quantity of parts and the inventory management, the supply chain management, the management of modernizations and the tracking of structural condition of spare parts. [3], [4]

The participation in inventory pooling may lead to the following advantages. The first advantage is the utilization of experiences and synergies as well as economies of scale of large MRO service providers and thus reducing operating costs. In particular this applies to airlines with smaller fleets. Another advantage is an increased availability of components away from the home base and thereby higher aircraft operational capability. Finally inventory pooling may lead to predictable maintenance costs and usage-based pool contributions (e.g. based on flight hours or flight cycles). [4]

2.2   Challenges within the Framework of Inventory Pooling

A main challenge in the processes of MRO service providers is the calculation of the optimal stock level of the pool components. The stock level has an influence on the service level and therefore on the customer satisfaction and on the other hand on the profitability of the processes. The basis of an optimal inventory planning for the supply of spare parts is the quality of the input parameters used for the calculation. The optimal stock level is highly influenced by the demand of the customers. The demand is furthermore influenced by different impact factors, which can be divided in four categories. Impact factors related to the primary product, impact factors related to the spare part, impact factors related to the maintenance and impact factors related to the market situation and other surroundings (Fig. 2) [5].

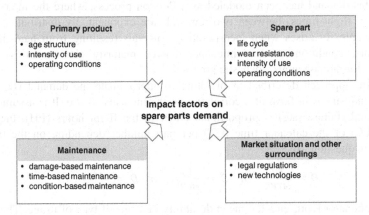

Fig. 2. Impact factors on spare parts demand [5]

Primary product-related factors include the age structure of the primary products, the intensity of use and the operating conditions. In addition to the life cycle of the primary products, the life cycle of the spare parts is important. An increased life cycle of the spare parts leads to a lower demand. In this case as well, factors such as wear resistance, usage and operating conditions play through its own activities an important role. The MRO service provider has also an impact on the spare parts requirements. The MRO service provider can use different maintenance strategies which also could have an influence on the demand of spare parts: the damage-based, the time-based and the condition-based maintenance strategy. In the first case parts are replaced after a defect. In the second case parts are replaced according to specified time intervals, independently of their condition. In the third case parts are checked as part of inspections and are replaced if necessary. Finally the spare parts demand is also influenced by the market situation, e.g. legal regulations or the introduction of new technologies. [5]

3 Demand Control Loops for a Global MRO Spare Parts Management

The main objective of this research project is the development of demand control loops for a global MRO spare parts management. For this purpose different sub objectives have to be achieved. The first sub objective is the calculation of the mean durability of different parts and the second sub objective is the analysis of the requirements for an organizational implementation. In the following part of this paper the sub objectives are described.

3.1 Calculation of the Mean Durability of Different Parts

The failure of LRU parts leading to unscheduled removals can be modeled as stochastic renewal process, where often the demand is rather sparse. Historically the distribution of this demand has been modeled as a Poisson process, where the inter-arrival times (e.g. flight times) between two removals are exponentially distributed. Additional complexity arises when incorporating removals resulting from hard-time requirements, condition-based maintenance and/or maturity characteristics of the material (non-homogenous stochastic process).

A basic approach described in literature to approximate the demand (D) in the aviation industry is in form of a correlation to the intensity of use. It is assumed that the demand (failure rate) is proportional either to the flight hours (FH), the flight cycles (FC) or the calendar time (CT) per part number depending on the type of material in question. [6]

$$D = \frac{FH}{MTBR} \quad or \quad D = \frac{FC}{MCBR} \quad or \quad D = \frac{CT}{MDBR} \tag{1}$$

The denominator represents the mean durability in terms of type of usage. The Mean Time Between Removal (MTBR), the Mean Cycles Between Removal (MCBU) and the Mean Duration Between Removal (MDBR) can be differentiated.

Due to the sparsity of the data, there are two major challenges in this approach that will be analyzed in this research work. Firstly, the mean durability is often calculated from historic data. However, the finite observation window cuts off a significant amount of data and therefore interferes with the data. Given this fact Zhao [7] has shown, that the stochastic distribution of demand strongly influences the method of calculating the mean in (1). He shows that the calculations (1) are of good quality only for the Poisson distribution assumption.

Secondly, the influences of additional factors will be examined as part of the research work in this project. A distinction between measurable impact factors and categorical impact factors is useful. Measureable impact factors are e.g. the number of flight hours, the number of flight cycles and the calendar time between the appearances of maintenance events. Categorical impact factors are e.g. the aircraft type, the operator, regional influences of climatic conditions, seasonal influences or the usage profile of the customer (e.g. long-distance or short-distance) [8]. The identified impact factors have to be checked by relevance and suitability. Furthermore the dependencies between the impact factors have to be analyzed.

The influence of the age of the primary product is exemplarily shown in Fig. 3. In an analysis of different ATA chapters (Air Transport Association), a standard numbering system, a dependency of the failure rate and the age in flying hours has been determined. [9] An analysis on the basis of the ATA chapter is probably no appropriate reference level as different material numbers are assigned to the ATA chapters. The appropriate reference level has therefore to be analyzed.

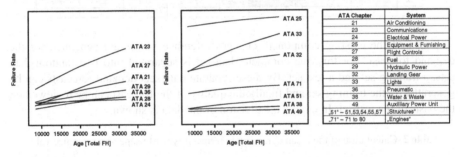

Fig. 3. Influence of the age of an aircraft on the failure rate of components [9]

For a forecast of the future demands the historical plan demands have to be constantly matched with the actual demand. By the permanent matching of the plan demand with the actual demand the control loops can be established. In the first step the identified relevant impact factors are set by the initially calculated value and should constantly be optimized. Approaches for forecasting methods in this context can exemplary be found in [10], [11], [12], [13], [14].

Of special importance is the measurement of the forecast quality. Table 1 shows an excerpt from the existing data base used in this project (data anonymized, values changed). Each line represents a change of a component. The table contains the changes of components and their material properties and their exchange properties.The material properties are the material code, the material group and the material number. The material code describes a technical function in an aircraft. In a material group several material numbers are combined, which are completely interchangeable.

The level of detail increases from the material code up to the material number. The previously described ATA chapter is in the detail level several steps above the material code. These three groups are chosen to illustrate the approach. Even more detailed material properties, for example the serial number, are available in practice. In addition to the material properties the exchange properties are shown in table 1. These are on one hand measureable impact factors such as the flight hours, the flight cycles and the calendar time and on the other hand the categorical impact factors such as the operator and the aircraft type, which are listed as examples. For each component change this information is recorded.

Table 1. Example of the structure of the data base

number	material code	material group	material number	operator	aircraft type	...	flight hours	flight cycles	calendar time
1	material code 1	material group 1	material number 1	operator 1	A330	...	13245	2835	39120
2	material code 1	material group 1	material number 1	operator 2	A330	...	9682	4494	29760
3	material code 1	material group 1	material number 1	operator 2	A340	...	9007	3452	19608
4	material code 1	material group 1	material number 2	operator 3	747	...	14864	1183	16533
5	material code 1	material group 2	material number 3	operator 1	777	...	1617	1306	5808
6	material code 1	material group 2	material number 3	operator 2	A320	...	7420	6387	26808
7	material code 1	material group 2	material number 4	operator 1	747	...	8979	7362	32880
8	material code 1	material group 2	material number 4	operator 3	A320	...	4950	4020	27600
9	material code 1	material group 2	material number 4	operator 2	A330	...	10870	9000	38400
10	material code 1	material group 2	material number 4	operator 2	A330	...	9703	6973	29488
11	material code 1	material group 3	material number 5	operator 1	747	...	8979	7362	32880
12	material code 1	material group 3	material number 5	operator 3	A320	...	4950	4020	82800
13	material code 1	material group 3	material number 5	operator 3	747	...	8501	7103	29976
14	material code 1	material group 3	material number 6	operator 2	747	...	5194	4471	18766
...	...	...	...	...	...	...	...	...	...

Based on the existing component changes reference values are generated for the demand forecast. For this, the complete data set is separated into two random data sets, a training set and a test set. By these separate data sets demand forecasts can be generated by the training set and finally the quality of the forecast can be reviewed on the basis of the test set. In table 2 the division of the data is shown.

Table 2. Calculation of the mean durability in terms of type of usage as a reference value

number	material code	material group	flight hours	flight cycles	calendar time	set by chance		MTBR	MCBR	MDBR
									calculated	
1	material code 1	material group 1	13245	2835	39120	training		11464	3665	34440
2	material code 1	material group 1	9682	4494	29760	training				
5	material code 1	material group 2	1617	1306	5808	training				
7	material code 1	material group 2	8979	7362	32880	training		7155	5889	25696
9	material code 1	material group 2	10870	9000	38400	training				
12	material code 1	material group 3	4950	4020	82800	training		6726	5562	56388
13	material code 1	material group 3	8501	7103	29976	training				

number	material code	material group	flight hours	flight cycles	calendar time	set by chance		D_{MTBR}	D_{MCBR}	D_{MDBR}
3	material code 1	material group 1	9007	3452	19608	test		0,8	0,9	0,6
4	material code 1	material group 1	14864	1183	16533	test		1,3	0,3	0,5
6	material code 1	material group 2	7420	6387	26808	test		1,0	1,1	1,0
8	material code 1	material group 2	4950	4020	27600	test		0,7	0,7	1,1
10	material code 1	material group 2	9703	6973	29488	test		1,4	1,2	1,1
11	material code 1	material group 3	8979	7362	32880	test		1,3	1,3	0,6
14	material code 1	material group 3	5194	4471	18766	test		0,8	0,8	0,3
							$\sum$	7,3	6,3	5,2

In this example the material group is chosen as a reference. Based on the material group the MTBR, MCBR and MDBR are calculated in the training set. With the values determined in the training set, the resulting changes in the test set according to formula (1) are calculated. These values are compared to actual changes, which in this specific test set turn out to be 7. In comparison 7.3 changes are determined with the calculated MTBR based on the training set. Furthermore 6.3 changes are determined with the calculated MCBR and 5.2 changes are identified with the calculated MDBR. Thus, the best forecast value is calculated by the use of the MTBR. In other words, the flight hours have the most significant impact on the number of changes. These values have to be validated by repeated random separation of the data into a training and a test set. By combining different material and exchange properties other influencing factors can be analyzed. The combination of (material group x operator), (material group x aircraft type) or (material group x operator x aircraft type) are only a few possible combinations in this example.

3.2   Analysis of the Requirements for an Organizational Implementation

The analysis of the requirements for an organizational implementation is another topic in the research project. Different departments of an organization have varying requirements regarding the use of the calculated demands. E.g. a repair shop needs the demand to schedule the work orders or the technology management uses the information in the context of the reliability analysis. To determine the Repair Float Quantity (RFQ) this information is used in the materials planning. It should be examined whether it is possible to develop an universal approach which generates the corresponding varying values for the different departments on the basis of a consistent data selection.

4   Summary

The efficient delivery of spare parts during the entire life cycle of the product is a differentiating quality characteristic in competition that leads to improved customer loyalty and, therefore, strengthens the company in the market. In the field of aviation the competition and cost pressures in the MRO sector increased strongly in recent decades. The main goal of a MRO service provider is to ensure on-time supply of spare parts and a main challenge in the processes of MRO service providers is the calculation of the optimal stock level of the pool components which is influenced by different impact factors. The main objective of this research project is the development of demand control loops for a global MRO spare parts management. Due to the sparsity of the data, there are two major challenges in this approach that will be analyzed in this research work. Firstly, the calculation of the mean durability of components and the integration of the influences of additional factors like regional influences of climatic conditions. Finally the requirements for an organizational implementation are another topic in this research project.

Acknowledgements. The results presented in this paper were developed in the research project "Demand control loops for a global component spare parts management". This research project is part of the regional aviation research program LUFO II-2 funded by the German Federal State of Hamburg (Behörde für Wirtschaft, Verkehr und Innovation).

References

1. Dombrowski, U., Schulze, S., Vollrath, H.: Klassifizierung kritischer Elektronikbauelemente unter Lebenszyklusaspekten. Automotive 11, 34–37 (2009)
2. Ghobbar, A.A., Friend, C.H.: Sources of intermittent demand for aircraft spare parts within airline operations. Journal of Air Transportation Management 8, 221–231 (2002)
3. Schmidt, T., Laucht, O., Bauer, A.: Mehrwert schaffen durch Fokussierung auf das Servicegeschäft. In: Barkawi, K., Baader, A., Montanus, S. (eds.) Erfolgreich mit After Sales Service: Geschäftsstrategien für Servicemanagement und Ersatzteillogistik, pp. 95–111. Springer, Heidelberg (2006)
4. Hinsch, M.: Industrielles Luftfahrtmanagement: Technik und Organisation luftfahrttechnischer Betriebe. Springer, Berlin (2010)
5. Loukmidis, G., Luczak, H.: Lebenszyklusorientierte Planungsstrategien für den Ersatzteilbedarf. In: Barkawi, K., Baader, A., Montanus, S. (eds.) Erfolgreich mit After Sales Service: Geschäftsstrategien für Servicemanagement und Ersatzteillogistik, pp. 250–270. Springer, Heidelberg (2006)
6. Linser, A.: Performance Measurement in der Flugzeuginstandhaltung. Dissertation. Universität, Hochschule für Wirtschafts-, Rechts- und Sozialwissenschaften (HSG), St. Gallen (2005)
7. Zhao, Y.: Parametric interference from window censored renewal process data. Dissertation. Ohio State University (2006)
8. Bauer, A.: Lebenszyklusorientierte Optimierung von Instandhaltungssystemen für hochwertige Investitionsgüter. Dissertation. Shaker, Aachen (2002)
9. Wagner, M., Fricke, M.: Estimation of daily unscheduled line maintenance events in civil aviation. In: 25th International Congress of Aeronautical Science, Hamburg (2006)
10. Luxhøj, J.T., Trefor, P.W., Shyur, H.-J.: Comparison of regression and neural network models for prediction of inspection profiles for aging aircraft. IIE Transactions 29, 91–101 (1997)
11. Ghobbar, A.A., Friend, C.H.: Evaluation of forecasting methods for intermittent parts demand in the field of aviation: a predictive model. Computers & Operations Research 30, 2097–2114 (2003)
12. Regattieri, A., Gamberi, M., Gamberini, R., Manzini, R.: Managing lumpy demand for aircraft spare parts. Journal of Air Transport Management 11, 426–431 (2005)
13. Bevilacqua, M., Braglia, M., Frosolini, M., Montanari, R.: Failure rate prediction with artificial neural networks. Journal of Quality in Maintenance Engineering 3, 279–294 (2005)
14. Louit, D.M., Pascual, R., Jardine, A.K.S.: A practical procedure for the selection of time-to-failure models based on the assessment of trends in maintenance data. Reliability Engineering and System Safety 94, 1618–1628 (2009)

The Value and Management Practices of Installed Base Information in Product-Service Systems

Nicola Saccani[1], Andrea Alghisi[1], and Jukka Borgman[2]

[1] Dept. of Mechanical and Industrial Engineering, University of Brescia, Brescia, Italy
{nicola.saccani,andrea.alghisi}@ing.unibs.it
[2] School of Science, Department of Computer Science and Engineering,
Aalto University, Espoo, Finland
Jukka.Borgman@aalto.fi

Abstract. Increasing competitive pressures have pushed manufacturers to increase the value of their offerings through the provision of Product-service systems. This shift results in an increased complexity of offerings and a higher degree of risk and responsibility taken by manufacturers concerning product availability, performance and product-enabled processes.

The paper investigates the impact and potential benefits of installed base information management practices on the offering of Product-Service Systems. A case study concerning an underwater system in a cruise vessel is presented: the data collected were used to develop a simple decision analysis tree, which allows to estimate the value of installed base information in the studied case.

Keywords: Product-Service System, installed base information management, decision analysis method.

1 Introduction

1.1 Context and Definition

In the last decades, growing competitive pressures and increased customer expectations have pushed western manufacturers to extend their offerings through the provision of value-adding services to their customers [1]. Operations management scholars have delineated three main rationales for this shift. First, manufacturers can gain a stable stream of revenue by providing services for their installed base [2]. Second, manufacturers can achieve a sustainable competitive advantage providing advanced services that aim to support their customers and product's enabled processes [3]. Third, customers are demanding more services and opportunities to reduce operational risks [3, 4]. The term Product-Service System describes the ever increasing integration between products and services and the shift from value in exchange to value in use [5].

However, evidence from research and business practice suggests that the transition toward the provision of PSS implies challenges that could neutralize the opportunities

C. Emmanouilidis, M. Taisch, D. Kiritsis (Eds.): APMS 2012, Part II, IFIP AICT 398, pp. 415–421, 2013.

given by service offerings and even reduce firms' profitability and value [4, 6–10]. In this challenging context, the adoption of procedures and technologies aimed to collect, organize and exploit the information related to the installed based and the usage of products and services by the customers can act as enablers and means to overcome or mitigate the increasing risks for manufacturers [1, 2, 4, 9, 11, 12].

1.2   Objective

The study has two main objectives. The first one is to investigate how installed base information management (IBIM) practices impact on PSS delivery processes, while the second one is to quantify the value of installed base information (IBI) from the perspective of a customer. A survey has been conducted to gain an understanding on how the offering of different PSS types is linked with the typologies of data collected from the installed base, the collection methodologies and information systems. In order to achieve the second objective, a pilot case study was conducted through semi-structured interviews with a company using an underwater system in a cruise vessel.

2   Background

2.1   Literature Review

Strategic Aspects of Servitization vs. IBIM
Ala-Risku defines "installed base" as *a collective noun for currently used individual products sold or serviced by the focal firm* [13]. This definition is most suited for our purposes than others found in literature – e.g. [2] for whom installed base is just a cumulative equivalent of market share – since it suggests that *every single product* sold and serviced by the firm can be a valuable source of information. In this study, we also define installed base information (IBI) as *all technical and commercial data related to installed base and needed for operation or optimization of industrial services*. Examples of IBI include as-maintained structure of a product individual, its usage, maintenance activities and the customer process the piece of equipment is located in. Installed base information management (IBIM), instead, *represents the set of practices that companies adopt to collect, analyze, use and share data concerning installed products and their utilization*. For instance, the Rolls-Royce case, with its "Power by the hour" blueprint, provides an example of how the collection and analysis of IBI enables the provision of PSS and also the transition towards a new business model that meet customer needs [4, 10, 14]. In fact, Rolls-Royce has changed its business model from transactional to relational and delivers value in use instead of value in exchange. Thanks to the adoption of installed base information systems such as real-time remote monitoring technologies, Rolls-Royce has mitigated the increased operational risks that such a business model implies for the manufacturer.

The potential of IBIM for the provision of PSS has been recently addressed by [9] who claims that IBI collection systems and data analysis methods are to be considered respectively as fundamental resources and capabilities for manufacturers in order to successfully offering innovative solutions characterized by a strong relationship between products and services.

Impact of IBIM on Service Processes (Service Provider Perspective)
Despite these multiple evidence and practitioners growing interest in the management of information generated during products' lifecycle [15], a preliminary literature analysis unveils the lack of a comprehensive approach in studying the IBIM phenomenon [13], since several studies focus on technological aspects rather than managerial ones. Indeed, there is a paucity of studies investigating the relationship between IBIM practices and operations management activities related to the provision of PSS as well as investigating how IBIM enables the transition towards relationship-based business models. A few exceptions can be cited. [16] analyzes how the exploitation of IBI positively impacts on the spare parts forecasting and management performance. [10] focus on how product condition monitoring technologies such as Product Health Monitoring can facilitate the transition to service-based business models allowing manufacturers to handle increased risks.

This study is aimed to contribute in filling such a gap in the literature. One way to address the issue is to understand how making the benefits of IBIM tangible to customers can impact on the PSS offering and the overall business relationship between the PSS provider and its customers.

3   Methodology

3.1   Case Study

We conducted an explorative and descriptive case study [17] on a remote monitoring service provider and a cruise line company. The interviews were recorded and transcribed for analysis. Access to the cruise line company was through the service provider and we interviewed operations manager at the customer. Where feasible, data were double-checked from other informants of the service provider. At the end, all data was validated by presenting it to the service provider business development management.

Data collected have been the input to estimate the value of IBI, assessed through the decision analysis method [18]. The method is based on statistical and probabilistic mathematics and utilizes a decision tree to illustrate available decision options and monetary rewards and losses connected to each option. When comparing each option, *expected monetary value (EMV)* is computed multiplying the payoff (monetary return) of an option by its probability.

3.2   Survey

An exploratory survey has been conducted using on-line questionnaire on a sample of medium and large companies that operate in Italy, about their IBIM practices. Respondents (29) are mainly service managers, CEOs or technical managers. The questionnaire, developed from the analysis of literature, has been structured as follows:

- A first set of questions aims to evaluate firms maturity in terms of PSS provision and concerns firms' perception of the importance of competitive factors (price of the offering, innovation of the offering, personalization of the offering, during-the-sale services, after-sale services and the total cost of ownership), percentage of turnover gained from services, composition of the service portfolio and accounting nature of the service business unit.
- A second set of questions aims to delineate installed base information management practices in terms of typologies of data that are collected from the installed base. Considered typologies are resource consumption, product functioning parameters, product use configuration, level of utilization of the product, product geographical positioning, customer satisfaction about the product and technical assistance, history of maintenance activities. The second question of this set deals with data collection methods (e.g. collection on paper, manual insertion in information system or automated). Once collected, data can be handled and managed using different information system such as custom database solutions, ERP (Enterprise Resource Planning), CRM (Costumer Relationship Management), PLM (Product Lifecycle Management) or PDM (Product Data Management).
- A third set of questions investigates both the benefits from IBIM practices as well as the obstacles to its adoption.

4   Findings

4.1   Quantifying Value of Installed Base Information

A recurrent theme across companies is: *how to quantify value of IBI?* The case company wanted to quantify the value of IBI in order to answer two major questions. First, how much a service provider should invest in IBI collection, management and related IT tools? In practice, the value could be used in investment calculations of IT tools and the justification would come from increased internal process efficiency, or better maintenance scheduling, for example. Second, how to communicate the value of IBI to customers e.g. to support the sales of remote monitoring-type of services? Remote monitoring data may indicate in advance if some major problem is developing, and corresponding corrective activities can be performed during planned dry dockings, instead of leading to unplanned dry-dockings. The cost of an unplanned dry-docking to the cruise line customer usually ranges between $1 to 3 million, but can be as high as $7 million. The analyzed customer had 29 unplanned dry-dockings in 10 years with 4 vessels. Based on this data, the probability of a vessel to have an unplanned dry docking during a one-year period is (29/10)/4= 0.725.

In Fig. 1, a decision tree allows to compare two options for potential customers of remote monitoring services. In the upper branch, the customer purchases a vessel without remote monitoring leading to an annual dry docking probability of 0.725, each dry docking bearing a cost of $2 million (an average of the observed 1 to 3 million $). In the lower remote monitoring branch, annual estimated price of remote monitoring services $ 300 000 is counted in first. Then the original dry-docking probability of 0,725 is reduced due to remote monitoring capability of detecting 80% of developing faults in advance. The figure of 80% is not the actual detection capability of the remote monitoring, but an illustrative number to demonstrate the use of the method.

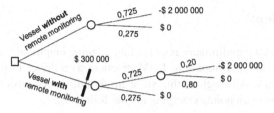

Fig. 1. Decision tree of purchasing a vessel with or without remote monitoring service

Following the final cost of each branch and its probability, resulting expected monetary value of each option yields:

$$EMV_{without}=0,725 * (-\$ 2\ 000\ 000) + 0,275 * (\$0) = -\$1\ 450\ 000$$
$$EMV_{with}= 0,725 * 0,20 * (-\$ 2\ 000\ 000) + 0,725 * 0,80 * (\$0) - \$300\ 000 = -\$590\ 000$$

With these parameters, the annual added value of the information gained by remote monitoring is the difference $1 450 000 - $590 000 = $860 000.

4.2   Preliminary Survey Findings

The sample size does not allow to perform inferential analysis, however some interesting evidence about IBIM practices emerged from descriptive analysis. First, we found that in general after-sales services is considered the most important competitive factor. However, the companies that implement new service-led business models, such as the pay-per-use, consider the total cost of ownership as the most important factor.

The second finding relates to the research gap highlighted in the literature review. In fact, only 17% of respondents indicate the adoption of new service-led business model as a "benefit" of IBIM. Such firms collect higher range and volume of data from products (e.g. geographical position, work hours, number of working cycles, typology of activities, functioning parameters such as vibration or temperature and resources consumption).

The third finding concerns information collection methods and systems: automated systems are still scarcely diffused being adopted by 2 out of 29 respondent. While several firms that implement traditional business models are still collecting data using paper, all the firms that implement service-led business model have adopted information systems to support the data collection. Most respondents (69% of the sample), instead, rely on ad hoc solutions such as spreadsheets or in-house developed databases. Information systems as ERP, CRM and PLM have lower adoption rates, 41% for both ERP and CRM and only 7% for PLM. However, firms that implement service-led business models declare doubled CRM and ERP adoption rates and a three times higher PLM adoption rate in comparison to company that implement traditional business models (60% against 37% for ERP and CRM, and 20% against 4% for PLM).

5   Conclusions

This paper presents the preliminary results of an ongoing empirical research that aims to understand the role and impact of IBIM practices as a driver in the transition towards PSS offerings. Although at this stage no definitive conclusion can be drawn from this study, the main points emerging are the following:

i.) the role of IBIM as an enabler in the transition from product to services is still under-investigated in the literature from a business strategy perspective, but also in term of value for the customer it can generate, or in the way it can influence service delivery processes;

ii.) the survey findings suggest that IBIM can be an enabler in the transition towards service-based business models, or at least that companies that implement service-based business models rely (also) on IBIM practices supporting the development and provision of their offerings;

iii.) IBIM is not relevant only for the company delivering the PSS, but rather it can increase the value of the PSS for its customers. Quantifying (with simple enough but robust methods such as decision analysis applied in the case study) the value the customer can gain from IBIM makes tangible the impact of PSS, and supports communication of the new business models towards customers.

Acknowledgments. The research presented in this paper stems from the activity of the ASAP Service Management Forum (www.asapsmf.org), a research and dissemination initiative involving researchers from five Italian universities and several companies, about product-service systems, servitization of manufacturing and service management. The authors also wish to thank researchers in the Future Industrial Services (FutIS) research program in Finland for collecting data for the case study.

References

1. Wise, R., Baumgartner, P.: Go Downstream: The New Profit Imperative in Manufacturing. Harvard Business Review 77, 133–141 (1999)
2. Oliva, R., Kallenberg, R.: Managing the transition from products to services. International Journal of Service Industry Management 6, 160–172 (2003)
3. Mathieu, V.: Service strategies within the manufacturing sector: benefits, costs and partnership. International Journal 12, 451–475 (2001)
4. Neely, A.: Exploring the financial consequences of the servitization of manufacturing. Operation Management Research, 103–118 (2009)
5. Baines, T.S., Lightfoot, H.W., Benedettini, O., Kay, J.M.: The servitization of manufacturing: A review of literature and reflection on future challenges. Journal of Manufacturing Technology Management 20, 547–567 (2009)

6. Gebauer, H., Fleisch, E., Friedli, T.: Overcoming the Service Paradox in Manufacturing Companies. European Management Journal 23, 14–26 (2005)
7. Fang, E.E., Palmatier, R.W., Steenkamp, J.E.M.: Effect of Service Transition Strategies on Firm Value. Journal of Marketing 72, 1–14 (2008)
8. Martinez, V., Bastl, M., Kingston, J., Evans, S.: Challenges in transforming manufacturing organisations into product-service providers. Journal of Manufacturing Technology Management 21, 449–469 (2010)
9. Ulaga, W.: Hybrid Offerings: How Manufacturing Firms Combine Goods and Services Successfully. Journal of Marketing (2011)
10. Greenough, R.M., Grubic, T.: Modelling condition-based maintenance to deliver a service to machine tool users. The International Journal of Advanced Manufacturing Technology 52, 1117–1132 (2010)
11. Auramo, J., Ala-risku, T.: Challenges for Going Downstream. International Journal of Logistics Research and Applications 8, 1–22 (2005)
12. Cohen, M.A., Agrawal, N., Agrawal, V.: Winning in the aftermarket. Harvard Business Review 84, 129–138 (2006)
13. Ala-Risku, T.: Installed Base Information: Ensuring Customer Value and Profitability After the Sale. Industrial Engineering (2009)
14. Davies, A., Brady, T., Hobday, M.: Charting a Path Toward Integrated Solutions. MIT Sloan Management Review 47 (2006)
15. Dutta, S.: The Evolution of Remote Product Service and the Emergence of Smart Services (2009)
16. Dekker, R., Zuidwijk, R., Jalil, N.: On the use of installed base information for spare parts logistics: A review of ideas and industry practice. Intern. Journal of Production Economics (2011)
17. Yin, R.K.: Case study research: design and methods. Sage Publications, Inc. (1994)
18. Raiffa, H.: Decision analysis: introductory lectures on choices under uncertainty. MD Computing Computers in Medical Practice 10, 312–328 (1968, 1970)

Reference Decision Models in the Medico-social Service Sector

Henri Kromm[1] and Yves Ducq[2]

[1] Acthan Expertises, 18 Rte de Beychac, 33750
Saint Germain du Puch, France
hkromm@acthan-expertises.com
[2] University of Bordeaux – IMS – UMR 5218 CNRS – 351 cours de la Libération – 33405
Talence cedex - France
yves.ducq@u-bordeaux1.fr

Abstract. This paper aims at defining a dedicated method to analyse existing systems and to implement target models for social and medico-social structures in France. Based on GRAI Method, one proposes generic models for decisional systems and processes. The first application presented here proves that reference models could be used to identify strengths and weaknesses but also specific performance indicators more adapted than existing ones. The main observed results are an improvement of the added value of service and an optimization of strategic management tools. In a second time, we demonstrate that it is necessary to specify reference models for each kind of the 15 structures in order to take into account the people particularisms on one hand and to improve information system to answer efficiently to user needs and institutional requests on the other hand.

Keywords: performance indicators, business models, medico-social sector, modeling, decisional system, process models, quality management.

1 The Medico-social Service Sector

1.1 Context

The French social and medico-social service sector is governed by the Social Action and Family Code (*Code d'Action Sociale et des Familles*) revised in 2002 [1]. The L312-1 article [2] describes the organisation of the field, as well as its ad hoc actors. A typology of 15 potential actors can be drawn like: Institutions or departments usually dealing with young people under 18 or 21, Institutions or special schools acting as main providers of adapted education and social or medico-social care to young people under 18, Health, welfare and social action centres, Institutions or departments implementing the educational measures ordered by Court concerning delinquents under 18 or under 21, etc.

The field is made up of 35,000 structures and employs nearly three million people as well as volunteers and family caregivers in France. Since 2002 France has been engaged in a pro-active policy of professionalisation of the field which consists in:

C. Emmanouilidis, M. Taisch, D. Kiritsis (Eds.): APMS 2012, Part II, IFIP AICT 398, pp. 422–429, 2013.
© IFIP International Federation for Information Processing 2013

✓ setting up long-term schemes (about disability, cancer, Alzheimer disease, etc),
✓ favouring the empowerment of all actors involved through the tutelarization of structures, institutions and departments by specialized agencies: the National Agency for Performance *(ANAP)*, the National Agency for Assessment *(ANESM)*, Regional Health Agencies *(ARS)*...

The whole medico-social service sector has integrated simultaneously the concept of continuous quality improvement, finding its main inspiration in the actions applied in the health sector.

1.2   Issues at Stake

The major issues are of two types. Firstly, the organisational challenges resulting from the complexity of medico-social structures. They are caused by the numerous processes implemented for the completion of planned activities and also by the nature of the service provided which affects the beneficiaries themselves in their personal fulfilment.

Secondly, the issue of management related to the very strong increase of requests by institutions to implement continuous quality improvement [3]. This includes the development of an assessment cycle combining self-assessment and external assessment by an independent organisation. The authorization for an institution to work depends on the completion of the whole assessment cycle which consequently influences the whole management of the structures.

Actually, numerous structures have kept traditional organisation methods and find it difficult to meet the expectations of/respond to requests by supervisory authorities [4].

The challenge of our work is thus to provide a method and a reference model for the implementation of a management structure adapted to the social and socio-medical service sector which could also integrate all its environmental evolutions. The objective is to build a reference model of the system which should lead to an implementation process associated to the ad hoc management tools (performance indicators).

1.3   Structuring Measures and Reference Frames

To support the different actors in their action, ANESM has created guidelines and recommendations in addition to the existing reference frames applying to each sector of activity. In fact, each federation, sector or grouping of structures has developed its own assessment tools in order to take into account the specific contexts and issues at stake for each of them: ISO Standards [5], the *Angélique* referential [6], the gerontology quality policy *EVA* [7], auto evaluation framework for public services [8], etc, are examples of the numerous evaluation tools and processes which can be used by the managers of socio-medical structures. In this context, it seems indispensable to move towards an harmonisation of reference frames in order to guarantee the quality of analysis and the homogeneity of results on the one hand, to facilitate the integration of the new standards and professional recommendations regularly emerging on the other hand.

Besides, as aptly pointed out by [9], one confirms the necessity not to tend to reference frames (by sector or not), but rather toward operational models which take into account the type of users/beneficiaries, their needs and the specificities of the structure involved.

1.4   The Medico-social Service System

The classical production system [10] is characterised by: the resources which are going to carry out the transformation processes of the product, the products circulating in the system on which operations of added value are made, the issues of synchronisation and coordination of the availability of the resources and the products, an environment with a strong influence on the evolution of the system.

A number of strong specificities can be noted:

A very special customer: The customer is also a "product "of the system, if you consider the services provided as applying fully to their user. In fact, in some types of institutions (residential care homes, 'Etablissement Hospitalier pour Personnes Agées Dépendantes (EHPAD)' nursing homes, ...), the user is not necessarily supposed to get out of the place. Thus, as opposed to what happens in the education system, the user may have to stay permanently in the department. We can also consider the case of the users of medico-social services who, even if strongly encouraged to play an active role in their lives (through personalised projects for example), do not always have the capacities to become fully involved in their health paths [11].

Very strong institutional and legal constraints

Two categories can be considered:

1. Budgetary constraints as formalised in Tripartite Agreements and/or Aims and Means Contract (CPOM: Conventions d'Objectifs et de Moyens),
2. Constraints related to issues raising ethical concern such as the fight against mistreatment or the fight for the respect of the user's rights and freedoms.

These constraints shape all professional practices and lead to governance and management processes which are specific to the sector [12], [13]: evaluation cycles, activity traceability (healthcare and organised activities), etc.

One of the specificities is that some parts of the support activities are difficult to assess: the evaluation of the effectiveness of the actions relies on the analysis of the professional who undertakes them.

Erratic flows

The movements of the users are also quite specific. They are rare and connected to:

1. Either the necessity for a professional to intervene (e.g. operation) or the completion of a given action (e.g. catering/meals),
2. Either a choice from the user, sometimes with no particular objective, to move to a specific place as users called "outpatients" could do.

Indeed moves are often erratic and the issues of people's movement and logistics focus more on the safety of places and the observance of hygiene rules than on the optimisation of logistics flows themselves.

Specific care: Healthcare for a user also requires assistance and safety at all times [11]. That is why institutions must constantly question their practices in order to guarantee optimal service quality, including when the user is in a more « private » area. In the health system, the main objective remains the recovery of the patient. Other objectives are contingent on the health system (pain relief, end of life care), but generally, the patient is meant to get out of the system cured. Concerning the users of the medico-social service system, if they can legitimately expect to come back to an ordinary background (home, workplace), they do not have the objective to be "cured" from their disability or to become younger. This fundamental aspect has a strong and double impact. First, it has an impact on activities for each profession: as opposed to what happens in the health system, the technical part of work is not always predominant, and the assistance and care to the users are generally more important than the sheer technical gestures that could be provided to them. Second, it has an impact on the professionals of the sector themselves who can quickly become worn-down by the impression that their work is ineffective. This second impact has a direct effect on the management methods used in the social and medico-social service sectors.

2   Business Modelling Applied to the Social Sector

2.1   Method and Reference Decision Model

Using the GRAI method [14], we consider the medico-social structure as an entity which connects the three classical subsystems.

The decision system offers the following functions in the basic version:

✓ Managing human resources,
✓ Managing infrastructures,
✓ Managing accountancy and cash-flow,
✓ Planning / synchronizing.

Concerning the "activity-oriented" functions, we notice a recurrence of some functions such as:

✓ Managing healthcare;
✓ Managing organised activities and assistance;
✓ Managing hospital accommodation and catering.

The physical system enables to model all activities (in the form of processes) implemented by a structure. Once again, the activities are usual ones and include all the skills of social workers, medical and paramedical staff: organised activities, psychology, healthcare, administration, etc.

Last, the information system is paramount when considering the growing issues of traceability of actions in terms both of how they are carried out and of which budget they are charged to. The typical decision grid (figure 1) for a nursing home can be found below: it is one of the reference models for decisional systems. The decision-making process is decentralised for the « activity-oriented » functions requiring specific skills (healthcare, organised activities, etc.). It remains centralised in the hands of institution management teams, particularly for the support and development functions (Human Resources, partnerships) as well as budget and reporting.

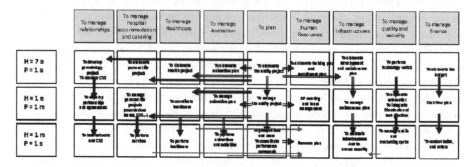

Fig. 1. The reference decisional GRAI grid for a nursing home

Long-term governance remains strongly bound to the environment of the system. Indeed, the development of institution relies on budget planning which is largely supervised by government-controlled organisations (Departmental Councils and Regional Health Authorities in particular). Budgets are closely connected to funding (subsidization) conditions for the institutions, and development strategies are consequently devised collaboratively with institutional partners.

The decision grid conceptualizes the monitoring of implemented processes, such as 'welcoming patients', 'providing care' for instance. Numerous models of processes were built based on GRAI diagram and GRAI actigram such as "welcoming process", or "emergency reception process.

Each step of the process is controlled by specific procedures. For example, we notice that the development of a personalised project is a fundamental step and that numerous documents rule this process: National Agency for Assessment *(ANESM)* recommendations, professional standards, etc. These reference models were used to specify action plans for the nursing home described here after.

2.2   Management and Performance

As a rule, governance relies on a certain number of indicators. The most well-known apply to the level of dependency (PATHOS tool) dealt with by the institutions:

✓ PMP for *Pathos Moyen Pondéré* (PATHOS tool Weighted Average Dependency) [15] is a cost indicator in medical and technical care for a given population,

✓ GMP for *GIR (Groupe Iso-Ressources) Moyen Pondéré* (AGGIR Weighted Average Autonomy) [16] is an indicator of the level of autonomy of a given population calculated by applying the AGGIR grid to each individual people in the group considered.

These indicators allow decision makers in particular to address supervisory authorities in order to negotiate the budgetary allocation keys and the aid amounts. After that, numerous indicators (statistics) make the answers to give to the authorities clearer, but we notice that institutions rarely read the results with enough precision to infer the relevant levers of action in terms of professional practices.

1. About healthcare, we can mention: the number of bedsores, the number of injections, the average duration of care, by patient, etc.
2. For institutions providing accommodation: the occupation rate, the turnover rate, the checking out rate (with causes/justified), the depth of the waiting list, etc.

The indicators give results which are essentially statistics referring to specific activities. However, they are rarely put in perspective with the (often qualitative) objectives of the institution: the social culture of the sector is a natural restraint to this initiative. Besides, the indicators asked for by the institutions and the supervisory authorities being statistic indicators too, institution management teams often stop at this first level of performance assessment. The method of management is thus evolving towards a more budgetary approach, which creates tensions with the operational level which would prefer a user-centred type of management based on the quality of the service rather than financial aspects [17].

An indicator often required by supervisory authorities can be quoted as an example: the number and variety of partnerships signed by an institution. Yet we know that the number of partnerships does not prove the relevance of the cooperation and collaboration actions undertaken in comparison with the objectives pursued for the beneficiary. It seems more appropriate to use an indicator such as the "degree of activity of all the stakeholders for the benefit of a user": This enables to evaluate the relevance of undertaken actions contributing to mobilise professionals for the benefit of a user in order to maintain and/or improve his/her autonomy.

2.3   Implementation Process

The modelling of an institution applies following a classical modelling and development process in five steps:

1. Definition of objectives and goals,
2. Elaboration of existing system models,
3. Diagnostic of models,
4. Elaboration of target models,
5. Elaboration of action plan.

The modelling phase corresponds to a phase of abstraction which enables to translate the way an institution works, the way it is organised, and the processes it uses into understandable and analysable models. This analysis leads us to build an operating mode conceptualized by a set of models called 'target models'. The implementation of these models is conducted through a prioritized action plan.

Under no circumstances can this action plan be established on the sole and only basis of modelling, as the opinion and validation of the professional(s) involved is fundamental. The target models are used only for the justification of proposed actions and solutions.

3   Application to the Case of an EHPAD Nursing Home

We are applying this method to a public nursing home (*EHPAD*) of 55 beds. The level of dependency (*GMP*) is of 783 and the level of medication (PMP) of 200.

The institution is in a standard average according to the AGGIR and Pathos grids. In the context of the decree on external evaluation, this institution is making a request for external evaluation at the end of the self-evaluation conducted previously. The previous method was applied with some adaptations due to the specific context of legal external evaluation. One elaborates models of the physical system, called 'professional practices', the information system called 'organisation' and the decision system called 'management, cooperation and professional networks'. The figure 3 shows the process model for user welcoming.

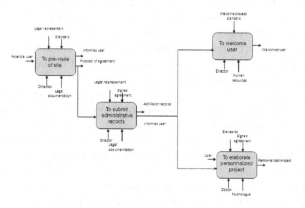

Fig. 2. Process model to welcome users

The analysis of models, based on specific GRAI rules, knowledge on best practices and ANESM guidelines, enables to establish a level of control over good practices for the different points and consequently to identify the areas for potential improvement. The analysis of the correlation between the means and needs shows a discrepancy between the resources available and the expectations: the growing number of internal projects has caused high expenses which have led to a mission drift for the professionals involved. As far as models are concerned, this results in too many functions for the same people: quality management (management of projects) and management of cooperation and external relations. This excess of roles to play generates a high activity which places a strain on the structure due to the growing mobilisation of professionals to the detriment of the closeness with beneficiaries.

Another way of analysis was the definition of specific indicators well-adapted to the nursing home such as well-feeling rating or dependency degree evolution. These indicators were consolidated into scorecard and adapted to each function described with the GRAI grid.

4   Conclusions

In this paper, we have defined the main characteristics of social and medico-social services organisations in order to put forward clear possible models. The implementation of the GRAI method enables to elaborate models specific to the different activities in this sector.

A set of models could be developed to demonstrate the applicability of the method to this context and the interest it represents to build specific reference models adapted to the type of users for these institutions. The creation of reference models for each sector constitutes a basis for the development of tools and methods to assist in the management of social and medico-social services institutions: systems of dedicated performance indicators, reference processes, guides of managerial and organisational good practices, adapted information systems, etc., are examples of tools that we will be able to define and implement. This leads us to think that there is a real opportunity of development and research in this evolving sector.

References

1. CASF-2002 - Code d'action sociale et des familles de, dernière version en vigueur, http://www.legifrance.gouv.fr/ (Octobre 29, 2011)
2. Loi 2002-2 de rénovation de l'action sociale et médico-sociale, http://www.legifrance.gouv.fr/
3. Loi Hôpital, Patient, Santé, Territoire du 22 Juillet 2009, http://www.legifrance.gouv.fr/
4. Décret 2007-975 du 15 mai 2007 fixant le contenu du cahier des charges pour l'évaluation des activités et de la qualité des prestations des établissements, http://www.anesm.sante.gouv.fr/
5. Blanc, D.: Santé et social: L'ISO 9001 à votre portée; Editions AFNOR (2008)
6. Gouley, C.: Evaluation de la Qualité: EVA, référentiel d'évaluation externe de la qualité des EHPAD. La revue hospitalière de France (2002)
7. Ministère de l'Emploi et de la Solidarité: Guide d'accompagnement de l'outil d'auto-évaluation de la qualité en EHPA - Application ANGÉLIQUE (2000), http://www.travail-solidarite.gouv.fr/ IMG/pdf/outil_auto_eval.pdf
8. European Institute of Public Administration: The common assessment framework: Improving an organisation through self-assessment. CAF resource Center (2002)
9. Ardoinot, J., Ladsous, J.: revue Lien Social, N° 751 rubrique rebonds (Avril 28, 2005)
10. Ducq, Y., Doumeingts, G.: Enterprise Modelling techniques to improve efficiency of enterprises. International Journal of Production Planning and Control 12(2) (2001)
11. ANESM: recommandation de pratiques professionnelles de l'ANESM – « Expression et participation des usagers dans les établissements relevant du secteur de l'inclusion sociale » (2008)
12. ANESM: recommandation de pratiques professionnelles de l'ANESM – « Mission du responsable d'établissement et rôle de l'encadrement dans la prévention et le traitement de la maltraitance » (2008)
13. ANESM: recommandation de pratiques professionnelles de l'ANESM – « Mise en oeuvre d'une stratégie d'adaptation à l'emploi des personnels au regard des populations accompagnées » (2009)
14. Ducq, Y., Vallespir, B.: Definition and aggregation of a Performance Measurement System in three Aeronautical workshops using the ECOGRAI Method. International Journal of Production Planning and Control 16(2) (2005)
15. Vétel, J.M., Leroux, R., Ducoudray, J.M., Prévost, P.: Le système PATHOS. La revue de gériatrie. Tome 24(6) (1999)
16. Aggir: Formulaire - Cerfa n°11510*01 disponible sur: http://vosdroits.service-public.fr/R21010.xhtml
17. Chemin, C., Gilbert, P.: L'évaluation de la performance, analyseur de la gouvernance associative. Politique et Management Public 27(1) (2010)

Service Model for the Service Configuration

Jose Angel Lakunza, Juan Carlos Astiazaran, and Maria Elejoste

Design and Production Process Business Unit, Ikerlan S.Coop. Technological Center, Spain
{Jalakunza,jcastiazaran,melejoste}@ikerlan.es

Abstract. Service is a concept difficult to define. It has been extensively used in different contexts. According with literature a service can be seeing: as an activity or as an output of a process.

By service customization we mean the definition and adaptation of a service according to the customer' requirements, when this customization process is carried out in a systematic way.

A company can respond to user needs diversity offering services than can be customized easily, and/or increasing the service variety offered to the market. The increasing in the service offer variety raises also the variety and complexity in the company transactions that involves cost increments for these transactions. Therefore, the challenge will be to extend the range of services offered to the market maintaining the efficiency, that is similar to the Mass Customization concept.

Keywords: Service configuration, Service model, Service personalization.

1 Introduction

The importance of service industry in the economy is growing ([3]). Customers are demanding services that meet their needs. The differences between goods and services are fuzzy as it has been argued that products always contain a service dimension. Human needs are satisfied not only with physical goods but also services.

Different authors argue that research on service customization is sparse and needs to be developed in depth ([2]). In the other hand, due to the service nature, it should be adapted to the customer needs.

Our research goal has been focused on the service customization. The main research questions we try to answer are:

- **What are the different configuration moments in the service life cycle?**
- **How can we define a generic "Service Family" model?**

First we made a literature review on the service concept. Next, we developed a service classification. After that, we focused on the definition of a generic model for the services that might be configured taking into account the customer needs. And finally, we analyzed the applicability of configuration along the service life.

C. Emmanouilidis, M. Taisch, D. Kiritsis (Eds.): APMS 2012, Part II, IFIP AICT 398, pp. 430–437, 2013.
© IFIP International Federation for Information Processing 2013

2   Literature Background

Service is a difficult term to define, because it is extensively used in different contexts. This difficulty has been widely mentioned in the literature by different authors ([3], [9]), and using different definitions for the service concept ([11], [3]).

According to [8] two main streams can be identified in the service definition literature: from the service provider's view as an activity (service) and from the customer view as an output of a system (service result).

Reference [9] mentions these different approaches. The provider sees the service offering in terms of process, related to service operation. On the other hand, the customer views it as a service outcomes. As an output a service represents what a customer receives. As an activity it represents how a customer receives the service.

According with [6], configurable services are services that can be customized to individual specifications by means of a set of options to meet a predetermined range of customers needs. Some examples can be: insurance agreements; machinery maintenance contracts; mobile subscriptions; traveling trips; etc.

Increasing the service offering in order to allow the service customization, increases the complexity of the company's operations. The challenge is to broaden the range of the services offered without risking performance [13] that seems similar to the Mass Customization concept as was established in [16].

Taking into account the active role of the customer, a service model has to be customer oriented . It is easily realized that a natural way of customizing a service is along the course of customer service experience.

Modularization as a way to customize services seems not to be a wide research subject. Nevertheless, using and matching modules in response to customer needs has been proposed in [14] and [15]. Reference [4] discusses the pros and cons of breaking down a service into its components. For that the designer should identify the different service elements and check them against the customer' needs. That means that modularity is an area for future research in service development [12]. Modularization seems as one way to achieve service customization.

Literature describing the support of existing configurators in the service configurations is very limited. The ILOG JConfigurator [10] and the CAWICOMS Workbench [1] are examples of product configurators that support the configuration of both goods and services.

3   Process Map

The figure 1 represents the process map that can be executed along the service life cycle. As we can see, we have defined three different process levels depending in the time horizon for the process:

- *Process level with large time horizon.* The input for the process is the market requirements and the output is also the offer to the market. At this level we can distinguish the process for the service strategy definition and the process for the service framework definition for the market (for instance the definition of the city bus lines and timetables).

- *Process level with a medium time horizon.* In this case the input for the process is the customer needs and output for the process is the service level agreement (SLA) for the customer. At this level we can see the process for the development of the SLA bid and the process for the development of the service platform. Both processes are framed by the framework defined in the previous level (for instance the definition of the car insurance conditions for a customer).

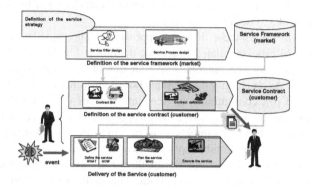

Fig. 1. Process Map

- *Process level with a short time horizon.* In this case the input is an event for the customer and the output is the executed service for the customer. At this level we can see the following activities in the process for the delivery of the service: definition of the facts for the service and the activities needed to execute the service (WHAT & HOW); definition of the resources to execute the service (WHO); and the execution of the service itself. These activities are framed by the framework (contract) defined in the previous level (for instance the response for a car accident from the insurance company).

4   Service Configuration

In order to answer the possed question **what are the different configuration moments in the service life cycle?**, we have identified two different service contexts from the point of view of the service configuration: services without SLA definition and services that need SLA definition.

4.1   Configuration of Services without SLA Definition

When the company doesn't define a service level agreement (SLA) for the customer, the service framework is the same for any customer that wants the service. That means the company has defined a general framework for the service offer.

In this case, firstly the company defines a general framework for the service, and after that, the company sells an instance of service to a customer, according with the specifications required for the customer.

The configuration of the service is carried out during the sale and specification definition of the service from the required needs of the customer. This service configuration takes into account the service offer defined previously by the company. In fact in this moment the process needed to answer to the customer requirement is configured (HOW) and also the type of resources needed to execute the process.

In this scenario of services, there is only a configuration possibility for the service: at the moment of specification definition and sale of the service. An example of this service could be the mail service. In this case the customer defines the specifications for the mail at the same moment that pays for the service.

4.2   Configuration of Services with SLA Definition

In the field of services, there are a lot of examples in which is necessary to define previously a service level agreement (SLA) for the customer, establishing the characteristics of the service to be provided in the future to the customer. Some examples are insurance services, maintenance services, etc.

In these cases of services we can distinguish three different moments along the service life cycle:

1. Service offer definition for the market.
2. SLA definition and sale for the customer
3. Customer event turn up and service execution for the customer

How does it works in the case of car insurance?. In a first moment, the company defines the overall service offer for the insurance of a car (1). Next, the customer in collaboration with the company defines a specific SLA for the insurance of the customer's car, mentioning all the options covered by the company (2). Once the SLA has been established, as response to any kind of event suffered by the customer (an accident, a car breakdown, etc.), the company provides the customer with the adequate service (3).

In this scenario, two different service configuration moments can be identified along the service life cycle:

- A first moment is the configuration of the SLA itself, taking into account the customer requirement for the SLA and the overall service offer defined for the company. This kind of configuration is quite similar to the used for the configuration of goods. Defines WHAT is going to be provided by the company. For instance when a customer establish with the insurance company the SLA for the car insurance
- In a second moment the company, as a response to a customer event, configures the service process to be execute (HOW), and the kind of resources to be used, taking into account the framework posed by the SLA. For instance when the customer suffers and accident with his car and the insurance company provides the adequate service

4.3   Service Execution Planning

Apart from the configuration of the service contract (WHAT the contract covers) and when an event happens, HOW is going to be delivered the service (the configuration of the process for the service), taking into account the event characteristics and the service contract defined for the customer and the defined type of resources to be used for the execution of the process.

Alter this definition and in order to execute the defined service in response to an event, we must to define exactly which are the resources to be used in the service process (WHO) and when this resources are going to be used (the scheduling). That means two different activities:

- *To find resources in the supplier's network:* from the information generated as result of the service configuration (HOW the service will be executed and the type of resources needed for the execution of the service) and taking into account the resources available in the network of suppliers, its finds the appropriate resources for the service execution.

- *To allocate resources for the service process:* once identified the resources, these will be allocated to the corresponding service process activity and the scheduling will be defined. As result of this we will have the customized service process with the allocated resources plus the execution scheduling for the service.

5   Service Model

According with [4], the service should describe *what* are the customer needs, *how* this is going to be achieved, and *with what* kind of resources. The breakdown of a service into its components, allows the designer to check them against the customers' needs. This approach is necessary in order to customize services in a mass customization schema.

Reference [14] is using product platform concepts that have been used for physical products. Applying modularization techniques to the service is seen as one way to achieve service customization. As in the case of goods, modules can be combined in response to specific customer needs. Usually these service modules are seen as work tasks, parts of processes or groups of activities.

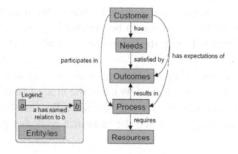

Fig. 2. Conceptual model of services

The figure 2 shows a high level conceptualization of service proposed in [5] as the result of the service literature analysis.

The aim of our work has been to apply the ideas of Product Family Architecture (PFA) developed in [7] in the field of services, in order to define a service architecture that can be used by a service configurator. Our approach for the definition of this service architecture is based in the analysis of the different moments identified in the service life:

- Definition of the service offer to be provided by the company.
- Definition of the processes to be carried out inside this service offer
- Sale of a service contract
- Specification of the service to be provided to the customer as response to an event
- Planning and scheduling of the service

As the result of our work we propose a service model to answer the question *how can we define a generic service model that represents a "Service Family"?*.

Our proposal for the conceptual service model derives from that proposed in [5].

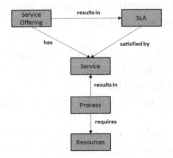

Fig. 3. Conceptual model proposed

In this model each one of the elements that appear in the figure 3 is defined as:

- *Service Offering*: framework offered by the company to the market (service family).
- *SLA (Service Level Agreement)*: represents the negotiated agreement between the customer and the service provider.
- *Service*: service element that can be offered by the company to a customer. This service element will be the results of a process.
- *Service Process*: Services are produced by processes. It represents the set of activities to be carried out to give a service to a customer.
- *Resource*: element needed to execute the process associated to a service. Resources can be material or human.

The service offering framework for a company represents the company offer to the market that can be customized to the customer needs. This customization of the service offered to a customer will be embodied in as a Service Level Agreement. It records a common understanding about services, priorities, responsibilities, guarantees, and warranties.

This service offering and its instances (SLA) is made up of elementary services.

Each elementary service will be characterized by several parameters. Every parameter will be constrained to a domain of values. In some cases and as a decision of the company, a parameter will have a fixed value that cannot be changed for the customer.

Each elementary service belongs or not to the service offering depending on a condition or rule.

Moreover, in the proposed model we can establish dependence relationships of different types between the services that take part of the service offering.

How the service can be seen depends on the point of view of the user. The point of view of the customer and the point of view of the company are not the same. Also from the company point of view there are differences between design and production.

From the customer point of view, the service will be defined by its different functions and options and by the list of parameters and value domain for each one.

On the other hand, form the company point of view the service will be defined by the processes, activities and resources needed to deliver the service.

According to this, each elementary service has been broken down into service modules (problems to be solved) and each one will be solved following different variants (service variant).

Each one of the defined service variants will have a process variant to be executed and also needs a resource to deliver the service variant. The set of process variants makes the whole process for the service.

Furthermore, each process variant will be made up of tasks that are broken down into activities.

Taking into account this model, the customization of a service entails the selection of the different service modules needed for the service and for each one of the modules, the selection of the service variant to be delivered to the customer. The sum of these selected variants will put together the service to be delivered.

6   Conclusion

As result of our research goal, we have answered the main research questions posed:

- **how can we define a generic "Service Family" model?;**
- **what are the different configuration moments in the service life cycle?.**

Answering the first question we have defined a service architecture that allows the model of services that can be customized to the customer needs and that takes into account the two aspects posed by the literature: service as an outcome and service as a process.

To answer the second question we have identified the different moments for the service configuration in the two different scenarios of the service: service without contract and service with contract.

These developments has been tested, during the 2012, in lab cases and later on will be tested in real cases of services.

As future work we are going to go deeply into the following:

- To adapt the configurator tool developed for the configuration of goods (physical products) to the configuration of service contracts.
- To develop new configurator tool for the configuration of the service processes to be executed by the service provider company, as answer to the event.

As result of this work, we have been able to apply this approach to a company leader in the Spanish lift sector, that provides maintenance services. In this scenario the maintenance service is a complex task for the company: the process depends on the lift; it changes with the year month and each maintenance worker must to carried out the maintenance of a big amount of lifts.

We have modeled the maintenance service and using a configurator tool, we have provided the maintenance worker with a tool that automatically creates the maintenance process to be carried out for each specific lift. That helps the worker in the execution of the maintenance service.

References

1. Ardissono, L., Felferling, A., Friedrich, G., Goy, A., Jannach, D., Schafer, R., Zanker, M.: A Framework for the Development of Personalized, Distributed Web-Based Configuration Systems. AI Magazine 24(3), 93–108 (2003)
2. Borenstein, D., Silveira, G., Fogliato, F.S.: Mass Customization: Literature review and research directions. International Journal of Production Economics (2001)
3. Fitzsimmons, J.A., Fitzsimmons, M.J.: Service Management – Operations, Strategy, and Information Technology, 4th International edn. McGraw-Hill (2004) ISBN 0-07- 121457-7
4. Goldstein, S.M., Johnston, R., Duffy, J.A., Rao, J.: The service concept: the missing link in service design research. Journal of Operations Management (2002)
5. Heiskala, M.: A conceptual model for modeling configurable services from a customer perspective, Master's Thesis, Helsinki University of Technology (2005)
6. Heiskala, M.: Modeling configurable services. Information and Comunication Technology Enabled Commerce, ICTEC (2007)
7. Jiao, J.: Design for Mass Customization by Developing Product Family Architecture, GMRG thesis (1998); Young, M.: The Techincal Writers Handbook. University Science, Mill (1989)
8. Jiao, J., Ma, Q., Tseng, M.M.: Towards high value-added products and services: mass customization and beyond. Technovation 23(10) (2003)
9. Johns, N.: What is this thing called service. European Journal of Marketing 33(9) (1999)
10. Junker, U., Mailharro, D.: Preference Programming: Advanced Problem Solving for Configuration. AI EDAM 17(1), 13–29 (2003)
11. Kotler, P.: Marketing management: analysis, planning implementation and control. Prentice Hall, London (1994)
12. Ma, Q., Tseng, M.M., Yen, B.: A generic model and design representation technique of service products. Technovation 22(1), 15–30 (2002)
13. Martines-tur, V., Peiro, J., Ramos, J.: Linking service structural complexity to customer satisfaction – The moderating role of type ownership. International Journal of Service Industry Management 12(3), 295–306 (2001)
14. Meyer, M.H., DeTorre, A.: PERSPECTIVE: Creating a platform-based approach for developing new services. The Journal of Product Innovation Management (2001)
15. Peters, I., Saidin, H.: IT and mass customization of services: the challenge of inplementation. International Journal of Information Management 20(2), 103–119 (2000)
16. Pine II, B.J.: Mass Customization: The New Frontier in Business Competition. Harvard School Business Press, Boston (1993)

Benefits and Risks in Dynamic Manufacturing Networks

Ourania Markaki, Panagiotis Kokkinakos, Dimitrios Panopoulos,
Sotirios Koussouris, and Dimitrios Askounis

Greek Interoperability Center, Decision Support Systems Laboratory, School of Electrical and
Computer Engineering, National Technical University of Athens, Greece
{omarkaki,pkokkinakos,dpano,skous,askous}@epu.ntua.gr

Abstract. More and more manufacturing enterprises realize that, by operating
as single enterprises in traditional supply chains, they cannot cope with the
challenges of the modern demanding environment, and that they need to adopt
new and innovative strategies in order to remain competitive. The establishment
of Dynamic Manufacturing Networks (DMNs) brings together various innovations, such as just-in-time delivery, flexible manufacturing, organizational
streamlining, and total quality, and emerges therefore as an advanced reaction
of collaborating enterprises to the constantly changing business environment
and its characteristics. This paper aims to expose the benefits and risks involved
in such networks, and create thereby the foundation for elaborating further on
the key factors that could be utilized for attracting organizations and enterprises
into embracing the vision of DMNs, supporting thus not only industrial organizations and practitioners interested in implementing such solutions, but also
scholars and researchers who study these new forms of business.

Keywords: Dynamic Manufacturing Network, DMN, Benefits, Risks.

1 Introduction

Survival and growth of enterprises in the intense competitive and innovation-driven
environment of the 21st century are beyond any doubt determined by their ability to
continuously improve their performance, skills and the complete set of operations,
both internally and externally. Today's manufacturing landscape is characterized by
dramatic and often unanticipated changes in demand, rapid change and increased use
of technology, short product lifecycles, time compression, complexity and fierce
global competition [1]. In this competitive environment, the manufacturing enterprise
must develop and implement new and innovative strategies in order to succeed.

In the light of remaining flexible and competitive, the manufacturing enterprise
witnessed during the last decades a progression of initiatives targeting the improvement of its operation. In the 1980s, many companies focused on Total Quality Management (TQM) [2]. Later, they implemented factory automation in various "islands"
on the factory floor and afterwards they focused on how to integrate these "islands of
automation" [3]. Flexibility became a key component, while agility took the former
concept one step further by embodying as well the ability to respond to unanticipated
change. The next step of improvement was to extend beyond the factory, to suppliers.

C. Emmanouilidis, M. Taisch, D. Kiritsis (Eds.): APMS 2012, Part II, IFIP AICT 398, pp. 438–445, 2013.
© IFIP International Federation for Information Processing 2013

Supply chain management has had a similar progression over the years in the interest of reducing costs, improving quality and shortening delivery cycles [4]. In the 1980s, improvements were focused on solving specific quality problems, and shifting inventory risk from the large company to the supplier base was the primary strategy applied during this period, while the early 1990s were characterized by cross-functional teams of primes and suppliers working to improve process capability and implement compatible systems interfaces with a limited contribution of suppliers' engineering knowledge to new product development.

Nowadays, competition and other pressing market situations, such as fluctuating demand or market saturation have greatly intensified to the point where manufacturing enterprises and supply chain initiatives must yield greater improvements than ever before. As indicated by the outcomes of recent business reports [5], large enterprises have yet exhausted most of the efficiencies available within their existing supply chain, so that further gains require structural changes that streamline the flow of supply and eliminate product and portfolio complexity that do not provide or protect value. These changes call for a dynamic and holistic approach that takes into consideration all aspects of the entire supply chain from a systems view [6].

An increasingly popular approach for enterprises striving to cope with the challenges of today's rapid changing and demanding environment has been the concept of "upgrading" their supply chains to Dynamic Manufacturing Networks (DMNs). The DMN concept evolves and particularizes the notion of virtual organizations [7] in the manufacturing sector, as it is a dynamic alliance of manufacturing entities collaborating for gaining mutual benefits [8-10]. Compared to a virtual organization however, a DMN is a real formation, though with loose ends and a quite flexible structure, which includes geographically dispersed OEMs and a pool of potential suppliers of various tiers. For an enterprise, participating in (or forming) a DMN can be considered as a systematic way for cultivating extended co-operation with other members of its supply chain, and calls for modifications in its modus operandi, while it necessitates the network's dynamic management [11-13], so as to enable real-time communication and active collaboration among the different network nodes.

This new modus operandi offers the enterprise a number of important benefits in the directions of enhancing manufacturing capacity and operational procedures, enlarging market share and improving viability and profits, but is also associated with a series of risks –the most important being related with information security and trust– which have to be identified and mitigated. In this context, this paper aims to present benefits and risks that accrue from the formation of DMNs under the prism of the end-to-end DMN management methodology, developed within the context of the IMAGINE FP7 project. The remaining of this paper is thus structured as follows: Section 2 introduces the concept of DMNs in IMAGINE, along with the key drivers for their establishment and outlines the respective DMN management methodology. Section 3 exposes the anticipated DMN benefits identified, while Section 4 provides insight on the associated risks and the respective mitigation strategies. Finally, Section 5 summarizes the ideas presented and concludes the work.

2   DMN Concept, Business Incentives and IMAGINE Methodology

The main idea behind DMNs is to achieve market differentiation through focusing on the core competencies and obtaining all other activities from outside, i.e. from other DMN members. The prospects of improving competitiveness, productivity and quality, enhancing efficiency and responsiveness to market demands, and exploring possibilities to lower overheads and costs are considered [14-15] as the most important driving forces for an enterprise to overcome its traditional operation and adopt a collaborative way of thinking and dealing with suppliers and partners, and are at the same time the benefits anticipated regardless of the scheme or scope of the DMN.

The term Dynamic Manufacturing Network denotes a permanent or temporal coalition, comprising production systems of geographically dispersed SMEs and/or OEMs that collaborate in a shared value-chain to conduct joint manufacturing [8]. Each member of the network produces one or more product components that can be assembled into final service-enhanced products under the control of a joint production schedule. Production schedules are monitored collectively to accomplish a shared manufacturing goal, while products are composed, (re-) configured and transformed on demand through dynamic and usually ad-hoc inter-organisational collaborations that can cope with evolving requirements and emergent behaviour.

From an operational point of view, this complex context of collaborations and interactions among enterprises and their suppliers, partners and customers is coordinated by a sophisticated IT platform and the respective DMN end-to-end management methodology [8]. The former revolves around the DMN lifecycle – comprising the DMN configuration, design, and monitoring and management phases - and is based on a Blueprint Model which gathers, consolidates and integrates manufacturing data and processes in order to develop actionable insights that help manage enterprise resources, product life cycles, supply chains, partner relationships, operational planning, manufacturing process execution, compliance regulations and safety issues for the DMN lifecycle, and thereby maximise the performance of participating enterprises. This model is a declarative meta-model that aggregates and modularises production, manufacturing operations and logistics information, distilled from Manufacturing Integration Standards, such as the ISA-88 and ISA-95 and the Open Applications Group Integration Specification (OAGIS), reference models such as the Supply Chain Operations Model (SCOR), and the Business-to-Manufacturing-Markup-Language (B2MML), and consists of four interrelated blueprints supporting information sharing, collaboration, enterprise-wide visibility and interoperability as follows:

- the Partner Blueprint, which provides business and technical information to facilitate partners' selection by a specific contractor,
- the Product Blueprint, containing all components necessary, such as machines, tools, personnel skills, materials, other equipment, for producing a product, as well as other entities necessary for the manufacturing work,
- the Quality Assurance Blueprint, used to capture metrics for operations analytics and associate these with the end-to-end manufacturing processes, and

- the end-to-end Process Blueprint, which ties together the many discrete processes associated with all aspects of product development while providing the ability to adapt to changing conditions and environments.

The idea of the DMN, as defined in the IMAGINE project along with the concept and applicability of the DMN management methodology and Blueprint Model are the keys for materialising a series of anticipated DMN benefits, which are presented in Section 3, and mitigating the associated risks, exposed in Section 4 of this paper.

3   Expected DMN Benefits

Every DMN, regardless of its size and formation, has the same closely defined mission which is to enhance the entire value creation process of products and services and consequently to create extra profit and other benefits for all DMN members. In the context of the IMAGINE methodology, the expected DMN benefits can be classified in three categories, namely *Time savings, Cost reduction* and *Enhancement of operations*: *Time savings* are mainly associated with the time-to-market reduction, the optimized design of end products and individual components, collaborative product development, the network-optimized production planning and scheduling, the fast selection of suppliers for each project/product and the corresponding rapid network set-up, the instant reconfiguration of the suppliers' network, the automated communication and data exchange with suppliers/clients and partners, as well as the increased visibility and access speed to information and network/manufacturing data. On the other hand, *cost savings* may include the cost-optimized selection of suppliers, the reduction of inventory costs, the cost-optimized management of resources, as well as the decrease of marketing expenses. The last category of benefits, concerned with *operations' enhancement* includes these kinds of gains that are associated with improvements in the way that each individual enterprise and consequently the whole network operate, and can be indirectly linked either to time/cost reductions or to profitability rise for the whole network. This type of benefits in fact enumerates: a clear focus on core competences, product/services co-creation, cost/risk sharing with collaborating partners, real-time monitoring of product development and manufacturing operations, reduction of design and production flaws, optimal selection of suppliers and collaborators, improved quality throughout the complete product lifecycle, know-how exchange, access to new customers/markets, and diverse enterprise IT systems' integration for better, holistic and more efficient production.

Despite the above-mentioned long list of benefits, the decision of joining a DMN is still an important one for any enterprise, since it is related to many changes not only to the way the enterprise collaborates with the external environment, but also to the way that almost all the internal processes are being performed. This is why such a decision should always be based on real estimations of the expected benefits, taking into consideration good practices and success results achieved in previous collaboration cases, as specified through an extensive literature review:

As far as cost savings are concerned, research [16-17] shows that in a typical manufacturing sector like automotive, amazingly only 30% of the cost of the final product has to do with "value activities". The other 70% are the costs and overheads of running a major manufacturer in its current form. The scope for cost savings through collaborating in a DMN is therefore huge.

Previous experience on networked manufacturing as presented in several studies proves moreover that if manufacturing networks run properly they can generate up to 30% additional profit per member after the initial settling in period [17-18]. As seen in Table 1, this has to do with an estimated reduction of up to 25% concerning total manufacturing and operational costs, as well as a maximum of 20% reduction concerning costs, incurred due to poor quality issues. Additionally, increased profitability is also linked with the expected rise of productivity in a well-established DMN that can reach up to 30%, according to cases examined in past studies [16]. Another important fact is that not only profits grow higher but also at the same time the financial exposure of partners may be decreased by 25%. In fact, the overall reduction of required investments by the DMN members, whether the former regard IT infrastructure, knowledge or machinery, is estimated at a maximum of 20% [19].

Furthermore, very good results are expected, by joining a DMN, on the product development operations. Previous applications of collaborative product development processes like those in DMNs have proved that a reduction of lead-time and cost up to 30% and 50% respectively are realistic goals which can be achieved [20].

Finally, a carefully established and well-managed DMN can lead to a very efficient operation of all of its members. This is proved not only by the financial results, previously presented, but also by the improvement on the values of several metrics related to the operation of each individual enterprise and of the supply chain as a whole.

Table 1. Expected Benefits following a DMN formation

Metric	Improvement up to
Total Profitability	⇑ 30%
Total operational & manufacturing cost	⇓ 25%
Cost due to quality issues	⇓ 20%
Total productivity	⇑ 30%
Financial exposure of partners	⇓ 25%
Required investments by partners	⇓ 20%
Product development lead time	⇓ 30%
Product development cost	⇓ 50%
Time for contractual formalization	⇓ 50%
Time-to-market	⇓ 25%
Manufacturing lead time	⇓ 20%
Co-operation processes efficiency	⇑ 30%
Product cycle times	⇓ 50%
Life cycle costs	⇓ 30%
Maintenance costs	⇓ 30%

According to the literature on virtual enterprises and manufacturing networks the following achievements can be expected: reduction of time required for co-operation contractual formalization up to 50% [21], reduction of time-to-market up to 25% [21], [22], reduction of lead time up to 20% [21], [23], improved efficiency of co-operation processes (manufacturing network design, re-configuration and re-engineering) up to 30% [21], decrease of product cycle times up to 50% [18], of life cycle costs up to 30% [22], and of maintenance costs up to 30% [18].

It has to be noted that the figures presented in this paragraph are mostly based on specific examples/cases analyzed in the literature and cannot be considered as reference values for all cases. However, they provide a direction with regard to the objectives that should be set and expected when establishing a Dynamic Manufacturing Network and a good starting point for quantifying the above-mentioned anticipated DMN benefits, which are to be assessed along the course of the IMAGINE project.

4   Potential DMN Risks

Inarguably, the introduction of any new innovation does not come without any risk for possible adopters. According to Hallikas et al. [24], functions that generate the possibility of beneficial effects or profit often include risks. The same applies for the idea of walking away from typical, long operating models of traditional supply chains and moving to new models of virtual factories and the DMN concept in particular. The risks that may be encountered in a DMN are in fact associated with:

Information Security and Trust. Information leaks due to unwanted and malicious attacks, and disclosure of corporate practices and other critical or strategic importance data can prove to be very harmful for an enterprise, and can be mitigated by applying efficient security and efficient mechanisms, that impede unauthorized access and define different access rights for different partners, as well by signing contractual agreements with special clauses on information confidentiality.

Poor Configuration, Design and Management of the Network. This makes up a risk which may come up as a result of the provision of non-valid, deficient or even outdated information for carrying out partner searches and negotiations in the first place, as well as for coordinating the complex grid of multiple and diverse actors, functions, processes and flows of information involved thereafter. This risk may prove to be fatal even for the network's survival and can be addressed by granting dynamic, and therefore accurate information on the actual manufacturing and delivery capacity of each DMN member, as well as global visibility across the whole network so as to constantly fine tune its performance.

DMN dissolution when key partner drops out of the network. Withdrawal of a key supplier/manufacturer could jeopardize the success of a project, resulting even in the network's dissolution. Thus, it should be foreseen as a risk in the contracts signed upon the establishment of the DMN, so as to legally bind DMN members not to be able to waive their DMN responsibilities and obligations at will.

Transition issues related to resistance to change, modifications to procedures and IT systems. The transition from an isolated to a collaborative manufacturing model is not easy and may be accompanied by modifications in the procedures followed and the systems used as well as the employees' resistance. This risk is addressed by introducing a set of adapters that interconnect the IT systems of all DMN members to the DMN platform, and facilitating the unhampered exchange of information, enabling thereby smooth transition for both processes and people.

Competitive threats after a partner's withdrawal or the dissolution of the DMN. The risk of important R&D knowledge misuse for gaining competitive advantage over former collaborators, in case a member exits the DMN or the former is dissolved, can be mitigated by signing legal agreements that explicitly define the use and exploitation of intellectual property and knowledge generated during the operation of the DMN.

Loss of DMN/ Partners' Reputation. A partner's inability to deliver as planned may affect the operation and damage the reputation of the overall DMN structure. Such a risk is to be mitigated pro-actively by allowing selection of the most appropriate partners as well as early detection of any deviation in the production plan, and triggering the network's reconfiguration with zero or minimal damage to the DMN reputation.

5   Concluding Remarks

The identification and analysis of the associated benefits and risks is the first step for identifying key factors that could be utilized in order to attract organizations and enterprises into embracing the vision of DMNs. In this context, and as a concluding remark, attention should be drawn to the fact that in most cases the drivers for setting up or for participating in a DMN are practically a mixture of several of the benefits identified, as well as to the observation that both the benefits and risks specified may have a different impact on DMN enterprises with different goals and expectations. This is something that should be taken into account when forming the DMN and setting the rules and norms for managing and operating it efficiently.

Acknowledgements. The research leading to these results has been supported by the EC 7th Framework Programme under the project "IMAGINE - Innovative end-to-end management of Dynamic Manufacturing Networks" Grant Agreement No. 285132, (http://www.imagine-futurefactory.eu).

References

1. Shi, Y., Gregory, M.: International Manufacturing Networks – to develop global competitive capabilities. Journal of Operations Management 16, 195–214 (1998)
2. Powell, T.C.: Total Quality Management as Competitive Advantage: A Review and Empirical Study. Strategic Management Journal 16, 15–37 (1995)
3. Davenport, T.: Putting the Enterprise into the Enterprise System. Harvard Business Review, 121–131 (1998)
4. Yoon, S.C., Makatsoris, H.C., Richards, H.D. (eds.): Evolution of Supply Chain Management: Symbiosis of Adaptive Value Networks and ICT. Springer (2004)

5. Payne, T.: Supply Chain Functional Excellence Key Initiative Overview. Gartner Inc. (2012)
6. Shi, Y.: A Roadmap of Manufacturing System Evolution-From Product Competitive Advantage towards Collaborative Value Creation. In: Yoon, S.C., Makatsoris, H.C., Richards, H.D. (eds.) Handbook Evolution of Supply Chain Management, pp. 341–365. Springer (2004)
7. Katzy, B.R., Schuh, G.: The Virtual Enterprise. In: Molina, A., Sánchez, J.M., Kusiak, A. (eds.) Handbook of Life Cycle Engineering: Concepts, Methods and Tools, pp. 59–92. Springer (1999)
8. IMAGINE Project: Innovative End-to-end Management of Dynamic Manufacturing Networks. Description of Work (2011), http://www.imagine-futurefactory.eu
9. Viswanadham, N.: Partner Selection and Synchronized Planning in Dynamic Manufacturing Networks. IEEE Transactions on Robotics and Automation 19(1), 117–130 (2003)
10. Papakostas, N., Efthymiou, K., Georgoulias, K., Chryssolouris, G.: On the Configuration and Planning of Dynamic Manufacturing Networks. Logistics Research Journal, 1–7 (2012)
11. Accenture: Developing Dynamic and Efficient Operations for Profitable Growth - Research Findings from North American Manufacturers (2012)
12. Williams, G.P.: Dynamic Order Allocation for Make-to-order Manufacturing Networks: An Industrial Case Study of Optimization under Uncertainty. Massachusetts Institute of Technology (2011)
13. University of St. Gallen: Global Manufacturing Networks (2012)
14. Cunha, M.M., Putnik, G.: Agile Virtual Enterprises: Implementation and Management Support. Idea Group Inc. (IGI) (2006)
15. Cueni, T., Seiz, M.: Virtual Organizations - the next Economic Revolution? Swiss Federal Institute of Technology, Lausanne, EPFL (1999)
16. Chalmeta, R., Grangel, R.: Performance Measurement Systems for Virtual Enterprise Integration. Int. J. Computer Integrated Manufacturing 18(1), 73–84 (2005)
17. Thompson, K.: Achieve Supply Chain Agility through Virtual Enterprise Networks. Case Studies in Collaboration (2005), http://www.bioteams.com (retrieved January 04, 2012)
18. Landeg, B., Ash, S.: Implementation of Airbus Concurrent Engineering. In: 85th AGARD SMP Meeting on "Virtual Manufacturing", Aalborg (1997)
19. Thompson, K.: A kick-start plan for setting up a Virtual Enterprise Network in 6 weeks. Case Studies in Collaboration (2005), http://www.bioteams.com (retrieved January 04, 2012)
20. Karlsson, L., Löfstrand, M., Larsson, A., Törlind, P., Larsson, T., Elfström, B.O., Isaksson, O.: Information driven Collaborative Engineering: Enabling Functional Product Innovation. In: 3rd International Workshop on Challenges in Collaborative Engineering, CCE 2005, Sopron (2005)
21. Santoro, R., Conte, M.: Evaluation of Benefits and Advantages of the Virtual Enterprise approach adoption for Actual Business Cases. In: 8th International Conference on Concurrent Enterprising, Rome (2002)
22. Renton, W.J., Rudnick, F.C., Brown, R.G.: Virtual Manufacturing Technology Implementation at Boeing. In: 85th AGARD SMP Meeting on "Virtual Manufacturing", Aalborg (1997)
23. Kingsbury, A.: Use of Virtual Prototyping in Design and Manufacturing. In: 85th AGARD SMP Meeting on "Virtual Manufacturing", Aalborg (1997)
24. Hallikas, J., Karvonen, I., Pulkkinen, U., Virolainen, V.M., Tuominen, M.: Risk Management Processes in Supplier Networks. Int. J. Production Economics 90, 47–58 (2004)

Dynamic Manufacturing Networks Monitoring and Governance

Panagiotis Kokkinakos, Ourania Markaki, Dimitrios Panopoulos,
Sotirios Koussouris, and Dimitrios Askounis

Greek Interoperability Center, Decision Support Systems Laboratory, School of Electrical and
Computer Engineering, National Technical University of Athens, Greece
{pkokkinakos,omarkaki,dpano,skous,askous}@epu.ntua.gr

Abstract. "Monitoring and Governance" is the most important phase of every
Dynamic Manufacturing Network (DMN) lifecycle and aims at managing and
controlling in a continuous way the operations of the network, resulting either
in "small and corrective" actions towards the network's operation optimisation
or to "larger and structural" changes, which are fed back to the initial phases of
the network's lifecycle, for reconstructing the network towards better results.
The study at hand aims to review current approaches for controlling and monitoring plant operation or traditional supply chains, and to examine thereby their
maturity and adequacy for the management and monitoring of dynamic manufacturing networks, leading to useful conclusions with regard to the requirements and challenges encountered in this particular phase of the DMN lifecycle.

Keywords: Manufacturing Network, Operations Management, Monitoring,
Governance, Dynamic Manufacturing Network, DMN.

1   Introduction

Trying to adapt to the given and ongoing global economic crisis, the indus-
trial/manufacturing sector pursues to minimize costs and, at the same time, to increase
the effectiveness of external and internal procedures, as well as the customers' satisfaction through high quality products/services. The formation of Dynamic Manufacturing Networks (DMNs, which elsewhere and depending on the context, might also
be referred as Virtual Enterprises) [2] is the natural evolution of typical supply chains
that aim to respond to these challenges. DMN is a newly introduced term, coined to
express the establishment of dynamic alliances among manufacturing companies in
the direction of virtual enterprises for gaining mutual benefits. DMNs constitute a
demand-driven (yet long-lasting) formation of enterprises for a certain purpose [1].
For this purpose, the interconnection and effective communication among the various
systems of every participating enterprise is considered a precondition. This communication is not limited to systems serving the same goal (e.g. ERP systems), but includes
shop floor production systems, as well as top-level management systems. The general
rationale behind forming such networks is to reduce both costs and time to market,

C. Emmanouilidis, M. Taisch, D. Kiritsis (Eds.): APMS 2012, Part II, IFIP AICT 398, pp. 446–453, 2013.
© IFIP International Federation for Information Processing 2013

while increasing flexibility, gaining access to new markets and resources, and utilizing collective intelligence on methodologies and procedures. The notion of a DMN includes the configuration of a network consisting of a large number of closely integrated and interdependent projects, which are executed over a wide geographic spread, across different time zones, and involve large numbers of staff. As it is understandable, this whole process, apart from being very difficult to be performed, affects also a wide range of stakeholders whether they are members of the network or not.

Although research has delivered a lot of methodologies for controlling plant operation and for monitoring production systems' effectiveness, there are no mature methodologies and tools fully appropriate for managing and monitoring DMNs. Today, various platforms exist (e.g. Transportation Management Systems, Material Resource Planning, Warehouse Management Systems), but as Westphal et al. note [3], there is a lack of approaches and tools specifically developed for dynamic networks that consist of distributed, independent, and heterogeneous members. Current approaches cannot deliver acceptable results without strong modifications and one has to investigate to what extent they can meet the different requirements set by such dynamic alliances.

DMN Monitoring and Governance can be split in the following four sub-phases:

- Real Time Data Collection and Network Monitoring.
- Operational Level DMN Governance.
- Network Performance Measurement and KPIs Monitoring.
- Network Performance Evaluation and DMN Reformation.

The focus of this study primarily lies on the definition of appropriate methods and ICT tools supporting the efficient Monitoring and Governance of Dynamic Manufacturing Networks. The four aforementioned sub-stages are discussed and analyzed, while conclusions are drawn with respect to the whole DMN process.

2 Real Time Data Collection and Network Monitoring

Industries and manufacturing organizations in general constantly face the challenge of organizing, checking and monitoring their activities. Especially nowadays, where saving time and reacting as fast as possible to emergencies and changes of demand constitute vital parameters to such kind of organizations, enterprise network monitoring is becoming of outmost importance. Its main task is to support avoiding severe economic losses resulting from unexpected process failures by improving the network's reliability and maintainability [20].

Monitoring an event-driven [11] and complicated system, such as an enterprise or an industrial network, is based on real time collection, exchange and processing of information. It can be taken as granted that the processing speed, as well as the great volume of data, constitute barriers towards an effective and stable solution. However, the advances in network technology and data collection, storage and processing in the dispersed manufacturing approach and the flexible and powerful virtual enterprise approach are rapidly emerging [14]. Processes take place in several locations and new business opportunities can rise, both for suppliers and producers. Similar approaches can be met as performance measurement and performance management [25].

In order to overcome interoperability and data exchange problems, that are highly possible to come up in such complex procedures, a number of standards such as Product Data Exchange Specification (PDES), Standard for Exchange of Product (STEP) and Initial Graphic Exchange Specification (IGES) have been established.

The architecture of a virtual enterprise network basically consists of three layers: the network/platform layer, the service layer and the application layer. At the network level, the architecture defines the data formats and communication protocols that enable clients to exchange information and services. The service layer is a middle layer of reusable building blocks and runtime services that facilitate the development and use of end-user applications. Network security is incorporated in the design. The application layer includes information searching, collaborative engineering such as co-design, co-prototyping, and electronic commerce.

Numerous technologies and approaches have been recognized in order to support the aforementioned structure. Complex event processing (CEP), the agent-based models approach [15], Sequential Probability Ratio Test (SPRT) [22], artificial neural networks (ANNs) [21] constitute well-known and widespread alternatives.

3   Operational Level DMN Governance

This sub phase deals with the processing of the data retrieved during the monitoring phase and the decisions that should be taken and communicated in the responsible network points for easing out any abnormalities identified. As such, the main tasks performed in this phase deal with issues resolution, communication of the necessary actions to the DMN network nodes and coordination of the overall network in order to bounce back into an effective and productive state.

As noted by Douglas and Padula [5], *"governance refers to the set of rules, restrictions, incentives and mechanisms applied to coordinate the participants in an organization"*, while Theurl [24] calls it *micro-governance* and notes that, under rules, one must include procedures for cooperation, management, decision making, conflict resolution and ways to adapt the operation. Operational Level DMN governance implies the need of control and management actions in real time, which requires the appropriate mechanisms for collecting and analyzing the data from the different nodes in real time (or close to real time).

According to [1], a common mistake performed is the perception that there is direct relation of the behavior and the management activities of virtual organizations to these single organizations. Sydow [23] argues that the management of an inter-organizational network implies significant changes to the functions and management practices, compared with those used in hierarchical organizations and corporations. The possibility to optimize the coordination of the value network is better in the single-organization environment, whereas multi-organization environments focus on collaboration and feasible, but not optimal, ways to coordinate the network [19]. Based on the same study, the possibility to effectively manage a value network is also dependent on the quality of the available information, and ICT is playing a very important role in this direction, trying to bring the various systems together.

Although many propositions have been made in order to address the network complexity [8], [16], probably the most important interoperability constraint faced today deals with the inability of systems to directly use these standards and build touch points for interacting directly with the other systems. This need is addressed by the introduction of the Enterprise Service Bus (ESB) concept, which is a software architecture model used for interconnecting different software applications in a Service Oriented Architecture [3]. A well-designed ESB for manufacturing applications would be able to bring together the PLM and ERP capabilities of systems, thus allowing governing the network. Adapter modules are responsible for providing a layer of abstraction between the servers and the component business or manufacturing systems (nodes) in the ESB, e.g., ERP, cPLM, product data and workflow systems. To promote interoperability, execution in this type of architecture occurs among component system adapters within the ESB. The component adapters facilitate point integration of component systems by adapting legacy systems and applications and other back-end resources such as databases, ERP, MES (Manufacturing Execution Systems), and PLM, to the ESB so that they can express data and messages in the standard internal format expected by the ESB.

4   Network Performance Measurement and KPIs Monitoring

This sub-phase includes measurement of the performance of the DMN by taking into consideration specific methodologies, directives and indicators for measuring and evaluating the effectiveness of the network, not only in operational but also in conceptual and strategic level. The most important business processes are – in general – those related to Production procedures, Supply Chain operations, Human and Physical Resources management, Product Development, Sales and Financial Management.

Generally, the challenge in network performance measurement is the necessity to transfer highly complex real-world processes to a simplifying processes model, to derive performance information from the model, and to transfer these results back to the real world [6]. The drawback of the several "traditional" approaches in performance measurement (e.g. Benchmarking, Six Sigma, EFQM, SCOR) is their orientation to single processes or functions, focusing on few certain perspectives, so they are not so appropriate for evaluation in strategic level. In all the recent studies [25], [7], [12], [4], [10], [18] several aspects of collaboration performance and potential performance indicators can be identified. Selected sets of KPIs measuring flexibility, reliability, and prompt-ness/speed are taken as defined in traditional approaches (SCOR, BSC). Westphal et al. [26] goes a step further and proposes a generic structure that organises the different aspects, while it also supports the integration of collaboration performance in existing performance measurement approaches.

In any case, it is obvious that measurement and monitoring of "combined" KPIs is the key for evaluating a DMN's performance and taking strategic decisions for altering the network's structure and/or operation. Ibis Associates [9] also provide a set of the most commonly used KPIs in manufacturing and engineering enterprises.

5   Network Performance Evaluation and DMN Reformation

"Network Performance Evaluation" includes the analysis and evaluation of the latter towards deciding on whether a reconfiguration of the network is necessary in order to maximize the anticipated results (e.g. risk/opportunity assessment, optimization of the DMN organizational structure, evaluation of the DMN management approach, inheritance management etc.). Contrary to the "Real Time Data Collection" and the "Network Performance Monitoring" sub-phases, "Network Performance Evaluation" involves considerably the human aspect and relies to a large extent on management experiences previously acquired.

The reconfiguration of the network's organizational structure is possible and justifiable as a result of the fluidity and changing nature of a DMN and should be performed in the light of optimizing the network structure and enabling better accomplishment of its objectives. The type of the DMN organizational structure is interdependent to the DMN management approach, discussed in the following paragraph, while it should also basically determine the framework for knowledge management.

As already outlined, "Monitoring and Governance" is the last phase of the DMN lifecycle, which aims at monitoring and controlling the operation of the network in a continuous way, resulting either in "small and corrective" decisions towards the network's operation optimization or to "larger and structural" changes, which are fed back to the DMN "Network Configuration" phase. Despite the fact that the nature of a DMN is prone to change and evolution, such a network is practically a strategic alliance among enterprises that poses a great deal of advantages for its members, so that it is in their best interest to maintain its operation. Yet, although less likely to occur, one of the possible stages in the DMN lifecycle is the DMN dissolution.

In the unusual event of DMN dissolution, there is a need to plan the transfer of the knowledge collected within the DMN to its members or another entity based on defined agreements. Such knowledge may include devised practices, developed products and processes, warranties, Intellectual Property Rights, knowledge about customers and markets, working and sharing principles, partners' performances, performance metrics, and other information possibly important for future activities [1]. In this case it is necessary to process the information first to obtain an utilizable format instead of transferring all available raw data. As far as network performance metrics and KPIs are concerned, typical processing includes among others the calculation of means, maximum and minimum values as well as standard deviations. The number of measured values and the target values improve the picture. The DMN inheritance management is intended to support future endeavors of the DMN partners in terms of [2]:

- improving their preparedness and thus supporting the faster creation of DMNs;
- making DMNs more effective and reliable in terms of both time and costs and improving or ensuring quality;
- decreasing DMN management efforts through increased trust and strengthened relationships;
- supporting decision-making and tracking of DMN problems or deviations;
- enabling higher chances of success in competitive bidding, because of customer knowledge and closer customer relationships.

6   The IMAGINE Project Approach

IMAGINE[1] is an R&D project, funded by the European Commission under the "Virtual Factories and Enterprises" theme of the 7th Framework Programme. The project targets the development and delivery of a novel comprehensive methodology and the respective platform for effective end-to-end management of DMNs in an innovative plug and produce approach, and aims at supporting the emergence of a powerful new production model, based on community, collaboration, self-organization and openness rather than on hierarchy and centralized control.

The DMN lifecycle, as defined by IMAGINE, is structured as an iterative closed-loop, network manager assisted methodology that enables automation of repetitive steps, while retaining the flexibility to allow product variants, value adding network re-configurations, and end-to-end processes customizations. The IMAGINE framework relies on end-to-end integrated ICT solutions that effectively enable the management of networked manufacturing supply chains. The IMAGINE solution is market-oriented with focus on value chain streamlining and support for innovative business models. Processes are streamlined looking for the flexibility to adapt to take advantage of the unique capabilities inherent at each individual company, and to adapt easily to changing circumstances and emerging markets.

The three major phases that constitute the IMAGINE Lifecycle are: i) Network Analysis and Configuration that deals with the formation of the DMN upon the receipt of a new order and the validation of its capability to carry out the necessary production ii) Network Design, which focuses on modelling and developing the coordination plan of the various manufacturing processes, and finally iii) Network Execution Management and Monitoring. Network Execution Management and Monitoring aims to include process and production tracking, performance analysis (based mainly on carefully selected KPIs), labour management, resource availability management, movement, storage and tracking of materials, as well as repair adaptation and tuning – leading eventually to Network refinement and improvement.

The DMN collaboration platform of IMAGINE will provide the technical backbone to support the proposed life cycle and integrate virtually all the aspects of the virtual manufacturing network and processes.

7   Conclusions

As presented in the document at hand, according to current approaches, three consequent key phases are considered in the lifecycle of a DMN: a) Network Configuration, b) Network Design, and c) Network Monitoring and Governance. The present study focused on the last phase which is the most crucial for the operation and the sustainability of the network. It can be taken for granted that, no matter how efficient and effective a Dynamic Manufacturing Network can be, the monitoring and governance of such a multi-disciplinary formation is a real challenge, as poor performance in

---

[1] http://www.imagine-futurefactory.eu

management and monitoring could easily cost huge amounts of money and time, while it could even result in the collapse of the network.

As stated above, the last phase of the DMN lifecycle claims the responsibility for monitoring and governing end-to-end process performance and detecting events that may affect the execution of the manufacturing operations. Analyzing process efficiency and effectiveness and aligning processes with enterprise goals and objectives involves reacting to critical business events, correlating event data and updating the, during the Network Design phase defined, key performance indicators (KPIs).

The IMAGINE Project proposes a novel, integrated solution-focused manufacturing environment that involves global supply chain management, product-service linkage and management of distributed manufacturing assets. It enables companies to improve visibility and optimize supply network performance by connecting key people, processes and information across the production lifecycle into a collaborative manufacturing environment, while providing continual refinement and improvement of end-to-end processes through the constant measurement, evaluation and improvement of processes and resource consumption patterns.

Acknowledgements. The research leading to these results has been supported by the EC 7th Framework Programme under the project "IMAGINE - Innovative end-to-end management of Dynamic Manufacturing Networks" Grant Agreement No. 285132.

References

1. Camarinha-Matos, L.M., Afsarmanesh, H., Ollus, M.: ECOLEAD: A Holistic Approach To Creation And Management Of Dynamic Virtual Organizations. In: Camarinha-Matos, L.M., Afsarmanesh, H., Ortiz, A. (eds.) Collaborative Networks and Their Breeding Environments. IFIP, vol. 186, pp. 3–16. Springer, US (2005)
2. Camarinha-Matos, L.M., Afsarmanesh, H., Ollus, M.: ECOLEAD and CNO base concepts. In: Camarinha-Matos, L.M., Afsarmanesh, H., Ollus, M. (eds.) Methods and Tools for Collaborative Networked Organizations, vol. VIII, pp. 3–32. Springer (2008)
3. Chappell, D.: Enterprise Service Bus. O'Reilly Media (2004)
4. Colotla, I., Shi, Y., Gregory, M.J.: Operation and Performance of International Manufacturing Networks. International Journal of Operations and Production Management 23(10), 1185–1206 (2003)
5. Douglas, W., Padula, A.: Governance and Management of Horizontal Business Networks: An Analysis of Retail Networks in Germany. International Journal of Business and Management 5(12) (December 2010)
6. Eschenbaecher, J., Seifert, M.: Predictive Performance Measurement in Virtual Organisations. In: Camarinha-Matos, L.M. (ed.) Emerging Solutions for Future Manufacturing Systems. IFIP, vol. 159, pp. 299–307. Springer, New York (2005)
7. Graser, F., Jansson, K., Eschenbächer, J., Westphal, I., Negretto, U.: Towards performance measurement in virtual organizations – potentials, needs and research challenges. In: Camarinha-Matos, L.M., Afsarmanesh, H., Ortiz, A. (eds.) Collaborative Networks and their Breeding Environments. IFIP, vol. 186, pp. 301–310. Springer, New York (2005)
8. Hill, T.: Manufacturing strategy: Text and cases, 2nd edn. Palgrave, Hampshire (2000)
9. Ibis Associates, Key Performance Indicators (2011), http://www.ibisassoc.co.uk (accessed November 12, 2011)

10. Jähn, H.: Value-added process-related performance analysis of enterprises acting in cooperative production structures. Production Planning and Control 20(2), 178–190 (2009)

11. KAP, Deliverable 5.1 - Requirements and State-of-the-art for Monitoring, Analysis and Mining of Event Streams (2011), http://kap-project.eu/fileadmin/KAP/user_upload/ Deliverables/D5.1.pdf (accessed November 12, 2011)

12. Kaplan, R., Norton, D.: Balanced Scorecard, Boston (1996)

13. Katzy, B., Schuh, G.: The Virtual Enterprise. In: Molina, A., Sanchez, J., Kusiak, A. (eds.) Handbook of Life Cycle Engineering: Concepts, Methods and Tools, pp. 59–92. Kluwer Academic Publishers (1998)

14. Lau, H.C.W., Wong, E.T.T.: Partner Selection and Information Infrastructure of a Virtual Enterprise Network. International Journal of Computer Integrated Manufacturing 14(2), 186–193 (2010)

15. Gou, H., Huang, B., Liu, W., Li, X.: A Framework for Virtual Enterprise Operation Management. Computers in Industry 50(3), 333–352 (2003)

16. Olhager, J., Rudberg, M.: Linking manufacturing strategy decisions on process choice with manufacturing planning and control systems. International Journal of Production Research 40(10), 2335–2352 (2002)

17. Putnik, G., Cruz-Cunha, M.M., Sousa, R., Avila, P.: Virtual Enterprise Integration: Challenges of a New Paradigm. In: Putnik, G.D., Cruz-Cunha, M.M. (eds.) Virtual Enterprise Integration: Technological and Organizational Perspectives, pp. 1–30. Idea Group Inc. (2005)

18. Romero, D., Molina, A.: VO breeding environments & virtual organizations integral business process management framework. Information Systems Frontiers 11(5), 569–597 (2009)

19. Rudberg, M., Olhager, J.: Manufacturing Networks And Supply Chains: An Operations Strategy Perspective. Omega 31, 29–39 (2003)

20. Salvadori, F., de Campos, M., Sausen, P.S., de Camargo, R.F., Gehrke, C., Rech, C., Spohn, M.A., Oliveira, A.C.: Monitoring in Industrial Systems Using Wireless Sensor Network With Dynamic Power Management. IEEE Transactions on Instrumentation and Measurement 58(9), 3104–3111 (2009)

21. Sari, B., Amaitik, S., Kilic, S.E.: A Neural Network Model for the Assessment of Partners Performance in Virtual Enterprises. The International Journal of Advanced Manufacturing Technology 34(7-8), 816–825 (2006)

22. Singer, R.M., Gross, K.C., King, R.W.: Applications of pattern recognition techniques to online fault detection. In: Probabilistic Safety Assessment and Management Conference (PSAM), San Diego, CA (1993)

23. Sydow, J.: Management von Netzwerkorganisationen: Zum Stand der Forschung. In: Sydow, J. (ed.) Management von Netzwerkorganisationen, pp. 387–472. Gabler, Wiesbaden (2006)

24. Theurl, T.: From corporate to cooperative governance. In: Theurl, T. (ed.) Economics of Interfirm Networks, pp. 149–192. Mohr Siebeck, Tübingen (2005)

25. Westphal, I., Mulder, W., Seifert, M.: Supervision of Collaborative Processes in VOs. In: Camarinha-Matos, L.M., Afsarmanesh, H. (eds.) Methods and Tools for Collaborative Networked Organizations, pp. 239–256. Springer, Boston (2008)

26. Westphal, I., Thoben, K.D., Seifert, M.: Managing collaboration performance to govern virtual organizations. Journal of Intelligent Manufacturing 21(3), 311–320 (2010)

The Insignificant Role of National Culture in Global Lean Programmes

Torbjørn H. Netland[1,2], Miguel Mediavilla[3], and Ander Errasti[4]

[1] NTNU, Trondheim, Norway
[2] Georgetown University, Washington DC, USA
[3] BSH Gmbh, Munich, Germany
[4] University of Navarra, San Sebastián, Spain
torbjorn.netland@iot.ntnu.no

Abstract. Large corporations are increasingly implementing lasting corporate improvement programmes based on lean thinking in their global production networks. The aim is to improve operational efficiency by sharing best operational practices and foster continuous improvement among all subsidiaries. However, it remains an open question why implementation success differs substantially across cultures and sister plants for most companies. We review the existing literature on improvement programmes and culture, and compare the current state of the art with unique quantitative data from 80 factories belonging to two global manufacturing companies. We surprisingly find no explanatory power in national culture (measured with Hofstede's model) and propose that other factors such as the organisational culture and the strategic role of the plant matters far more.

Keywords: Company-specific Production Systems, National Culture, Organisational Culture, Global Production, Lean.

1 Introduction

In order to improve the efficiency and effectiveness of operations worldwide, companies have increasingly embarked on corporate-wide improvement programmes. Inspired by the great success of Toyota's global deployment of the Toyota Production System (TPS), companies have developed company-specific variants of the TPS [1]. However, success does not come free of challenges. A particular challenge for multinational companies is to implement the same type of thinking with its methods and tools in a diverse world of different needs, cultures and beliefs.

According to Hofstede and Hofstede [2] national culture is the "collective programming of the mind" that make one nation distinctive different from another. Such national cultures are extremely hard to change because they are institutionalised in the societies. There is much research that investigate the impact of national culture on different improvement programmes [e.g. 3, 4, 5], but our literature review shows that the current research is largely inconclusive in which specific cultures are favourable for the programme implementation. We also find that there is abundance of research that

C. Emmanouilidis, M. Taisch, D. Kiritsis (Eds.): APMS 2012, Part II, IFIP AICT 398, pp. 454–462, 2013.

use perception-based surveys to empirically investigate the link between Hofstede's five cultural dimensions and process improvement, but real-life case studies that make use of factual performance data are rare or absent in the current literature.

We contribute to literature and practice by—once again—investigating the role of national culture in improvement programme efforts. First we want to investigate if the usual assumption that Hofstede's 5D model can explain performance differences is waterproof. We therefore ask: *Do Hofstede's cultural dimensions explain differences in XPS implementation?* (RQ1). We investigate these two questions empirically through real-life case studies, where we make use of rare and original data to test and explore the findings in previous studies.

We acknowledge that other factors can either triumph disadvantages in national cultures or impede favourable national cultures, and we therefore include a second research question: *What other factors are likely to explain differences in XPS implementation?* (RQ2). This second research question is subject to discussion in our post-hoc analysis.

2   Literature Review

An XPS follows the belief that there are "best practices" that are applicable in all nations [6]. But because cultures differ, practices are likely to differ across cultures. Therefore, many authors argue that a *contingency approach* is needed , where a good *fit* between the context and adapted practices is needed for good performance. Thus, the local culture in which the subsidiary operates influences the receptiveness of the XPS, and hence its implementation success. It is suggested that some cultures have more favourable traits for improvement programmes than others [7]. The question arises: Which cultures are better for the implementation of an XPS?

This question has been abundantly investigated in operations management research. Popular approaches in this research is to operationalise national culture based on Hofstede's [8, 9] well-defined and much used types of culture attributes [3, 5, 7, 10, 11], or the extension known as the GLOBE-framework [4, 12, 13]. In his seminal study of 116.000 employees in IBM in 50 countries from 1967-1973, Hofstede [9] suggested four cultural dimensions: High versus low power distance, individualism versus collectivism, high versus low uncertainty avoidance, and masculinity versus femininity. Later he added long-term versus short-term orientation as a fifth and final dimension. These five culture types are summarised in Table 1.

Table 1. Hofstede's 5 dimensions for national culture

Dimension	Description (Source: http://geert-hofstede.com)
Power distance (PDI)	The extent to which the less powerful members of institutions and organisations within a country accept that power is distributed unequally.
Individualism (IDI)	In Individualist societies people look after themselves while in Collectivist-societies people belong to "in-groups" that care for them.
Masculinity (MAS)	The fundamental issue is what motivates people; wanting to be the best (masculine society) or liking what you do (feminine society).
Uncertainty avoidance (UAI)	The extent to which the members of a culture have created beliefs and institutions that try to avoid risks and uncertainty.
Long-term orientation (LTO)	The extent to which a society shows a pragmatic future-oriented perspective rather than a conventional historical short-term point of view.

We reviewed the literature that investigates the effect of cultural dimensions on improvement programmes using Hofstede's 5D model or the same dimensions collected from the GLOBE framework. The review is summarised in Table 2.

Table 2. Review of the effect of cultural dimensions on improvement programmes

Paper	Data*	Programme	Culture	# Countries	# Plants	PDI	IDI	MAS	UAI	LTO
Wiengarten et al. [10]	GMRG survey	Quality practices	Hofstede 4D	15	960	0	-	-	-	ni
Cagliano et al. [11]	IMSS survey	Work org	Hofstede 4D	21	660	-	+/-	-	-	ni
Flynn & Saladin [10]	WCM survey	Baldrige Quality Award	Hofstede 4D	5	164	+	-	+	+	ni
Lagrosen [3]	Survey 1 MNC	TQM	Hofstede 4D	30	47	ns	+/-	ns	-	ni
Power et al. [14]	GMRG survey	Quality, lean, TQM etc.	Individualist vs collectiv.	9	639	ni	-	ni	ni	ni
Galperin & Lituchy [15]	Case study	TQM	Individualist vs collectivist	2	10	ni	-	ni	ni	ni
Kull & Wacker [6]	GMRG survey	Quality practices	GLOBE	3	222	0	ni/0	ni	+	0
Naor et al. [16]	HPM survey	Cost/quality/deli very/flexibility	GLOBE	6	189	-	-	ni	+	+
Vecchi & Brennan [15]	IMSS survey	Quality practices	GLOBE	24	711	+	+/-	-	-	-
				Σ		?	-	?	?	0

* *GMRG = Global Manufacturing Research Group | IMSS = International Manufacturing Strategy Survey | WCM = World Class Manufacturing Project | HPM = High Performance Manufacturing Project.*
+ / - / 0: The impact of the cultural dimension on implementation performance: ni= Not investigated | ns= No significance.

There is mixed evidence for four out of the five cultural dimensions in the literature. The research to date suggests that the only dimension that for sure increases implementation of quality practices is low individualism, also referred to as a collectivist culture. The studies that use the GLOBE framework instead of Hofstede's model find that this picture should be nuanced: First, Kull and Wacker [4] found that *institutional* collectivism has no specific affect on implementation and argue the same for *in-group* collectivism. Second, Vecchi and Brennan [12] found that in-group collectivism do positively affect implementation while the opposite effect is found for institutional collectivism. Third, Naor et al. [13] find that both types of collectivism weakly but positively influence performance. Thus, the only thing we can say for sure across these studies is that *in-group collectivism seems to positively influence improvement programme implementation*. Several authors find that the coexistence of several cultural dimensions however substantially mediates the effect of collectivism. These studies find that different cultures have different strengths and weakness when it comes to implementing global lean programmes and suggest that there is not one unique culture type that fits perfect [16]. The conclusion from our review must be that there is great confusion in literature on if and how the different cultural dimensions affect the implementation of improvement programmes with the notable exception of in-group individualism.

3   Methodology

To investigate the role of national culture on XPS implementation we chose an explorative multiple-case approach [17]. Data and experiences from 80 plants belonging to two global players in different industries are utilised. In particular we build on quantitative assessment data that are collected throughout the two case companies in a rigid and standardised way. In our post-hoc analysis we also take advantage of our visits to most of the plants in the sample.

3.1   Case Companies

Company A is a worldwide operating appliances corporation and is headquartered in Germany. The company has over 40 factories operating in Europe, the USA, Latin America and Asia, and employing approx. 40,000 people. Company A's XPS has been implemented in 34 plants in 7 countries since the beginning of 2007. The assessment data for company A have been collected through on-site audits based on a standardised questionnaire.

Company B is a major player in the transportation industry and is headquartered in Sweden. It has more than 60 plants all over the world. Company B's XPS has been implemented in more than 50 plants since 2007. The maturity assessment data for company B have also been collected through on-site reviews based on a standardised questionnaire.

3.2   Operationalisation of the Variables

Case A and B have provided the authors with original XPS assessment data. This data is based on structured and thorough assessments of the implementation of XPS in the companies. The assessments are carried out by trained assessors that follow standard assessment schemes over several days. For each plant in the sample, a score summarises how much the plant has implemented lean methods and tools. Even if the content is basically similar and largely resembles that of lean thinking, the XPS scoring process is different between the companies. We therefore normalised the data across the cases using z-scores. The sample covers 23 countries. Figure 1 summarises the XPS implementation z-scores for the countries included in our sample.

We controlled for differences between the MNCs by analysing the countries that are part of both samples (9 plants in US, 9 in Germany, 6 in France, 8 in China, and 4 in Poland). We found a very good fit between the datasets for these countries, which justifies discussing the two datasets as one. As a consequence we merged the results for the same countries from both MNCs into one z-score using the simple mean of the two z-scores.

To operationalise the national culture, we use Hofstede's 5D indexes [e.g. 2, 10]. This index comes with pre-defined and tested measures for most countries in the world. These scores are publicly available through the web-page http://geert-hofstede.com.

458   T.H. Netland, M. Mediavilla, and A. Errasti

z-scores XPS implementation

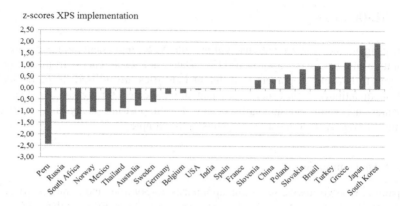

Fig. 1. Z-scores for XPS implementation across the 23 countries in the sample

4   Discussion

4.1   Do Hofstede's Cultural Dimensions Explain Differences in XPS Score?

The correlation analysis given in Table 3 finds no significant correlation between Hofstede's five cultural dimensions and XPS implementation. The only dimension that is significant at a 10 % level is long-term orientation which positively influences implementation.

Table 3. Correlations between z-scores and Hofstede's 5D model

Indep. variable*	PDI	IDI	MAS	UAI	LTO
Pearson's r	.131	-.155	.313	.251	.463
Significance	.552	.480	.145	.248	.071
N	23	23	23	23	16

Correlations with dependent variable XPS implementation z-scores.

In support of the finding that national culture seems not to explain too much, we also find quite large difference between plants in some of the countries. This is particular true for countries such as Sweden, France and Germany where we both find good and less good performing plants.

It seems like Hofstede's 5D model has limited explanatory power in the implementation of XPSs in our two case companies. We do not even find significant support for the only dimension that previous literature agrees matters [7, 10, 13, 14]: low degree of individualism, i.e. collectivism. (The only sign of support, even if not significant, is that IDI is as expected the only factor that loads negatively on XPS implementation). If this is the case in our two MNCs, it is probably also the case in other MNCs. We cannot conclude that the national cultures have no effect, but our first proposition will be: (P1) *Whatever the effect of Hofstede's cultural dimensions on XPS implementation are, there are other factors in the plants that by far triumph these cultural dimensions.*

4.2   What Other Factors Can Explain Differences in XPS Implementation?

We now proceed with our post-hoc analysis for some alternative explanations for the XPS implementation in our cases (c.f. Figure 1).

A first possible explanation for differences in performance is naturally *organisational culture*. There are numerous studies that establish that the successful transfer of management and operational practices is less dependent on the national culture than on the organisational culture [13, 18]. It has long been established that it is possible to successfully implement lean production in cultures very different from the Japanese [18, 19]. Deal and Kennedy [20] define organisational culture as "the way things get done around here". As demonstrated with this definition, organisational culture is not clear-cut. In general, it lacks good operationalisation in the literature and is so multi-faceted that we still do not know exactly how to build organisational cultures that sustain high XPS performance. Our field studies in the case companies clearly indicate that organisational culture is of major importance, but our quantitative data do not allow any analysis of this sort. We can only keep this as a proposition for further research: (P2) *A plant's organisational culture can triumph any effects of national cultures in the implementation of an XPS.*

A second possible explanation is the strategic role of the plant. Ferdows [21] suggested that plants can have different roles based on their strategic importance. While the concept of factory roles have been subject to testing and refining [22, 23], only few studies explicitly investigate the link between factory role and improvement programmes [24]. Mediavilla *et al.* [24] found some evidence that the lower the plant role, the more actively the plants try to implement the improvement programme with the purpose of increasing its role. Consequently, this would also mean that the higher the role of the plant the more ambivalent the plant would be to implement the programme. The reasoning for this will be that plants that are specifically put up for the purpose of offshored production compete solely on the basis of their operational competitiveness. We find partial support for this proposition in our data, with low-role plants that perform well with XPS implementation in China, Poland, Slovakia, Brazil, Turkey and Greece. Also the fact that high-role plants in Sweden, Germany, France, USA and Belgium seem to cluster around and above the average support this. However, it does not explain that the high-role plants in South Korea and Japan perform best of all, and that low-role plants in Peru, Russia, South Africa, Mexico and Thailand perform well below average. Possible explanations for the latter might be proprietary markets and a high degree of plant autonomy in these countries, or simpler explanations like the learning curve effect. As globalisation increases also in these countries we might see a change in the future. With the need for more research we conclude with our third proposition: *(P3): The lower the role of the plant in the global network, the higher the external and internal pressure for XPS implementation will be.*

5   Conclusions

In the literature review we found mixed evidence on which cultural dimensions impact XPS implementation, and our analysis suggest this has a good reason; the impact of national culture on global lean programmes is insignificant. Cultural dimensions, such as the ones summarised by Hofstede, explain little of the successful implementation of global lean programmes. Instead we should search for other explanatory factors that far outweigh the impact of national culture. The literature to date has suggested that organisational culture is one such important factor; we suggest the plant role is another factor that deserves more attention in future research.

5.1   Implications for Researchers

If we are right, researchers should reduce all the work that goes into analysing the link between global manufacturing surveys and cultural dimensions based on Hofstede. Even if that type of research is relatively easy to conduct and get published, its contribution to practice is more confusing than helpful. Correspondingly more research is needed to explore the three other propositions we set forward. So far, most published research seems to fall into one type of research designs: Large multinational surveys based on perceptual answers from a single or few respondents in each plant. We call for more research that utilise real plant performance data like we do here. We also encourage collaborative studies with between practitioners and researchers. We think that can help resolve the gridlock picture of cultural impact on global lean programmes. Longitudinal case studies are in consequence a preferable research strategy.

5.2   Implications for Managers

With the realisation that managers cannot change the national culture but *can* impact the other factors that we suggest impact XPS implementation even more, our findings are in fact good news for global managers. If our second proposition is right, managers can delimit negative traits and enhance positive traits in the national culture if such exist, by building supportive organisational cultures for different contexts. There is available a vast literature on critical success factors for improvement programmes. If our third proposition is right, global managers would know what XPS performance to expect from each plant based on their role. Thus, resources can more economically be employed where needed in the network.

5.3   Limitations

Our data have several limitations which is why we conclude with propositions and not assertions. First, the numbers of plants in each of the countries we investigate vary from 1 to 10; a cursory look at our results show that the more plants you include from one country the closer to the mean that country ends. Therefore caution should be taken when analysing the end points in our country scale. This, however, lends support to our first proposition that national culture is insignificant. Second, the assessment data—even if rigid and robust—does only tell *how much* of the XPS a plant has implemented, not *how well* the plant is performing. In the real world, companies ultimately compete with performance and not implementation of lean programmes, even if a positive correlation between them is expected. Third, it should also be noted that other classifications for national culture exist, and might provide better explanations for XPS implementation than Hofstede and GLOBE that we base our analysis on her. We leave the task of addressing our limitations to future research.

References

1. Netland, T.H.: Exploring the phenomenon of company-specific Production Systems: One-best-way or own-best-way? International Journal of Production Research (2012), doi:10.1080/00207543.2012.676686.
2. Hofstede, G., Hofstede, G.J.: Cultures and organizations: software of the mind, vol. XII, p. 434s. McGraw-Hill, New York (2005)
3. Lagrosen, S.: Exploring the impact of culture on quality management. International Journal of Quality & Reliability Management 20(4), 473–487 (2003)
4. Kull, T.J., Wacker, J.G.: Quality management effectiveness in Asia: The influence of culture. Journal of Operations Management 28(3), 223–239 (2010)
5. Newman, K.L., Nollen, S.D.: Culture and Congruence: The Fit between Management Practices and National Culture. Journal of International Business Studies 27(4), 753–779 (1996)
6. Laugen, B.T., et al.: Best manufacturing practices: What do the best-performing companies do? International Journal of Operations & Production Management 25(2), 131 (2005)
7. Flynn, B.B., Saladin, B.: Relevance of Baldrige constructs in an international context: A study of national culture. Journal of Operations Management 24(5), 583–603 (2006)
8. Hofstede, G.: Think Locally, Act Globally: Cultural Constraints in Personnel Management. Management International Review 38, 7 (1998)
9. Hofstede, G.: Culture's consequences: International differences in work-related values. Sage, Beverly Hills (1980)
10. Wiengarten, F., et al.: Exploring the impact of national culture on investments in manufacturing practices and performance. International Journal of Operations & Production Management 31(5), 554–578 (2011)
11. Cagliano, R., et al.: The impact of country culture on the adoption of new forms of work organization. International Journal of Operations & Production Management 31(3), 297–323 (2011)
12. Vecchi, A., Brennan, L.: Quality management: a cross-cultural perspective based on the GLOBE framework. International Journal of Operations & Production Management 31(5), 527–553 (2011)
13. Naor, M., Linderman, K., Schroeder, R.: The globalization of operations in Eastern and Western countries: Unpacking the relationship between national and organizational culture and its impact on manufacturing performance. Journal of Operations Management 28(3), 194–205 (2010)
14. Power, D., Schoenherr, T., Samson, D.: The cultural characteristic of individualism/collectivism: A comparative study of implications for investment in operations between emerging Asian and industrialized Western countries. Journal of Operations Management 28(3), 206–222 (2010)
15. Galperin, B.L., Lituchy, T.R.: The implementation of total quality management in Canada and Mexico: a case study. International Business Review 8(3), 323–349 (1999)
16. Zu, X., Robbins, T.L., Fredendall, L.D.: Mapping the critical links between organizational culture and TQM/Six Sigma practices. International Journal of Production Economics 123(1), 86–106 (2010)

17. Yin, R.K.: Case study research: design and methods, vol. XVI, p. 181s. Sage, Thousand Oaks (2003)
18. Krafcik, J.F.: Triumph of The Lean Production System. Sloan Management Review 30(1), 41–51 (1988)
19. Womack, J.P., Jones, D.T.: Lean thinking: banish waste and create wealth in your corporation, p. 396s. Free Press, New York (1996)
20. Deal, T.E., Kennedy, A.A.: Corporate cultures: the rites and rituals of corporate life, vol. VII, p. 232s. Addison-Wesley, Reading (1982)
21. Ferdows, K.: Making the most of foreign factories. Harvard Business Review 75(2), 73 (1997)
22. Maritan, C.A., Brush, T.H., Karnani, A.G.: Plant roles and decision autonomy in multinational plant networks. Journal of Operations Management 22(5), 489–503 (2004)
23. Vereecke, A., Dierdonck, R.V., Meyer, A.D.: A Typology of Plants in Global Manufacturing Networks. Management Science 52(11), 1737–1750 (2006)
24. Mediavilla, M., Errasti, A., Domingo, R.: Framework for evaluating and upgrading the strategic plant role. Case study within a global operations network. DYNA Engineering and Industry 86(4), 405–451 (2011)

Methodology to Identify SMEs Needs of Internationalised and Collaborative Networks

Beatriz Andrés and Raúl Poler

Research Centre on Production Management and Engineering (CIGIP),
Universitat Politècnica de València (UPV)
Plaza Ferrándiz y Carbonell, 2, 03801 Alcoy, Spain
{beaanna,rpoler}@cigip.upv.es

Abstract. This paper provides a methodology to support researchers in the identification of SMEs needs encountered when establishing collaborative processes within non-hierarchical manufacturing networks. Furthermore, the methodology also determines the needs when non-hierarchical networks internationalise their processes and operations to overcome globalisation and competitive environments. The major goal of this study is to provide a methodology to enable researchers to underline factors of SMEs integration with particular emphasis on the internationalisation of operations and the establishment of collaborative processes with networked partners. The provided methodology is the first step to develop a future empirical study to explore the findings of the literature review applied to SMEs and to identify the enterprises needs appeared when internationalised and collaborative processes are established in non-hierarchical networks.

Keywords: SMEs, non-hierarchical networks, internationalisation of operations, collaborative needs.

1 Introduction

The nature of the modus operandi in small and medium enterprises (SMEs) is changing by means of partnerships with other companies in complex value chains now globally extended [1]. Firms' competitiveness has experienced several changes over the last years. This tendency changes the way how SMEs work and relate [1]. As a result, the Non-Hierarchical manufacturing Networks (NHN) concept has emerged implying a decentralised decision making perspective and commitment of all companies without losing their authority in decision-making.

Competitive and global environments have also allowed changing the way how SMEs operate within a network through the internationalisation. Globalisation forces that the operations network design must encompass multiple regions that are becoming more widespread, forcing networks to cope with greater complexity [2]. Internationalisation is defined as the creation and management of production facilities in foreign countries to benefit from tariff preferences, lower labour costs, subsidies and lower logistics costs, as consequence a common approach to internationalisation aims

C. Emmanouilidis, M. Taisch, D. Kiritsis (Eds.): APMS 2012, Part II, IFIP AICT 398, pp. 463–470, 2013.
© IFIP International Federation for Information Processing 2013

to reduce costs and increase competitiveness in the short term [3]. Nowadays, companies are more internationalised due to the extension of the value chain configurations beyond national borders. Nevertheless, the internationalisation starting up process is a difficult decision to make, because it implies risks especially for SMEs whose capabilities and resources are insufficient. Many SMEs fail in foreign markets due to the production management of internationalised networks requires a greater collaboration to achieve optimal degrees of quality, flexibility and costs [4].

Regarding the networks under study (NHN), the evolution from a traditional hierarchical network, based on centralised decision making, to a NHN implies that SMEs have to face new challenges. The literature review carried out by [5] identifies and structures the emerging needs of SMEs that decide to establish collaborative relationships in a NHN. Besides, if SMEs establish in their strategy the internationalisation of operations, collaborative problems SMEs have to face are increased within the NHN. Consequently internationalisation in NHN enlarges collaborative problems that SMEs have to face within a network; therefore, problems arising from the internationalisation must be added to those existing in the establishment of collaborative processes already defined by [5-6]. In the light of this, a number of needs must be identified and subsequently addressed regarding (i) the establishment of collaborative relationships amongst NHN partners characterised by decentralised decision making and (ii) the internationalisation of operations.

Considering the reasons above stated a generic methodology to identify the SMEs obstacles to overcome when establishing collaborative relationships among national and international partners is provided in order to structure the SMEs needs that appear when they decide to participate in collaborative and international manufacturing networks. The proposed methodology allows sequencing the actions to be taken in order to identify the weaknesses that can appear in SMEs when they decide to belong to an internationalised and collaborative NHN. Taking into account the literature review developed by [5], it can be said that there is an absence of a unified approach to assist the process identification of needs for international and collaborative networks. Therefore, this paper develops a methodology in order to fill this identified gap.

2   Methodology Background

This section provides the methodology background based on a questionnaire to allow SMEs identifying the needs they find when establishing collaborative relationships. Regarding the methodology, two levels are considered (i) network level that consists of all nodes in the NHN and (ii) local level that consists of each SME [7]. The methodology takes into account the local SME level comparing with needed requirements at network level. Participating SMEs must identify in which processes are involved within the NHN and the roles and responsibilities they assume.

SMEs adopting internationalised processes establish relationships with SMEs with limited number of responsibilities, decision making, participation in network operations and resources. From the collaborative NHN point of view, participating SMEs have higher expectations in their foreign SMEs and, therefore, try to get a lot more of them. Thus, internationalisation of operations in a collaborative perspective does not only reduces costs advantages, but also provide access to a global production and distribution network closer to potential markets, with easy access to customers, suppliers, or workers with specific skills. In collaborative NHN partners have greater management capacity and autonomy in decision making than just operational management of production, including: product and process development, decision making in procurement and purchasing, technical support, etc. [8]. The evolution of a SME from an isolated perspective to an integrated perspective within a collaborative NHN, benefits synergies between enterprises, reduce costs, increase reliability of delivery and reduce the learning curve of other members of the network operations [9]. The internationalisation process within collaborative NHN is a difficult decision making due to consists of wide range of SMEs. In the light of this, this paper allows to identify limited resources and capabilities of SMEs when they decide to establish the internationalisation of operations in collaborative NHN.

In the provided methodology, the weaknesses that can be identified in networked SMEs are clasified through a 4-dimensions analysis: (i) *strategy*, (ii) *technology*, (iii) *partners* and (iv) *product* (Fig.1). This 4-dimensions are considered taking into account the PEST factors analysis (Political, Economic, Social and Technological) as the identification of the overall environmental factors that affect companies [10]. All dimensions are related and linked to each other and establish the most important pillars to identify the SMEs needs. The analysis is performed in parallel for the two identified levels: (i) the environment that characterizes the collaborative NHN based on internationalisation of operations and (ii) the specific context of SMEs, regarding SMEs features and capabilities to cope with collaborative NHN requirements (Fig.1).

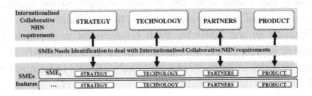

Fig. 1. 4-Dimension Analysis at Network and Local level

The *SMEs environment* (external view) characterises the collaborative environment within the network they belong to: (i) Strategy Dimension: decisions are based in network design, decision making system, strategies and Performance Management System (PMS) design, (ii) Technology Dimension: decisions are related with needed technologies and systems to address the exchange of information and knowledge, process connection, interoperability and security systems for exchanging information,

(iii) Partners Dimension: treats about coordination, contract negotiation, sharing costs and benefits, relationships with partners through collaborative arrangements, orders management and alignment of strategies and (iv)Products Dimension: decisions are aimed at establish collaborative forecast, planning and replenishment, production scheduling, inventory management and product design.

The *specific context* (internal view), characterises the SMEs features: (i) Strategy Dimension: takes into account the SME location strategy, decision-making system, performance management, degree of strategy alignment with the global network strategy, (ii) Technology Dimension: identify the SME capability for technological and scientific innovation, technological innovation infrastructure, scientific and technological knowledge level, (iii) Partners Dimension: analyse the SMEs capability and bargaining power, trust, risk, equity, uncertainty, participation in company, profits, collaborative relationships with partners and threats of vertical integration forward or backward and (iv) Product Dimension: deal with SMEs acceptance of sharing product information, product storage and product importance for the NHN.

3   Methodology

A methodology to identify the degree of adaptation with SMEs partners that belong to collaborative NHN is provided in this section (Fig. 2). Through the degree of adaptation SMEs can identify the problems they have to overcome to fulfil the internationalised collaborative NHN requirements. Therefore, the methodology allows networked partners to determine the adaptability between the two scenarios: local characteristics (SME) and network requirements (NHN) when establishing internationalisation of operations. The methodology sequence allows to consider first of all if the SME is willing to participate in a collaborative NHN and to internationalise his operations. Once the mission and vision from the network is defined the methodology starts working with the internal and external analysis that will allow experts to define the degree of adaptation of the SME for each requirement at network level. Finally, through the degree of adaptation, specialists will be able to identify the SMEs needs and weaknesses in order to be overcame and enable SMEs to be ready to start collaborative relationships in international NHN.

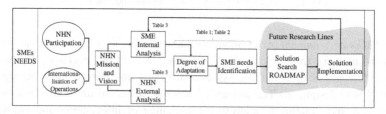

Fig. 2. Methodology Scheme to identify the SMEs needs

Table 2 allows identifying the degree of adaptation and the emerging needs of SMEs in establishing collaborative relationships in NHN. The *Degree of Adaptation* represented in the Table 1 scales via 1 to 10, how the SMEs features fit into the needs of the collaborative NHN. Questionnaire provided in Table 3 allow the SMEs to easily identify the appropriateness and the SMEs degree of adaptation regarding the requirements of the internationalised collaborative NHN. The questions enable SMEs to identify the degree of adaptation in Table 2 and; therefore, the problem to overcome. Thus, each numbered question (Q_x) is associated to each problem and allows experts to determine the degree of adaptation of each SME in relation to collaborative NHN needs (Table 2).

Table 1. Degree of Adaptation Legend

Degree of Adaptation	Definition	Explanation
0	Very Weak	The SME does not have capabilities and resources to belong to a collaborative NHN
1	Weak	The SME capabilities and resources do not favour the collaborative NHN requirements
3	Moderate	The SME capabilities and resources slightly favour the collaborative NHN requirements
5	Good	The SME capabilities and resources favour the collaborative NHN requirements
7	High	The SME capabilities and resources of tightly fit with the requirements of the collaborative NHN
9	Very High	The SME capabilities and resources are equal to the requirements needed within the collaborative NHN
		2, 4, 6, 8 are mediate values

Table 2. Degree of Adaptation to identify SMEs needs based on 4-Dimensional Analysis (S: Strategic, T: Tactical, O: Operational)

	Collaborative NHN	Adaptation Degree	SME	PROBLEM TO TACKLE	LEVEL
STRATEGY	Network Design	Q: 1	SME location	Network Design	S
	Strategy	Q: 2	Alignment Degree	Strategy Alignment	S
			SME Objectives		
			Market Position		
		Q: 3	Participation in other Networks	Partner Selection	S
	Decentralised Decision Making	Q: 4	Decision System Making	Decision System Design	S
	PMS collaborative KPIs	Q: 5	SME PMS KPIs	PMS Design	S
TECHNOLOGY	Technologies to address the collaborative exchange of information and knowledge	Q: 6	Capability for technological and scientific innovation	Information Exchange	O
			Level of technical sophistication		
			Level of scientific and technological knowledge	Knowledge Management	T
				Uncertainty Management	
	Process Connexion	Q: 7	Technology Innovation	Process Connexion	O
	Interoperability	Q: 8	Infrastructures	Interoperability	O
PARTNERS	Strategy Alignment	Q: 9	SME Strategy	Partners Collaboration	S
			Vertical Integration Threat	Partners Selection	S
	Contracts Negotiation	Q: 10	Capacity and Power Negotiation	Contracts Negotiation	T
	Share costs and benefits Equity Partners Involvement	Q: 11	SME Profits comparing with the collaborative partner within the NHN	Share Profits and Costs	T
			Trust Uncertainty		
	Partners relationships through collaborative mechanisms	Q: 12	Collaboration Mechanisms	Collaboration Mechanisms Design	S/T
	Order Promising Process	Q: 13	Orders's Management	OPP	O
	Information	Q: 14	Willingness for information exchanging	Information Exchange	

Table 2. cont. Degree of Adaptation to identify SMEs needs based on 4-Dimensional Analysis (S: Strategic, T: Tactical, O: Operational)

Collaborative NHN		Adaptation Degree	SME	PROBLEM TO TACKLE	LEVEL
PRODUCTS	Product	Q: 15	Product Importance for the NHN	Product Design	S
	Collaborative Forecast	Q: 16	Forecast System	Collaborative Forecast	T
	Collaborative Planning	Q: 17	SME Planning	Operation Planning	T
	Collaborative Replenishment	Q: 18	SME Replenishment Order Management	Replenishment	T
	CPFR	Q: 19	Willingness for information exchanging	Information Management	T
	Collaborative Scheduling	Q: 20	Production Scheduling Production Lines	Scheduling	O
	Inventory Management	Q: 21	Product Stocking Lotsizing	Inventory Management	O

(Q$_x$: question developed in Table 3)

Being from 0 to 3 degrees of adaptation implies that the SMEs capabilities and resources do not encourage the requirements needed to participate in a collaborative NHN for establishing internationalisation processes. Besides, for those problems whose degree of adequacy is between 0 and 5 SMEs should seek on solutions to favour a higher adequacy (between 6 and 10).

This classification allows networked partners know what their weaknesses are and where they must improve to efficiently belong to a collaborative NHN based on decentralised and internationalised decisions.

Table 3. Questionnaire for identifying SMEs Needs based on 4-Dimensional Analysis

	Questions	PROBLEM TO TACLKE
STRATEGY	**Q 1.** How much adapts the SME location with the NHN design? The collaborative NHN is divided into different processes: (i) procurement (ii) production, (iii) distribution and (iv) marketing and sales. Each process is designed in a particular location. What process is identified in your SME? Is the SME location corresponding with the determined in the NHN design?	Network Design
	Q 2. What is the degree of alignment: between the SME strategy and the NHN overall strategy? between the SME the objectives and the global goal? Are the objectives of the SME aligned with the objectives defined at NHN level?	Strategy Alignment
	Q 3. Is the SME linked to other networks? In which extent can the SME achieve the collaborative NHN objectives and strategies without affecting other networks the SME belong to? Have the partners the proper features to adapt to collaborative and internationalisation requirements?	Partners Selection
	Q 4. Does the SME decision making system adaptable to a decentralized decision making system what characterises the collaborative NHN?	Decision System Design
	Q 5. Can the SME Performance Measurement System (PMS) be redesigned to measure parameters needed to calculate the overall performance of the NHN? Can the KPIs be redesigned to make them adaptable to a NHN? Does the SME able to measure the collaborative and internationalisation of operations success?	PMS Design
TECHNOLOGY	**Q 6.** Does the SME have the suitable technologies needed to meet the information and knowledge exchange required in an internationalised collaborative NHN? What are the SME scientific and the technological innovation capabilities? What level of scientific and technological knowledge has the SME? What is the SME level of technology sophistication to implement new IT/IS?	Information Exchange / Knowledge Management / Uncertainty Management
	Q 7. Does the SME have available resources and expertise to successfully implement tools to achieve the process connection in internationalised and collaborative networks? Does the SME have technological innovation infrastructure?	Process Connexion
	Q 8. Does the SME have information systems (IS) ready to establish interoperability between the IS of the NHN collaborative partners (international and national)?	Interoperability

Table 3. cont. Questionnaire for identifying SMEs Needs based on 4-Dimensional Analysis

	Questions	PROBLEM TO TACLKE
PARTNERS	Q 9. Is the SME strategy aligned with the strategies of the NHN partners? Is there a threat of vertical integration for the SME's partners?	Partners Selection
	Q 10. Does the SME have defined negotiation protocols with other partners? Does the SME have capacity, bargaining power and tools to negotiate?	Negotiation Contracts
	Q 11. Is the SME willing to equally share profits among the NHN collaborative partners? Does the SME trust to share profits? What are the SME profits in relation to the collaborative partners? How are the profits measured in the SME? Is the SME measurement system consistent with the NHN profits measurement?	Share Costs And Profits
	Q 12. Does the SME establish collaborative mechanisms? Does the SME have know how to use collaborative mechanisms to establish closer relationships among internationalised NHN members?	Collaboration Mechanisms
	Q 13. How is done the Order Promising Process (OPP) within the SME? Can the SME OPP be connected with inventory and production capacities of other NHN partners? The OPP within the SME, could be connected with other NHN partners?	Order Promising Process
	Q 14. Is the SME willing to share information amongst NHN collaborative partners? Does the SME distinguish private from public information?	Information Exchange
PRODUCTS	Q 15. How important is, for the internationalised collaborative NHN, the product manufactured by the SME?	Product Design
	Q 16. Does the SME trust enough to share or accept the downstream partner's forecast data? Does the SME works with POS data? Which security system to exchange information uses the SME?	Collaborative Forecast
	Q 17. Does the SME have a collaborative planning system? What sort of planning system uses the SME? Can be adapted to the collaborative system within the NHN? Is the SME willing to share data plan information with other members of the collaborative NHN?	Operation Planning
	Q 18. Does the SME use a replenishment system managed by the supplier? Does the SME perform a collaborative replenishment process amongst national and international partners?	Replenishment
	Q 19. Does the SME use a collaborative planning, forecast and replenishment system? Is the SME willing to jointly manage the information with NHN partners?	Information Management
	Q 20. Does the SME use a distributed scheduling? Is the scheduling processes collaboratively done among NHN partners? What SME production lines are included in the NHN?	Scheduling
	Q 21. How is the SME inventory management performed? Does the supplier manage the SME inventory? Does the SME have any inventory management system? Is the SME willing to jointly manage the inventory within NHN partners?	Inventory Management

4   Conclusions

In this paper, a methodology to identify the weaknesses of SMEs arising from participating in a NHN is provided. The methodology assesses the current state of SMEs in
order to be known by themselves and by their networked partners. The SMEs needs
identification provides an important improvement in order to establish decentralised
decisions within networks characterised by the internationalisation of operations.

Next steps regarding the methodology are focused on the implementation of a
questionnaire to obtain a representative sample of SMEs, in order to identify the major gaps affecting the collaborative and internationalised processes. In this context the
main objectives to carry out are (i) to apply the methodology through a questionnaire
in order to determine what are the problems and needs encountered in SMEs when
establish collaborative processes when they decide to internationalise their operations
and (ii) to provide researchers a global vision of the SMEs current situation in order to
give an insight to start a series of solution proposals to enable the SMEs participation
in collaborative and internationalised NHN. The distributed questionnaire will allow
the subsequent search of solutions to reduce the SMEs weaknesses. Therefore,
through the provided paper experts should be able to assess the SMEs current capabilities that will define their preparation, readiness and potential benefits to face a
membership in a NHN based in internationalisation of operations. Finally, upcoming
work is leaded solve the encountered SMEs needs to establish collaborative

relationships characterized by decentralised decision making; and propose the best solution to overcome the problems within the international, collaborative and decentralised context.

References

1. Camarinha-Matos, L., Afsarmanesh, H., Galeano, N., Molina, A.: Collaborative networked organisations – Concepts and practice in manufacturing enterprises. Computers & Industrial Engineering 57(1), 46–60 (2008)
2. Corti, D., Egaña, M.M., Errasti, A.: Challenges for off-shored operations: findings from a comparative multi-case study analysis of Italian and Spanish companies. In: Proceedings 16th Annual EurOMA Conference (2009)
3. Mediavilla, M., Errasti, A., Domingo, R.: Framework for assessing the current strategic factory role and deploying an upgrading roadmap. An empirical study within a global operations network. Dirección y Organización 46, 5–15 (2012)
4. Martínez, S., Errasti, A., Santos, J., Mediavilla, M.: Framework for improving the design and configuration process of a global production and logistic network. In: Emmanouilidis, C., Taishch, M., Kiritsis, D. (eds.) APMS 2012, Part II. IFIP AICT, vol. 398, pp. 471–478. Springer, Heidelberg (2013)
5. Andrés, B., Poler, R.: Análisis de los Procesos Colaborativos en Redes de Empresas No-Jerárquicas. In: Ros, L., Fuente, V., Hontoria, E., Soler, D., Morales, C., Bogataj, M. (eds.) Ingeniería Industrial: Redes Innovadoras. XV Congreso de Ingeniería de Organización, CIO 2011 Libro de Actas, Cartagena, Spain, September 7-9, pp. 369–373 (2011)
6. Andrés, B., Poler, R.: Relevant Problems in Collaborative Processes of Non-Hierarchical Manufacturing Networks. In: Prado, J.C., García, J., Comesaña, J.A., Fernández, A.J. (eds.) 6th International Conference on Industrial Engineering and Industrial Management, Vigo, Spain, July 18-20, pp. 90–97 (2012)
7. Alfaro, J.J., Rodríguez, R., Ortiz, A., Verdecho, M.J.: An information architecture for a performance management framework by collaborating SMEs. Computers in Industry 61(7), 676–685 (2010)
8. Ferdows, K.: Making the most of foreign factories. Harvard Business Review, 73–88 (March-April 1997)
9. Flaherty, T.: Coordinating International Manufacturing and Technology. In: Porter, M. (ed.). Harvard Business School Press (1986)
10. McGee, J., Thomas, H., Wilson, D.: Strategy: Analysis and Practice. McGraw-Hill, New York (2005)

Framework for Improving the Design and Configuration Process of Global Operations

S. Martínez[1], A. Errasti[1], J. Santos[1], and M. Mediavilla[2]

[1] Engineering School, Tecnun, University of Navarra, San Sebastián, Spain
{smartinez,aerrasti,jsantos}@tecnun.es
[2] BSH Bosch und Siemens Hausgeräte GmbH, Munich, Germany
Miguel.Mediavilla@bshg.com

Abstract. In the current dynamic, volatile and competitive playground, the design and managing of global production and logistic networks has become a crucial issue even for SMEs, although with the difficult added that they have limited resources. Thus, how dealing with these complex production networks present a real challenge for this kind of companies. In order to do so, it is necessary to provide business managers a useful guideline to face the internationalization process in an effective way. Therefore, the aim of this paper is to propose a framework, which takes into account the three main problems (new facilities implementation, global supplier network and multi-site network) related to Operations configuration, to aid managers in the different stages of the decision making and propose useful principles, methods and techniques depending on the problem.

Keywords: Internationalization, SMEs, SBUs, Operations Strategy.

1 Introduction

Internationalization of production and logistics networks is a phenomenon that has gained momentum over the last decade as a consequence of the evolution of the competitive environment. Many manufacturing companies, in fact, have increased their international presence to remain competitive.

The internationalization of operations can take different forms and includes the development of new configurations such as international distribution systems, networks of global suppliers, and multi-site and/or fragmented manufacturing networks.

However, the starting up and supplier development process are some of the most difficult decisions to make, because it implies a lot of risks not only for multinational companies, but also and especially for SMEs (Small Medium Enterprises) and SBUs (Strategic Business Units) from Industrial Divisions, which resources are limited.

Many SMEs and SBUs of industrial divisions with local success fall down in foreign markets. Although, these are immersed in the globalization process, many of them are in the initial phase of internationalization in emerging market economies as well as in countries in transition, and need to be prepared for the challenges of new market economies [1].

C. Emmanouilidis, M. Taisch, D. Kiritsis (Eds.): APMS 2012, Part II, IFIP AICT 398, pp. 471–478, 2013.

Due to the rapid changes that have occurred during the last decades, almost every company or enterprise is affected by at least some kind of international challenge. Nevertheless, in the case of SMEs they have to cope with more difficulties because of having limited resources, limited market knowledge, limited use of networks and limited international experience of the entrepreneurs [2], and the same complications can affect to SBUs too. Consequently, the SMEs and SBUs internationalization process merits great attention.

Therefore, facing the management of a production logistic network in different countries is an enormous challenge which requires a greater coordination to get optimal levels of quality, flexibility and cost [3]. Summarizing, whilst all type of organisations are facing significant challenges for managing increasingly complex global operation, current literature on global operation networks is still limited in its scope [4-5]. Even more if it is considered SMEs and SBUs.

This paper shows the new improved version of the GlobOpe (Global Operations) Framework, which was exposed in the last APMS Conference, held in Stavanger (Norway) [6].

2   Research Problems and Gap

2.1   New Production Facility Implementation

The implementation of a production plant is the strongest step of any organization that seeks to internationalize [7], and for that besides the obvious economic investment, the establishment and subsequent management of the production facilities require a broad range of knowledge and skills related to operations management such as: establish agreements with local logistics suppliers, manage the expatriate staff, modify products and services to suit local requirements, etc.

On the other hand, some companies try to minimize the problems associated with the establishment through the acquisition of existing resources. In these cases, there might be a number of contingencies, for example: the integration into the operating practices of the organization, incompatibility of the acquired information systems, etc.

2.2   Supply Network Design and Sourcing

Purchasing has evolved in the past few decades from a passive administrative role into a strategic function that contributes to creating a competitive advantage as much as other business functions [8]. This development is logical, given that purchases represent a large percentage of the final cost of the product and are of crucial importance for its quality and performance.

Hence, considering the definition of global or international purchasing given by [9] as "the activity for searching and obtaining goods, services and other resources on a possible worldwide scale, to comply with the needs of the company and with a view to continuing and enhancing the current competitive position of the company. The global purchasing includes all phases of the purchasing process, from before the definition of the specification list, through supplier selection and buying to the follow-up and evaluation phase. Furthermore, the global purchasing management is one of the first steps to define and design a global supply chain development [10].

Errasti [11] in his book about purchasing management identifies and explains in depth which are the challenges, risks and characteristics of the new purchasing function, some of them are: define the strategy in the supplier market, search for new suppliers, collect suppliers' value-added proposals and develop appropriate suppliers, integrate marketing and supply strategies in shorter product life cycles, define the contract management in the contract life cycle, negotiation power, face the different supply chain configurations, etc. For instance, in terms of supply chain configurations, it can be seen that nowadays in a multisite and fragmented production system, where the supplier network is composed of local or domestic suppliers and offshore suppliers and manufacturing facilities, these offshore suppliers and facilities need the coordination of quality control and the supply network with different delivery times and procurement reliability [12].

2.3   Research Gap

Although, there are many researchers about Global Operations, practical experiences have shown that strategy-specific checklists are needed, which might raise awareness of the real success factors of the pursued goal and avoid unpleasant surprises [13]. Moreover, different researchers [14-15] state the need to build models or frameworks of international manufacturing systems that help managers to design and manage their networks, which should take into account the requirements for the next generation of factories such as agility, flexibility, modularity, adaptability, etc. [16].

Hence, the examination of the literature revealed that there is a lack of methods and techniques to accomplish the design and configuration process of a global production and logistic network.

3   Research Methodology

There are many researchers who view the use of a mixture of methods as desirable, particularly in terms of developing valuable theory form observation and empirical analysis [17-18]. The important point is to choose the most appropriate methods for the investigation of the defined research question [19]. Then, a combination of different research methodologies have been chosen with the objective of reinforcing the week points of one method with the strengths of others. With these aims in mind and due to lack of space, the next table just mentions which have been the steps given by the researchers:

Table 1. Roadmap of research methodology to build, test and verify the GlobOpe Framework

Stage	Research Technique	Purpose or scope
1	Literature review	Identify the gaps
2	Constructive research [20]	Develop the GlobOpe Model for New Facilities Implementation (NFI)
3	Action research (in a wind turbine manufacturer) [21-22]	Test and verify the GlobOpe Model for NFI
		First thoughts about the necessity to expand the model
4	Literature review	Develop and improve the GlobOpe Model for Global
	Case study [23]	Supplier Network Configuration (GSNC)
5	Action research (in two textile industries)	Test the GlobOpe Model for GSNC
6	Multiple case studies and triangulation	Verify and refine both models

4   Theory Building: GlobOpe Framework

4.1   Scope

The Framework called GlobOpe bears in mind the Operations Strategy key decisions that need to be made regarding a global production and logistic network configuration and design in the internationalization process. These key decisions are the following five: supply sources location (own and not own); strategic role; make or buy decisions; service delivery strategy and global operations network.

4.2   Approach

The methodology aids to determinate the problems specifications with the users help and it allows homogenizing the whole information. There are many modeling techniques, each one with special characteristics. According to the methodologies classification [24-25], the GlobOpe Framework covers the strategic and tactical horizon, the physic and decisional model nature and also the analysis, design and implementation stages.

4.3   GlobOpe Framework

The framework is centred in the most advanced stage of a company in terms of becoming global. According to the volume of international sales and the international production, the companies can be classified as: global, local, offshorer and exporter companies [26]. Nevertheless, companies are not tied to one of these strategies during their whole life cycle. Thus, they could change and adapt them. There are different behaviors and paths can be followed to achieve a rating of global competitor, but the GlobOpe Framework is focused on helping companies in the internationalization process, that is to say, to move from exporter to global.

Hence, the goal of the GlobOpe Framework is the design and configuration process of a global production and logistic network, which can be a useful management tool for SMEs and SBUs steering committees responsible for the Global Operations effectiveness and efficiency [27].

The framework intends to fill the gap left by the other ones which are really useful in a stable environment but they are not suitable in a market dynamic environment [28] where new facilities implementation [13, 16, 29] supplier network development [10, 30, 31] and multi-site network [14, 32] are needed.

Keeping in mind the GlobOpe presented in the previous APMS Conference [6] and after different project and researcher carried out, the researchers realize that the GlobOpe Framework needs to be enlarged. Therefore, the new GlobOpe Framework considers that there are three main problems related to Operations configuration in which the above decisions should be reviewed: new facilities implementation, global supplier network configuration and multi-site network configuration, so for each of them the researchers have developed a specific model. However, in this paper are only briefly exposed the first two pillars of the Framework.

GlobOpe Model for New Facilities Implementation
When assessing production locations abroad, companies tend to underestimate the necessary ramp up times [13] for securing process reliability, quality and productivity. Nevertheless, in order to manage such a ramp up with a high degree of precision, first a planning period phase is necessary, starting with the design of the product, the process and the supply chain network [33].

Therefore, the main goal to be achieved with this model is to manage the ramp up process with a high degree of precision and reduce ramp up delays in time and volume. With this aim in mind, when designing the model, the researchers have taken into consideration the following assumptions:

- Business Strategy should be aligned with Operations Strategy [34].
- A close coordination between agents in the supply chain due to the multiple possible configurations [12].
- Apply concurrent engineering: a planning period phase is necessary, starting with the design of the product, the process and the supply chain network in a parallel way [35].
- The physical and productive design should be adaptive.
- The process and management system have to be adapted to local characteristics [36].
- The shop floor management process has to be progressive [37] (start up, team and equipment stability, improvement and excellence).
- Think about the productive process strategy (fragmented or not). In case to be fragmented a decoupling point [38] could be needed to assure it.
- Supplier network design and configuration is the bottleneck in the ramp up process.

Ultimately, bearing in mind the life cycle of a company, this model shows which are the analysis, operational, stability, improvement and excellence decisions that should be made and propose useful principles, methods and techniques in order to accomplished these decisions in an effective and efficient way.

GlobOpe Model for Global Supplier Network Development
There are companies, which have expanded their operations throughout the world. The purchasing is one of them, however, global purchasing can be the result of a reactive, opportunist decision to decrease the purchasing cost of one item, but it can also be a strategic and coordinated effort to pro-actively enhance the competitive position of the company. Consequently, in this case, the main goal to be reached with this model is to develop and design an accurate and reliable supply network. So that, when designing the model, the researchers have been aware of the following assumptions:

- The starting point is the suppliers' network design, which is considered as the bottleneck in the ramp up process.
- The global purchasing management is one of the first steps to define and design a global supply chain development [10].
- The global sourcing strategy has to be aligned with organizational design [39].
- Keeping in mind the five purchasing stages propose by Trent and Monczka [30] the researches define and summarize them in three stages, the first one is when company only purchase in domestic or local markets, the second is when the companies engage a close international purchasing strategy and the last one is when they develop a worldwide purchasing strategy.

In short, this model proposes purchasing policies or principles, levers or methods and techniques (for each stage) for aiding the decision process and identifying which are the next steps that the company needs to go through the next stage in the purchasing internationalization process.

5   Contribution

The framework developed is theoretically grounded and combines practical relevance and practical utility with theoretical novelty, all being criteria for evaluating the quality of constructive research [40].

For this reason, the GlobOpe Framework might be a practical guideline to help managers in the decision making in order to define the efficient and effective roadmap for their company depending on the problem that they have to face. On the one hand, the GlobOpe Model for New Facilities Implementation along with the principles and tools proposed could aid to increase effectiveness and decrease ramp up delays. It also allows managing the design and configuring the facilities supply network with a high degree of precision. On the other hand, the GlobOpe Model for Global Suppliers Network Configuration could be used as an assessment tool for a Steering Committee to help them in the global supplier development.

References

1. Szabó, G.G.: New institutional economics and agricultural co-operatives: a Hungarian case study. In: Karafolas, S., Spear, R., Stryjan, Y. (eds.) Local Society & Global Economy: The Role of Co-operatives. Naoussa: Editions Hellin, ICA International Research Conference, pp. 357–378 (2002)
2. Kalinic, I., Forza, C.: Rapid internationalization of traditional SMEs: Between gradualist models and born globals. International Business Review (2011)
3. De Meyer, A., Nakane, J., Miller, J., Ferdows, K.: Flexibility: the next competitive battle the manufacturing futures survey. Strategic Management Journal 10, 135–144 (1989)
4. Corti, D., Egaña, M.M., Errasti, A.: Challenges for off-shored operations: findings from a comparative multi-case study analysis of Italian and Spanish companies. In: Proceedings 16th Annual EurOMA Conference, Gothenburg (2009)
5. Laiho, A., Blomqvist, M.: International Manufacturing Networks: a literature review. In: Proceedings 17th Conference EurOMA, Porto (2010)
6. Martinez, S., Errasti, A.: Framework for International Manufacturing Network Design and Configuration: An Empirical Study in the Wind Sector. In: APMS Conference, Stavanger (2011)
7. Barnes, D.: The complexities of the manufacturing strategy formation process in practice. International Journal of Operations & Production Management 22(10), 1090–1111 (2002)
8. Alinaghian, L.S., Aghadasi, M.: Proposing a model for purchasing system transformation. In: Proceedings 16th Conference EurOMA, Glasgow, Scotland (2006)
9. Van Weele, A.J.: Purchasing and Supply Chain Management. Thompson Learning, London (2005)
10. Leenders, M., Fearon, H.E., Flynn, A.E., Johnson, P.F.: Purchasing and Supply Management. McGraw Hill/Irwin, New York (2002)
11. Errasti, A.: Gestión de compras en la empresa, ediciones Pirámide, Grupo Anaya, Madrid, p. 280 (2012)
12. Meixell, M., Gargeya, V.: Global Supply Chain Design: A literature Review and A Critique. Transportation Research Part E 41, 531 (2005)
13. Kinkel, S., Maloca, S.: Drivers and antecedents of manufacturing offshoring and backshoring. A German Perspective. Journal of Purchasing & Suppply Management 15, 154–165 (2009)
14. Vereecke, A., Van Dierdonck, R.: The strategic role of the plant: testing Ferdow´s model. International Journal of Operations and Production Management 22, 492–514 (2002)
15. Shi, Y.: Internationalization and evolution of manufacturing systems: classic process models, new industrial issues, and academic challenges. Integrated, Manufacturing Systems 14, 385–396 (2003)
16. Azevedo, A., Almeida, A.: Factory Templates for Digital Factories Framework. Robotics and Computer-Integrated Manufacturing 27, 755–771 (2011)
17. Gill, J., Johnson, P.: Research Methods for Managers. Paul Chapman Publishing, London (1991)
18. Mingers, J., Brocklesby, J.: Multimethodology: towards a framework to mixture methodologies. Omega: International Journal of Management Science 25(5), 489–507 (1997)
19. Karlsson, C.: Researching Operations Management. Routledge, UK (2009)
20. Meredith, J.: Theory building through conceptual methods. International Journal of Operations and Production Management 13(5), 3–11 (1993)

21. Westbrook, R.: Action Research: a new paradigm for research in production and operations management. International Journal of Operations and Production Management 15(12), 6–20 (1995)
22. Voss, C., Tsikriktsis, N., Frohlich, M.: Case Research in operations management. International Journal of Operations and Production Management 22(2), 195–219 (2002)
23. Yin, R.K.: Case Study Research: Design and methods, 4th edn. SAGE Publications, Inc. (2009)
24. Erkes, K., Clark, M.: Public Domain Report Number 1, Rapport pour le domaine publique du projet Européen ESPRIT 418, Avril (1987)
25. Roboam, M., Doumeingts, G., Dittman, K., Clark, M.: Public Domain Report Number 2. Rapport pour le domaine publique du projet Européen ESPRIT 418 (September 1987)
26. Luzarraga, J.M.: Mondragon Multi-Location Strategy- Innovating a Human Centred Globalisation Mondragon University, Oñati, Spain (2008)
27. Errasti, A.: International Manufacturing Networks: Global Operations Design and Management. Servicio Central de Publicaciones del Gobierno Vasco, San Sebastian, Spain (2011)
28. Mediavilla, M., Errasti, A.: Framework for assessing the current strategic plant role and deploying a roadmap for its upgrading. An empirical study within a global operations network, APMS, Cuomo, Italy (2010)
29. Abele, E., Meyer, T., Näher, U., Strube, G., Sykes, R.: Global production: a handbook for strategy and implementation. Springer, Heidelberg (2008)
30. Trent, R.J., Monczka, R.M.: Pursuing competitive advantage through integrated global sourcing. Academy of Management Executive 16(2), 66–80 (2002)
31. Gelderman, C.J., Semeijn, J.: Managing the global supply base through purchasing portfolio management. Journal of Purchasing and Supply Management 12, 209–217 (2006)
32. Ferdows, K.: Making the most of foreign factories. Harvard Business Review, 73–88 (March-April 1997)
33. Kurtila, P., Shaw, M., Helo, P.: Model Factory concept-Enabler for quick manufacturing capacity ramp up (2010)
34. Monczka, R.M., Handfield, R.B., Guinipero, L.C., Patterson, J.L.: Purchasing and Supply Chain Management, 4th edn. South-Western Cengage Learning, USA (2009)
35. Errasti, A., Oyarbide, A., Santos, J.: Construction Process Reengineering. In: Proceedings of Faim, Bilbao, Spain (2005)
36. Errasti, A., Egaña, M.M.: Internacionalización de operaciones: estado del arte, Cluster de movilidad, logística y transporte, San Sebastian (2009)
37. Taylor, D., Brunt, D.: Manufacturing operations and supply chain management: The lean approach. Cengage learning, United Kingdom (2010)
38. Wikner, J., Rudberg, M.: Integrating production and engineering perspectives on the customer order decoupling point. International Journal of Operations and Production Management 25(7), 623–664 (2005)
39. Trent, R.J., Monczka, R.M.: Understanding integrated global sourcing. International Journal of Physical Distribution and Logistics Management 33(7), 607–629 (2003)
40. Kasanen, E., Lukka, K., Siitonen, A.: The constructive approach in management accounting research. Journal of Management Accounting Research 5, 243–264 (1993)

What to Offshore, What to Produce at Home? A Methodology

Marco Semini[1], Børge Sjøbakk[1], and Erlend Alfnes[2]

[1] SINTEF Technology and Society, Industrial Management,
P.O. Box 4760 Sluppen, N-7465 Trondheim, Norway
{marco.semini,borge.sjobakk}@sintef.no
[2] Department of Production and Quality Engineering,
Norwegian University of Science and Technology, NTNU
erlend.alfnes@ntnu.no

Abstract. Ever-increasing cost pressure and global competition has forced many Western manufacturing companies to offshore some or all of their production; i.e. to establish a manufacturing operation/facility in a low-cost country that replaces a facility in the country of origin. Literature concludes, however, that businesses do not make offshoring decisions in a systematic manner. This emphasizes the need for models, methodologies and tools supporting companies in making sound offshoring decisions. This paper proposes such a methodology for one of the crucial questions many offshoring companies face: For which products should production be offshored, for which should it be kept back? The proposed methodology consists of five steps: (1) Identify constants and variables (scoping); (2) Determine and characterize product groups; (3) Perform a strategic (qualitative) analysis; (4) Perform a financial (quantitative) analysis; and (5) Take a decision. The paper briefly describes each step, with a focus on the first three steps.

Keywords: Offshoring, facility strategy, global manufacturing, methodology.

1 Introduction

Ever-increasing cost pressure and global competition has forced many Western manufacturing companies to offshore, i.e. move some or all of their operations to low-cost countries, such as China or India, where manual labor continues to be as much as ten times cheaper than in Western Europe or the U.S. Besides lower factor costs, decisions to offshore are usually driven by closeness to (new) markets; access to foreign distribution channels, materials and goods; and securing of knowledge (Kinkel and Maloca 2009).

Offshoring is a highly complex process which entails a vast amount of decisions to be taken. In fact, most – if not all – decision categories within operations strategy as identified by Beckman and Rosenfield (2008) need to be addressed: Vertical integration, process technology, capacity, facilities, sourcing, business processes and policies, supply chain coordination, information technology and operations capabilities

C. Emmanouilidis, M. Taisch, D. Kiritsis (Eds.): APMS 2012, Part II, IFIP AICT 398, pp. 479–486, 2013.

development. When a company has decided to engage in offshoring, making good decisions in such strategic areas will significantly impact whether the company will fail or succeed with the endeavor. Literature concludes, however, that "businesses don't make decisions about offshoring systematically enough" (Aron and Singh 2005). At the same time, literature aiming to help companies address offshoring-related issues is scarce. This emphasizes the need for models, methodologies and tools supporting companies in making sound offshoring-related decisions.

This paper proposes a methodology for a crucial question many offshoring companies face: For which products should production be transferred to a low-cost facility, for which should it be kept back? In other words, should some products still be produced at the domestic plant, and – if so – which? This is a complex and difficult decision affecting many operations strategy decision categories, short-term and long-term considerations can pull in different directions, and it is highly affected not only by business-economical, but also political and personal considerations. The authors take the stance that a structured, rational and holistic approach to this decision increases the chance that it supports sustainable development of the business and reduces short-term focused, opportunistic behavior.

The remainder of this paper is structured as follows: First, the research method employed is described briefly. This is followed by a chapter briefly reviewing relevant literature and concluding that there is a need for more practical guidelines and methodologies on which products to produce where. Thereafter, we present the case company, i.e. the problem holder together which the proposed methodology was developed. Next, the five-step methodology is described, with focus on how the first three steps were carried out together with the case company. Finally, conclusions, including limitations and opportunities for further research are presented.

2   Research Method

The proposed methodology has been developed through utilizing the action research method. In action research, one seeks to generate new knowledge for both a problem owner and an action researcher through doing collaborative problem solving while having a research interest in mind (Greenwood and Levin 2007). As such, action research relies on the researcher(s) actively taking part in the context of his/her research interest area, offering a good insight to the problem and the problem holder (Gummesson 1991). This approach differs from many other research methods, which typically investigate the problem from the outside.

Like any other research method, action research has some shortcomings, especially regarding the reliability of the results. We acknowledge that the idiosyncratic context of the researchers and the problem holder impede the possibility to fully replicate the research and its results. Therefore, in order to achieve as high reliability as possible, we have documented the researchers' relation to the problem holder and how the methodology was developed (see chapter 4 and 5, respectively).

3   The Product Offshoring Decision

Faced with significantly lower factor costs; closeness to new markets; access to foreign distribution channels, materials and goods; and securing of knowledge many companies choose to relocate parts their production (Kinkel and Maloca 2009). When making this decision, a company has multiple alternatives. It may choose to keep the production internally or have an external actor take on the responsibility, and the production may be either domestic or international (Monczka et al. 2005, Jahns et al. 2006). When activities are kept within the company, but moved to foreign markets, the term "captive offshoring" (Monczka et al. 2005), or just "offshoring", is used. For the purpose of this paper, we define "offshoring" as the situation of establishing a manufacturing operation in a low-labor-cost country that replaces a facility in a high-wage country (Hogan, 2004).

Relevant literature regarding offshoring encompass topics such as empirical investigations of how offshoring and outsourcing decisions are made (e.g. Lewin and Peeters 2006, Kedia and Mukherjee 2009) and the extent of offshoring in practice (e.g. Mol et al. 2004, Lewin and Peeters 2006, Kinkel and Maloca 2009); design and configuration of global manufacturing networks (e.g. Ferdows 1997); the importance of co-locating functions (e.g. Bartmess and Cerny 1993, Ulrich and Ellison 2005); global versus local sourcing (e.g. Kotabe and Murray 2004, Gelderman and Semeijn 2006, Trautmann et al. 2009); capacity expansion (e.g. Julka et al. 2007) and facility location (e.g. Dou and Sarkis 2010, Kedia and Mukherjee 2009). Several authors concentrate on the drivers and risk of offshoring (Schoenherr et al. 2008; Lampel and Bhalla 2011) – often, they take a stance for or against the necessity of offshoring. Some authors discuss the common pitfalls in offshoring (Aron and Singh 2005). They find that companies tend to focus too much on location and factor costs, do not evaluate all risk factors, and think that it is a matter of all or nothing.

Our review of the literature revealed some guidelines and methodologies supporting the relocation of production. However, such methodologies typically consider the make-or-buy decision and the logic of outsourcing (i.e. transferring production to an external actor) (e.g. Cousins, Lamming et al. 2008; Dou and Sarkis 2009; Tayles and Drury 2001), together with capacity strategy issues (e.g. Slack and Lewis 2008). Common for these methodologies is that they typically do not consider all product characteristics that may influence the offshoring decision. As such, there is a need to combine existing guidelines and methodologies on offshoring/outsourcing with other relevant literature in order to reach a structured, rational and holistic approach to the decision of what to produce where.

4   The Case Company

The present research has been carried out in collaboration with a Norwegian manufacturing plant. The plant designs, produces and delivers electronic high-tech equipment for the maritime industry worldwide. The total yearly production volume is approximately 60'000-70'000 items, delivered directly to shipyards, to suppliers of the yards and – in the aftermarket – to shipowners for repairs and upgrades. The market is constantly moving more to the East, especially the shipbuilding nations China and Korea, but there are still considerable volumes sent to European locations as well.

Until 2008, all production of these items was performed by the Norwegian plant. There is, however, an increasing need to reduce costs and follow the market to stay competitive in an increasingly global and fierce competition. This made the case company establish a manufacturing facility in the Shanghai area. In the process of transferring operations to this plant, the company realized that deciding which products to offshore involves trade-offs of more than costs and other easily quantifiable and comparable factors. It was concerned with a holistic, thorough analysis of all relevant aspects. The plant raised this issue to the authors, requesting a practical, but still systematic approach to decide which products to offshore, which to keep back. It should provide the managers with arguments supporting their decisions and, thereby, increase their confidence in them. It led the researchers to the development of the methodology presented in this paper, which is further described in the next chapter.

5   A Methodology for Product Offshoring

As explained, the purpose of the proposed methodology is to guide manufacturing plants in deciding which products to transfer to foreign subsidiaries and which to keep producing at the domestic plant. It has been developed for and tested at the case company presented, and it is therefore presented here by reporting its use in this context. In order to assure a comprehensive assessment, we considered it as important that all relevant business functions at the case company were represented when we performed critical steps in the methodology, such as production, product development, process development, purchasing and marketing/sales. The methodology consists of the following steps, which will be described below: (1) identify constants and variables (scoping); (2) determine and characterize product groups; (3) perform a strategic (qualitative) analysis; (4) perform a financial (quantitative) analysis; and (5) take a decision.

Step 1: Identify Constants and Variables (Scoping). First, we had to make sure all involved parties agreed on contextual parameters (fixed), decision variables (to be decided upon), and consequences of the decision (indirect decision variables). This is important in order to focus the assessment on the key question; avoiding circular argumentation and assuring that all parties base it on the same premises. In particular, the following was considered as fixed framework conditions within the present methodology: Macro-economic factors and developments, business strategy, product specter and product/market characteristics, available process technologies for these products (e.g., level of automation), as well as plant locations and overall plant-locational characteristics such as culture and industrial traditions. Overall business functions performed at each plant were also considered as given. For example, product and process development were assumed to be located in Norway, sourcing of mechanical components in China and distribution at both plants.

Furthermore, we selected a range of products for which the offshoring question was particularly relevant, and we clearly demarcated which steps of the production process were included in the analysis, i.e. were candidates for offshoring (e.g. assembly). These products/process steps did not share materials or resources with the remaining products and process steps, for which we considered the location to be given. The decision variables were thus where to locate the selected process steps for the selected product range. Finally, we considered plant capacities, equipment and capabilities to a reasonable degree variable and depending on the decisions variables.

Step 2: Determine and Characterize Product Groups. The degree to which offshoring leads to benefits or implies risks depends on product characteristics. A basic element of the proposed methodology is therefore that it matches product characteristics to plant-locational characteristics. We have compiled a "checklist" of relevant product characteristics (Table 1). Based on this "checklist", we defined a number of product groups, each of which was largely homogeneous with respect to such characteristics. Group technology (Burbidge 1975) can provide the theoretical foundation for this. For each such product group, it should be possible to determine a suitable production location. As we realized, it was crucial to assure a common understanding of these product groups, if a consensus was to be achieved on where to produce them.

Table 1. Product characteristics of relevance when deciding whether to offshore or not

---

Market requirements (importance of ...)
- Quality, low price, availability (lead time and delivery precision)
- Level of customization and product change, product variety
- Level of innovation and life cycle stage
- Special features (need for special purpose and/or high-quality components)
- Asian or Western origin

Demand in each region

Produceability (Labor and process)
- Complexity of specifications, (level of) skills required for production
- Process requirements (resources and capabilities)
- Level of manual work (either because too low volume or difficult to automate)

Unit Transportation costs, inclusive taxes and tariffs

Inventory carrying costs (heavily affected by product value)

Required raw materials and components

Step 3: Perform a Strategic (Qualitative) Analysis. In this step, we qualitatively assessed the consequences of offshoring each of the identified product groups. We compiled a "checklist" of relevant aspects (Table 2) and used it to compare offshoring to continued domestic production. This was done in a workshop with key informants from the case company. In a combination of group and plenary work, we gave each aspect of Table 2 a score, separately for each product group. This led to fruitful discussions and identification of key arguments for and against offshoring. It also led to a preliminary conclusion for each product group. We then combined the results and assessed the resulting scenario as a whole with respect to shared materials, resources and capabilities.

Table 2. Aspects affecting the product offshoring decision

Factor costs	How are factor costs affected? Direct and indirect labor cost seems to be the most common offshoring driver (Kinkel & Maloca 2009). Other factor costs include material, capital and energy. Factor costs are often too significant to stay in a developed market and remain competitive (Beckman and Rosenfield 2008).
Outbound logistics	How is distribution affected, in terms of transportation costs, lead times, responsiveness, delivery precision, import taxes and tariffs, inventory carrying costs and value chain coordination? Whether the effects are positive or negative depends highly on the location of the main market. Market proximity is an important driver for offshoring (Kinkel & Maloca 2009).
Plant and equipment utilization	How is capacity utilization at each plant affected if the products are offshored? How easily can capacities be adapted to production volumes (flexible/inflexible resources)? Can plant overhead costs be justified for such volumes, if this is deemed necessary? It may be easier to argue for offshoring if capacity is well-utilized at the domestic plant.
Plant capabilities	How capable is the foreign plant of producing products with the given specifications and process requirements? The more complex the specifications/process, the higher typically is the level of skills and competences required. The ability to produce the required quality also needs to be considered, as well as, for example, labor effectiveness and flexibility.
Inbound logistics (purchasing)	How is inbound logistics affected? This aspect addresses the acquisition of raw materials and components. How are the costs, lead times, availabilities and responsiveness of potential suppliers to the foreign plant? How is product quality, in terms of functionality, robustness and health and environment? The costs needed to assure a satisfactory level of quality also need to be considered.
Transfer and start-up costs	What are the transfer and start-up costs? The costs and challenges associated with moving and investing in equipment, ramping up production, capturing and transferring knowledge, establishing organizational structures and policies, selecting suppliers etc. may vary with different offshoring alternatives. Companies seem to underestimate such costs.
Proximity to product development	What is the risk of hampering innovation and customization due to distance between product development and production? Geographic dispersion can make communication more difficult. The higher the need for informal, "unstructured" technical dialogue, the more important is geographical proximity between production and product development.
Intellectual property	What is the risk of intellectual property leaking and competitors building similar products, in turn reducing the company's competitive advantage? Even in captive offshoring, sensitive information and knowledge can leak through employee turnover. Employee turnover rates, intellectual property rights legislation in the foreign country and how to safely transfer specifications need to be considered.
Other	Additional aspects of relevance may be identified in each particular case. In our study, the following issues were brought up: Market capturing/positioning; problems with "bringing home profit", i.e. transferring profit back to the home country; customer requests for price reductions due to production in low-cost country, or even customer refusals to buy such products.

Step 4: Perform a Financial (Quantitative) Analysis. In step 4, a quantitative cost analysis is performed. While ideally, all relevant costs should be included (see Platts and Song 2010 for an overview), such an analysis in practice often focuses on cost types that can be reasonably well estimated, such as direct costs and some types of indirect costs. While it must be kept in mind that such easily quantifiable costs only stand for a part of the total cost of offshoring, a quantitative analysis can still provide a strong argument for a decision and increase confidence in it.

Step 5: Take a Decision. In combination, the results from the qualitative and quantitative assessment should provide a solid basis for the management board to take the final decision. It should however be kept in mind that only offshoring is considered, with plenty of framework conditions considered as given (as specified in step 1). Offshoring should be compared to other cost-reducing initiatives, such as automation and other process improvements at the domestic plant, product redesign according to design for manufacturing principles, product outsourcing or phasing-out etc.

6   Conclusions

This paper has presented a methodology for taking sound product offshoring decisions. It can be considered as a standardization of a strategy process. It must be repeated regularly as relevant aspects of the business and environment, such as those identified in step 1, change. It should also be kept in mind that in general, there is not one correct answer to the offshoring question. Competitive advantage comes not only from making good offshoring decisions, but equally from how these are implemented.

Feedback from the case company's managers supports the usefulness and validity of the proposed methodology. Some limitations still need to be mentioned. First, it has so far been mainly developed for and tested at a single case company; there is a need for additional case studies and subsequent improvement of the methodology. Second, it must be emphasized that it is a heuristic, i.e. it does not guarantee to find the "best" solution. It puts emphasis on ease of application and fostering company-wide awareness of the trade-offs in offshoring decisions.

Acknowledgements. We thank the MARGIN project and the SFI Norman research program for support of the research presented in this paper.

References

Aron, R., Singh, J.V.: Getting Offshoring Right. Harvard Bus. Rev. 83(12), 135–143 (2005)

Bartmess, A., Cerny, K.: Building Competitive Advantage through a Global Network of Capabilities. Calif. Manage. Rev. 35(2), 78–103 (1993)

Beckman, S.L., Rosenfield, D.B.: Operations Strategy: Competing in the 21st Century. McGraw-Hill/Irwin, Boston (2008)

Burbidge, J.L.: The Introduction of Group Technology. Heinemann, London (1975)

Cousins, P., et al.: Strategic Supply Management: Principles, Theories and Practice. Prentice Hall (2008)

Dou, Y.J., Sarkis, J.: A Joint Location and Outsourcing Sustainability Analysis for a Strategic Offshoring Decision. Int. J. Prod. Res. 48(2), 567–592 (2010)

Ferdows, K.: Making the Most of Foreign Factories. Harvard Bus. Rev. 75(2), 73–88 (1997)

Gelderman, C.J., Semeijn, J.: Managing the Global Supply Base through Purchasing Portfolio Management. J. Purch. Supply Manag. 12(4), 209–217 (2006)

Greenwood, D., Levin, M.: Introduction to Action Research, 2nd edn. Sage Publications, Thousand Oaks (2007)

Gummesson, E.: Qualitative Methods in Management Research. Sage Publications, Inc. (1991)

Hogan, G.: Going Offshore's Easy Right? Manuf. Eng., 75–84 (December 2004)

Jahns, C., Hartmann, E., Bals, L.: Offshoring: Dimensions and Diffusion of a New Business Concept. J. Purch. Supply Manag. 12(4), 218–231 (2006)

Julka, N., et al.: A Review of Multi-Factor Capacity Expansion Models for Manufacturing Plants: Searching for a Holistic Decision Aid. Int. J. Prod. Econ. 106(2), 607–621 (2007)

Kedia, B.L., Mukherjee, D.: Understanding Offshoring: A Research Framework Based on Disintegration, Location and Externalization Advantages. J. World Bus. 44(3), 250–261 (2009)

Kinkel, S., Maloca, S.: Drivers and Antecedents of Manufacturing Offshoring and Backshoring—a German Perspective. J. Purch. Supply Manag. 15(3), 154–165 (2009)

Kotabe, M., Murray, J.Y.: Global Sourcing Strategy and Sustainable Competitive Advantage. Ind. Market. Manag. 33, 7–14 (2004)

Lampel, J., Bhalla, A.: Living with Offshoring: The Impact of Offshoring on the Evolution of Organizational Configurations. J. World Bus. 46(3), 346–358 (2011)

Lewin, A.Y., Peeters, C.: Offshoring Work: Business Hype or the Onset of Fundamental Transformation? Long Range Plann. 39(3), 221–239 (2006)

Mol, M.J., et al.: A Technological Contingency Perspective on the Depth and Scope of International Outsourcing. Journal of International Management 10(2), 287–305 (2004)

Monczka, R.M., et al.: Outsourcing Strategically for Sustainable Competitive Advantage. CAPS Research Report. 1, 99 (2005)

Platts, K.W., Song, N.: Overseas Sourcing Decisions - the Total Cost of Sourcing from China. Supply Chain Manag. 15(4), 320–331 (2010)

Schoenherr, T., Rao Tummala, V.M., Harrison, T.P.: Assessing Supply Chain Risks with the Analytic Hierarchy Process: Providing Decision Support for the Offshoring Decision by a Us Manufacturing Company. J. Purch. Supply Manag. 14(2), 100–111 (2008)

Slack, N., Lewis, M.: Operations Strategy, 2nd edn. Pearson Education, Harlow (2008)

Tayles, M., Drury, C.: Moving from Make/Buy to Strategic Sourcing: The Outsource Decision Process. Long Range Plann. 34(5), 605–622 (2001)

Trautmann, G., Bals, L., Hartmann, E.: Global Sourcing in Integrated Network Structures: The Case of Hybrid Purchasing Organizations. Journal of International Management 15(2), 194–208 (2009)

Ulrich, K.T., Ellison, D.J.: Beyond Make-Buy: Internalization and Integration of Design and Production. Prod. Oper. Manag. 14(3), 315–330 (2005)

Idiosyncratic Behavior of Globally Distributed Manufacturing

Stanislaw Strzelczak

Warsaw University of Technology, Faculty of Production Engineering, Warsaw, Poland
s.strzelczak@wip.pw.edu.pl

Abstract. The paper presents results of empirical research, which explores systemic background of increasing turbulences and disruptions within globally distributed manufacturing networks. Among the identified factors three have biggest impact: (1) the level of completeness and connectivity of the networks, i.e. topological characteristics of the manufacturing network (2) the herd behavior of clients and decision makers, which enhances or tames the demand due to occasional asymmetry of their perception of the demand (3) the diversity of operational environments within the network, which itself may be a dominant factor of turbulences or even disruptions of the operational processes. It means that in some circumstances, the internal resources of companies may have limited value as a countermeasure against the unlikely effects of turbulences and disruptions. The research has also identified some other factors of idiosyncratic behavior of globally distributed manufacturing, which are rooted in some particular operational policies.

1   Introduction

The industrial practice of recent years brings more and more examples of idiosyncratic behavior of globally distributed manufacturing networks [6, 12]. In some circumstances industrial supply chains present surprisingly sensitive reactions to the disruptive events or even minor changes in the business environment, like reversing trend of demand. Disruptions and turbulences are becoming more and more frequent, like the catastrophic events, which often trigger them. In extreme cases we can observe long lasting breakdowns of business continuity or even bankruptcy avalanches. The existing theories, which are mostly rooted in the industrial dynamics [14], the bullwhip effect related research [1] and enterprise risk management [11], when confronted with the empirical evidence, provide only limited explanation to the increasingly frequent phenomena, as a limited scope of probably factors of idiosyncratic behavior is usually considered in the literature [15].

The purpose of the research presented in this paper was to investigate the reasons and mechanisms, which influence emergence and dynamics of idiosyncratic phenomena in manufacturing networks, with a special reference to the circumstances and qualities, which are typical for globally distributed manufacturing networks, like cross-border effects, increased and more variable lead times, or diversified business environments.

C. Emmanouilidis, M. Taisch, D. Kiritsis (Eds.): APMS 2012, Part II, IFIP AICT 398, pp. 487–494, 2013.

To avoid disadvantages of the earlier research, presented in the available literature, a holistic methodological approach was presumed from the early beginning, including hybrid and multi-perspective modeling. A particular attention was given to the explanation of complexity of all existing reasons of idiosyncratic behavior, by empirical evidence. This was protected by a range of research approaches, ranging from case studies and interviewing, through analysis of operational records from the ERP databases, to a hybrid modeling.

2   Existing Knowledge

The existing theory presents two major explanations of unsteady behavior of industrial networks, both linked to demand information distortion backward supply chains:

1. Misperception of feedback in the closed loops of decision making, typically enhanced by some operational factors, like lot-sizing, etc. [13],
2. Behavioral causes, e.g. shortage gaming by decision makers [5].

The theory suggests, that the most steady demand patterns can be observed at the end of supply chains, while the final customers are not considered as a major source of disruptions and operational risks. It also means that it is taken for granted, that the distortion of demand information normally increases backward supply chain. Typically the available publications discuss behavioral effects without any consideration of the social context or the social dynamics. Particularly, the impacts of communication within industrial networks or other impacts of external environment, like the media, which all together may possibly cause misperceptions, herd behaviors and other behavioral impacts resulting in deviation of decision making from its normal mode, are not being considered in the production management literature. It is also worth to notice, that the conclusions from the research around prospect theory were not considered by the production management literature [2].

In recent several years numerous publications exploited different frameworks of operational risk management. The factors of risk are being classified in different ways and risk prevention and mitigation policies proposed [e.g. 4, 3, 9, 10, 16], together with some relevant performance measurements [8]. It is notable, that this stream of literature actually applies a particular research perspective. The explored phenomena are being considered as affecting a single company, and locally applied countermeasures are the focus of considerations. This happens, despite the considered factors are located not only inside a company, but also outside, in the supply chain. Furthermore, some external determinants, like oscillating or even disrupting exchange rates, or – surprisingly – the effects of global spread or off-shoring of production processes (e.g. longer and more variable lead times), got very limited attention in the literature as a factor of turbulences within industrial networks.

To resume, due to a reductionism of the research methodologies in the literature, a question is justified, if some important factors were ignored, e.g. some exogenous determinants or structural qualities or social behaviors or systemic factors. The above doubts established the starting point of the presented research.

3   Methodology and Data

The formulated problem demanded for a research, which could identify all actual reasons of idiosyncratic behavior of globally distributed manufacturing networks. Hence, a holistic model approach was needed and an access to a relevant data. Employing a causal texture framework for organizational environments [7], the below ontological model of problem domain has been developed, which eliminate the methodological shortcomings of former research (Fig.1). It recognizes environmental heterogeneity, different types of determinants and different types of interdependencies, which may trigger or enhance idiosyncratic phenomena.

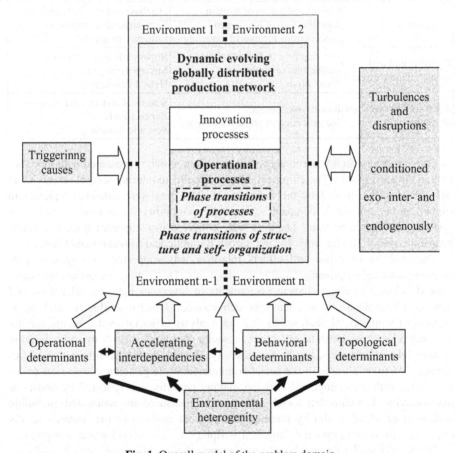

Fig. 1. Overall model of the problem domain

After consideration of possibilities to access relevant data, three approaches for empirical data collection were assumed, to protect reliability and relevance of final results of the research, and particularly to support later modeling and simulations:

- field observation or case studies, including case studies of turbulent phenomena within network context, like disruption avalanches;
- semi-structured interviewing and questionnaire research;
- exploration of databases of the ERP systems of networked companies, as well as other available statistical data.

Table 1. Structure of the research

Phase of research	Scope of research	Methods and tools
Initial (conceptual)	Initial problem conceptualization Identification of factors and elements of the problem domain	Analysis of literature Questionnaire research Semi-structured interviews
Ontological	Conceptualization of domain Identification of interdependencies Assumptions for hybrid modeling	Database and statistics analysis Semi-structured interviews Influence diagrams
Experimental and monographic research	Development of hybrid models Calibration of models Simulations	Bayesian-Belief Networks Management games Hybrid simulations
Analysis and synthesis of results	Results assessment Identification of phase transitions	Statistical and spectral analysis Expert panels Scenario modeling

The further research was run according to a plan, which is presented with more details in the above table. The empirical data were collected during several research and advisory projects, leaded by the main author. The data were collected typically in supply chains, not single companies, to get the possibility for empirical analysis of systemic driven phenomena. The data were collected in companies from five European countries (UK, Germany, Poland, Czech Republic and Slovakia) and China.

The analysis of cause and effects relations was supported by cognitive pre-mapping and development of influence diagrams. Descriptive measurement scales were developed to enable hybrid assessments of leverages between behavioral and material phenomena. A particular approach was developed to enable researching of impacts of some social phenomena. E.g. an analysis of social modes accompanying herd behaviors, which can be reflected in a social communication or by some decision making related behaviors, can be run this way. We can do it by confrontation of frequencies of some phrases in the social communication (e.g. at some web-sites or forums etc.) with the changes of decision making patterns, e.g. reflected by under- or over-ordering. It means that social modes can be measured and monitored, including follow-up of social media by Internet. A statistical analysis of the research results (Pearson – for correlations and Cronbach's Alpha – for reliability) was also applied.

The hybrid modeling was based upon agency theory. However, use of AnyLogic package, enabled to incorporate behaviors and social interactions of agents. Because of that modeling of social dynamics within the production networks and between the agents and environment became possible. E.g. it became possible to model increasing fears or euphoria, leading to herd behavior of decision makers. Different operational strategies and policies could be also considered this way, e.g. comparison of lean manufacturing networks and networks with high level of connectivity, like the cluster-based networks, or comparison of push- and pull-flow based control, etc.

4   Results of the Research

The first two stages of the research confirmed, that idiosyncratic behavior of globally distributed manufacturing networks is a systemic phenomena driven by inter- endo- and exogenous interdependencies, and determined by following factors:

- triggering causes:
  - turbulences in the environment,
  - disruptions, which immediately influence operation of network etc.,
  - deviations of processes or some operational characteristics,
- enabling causes:
  - accelerating interdependencies: exo-, inter- and endogenous,
  - heterogenic environment (or its segments), process flow barriers between them,
- conditioning causes:
  - network topology:
    o topology of flows,
    o topology of technical and organizational tiers,
  - behavioral determinants:
    o profile of inter-organizational behaviors,
    o profile of asymmetric perception of demand during purchasing decisions,
  - operational determinants:
    o profile of operational liquidity,
    o profile of operational policies,
    o profile of operational risks.

The research provided empirical evidence for a thesis, that among the different non-behavioral factors three have the biggest impact on idiosyncratic phenomena:

- the level of completeness and connectivity of the networks, which is related to the freedom of choosing alternative vendors or distribution channels,
- the diversity of operational environments within the network, which is related to diversification of operational characteristics of different segments of the network,
- the profile of operational liquidity[1], which is related to ability to cope with changing market demand and availability of supplies, that is depending not only to the internal resources and contingencies, but also to the internal operational flexibility.

The research has also shown some other factors of turbulent behavior of manufacturing networks, which are rooted in particular operational policies[2]. Oppositely, it has shown that common contingencies, like inventories, may have limited role as countermeasures against disruptions or turbulences, depending on some circumstances.

---

[1] To be distinguished from financial liquidity.

[2] Not discussed in this paper due to its limited size.

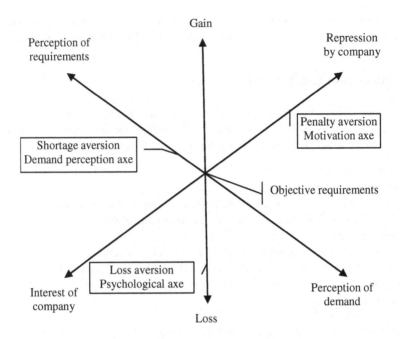

Fig. 2. Asymmetric perceptions behind operational purchasing decisions

The research of behavioral causes of idiosyncratic phenomena in manufacturing networks suggest, that a particular mechanism is underlying misperception of demand and later its distortion, which is different than that described in the literature of bullwhip effect and by the theory of prospect. It is presented at Figure 2. Three asymmetries work together which may deviate perception of purchasing requirements from the actual objective level: fear of loss by a company, fear of a material shortage and fear personal loss due to some penalty from a company, depending on the motivation system. The fear of material shortage (or surplus) can be substantially enhanced by communication with the environment: clients and vendors or the overall environment, particularly markets. Occasionally a herd behavior of clients and/or decision makers may arise, like panic or euphoria, which may enhance or tame the demand or supplies. If the speed of communication is high, like it happens with the Internet based media, and if the change of supplies or demand is not limited by availability of some resources, the turbulence within the network maybe extremely rapid, high and long lasting. Its growth is driven by an accelerating interdependence of modes at markets and decision-making behaviors. Due to increasing openness of social communication this phenomena may have a growing impact on manufacturing industries and economies in the near future. To continue, it is interesting, that the research has confirmed, that by a comparison of operational records from the ERP databases and the records of media or business communication (e.g. content of particular websites or forums, etc.), we can follow and confirm correlation of changing asymmetries of the demand perceptions and changing modes of markets or other communities (like the communities of decision makers within one network).

The results of both, case studies and hybrid modeling have confirmed that disruptions and turbulences propagate within networks, like avalanches in different directions, depending on the triggering causes and environmental factors. This means that the explanations of bullwhip effect by existing theories cannot be recognized as a relevant framework for a full explanation of the discussed phenomena.

Although the results presented in this paper were obtained on the basis of research and advisory projects, done in industrial companies, which operate in the EU and China, they obviously apply to other sectors regions. Nevertheless, the proposed methodology and the research results should be considered as initial. They need to be verified and developed by a further empirical and conceptual research.

5   Conclusions and Summary

The obtained results have extended available knowledge on the reasons and mechanisms of disruptions and turbulences within globally distributed manufacturing networks. Systemic factors of disruptions and turbulences have been identified and the model of their impact has been proposed and justified. Among the identified factors two may have a growing impact in the future: the herd behavior of decision makers driven by growing possibilities of social communication and the diversity of network environments due to the increasing globalization.

The obtained results put a question mark against common operational strategies, particularly these, which are rooted in the concept of lean manufacturing. Lean networks are typically characterized by a minimized number of clients and vendors as well as by limited contingencies of resources, like capacities or inventories. Using the results of the research we can argue that lean networks are particularly exposed to disruptions and turbulences and by leaning the network we increase its potential for idiosyncratic behaviors. Similarly, according to the obtained results, the global spread of manufacturing networks, due to increased diversity of operational environments and due to deteriorated operational characteristics, is normally enhancing idiosyncratic performance of manufacturing networks, which up to now was not considered within operation strategy processes. Particularly, the operational strategies and policies should consider differences of operational environments along the supply chains, mostly these, which influence operational liquidity and connectivity. There are good reasons to advocate for further research aimed at methodologies and assessments which could facilitate these shortcomings.

Referring to the possible practical implementations of the obtained results, two possible mainstreams seem to have major role: executive education and consultancy. Using the existing experience it is possible to propose and justify some frameworks means, which can be used to improve strategic planning of operations and managing the performance of globally distributed production networks, by harmonization of strategies, systems and cultures. However, a major difficulty cannot be easily avoided. The companies tend to perceive reality from the perspective of their interior, while the discussed phenomena has evidently systemic roots and should be considered from a network perspective, including interactions with the business environment.

To resume, it is worth to note some novelty of the research and obtained results. The material and cultural phenomena and processes within industrial networks were considered simultaneously. This enabled new modeling approaches, and much more relevant explanations of the discussed phenomena were obtained, than before. The results suggest new types of threats and perils, which may follow lean networking, global outsourcing and off-shoring. Finally, a new way of parallel researching of social phenomena observed in media and operational processes observed in the operational databases was proposed.

References

1. Bhattacharya, R., Bandyopadhyay, S.: A review of the causes of bullwhip effect in a supply chain. The International Journal of Advanced Manufacturing Technology 54(9-12), 1245–1261 (2010)
2. Camerer, C., Loewenstein, G., Rabin, M. (eds.): Advances in behavioral economics, pp. 689–723. Princeton University Press, Princeton (2004)
3. Chopra, S., Sodhi, M.S.: Managing risk to avoid supply-chain breakdown. Sloan Management Review 46(1), 53–62 (2004)
4. Christopher, M., Holweg, M.: "Supply Chain 2.0": managing supply chains in the era of turbulence. International Journal of Physical Distribution and Logistics Management 41(1), 63–82 (2011)
5. Croson, R., Donohue, K.: Behavioral causes of the bullwhip effect and the observed value of inventory information. Management Science 52(3), 323–336 (2006)
6. Dowell, A.: Effects of Triple Disaster Will Reverberate for Months. The Wall Street Journal (March 28, 2011)
7. Emery, F.E., Trist, E.L.: The causal texture of organizational environments. Human Relations 18(1), 21–32 (1965)
8. Fransoo, J., Wouters, M.: Measuring the bullwhip effect in the supply chain. Supply Chain Management: An International Journal, 5 5(2), 78–89 (2000)
9. Jüttner, U.: Supply chain risk management. Understanding the business requirements from a practitioner perspective. International Journal of Logistics Management 16(1), 120–141 (2005)
10. Kleindorfer, P.R., Saad, G.H.: Managing disruption risks in supply chains. Production and Operations Management 14(1), 53–68 (2006)
11. Pfohl, H.-C., Köhler, H., Thomas, D.: State of the art in supply chain risk management research: empirical and conceptual findings and a roadmap for the implementation in practice. Logistics Research 2(1), 33–44 (2010)
12. Schäfer, D.: Lack of parts hits VW production. Financial Times (January 20, 2011)
13. Sterman, J.D.: Misperceptions of feedback in dynamic decision making. Organizational Behavior and Human Decision Processes 43(3), 301–335 (1989)
14. Sterman, J.D.: Business dynamics. McGraw-Hill (2000)
15. Strzelczak, S.: Reducing turbulences in industrial supply chains. In: Koch, T. (ed.) Learn Business System and Beyond. LNBIP, vol. 257, pp. 393–402. Springer, Boston (2008)
16. Wagner, S.M., Bode, C.: An empirical investigation of supply chain performance along several dimensions of risk. Journal of Business Logistics 29(1), 307–325 (2008)

Improving the Industrialization of a New Product in an International Production Network: A Case Study from the Machinery Industry

Donatella Corti and Saransh Choudhury

Dept of Management, Economics and Industrial Engineering,
Politecnico di Milano P.zza Leonardo da Vinci, 32, 20133 Milano, Italy
donatella.corti@polimi.it, saransh.choudhury@imim.polimi.it

Abstract. The paper deals with cross-functional disciplines affecting product industrialization in companies organized around an international production network. Aim of the paper is the development of a framework to support a company along the industrialization process taking into consideration that more than one plant located globally could be affected by the introduction of a new product. The framework is based on the use of the general morphological analysis and can be used at both strategic and tactical level by managers in medium sized manufacturing enterprises. The framework is tailored to a case study company and then some operational guidelines are provided to develop the industrialization framework for other organizations.

Keywords: global operations, machinery, industrialization process, new product development.

1 Introduction

A new product generally takes a tangible form after market survey, concept validation in research laboratory, followed by development and testing. A number of activities need to be carried out at all stages of the product life-cycle to ensure that products are manufactured at desired locations, at targeted cost, on schedule, and with the features demanded by customers. Based on literature review and interaction with practitioners in industry, these activities were found to be interchangeably called commercialization, industrialization, localization or product launch (Swink and Song, 2007; Song and Montoya-Weiss, 1998). In absence of a common definition, in this paper industrialization is defined as all upstream activities aimed at designing the production process of new products at the desired manufacturing location (including offshore plants).

Globalization and the emergence of developing countries have meant that product development, manufacturing and marketing decisions happen in far-flung geographical locations (Abele et al., 2008). The process of industrialization becomes further challenging due to physical distance between manufacturing facilities and development centre, language barriers and cultural differences across locations. Companies

C. Emmanouilidis, M. Taisch, D. Kiritsis (Eds.): APMS 2012, Part II, IFIP AICT 398, pp. 495–502, 2013.
© IFIP International Federation for Information Processing 2013

would like to have a standard quality of products irrespective of the location where the new product is produced and to take advantage of cost savings associated with offshore manufacturing. The aim of this paper is the development of a framework that could structure the industrialization process of an Italian medium sized company producing capital goods and with an international production network. An attempt is done to generalize the empirical findings and some guidelines are provided to support companies in a similar context to develop their own industrialization process.

2 Literature Review

For a review on industrialization some contributions can be found in the literature dealing with supply chain management and New Product Development (NPD).

Cooper et al. (1997) developed a supply chain framework to increase the understanding of supply chain. They suggested that the SCM framework consists of three main elements: the structure of supply chain, the supply chain business processes, and supply chain management components. Lambert et al. (1998) extended this framework by providing options for managing the links across the supply chain. Spens and Bask (2002) after applying the framework by Lambert et al. (1998) to the Red Cross blood transfusion service, concluded that in its original form was too complex to map the supply chain, as too many levels and components had to be considered simultaneously. Consequently, they suggested that the framework could be further developed and simplified by concentrating on main processes and components. Pero et al. (2010) created a framework for NPD and supply chain. They carried out case study analysis at four companies to study the effect of product design features - modularity, variety and innovativeness on supply chain performance. They concluded that if a product is highly modular, high level of variety and innovativeness might be tolerated. If the product has an integral architecture and the product is highly innovative, it is necessary to sacrifice variety. Hicks et al. (2000) studied the unique supply chain management in low-volume engineer to order (ETO) product organizations. They concluded that the low volume ETO companies have limited influence over buyers.

Eppinger and Chitkara (2006) provided a framework for global product development and listed the key success factors that help companies overcome its challenges. Abele et al. (2008) presented their extensive study of global production dealing with areas of drivers for international manufacturing, selection criteria of sites, manufacturing network design, technology usage, ramp up suggestions, sourcing guidelines and alignment of R&D. From the analysis of the existing frameworks, it can be drawn that:

- there are no frameworks specifically meant to aid the industrialization process of products in either bigger or smaller companies;
- most of the available frameworks deal with the broader issues of supply chain development and NPD, whilst limited attention is paid to industrialization.

To sum up, there are two types of research contributions: frameworks with strategic issues, but at very high level of abstraction and with little guidance for the practitioners; and research dealing with specific areas of industrialization, but without consideration of upstream and downstream processes. In absence of a unified framework supporting the industrialization process as a whole for international production network, first step towards the development of the proposed framework is the identification of activities to be included in the process of interest.

2.1   The Activities and Processes Impacting Industrialization

The industrialization of a product is a cross functional activity requiring inputs from different functional departments. Since a clear definition of industrialization is missing, the choice of activities which have been discussed here are based on literature review, interaction with practitioners and author's experience as a practitioner in industry. The list of selected activities and the available options follows.

- *New product development process.* It can be carried out using a stage gate process, a phased review method or without use of any formal NPD process. In a stage gate method, the NPD process is divided into many stages. Each stage requires execution of a specific set of activities by different members of the cross functional team (CFT). Each stage is followed by a gate, a meeting of the CFT and the management sponsors. During the gate meeting, the activities of the previous stage of the NPD process are reviewed. The financial projections and technical specification of the new product or service under development are reviewed. A decision is taken by the sponsors to allow the project to move to the next stage of the development process (Cooper, 1990, 2008). In the phased review method NPD is broken down into activities which are assigned to different functional departments. The responsibility of each functional department ends when semi completed work in progress is handed over to the internal customer within the organization. As a result, there is no commitment to the project from beginning to end by any one group.
- *Team Structures.* NPD as well as industrialization in organizations may be carried out using very different team structures and collaboration techniques. They may be classified as CFT, 'pseudo CFT' and department driven development. Team structure impacts the efficiency and effectiveness of industrialization and NPD process.
- *Product design consideration.* The design approach can broadly be classified as modular, platform and integrated (or customized). The product architecture has a profound impact on the industrialization of products.
- *Knowledge management.* Knowledge can be classified into two broad categories – explicit and tacit knowledge (Nonaka and Takeuchi, 1995). Explicit knowledge can be relatively easily transferred, shared and explained (Killing, 1980). On the contrary, tacit knowledge is ingrained in action and is linked to concrete contexts.
- *Make-or-buy decisions.* For industrialization of new products, organizations have to take a decision to make products parts and assemblies in-house or to buy it from suppliers. The decision impacts the preservation of a company's core competences.
- *Vendor Selection.* The vendor selection for product industrialization refers to the distribution among existing or new vendors of the new business opportunities generated by the industrialization.

- *Supplier relationship.* The relationship with suppliers affects the ease with which new products can be industrialized because of reliability and flexibility on the part of the suppliers. A first approach suggested by Kraljic (1983) prescribes supplier relationship based on strategic importance of the specific component and the complexity of the supply market. Based on the evaluation, a type of supplier relationship is chosen. In alternative, it is possible to start by evaluating the type of relationship and the attractiveness of the supplier (Olsen and Ellram, 1997). Based on the above evaluation, parts are assigned to suppliers.

3   The Proposed Framework

The development of the industrialization framework for the case study is done using general morphological analysis adapted to the field of interest. Fritz Zwicky pioneered the development of General morphological analysis (GMA) as a method for investigating the totality of relationships contained in multi-dimensional, non-quantifiable problem complexes (Zwicky, 1969) and was further used by Ritchey (1998) in several applications. The industrialization of products for a multinational company deals with different functions, geographies, cultures and knowledge bases, a qualitative GMA was considered an appropriate tool, even tough the GMA has been never used in this field. In particular, GMA was used to identify the activities of industrialization and then to list the corresponding methodologies. Then the total number of configurations possible by choice of one methodology for each activity was reduced by use of cross consistency assessment (CCA). The output of GMA is a set of possible configurations for industrialization of products. For sake of operational usefulness, the number of configurations has been further refined by introducing certain drivers that may reflect the product and corporate strategy of the company. A guideline for the extension of the use of the framework for other firms is also provided.

4   The Case Study: CM S.p.A

CM S.p.A is a medium sized Italian industrial machinery manufacturer employing approximately 1200 people around the world. The company has two development centers in Italy, each focusing on a specific family of products and four assembly facilities (two in Italy, one in South America and one in China). The development centers design machines and produce the first prototype. Most of the products are made according to an engineer to order (ETO) approach. The pace of innovation is slow to medium. The lead time for a customer order varies from five to eight months. For the product industrialization, the company has in place what can be defined as a stage gate method. During the stage gate meeting that takes place once a month, the senior and middle management reviews the product, but the project team members who carry out the actual work are not present. The project team was not structured as well as the responsibilities assignment. The platform design approach is used for new product design. The knowhow of the employees in development centers as well as in assembly is not codified. The knowledge in areas such as design, assembly, and testing of machines is passed on from one generation of employees to the other orally and by observation. This implies that the organization does not have structured manufacturing processes for assembly of prototypes at its facilities in Italy. Make-or-buy decisions are made without following a structured procedure by individuals in development and procurement functions at different stages of the product lifecycle. All assemblies are done in-house. The supplier selection is ad-hoc and varies across geographies: is driven by cost only in Italy, while in China quality is the most important factor. The relationship with all vendors is also managed in an ad-hoc fashion. The company signs annual rate contract with some important vendors, but a formal classification of products and management of relationship is not carried out. The current state represented by a lack of standardization can be attributed to the explosive growth without attention to standardized processes in the last two decades. The growth of CM S.p.A. was a result of a very important patent that transformed the industry. Main challenges for the industrialization process can be summarized as follows:

- variation in product quality at different manufacturing locations;
- asymmetrically dispersion of knowledge across locations;
- no proper product architecture for global sourcing and global industrialization;
- long lead times for NPD and industrialization.

4.1   Framework Development for CM S.p.A

The first step of the industrialization process was the creation of the industrialization Zwicky box (IZB) that lists all the activities that impact on industrialization (see Table 1). The first column in the IZB lists the industrialization activities and for each one, the corresponding methodologies are put in the right side of the table.

Table 1. – Zwicky industrialization box (IZB)

Activity	Methodologies
NPD process	Stage Gate method
	Phased Review method
	No formal NPD method
Team organization	Cross functional team (CFT)
	Pseudo CFT
	Individual department driven development
Product design consideration	Integrated product Design
	Platform product design
	Modular product design
Tacit knowledge transfer	Codification and sharing of important processes
	Intra company personnel transfer
Make-or-buy decisions	Strategy driven make-buy decision
	Maximization of contribution margin
	Process Technology driven
	Integrated make-buy decision
Vendor selection	Data envelopment analysis (DEA)
	Simple multi criteria rating technique (SMART)
	Analytic Hierarchy Process (AHP)
Supplier relationships	Exploit, balance or Diversify (Kraljic Martix)
	Relationship management (Olsen matrix)

With the above IZB, the total number of possible configurations is 1296 (3x3x3x2x4x3x2). A configuration is defined as a set of choices including one methodology for each of the activity constituting industrialization as defined in the current research. The next step has been the cross consistency assessment (CCA) to reduce the number of industrialization configurations to get a manageable number. Using the CCA, pairs of activities are checked for logical, empirical or normative contradictions (Ritchey, 1998). Logical contradictions are those that are based on the nature of the concepts involved. Empirical contradictions are those relationships judged to be highly improbable or implausible on empirical grounds. Normative contradictions are relationships ruled out on e.g. ethical or political grounds. A detailed analysis of all the contradictions found for the CM case study does not find space in here, but after CCA the total number of configurations was reduced to 24. Among the remaining, the number of configurations which do not reflect the company's product and corporate strategy were eliminated based on the drivers explained in the next section. For instance, a configuration containing Phased review method and pseudo CFT was eliminated as the organization's senior management has taken a strategic decision to develop the products using a stage gate method. The international nature of operations requires that the company's decision making should be based on objective data which can be audited and compared across locations. Thus the supplier relationship has to be based on the use of the Kraljic matrix (Kraljic, 1983). As a result of the GMA and the reduction of configurations guided by drivers, the final industrialization framework that is considered most suitable for CM S.p.A. is the one shown in Table 2.

Table 2. – Zwicky industrialization box (IZB) adapted to the CM case

Industrialization Framework						
NPD process	Team	Product Design	Knowledge transfer	Make-or-buy decision	Vendor Selection	Supplier relationship
Stage Gate method	CFT	Modular product	Codification and sharing of important processes	Strategy driven make-buy decision	SMART	Exploit, balance or Diversify (Kraljic Matrix)
Stage Gate method	CFT	Modular product	Intra company personnel transfer	Strategy driven make-buy decision	SMART	Exploit, balance or Diversify (Kraljic Matrix)

The suggestions provided in the research will require time and effort for implementation at CM S.p.A. However, the immediate impact that was observed in the company was a review of the product design strategy and the set up of a new industrial engineering department for industrialization of products. Also, the activities at each stage of the NPD process and the gates are being standardized using a RACI (Responsible, Accountable, Consult, Inform) matrix.

5   Generalization of the Framework

An attempt of generalization can be done in order to derive a procedure that could support a company along the industrialization process. Even though a single case study has been used, the literature review used for the framework development in CM has been wide enough to identify how some considerations can be extended to similar context. In particular, what follows is valid for medium sized companies operating in the B2B industry and offering complex products. Further empirical analysis should be carried out in order to better identify the impact of cultural elements on the framework, in particular for the "tacit knowledge transfer" activity. Nonetheless, since the level of the framework is quite aggregate, it is reasonable to think that the same set of methodologies can be generalized, whilst what depends on the local culture is how the methodology is implemented. A stepwise procedure has been identified:

- STEP 1: Start with the industrialization Zwicky box as in Table 1. More methodologies for each relevant activity could be added according to the needs.
- STEP 2: Carry out cross consistency assessment to reduce the number of configurations based on the three types of contradictions – logical, empirical and normative. Contradictions may vary across companies and thus must be carefully analyzed to reduce number of configurations.
- STEP 3: Choose or reject certain methodologies for industrialization activities based on drivers for industrialization. Drivers that may be considered during the choice of methodologies are summarized in Figure 1.

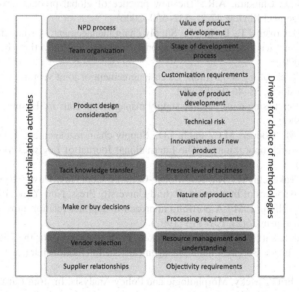

Fig. 1. – Industrialization activities and drivers for choice of methodologies

6   Conclusion

This research work provides a framework for industrialization of products across an international production network of an Italian medium sized machinery manufacturer and identifies a methodology for the framework development for similar companies.

From a practical point of view, the framework proposal should guarantee the coherency of the different strategies across functions leading to an improvement of efficiency and effectiveness of the NPD and the industrialization process. From an academic point of view, the proposed methodology can act as a starting point for future research in this area. As a further development of this work, the preparation and implementation of the industrialization framework in more cases is advisable in order to validate the GMA and the drivers used in the current research.

References

1. Abele, E., Meyer, T., Näher, U., Strube, G., Sykes, R.: Global Production – A Handbook for Strategy and Implementation. Springer, Berlin (2008)
2. Cooper, R.: Jun.: Stage-gate systems: A new tool for managing new products. Business Horizons 33(3), 44–54 (1990)
3. Cooper, M.C., Lambert, D.M., Pagh, J.D.: Supply chain management: More than a new name for logistics. The International Journal of Logistics Management 8(1), 1–14 (1997)
4. Cooper, R.G.: May: Perspective: The Stage-Gate ® Idea-to-Launch Process Update, what's new, and Negev systems. Journal of Product Innovation Management 25(3), 213–232 (2008)
5. Eppinger, S.D., Chitkara, A.R.: The new practice of global product development. MIT Sloan Management Review 47(2), 532–550 (2006)
6. Hicks, C., McGovern, T., Earl, C.F.: Supply chain management: A strategic issue in engineer to order manufacturing. International Journal of Production Economics 65(2), 179–190 (2000)
7. Killing, P.: Technology acquisition: License agreement or joint venture. Columbia Journal of World Business, 38–46 (Fall 1980)
8. Kraljic, P.: Purchasing must become supply management. Harvard Business Review 61(5), 109–117 (1983)
9. Lambert, D.M., Cooper, M.C., Pagh, J.D.: Supply chain management: Implementation issues and research opportunities. The International Journal of Logistics Management 9(2), 1–20 (1998)
10. Nonaka, I., Takeuchi, H.: The Knowledge-Creating Company: How Japanese Companies Create the Dynamics of Innovation. Oxford University Press, New York (1995)
11. Olsen, R.F., Ellram, L.M.: A portfolio approach to supplier relationships. Industrial Marketing Management 26(2), 101–113 (1997)
12. Pero, M., Abdelkafi, N., Sianesi, A., Blecker, T.: A framework for the alignment of NPD and supply chains. Supply Chain Management: An International Journal 15(2), 115–128 (2010)
13. Ritchey, T.: Fritz Zwicky, Morphologie and Policy Analysis. In: 16th Euro. Conference on operational Analysis, Brussels (1998)
14. Song, X.M., Montoya-Weiss, M.M.: Critical development activities for really new versus incremental products. Journal of Product Innovation Management 15(2), 124–135 (1998)
15. Spens, K.M., Bask, A.H.: Developing a framework for supply chain management. The International Journal of Logistics Management 13(1), 73–88 (2002)
16. Swink, M., Song, M.: Effects of marketing-manufacturing integration on NPD time and competitive advantage. Journal of Operations Management 25(1), 203–217 (2007)
17. Zwicky, F.: Discovery, Invention, Research Through the Morphological Approach, 1st American edn. Macmillan (1969)

Optimize Resource Utilization at Multi-site Facilities with Agent Technology

M.K. Lim[1] and H.K. Chan[2]

[1] Centre for Supply Chain Improvement, University of Derby, Derby, U.K.
m.lim@derby.ac.uk
[2] Norwich Business School, University of East Anglia Norwich Research Park, Norwich, UK
h.chan@uea.ac.uk

Abstract. Many enterprises expanded their manufacturing environment from localised, single-site facility to more globalised, multi-site facilities. This paper proposes a multi-agent system, using its characteristics of autonomy and intelligence, to integrate process planning and production scheduling across different facilities, so as to secure the most efficient and cost-effective plan and schedule to meet the demand. A currency-based agent iterative bidding mechanism is developed to facilitate the coordination of agents. A genetic algorithm is employed to tune the currency values for agent bidding. In this paper, a case study is used for simulation in order to demonstrate the effectiveness and performance of the proposed agent system.

Keywords: Multi-agent system, multi-site manufacturing, genetic algorithm.

1 Introduction

Due to rapid expansion of market, vigorous acquisition and new facility development have taken place among manufacturing enterprises. The manufacturing has evolved from localized, single-site facility to more globalised, multi-site facilities [1]. Process planning and production scheduling are two manufacturing functions traditionally treated as separate operations and majority of works predominantly focuses on single-site facility and the methodologies are not designed for multi-site optimization. In the literature, multi-site research specifically in integrated process planning and production scheduling is rather limited, and hence the focus of this paper. Furthermore, multi-agent system (MAS) is a popular and promising tool for solving complex problems, such as in multi-site research, but yet its application in this area, particularly related to integrated process planning and scheduling, is rare. Therefore, this paper will investigate the performance and effectiveness of employing MAS to optimize process planning and production scheduling within multi-site manufacturing environment.

This paper is organized as follows. Section 2 reviews the literature in process planning and production scheduling and the use of MAS in this domain. Section 3 defines the case study used and Section 4 describes the agent model and currency-based agent iterative bidding mechanism for multi-site resource optimization. Section 5 explains

C. Emmanouilidis, M. Taisch, D. Kiritsis (Eds.): APMS 2012, Part II, IFIP AICT 398, pp. 503–510, 2013.
© IFIP International Federation for Information Processing 2013

the genetic algorithm for currency tuning to facilitate agent bidding, and followed by simulation analysis in Section 6. Finally, a conclusion will be given in Section 7.

2   Literature Review

2.1   Process Planning and Production Scheduling

In order to have an efficient process planning and scheduling, it is necessary to have simultaneous assessment of process planning and scheduling decisions [1]. There are a number of approaches to integrated process planning and production scheduling that can be found in the literature. These approaches can be classified into non-linear process planning (NLPP), closed-loop process planning (CLPP), and distributed process planning (DTPP) [2]. NLPP generates possible alternative plans for each part prior to actual shop floor production. All the possible plans are ranked according to the process planning criteria. For an efficient planning and scheduling, it is vital to have feedback from the shop floor and CLPP provides such feedback by taking into account of the shop floor status at that time [3]. DTPP performs in parallel and in two phases. The first phase is pre-planning, i.e. process planner analyses the operations to be carried out based on product data. The second phase is final planning, whereby the operations will be matched against the capability of the available resources.

All these research works predominantly applied on single-site facility; very limited attention has been paid to optimizing process planning and production scheduling within multi-site manufacturing environment. Most research in multi-site has been focusing on more strategic issues, e.g. with regard to integrating production planning with distribution systems [4]. Chung et al. [5] applied a modified genetic algorithm for process planning and scheduling in multi-factory environment. The aforementioned works have limited focus on ways to optimize resource utilization within multi-sites, taking into account of the complexity of multi-site environment. To assist decisions making for multi-site optimization, MAS has been suggested by Wang and Chan [6] as a promising tool and their future research work.

2.2   Multi-Agent System (MAS)

The system consists of a group of intelligent autonomous agents interacting with each other to achieve a global goal, while bearing their own objectives to fulfill [7]. The agent's characteristics of intelligence and autonomous decision-making have attracted a large number of researchers using it to solve complex problems in manufacturing domains [8]. However, these works are mainly on research domains related to single-site manufacturing facility. There is a small number research works using agent concept in multi-site manufacturing facilities [9]. Based on the literature, most agent-based research focuses on strategic issues, e.g. improving communication/information sharing between multi-plants, but less on operational issues, such as integrating operational functions (e.g. process planning and production scheduling) to optimize the resources in multi-site facilities. This paper is aimed at addressing this gap.

3   Case Study

The make-to-order enterprise has two manufacturing facilities and recently acquired a new facility at a nearby location. All these facilities operate on cellular manufacturing systems whereby machines are grouped into cells based on the type of manufacturing processes offered. Each cell in each facility has different manufacturing attributes, such as machine capability (e.g. productivity, tolerance precision, quality, reliability) and availability, machine setup, production cost, shop floor layout, etc.

When a customer places an order, the challenge is how to take advantage of owning these facilities by sharing the available resources, so as to secure the most efficient and cost-effective process plan and production scheduling to fulfil the order. This process and scheduling plan should optimize the overall utilization of resources in multi-site environment at the lowest (transportation and production) cost possible. In this study, we predominantly consider operations between the multi-site manufacturing facilities (mainly on transportation) and within each facility (production-related) with certain constraints.

4   An Agent Model for Multi-site Manufacturing Facilities

4.1   Agent Model

In this study, the key entities in the multi-site manufacturing environment are represented by agents (Fig. 1). There is an order agent representing an order placed by a customer. A job agent represents a job (i.e. a series of operations to produce a batch of components ordered) to be performed, the responsibility of which is to identify the most appropriate manufacturing resources to fulfill the order. Each facility will be assigned with one job agent. In each facility, each machine in the cells is represented by a machine agent. These machine agents will interact with each other in order to find a group of machines to produce the components from within the same facility. In order to explore the possibility of obtaining better machines, the agents will extend their search to look for alternative machines in other facilities. A transportation agent represents the available transportation between the facilities. When there is a need to transport WIP between these facilities, the transportation agent will provide the necessary information and determines if the service requested is available.

4.2   Currency-Based Iterative Agent-Bidding Mechanism

A currency-based iterative agent bidding mechanism is proposed to perform dynamic integration of process planning and production scheduling in multi-site environment. The bidding process begins when the order agent informs job agents of a new order, and the job agent announces the job to all machine agents in their respective facility to bid. The announcement includes the information in relation to the machining operations required for the job and the virtual currency value assigned to each operation. Machine agents that have the technical capability to perform the first operation will come forward to become 'leaders', whose responsibility is to search for other machines to perform the remaining operations. The leaders then announce the second operation to all machine agents within the same facility, including the leaders themselves. To offer better bids, the machine agents may reschedule and optimize their machine buffer by shifting jobs if other operations' due dates are not violated. This aims to produce optional (and hopefully, better) bids.

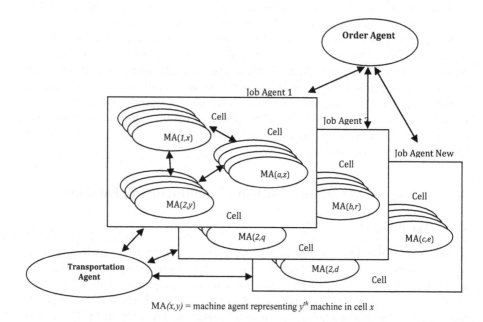

MA(x,y) = machine agent representing y^{th} machine in cell x

Fig. 1. Agent model

Machine agents construct their bids in production cost and lead time. Individual machine cost and lead time is a sum of various elements, defined from operational data.

$$C_i = C_{ti} + C_{wi} + C_{si} + C_{pi} + C_{ri} \qquad (1)$$

where

$$C_{ti} = C_{ti/d}(D)$$

$$C_{pi} = C_{pi/t}\left(\frac{V_{removed}}{MRR}\right)$$

where C_{ti} = transportation cost from the preceding machine (unit of cost) $C_{ti/d}$ = transportation cost / unit of distance (unit of cost), D = distance from the location of preceding machine (m), C_{wi} = holding cost (unit of cost), C_{si} = setup cost (unit of cost), $V_{removed}$ = volume to be removed in order to produce the feature (mm^3),

MRR = material removal rate (mm³ / unit of time), C_{pi} = processing cost (unit of cost), $C_{pi/t}$ = processing cost / unit of time (unit of cost), C_{ri} = rescheduling cost (unit of cost).

The individual lead time is populated as:

$$T_i = T_{ti} + T_{wi} + T_{si} + T_{pi} \qquad (2)$$

Where

$$T_{ti} = T_{ti/d}(D)$$

$$T_{wi} = \sum_{j=1}^{n} t_{wi[j]}$$

Where T_{ti} = transportation lead time from preceding machine (unit of time), D = distance from the location of preceding machine (m), $T_{ti/d}$ = transportation lead time / unit of distance (unit of cost), T_{wi} = waiting time at buffer, i.e. queuing time/bottlenecks (unit of time), $\sum_{j=1}^{n} t_{wi[j]}$ = total waiting time of n jobs scheduled in the job buffer before the currently bidding job (unit of time), T_{si} = setup time (unit of time), T_{pi} = processing lead time (unit of time), $V_{removed}$ = volume to be removed in order to produce the feature (mm³), MRR= material removal rate (mm³ / unit of time).

As to whether to forward a bid for an operation, the machine agents will base on the amount of virtual profit earned which is above a set threshold value. By shifting jobs in the job buffer, a machine agent may put forward more than one bid as long as the virtual profits are above the set threshold. When the bids are received, the leader will select winning bid that provides the shortest lead time. This process is continued until whole set of operations to be performed is concluded. Job agent evaluates the resulting job plan for due date adherence which can be denoted as follow:

$$T = \sum_{i=1}^{n} T_i^{win}, \qquad C = \sum_{i=1}^{n} C_i^{win} \qquad (3)$$

The job agent evaluates the bids with the aim of fulfilling the due date D and achieving minimum total production cost C:

$$Min\left(C = \sum_{i=1}^{n} C_i \right)$$

$$T = \sum_{i=1}^{n} T_i \leq D \qquad (4)$$

If the due date is not fulfilled (i.e. T > D), or the cost is not considered minimum, the virtual currency allocated to operations will be tuned in the next iteration to look for a better plan. If the due date cannot be fulfilled after a predefined iteration, the leader will search across different facilities to find optimal plan, which is then forwarded to order agent to decide.

Based on Eq. 3, the order agent will award the job to the outstanding machine group and this will be conveyed to the machine agents through the respective job agent. The machine agents in the group will then update their loading schedules.

5   Genetic Algorithm (GA) for Currency Values Tuning

In this study, GA is used by the job agents to tune the currency values iteratively in order to search for better and better process plans and schedules. The following describes the GA process:

1. Gene coding: A population of chromosomes (POP_SIZE) and a generation number (GEN) are determined. The genes in each chromosome represent the currency values allocated to the features in a component.
2. Evaluation of fitness function (announcement to machine agents): The job agent evaluates the bids from the machine agents for the best solution at this iteration.
3. Selection of chromosomes ("select-all" strategy): All the chromosomes have equal opportunity to be selected for crossover and mutation operations.
4. Crossover process, then Mutation process
5. Re-announcement to machine agents: The offspring chromosomes in the new population (achieved through above steps) are announced to machine agents, and chromosome which the bid carries the least production cost and satisfies the product due date, is recorded as the best solution found at this iteration. Steps 3-5 are repeated till the Gen number is achieved.

6   Simulation and Discussions

The MAS proposed in this study was implemented on Java Platform. Two orders, with details about features to produce in sequence, were placed at interval times to produce a batch of parts each, namely PA and PB. The currency values were an estimate based on history data. The simulation of iterative mechanism commences with the order agent analyzing the process requirements, and followed by announcing the jobs of producing PA to all job agents and let them coordinate with the machine agents to find the best machines to perform the jobs. This process repeats for PB.

The best bid (which was considered to be near-optimum) for part PA received by the order agent has a production cost of 1465 units and lead time of 942 units put forward by the job agent of Facility B, Fig. 2. When the leader extended its search to other facility, no overall best bid was obtained.

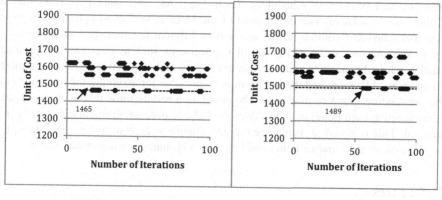

(a) Within Facility B   (b) Across all facilities

Fig. 2. Bids received for part PA by job agent at each GA iteration in Facility B

The same GA parameters were used for the next order placed to produce a batch of 80 units of part PB. The overall best bid received to produce part PB has a production cost of 2308 units and lead time of 1448 (Fig. 3). It was found that the best bids received by the job agents were the same as presented in figures above, however the simulation time has increased approximately triple of the generation size of 100 iterations. The bids received at each iteration are spread out as previous runs shown above.

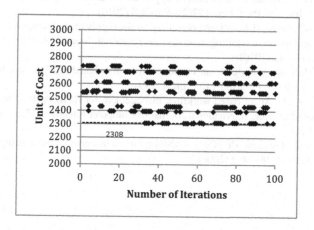

Fig. 3. Bids received for part PB by job agent at each GA iteration in the new facility (for across all the three facilities)

7   Conclusions

This paper proposed a multi-agent system (MAS) to optimize the resources within a multi-site manufacturing environment, in particular through the integration of process planning and production scheduling. Each agent has individual objectives and a global goal to achieve. The global goal of the MAS is to find an optimized process plan and schedule (within a facility and across different facilities) that gives the lowest production cost while satisfying all requirements such as due date and product quality, while the machine agent's objective is to win the operation jobs and optimize its machine utilization, and the job agent is responsible for assigning the operations to the outstanding group of machines. The simulation results show that as the currency being tuned at each iteration and so does the bidding process, different bids were constructed. This is aimed at increasing the opportunity to explore wider non-elite solution spaces, so as to finding better and better bids optimizing resource utilization.

References

1. Chan, F.T.S., et al.: Solving distributed FMS scheduling problems subject to maintenance: genetic algorithms approach. Robotics and Computer-Integrated Manufacturing 22(5), 493–504 (2006)
2. Larsen, N., Alting, L.: Simultaneous engineering within process and production planning, Australia (1990)
3. Khoshnevis, B., Chen, Q.M.: Integration of process planning and scheduling functions. J. of Intelligent Manufacturing 2(3), 165–175 (1991)
4. Alvarez, E.: Multi-plant production scheduling in SMEs. Robotics and Computer-Integrated Manufacturing 23(6), 608–613 (2007)
5. Chung, S., et al.: Application of genetic approach for advanced planning in multi-factory environment. Int. J. of Prod. Eco. 127(2), 300–308 (2010)
6. Wang, W.Y.C., Chan, H.K.: Virtual organization for supply chain integration: Two cases in the textile and fashion retailing industry. International Journal of Production Economics 127(2), 333–342 (2010)
7. Ferber, J.: Multi-agent systems: an introduction to distributed artificial intelligence. Addison-Wesley Longman Publishing Co., Inc. (1999)
8. Zhang, Y.F., et al.: Agent-based workflow management for RFID-enabled real-time reconfigurable manufacturing. International Journal of Computer Integrated Manufacturing 23(2), 101–112 (2010)
9. Wong, T., et al.: Dynamic shopfloor scheduling in multi-agent manufacturing systems. Expert Systems 31(3), 486–494 (2006)

Proposing an Environmental Excellence Self-Assessment Model

Peter Meulengracht Jensen, John Johansen, Brian Vejrum Waehrens,
and Md. Shewan-Ul-Alam

Center for Industrial Production, Aalborg University, Fibigerstaede 10, 9220 Aalborg
pmjensen@grundfos.com, {jj,bvw}@production.aau.dk,
mshewa11@student.aau.dk

Abstract. This paper presents an Environmental Excellence Self-Assessment (EEA) model based on the structure of the European Foundation of Quality Management Business Excellence Framework. Four theoretical scenarios for deploying the model are presented as well as managerial implications, suggesting that the EEA model can be used in global organizations to differentiate environmental efforts depending on the maturity stage of the individual sites. Furthermore, the model can be used to support the decision-making process regarding when organizations should embark on more complex environmental efforts to continue to realize excellent environmental results. Finally, a development trajectory for environmental excellence is presented.

Keywords: Environmental Sustainability, Self-Assessment, Global Operations Management.

1 Introduction

Not only customers, but also various stakeholders, for example, legislatures, non-governmental organizations (NGOs) and media, all contribute to the fact that sustainability, especially environmental sustainability, has gradually established itself as a key competitive parameter [1]. Issues such as increasing utility prices, scarcity of resources, and climate changes have caused the environmental sustainability agenda to move into the boardroom [2].

However, several studies report that while companies understand well the philosophy and logic underpinning sustainability (e.g. triple-bottom line and balanced results), few companies manage to incorporate environmental sustainability into organizational practices in a coherent and systematic manner [3]. Environmental sustainability efforts often appear as a hodgepodge of sporadic initiatives without any considerable effect on or contribution to the competitive advantage of the company [4]. This poses a great risk, since companies could lose competitive territory in the globalized economic landscape [1].

2 Empirical Background and Initiating Problem

This study is carried out in collaboration with a Danish multinational manufacturing company; a privately owned organization, with sites in more than 45 countries that

C. Emmanouilidis, M. Taisch, D. Kiritsis (Eds.): APMS 2012, Part II, IFIP AICT 398, pp. 511–518, 2013.
© IFIP International Federation for Information Processing 2013

employ 15,000+ worldwide. The company is considered one of the frontrunners at deploying environmental sustainability. Despite achieving noteworthy environmental results, the case company is similar to others facing difficulties incorporating its efforts systematically. The challenges can be viewed from two perspectives.

From a corporate perspective, there is a need to differentiate efforts and apply more sophisticated solutions at more advanced sites and more basic solutions at more immature sites. There is no "one-size-fits-all" in the global context, yet complete individualization is impossible/inappropriate from a managerial/resource-efficiency point of view.

From a local perspective, there is a need to prioritize and implement the "right" solutions given for the site context and situation and to obtain results that match the resources invested. Management concern is raised whether invested resources match the realized results.

The case company has previously struggled with similar challenges within the field of quality management (QM) and has experienced increases in quality performance by deploying the European Foundation of Quality Management Business Excellence Model (EFQM model) [5], which is now deeply rooted as the overall management framework in the organization.

3   Theoretical Background

The EFQM model has been reviewed and revised during the past 20 years [6] and now takes a society-wide perspective on QM and strives to promote "business excellence," that is, improved company-wide performance across the organization, by focusing on customers, people, society and key results [5].

The EFQM model serves as a self-assessment framework to undertake continuous improvement [7] by measuring progress toward the organization's long-term vision and assessing which activities are going well and which have stagnated [8]. In order to do so, the EFQM model consists of the following key elements [5]:

1. Five enabler criteria and four results criteria
2. Definitions and descriptions of the enabler and results criteria
3. A self-assessment approach based on "RADAR" logic
4. A mechanism for quantifying the organization's current state, or "maturity level," and quantifying areas for improvement

4   Research Objective

Taking the EFQM model as a structural starting point, the objective of this paper is to present and discuss an Environmental Excellence Assessment (EEA) Framework. The purpose of the EEA is to serve as a framework for undertaking continuous improvement activities, to increase environmental performance within the case company, and to overcome managerial challenges previously described. The outlook is that the EEA framework can in future assist similar companies facing similar challenges. This paper briefly presents the EEA model itself in order to provide an overview and then continues to discuss possible scenarios for deploying the model.

5   Methodology

This study is part of a three-year research collaboration following a design science approach [9] undertaken as action research [10] and a joint collaboration between the case company and the research institution. The conception of the EEA model is a result of working closely with and within the case company for more than two years, a student MSc-thesis project, and an extensive literature study focusing on environmental sustainability. Furthermore, required inputs to the EEA model conception were provided by a three-day introductory course in the EFQM Business Excellence Model, and presentations, workshops, and discussions with key stakeholders in the case company. The literature study and the stakeholder presentations/workshops served to theoretically and empirically validate the content of the model within the constraints of action research, the embryonic stage of the EEA model development process, and the evolving nature of the environmental sustainability field.

5.1   Limitations

This paper does not go into detail describing logical underpinnings for the various criteria and sub-criteria of the EEA. These are presented in table form, to provide the reader an overview. Furthermore, the EEA follows the same principles and approach for self-assessment as the EFQM model. These are not described in this paper. The paper's purpose is solely to discuss prospects for deploying the EEA to solve the challenges facing the case company.

6   Environmental Excellence Assessment (EEA) Model

The proposed EEA model consists of five environmental enabler criteria and four environmental results criteria, as depicted in Figure 1. Table 1 provides an overview of EEA model criteria, definitions, and sub criteria.

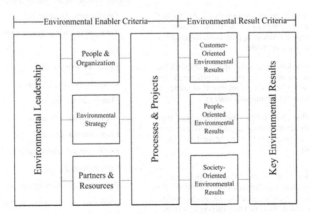

Fig. 1. The EEA Model

Table 1. Overview of criteria, definitions, and sub-criteria for the EEA model

Enabler Criteria

	Definition	*Sub-Criteria*	
Environmental Leadership	Organizations with excellent environmental performance have leaders who communicate a clear purpose for working with environmental sustainability. They provide a clear direction and build organizational commitment through demonstrating the associated business opportunities.	1a	Define the vision, purpose, and rationale
		1b	Environmental management system deployment
		1c	Stakeholders engagement
		1d	Reinforce a culture of green thinking
		1e	Provide the prerequisites for change
Environmental Strategy	Organizations with excellent environmental performance realize their environmental vision by implementing an environmental strategy. The strategy is based on the identification of issues with significant environmental affect and aligned with overall business strategy and stakeholder expectations.	2a	Embed environmental impact analysis
		2b	Understand internal strengths/weaknesses
		2c	Policy deployment
		2d	Strategy alignment
		2e	Strategy communication and implementation
People & Organization	Organizations with excellent environmental performance ensure that their people's competencies and skills are continuously developed. They ensure fit between competencies, resources, and responsibility. They communicate, care for, reward, and recognize environmental achievements.	3a	Competence development
		3b	Alignment, involvement & empowerment
		3c	"Fit" competence, responsibility & responsibility
		3d	Constructive communication & cooperation
		3e	Reward & recognition
Partners & Resources	Organizations with excellent environmental performance manage their partners, suppliers, technological resources, and material flows in order to implement environmental strategy and increase their environmental performance.	4a	Supplier and partner management
		4b	Environmental budgets
		4c	Building management
		4d	Technology management
		4e	Information technology deployment
		4f	Material and utility management
Processes	Organizations with excellent environmental performance redesign their processes to improve environmental performance. This includes management, business, and support processes.	5a	Management process redesign
		5b	Business process redesign
		5c	Support process redesign
		5d	Project management

Result Criteria

	Definition	*Examples include but are not limited to*
Customer Results	Results that put the organization in a better position to market its products or services. Results are communicated through appropriate challenges to customers and stakeholders.	Environmental certification Transparent environmental product data Case stories
People Results	Results that demonstrate that the organization has the commitment of the entire organization and continuously increases capabilities required to implement the environmental strategy.	Employee awareness Competence development Managerial acceptance
Society Results	Results that demonstrate that the organization reduces its environmental impact and demonstrate that they actively strive to go beyond regulatory compliance.	Organizational reputation Environmental awards Environmental-related media coverage
Key Results	Results are a set of environmental performance indicators that are measurable and that the organization uses to measure its environmental performance and associated financial opportunities.	Consumption and cost Payback times on environmental projects Environmental effect on environmental projects Accreditation and certification

7 Possible Outcomes of Deploying the EEA Model

Considering that the EEA model consists of a set of enabler criteria and a set of results criteria, the following four outcomes of its deployment are possible:

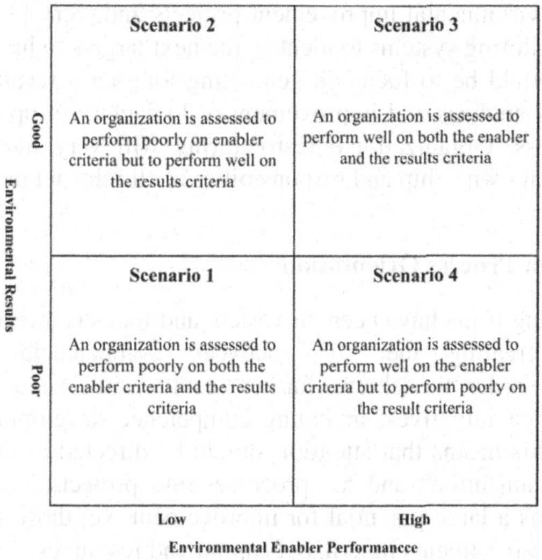

	Scenario 2	Scenario 3
Good	An organization is assessed to perform poorly on enabler criteria but to perform well on the results criteria	An organization is assessed to perform well on both the enabler and the results criteria
	Scenario 1	**Scenario 4**
Poor	An organization is assessed to perform poorly on both the enabler criteria and the results criteria	An organization is assessed to perform well on the enabler criteria but to perform poorly on the result criteria
	Low	**High**

(Vertical axis label: Environmental Results; Horizontal axis label: Environmental Enabler Performance)

Fig. 2. Possible outcomes for deploying the EEA Model

Based on interaction and discussion with the case company, these four scenarios will be discussed in light of the challenges facing various company sites worldwide.

7.1 Type 1 Sites: No Integration

Here, no/few efforts are dedicated to creating environmental results, and as a consequence, environmental performance is lacking. Causes are likely to be rooted in poor performance in leadership (enabler criteria 1) and strategy (enabler criteria 2). It should be evident that there is no management commitment, focus, and direction for working on environmental sustainability. These are considered prerequisites for dedicating resources to work on environmental sustainability and undertaking improvements.

In light of the challenges experiences by the case company, we suggest that corporate and local efforts should be dedicated to forming environmental vision and implementing an environmental strategy for the organization. Furthermore, attention should focus on assistance with deploying a functional environmental management system to serve as a backbone and framework for undertaking environmental tasks.

The next immediate step would be identification of simple "low hanging fruit," from which the organization can generate noteworthy results with little dedicated effort.

7.2 Type 2 Sites: Project Orientation

Here, few systematic efforts are taking place, yet the organization achieves noteworthy environmental results. It is likely that this is the result of focusing on low-hanging fruit, largely by isolated environmental departments in different locations. Focus is likely to be centered on enabler criteria 4, "partners and resources," for example, through retrofitting buildings and production technology and managing the organization's resources/utility flow.

In this situation, corporate and local efforts should be directed toward continuous identification of environmental improvement projects and, very likely, installation of environmental monitoring systems to identify the next targets to hit.

The next step would be to focus on generating long-term results through process integration, such as analysis and improvement of logistical set-up or the production-development process. Organizational restructuring will very likely be required to create environmental ownership and responsibility in all relevant processes.

7.3   Type 3 Sites: Process Orientation

Here the low-hanging fruits have been harvested, and focus is directed toward process integration and creating the "fit" between competencies, resources, and responsibilities. In order to achieve further results, sites should focus on larger organizational-change initiatives, including competence development, restructuring, and recruitment. This means that attention should be directed toward enabler criteria 3, "people and organization" and 5, "processes and projects." It is likely that the organization still has a large potential for improvement, yet those improvements will come at fairly high investments in terms of capital and resources.

Corporate and local efforts should therefore be directed toward cooperation on these complex change initiatives, which are likely to require changes at several levels in the organization, such as performance metrics, objectives, headcount, process-design, etc.

7.4   Type 0 Sites: Perplexity

Here, dedicated and extensive efforts are taking place, yet the results are missing. This is a very unfortunate, but common, situation. It is likely that efforts taking place are scattershot (or a hodgepodge of activities), with little prioritizing based on the situational context of the organization. This scenario has several likely causes. First, lack of sound, integrated leadership and strategy. In addition, ambitions to undertake "high-profile" initiatives with news value and branding potential might cause the organization to down prioritize effective initiatives that hold less or no branding value, so-called "dirty low-hanging fruit."

Corporate and local efforts should be directed toward reviewing organizational leadership and strategy and toward systematically analyzing whether buildings, technologies, etc. have been optimized to support generating environmental results.

8   Discussion of the EEA Model

Expected benefits from deploying the EEA are promising, particularly because the EEA model provides insight into which one of the four types each site currently falls into. As mentioned, relevant next steps for the types differ, and the approach, tools, competence requirements, focus, etc. also differ depending on whether the site is a

Type 1, 2, 3, or 0. The role of corporate management will differ significantly depending on whether it is striving to assist a Type 1 site, just embarking on integrating environmental sustainability, or a Type 3 site, needing to define how environmental sustainability can provide business value from a strategic and operational procurement perspective.

Furthermore, by deploying the EEA, local management can get an overview of whether to embark on complex, large-scale, business-process re-engineering programs or whether to prioritize efforts to retrofit existing equipment and building technologies.

The intention is that deploying the EEA will yield a more nuanced understanding of the current stage of environmental maturity at individual sites, and, based on that understanding, corporate and local efforts can be customized for each of the four types, thus avoiding both "one-size-fits-all" solutions and myriad individualized solutions.

8.1   Road-Mapping the Path to Environmental Excellence

As described in the introduction, most companies struggle to realize results in line with their ambitions and efforts [3] and fail to integrate environmental sustainability strategy with business strategy [4]. Reviewing the four possible site types identified by the EEA has led to the conclusion that one cause of this failure is very likely that these companies find themselves in the perplexing situation faced by Type 0 sites. The EEA provides organizations with a development trajectory, or "path," for realizing environmental results, moving from "no integration" (Type 1) to "project orientation" (Type 2) to "process integration" (Type 3), while avoiding/escaping from "perplexity" (Type 0). Figure 2 depicts this proposed development trajectory, including characteristics of the four types.

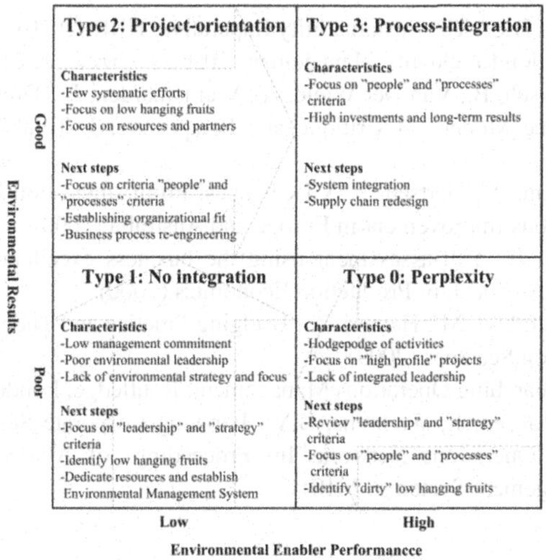

Fig. 3. An environmental excellence development trajectory based on site categorization as a result of deploying the EEA model

9   Conclusion and Contribution

This paper presents an Environmental Excellence Self-Assessment (EEA) model that can help diagnose organizational improvements that need to be undertaken in order to realize environmental results. Prospects for deploying the model are promising, since the EEA model can be expected to provide a nuanced understanding of the current stage of maturity at individual sites. Based on this understanding, corporate and local management efforts can be prioritized in order to implement solutions that will yield results in line with efforts. This paper adds to the body of literature on environmental sustainability and responds to a call made [3 and 11] to move beyond the tool-focused regime and address environmental sustainability as an organizational issue. The paper addresses the issue of how a focused self-assessment on environmental sustainability can be used as a "differentiated management mechanism." The EEA model has yet to be empirically tested, and therefore the validity of the model is fairly low at this embryonic stage of development. However, it is expected that the model will be deployed in the case company in the immediate future and experience will show whether the EEA model lives up to its potential.

References

1. Porter, M.E., Kramer, M.R.: Strategy & Society: The Link Between Competitive Advantage and Corporate Social Responsibility. HBR (2006)
2. Pagell, M., Wu, Z.: Building a More Complete Theory of Sustainable Supply Chain ManagementUsing Case Studies of 10 Exemplars. J. of Sup. Chain Man. (2009)
3. Bowen, F.E., Cousins, P.D., Lamming, R.C.: Horses for Courses: Explaining the Gap between the Theory and Practice of Green Supply. Greener Management International (2001)
4. Lubin, D.A., Esty, D.C.: The Sustainability Imperative. HBR (2010)
5. European Foundation for Quality Management, http://www.EFQM.org
6. Williams, R., Bertsch, B., Van Der Wiele, A., Van Iwaarden, J., Dale, B.: Self-Assessment Against Excellence Models: A Critique and Perspective. J. Total Quality Management (2006)
7. Boer, H., Chapman, A., Gertsen, F.: CI Changes: From suggestion box to organizational learning. Continuous Improvement in Europe and Australia (2000)
8. Ritchie, D., Dale, B.: Self-assessment using the business excellence model: a study of practice and process. Int. J. of Production Economics (2000)
9. Holmström, J., Ketokivi, M., Hameri, A.: Bridging Practice and Theory: A Design Science Approach. Decision Sciences (2009)
10. Karlsson, C.: Researching Operations Management. Routledge, London (2009)
11. Jensen, P.M., Johansen, J., Wæhrens, B.V.: Pursuing Corporate Sustainability Synergies within a Global Operations Network. In: Proceedings of APMS 2010: Advances in Production Management Systems (2010)

Method for Quality Appraisal in Supply Networks

João Gilberto Mendes dos Reis[1,2] and Pedro Luiz de Oliveira Costa Neto[1]

[1] Paulista University (UNIP), PPGEP, São Paulo, Brazil
`politeleia@uol.com.br, betomendesreis@msn.com`
[2] Federal University of Grande Dourados (UFGD), Department Production Engineering,
Dourados, Brazil
`joaoreis@ufgd.edu.br`

Abstract. The study of supply networks or supply chains is an emerging theme in the world of Production Engineering. The complexity of how companies relate to their networks cannot be resolved through a single management strategy anymore. At the same time, quality can no longer be seen as something inherent to individual companies. This paper studies the alignment of three important aspects: product type (functional or innovative) network strategy (agile, responsive, flexible or lean), Quality Management System - QMS (Hashin Kanri, Total Quality Management, Six Sigma and / or ISO Standards). To do this developed a method that aims to check the alignment mentioned and suggest to companies the quality management system best suited to each situation. The method presented an accuracy of over 90% in its use in research conducted.

Keywords: Supply Networks, Supply Network Strategies, Quality Management Systems, Innovative and Functional Products.

1 Introduction

Relationships between companies have become consolidated as these understand the need to operate in networks to be able to compete in current markets. For this purpose, and also seeking to maintain competitiveness in their markets, the companies have had to appraise and also position themselves inside the supply networks, including the flow of their products and services within these chains, seeking to respond to all the demands made by the clients.

Within this context, we can also conclude that these supply networks have different strategies according to the approach adopted by this net, or, in other words, the search for the elimination of waste, the capacity to make the processes more flexible, the ability of responding to the markets and also agility in serving the volatile markets. In essence, these strategies refer to the characteristics of the products made by the chain, that can be of the innovative or functional kind.

The success of the supply networks lies in the identification of the type of product which is delivered to the consumer, as it is therefore possible to establish the correct chain strategy to be adopted and also the application of the most appropriate QMS to be used.

C. Emmanouilidis, M. Taisch, D. Kiritsis (Eds.): APMS 2012, Part II, IFIP AICT 398, pp. 519–526, 2013.
© IFIP International Federation for Information Processing 2013

In this way, this work seeks to present a method for the appraisal of quality in supply networks, that checks the alignment between these three aspects. The purpose of this method is to allow the organisations to appraise if their supply networks are using the appropriate approach in relation to the chain strategy and also the quality management system.

2   Methodology

Methodologically, this work has been divided into a sequence of phases, as shown below:

- First, there was a review of the relevant literature, seeking to understand the aspects and strategies that involve the supply networks, as also the concepts of quality, their applications and consequences.
- Next, a method was established to identify the functional or innovative characteristic of the product, its supply network strategy and also the most appropriate quality system for this strategy.
- Then, there was the production of a form with the questions to be aimed at the organisations and also the collection of management and accounting data from the companies.
- The fourth part was the application of the method to thirteen organisations, in order to identify the alignment between the type of product, chain strategy and quality, checking to see if this is in agreement with what the method proposes and also its discussions.

3   Background

3.1   Supply Networks Strategies

A supply network seeks, by means of a relationship between organisations, in other words suppliers and clients, to deliver their products and services to the end consumer. The process of management this Supply Networks or Supply Chains is known as Supply Chain Management (SCM).

SCM is the management of the interconnection between companies that establish relationships with each other, through upstream and downstream links between the different processes, which add value in the form of products and services for the final customer [1].

Thus, this is more than just a case of cost management, as this affects other aspects such as performance, speed and reliability of deliveries, the quality of the products and, finally, the flexibility with which the network can make adaptations [2]. At present, it is possible to divide the supply network strategies into four distinct strategies.

Lean Supply Network. The concept of lean thought consists of developing a continuous flow of value to eliminate all the waste, including the waste of time [3].

This thought may be brought out in the Toyota Production Systems (TPS), whose focus is on the reduction and elimination of waste [4]. TPS became known to other Japanese companies, and in the 1980s it took the West by storm, becoming known as Just in Time (JIT). One of the key characteristics of the business environment is that competition also takes place between the supply networks and not only between organisations [5]. Similarly, the elimination of waste, as also the effects of Lean Manufacturing (LM), does not occur only in one organisation but rather in a network of companies. Thus, this advancement of lean techniques for the whole network has become known as Lean Supply Network (LSN) or Lean Supply Chains (LSC).

Flexible Supply Network. Manufacturing companies, up against keen competition, have developed the skill to deal with external and internal uncertainties, making use of flexibility [6]. This is a target to be sought within organisations. The concept of flexibility, like that of Lean Production, has its main showcase of ideas in TPS, as flexibility is a constituent element of JIT. Thus, flexibility may be defined as the skill in changing or reacting with minimal loss of time [7]. A supply chain cannot be something that cannot be changed, and it is necessary that it has the ability to impart quick flexibilisation of its operations, whether of production, logistics, marketing or supplies, which is possible through the circulation of information through the different links of the chain. Thus, the use of flexibility in supply chains has created the strategy known as Flexible Supply Chain (FSC), in some cases defined as Supply Chain Flexibility (SCF) or in this paper Flexible Supply Network (FSN). The idea behind this type of strategy is the reduction of risk through the use of characteristics of flexibility throughout the network.

Responsive Supply Network. Responsiveness consists of a skill of intentionally reacting, within an appropriate time scale, to the demands and changes in the market, thus maintaining a competitive edge [8]. Responsiveness is a strategy that consists of its response time, meaning that the shorter the response time for the chain in meeting the needs of the clients, the more responsive the chain shall be. Thus, those organisations that compete in volatile markets and/or where the client is not willing to wait, can obtain a sustainable competitive advantage through the reduction of their process times, whether the processes are productive, logistic or through obtaining raw materials. What allows a network to be more responsive is the good use of the competitive advantages based on time, using systems that are responsive and fast [5]. The responsive chains are known as Responsive Supply Network (RSN) or Responsive Supply Chains (RSC).

Agile Supply Chains. Among the different supply network strategies, one may be considered the most important among them, which is the case of agile supply chains. Agility is the skill of companies involving an organisational structure, information systems, logistic processes and, in particular, knowledge management [9]. The idea of agility within the concept of SCM focuses on the context of response to the market, being led by demand, with one main characteristic being that of a shorter lead time, based on information [10]. This kind of supply chains are known as Agile Supply Network (ASN) or Agile Supply Chains (ASC).

3.2   Supply Chain Management Quality

Quality can be defined as conformity with the requirements [11]. Quality cannot exist if the requirements are not met; someone could wish to have quality of life, but this would be generic were it not for the establishment of specific requirements such as appropriate income, health, education and other measurable aspects [11]. Among the different processes of quality management, we could highlight: TQM (Total Quality Management), Six Sigma, ISO Standards and Hoshin Kanri.

Feigenbaum, who is one of the most important quality gurus, says that the quality of products and services to the consumer varies according to the life cycle of the product [12]. Thus, it is possible to identity four well-defined phases: innovation, the period in which the product is innovative and the consumer's demand for quality is less due to the fact that this is an innovation being implemented; conspicuous consume, the period in which the consumer seeks the visibility of the product (beauty and aesthetic characteristics) where the demand for quality is higher than in the previous phase, but still susceptible to faults; general use, where the use of the product becomes more widespread and there is the start of complete demand for quality; and commoditisation, the stage in which the products are part of people's lives, with the sale price of the product is low and the quality demands are at a maximum, meaning that in this stage there is no tolerance of faults and defects[12].

In the study of the literature on the issue, we see that there are very few texts that study the quality of supply networks; among the works found we can mention some research that has been used to understand the theme and also for the execution of this work: [13], [14], [15], [16], [17].

3.3   Functional and Innovative Products

The supply networks suffer from the excess of some products and the shortage of others, through the inability to predict demand and that an effective supply chain strategy is more than just considering the nature of demand for the company products [18].

Fisher classifies the products, based on the demand standards, in two different categories [18]:

Functional Products. These are the products which satisfy basic needs of the consumer, which do not change much over time, having predictable and stable demand and long life cycles. This stability generates competition, which leads to low profit margins.

Innovative Products. These are the products which, through innovation and technology, become popular in certain periods and therefore generate, for the consumers, an additional attraction for the purchase of these products, which increases the profit margins. However, their demand is unpredictable, their life cycle is short (a matter of months) and also they suffer from imitations by other companies, which either reduce or eliminate the original competitive edge, meaning that the company shall have to live based on cycles of innovations.

4   Method Development

The method that has been developed for research consisted of four phases:

1. *Research of Data*: The first stage of the method is that of collecting the input data. In this work, the data were collected through a specific form assigned to managers of participating companies and also data available on the market, about participating companies, such as management reports and accounting spreadsheets.

2. *Identification of Products*: The identification of whether the products are functional or innovative is made through the use of Table 1, where the corresponding answer is marked for each column. A number of five or greater for the column of functional products or the column of innovative products allows one to identify if the product is functional or innovative.

Table 1. Innovative x functional products

Item	Features	Functional Products	Innovative Products
1	Aspects of demand	Predictable	Unpredictable
2	Product life cycle	More than 2 years	Up to 2 years
3	Contribution margin	Up to 20%	More than 20%
4	Product variety	Low	High
5	Average margin of error in the forecast at the time production is committed	Up to 10%	More than 10%
6	Average stockout rate	Up to 2%	More than 2%
7	Average forced end-of-season markdown as percentage of full price	Up to 10%	More Than 10%
8	Lead time required for made-to-order products	3 weeks or more	Up to 2 weeks

3. *Identification of chain strategy*: Once the nature of the products has been identified, then the third stage seeks to establish the chain strategy to be used for this type of product. Once again making use of the data collected about uncertainty in supplies and also of demand, there is the application of the Table 2 which is based in the observations made by Lee [19], thus finding the most appropriate chain strategy.

Table 2. Supply uncertainty x demand uncertainty

| | | Demand Uncertainty | |
		Low (Functional Products)	High (Innovative Products)
Supply Uncertainty	Low (Stable Process)	Lean Supply Network	Responsive Supply Network
	High (Evolving Process)	Flexible Supply Network	Agile Supply Network

4. *Establish a correlation between the variables and also identify the quality management system which is suitable for the supply chain:* Once the type of product and the chain strategy have been identified, the types of products are linked to the supply chain strategy, the quality stage and the QMS. The result shows the ideal quality system to be applied (Table 3).

Table 3. Relationship between type of product, supply chain strategy, quality stage and QMS

Items	ASN	RSN	FSN	LSN
Type of Product	Innovative	Innovative	Functional	Functional
Supply Network Strategy	Agile	Responsive	Flexible	Lean
Stage of Quality	Innovation	Conspicuous Consume	General Use	Commoditization
Quality Management System Hint	*Hoshin Kanri*	*Hoshin Kanri* Total Quality Management	Six Sigma Total Quality Management Standards ISO (Second Part Audit)	Six Sigma Total Quality Management Standards ISO (Third Part Audit)

5   Discussion and Research Results

The method presented was applied to thirteen organisations from several different segments: one manufacturer of electrical equipment, one of plastic products, two of technology, one of foodstuffs, two of metallurgy and steel production, one from the automotive industry, two from the medical and diagnostic equipment segment and three producers of electronic goods. The field research took place in the second half of 2011. To check if the products were functional or innovative at the companies, products were chosen for each institution with similar characteristics, as the method requires the identification of the product to be analysed. Applying the concepts of Table 1, nine companies presented functional products, while only four were dealing with innovative products.

Once the type of product was identified, there was then the assessment of the most appropriate network strategy for each company, listing the uncertainties of demand and supply, and also checking the characteristics of the product, based on Table 2.

Thus, it was confirmed that 46% of the companies should use a lean strategy, 23% should use a flexible strategy, 15.5% a responsive strategy and another 15.5% an agile strategy.

In the form, there was the inclusion of one question in order to identify if the respondents perceived the type of supply chain strategy adopted by the organisations. The results showed that only two respondents managed to precisely identify the chain strategy used by their supply chain.

In relation to the QMS that the companies adopt, these have been analysed from two different angles, first considering the organisation under study and then considering this company's suppliers of raw materials, equipment and services.

The companies have said that they apply the ISO 9001:2008 standard. Evidently this standard is well known throughout the world and hence it is applied by most companies. In many segments, this standard is even mandatory for the suppliers. The other quality management systems were mentioned in an equivalent way, but none of them was present in more than 30% of the sample. Some organisations say that they use other specific quality assurance systems for the segment in which they are present. In all, 77% of the companies researched consider their management system to be excellent or good.

The second analysis was in relation to the quality management systems which they demanded from their suppliers of raw materials, equipment and services. To make sure of the quality of suppliers of products and services, the companies surveyed mostly used internal systems for the certification of suppliers and also created indices for the monitoring thereof. Other companies used ISO certification as a way of ensuring this quality. Only two companies said that they had distinctive systems to make sure of the quality of suppliers of products (raw materials and equipment) and service suppliers. For the first situation, they use ISO 9001:2008 while for the second situation they use performance indicators.

Finally, in relation to the correct alignment between product type, chain strategy and QMS, it was observed that the most appropriate systems to be implemented for the chain strategy of each organisation are not being applied in practice, there being a predominance of the application of ISO, regardless of the chain strategy used. TQM and Six Sigma are sometimes applied together and other times individually, but there is no prevalence for the companies as a whole. In relation to Hashin Kanri, we see that most companies are unaware of its scope, and this is directly reflected in the low usage of this type of QMS.

Through the data collected in the research, it was possible to reach the conclusion that, for the companies dealing with functional products, there is a correct application of QMS, in relation to the type of product made and the chain strategy to be used. However, in the case of innovative products there is some difficulty in using the correct QMS due to the high degree of uncertainty to which the organisations have been subjected and also the lack of awareness of the most efficient quality techniques for this type of stage, as mentioned by Feigenbaum [12] and demonstrated in this work.

6   Conclusions

This work developed a method to check the alignment between type of product, chain strategy and quality management system which can allow organisations, on achieving their correct alignment, to obtain sustainable competitive advantage.

References

1. Slack, N., Chambers, S., Johnston, R.: Operations management. Prentice-Hall, Upper Saddle River (2010)
2. Corrêa, H.L.: Management supply networks. Atlas, São Paulo (2010) (in Portuguese)
3. Naylor, J.B., Mohamed, M.N., Berry, D.: Leagility: integration the lean and agile manufacturing paradigms. International Journal Producton Economics 62, 107–118 (1999)
4. Agarwal, A., Shankar, R., Tiwari, M.K.: Modeling the metrics of lean, agile and leagile supply chain. European Journal of Operations Research 173, 211–225 (2006)
5. Christopher, M.: Logistics & supply chain management. Prentice-Hall, Harlow (2005)
6. Gong, Z.: An economic evaluation model of supply chain flexibility. European Journal of Operation Research 184, 745–758 (2008)
7. Upton, D.M.: The management of manufacturing flexibility. California Management Review 36, 72–89 (1994)
8. Holweg, M.: The three dimensions of responsiveness. International Journal of Operations and Production Management 25, 603–622 (2005)
9. Christopher, M.: The agile supply chain: competing in volatile markets. International Marketing Management 29, 37–44 (2000)
10. Christopher, M., Lowson, R., Peck, H.: Creating agile supply chains in fashion industry. International Journal of Retail and Distribution Management 32, 367–376 (2004)
11. Crosby, P.B.: Quality is investment. José Olympio, Rio de Janeiro (1994) (in Portuguese)
12. Feigenbaum, A.V.: Total quality control. Makron Books, São Paulo (1994) (in Portuguese)
13. Robinson, C.J., Malahotra, M.K.: Defining the concept of supply chain quality management and its relevance academic and industrial practice. International Journal of Production Economics 96, 315–337 (2005)
14. Sila, I., Ebrahimpour, M., Birkholz, C.: Quality in supply chains: an empirical analysis. Supply Chain Management 6, 491–502 (2006)
15. Foster Jr., S.T.: Towards an understanding of supply chain quality management. Journal of Operations Management 26, 461–467 (2008)
16. Kaynak, H., Hartley, A.: A replication and extension of quality management into supply chain. Journal of Operations Management 26, 468–489 (2008)
17. Carmignani, G.: Supply Chain and Quality Management. Business Process Management Journal 15, 395–407 (2009)
18. Fisher, M.: What is the right supply chain for your product? Harward Business Review, 105–115 (March-April 1997)
19. Lee, H.L.: Aligning supply chain strategies with product uncertainties. California Management Review 44, 105–119 (2002)

Chinese SMEs' Sourcing Practices and Their Impact on Western Suppliers

Matthias Wandfluh, Christian Schneider, and Paul Schönsleben

ETH Zurich, BWI Center for Industrial Management, Zurich, Switzerland
{mwandfluh,cschneider,pschoensleben}@ethz.ch

Abstract. Whereas many countries are still suffering from the aftermath of the financial crisis, China's continuous economic growth offers an opportunity for Western companies to reach their growth targets. More and more, Western companies are starting to see Chinese companies not only as sourcing partners but also as potential customers (B2B). While internationally operating Chinese companies are used to purchasing goods from Western companies, for Chinese SMEs this process constitutes a huge challenge. By addressing buyer-supplier relationships from the point of view of Chinese SMEs as buyers, this paper approaches an often neglected topic. Based on an interview series conducted with representatives from Chinese companies, this paper discusses the sourcing behavior of Chinese SMEs and the change of supply base over time. The paper offers valuable insights for Western suppliers and Chinese buyers on how to build and improve their relationship and on how to strengthen their competitive position.

Keywords: Supply Chain Management, China, SME, Change of Supply Base.

1   Introduction

The Chinese market is gaining enormous attention from internationally operating Western companies. Increasing cost pressure due to growing global competition encouraged Western companies to push sourcing components in low wage countries like China. However, industrial Western companies are starting to see Chinese companies not only as sourcing partners but also as potential customers (B2B). The evolving market potential in China is an opportunity for Western companies to compensate the often unsatisfactory growth of Western markets.

While most studies focus on raising export figures of China (see e.g. [1]), also import figures increased during the last years. Looking at specific commodities, the enormous potential of the Chinese market emerges (see figure 1). For mechanical and electrical products for example, the export volume increased by 15.8 percent annually between 2006 and 2011 whereas the import volume reached an annual increase of 12.9 percent. In the commodity of high and new technology products, the annual growth of import volume was 14.2 percent and thus even exceeded the annual growth of the export volume (14.0 percent).

C. Emmanouilidis, M. Taisch, D. Kiritsis (Eds.): APMS 2012, Part II, IFIP AICT 398, pp. 527–534, 2013.
© IFIP International Federation for Information Processing 2013

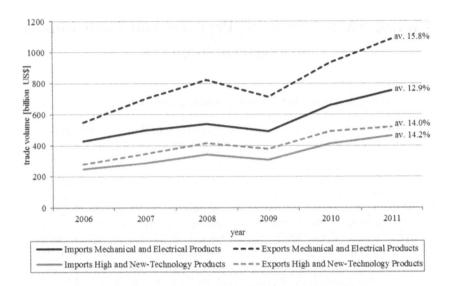

Fig. 1. Import figures of Chinese companies by commodity[1]

As these figures show, Chinese companies do not only export goods to Western countries, more and more especially in the area of high-tech products they also purchase goods from Western suppliers. This trend is not only caused by large international companies in China, also Chinese SMEs, representing more than 99% of the Chinese companies [2], are increasing their import activities. Although official figures are sketchy and the definition of a SME in China is quite complex and depend on the industrial sector [3], Liu argues that up to 70 percent of all import and export activities are performed by SMEs [4]. Due to various problems as difficulties to access credits or limited technological and managerial capabilities [3], in comparison with larger companies they have other needs which in literature so far are often neglected. Apart from the fact that most studies mainly focus on large international companies, many studies have just analyzed the supply chains characterized by Western buyers and Asian suppliers (see e.g. [5–7]) or discussed entry strategies for Western companies going to China (see e.g. [8, 9]). This exploratory study follows another approach and highlights the requirements and procedures of buyers of Chinese SMEs when purchasing from Western suppliers. For that purpose, this paper analyzes the sourcing processes of Chinese SMEs and characterizes the process of supplier substitution from Western to local suppliers.

2   Background and Research Questions

The sourcing process of a company strongly depends on its organizational setup. While in large, global companies the purchasing department may have different shapes, SMEs mostly have a central purchasing department and the responsibility lies

---

[1] Data from "BRICS Joint Statistical Publications 2012".

in the hands of very few persons having limited knowledge, limited capacity and limited access to technology (see e.g. [2, 10, 11]). While previous studies focused on differences between different types of local suppliers [12] or on Chinese subsidiaries of Western companies as buyers [13], there is to our best knowledge no information available on how sourcing processes in Chinese SMEs differ according to the location of their suppliers. Our first research question is therefore the following:

- R1: Do Chinese SMEs apply different sourcing processes when sourcing from local suppliers as compared to Western suppliers?

As important as the sourcing process is the composition of the supply base. The occurring performance improvement of local supplier especially regarding quality might result in a change of the supply base towards more local suppliers. Although this trend is well known in practice, in research there is hardly evidence on what are the drivers for this change. Especially how this trend appears in Chinese SMEs is not known. Therefore, our second research question is the following:

- R2: How does the supply base of Chinese SMEs change over time and what are the drivers for this change?

3   Methodology

The results of this paper are based on six exploratory case studies conducted with Chinese companies headquartered in the Shanghai area (see table 1). Ensuring the comparability of the observed cases, they all belong to the industry of mechanical and plant engineering. All companies purchase a wide range of products: from very simple ones to high-tech products. The chosen method of data collection are semi-structured interviews. The interviews were carried out in summer 2011 with high-ranked executives of the respective company (CEOs or chiefs of purchasing/engineering). The case studies consist of two parts. The first part deals with the characteristics of Chinese SMEs as buyer, their specific requirements concerning procurement and their purchasing processes. The second part focuses on the selection of the supply base and the factors inducing change over time.

Table 1. Case study sample

No.	Years operating	Turnover 2010	Employees (thereof in Sourcing)
1	8	5 Mio. USD	22 (2)
2	14	5 Mio. USD	40 (3)
3	28	25 Mio. USD	50 (3)
4	13	22 Mio. USD	260 (10)
5	8	11 Mio. USD	80 (4)
6	11	10 Mio. USD	40 (10^2)

---

[2] Number of employees in management, including sourcing.

4   Results

In this section, the results of the case study research regarding the differences in sourcing processes for Western and local suppliers and the change of the supply base over time are presented. Furthermore, the impact for both, Western suppliers and Chinese SMEs as customers, is derived.

4.1   Chinese SME's Sourcing Processes

Compared to large, international companies, purchasers of Chinese SMEs have different needs. In addition to the restricted capacity (see table 1), limited know how and insufficient technology access, many interviewees argued that the main differences lie in high flexibility requirements. These constraints and requirements face different characteristics of Western and local suppliers affecting the sourcing processes on strategic as well as on operative level and leading to a separate sourcing process for Western and local suppliers. The most significant differences identified during our research are described in the following.

Strategic Sourcing
Before supplier negotiations start, the buyer has to identify possible suppliers. For Chinese SMEs it is hard to find new Western suppliers. Problems often mentioned are language barriers, long distances to possible suppliers and difficulties in identifying skills of possible suppliers. When searching for Western suppliers, Chinese SMEs mainly focus on internet searches, visited exhibitions and recommendations of peers. The process is very similar to searching local suppliers. Once a possible supplier is identified, usually a supplier qualification takes place. Whereas Chinese suppliers are audited very properly, Western suppliers often are not visited at all. The most frequent argument for this circumstance is the high (travelling) costs associated with visiting Western supplier for qualification. If at all, Western suppliers are visited in the context of attending an exhibition or another event taking place in the same area. This is also valid for regular supplier audits, while local suppliers are visited regularly in a given period, Western suppliers in general are not audited at all as the buyer has more trust in the good quality. However, if the required quality is not reached, Chinese buyers do not hesitate to change the supplier.

Compared with local suppliers, communication with Western suppliers proves more challenging. While several Western suppliers have local sales offices or even local production facilities, others can only be contacted by a third-party agency or through headquarter. This may cause long communication paths and thus little flexibility. Furthermore, this may result in difficulties because of different languages and cultures. Local offices simplify the communication; flexibility however hardly improves because most of the sales offices are guided by headquarters. The differences in communication are also reflected in the personal relationships to the suppliers, which are often closer and less formal to local suppliers as compared to Western suppliers. However, most of the interviewed companies argue that this strongly depends on the organizational setup of their supplier. For suppliers running a local office with local sales persons, the language and cultural barriers dissolve, leading to comparable types of communication and relationships. Especially for complex products needing additional consulting, the interviewed Chinese SMEs often see local support as a necessity in order to select right components and install them professionally. Close collaborations with local suppliers may also manifest in R&D collaborations. In contrary to most Western suppliers, local suppliers sometimes do not have their own R&D department. Depending on the complexity of the components and the available know how of the supplier, deeper R&D collaboration might be essential to enable the supplier to produce the product at the needed quality. On one hand this is seen as an additional burden compared to Western suppliers, however, it ensures the flexibility of local suppliers and the realization of product requirements.

Operative Sourcing

Looking at the operative level of sourcing, since most goods are delivered by sea freight the transportation lead time for Western suppliers is significantly higher than for local suppliers. More astonishing, the interviewees argued that also the production lead time of local suppliers is lower. The reason for this is seen in the higher flexibility of the local suppliers and the higher relevance of the Chinese SME as customer for these suppliers. Whereas Chinese SMEs usually deal with large international Western companies supplying many companies in various countries, local suppliers in the corresponding fields are in general smaller and thus buyers have more weight. Regarding supplier integration, the degree of integration for Western suppliers is significantly lower. From an ERP software point of view, the analyzed SMEs don't integrate the suppliers at all, also within their own company they use rather simple software tools. However, looking at other types of integration as for example sharing of production plans, forecasts and demand figures or customization of packaging, the local suppliers are better integrated into business processes and regular meetings with local suppliers strengthen this integration.

Differences are also seen in the process of problem solving. The interviewed persons indicated that problem solving with local suppliers is less formal and faster than with Western suppliers. This is only partly due to the fact that the distance between supplier and buyer is much longer. The basic attitude of the interviewees was that Western suppliers spent more time on clarifying the responsibilities than solving the problem. Although this statement is to be treated with caution, it says that local suppliers are in general faster in reacting to problems and tend to accept responsibility easier. However, once the problem is approached, they mentioned Western suppliers come up with more sustainable solutions.

4.2   Change of Supply Base

The analysis of the way Chinese SMEs evaluate the supplier performance has shown that, while Western suppliers perform better in the target area quality, local suppliers outperform in the areas delivery, flexibility and costs. If Western suppliers therefore are not able to improve in other target areas, the improving quality performance of local suppliers may result in change of the supply base over time. This trend was confirmed by the interviewed Chinese SMEs. The factors influencing the change of supply base are discussed in the following. The study shows while for example at a new product launch the share of Western components comparatively high, it significantly decreases during the following years, Western supplier's components are more and more replaced by local substitutes (see figure 2a). The shape of the supply base curve depends on three impact factors: speed of adaptation ($t1 - t0$), initial share of Western Supplier's components ($s0$) and minimum share ($s1$). In order to sell more components, Western suppliers thus have the possibility to delay the speed of adaptation ($t1' - t0$) or to increase the initial ($s0'$) respectively the minimum share ($s1'$) (see figures 2b, 2c, 2d).

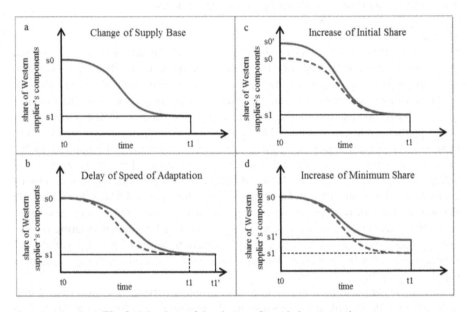

Fig. 2. Adaptions of the change of supply base over time

The speed of adaptation depends on various factors. On one hand, the availability of local substitutes having the corresponding certifications respectively the time needed to deliver the components at similar quality are the main boundaries for a fast adaptation. Having a good relationship and collaboration with the Western supplier may decrease the pressure for a fast change. The initial share provided by Western suppliers strongly depends on product requirements and the availability of local substitutes. However, having already delivered components for previous products, Western suppliers initially are often preferred to local suppliers because of simpler product launches. Particularly for complex components needing additional consulting Western suppliers are favored. Quite often Western suppliers, although they are replaced for the initial product, receive again a delivery contract at new product launches. The availability of local suppliers and the competitiveness of Western suppliers (especially regarding price) compared to local suppliers influence the minimum share of Western supplier's components to a great extent. However, especially for high tech products, it is often the end customer defining specific core components and the corresponding manufacturer. While for many components Chinese SMEs can choose freely which supplier to select, the core components are bound to a (Western) supplier. For these core components Chinese SMEs as buyers and their customers are often willing to accept additional purchasing costs.

Western suppliers may pursue different strategies to fit the requirements of Chinese SMEs and to avoid being replaced by local suppliers. The most mentioned factor ensuring long term relationships was the availability of local contact persons speaking the same language. This also simplifies the purchasing processes as described in section 4.1 and facilitates communication to a great extent. In some cases change of supply base may not necessarily lead to reduced quantities delivered by Western suppliers. Although many components of Western suppliers are partly replaced over time, some interviewees argued that the overall growth in sales is higher than the replacement rate. For Western suppliers, this can result in increasing sales rate while the percentage share of components delivered decreases.

5   Conclusion

While many previous studies focused on how to source from China, this exploratory study analyzes the needs and the purchasing processes of Chinese SMEs as buyers and the resulting requirements for Western companies. By addressing buyer-supplier relationships from Chinese buyers' point of view, this paper approaches a so far often neglected topic and contributes to research as well as practice. The case studies show that purchasing processes for Western and local suppliers differ strongly. While the collaboration with local suppliers is closer and less formal, long distances as well as language and cultural barriers burden the relationship to Western suppliers. Whenever possible, Chinese SMEs prefer working with local contact persons. Especially when they purchase high tech components from Western suppliers, there might be a great need for additional consulting and support in selection and installation of components and product development.

Due to increasing cost pressure, Chinese SMEs are forced to decrease the purchasing costs. Particularly if Western suppliers are not competitive regarding price and if local substitutes are available, it is only a matter of time until the Western suppliers are replaced. In this study we characterized this trend and identified various factors influencing adaptation time, initial and minimal share of components provided by Western suppliers. Frequently mentioned factors were availability of local suppliers, product or customer requirements, consulting by supplier and relationship to suppliers. While some of these factors cannot be affected by the suppliers, others strongly depend on the supplier's adaptability.

The findings offer valuable insights for Western companies trying to attract Chinese customers and competing against Chinese suppliers. Focusing on Chinese SMEs, the paper discusses an increasingly important topic. The practical implications can be used by both parties as a reference on how to build and improve their relationship and on how to strengthen their competitive position. The findings should be used as a basis for further, more generalizable research extending the results to other (Asian) countries and to other industries.

References

1. Wang, J., Ngoasong, M.Z.: The internationalization process of Chinese SMEs: does globalizing wholesale markets play a role? Strategic Change 21, 143–157 (2012)
2. Singh, R.K., Garg, S.K., Deshmukh, S.: The competitiveness of SMEs in a globalized economy: Observations from China and India. Management Research Review 33, 54–65 (2009)
3. Cunningham, L.X.: SMEs as motor of growth: A review of China's SMEs development in thirty years (1978-2008). Human Systems Management 30, 39–54 (2011)
4. Liu, Y.: Chinese SMEs: Successful Factors, Constraints and Future Prospects. The Keizai Ronkyu 142, 47–60 (2012)
5. Ruamsook, K., Russell, D.M., Thomchick, E.A.: Sourcing from low-cost countries: Identifying sourcing issues and prioritizing impacts on logistics performance. The International Journal of Logistics Management 20, 79–96 (2009)
6. Hall, C.: When the dragon awakes: Internationalisation of SMEs in China and implications for Europe. CESifo Forum 8, 29–34 (2007)
7. Carter, J.R., Maltz, A., Yan, T., Maltz, E.: How procurement managers view low cost countries and geographies: a perceptual mapping approach. International Journal of Physical Distribution & Logistics Management 38, 224–243 (2008)
8. Meyer, K.E., Estrin, S., Bhaumik, S.K., Peng, M.W.: Institutions, resources, and entry strategies in emerging economies. Strategic Management Journal 30, 61–80 (2009)
9. Johnson, J., Tellis, G.J.: Drivers of success for market entry into China and India. Journal of Marketing 72, 1–13 (2008)
10. Gunasekaran, A., Marri, H., McGaughey, R., Grieve, R.: Implications of organization and human behaviour on the implementation of CIM in SMEs: an empirical analysis. International Journal of Computer Integrated Manufacturing 14, 175–185 (2001)
11. Vos, J.P.: Developing strategic self-descriptions of SMEs. Technovation 25, 989–999 (2005)
12. Millington, A., Eberhardt, M., Wilkinson, B.: Supplier performance and selection in China. International Journal of Operations & Production Management 26, 185–201 (2006)
13. Schneider, C., Finke, G., Sproedt, A., Alard, R., Schönsleben, P.: Enabling Manufacturing Competitiveness and Economic Sustainability. In: Proceedings of the 4th International Conference on Changeable, Agile, Reconfigurable and Virtual production (CARV 2011), pp. 384–390 (2012)

Game Theory Based Multi-attribute Negotiation between MA and MSAs

Fang Yu, Toshiya Kaihara, and Nobutada Fujii

Graduate School of System Information, Kobe University
1-1 Rokkodai, Nada, Kobe, Hyogo, 657-8501, Japan
yufang@kaede.cs.kobe-u.ac.jp, kaihara@kobe-u.ac.jp
nfujii@phoenix.kobe-u.ac.jp

Abstract. This paper focuses on the multi-attribute negotiation between Manufacture Agent (MA) and Material Supplier Agent (MSA) of supply chain network (SCN). A modified two-stage negotiation protocol is proposed based on the two-stage negotiation protocol proposed in the previous work. The negotiation between MA and MSAs, where the quantity of the order of MA depends on the demand of Consumer Agent (CA), are discussed to decide the final supplier and the final strategies. The strategies of the negotiation are the wholesale price of the product, the quantity of the order, and the lead time. The final solution is solved by finding the Stackelberg equilibrium of MA-Stackelberg game. Numerical case is provided to illustrate the proposed protocol.

Keywords: Multi-agent, supply chain, negotiation, game theory.

1 Introduction

A Supply Chain (SC) can be defined as a system consists of suppliers, manufacturers, distributors, retailers, and customers, where materials flow downstream from suppliers to customers and information flows in both directions [1]. Game theory is a powerful tool for analyzing situations in which the decisions of multiple agents affect each agent's payoff [2]. It has become a primary methodology used in supply chain network (SCN) related problems.

Related to the topic, a lot of researches have been done. *Hall et al.* [3] modeled the manufacturer's capacity allocation problem of the SC with a manufacturer and several distributors. [4] considered a profit-maximizing retailer using Stackelberg game and Nash equilibrium. A game theoretic model of a three-stage supply chain consisting of one retailer, one manufacturer and one subcontractor was developed to study ordering, wholesale pricing and lead-time decisions in [5]. *Sinha et al.*[6] analyzed the coordination and competition issues in a two-stage SC distribution system where two vendors compete to sell differentiated products through a common retailer in the same market. *Xia* [7] studied the market competition and pricing strategies for suppliers in a SC with two competitive suppliers and multiple buyers. In the previous research, the single attribute negotiation between one Manufacture Agent (MA) and multiple Material Supplier

C. Emmanouilidis, M. Taisch, D. Kiritsis (Eds.): APMS 2012, Part II, IFIP AICT 398, pp. 535–543, 2013.
© IFIP International Federation for Information Processing 2013

Agents (MSA) has been discussed [8]. It was assumed that the quantity of the order of MA was fixed. However, in the real market, the quantity of MA is not fixed and it related to the demand of Consumer Agent (CA). Thus, this research extends to the multi-attribute negotiation between one MA and multi-MSA, where the demand is based on the selling price of MA. In particular we focus on the situation of MA monopolies or oligopolies, as it is often the case in the trading business.

This paper is organized as follows: section 2 describes negotiation model and settings used in this research; section 3 describes the modified two-stage negotiation protocol; numerical example and analysis are given in section 4. In conclusion, the contributions and the directions of the future work are commented.

2   Model

All the used notations are shown as follows:

$\alpha_{j'}^{Max}$	maximum percentage of profit of MSA j'		
β^{Max}	maximum percentage profit of MA		
$\delta_{LT,w}^{M}$	concession function of lead time of MA		
$\delta_{Q,w}^{M}$	concession function of quantity of MA		
$\delta_{w,LT}^{M}$	concession function of wholesale price of MA		
$\delta_{w,Q}^{S}$	concession function of wholesale price of SF_j		
$\delta_{w,LT}^{S}$	concession function of wholesale price of SF_j		
γ_j	productivity of SF_j	$\pi_j[k]$	profit of MA at k
$\pi_j^S[k]$	profit of SF_j at k	$\pi_j^{SM}[k]$	profit of SF_j takes strategy of MA at k
AC_j	combined ability of SF_j	PCA_j	maximum price of SF_j
cf	fixed cost per order of MA	PCI_j	minimum price of SF_j
cp_j	unit production cost of SF_j	PMA	maximum price of MA
cs_j	set-up cost per order of SF_j	$ps_j[k]$	selling price of MA at k
cst	shortage cost of MA	$Q_j^S[k]$	quantity of SF_j at k
$D_j[k]$	demand of CA at k	$Q_j^M[k]$	quantity of MA at k
f_Q	function of quantity of SF_j	sv	salvage value of unsold product of MA
h^M	holding cost of MA	TN	deadline of the negotiation
h^S	holding cost of SF_j	TS	time of each negotiation round
$LT_j^M[k]$	lead time of MA at k	$w_j^M[k]$	wholesale price of MA at k
$LT_j^S[k]$	lead time of SF_j at k	$w_j^S[k]$	wholesale price of SF_j at k

This research considers the multi-attribute negotiation between one MA and multiple MSAs, where MA should determine the quantity of his order based on the demand of CA. The negotiations between one MA and multiple MSAs, where the order requested by MA is too large for MSA to complete independently, have been discussed in the previous work[8]. It tried to find another way to resolve this problem which can maintain the integrity of the order. It assumed that the MSAs accepted only the orders which were able to fulfill independently, and tried to combine with the other MSAs as a coalition when the order was out of their abilities. Furthermore, it assumed that the quantity of the order of MA was fixed. However, in the real market, it must be related to the demand of CA. Thus, this research tries to extend the negotiation under fixed demand to the negotiation under the situation where the demand depends on the selling price of MA. Three main attributes considered in this research are the wholesale price of the product, the quantity of the order, and the lead time of the order. MA negotiates with the MSAs to reach agreements on the strategies of the three attributes. We assume that the demand of CA is in an additive form as (1), where $a, b > 0$. It depends on the selling price of MA. $ps_j[k]$ is the selling price of MA of the negotiation between SF_j at k.

$$D_j[k] = a - bps_j[k]. \qquad (1)$$

3 Negotiation Protocol

This research proposes a modified two-stage negotiation protocol based on the two-stage negotiation protocol proposed in [8]:

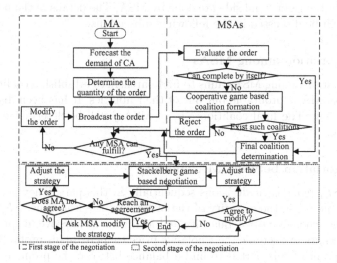

Fig. 1. Flowchart of modified two-stage negotiation protocol

Stage1: Negotiation among MSAs

- *Step 1:* MA forecasts the demand of CA, determines the initial price, quantity and lead time of the order which he wants to place, and then broadcasts the order to all the MSAs.
- *Step 2:* MSAs evaluate the order and check whether the order can be finished by themselves. If they can do it, themselves will be determined as the final coalition SF_j and fed back to MA; if they cannot do it, then they can negotiate with the other MSAs to build a coalition SF_j and feed back to MA. A cooperative game is used for coalition formation.

- *Step 3:* MA checks whether there exists any SF_j can fulfill the order, if there exists, goes to the second stage, if there does not exist, then MA modifies the order and re-broadcasts the order.

Stage2: Negotiation between MA and SF_j

- *Step 4:* MA starts to negotiate with SF_j. MA-Stackelberg game is introduced to find the final solution.
- *Step 5:* MA checks whether an agreement is reached, if the agreement is reached, negotiation ends, if the agreement is not reached, then MA checks whether he agrees with the strategies or not. If he agrees with it, he asks the MSA to modify his strategy, if he does not agree with it, then he adjusts his own strategy and gives a response.
- *Step 6:* MSA checks whether he agrees to modify his strategy or not. If he agrees to modify, he adjusts his own strategy, if he does not agree, then the negotiation ends and fails to find an agreement.

The flowchart of the modified two-stage negotiation is shown in Fig. 1. The processes in the left-hand side of the gray dash line are done by MA, and the processes in the right-hand side are done by MSA. The details of the negotiation protocol will be discussed in the following subsections.

3.1   Negotiation among MSAs

The negotiation among MSAs aims to find partners to establish a coalition when the order of MA is profitable but out of their abilities. It has been discussed in details in [8,9]. The final coalition SF_j of MSA j will be determined after the negotiation.

3.2   Negotiation between MA and SF_j

MA and SF_j make their decisions sequentially in this part. They negotiate on the wholesale price, the quantity of the order, and the lead time. SF_j wants to increase the wholesale price, quantity and lead time to improve his profit. However, MA wants to decrease the wholesale price to increase his profit. Therefore, the main point of this part is to find a balance between the profits of SF_j and MA.

The negotiation between MA and SF_j can be modeled as a Stackelberg game, where MA is indicated as a leader and SF_j can be seen as a follower. In the formulation of a Stackelberg game, it is usually assumed that players' profit functions are common knowledge [10]. Thus, MA can use this common knowledge to construct SF_j's most profitable responses to all the possible decisions. Then, MA's profit function from corresponding decisions based on all the SF_j's responses can be explored. In the end, MA makes a decision which can maximize his profit. SF_j then has a best response to matching the decision. We assume that both MA and SF_j are rational, thus, they do not want to deviate from this set of decisions, which is called Stackelberg equilibrium in the game theory. The strategies of MA and SF_j are determined in the following sections.

Determination of the Strategies of MA. From the analysis above, we can see that MA offers his strategies from low to high. The strategies of MA for SF_j at round k are $(Q_j^M[k], w_j^M[k], LT_j^M[k])$, where:

$$w_j^M[k] = w_j^M[k-1] + \frac{PMA - w_j^M[k-1]}{(TN - kTS)/TS} + \delta_{w,LT}^M(LT_j^S[k-1]) \tag{2}$$

$$\delta_{w,LT}^M(LT_j^S[k-1]) = \begin{cases} \theta_z^{wLT}, & \text{if } LT_{ij}^S[k-1] \le x_1^{LT} \\ \theta_{z-1}^{wLT}, & \text{if } x_{z-1}^{LT} < LT_{ij}^S[k-1] < x_z^{LT} \\ 0, & \text{if } LT_{ij}^S[k-1] \ge x_z^{LT} \end{cases} \tag{3}$$

$$Q_j^M[k] = D_j[k] + \delta_{Q,w}^M(w_j^S[k-1]) \tag{4}$$

$$LT_j^M[k] = LT_j^M[k-1] + \delta_{LT,w}^M(w_j^S[k-1]) \tag{5}$$

$$ps_j[k] = w_j^M[k](1 + \beta^{Max}). \tag{6}$$

At each round of negotiation, MA should determine strategies of all the three attributes. MA determines the value of the first attribute according to his preferential choice and we assume that MA in this research firstly determines his price. MA not only considers the concession which related to the remnant negotiation time at round k (the second item of (2)), but also takes the strategies of SF_j at $k-1$ into account (the third item of (2)). He can increase certain amount of price if SF_j can offer the product in shorter time. The quantity $Q_j^M[k]$ of MA depends on the demand of CA(the first item of (4)) and the increment according to the price of SF_j (the second item of (4)). If SF_j can offer lower price, MA will increase the total amount to buy. The lead time $LT_j^M[k]$ of MA related to the price of SF_j (the second item of (5)). If SF_j can offer lower price, MA will extend the lead time of his order. $\delta_{w,LT}^M$ is a piece-wise function as (3), it means when $LT_j^S[k-1]$ belongs to the range (x_{z-1}^{LT}, x_z^{LT}), MA will give a concession of the price at the value of θ_{z-1}^{wLT}. All the threshold values x_{z-1}^{LT} of each segment and the related mapping values θ_{z-1}^{wLT} are determined by himself. $\delta_{Q,w}^M$ and $\delta_{LT,w}^M$ have the same form as (3).

Determination of the Strategies of SF_j. Each SF_j tries to determine his strategies to maximize his profit. The higher value of the three attributes, the better. Thus, he replies his strategies from high to low. However, it is better to reach an agreement than does not reach an agreement. Thus, SF_j should also take the strategies of MA into account and then decide his strategies. The strategies of SF_j are defined as follows:

$$w_j^S[k] = w_j^S[k-1] - \frac{w_j^S[k-1] - PCI_j}{(TN - kTS)/TS} - \delta_{w,Q}^S(Q_j^M[k]) - \delta_{w,LT}^S(LT_j^M[k]) \tag{7}$$

$$Q_j^S[k] = f_Q(w_j^S[k]) \tag{8}$$

$$LT_j^S[k] = Q_j^S[k]/\gamma_j \tag{9}$$

$$f_Q(w_j^S[k]) = \begin{cases} \theta_Q^{max}, & \text{if } w_j^S[k] \le PCI_j \\ \theta_Q[k], & \text{if } PCI_j < w_j^S[k] < PCA_j \\ \theta_Q^{min}, & \text{if } w_j^S[k] \ge PCA_j \end{cases} \tag{10}$$

$$\theta_Q[k] = AC_j - \frac{[\frac{cs_j}{w_j^S[0]-cp_i} - AC_j]PCI_j}{PCA_j - PCI_j} + w_j^S[k]\frac{\frac{cs_j}{w_j^S[0]-cp_j} - AC_j}{PCA_j - PCI_j}. \tag{11}$$

SF_j firstly decides his price according to the strategies of MA. (7) means SF_j will give a discount if MA can increase the quantity of his order (the third item of (7)) or extend the lead time (the last item of (7)). The quantity (8) and lead time(9) of SF_j strongly depends on his productivity. Thus, all the three attributes constraint each other. $\delta_{w,Q}^S(Q_j^M[k])$ and $\delta_{w,LT}^S(LT_j^M[k])$ are also piecewise functions as (3) but has opposite tendency (threshold and related mapping values). $\theta_Q[k]$ is used to determine the minimum quantity to ensure the order will be profitable (for each order, minimum setup cost is needed).

Determination of the Final Equilibrium. MA has his own preferences for wholesale price, quantity and lead time and he is looking for the offer that best satisfies these preferences. Both MA and SF_j want to maximize their profits by choosing their preferred strategies. The profits of MA at k, where he agrees with the strategy of SF_j, is defined as:

$$\pi_j^M[k] = ps_j[k]D_j[k] + sgn(Q_j^M[k] - D_j[k])(Q_j^M[k] - D_j[k])sv - sgn(D_j[k]$$
$$-Q_j^M[k])(D_j[k] - Q_j^M[k])cst - w_j^M[k]Q_j^M[k] - \frac{cfD_j[k]}{Q_j^M[k]} - \frac{hQ_j^M[k]}{2} \tag{12}$$

where $sgn(x)$ equals to 1, if $x > 0$, otherwise it equals to 0.

We can see that in this model MA is the leader and he has more decision power. Thus, the objective of the Stackelberg game is to find the equilibrium which can maximize the profit of MA. It can be transformed into finding the agreements on the strategies of the three attributes and so to maximize the profit of MA. However, the strategies must be accepted by SF_j. Thus, the equilibrium of the negotiation between MA and SF_j can be determined as the strategies $(Q_j^M[k], w_j^M[k], LT_j^M[k])$ of MA at k. Moreover, these final strategies must meet the following conditions:

$$\max \{\pi_j^M[k]\} \tag{13}$$

$$\text{s.t. } \pi_j^{SM}[k] \ge \pi_j^S[k], \text{if } k < TN\text{-}1 \tag{14}$$

$$\pi_j^{SM}[k] > 0, \text{if } k=TN\text{-}1 \tag{15}$$

$$Q_j^M[k] \le AC_j[k] \tag{16}$$

where (14)-(15) are used for SF_j to evaluate the acceptability of the strategies, and these mean that the order must be profitable for SF_j. (16) means the order must be in ability of SF_j. $\pi_j^{SM}[k]$ is the profit of SF_j adopts the strategies of MA at k (as (2)-(5)), $\pi_j^S[k]$ is the profit of SF_j adopts his own strategies at k (as (7)-(9)). The agreement can be reached only if the profit of taking the strategies of

MA is greater than the one of taking his own strategies. Finally, MA decides the final supplier which can maximize his profit based on the equilibrium acquired from (13)-(16).

The characteristics of the proposed protocol are:

- The agreement can be reached as long as (14)-(16) are satisfied, no matter MA cannot reach an agreement with SF_j on the wholesale price or not.
- The agreement may not be reached even MA has reached an agreement with SF_j on the wholesale price.
- The attributes may not be monotone changing.

4 Numerical Case and Analysis

A numerical case is provided to illustrate the processes of the multi-attribute negotiation and how does the negotiation find the final equilibrium. Assume there is one MA and 5 MSA in SCN and all the used parameters are defined as Table 1.

Table 1. Parameter settings and threshold values of the concession functions

MSA (J=5)		MA		
$\gamma_j \sim U(100,300)$ $cp_j \sim U(7,8)$		$\alpha^{max}=0.5$ $h^M = 3$		$cst^M = 5$
$\beta_j^{min}=0.2$ $\beta_j^{max}=0.5$		$\alpha^{min}=0.3$ $psIn_i^M \sim U(13,14)$		$cf^M = 100$
$h_j^S=3$ $cs_j \sim U(200,300)$		$sv^M = 2$ $a \sim U(1000,2000)$		$b \sim U(0,100)$

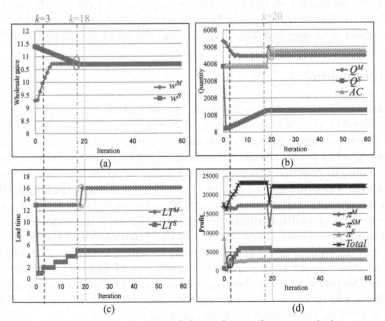

Fig. 2. The fluctuation of the multi-attribute negotiation

Firstly, we discuss about the details of the multi-attribute negotiation between one MA and one SF_j. We take the negotiation between MA and coalition $\{12\}$ as an example. The fluctuations of three attributes are shown as Fig. 2. We can see that:

- At $k = 3$, the profit of $\{12\}$ takes the strategies of MA is greater than takes his own strategies (see the area marked by ellipse in Fig. 2(d), where $\pi^{SM}[3] > \pi^{S}[3]$), that means (14) is satisfied. However, the quantity of MA is also greater than the ability of $\{12\}$ (see the quantity at $k=3$ of Fig. 2(b), where $Q^{M}[3] > AC[3]$), that means (16) is not satisfied. Therefore, the agreement is not reached and the negotiation goes by.
- At $k = 18$, MA reaches an agreement with $\{12\}$ on the wholesale price (see the area marked by ellipse in Fig. 2(a)) and (14) is satisfied. However, (16) is still not satisfied because $Q^{M}[18] > AC[18]$ from Fig. 2(b). Therefore, the agreement is not reached and the negotiation goes by.
- At $k = 20$, the wholesale price of MA keeps unchanging, but he makes a concession of his lead time (see the area marked by ellipse in Fig. 2(c)) and then (16) is satisfied (see the area marked by ellipse in Fig. 2(b), where $Q^{M}[20] < AC[20]$). Therefore, both constraints (14) and (16) are satisfied.

Then we can get final equilibrium between MA and$\{12\}$ is the strategies of MA at $k = 20$ where the strategies are $(10.704, 4489, 16)$. What we should pay attention to are: 1) The equilibrium not always exists; 2) The order MA may become out of ability of SF_j even it was in ability at the first time.

Similarly, we can get all the equilibriums and then MA decides the final supplier which can maximize his profit. In this case, the final supplier for MA is $\{32\}$ with the final strategies $(10.703, 6735, 16)$ and the profit equals to 25501.295.

5   Conclusion

The multi-attribute negotiation between MA and MSA, where the quantity of the order of MA depends on the demand of CA, was discussed in this paper. A modified two-stage negotiation protocol was proposed. MA-Stackelberg game was introduced to decide the final strategies by finding the Stackelberg equilibrium. A different criterion was proposed for MSA to decide whether accept the order or not. The strategies of MA at k was defined as final equilibrium if the constraints are satisfied. In this research, we only provided a method to find the equilibrium of multi-attribute negotiation. However, it cannot ensure the equilibrium always exists. There still exists the situation where the negotiation cannot find the equilibrium. For future work, we will take the dynamic coalition formation into account to improve the success rate of finding the equilibrium. Moreover, the performance of the proposed protocol will be discussed, including what effects will be caused by changing the parameter, what's the effect of the ability of MSA on the formation of the coalition.

References

1. Ganeshan, R., Jack, E., Magazine, M.J., Stephens, P.: A taxonomic review of supply chain management research, a chapter of Quantitative models for supply chain management. Kluwer Academic Publishers, USA (1999)
2. Cachon, G.P., Netessine, S.: Game theory in supply chain analysis, an invited chapter for the book "Supply Chain Analysis in the eBusiness Era". Kluwer (2003)
3. Hall, N.G., Liu, Z.X.: Capacity allocation and scheduling in supply chains. Operations Research 58(6), 1711–1725 (2010)
4. Martinez-de-Albeniz, V., Roels, G.: Competing for shelf space. Production and Operations Management 20(1), 32–46 (2011)
5. Xiao, T.J., et al.: Ordering, wholesale pricing and lead-time decisions in a three-stage supply chain under demand uncertainty. Computers & Industrial Engineering 59, 840–852 (2010)
6. Sinha, S., Sarmah, S.P.: Coordination and price competition in a duopoly common retailer supply chain. Computers & Industrial Engineering 59, 280–295 (2010)
7. Xia, Y.: Competitive strategies and market segmentation for suppliers with substitutable products. Eur. J. Oper. Res. 210, 194–203 (2011)
8. Yu, F., Kaihara, T., Fujii, N.: A Multi-agent based negotiation for SCN using game theory. In: Frick, J., Laugen, B.T. (eds.) APMS 2011. IFIP AICT, vol. 384, pp. 299–308. Springer, Heidelberg (2012)
9. Yu, F., Kaihara, T., Fujii, N.: Hierarchical-game based negotiation for supply chain network. In: The ASME 2012 International Symposium on Flexible Automation, St. Louis, MO, USA (2012)
10. An, N., Lu, J.-C., Rosen, D., Ruan, L.: Supply-chain oriented robust parameter design. International Journal of Production Research 45(23), 5465–5484 (2007)

Supplier Selection Criteria in Fractal Supply Network

Sameh M. Saad, Julian C. Aririguzo, and Terrence D. Perera

Department of Engineering and Mathematics
Sheffield Hallam University
Sheffield S1 1WB UK
s.saad@shu.ac.uk

Abstract. Original Equipment Manufacturers (OEMs) collaborate with their key suppliers in a new form of hands-on partnership. The Fractal supply network is distinct from the traditional supply chain because of the inherent congenital fractal characteristics. This paper uses the Analytic Hierarchy/Network Process (AH/NP) approach to provide a strict methodology and criteria ranking in the complicated decision-making process of exploring the suitability, selection and maintenance of few, albeit reliable and high quality suppliers prior to going into the Fractal Manufacturing Partnership (FMP). Selecting the right set of suppliers without undermining essential competitive factors and material costs is of strategic importance in forming this alliance and could help or hinder the inherent strength in the collaboration. The outcome from this research project is a simple, systematic, logical and mathematical guide to user of OEMs in making robust and informed supplier selection decision prior to going into FMP from a fractal supply network perspective.

Keywords: Fractal supply network, supplier selection.

1 Introduction

The vigorous competition in today's global markets has drawn attention on supply chains and networks [1]. Evolution in manufacturing and management, strategic alliances, technological changes and cycle time compression [2] make frugal resource management relevant [3]. Manufacturers tend to manage their suppliers in different ways leading to supplier development, supplier evaluation, supplier selection, supplier association, supplier coordination etc. [1] & [4], and management of the logistics involved plays a strategic role for organizations that keep pace with market changes and supply chain integration [2]. Alliances, collaborations and networks particularly between Original Equipment Manufacturers (OEMs) and their key suppliers to achieve competitive advantage especially in the face of global volatile and unpredictable markets is gaining popularity [5]. Involving suppliers from initial product development through to final assembly reduces product development time, manufacturing expenses and improves quality [5] by evaluating and managing the inherent logistics. OEMs increasingly hand over their non-core business to key suppliers who can demonstrate the expertise and capability necessary for the task. These key suppliers are responsible for designing, making and assembling their modular components on the

C. Emmanouilidis, M. Taisch, D. Kiritsis (Eds.): APMS 2012, Part II, IFIP AICT 398, pp. 544–551, 2013.
© IFIP International Federation for Information Processing 2013

assembly line, while co-owning the OEM's facility. The advantages of this new manufacturing formula have been reported to be tremendous. In FMP, OEMs focus on their core capabilities which include specification of envelop size and weight and overall supervision of the production process while handing over non-core business to key suppliers who can demonstrate the expertise and capability necessary providing the synergy and motivation required to form leaner core business units interacting to create mass customized products [5]. Selection of the right set of suppliers is of strategic importance in forming this alliance and could help or hinder the inherent strength in the collaboration.

Therefore, comprehensive framework is needed to facilitate supplier selection process and to cope with trends in various manufacturing strategies [5] & [6]. The basis considered for supplier selection include least invoice, implicit or explicit quality, delivery reliability, lot size, paper work, returns, transportation and expediting costs [3] & [7]. The traditional approach to this selection task in procurement situations and buyer-supplier relationships has been to maintain a competitive supplier base, keeping them at arm's length, and playing them off against each other [3] & [4]. Number of authors have developed and proposed various mathematical frameworks and system modeling such as [6], [8], [9], [10], [11] [12], [13] & [14] to assist in this process. This paper ventures explicitly into the FMP or the OEM/ supplier collaboration which has until now not been addressed comprehensively. The model proposed in this paper is simple, systematic, logical and mathematical using MAT LAB to create a user-friendly interface for the supplier selection to guide user OEMs in making robust and informed choices/ decision in the selection task.

2   Framework for Defining the Supplier Selection Criteria in FMP

Determining the buyer-supplier level of integration is the most important decision in the buyer-supplier selection process [15]. Likewise, the level of integration and closeness between manufacturers and suppliers in the FMP is of vital importance in the supplier selection process. The work by [6] is particularly significant and relevant to the FMP because it is not only investigates two basic possible qualitative and quantitative criteria, but most importantly, their approach could assist decision makers in determining the OEM-supplier integration level. This is vital in the long-term relationship inherent in the FMP. Quantitative criterion measures concrete quantitative dimensions such as cost whereas qualitative criterion deals with quality of design. Trade-offs are usually required to resolve conflicting factors between the two criteria [6]. In the FMP business partnership and integration is desired. The OEM fully interacts or cooperates with the suppliers in the long term. It is based on series of production silos arranged serially and highly coordinated with one another [5]. The suppliers are directly involved in the manufacturing process rather than supply and leave. High level of technology facilitates both OEM and suppliers to work towards the same strategic goals. This alliance warrants sharing of business related information to explore new markets with novel ideas and technologies. It also encourages more investment in R&D. It is note-worthy the different degrees of integration and how OEM-supplier integration has evolved from JIT, JIT11, modular sequencing, supplier parks to FMP [5].

2.1   AHP Modelling Procedure

The AHP was originally designed and applied by [16] [17] & [18]; for solving complex multiple criteria problems involving comparison of decision elements difficult to quantify [12] & [14]. It considers both qualitative and quantitative criteria in a hierarchical structure (ranking) for supplier selection. AHP divides a complex decision problem into a hierarchical algorithm of decision elements. A pair wise comparison in each cluster (as a matrix) follows, and a normalized principal eigenvector is calculated for the priority vector which provides a weighted value of each element within the cluster or level of the hierarchy and also a consistency ratio (used for checking the consistency of the data). The main theme is the decomposition by hierarchies, [19] finds that AHP is based on three basic principles, namely; decomposition, comparative judgments, and hierarchical composition of priority. The decomposition level breaks down complex and unstructured criteria into a hierarchy of clusters. The principle of comparative judgments is applied to construct pair wise comparison of all combinations of the elements in a cluster with respect to the parent of that cluster. The principle of hierarchical composition or synthesis is applied to multiply the local priorities of elements in a cluster by the 'global' priority of the parent, producing global priorities throughout the hierarchy.

2.2   Mathematical Formulation Leading to Supplier Selection

Based on the AHP approach, weights of criteria and score of alternatives are called local priorities which are considered as the second step of the decision process [9]. The decision making process requires preferred pair-wise comparison concerning weights and scores. The value of weights v_i and the scores r_{ij} are extracted from the comparison and listed in a decision table. The last step of the AHP aggregates the local priorities from the decision table by a weighted sum as shown on equation (1).

$$R_j = \sum_i v_i \times r_{ij} \qquad (1)$$

R_j represents the global priorities and is thus obtained for ranking and selection of the best alternatives. Assessment of local priorities based on pair-wise comparison is the main constituent of this method where two elements E_i and E_j at the same level of hierarchy are compared to provide a numerical ratio a_{ij} of their importance. If E_i is preferred to E_j then $a_{ij} > 1$. On the other hand the reciprocal property, $a_{ji} = 1/a_{ij}$, $j = 1,2,3,4,....,n$ and $i = 1,2,3...n$ always holds. Each set of comparison with n elements requires $[n \times (n - 1)] /2$ judgments [9]. The rest half of the comparison matrix is the reciprocals of those judgments lying above the diagonal and are omitted. The decision maker's judgments a_{ij} are usually estimations of the exact. Hence, a consistency ratio method was introduced by [16] to govern the consistency of judgments. If a decision maker states that criterion x is of equal importance to criterion y, then, $a_{xy} = a_{yx} = 1$, and if criterion y is extremely more important than criterion z, then, $a_{yz} = 9$, & $a_{zy} = 1/9$, then criterion z should be having the same weight to criterion z as criterion y does. However, the decision maker is often unable to express the consistency of the judgment and this could affect the analysis. Hence, [16] consistency method measures the inconsistency of the pair-wise comparison matrix and sets a threshold boundary which should not be exceeded. In the non-consistent case the comparison matrix A may be considered as a perturbation of the previous consistent case. When the entries a_{ij} changes only slightly, the Eigen values change in a similar fashion. The consistency index (CI) is calculated using equation 2.

$$CI = \frac{\lambda_{max} - n}{n - 1} \qquad (2)$$

where n is number of comparison elements, and λ_{max} is Eigen value of the matrix.

Then, the consistence ratio (CR) is calculated as the ratio of consistency index and random consistency index (RI). (RI) is the random index representing the consistency of a randomly generated pair-wise comparison matrix. The consistency ratio (CR) is calculated using equation 3.

$$CR(A) = \frac{CI(A)}{RCI(n)} \qquad (3)$$

If CR(A) < 0.1 (10%), the pair-wise comparison matrix is considered to be consistent enough. In the case where CR(A) > 0.1, the comparison matrix should be improved. The value of (RI) depends on the number of criteria being compared or considered.

3   Modelling the FMP Supplier Selection Process

The model sorts the decision problem in a hierarchical system of decision elements. Pair-wise comparison matrix of these elements is constructed, normalized principle Eigen vector is calculated for the priority vector which provides the measurement of weights (relative importance) of each element. Supplier selection criteria, sub-criteria and alternatives for the FMP have been formed based on relevant extensive literature [1], [6], [8], [9] & [20] reviewed and consulted for the project. They are grouped as either tangible or intangible depending on how perceptible or realistic they are and include the following; business criteria, manufacturing, quality assessment, performance assessment, organizational culture and strategy, personnel management, compatibility and information technology. The first four are considered tangible while the rest are intangible criteria.

3.1   Modelling Procedure

The general modeling procedure is summarized below:

(i)   Construct the hierarchy system, including several independent elements. The model has four levels of hierarchy - the overall goal, main evaluation criteria, sub-criteria and alternatives.

(ii)   Pair-wise comparison of criteria and alternatives is done to find comparative weights amongst the attribute decision elements. The mathematical modeling utilizes the 'slider' function of MATLAB GUI (Graphical User Interface) as comparative input tool. The quantified subjective decisions are stored in allo-cated cells. The outcome is a ranked priority order of criteria and ranked priority order of decision alternatives under each criterion.

(iii) Calculate the weights, test the consistency and calculate the Eigen vector of each comparison matrix to obtain the priority of each decision elements. Hence, for each pair-wise comparison matrix, the Eigen value of the matrix λ_{max} and Ei-gen vector w (w_1, w_2...w_n), weights of the criteria is estimated.

(iv)   The last step in the modeling is finding the overall priorities for decision alterna-tives. This is calculated by multiplying the priority for each alternative under each criterion by the weight of each criterion (local weights). The calculations is performed from the lower level to the higher level of hierarchy where the out-come of the step is ranked in order of the decision alternatives to aid the decision making process.

(iv)   Validation of the model is needed to test the logical and mathematical correct-ness and reliability of the model. To this end, the result from the case study by [9] is imported into the project. In [9], the authors use Data Envelopment Analy-sis (DEA) approach and this is embedded into the analytic hierarchy process me-thodology. The criteria, sub-criteria, and alternatives and the scores of the com-parisons are used as they are. The final outcome of the mathematical model is compared and the results show close comparison and validated to 0.07%.

FMP Supplier Criteria. Supplier selection criteria, sub-criteria and alternatives for the FMP have been formed based on relevant extensive literature [6], [8], [9], [20] & [22] reviewed and consulted for the project. These are considered while making op-timal supplier selection for the FMP. They are grouped as either tangible or intangible depending on how perceptible and realistic they are. They form the framework on figure 1, and include the following; business criteria, manufacturing, quality assess-ment, performance assessment, organizational culture and strategy, personnel man-agement, compatibility and information technology. The first four are considered tangible while the rest are intangible criteria.

The input of each element is recorded in a tabular form and the AHP output is cal-culated once the relevant data is collected and the consistency ratio is calculated along with the AHP weights. Each relevant elements of the model is compared quantitative-ly and the result is recorded for final calculations. Due to space limitation, results and discussion will be provided in the conference.

Overall Goal   Main Criteria Level 1   Sub-criteria Level 2

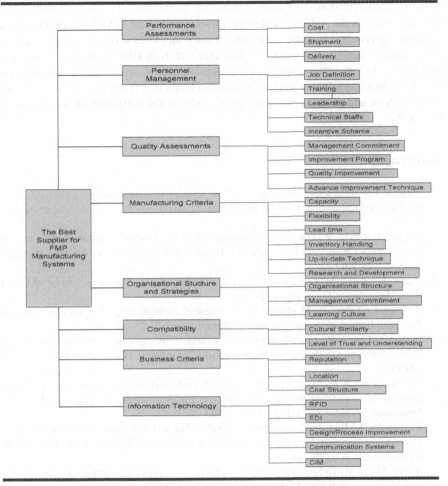

Fig. 1. Framework of supplier selection process

4   Conclusion

Selection and maintenance of high quality and reliable Suppliers is key component of successful implementation of the FMP. One objective of the selection process is determination of optimal supplier criteria particularly suited to the fractal manufacturing philosophy. The fractal company advocates a great learning, 'open book' culture and more sophisticated communication link between fractals in order to maintain the transparency of information and to facilitate continuous improvement program and Research and Development. This paper has reviewed conventional criteria used mainly in the buyer-supplier/ procurement selection process and short listed some important criteria which are relevant to the FMP. These criteria are classified as tangible and intangible criteria. A mathematical argument is put forward to justify the process of the supplier selection. To further evaluate the importance of each criterion to FMP, this study utilizes the AHP methodology implemented using MAT LAB programming language to generate a framework that robustly identifies different criteria most of which are conflicting, and suppliers. The approach is flexible enough to allow decision makers to make their choices in a qualitative manner while the framework transforms the decision into quantitative results and helps in selecting the right set of suppliers without undermining the inherent strengths in the collaboration as obtained in the FMP.

References

1. Chan, F.T.S.: Interactive selection model for supplier selection process: an analytical hierarchy process approach. International Journal of Production Research 41(15), 3549–3579 (2003)
2. Arvind, J., Gupta, P., Garg, S.: An Application of the Analytic Network Process to Evaluate Supply Chain Logistics Strategies. International Journal of the Analytic Hierarchy Process 3(2) (2011)
3. Akinc, U.: Selecting a set of vendors in a manufacturing environment. Journal of Operations Management 11(2), 107–122 (1993)
4. de Boer, L., Labro, E., Morlacchi, P.: A review of methods supporting supplier selection. European Journal of Purchasing Supply Management 7(2), 75–89 (2001)
5. Noori, H., Lee, W.B.: Fractal manufacturing partnership: exploring a new form of strategic alliance between OEMs and suppliers. Logistics Information Management 13(5), 301–311 (2000)
6. Sen, S., et al.: A framework for defining both qualitative and quantitative supplier selection criteria considering the buyer-supplier integration strategies. International Journal of Production Research 46(7), 1825–1845 (2008)
7. Lipovetsky, S.: Priority Eigenvectors in Analytic Hierarchy/Network Processes with Outer Dependence Between Alternatives and Criteria. International Journal of the Analytic Hierarchy Process 3(2) (2011)
8. Sevkli, M., et al.: Hybrid analytical hierarchy process model for supplier selection. Industrial Management & Data Systems 108(1-2), 122–142 (2008)
9. Sevkli, M., et al.: An application of data envelopment analytic hierarchy process for supplier selection: a case study of BEKO in Turkey. International Journal of Production Research 45(9), 1973–2003 (2007)
10. Ramanathan, R.: Data envelopment analysis for weight derivation and aggregation in the analytic hierarchy process. Computers & Operations Research 33(5), 1289–1307 (2006)
11. Tam, M.C.Y., Tummala, V.M.R.: An application of the AHP in vendor selection of a telecommunications system. Omega 29(2), 171–182 (2001)
12. Lami, I.M., Masala, E., Pensa, S.: Analytic Network Process (ANP) and Visualization of Spatial Data: the Use of Dynamic Maps in Territorial Transformation Processes. International Journal of the Analytic Hierarchy Process 3(2) (2011)
13. Kopytov, E., Demidovs, V., Petukhova, N.: Application of the Analytic Hierarchy Process in Development of Train Schedule Information Systems. International Journal of the Analytic Hierarchy Process (2011)

14. Amponsah, C.T.: Application of Multi-Criteria Decision Making Process to Determine Critical Success Factors for Procurement of Capital Projects under Public-Private Partnerships. International Journal of the Analytic Hierarchy Process 3(2) (2011)
15. Masella, C., Rangone, A.: Managing supplier/customer relationships by performance measurement systems. In: Proceedings of the 2nd International Symposium on Logistics, pp. 99–102 (1995)
16. Saaty, T.L.: The Analytical Hierarchy Process. McGraw-Hill, New York (1980)
17. Saaty, T.L.: Decision making with the analytic hierarchy process. Int. J. Services Sciences 1(1), 83–98 (2008)
18. Saaty, T.L., Vargas, L.G.: Models, Methods, Concepts and Applications of the Analytic Hierarchy Process. Kluwer Academic Publishers, Boston (2000)
19. Rao, R.V.: Evaluating flexible manufacturing systems using a combined multiple attribute decision making method. International Journal of Production Research 46(7), 1975–1989 (2008)
20. Chan, F.T.S., et al.: A decision support system for supplier selection in the airline industry. Proceedings of the Institution of Mechanical Engineers Part B-Journal of Engineering Manufacture 221(4), 741–758 (2007)
21. Ting, S.-G., Cho, D.I.: An integrated approach for supplier selection and purchasing decisions. Supply Chain Management-an International Journal 13(2), 116–127 (2008)
22. Perçin, S.: An application of the integrated AHP-PGP model in supplier. Measuring Business Excellence 10(6), 34–49 (2006)

A Test-Bed System for Supply Chain Management Incorporating Reverse Logistic

Shigeki Umeda

1-26 Toyotama-kami Nerima Tokyo 176-8534,
Japan
shigeki@cc.musashi.ac.jp

Abstract. Due to environmental and ecological responsibility, enterprises are
trying to reuse, remanufacture and recycle the used products to reduce the negative impact on environment. Reverse logistics is one of essential elements to
implement such sustainable supply chain system. This paper proposes simula-
tion-based test-bed system for supply chain management incorporating reverse
logistics.

Keywords: Supply chain management, Reverse Logistics, Simulation, Test-bed
system.

1 Introduction

Modern manufacturing enterprises need to collaborate with their business partners
through their business process operations such as design, manufacture, distribution,
and after sales service. A supply chain system is a chain of processes from the initial
raw materials to the ultimate consumption of the finished product spanning across
multiple supplier-customer links. It provides functions within and outside a company
that enable the value chain to make products and provide services to the customers.
Many discussions have been done [1].

In the last decade, due to environmental and ecological responsibility, enterprises
are trying to reuse, remanufacture and recycle the used products to reduce the negative impact on environment, especially the manufacturers of the electrical consumer
products. Electrical and electronic scrap also known as e-waste or e-scrap – has increased dramatically.

Requirements for corporate responsibility and sustainability are getting more urgent. The reverse logistics in supply chains is strongly related to all stages of a product development and is also a critical problem to all level of the industry.

Reverse logistics systems require taking back products from customers and the repairing, remanufacturing (value-added recovery), or recycling (material recovery) the
returned products.

The reverse logistics makes more complicated material-flows in supply chain.
There are different kinds of material-flows in a chain. One is forward-flow which
starts at part/material suppliers and reach customers. The other is reverse-flow which

C. Emmanouilidis, M. Taisch, D. Kiritsis (Eds.): APMS 2012, Part II, IFIP AICT 398, pp. 552–559, 2013.
© IFIP International Federation for Information Processing 2013

starts at customers and reach remanufacturer or recycler. Accordingly, introduction of reverse logistics in supply chain system would have profound effects on operations such as material-handling and procurement. This relationship is similar with arterial-flow and venous-flow in a human body.

System design and implementation of a "supply chain system with reverse-flow" would be extremely difficult in comparison with the cases without reverse-low. This is because considerations of reverse logistics would promote many issues in both configuration design phase and operations design phase. A generic method is needed to support supply chain system with reverse logistics.

System modeling technologies often provide useful operational analysis of system behaviors. The SCOR model is the most prominent process model in supply chain system [2]. This model provides a set of core models, which represents business processes in supply chain operations. The SCOR model includes five core models (PLAN, SOURCE, MAKE, DELIVER, and RETURN). Individual model describes activities in detail. Such macro-level models are, needless to say, useful for generic system descriptions at initial stage.

Modeling and simulation is one of the general purpose tools to optimize designs and operations of manufacturing and logistics systems. Especially discrete-event simulation provides predictions of system's behaviors potential status by "what-if scenario". Thus, simulations have been used as a powerful solution tool for various operational management problems, such as capacity planning, resource planning, lead-time planning, supplier selection, and outsourcing planning. The disadvantage of modeling and simulation is that system analysts need to implement simulation models of their own target system. This workload is very huge.

Analysts would be able to use modeling and simulation if typical generic simulation models are provided as a simulation model library in advance. In this case, the analyst chooses proper models in library, and customizes them as the need arises [3][4].

The objectives of this paper are (1) to propose a generic supply chain model with reverse logistics for product reuse, (2) to implement generic simulation models for the test-bed system by using generic models, and (3) to represent effectiveness of the proposed test-bed system by numerical examples. These models include component members, which enables to organize a supply chain system with reverse logistics. All models represent both material-processing logic and information-processing logic in the chain.

2   Reverse Logistics Models

2.1   Member Elements Model

First, we configured models that provide regular flow in a supply chain system. This feature is composed of elements, which include a Supplier, a Manufacturer, a Retailer, a Customer, and a Chain manager. Second, we also arranged components that realize reverse flow for product reuses. These elements are "Collector", "Remanufacturer", and "Recycler". A set of these elements would be a generic supply chain model with reverse logistics (Fig.1). Data descriptions of these elements include input (information/material), output (information/material), Pre-defined information, activities sequences, and performance measurement data. The summaries of activities of these elements are as follows.

Fig.1 represents a configuration of this model. This model is based on an analogy between arterial-venous blood flows in a human body and material-flow in a supply chain. Solid lines are production generation flow (arterial-flow), meanwhile, dashed lines are reverse logistics flow (venous-flow). Arterial-flows and venous-flow should be synchronized with each other. The system synchronizes venous flows with arterial flows. A set of simulation models represents above elements was implemented as a test-bed system for supply chain management incorporating reverse logistics.

- **Chain manager:** The major task of this element is to generate orders to elements which belong to an arterial flow in a chain: these are "Supplier", "Manufacturer", and "Retailer". This is a heterogeneous element in the chain. It predicts Customers' demands, and it gives orders to other members by using the predicted data. It keeps Customers' purchase data in a particular duration, and it uses them to predict demands in next ordering cycle. We developed an IDEF0-based hierarchical function model, that represents ordering process mechanisms in a chain [5].
- **Supplier:** This element is a start point of material flows in a chain. It generates parts by a sourcing order from Chain manager. And, it sends the parts to "Manufacturer" by using a transporter.
- **Manufacturer:** It receives parts from the Supplier and keeps them. When it receives an order from the Chain manager, it starts to generate products. After predefined lead-time, it sends the products to "Retailer" by using a transporter.

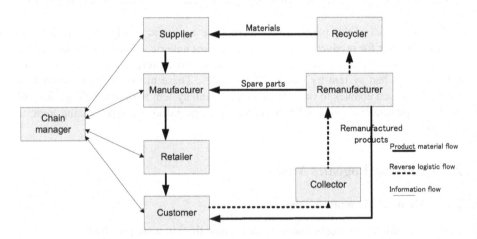

Fig. 1. Generic supply chain model with reverse logistics

- **Retailer:** The activities of this element are similar with Manufacturer. It receives products from Manufacturer, and it sends them to the Customer according as purchase orders.
- **Collector:** It reclaims used products from Customer, when he/she disposes the used product. And, it detaches reusable materials from the disposed product, and sends them to Remanufacturer.
- **Remanufacturer:** It produces remanufactured products by using materials from Collector. Examples of the remanufactured product are spare-parts. It provides the regenerated objects to Manufacturer.
- **Recycler:** It reclaims materials from wastes produced by Remanufacturer.

2.2   PUSH-Type and PULL-Type Reverse Model

Fig.2 represents configurations of reverse logistics models. These models are based on an analogy between arterial-venous blood flows in a human body and material-flow in a supply chain. Solid lines are production generation flow (arterial-flow), meanwhile, dashed lines are reverse logistics flow (venous-flow). Arterial-flows and venous-flow should be synchronized with each other. The system synchronizes venous flows with arterial flows. A set of simulation models represents above elements was implemented as a test-bed system for supply chain management incorporating reverse logistics.

The flow from Customer to Remanufacturer by way of Collector is a reverse logistics flow. There are two ways to control this flow: PUSH-type and PULL-type. Customer sends "used-products" to Collector, when Customer disposes them. The role of Collector is to distinguish reusable materials from the disposed products, and stores them.

One way is that Collector and Remanufacturer sends reverse products to Manufacturer in an orderly manner. This is PUSH-type flow, which is illustrated in Fig.2 (a). Another way is that Remanufacturer regenerates reverse products as the need arises in Manufacturer. The same logic is applied in between Remanufacturer and Collector. This is PULL-type flow. The implementation of this logic needs two pull signals, which is illustrated in Fig.2 (b). The first one is from Manufacturer to Remanufacturer, and the second one is from Remanufacturer to Collector. Collector acquires reusable materials from Customer with constant collection rate. Remanufacturer *pulls* materials from Collector, when it requires materials. Manufacturer also *pulls* materials from Remanufacturer as the need arise.

In PUSH-type, remanufactured products are sequentially pushed into Manufacturer, synchronizing with occurrence of reverse. Remanufactured product would be kept as material inventory in Manufacturer. In PULL-type, reverse products are stocked at Collector. These products stay at there, during no PULL signal from Remanufacturer. And, Remanufacturer does not work until it receives PULL signal. When high volumes of reverse products are generated, they are stopped at Collector.

When demand volume by Retailer increases, volume of used product flowed to Collector would rise. These are recycled by Remanufacturer, and are stocked as refreshed parts in Manufacturer's buffer. Meanwhile, in PULL-type, even if demand volume decreases, volume of used product flowed to Collector would move down.

Synchronized with the used product volume, the volume of spare parts and reuse materials would increase or decrease. When manufacturing order increases after low production continues, parts shortage is possibly occurred in Manufacturer.

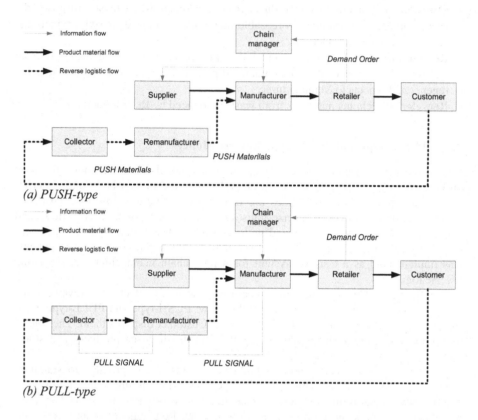

Fig. 2. Push-type and Pull-type reverse model

3   Simulation Examples

Based on the generic supply chain model described in 2.1 and 2.2, we implemented two types of model of reverse supply chain systems. One is Push-type reverse supply chain model, and another is Pull-type reverse supply chain model. In these models, Chain manager predicts market demands, and gives orders to both Supplier and Manufacturer in every week (5 working days).

Performance of reverse supply chain system depends on the "collection rate" of reusable materials from disposed products in market. In this case, we defined this value as 60%. Remanufacturer provides high performance; meanwhile Collector needs comparatively long lead-time to get reusable materials from the disposed product. Balance of these two reverse suppliers would be a key issue to determine whole of reverse supply chain system.

Other parameters of this simulation are lead-time and lot-size of chain members (Manufacturer, Retailer, Remanufacturer, Collector, and Deliverer). Chain manager generates the orders to Manufacturer and Supplier. Manufacturer and Retailer own almost same resource capacities. Meanwhile, Collector, Remanufacturer, and Retailer own almost similar resource capacities.

Operations during a hundred days are simulated, and the ordering cycle is a week (5 working days). Chain manager gives an operation order to Supplier and Manufacturer in every 5 working days. When the manager gives orders, he/she predicts demands in market by using exponential smoothing method. Each chain member gives transportation orders to Deliverer, when its operations are finished.

Figure 3 represents transitions of material volumes in the Push-type reverse supply chain. Retailer and Remanufacturer represent a steady state transition (Figure 3 (b) and (c)). Manufacturer represents a tendency that material increases, and Collector represents a material shortage state.

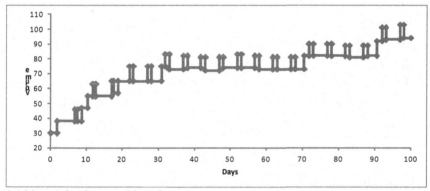

(a) Material volume at Manufacturer

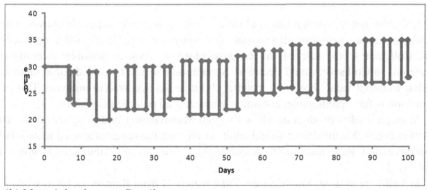

(b) Material volume at Retailer

Fig. 3. Material volume at chain members

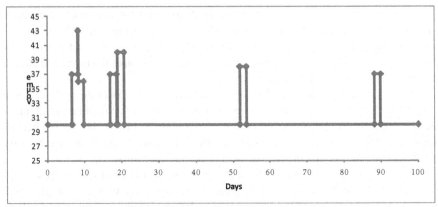

(c) Material volume at Remanufacture

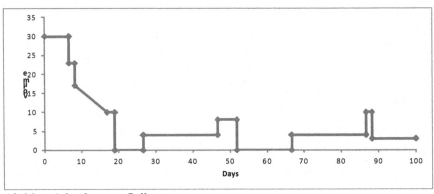

(d) Material volume at Collector

Fig. 3. (*continued*)

Collector needs independent lead-time to collect reusable materials. Nevertheless, Collector cannot withdraw all materials that consumer used. In this simulation scenario, Collector sends materials to Remanufacturer as soon as possible. Accordingly, materials in Collector would decrease. Simulation configures considerable input materials as initial value; however, material shortage has occurred in midterm. This phenomenon is fully predictable, considering operational policy in Collector.

Manager makes production plans for both Manufacturer and Supplier considering Market needs. Manufacturer would additionally own the remanufactured materials by Collector and Remanufacturer. Accordingly, materials in Manufacturer would be increased.

In Pull-type system, Manufacturer *pulls* materials from Remanufacturer, when it is needed, and Remanufacturer *pulls* materials from Collector. Accordingly Manufacturer does not own over-need material. Besides, the collected material would stay at Collector. The only way is that Manager would make plans considering predictions of recycled materials from Collector at any situation.

However, it is very difficult to predict how many recycled materials in any operational phases. We would have no choice without preparing materials at suppliers' buffers, considering available materials at suppliers in a chain. Simulations based on other scenarios would be needed to discuss this issue.

4   Conclusion and Future Research

The work described in this paper is the first step in simulation researches for reverse supply chain management. Recovery, recycling, or reuse of products will be important issues in current supply chain management. A formal study of SCM incorporating reverse logistics is critical. The proposed test-bed simulation system would be a useful tool for designing supply chain incorporating reverse logistics.

There are various types of supply and reverse chain management problems. Design and planning would be the most popular scope. When a system planner designs a supply chain or a manager reviews performance of the existing supply chain, he/she would attach importance supplier selection problem. It is a significant decision since it affects the system performance for a long time. From the supply chain performance viewpoint, it affects all the problems discussed above. Mature decisions would be needed.

First of all, we should organize problems in reverse supply chain management. Design and planning problems, suppliers/venders selection problems, and outsourcing planning problem would be discussed. These problems are interlinked. Among them, discussions of Push-type and Pull-type reverse models would the most important.

References

1. Daniel, A., Guide Jr, R., Jayaraman, V.: Supply Chain Management Incorporating Reverse Logistics. APICS Research paper Series (2000)
2. SCOR model, http://www.supply-chain.org/
3. Umeda, S., Lee, Y.T.: Integrated Supply Chain Simulation – A Design Specification for a Generic Supply Chain Simulation, NISTIR 7146, National Institute of Standards and Technology, US Dept. of Commerce (2004)
4. Umeda, S., Zhang, F.: Supply chain simulation: generic models and application examples. Production and Planning Control 17(2), 155–166 (2006)
5. Umeda, S.: Planning and implementation of information systems in supply chain systems. Journal of Society for Project Management 5(4), 42–48 (2003)

A Dyadic Study of Control in Buyer-Supplier Relationships

Anna Aminoff and Kari Tanskanen

Aalto University, School of Science, Department of Industrial Management and Engineering,
Espoo, Finland
{anna.aminoff,kari.tanskanen}@aalto.fi

Abstract. Control of supply chains has been discussed in supply chain literature from various viewpoints. While previous studies have generally examined
only buyer's perspectives of control, we expand on such previous research by
comparing both the buyer's and supplier's views. In this paper our objective is
to analyze why the control is distributed in a certain way in the buyer-supplier
relationship, and how does the distribution of control affect the buyer-supplier
relationship. We categorize the explanations for the distribution of control. We
argue that control in the buyer-supplier relationship might look different from
buyer's and suppliers' perspectives. We used a multiple case study methodology with six dyadic buyer-supplier relationships and conducted 43 interviews.

Keywords: Control, supply chain management, dyadic buyer-supplier relationship.

1 Introduction

Control of supply chains has been discussed in supply chain literature from various
viewpoints. While previous studies (for example [1-4]) have examined the control in
buyer-supplier relationships, these studies have generally examined only buyer's
perspectives of control. This research expands on such previous research by comparing both the buyer's and supplier's views of control. We adapted Heide and John's [2]
approach to control. They use a term *vertical control, and define it as the buyer's
control over supplier's decisions.* On the other words, the buyer has control or can
decide over processes that would otherwise be part of supplier's domain in basic market transaction, Having the proportional nature of control in the dyadic relationship in
mind, we aim at answering following research question: Why is control distributed in
a certain way in the buyer-supplier relationship? In this research, we are using multiple case study methodology. We have six dyadic buyer-supplier relationships, two
buyer companies and their three suppliers. We conducted totally 43 interviews.

2 Literature Review

TCA theory is most cited theory related to control and it is an integral part of both the
buyer–supplier and channel research traditions (for example [2], [7-8]). According to

C. Emmanouilidis, M. Taisch, D. Kiritsis (Eds.): APMS 2012, Part II, IFIP AICT 398, pp. 560–567, 2013.
© IFIP International Federation for Information Processing 2013

TCA, one means by which a firm can safeguard specific assets in the absence of vertical integration is to acquire vertical control over the exchange partner based on mutual commitment [2], [9-10]. Heide and John [2] see that control is not desirable per se, but it is subject to efficiency considerations and deliberate choice. They also argue that the presence of specific assets only creates an incentive to establish a vertical control and does not in itself endow the firm with the ability to actually structure the relationship in the desired fashion. As decision control is a zero sum phenomenon [11], an increase in decision control by other party necessarily comes at the other's expense, meaning that one party's ability to exercise decision control derives from other party's decision to relinquish it. The control relinquishment can either be voluntary strategic choice and efficiency considerations [2], [11] or based on power. Heide and John [6] argue that suppliers won't transfer decision control to buyer without some insurance that the achieved control will not be abused.

Next we will discuss shortly about power in a relationship. We rely our approach of power to SET, more specifically to Emerson's power-dependence theory [6]. Emerson's lot quoted definition of power is: 'The power of actor A over actor B is the amount of resistance on the part of B which can be potentially overcome by B. [6](p. 32). Power is an attribute of a relationship, not an actor, which means that buying organization in not 'powerful' in general, but only with respect to a particular supplier. Most treatments of power emphasize the critical role of dependence. Emerson formulated relationship between power and dependence: 'the relative dependence between two actors in an exchange relationship determines their relative power [6]. He also provided a general conception of dependence: 'The dependence of actor A upon actor B is (1) directly proportional to A's motivational investment goals mediated by B, and (2) inversely proportional to the availability of those goals outside of the A-B relationship. This means that dependence is determined by two factors; the need for a resource, that other party posses and the availability of alternative sources. Power-dependency theory argues that a firm's investment in specific assets may constrain its ability to acquire vertical control, because the presence of specific assets represents conditions of interfirm dependence [2]. Prior studies have explored the nature of dependence and control in buyer-supplier relationships see for instance [12], [13-15].

Control has bee discussed in the context of supply chain management literature by multiple authors (see e.g., [2], [3-5], [13-14], [16-18]). Many of the studies discuss the different control mechanisms, e.g. [1], [16], [20]. Control mechanisms are structural arrangements deployed to regulate partners' behavior. Two categories of control mechanisms have been distinguished: (1) formal control, which rely primarily (but not exclusively) on explicit contracts and (2) social control (or relational forms), which primarily relies on informal means [16], [21-22]. Most of the previous authors have adopted TCE as underlying paradigm, especially when discussing the antecedents that lead to the adoption of formal control [16]. Formal control mechanisms enhance cooperation and decrease opportunistic behaviors, since explicit contracts detail the roles and responsibilities of the partners, determine the deliverable, and specify the processes necessary to resolve unforeseeable problems [24-25]. Some authors suggest that formal control and social control mechanisms are substitutes

[22], [26] as others argue that formal and social control mechanisms are complementary [23], [27]. Interfirm trust is a primary foundation for the use of social control [1]. Social control mechanisms usually take the form of joint problem solving, participatory decision making, thorough information exchange, and fulfillment of promises [20].

Our approach to control relies on those of previous authors, but also differs slightly from mainstream discussion. We adapted Heide and John's [2] approach to control. They use a terms *vertical control, and define it as the buyer's control over supplier's decisions*. On the other words, the buyer has control (or can decide) over processes that would otherwise be part of supplier's domain in basic market transaction, like supplier's production process and manufacturing technology, ongoing design and engineering changes, supplier's level of inventory, selection of supplier's subsuppliers and supplier's quality procedures. Our main interest doesn't lie in the control mechanisms as such, but more what are the antecedents and consequences of control distribution.

3   Method

In this study, we adopted multiple case study method. We examined the issue of interest through a dyadic study having the buyer-supplier relationship as the unit of analysis. We explored six relationships, which include two buyer companies and six suppliers. We chose dyadic case study, because case studies allow developing frameworks by using data collected through direct interaction with subjects of interest. In the research design and analysis we follow the principles of Eisenhardt [28], and Yin [29]. We selected our cases based on two principles: theoretical sampling and access to data. We came up with two buyer companies and their three suppliers: one company was from the high-technology industry (OEM, a pseudonym), and another was from the pharmaceutical industry (PharCo, a pseudonym). We had multiple sources of data, which made the data rich; interviews, meetings with company representatives, documents and workshops. Having multiple respondents from different companies and utilizing multiple sources of data (interviews, company documents, and memos) put into practice the principle of data triangulation. Interviews were our main source of data, and we conducted totally 43 interviews, and one interview lasted from 45 min -2 hours.

The first buyer firm – OEM- is a large high technology equipment provider. All three suppliers selected in our study are also ranked in the top five of their respective industries worldwide. HiTecCo supplies OEM components that are technically demanding and critical for the performance of the end product. ContrMan is one of OEM's largest suppliers and it has several plants located near OEM's markets that create manufacturing capacity. CoCom is an original equipment manufacturer that is widely considered to be the technological leader in its field. PharCo is a European R&D-based pharmaceuticals and diagnostics company focused on the development of medicinal treatments and diagnostic tests for the global market. It is a relatively small player globally but well positioned within European markets. PacCo is a small local supplier of printed products and services for packages and advertisements. This firm has a long and stable relationship with PharCo. MedDev is a globally operated supplier of drug delivery, medical devices, and diagnostic disposables. MedDev became a major supplier for PharCo only a few years ago. BulkMf is a manufacturer of bulk actives for the pharmaceuticals industry. BulkMf is also a fairly new supplier for PharCo and is one of PharCo's first low-cost country suppliers.

4   Results

According to the advice of Yin [29] we conducted within-case analysis and, subsequently, cross-case analysis. The within and cross-case analyses show that the pattern of control, more specifically how control is distributed and why, is different across the six dyads. Here, we will discuss results of cross case analyses and elaborate findings over the cases. We will first make observations how the control is distributed in relationships. Next, we analyze the control distribution as follows. (1) Why it is distributed in certain way and we categorize these explanations. (2) Why the party is relinquishing the control and, (3) what are the control mechanisms.

Table 1 shows the results of cross case analyses. Overall, in all the dyads, both the buyer and the supplier have influence over the explored processes and none of the processes are decided purely by the buyer or by the supplier. This finding supports the fact that all the sample relationships are collaborative and deep in nature. Also, this means that we can't distinguish relationships as 'buyer controls' or 'supplier controls', but it is more complicated than that. In all but one case (OEM- ContrMan), the supplier has more control than the buyer, or the control is balanced. In all case relationships of PharCo, the control is balanced between buyer and the supplier. In multiple cases, the distribution of control differ between product groups in a relationship. For example, in OEM-BulkMf relationship, the buyer wants to secure the availability of some product groups by deciding the suppliers buffer inventory levels, as in some product groups the supplier may decide. Based on our interviews, the buyers were mostly quite satisfied with how control was distributed and didn't feel they would need more control over suppliers' decisions. Also this reflects the fact that relationships are collaborative in nature. Generally, buyers would like to have more control on selection of supplier's subsuppliers. We explored, that there are incongruencies in all dyads, how the buyer and the supplier see the control is distributed in a relationship. For instance, in PharCo-PacCo relationship, PharCo and PacCo see the control distribution to be totally different in multiple processes. In this relationship, the buyer sets strong unilateral pressure to develop the supply chain. Over the course of the study, PharCo simultaneously placed more competitive pressure on PacCo and developed supply chain processes more effective from its own point of view, which decreased the efficiency of PacCo's operations. This unilateral pressure affects how the supplier sees the control and might create problems to the relationship.

We analyzed the antecedents for the control distribution. The table 1 shows how the control is distributed and why. We mapped different explanations for control distribution in sample relationships, and categorized them as follows: (1) *Type of purchasing* influences strongly control distribution, and there is often a 'natural' distribution of control. In contract manufacturing type of purchasing, for example in the relationship between OEM-ContrMan, the buyer generally has much control, especially over design and engineering changes.

Table 1. Results of cross-case analyses

Relationship	OEM-HitecCo		OEM-CoCom		OEM-ContrMa		PharCo-PacCo		PharCo-MedD		PharCo-BulkM	
The company the answer	Buyer	Supplie	Buyer	Supplie	Buyer	Supplie	Buyer	Supplie	Buyer	Supplie	Buyer	Supplie
Power balance	Balanced		Supplier		Buyer		Buyer		Balanced		Supplier	
Specific assets	Med	High	Med	Med	Low	Med	High	High	Med	Low	Low	Low
Perception of trust	High	High	High	High	High	High	High	High	High	High	Modera	High
Average power	High		High		Medium		Medium		Medium		Medium	
Performance	Good	Good	Med	Med	Good	Med	Good	Med	Med	Med	Med	Low
Control distribution 1) 2)												
A. Supplier's production processes and	1.4	2.0	2.5	2.3	2.2	2.3	2.5	2.0	2.8	3.7	1.3	1.0
B. Ongoing design and engineering changes	3.2	4.0	3.3	3.3	5.8	6.7	3.5	7.0	5.5	6.2	2.5	1.0
C. Supplier's level of inventory	2.8	3.0	2.7	4.0	3.0	6.0	3.5	2.0	1.5	2.5	3.3	1.0
D. Selection of supplier's sub suppliers	2.0	1.5	2.5	2.7	5.4	6.3	2.5	1.0	2.3	2.6	2.3	3.0
E. Supplier's quality control procedures	1.7	3.0	2.8	2.7	3.8	4.0	6.5	4.0	5.5	4.2	3.0	3.0
Control mechanisms	Contracts, standards, monitoring, social control		Contracts, standards, monitoring, social control		Contracts, standards, monitoring, social control		Contracts, standards, monitoring, social control, supplier development		Contracts, standards, monitoring,		Contracts, standards, monitoring, supplier development	
Influence mechanisms:	Trust		Trust		Power		Power		Trust		Power	
Reasons for control distribution												
A. Supplier's production processes and manufacturing technology	Capabilities of partners		Capabilities of partners		Type of purchasing, Capabilities of partners		Capabilities of partners		Type of purchasing Capabilities of the partners		Capabilities of partners	
B. Ongoing design and engineering changes	Capabilites of partners, Type of purchasing		Capabilities of the partners, Type of purchasing		Type of purchasing, Capabilities of the partners		Capabilites of partners		Type of purchasing, Capabilities of partners		Capabilities of partners, Type of purchasing,	
C. Supplier's level of inventory (raw material, semi finished and finished components)	Supply chain efficiency, minimize the effort of the		Supply chain efficiency, minimize the effort of the		Supply chain efficiency, minimize the effort of the		Supply chain efficiency		Capabilities of partners		Supply chain efficiency	
D. Selection of supplier's sub suppliers	Buyer wants to influence to certain needs		Buyer wants to influence to certain needs		Type of purchasing Capabilities of the partners		Capabilities of partners, Buyer wants to influence to certain needs		Buyer wants to influence to certain needs		Capabilities of partners, Buyer wants to influence to certain needs	
E. Supplier's quality control procedures	Capabilities of partners		Capabilities of partners		Capabilities of partners		Buyer wants to influence to certain needs		Buyer wants to influence to certain needs		Buyer wants to influence to certain needs	

1) Vertical control measures the control buyer has achieved over.
2) Scale (1-7): 1= Entirely decided by the supplier, 7= entirely decided by the customer.

(2) *Capabilities of partners:* the partner with best capabilities decides / conducts the process. For instance, in OEM-HitecCo case, supplier mainly decides the production processes, but the buyer makes suggestions if it would like to have new technology. OEM sees that HitecCo has best capabilities in deciding the production process. (3) Buyer wants to *influence to specific needs* that are important to the buyer. For instance, for OEM, issues related to environment and ethics are important and OEM controls that supplier takes these issues into consideration. Authority requirements belong to this category. For example, authorities require that PharCo must have control over suppliers' quality procedures. (4) Buyer wants to *minimize the work* and

gives the control to the supplier, as in the case of consignment stock. As decision control is a zero sum phenomenon [11], an increase in control by other party necessarily comes at the other's expense, meaning that one party's ability to exercise decision control derives from other party's decision to relinquish it. Heide and John [2] argue that suppliers won't transfer decision control to buyer without some insurance that the achieved control will not be abused. We analyzed why supplier (or buyer) relinquished the control to the other party and identified following 'enablers' (see also table 2): (1) *Trust,* control relinquishment is a strategic choice. Partner relinquishes the control often due to efficiency considerations. When a trust is high in a relationship, one can trust the other party doesn't behave opportunistically. (2) *Power,* more powerful party can force the other party to relinquish the control. Many of the control mechanism used in our sample relationships are formal ones, written explicitly in contracts. Some mechanisms are related to relational norms, and are close to supplier development, as the buyer helps the supplier to develop processes. For example, PharCo has helped its suppliers to develop production processes. Also, buyer controls the supplier by having requirements for (ISO) standards and via auditing, also supplier's subsuppliers. Buyer might also specify the product that there is only one supplier, although it doesn't specify the 'name' of the supplier. Also, multiple control mechanisms can affect to one process. Many of the previous authors discuss about contracts as control mechanism (see for example, [1], [32], [36], [39]), but other explored mechanisms (helping the supplier to develop, standards) are mentioned more rarely.

5   Discussion and Conclusion

For the most part, previous studies have only examined the perspective of the buyer, and this study is one of the first to take a dyadic view. Traditionally, TCE has been adopted as a primary theoretical lens to explore the antecedents of control mechanisms in buyer-supplier cooperation, for example [2], [4], [13-14]. Our study provides empirical evidence that the approach of TCE, in which, control is used to safeguard specific assets, doesn't explain the control distribution in buyer-supplier relationships. Also, some previous authors, for example [23], have criticized TCEs approach to control and argue that transaction cost economics overstates the desirability of either integration or explicit contractual safeguards in exchange settings commonly labeled as hazardous. We found out that control is a complex concept. In most relationships, both buyer and supplier have control over processes, and the distribution of control may vary between product groups. It is not easy to determine, who controls the supply chain. We argue that control in the buyer-supplier relationship might look different from buyer's and suppliers' perspectives. One relevant explanation for these incongruencies in perceptions is the unilateral nature of the relationship, in where the buyer bases its action to the power. We categorized the explanations for control distribution and discussed the impact of power, trust and attractiveness. We argue that in bilateral relationships, trust enables the efficiency considerations of control distribution, and the partner who has best capabilities has the control over processes.

For business managers this paper gives new insights for managing the control in the supply chain. We note that business managers must consider how the other party sees the control, as there might be mismatches in perceptions. Managers also need to rethink the control in supply chains and analyze the explanations why the control is distributed in the way it is and if it is optimal for the supply chain. Also, we found out that a company can persuade the other party to relinquish the control by three ways unilateral power, award power by being more attractive business partner and/ or trust.

References

1. Jap, S.D., Ganesan, S.: Control Mechanisms and the Relationship Life Cycle: Implications for Safeguarding Specific Investments and Developing Commitment. Journal of Marketing Research (JMR) 37(5), 227–245 (2000)
2. Heide, J.B., John, G.: Do norms matter in marketing relationships. Journal of Marketing 56, 32–44 (1992)
3. Mol, M.J.: Outsourcing: Design, Process and Performance. Cambridge University Press, UK (2007)
4. Petersen, K.J., Handfield, R.B., Lawson, B., Cousins, P.D.: Buyer Dependency and Relational Capital Formation: The Mediating Effects of Socialization Processes and Supplier Integration. Journal of Supply Chain Management 44, 53–65 (2008)
5. Zhao, X., Huo, B., Flynn, B.B., Yeung, J.H.Y.: The impact of power and rela-tionship commitment on the integration between manufacturers and customers in a supply chain. J. Oper. Manage. 26(5), 368–388 (2008)
6. Emerson, R.M.: Power-Dependence Relations. American Sociological Review 27, 31–41 (1962)
7. Morgan, R.M., Hunt, S.: Relationship-Based Competitive Advantage: The Role of Relationship Marketing in Marketing Strategy. Journal of Business Research 46(11), 281–290 (1999)
8. Morgan, R.M., Hunt, S.D.: The Commitment-Trust Theory of Relationship Marketing. J. Market. 58(7), 20 (1994)
9. Williamson, O.E.: The Economic Institutions of Capitalism; Firms, Markets, Relational-contracting. Free Press, New York (1985)
10. Powell, W.W.: Hybrid Organizational Arrangements: New Form or Transitional Development? Calif. Manage. Rev. 30, 67–87 (Fall 1987)
11. Grossman, S.J., Hart, O.D.: The Costs and Benefits of Ownership: A Theory of Vertical and Lateral Integration. Journal of Political Economy 94(8), 691–719 (1986)
12. El-Ansary, A., Stern, L.W.: Power Measurement in the Distribution Channel. Journal of Marketing Research (JMR) 9(2), 47–52 (1972)
13. Provan, K.G., Skinner, S.J.: Interorganizational Dependence and Control as Predictors of Opportunism in Dealer-Supplier Relations. Academy of Management Journal 32(3), 202–212 (1989)
14. Frazier, G.L., Gill, J.D., Kale, S.H.: Dealer Dependence Levels and Reciprocal Actions in a Channel of Distribution in a Developing Country. J. Market. 53(1), 50–69 (1989)
15. Buvik, A., Halskau, Ø.: Relationship duration and buyer influence in just-in-time relationships. European Journal of Purchasing & Supply Management 7(6), 111–119 (2001)
16. Li, Y., Xie, E., Teo, H., Peng, M.W.: Formal control and social control in do-mestic and international buyer–supplier relationships. J. Oper. Manage. 28(7), 333–344 (2010)

17. Youngdahl, W., Ramaswamy, K., Verma, K.: Exploring new research frontiers in offshoring knowledge and service processes. J. Oper. Manage. 26(3), 135–140 (2008)
18. Narasimhan, R., Nair, A., Griffith, D.A., Arlbjørn, J.S., Bendoly, E.: Lock-in situations in supply chains: A social exchange theoretic study of sourcing arrangements in buyer–supplier relationships. J. Oper. Manage. 27(10), 374–389 (2009)
19. Stump, R.L., Heide, J.B.: Controlling Supplier Opportunism in Industrial Relationships. Journal of Marketing Research (JMR) 33(11), 431–441 (1996)
20. Fryxell, G.E., Dooley, R.S., Vryza, M.: After the Ink Dries: the Interaction of Trust and Control in Us-Based International Joint Ventures. Journal of Management Studies 39(9), 865–886 (2002)
21. Dyer, J.H., Chu, W.: The Role of Trustworthiness in Reducing Transaction Costs and Improving Performance: Empirical Evidence from the United States, Japan, and Korea 14(1) (January-February 2003), 57–68 (2003)
22. Dyer, J.H., Singh, H.: The Relational View: Cooperative Strategy and Sources of Interorganizational Competitive Advantage. The Academy of Management Review 23(4), 660–679 (1998)
23. Poppo, L., Zenger, T.: Do Formal Contracts and Relational Governance Function as Substitutes or Complements? Strategic Manage. J. 23(8), 707 (2002)
24. Rindfleisch, A., Heide, J.B.: Transaction cost analysis: Past, present, and future applications. J. Market. 61(10), 30 (1997)
25. Argyres, N., Mayer, K.J.: Contract Design as a Firm Capability: an Integration of Learning and Transaction Cost Perspectives. Academy of Management Review 32(10), 1060–1077 (2007)
26. Uzzi, B.: Social Structure and Competition in Interfirm Networks: The Paradox of Embeddedness. Adm. Sci. Q. 42(3), 35–67 (1997)
27. Mesquita, L.F., Brush, T.H.: Untangling Safeguard and Production Coordination Effects in Long-Term Buyer-Supplier Relationships. Academy of Management Journal 51(8), 785–807 (2008)
28. Eisenhardt, K.M.: Building Theories from Case Study Research. The Academy of Management Review 14, 532–550 (1989)
29. Yin, D.R.K.: Case Study Research: Design and Methods, 4th edn. Sage Publications, Inc. (2009)

A Fuzzy Decision Support System for Drawing Directions from Purchasing Portfolio Models

Davide Aloini, Riccardo Dulmin, and Valeria Mininno

University of Pisa, Pisa, Italy
{davide.aloini,riccardo.dulmin,valeria.mininno}@dsea.unipi.it

Abstract. This work presents a decision support system (DSS) enhancing users to effectively integrate classical purchasing portfolio approaches with additional strategic oriented priorities and information in order to effectively support the definition of purchasing directions and action plans.

With these aims, a fuzzy-based DSS is designed and implemented. The decision process gets inputs from the Kraljic (K) matrix and draws directives on the traditional Olsen-Ellram (O-E) portfolio model integrating additional information about the purchasing context to validate their feasibility and suitability. The fuzzy DSS is applied to a demonstrative case study of an American multinational company operating in the field of Electric Power Systems and Alternative Energy Systems.

Keywords: Decision support, Strategic Purchasing, Portfolio model, fuzzy logic, case study.

1 Introduction

The complexity of business decisions as concerning the definition of adequate purchasing strategies and the assessment of opportune Buyer-Supplier (B-S) relationships, does not allow for simple recommendations. In contrast with growing acceptance and usage of Purchasing Portfolio models (Kraljic 1983; Olsen and Ellram, 1997), a major and most severe criticism recently moved to their main rationale is the extreme simplification of the decision logic which is often based on just two basic dimensions (Gelderman, 2003; 2005; 2006).

By simplifying the issue of buyer–supplier relationships and other context-related dimensions, portfolio models fail to capture essential aspects, such as the impact of overall company business strategy, corporate purchasing policies, the context of networks (Dubois and Pedersen 2002), the interdependencies between products (Ritter 2000), and other relevant item features (e.g. product lifecycle) or the concern for a sustainable competitive advantage.

At the same time, purchasing portfolio models potentially suffer of arbitrariness and compensative processes due to related problems in item positioning. They are sensitive to the choice of the evaluation dimensions, factors and weights (Ramsay, 1996). Moreover, a large number of these variables are qualitative and need to be assessed subjectively by experts basing on their own experience or specific analysis of the business sectors.

C. Emmanouilidis, M. Taisch, D. Kiritsis (Eds.): APMS 2012, Part II, IFIP AICT 398, pp. 568–575, 2013.

This paper proposes a fuzzy-based decision model to define appropriate and feasible strategic purchasing directions and action plans. Combining these kind of analysis with additional information, as for example about the supply market (the relative contractual power), supplier capabilities, company purchasing policies, the paper suggests an integrated decision logic enhancing practitioners in refining recommendations which are drawn on the traditional portfolio models by Kraljic (1983) and Olsen-Ellram (1997). Moreover, Fuzzy Set Theory is used in the Decision Support System in order to deal with the aggregation of different variables and often subjective information (e.g. linguistic variables vs numerical indicators, objective performance indexes vs subjective judgment) and to reproduce approximate, knowledge based and not-compensative reasoning.

2   Research Objective

Purchasing portfolio approach is usually a three step process finalized to manage supplier relationships. The first step generally address a product-based classification of components (Kralijc 1983, Olsen and Ellram, 1997; Kamann and Van Nieulande 2010), the second regards the analysis of suppliers and buyer supplier relationships (Olsen Ellram, 1997; Bensau, 1999; Caniel and Gelderman, 2007), the last step is decisional and draws on the propaedeutic information gathered to establish strategies and recommendations.

In this paper, we refer to the most known O-E model (Olsen and Ellram, 1997) which goes through the following 3 steps (Nellore and Soderquist, 2000):

1. *analysis of the products and their classification* according to the difficulty of managing the purchase situation and the importance of the purchase similarly to Kraljic (1983);
2. *analysis of the supplier relationships* required to deliver the products according to the Relative Supplier Attractiveness and B-S Strength of the Relationship (Olsen and Ellram, 1997); and
3. *development of action plans* in order to match the product requirements with the supplier relationships.

To successfully accomplish this process, decision makers have to arrange the decision logic integrating all the required information at the right step. This includes an appropriate selection of the critical decision dimensions and variables of analysis; a correct operationalization of the selected variables, related measurement and data collection; an effective item positioning (classification of goods-services et/or B-S relationships); and finally the integration of additional or complementary information for action validity check and synthesis of recommendations.

In this perspective, portfolio models, have been mostly criticized by different authors and perspectives both for their measurement concerns, and for their limited applicability in practice (Kamann 2000; Nellore and Soderquist, 2000; Dubois and Pedersen 2002).

The present work focuses on the last three previous activities: it integrates in an overall process K and O-E matrixes, it develops a fuzzy-based implementation of the O-E matrix (Olsen and Ellram, 1997) in order to deal with the problem of positing suppliers correctly starting from subjective judgments and weights; and finally, it validates and refines out coming recommendations suggesting additional information to be included in the decision process.

3   Methodology

3.1   Model Architecture

The proposed decision model consists of two main stages (Fig.1).

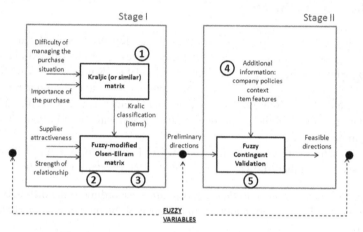

Fig. 1. A two stages (and five steps) decision logic

1. Firstly, it combines evidences of the current Buyer-Supplier relationships (according to a fuzzy implementation of the O-E matrix) with outputs from the analysis of purchasing items according to the Kraljic matrix (1983) perspective in order to define preliminary outputs (see step 1, 2, and 3 of O-E model).
2. In a second stage, instead, it completes the gathered information with additional considerations about specific company policies (e.g. localization: local vs global), purchasing item features (e.g. life cycle), and with other context related information about the purchasing situation (e.g. the relative contractual power between Buyer and Supplier, cross-supply level, level of shared investments on the suppliers/buyer side). This information is integrated into the decision model in order to provide a more effective and systematic validation of the outputs, and in case to refine recommendations basing on specific company contingencies to finally provide users with feasible and suitable action plans. In the steps 4 and 5, first the additional variables of analysis are selected and measured, and then preliminary outputs are refined accordingly by a fuzzy contingent validation.

In order to face with the related complexity and uncertainty which is distinctive in dealing with information often subjective in nature and up to the knowledge and experience of respondents, we considered fuzzy logic as potential useful and flexible way to deal with the measurement of variables and the item positioning, as well as to arrange a not-compensatory decision logic and support user during the process. Thus, we adopted fuzzy variables in order to set up the input data to the O-E matrix (Olsen and Ellram, 1997) and in order to define the related outputs. At this stage of the decision process, information about the purchasing situation (provided by Kraljic portfolio analysis) are added and taken into consideration within the Fuzzy Inferential System (FIS), in order to define preliminary directions. Fuzzy set theory is also adopted at the stage 2 to characterize the preliminary and final model outputs, the additional information here included and the overall decision logic.

3.2   Inputs, Outputs and Additional Control Variables

Inputs: Variables are defined according to Olsen and Ellram (1997) model. Two macro dimensions are adopted for each matrix as specified previously. A number of factors and sub-factors was assessed coherently in order to provide a complete measurement scale.

Outputs: The model presents a more analytic (multi-input-multi-output model) output structure in respect to the most traditional approaches. This is in order to offer practitioners better precisions and an easier interpretation of indications. Output variables (Table 1) are drawn, refined and completed accordingly the main directions provided by Olsen and Ellram (1997) and subsequent criticism (Kamann 2000; Nellore and Soderquist, 2000; Dubois and Pedersen 2002). Variables offer information about both strategic directions and macro actions to be implemented.

Table 1. O-E Matrix Outputs

(adapted from: Olsen and Ellram, 1997)

O-E directions
1. Strengthen the relationship (or diversify)
2. Improve supplier attractiveness and/or relation performance
3. Resource (allocation) level
4. Investment level
5. Timing horizon (short/long term)

Table 2. Additional Information

Additional/context information
1. Budget constrains
2.Uniformity constrains (Global vs local purchasing; single vs multi sourcing; Sustainability/Ethic; other purchasing policies)
3. Life cycle stage
4. Concurrent/shared investments
5. Allocated resource
6. Cross-supply level

Additional information (or control variables): Feasible and suitable actions should be evaluated in the light of some critical context-related information as for example that related to existing company constrains (budget, policies and other limitations to the supply base) or other influencing factors. This is particularly true when purchasing portfolio models are used to draw strategic directions at the Business Unit level since they usually need to be aligned with the Corporate directives.

In order to accomplish this last purpose, in the second decision step, the model integrates a number of variables (mostly subjective data) provided directly by the decision maker in order to validate the feasibility and suitability of preliminary directions. Specifically, two classes of information are considered: the first is related to "Corporate constrains", mainly budget and uniformity constrains (i.e. standardization and homogeneity in the supply process). These factors may limit investments (capital budget decisions), as well as influence criteria for the supplier selection process (the type of B-S relation, information exchange, integration level), and also impact on purchasing policies (sustainability, ethic, local/global and multi/single sourcing policies). The second class of information, instead, includes context-related factors which might limit the appropriateness and feasibility of proposed recommendations: the product life cycle stage, the level of current/shared investments (i.e. technology, specific asset, switching costs), the company resources currently allocated to the B-S relation, the company's network position, the level of cross supply. Details of selected variables are reported in table 2.

As an example, the product life cycle (plc) may affect and influence the out-coming strategic direction and action plans since the objectives of the B-S relations, the desirable performance, and also the available resource and risk change accordingly to the different plc-stages. Thus, an effective decision model should take into account this factor in order to provide really suitable recommendations.

4   Case Study

4.1   Context

The method was developed and applied to the case of a multinational company in the Power-electronic market. In the case study we refer to a specific implementation of the presented decision model in order to demonstrate the applicability of the proposed approach. A team of experts from the Company and University was built to run the project. For the purpose of this work, we assumed that the analysis of the purchasing situation (through the Kraljic matrix) was previously and adequately performed coherently with the evaluation objectives, as also we hypothesize that the adopted measures and the data collection process have been appropriately carried out. As a consequence, the focus of the paper is limited to the investigation of the Buyer-Supplier relationships (by O-E matrix) and on the additional information to be included in the decision logic (rules) to draw feasible and suitable strategies and action plans.

4.2   Data Collection

A highly qualified panel of academic experts and practitioners from the Sourcing and Purchasing functions was formed to select the most appropriate (and at the same time available) measures according to the OE dimensions, to define the relative weights, and to finally characterize the purchasing items/suppliers accordingly. Two questionnaires were assessed to obtain data. The first questionnaire addressed the importance scores of the selected attributes according to an AHP procedure while the second one was used for finding out the performance scores of suppliers. Respondents were asked to indicate the degree to which they agree with each statement on a 5-point fuzzy linguistic scale. A Delphi-based process was also adopted in order to achieve convergence of the experts' judgments.

Company experts was also involved in the DSS assessment and setting as concerning the definition of FIS rules, and the final model validation mostly by semi-structured interviews, focus group and observation on the field.

4.3   Model Design

The FIS design usually goes through the following steps:

1. Membership function design

In order to construct the fuzzy model, a number of semi-structured interviews was held. An open-ended questionnaire was used to conduct the interviews, including a set of questions to discuss the fuzzy variables and define their labels (linguistic values) and determine the fuzzy ranges of each value label whereas data were not available.

The model consists of input variables which attain the two main OE dimensions: Supplier Attractiveness and Strength of the Relationship. Some building factors are selected in collaboration with the company experts in order to assure data/knowledge availability to users and relevance of information into the company decision process. All the input variables are provided as 5-point linguistic scale by triangular fuzzy numbers. Then, factors are aggregated following a Ordered Weighted Average (OWA) procedure (Yager, 1988) considering weights which were defined by the Sourcing, Logistic and Quality managers according to a Delphi-AHP procedure (Okoli and Pawlowski, 2004; Saaty, 2006). An order relevant input to the model is the Item classification accordingly to Kraljic matrix, which is here modeled as a rule discriminator value (i.e. it modifies the rule base).

Preliminary outputs of the model as in Table 1 are modeled as a three level fuzzy scale. Specifically, they indicate to how extent the management should plan actions for strengthening the relation (high) or diversifying the supplier base (low); improving supplier attractiveness and/or performance; to how extend investing new assets/technology; allocating new resources into the relation; and also which is the time horizon of the relationship.

Control variables included in the second step of the decisional model are interpreted, as previously stated, as context-related variables or company constrains which may be due to the corporate policies and/or available budget (Table 4). They are modeled as 5-point linguistic scale by triangular fuzzy numbers as well.

2. Rule settings

In setting the decision rules of the FIS we used two common approaches in literature:

* Adopting a normalized or standard rule-base: firstly, we are here drawing on directions by the K and OE portfolio models.

• Codifying the experience and intuition of experts: rules were derived from the managerial procedures, from interviews using a carefully designed questionnaire, or often observing an actions to deduce if-then type rules. In this case, the approach is used to further investigate suitability and validity of preliminary OE direction according to the additional information provided.

The FIS uses the Mamdani inference method, once all the screening heuristics have been identified, they have to be transformed into proper fuzzy IF–THEN rules. More than 100 rules were finally defined and implemented in a FIS by the support of the Matlab Fuzzy rules editor toolbox.

For a purpose of clarity and due to space limitation, here we just present how the model works for a specific combination purchasing item/supplier. Once input factors are defined and evaluated, the fuzzy OE matrix is assessed. Judgments were aggregated into a single fuzzy index by a ordered weighted average (OWA). As a result, this procedure allows to assign a supplier to more than a single quadrant in the matrix according to a different membership degree and a fuzzy borderline which make classification more flexible and less restrictive (Fig. 2).

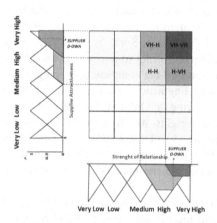

Decisional rules are expressed according to the following statements:

```
IF

    the Purchasing Item IS a (Kraljic class)

    AND

    Supplier Attractiveness IS (level)

    AND

    Strength of the Relationship IS (level)

THEN

    Strengthen the Relation  IS (level)

    Improve Supplier Attractiveness IS (level)

    Level of Investment IS (level)

    Level of Resource IS (level)

    Timing horizon of relation IS (level)
```

Fig. 2. Positioning on the fuzzy O-E matrix

Preliminary outcomes are finally refined in a second step considering the company constrains. The decision logic and fuzzy rules were set similarly to the previous ones.

3. Validation and/or Sensitivity Analysis

Model validation is currently in progress so that the DSS is still under refinement and liable to modifications. Managers and senior buyers from the company implementation team were involved in the process in order to test the proper operation of the fuzzy systems. With the support of experts, the validation of a number of cases is programmed in order to check model Completeness, Consistency, Redundancy and Interaction.

5   Conclusion

The main result of this work was the development of a decision support system enhancing users to effectively integrate traditional purchasing portfolio approaches with additional strategic oriented priorities/information in defining purchasing directions and action plans. A fuzzy-based decision model is proposed and implemented. The decision process gets inputs from the Kraljic matrix and draws directives on the traditional OE portfolio model integrating additional information about the purchasing context (company strategy, supply market, etc) to validate feasibility and suitability. The fuzzy DSS is applied to a demonstrative case study of an American multinational company operating in the field of Electric Power Systems and Alternative Energy Systems.

The DSS particularly helps decision makers in facing a number of common issues affecting the use of portfolio approaches, e.g. the Olsen-Ellram matrix, as such as:

- To deal with the assessment of subjective variables in order to get a correct and not arbitrary positioning of suppliers;
- To define appropriate rules for drawing feasible and suitable strategic directions and actions plans keeping into account additional information about strategic priorities or company policies.

References

1. Gelderman, C.J., Van Weele, A.J.: Handling MeasurementIssues and Strategic Directions in Kraljic's Purchasing Portfolio Model. Journal of Purchasing and Supply Management 9(5-6), 207–216 (2003)
2. Gelderman, C.J., Van Weele, A.J.: Purchasing Portfolio Models: A Critique and Update. The Journal of Supply Chain Management (Summer 2005)
3. Gelderman, C.J., Semeijn, J.: Managing the global supply base through purchasing portfolio management. Journal of Purchasing & Supply Management 12(4), 209–217 (2006)
4. Kraljic, P.: Purchasing Must Become Supply Management. Harvard Business Review 61(5), 109–117 (1983)
5. Okoli, C., Pawlowski, S.D.: The Delphi method as a research tool: An example, design considerations and applications. Inform. Manage. 42, 15–29 (2004)
6. Olsen, R.F., Ellram, L.M.: A Portfolio Approach to Supplier Relationships. Industrial Marketing Management 26(2), 101–113 (1997)
7. Yager, R.R.: On Ordered Weighted Averaging Aggregation Operators in Multi-criteria Decisions. IEEE Trans. on Systems, Man, and Cybernetics. 8(1), 183–190 (1988)
8. Zimmermann, H.J.: Fuzzy Sets, Decision Making, and Expert Systems, International Series in Management Science and Operations Research, Ignizio, University of Huston USA (1993)

A Mixed-Integer Linear Programming Model for Transportation Planning in the Full Truck Load Strategy to Supply Products with Unbalanced Demand in the Just in Time Context: A Case Study

Julien Maheut and Jose Pedro Garcia-Sabater

ROGLE – Departamento de Organización de Empresas, Universitat Politècnica de Valéncia,
Camino de Vera S/N, 46022 Valencia, Spain
juma2@upv.es, jpgarcia@omp.upv.es

Abstract. Growing awareness in cutting transport costs and minimizing the environmental impact means that companies are increasingly interested in using the full truck load strategy in their supply tasks. This strategy consists of filling trucks completely with one product type or a mixture of products from the same supplier. This paper aims to propose a mixed-integer linear programming model and procedure to fill trucks which considers limitations of stocks, stock levels and unbalanced demand and minimization of the total number of trucks used in the full truck load strategy. The results obtained from a case study are presented and are exported in a conventional spreadsheet available for a company in the automotive industry.

Keywords: Supply Chain Management, Automotive Industry, Full Truck Load, Case Study.

1 Introduction

In an increasingly globalized and internationalized world, Supply Chains (SCs) have had to adapt to remain competitive and become constantly more efficient, agile and flexible. SCs, and more specifically, all the companies involved in it, face a new problem: increasing complexity in managing products and in planning operations.

Increasing the variety of products manufactured or offered to customers directly influences planning tasks, currently deployed management methods and all the processes carried out to deliver the finished good. For example, models or tools designed and optimized for a definite and characteristic situation may no longer prove efficient and/or effective when product variety widens.

Increased complexity is one of the most difficult challenges for those companies currently working in tight environments because stocks are seen as wasteful and unnecessary costs if they exceed certain safety stock levels or coverage levels on days of demand, known as run-out time; that is, run-out time is the stocks coverage level of a specific product [1]. The proper calculation of these values is not only highly relevant

C. Emmanouilidis, M. Taisch, D. Kiritsis (Eds.): APMS 2012, Part II, IFIP AICT 398, pp. 576–583, 2013.
© IFIP International Federation for Information Processing 2013

when demand is irregular or when various products with short life cycles have different demand levels, but can be essential when demand is uncertain; this is precisely the case of the current economic crisis.

In the literature, the effect of variety on production planning, scheduling and the costs involved is a relatively developed theme [2]. Nonetheless, effects on transport tasks (shipping or supplying) have not been as well addressed to the best of our knowledge. Transportation planning is often approached from three perspectives and different backgrounds: strategic transport planning, tactical transport planning and operational transport planning.

At the operational level, the literature presents and identifies two main problem classifications: routing and truck-loading problems. However, the size of truck shipments may also be considered: partial shipments problems, less than truckload (LTL) shipments problems and full truck load (FTL) shipments problems. Historically, the automotive industry has used milk runs to resolve collection routes. Moreover, cross-docking systems [3] and, obviously, direct full load shipments [4] are also used.

Typically at the operational level, automotive assembly plants employ three different strategies to coordinate supply strategies [5]. Suppliers that supply low-volume products can receive direct shipments from a single supplier following the LTL strategy. Alternatively, shipments from multiple suppliers can be consolidated using milk runs in the LTL or the FTL strategy.

These three strategies are usually fixed according to the supplier because supply transport capacity contracts in the automotive sector are long-term contracts. They reserve a fixed transport capacity in each horizon and the carrier has to pay a fixed amount during each period, which is completely independent of the use of trucks. This long-term contracts policy is changing with new social conditions and environmental standards. For instance, optimizing fleet use has become one of the most important measurable performances.

In order to cut costs and minimize the environmental impact, the general trend in the automotive industry has been to reduce the number of actors in its own SC [6]. These SCs' first-tier companies have attempted to move toward a single supplier per product family. The direct consequence is that supply logistics has shifted toward the FTL strategy in which each provider supplies multiple products. The full-filling trucks problem has been traditionally solved with the help of a personalized, customized spreadsheet [4]. Moreover the "follower", which is the supplier contact, is responsible for planning and supervising truck loads; moreover, it is usually responsible for determining stock levels on both sides of the SC.

Each follower's working method might differ even within the same company as it takes into account not only actual product characteristics, but also different vehicle characteristics. With increasing product variety, which can form a product mix within a truck, the manual working method quickly reaches its limit and does not meet company expectations.

To overcome these problems, the literature offers a range of proposed solutions [7]. As Goetschalckx states in [8], Ford Motors Company and General Motors use full-size pickup truck models, but they are not described. In the automotive sector, the FTL strategy led to overdeliveries (serve in advance), as stated Garcia-Sabater et al. [4] in the case of motors distribution planning. Liu et al. [9] present 2-phase heuristic algorithms for the full truckloads multi-depot capacitated vehicle routing problem in carrier collaboration, but the consideration of different packaging for different products is not considered. Arunparam et al. [10] propose an algorithm for solving an integer-programming formulation of this vehicle-routing problem with full truckloads, but as in [9], a complex routing problem is considered. In the literature review, Boysen and Fliedner [3] offer an interesting literature review about cross-docking problems, but in our case study, only direct shipment by the FTL strategy must be considered. To the best of our knowledge, an MILP model for procurement planning that considers packaging and the FTL strategy which contemplates loss of truck capacity has never been proposed because of product mixture in the same truck. Other concerns in the automotive industry that our model includes are stocks limitations (minimum/maximum run out-times and total stock limits). These limitations in conjunction with stock levels, unbalanced demand and minimizing the total number of trucks used in the FTL strategy have never been considered, which implies a substantial combination of products to overcome truck capacity problems. This is precisely the aim of this paper: to propose an MILP that completes these types of trucks. Considerations such as time windows, routing and different truck capacities are not contemplated.

The rest of the paper is organized as follows. Section 2 offers a detailed description of the problem study. Section 3 proposes hypotheses to solve the problem, and then presents a mixed-integer linear programming (MILP) model to solve the problem. Section 4 presents a case study. Finally, the last section includes conclusions and future research lines.

2   Problem Description

An engine assembly plant is not only constituted by the assembly line of engines, but also by five component production lines. These lines constitute the so-called 5Cs (cylinder blocks, cylinder heads, camshafts, crankshafts, connecting rods). To produce these finished components, raw materials, whose origins are foundries, are produced in considerably large-sized batches. This raw material has to be purchased from suppliers and adjusted because the plant cannot hold substantial stock levels of materials at the entrance of component production lines.

The problem lies in deciding how to load the truck arriving from each supplier for the purpose of minimizing the total number of trucks over the year to keep the total stock below a maximum level and to also consider at least two alternative constraints:

— Maintaining a certain number of days of stock (called run-out time in days of demand) of raw material and a minimum safety stock for all the products.
— Considering maximum run-out times for products and considering stock restrictions because of limited storage capacity. This run-out time can be a maximum products demand peak, but also the stored holding value of the products controlled by the finance department.

Other considerations are taken into account. Because of paper's length restriction, those are not present in this extended abstract.

3 Modeling the Problem

3.1 Hypothesis

Product consumption is known and detailed for each period of the horizon. All the costs are assumed linear and known. The capacity of racks and all the trucks is also known. To avoid complicating the model presented herein, the same capacity for all trucks has been considered. Minimum and maximum run-out times are considered at all times for all products, or minimum and maximum stock levels values are determined by users and the respective stakeholders.

While minimizing costs and ensuring the planned run-out time, the following goals are pursued:

— Reducing the total number of trucks used during the horizon.
— Reducing capacity penalties.
— Reducing the level of obsolescence of the products in stock.

Penalties depend on the mixture of products loaded, but simplification is considered: from two different products loaded onto a truck, truck capacity will decrease by one unit for each new separate product loaded.

It is assumed that the truck should be completely filled with racks of products after taking into account the capacity loss due to the mixture of products. The minimum coverage defined must be guaranteed and cannot exceed the maximum coverage in days of demand.

The next section presents the mathematical MILP model which solves this problem.

3.2 MILP Model

Data Input Notation
The MILP model is specified as follows.

Table 1. Indexes and sets

$i \in P = \{1, \dots, n_p\}$	Products
$t = 1, \dots, T$	Periods (in day units)
$j \in J$	Trucks

Table 2. Parameter notation (1)

D_{it}	Demand of product i on day t
R_i	Number of products i that can be loaded in a rack
Y_i	Initial stock level of product i
K_j	Load capacity of truck j
s_i/S_i	Minimum/Maximum desired stock level of product i
$\underline{cob_i}/\overline{cob_i}$	Minimum/Maximum run-out times of product i (in day units)
M	Large number
C^α	Setup costs for using a truck
C^δ	Penalty costs for a truck's loss of capacity
C^λ	Cost of unbalanced stock

In modeling terms, we need to define two parameters:

— The maximum number of trucks available on day t.
— The run-out time for one product.

As this last parameter takes a different value to the minimum and maximum desired stocks levels for each product, a procedure to calculate a single parameter that fixes the minimum and maximum levels for each product in each period ($\underline{SM_{it}}/\overline{SM_{it}}$) has been created.

Table 3. Variable notation

$y_{it} \in \mathbb{Z}^+$	Stock level of product i on day t
$v_{ijt} \in \mathbb{Z}^+$	Number of products i loaded onto truck j on day t
α_{jt}	=1 if truck j is used on day t (0 otherwise)
$\lambda_t \in [0,1]$	Minimum level of balanced stock of all the products on day t
δ_{ijt}	=1 if one product i is loaded onto truck j on day t (0 otherwise)
$\varepsilon_{jt} \in \mathbb{Z}^+$	Variable that counts the number of the different variants loaded onto truck j on day t

Objective Function
The objective of the proposed model is to minimize total supply costs.

$$Z = Min[Costs] \tag{1}$$

$$Costs = \sum_t \sum_j \alpha_{jt} \cdot C^\alpha + \sum_t \sum_j C^\delta \cdot (\varepsilon_{jt} - 1) + \sum_t \lambda_t \cdot C^\lambda \tag{2}$$

The objective function (1), which consists in minimizing total supply costs, may be approximated as a linear function (2).

Constraints

$$y_{i,0} = Y_i , \forall i \tag{3}$$

$$y_{it} = y_{i,t-1} - D_{it} + \sum_j v_{ijt}, \forall (i,t) \tag{4}$$

$$\underline{SM}_{it} \le y_{it} \le \overline{SM}_{it}, \forall (i,t) \tag{5}$$

$$\left(1-\lambda_t\right) \leq \frac{\overline{SM}_{it} - y_{it}}{\overline{SM}_{it} - \underline{SM}_{it}}, \forall (i,t) \tag{6}$$

$$v_{ijt} - M \cdot \delta_{ijt} \leq 0, \forall (i,j,t) \tag{7}$$

$$\sum_i \delta_{ijt} \leq \varepsilon_{jt}, \forall (j,t) \tag{8}$$

$$\varepsilon_{jt} \geq 1, \forall (j,t) \tag{9}$$

$$K_j \cdot \alpha_{jt} - \left(\varepsilon_{jt} - 1\right) = \sum_i \frac{v_{ijt}}{R_i}, \forall (j,t) \tag{10}$$

The initial inventory levels of products are known (3). Classical continuity constraints (4) apply to the model. The stock level reached at the end of a period must be above a minimum level without exceeding a maximum level (5). Balancing stock levels is determined as a percentage according to the values of the stock level limits (6). With Constraint (7), we know if product i is loaded onto truck j on day t. Constraints (8) and (9) determine the number of variants loaded and the penalties associated with each truck used. Finally with Constraint (10), it is assumed that a truck's capacity in racks less its capacity penalty equals the racks loaded onto a truck.

4   Case Study

This study was particularly motivated by the problem faced by a company which assembles motors in Spain and sends its end products all over the world. The complete case study is presented in [4], but the 4 week procurement model had to evolve because stakeholders needed to consider new considerations like penalty for loss of capacity and the different run out-times of products. Given length constraints, a simple case study will be evaluated: five time periods, four products and three trucks will be considered. The different costs are: $C^\alpha = 60, C^\delta = 100, C^\lambda = 1000$. Tables 4 and 5 present the parameter values of the case study.

Table 4. Parameter values (I)

Product	R	Y	s	S	cob	$\overline{cob}$
1	8	160	150	300	1	2
2	6	100	0	200	2	6
3	8	0	0	50	2	6
4	7	50	50	100	1	2

Table 5. Parameter values (II)

Period	Product	D	$\underline{SM}$	$\overline{SM}$
1	1	150	186	300
1	2	80	0	157
1	3	0	14	50
1	4	50	51	100
2	1	186	181	300
2	2	0	0	157
2	3	14	0	50
2	4	51	52	100
3	1	181	155	300
3	2	0	78	157
3	3	0	0	50
3	4	52	59	100
4	1	155	170	300
4	2	78	79	200
4	3	0	15	50
4	4	59	64	100
5	1	170	150	300
5	2	79	0	200
5	3	15	0	50
5	4	64	50	100

Table 6. Results

PRODUCT	TRUCK	PERIOD	v
4	1	1	98
1	1	2	112
1	1	4	48
4	1	4	49
1	2	1	112
1	2	2	112
2	2	3	84
4	2	4	98
1	2	5	40
4	2	5	56
1	3	1	74
3	3	1	30
2	3	2	72
4	3	2	7
1	3	3	112
1	3	4	112
1	3	5	112

This model is solved by employing Gurobi Optimiser 4.5. The results show an average running time of 305 seconds per instance using an Intel Core i7 3.22 GHz processor, 24 GB RAM and Windows 7 as the OS. The procurement planning results are presented in Table 6.

As seen in the results, not all the trucks are needed in each period. Thanks to the procurement plan, we can see how capacity loss is considered and that each truck is fully loaded. Nevertheless, while implementing the real industry tool, the use of the MILP model is limited because computational times prolong exponentially when product and period numbers increase.

5   Conclusions

This paper presents an MILP model for planning supply planning in an engine assembly plant. The planning model allows different run-out times of products based on their fundamental characteristics and the arrival of loaded trucks in the FTL strategy by considering unbalanced run-out time to cover any changes in production planning and stock limits, plus truck capabilities which are penalized according to their load. A simple case study is proposed to demonstrate the applicability of the model.

A future research line would be to identify other strategies for loading trucks and to evaluate the best strategy in terms of transport costs against holding costs using real data. Another future research line would be to determine the minimum run-out time to be maintained in case of data uncertainty.

Acknowledgements. The work described in this paper has been partially supported by the Spanish Ministry of Science and Innovation within the Program "Proyectos de Investigación Fundamental No Orientada through the project "CORSARI MAGIC DPI2010-18243" and through the project "Programacion de produccion en cadenas de suministro sincronizada multietapa con ensamblajes/desemsamblajes con renovacion constante de productos en un contexto de inovacion DPI2011-27633". Julien Maheut holds a VALi+d grant funded by the Generalitat Valenciana (Regional Valencian Government, Spain) (Ref. ACIF/2010/222).

References

1. Bitran, G.R., Haas, E.A., Hax, A.C.: Hierarchical production planning: a single stage system. Operations Research 29, 717–743 (1981)
2. Sun, H., Ding, F.Y.: Extended data envelopment models and a practical tool to analyse product complexity related to product variety for an automobile assembly plant. International Journal of Logistics Systems and Management 6, 99–112 (2010)
3. Boysen, N., Fliedner, M.: Cross dock scheduling: Classification, literature review and research agenda. Omega 38, 413–422 (2010)
4. Garcia-Sabater, J.P., Maheut, J., Garcia-Sabater, J.J.: A two-stage sequential planning scheme for integrated operations planning and scheduling system using MILP: the case of an engine assembler. Flexible Services and Manufacturing Journal 24, 171–209 (2012)
5. Ben-Khedher, N., Yano, C.A.: The Multi-Item Replenishment Problem with Transportation and Container Effects. Transportation Science 28, 37–54 (1994)
6. Cousins, P.D.: Supply base rationalisation: myth or reality? European Journal of Purchasing Supply Management 5, 143–155 (1999)
7. Kiesmüller, G.P.: A multi-item periodic replenishment policy with full truckloads. International Journal of Production Economics 118, 275–281 (2009)
8. Goetschalckx, M.: Transportation Systems Supply Chain Engineering, vol. 161, pp. 127–154. Springer, US (2011)
9. Liu, R., Jiang, Z., Fung, R.Y.K., Chen, F., Liu, X.: Two-phase heuristic algorithms for full truckloads multi-depot capacitated vehicle routing problem in carrier collaboration. Computers Operations Research 37, 950–959 (2010)
10. Arunapuram, S., Mathur, K., Solow, D.: Vehicle Routing and Scheduling with Full Truckloads. Transportation Science 37, 170–182 (2003)

Improving the Application of Financial Measures in Supply Chain Management

Felix Friemann[1,*], Matthias Wandfluh[1], Paul Schönsleben[1], and Robert Alard[2]

[1] ETH Zürich, BWI Center for Industrial Management, WEINBERGSTRASSE 56, 8092 ZÜRICH, Switzerland
ffriemann@ethz.ch
[2] University of Applied Sciences, Promenade 26, 5200 Brugg, Switzerland

Abstract. Many companies (especially SMEs) still feel poorly prepared and notice a deficiency of financial know-how when facing situations such as limitations in working capital. To reduce the amount of capital employed, close linkage of financial measures to the daily operations within the companies is required. Yet, supply chain performance measures are often not directly linked to overall financial targets (e.g. cost of capital vs. service level). This paper proposes taking financial parameters into consideration when making supply chain management decisions. It outlines supply chain finance (SCF) solutions available to bigger corporates, analyses current financial metrics for supply chain management and proposes concepts for a greater linkage between finance and supply chain performance measures. Finally, this paper will also reveal gaps where current concepts and metrics have limitations and future research is needed.

Keywords: supply chain management (SCM), financial measures, metrics.

1 Introduction

1.1 Motivation

Within the last decades Supply Chain Management (SCM) gained enormous attention. It is no secret that it gives many companies great competitive advantage or even decides over success or failure of a product. That is why countless research efforts could be noted within this sector and it is an inherent part in the education of logistics managers. Even though progress in terms of optimizing and synchronizing material and information flows in SCM has been made, financial flows are insufficiently elaborated in practice by supply chain managers and their impact is not clarified. Since the targets are not aligned, finance managers limit supply chain operations in a sometimes unfavorable way and supply chain managers primarily focus on operational targets neglecting their financial impacts. Many companies (especially SMEs) still feel poorly prepared and notice a deficiency of financial know-how when facing

---

* Corresponding author.

C. Emmanouilidis, M. Taisch, D. Kiritsis (Eds.): APMS 2012, Part II, IFIP AICT 398, pp. 584–591, 2013.

situations such as limitations in working capital after the upturn following the latest financial crisis. After the production capacities and assets were reduced, the need for investments in new production assets and financing raw materials to serve the increased demand led to difficulties. Another example are the increasingly turbulent fluctuations in the currency and raw material markets that make it more difficult for global companies to forecast the financial flows. Deeper knowledge integration of financial concepts in the decision-making process of supply chain managers is expected to be a major competitive advantage allowing to create more robust and better performing supply chains.

1.2   Problem Statement

A current study in Germany shows that many medium-sized companies rely on traditional solutions when financial resources are needed. The vast majority (84 %) asks for loans from a bank and only 31 % of the medium-sized companies work on reducing their working capital [1].

This paper shall serve as a starting point for making supply chain finance (SCF) concepts more accessible for practitioners especially in SMEs. This will specifically be done by a closer linkage of financial know-how to the supply chain management measures. Until now, financing concepts are mainly implemented by the finance department of a company. The target values of finance managers are (beside others) to reduce the cost of capital within the supply chain. However, supply chain managers are primarily rated for performance measures like delivery reliability, fill rates or their own costs. A closer linkage between these different target values is needed to improve overall performance. This paper will outline a recommendation and reveal gaps where current concepts have deficiencies and future research is needed.

1.3   Methodology

This research is based on a literature research as well as on interviews with representatives from Swiss banks and industry. The methodology follows the following three steps. First, an overview about current application of SCF concepts is presented. Second, approaches for linking financial to supply chain performance measures are analyzed. In a third step, the potential gap between existing metrics and desired requirements are deduced and a new approach is outlined.

2   Application of Financial Measures within SCM

In this chapter, a short overview regarding the usage of financial methods within the SCM discipline will be given. For this reason, a common understanding of the term SCF will be provided in the first subchapter. Then, the cash-to-cash cycle as an important measure for the net working capital will be explained. At the end, an overview over existing SCF solutions in the market will be developed.

2.1   Definition of Supply Chain Finance (SCF)

Unfortunately, there is no distinct definition of SCF in the literature. By the banks, it was often used as a term for buyer-centric solutions and reduced on specific tools (reverse factoring[1] in specific). Lamoureux and Evans define SCF as a sub-set of trade finance (meaning both the supplier and the buyer side). This means a combination of technology solutions and financial services that closely connect global value chain anchors, suppliers, financial institutions and, frequently, technology service providers [2]. This definition is wider, but still not wide enough since SCF doesn't e.g. necessarily need financial providers or technology service providers. Moreover, in this paper SCF will be defined in a more general way as a concept encompassing any financing solution that supports the buyer or seller side of the supply chain to a considerable extent (accordingly to [3], [4]). This includes for example all concepts a supply chain manager applies that influence the financial measures of the buyer, seller or his own company.

In the next subchapter, the application of the cash-to-cash cycle as an important metric as well as its strengths and weaknesses will be explained.

2.2   Net Working Capital and the Cash-to-Cash Cycle

On average, the working capital accounts for 25 % of the turnover for companies listed in the Swiss Performance Index (SPI) [5]. Consequently, reducing the working capital has been on the agenda of many companies for a long time. Working capital is defined as the current assets of a firm minus its current liabilities [6]. Wagner and Locker specify the assets as accounts receivable plus inventory [5]. One key focus of SCM in the last years consequently is to reduce inventories (e.g. by just-in-time deliveries). The impact of decisions on accounts payable or receivable is not a key interest for many supply chain managers even though the accounts payable are directly influenced by e.g. vendor Managed Inventory (VMI) concepts where the supplier maintains the customer's inventory.

Looking for measures for the working capital, the cash-to-cash cycle has been often used as an indicator / measure for the net working capital that is needed by a company [7]. It bridges inbound material activities with suppliers, manufacturing operations and outbound sales activities with customers [8]. The cash-to-cash cycle can be calculated by Days Sales Outstanding (DSO) plus Days Inventory Outstanding (DIO) minus Days Payables Outstanding (DPO). Measures to improve the cash-to-cash cycle are therefore to reduce DSO and DIO and extend DPO.

This concept has been very successful for specific companies. One of the most prominent examples is the Dell Computer Corporation. In 2001, Dell had four days of inventory supply, 32 days of sales in accounts receivable, and 66 days in accounts payable adding up to a negative cash-to-cash cycle of 30 days [7]. For comparison:

---

[1] With reverse factoring (RF), early payment is provided by a bank or factoring company to a supplier against a rate based on the buyer's creditworthiness by selling confirmed invoices from the supplier to the factor. After the payment term the buyer pays the invoiced amount to the bank or factoring company [14].

European companies had a positive cash-to-cash cycle of 58,6 days in the same year [9].

But using the cash-to-cash cycle as the only metric has some drawbacks. The risks are e.g. rising costs and a higher probability of disruptions along the supply chain. This is due to the fact that while the stronger supply chain partner (which generally has the better credit rating) is able to e.g. reduce its DSO and therefore the needed working capital, the less powerful supply chain partners face worse conditions and their working capital employed is going up. When this moves on along the supply chain, it can lead to rising costs and serious problems at some point for smaller players. The effects of using the cash-to-cash cycle as a main metric for SCM measures are analysed by e.g. Losbichler and Rothböck [9] or Seifert and Seifert [10].

Due to these reasons, other measures to improve the financial situation of a company need to be analysed. In the next subchapter a brief outline over the range of available SCF solutions is given. It must be noticed that these solutions are mainly offered to bigger corporates since a critical turnover and market position is often essential to benefit from an implementation and recover the implementation and administration costs.

2.3   Range of Commercial SCF Solutions

The benefits for larger companies implementing SCF concepts with their suppliers or buyers include: 1) Reduced risks (by stabilizing their supply chain partners), 2) reduced costs along the supply chain (by e.g. lowering the working capital) and 3) enhanced capabilities of their supply chain (by e.g. providing cash to their supply chain partners that they can invest in new assets). That is why most major manufacturing and retail companies, for example, have a high degree of familiarity with SCF programs and are either considering or already using such a solution [4]. Therefore, different vendors offer various solutions to exploit these potentials (see e.g. [11], [3]). Among others, Yunqi especially mentions the advantages of online supply chain finance systems [12].

Banks traditionally marketed the term SCF and are offering a wide range of solutions. Beside others, these encompass factoring solutions (by selling the accounts receivable to a factor at a discount [13]) resp. reverse factoring, inventory finance, commodity finance or receivables finance.

Non-bank solution providers also exist and offer highly automated electronic platforms. These platforms involve several banks (or investors) that can provide the cash needed for various solutions. The relationship to the financial institutions is often not as strong, but a company might benefit from a greater competition between the funding providers.

Beside these platform solutions, concepts that do not involve a bank at all complement the portfolio. One example is dynamic discounting where a company enables its suppliers to choose when to receive the payment on outstanding invoices. The earlier the payment is received, the greater the discount the supplier has to accept [4]. In case the buyer has better access to capital, this might be a beneficial solution for all parties involved.

This chapter covered the definition of SCF, the introduction of the cash-to-cash cycle as a common metric to measure the net working capital and a short overview regarding the range of SCF solutions that larger businesses can choose of. The next chapter will now deal with solutions applicable to SME and especially implementable in the performance metrics of supply chain managers.

3   Linking Finance and Supply Chain Performance Measures

An implementation of before mentioned solutions often requires powerful market players who want to tighten their supply chain by supporting their buyers or suppliers. Even for them, onboarding suppliers can be difficult (see e.g. [14]). Within the supply chain, only a limited amount of information is shared due to several reasons (e.g. lack of trust, transparency). But especially SMEs with more restricted resources might have difficulties to participate when no larger player is interested in such a program. In these cases, the broad range of solutions that banks or platform providers offer is remarkably narrowed down.

Still, it can be beneficial if the SCF solutions are directly implemented in the SCM operations. Selected examples will be shown below. After that, a path is outlined to improve the application.

3.1   Financial Measures in Inventory Management

Existing approaches for a greater linkage between finance and supply chain performance measures exist e.g. in the area of inventory management. In 2004, Buzacott and Zhang stated that the financial situation impacts optimal inventory decisions when using asset-based financing (a lender loans money to the customer based on his assets) [15]. This is because the amount of money a company can borrow for financing inventories depends on the value of the inventory itself (only a specific percentage of the inventory-value depending on various factors will be provided by e.g. the bank). The variables are the following. A bank must decide the interest to charge and the loan limit whereas the retailer needs to decide the amount of capital to borrow within the limit and the amount of inventory to order. Buzacott and Zhang model the available cash dynamically in each period. A deterministic model is developed to understand how asset-based financing influences inventory decisions and the ability to grow for a company. Besides, a stochastic model analyzes the motivation of asset-based financing and impact of demand uncertainty. The demand uncertainty is important because it is one reason why the lender might not be able to pay back the loan (when the demand is smaller than expected). They state that their model is especially useful for start-ups facing financial restrictions. This argumentation follows the proposition of this paper that especially smaller companies might benefit from innovative SCF solutions.

With asset-based financing, Buzacott and Zhang focus on short-term debts. Protopappa on the other hand considers long-term interrelations [16]. She states that payment delays impact profit margins and motivates a joint consideration of financial and operational objectives since financial flows are often treated separately from the physical product flow nowadays. Therefore, a model is presented to understand the trade-off between operational and financial parameters in order to answer questions like how working capital targets affect ordering policy and the trade-off between financial and operational measurements. She analyses the interrelation between inventory level, service level, return on working capital investment, cash flows and working capital requirements. In short, operational and financial performance measures. The analysis is done by a mathematical model within various environments (single / multi-product, various product characteristics, multi-echelon supply chain with joint working capital restrictions, etc.). She concludes that offering more tight payment delays on the customers may have counterproductive outcomes on the performance of the SC due to increased costs on the customers.

These examples proof the positive performance when inventory decisions depend on both operational and financial measures. Still, the supply chain manager must be perfectly equipped with the needed financial know-how and information. Besides, financial measures must be included in his personal objectives. Since this is often not the case, other ways are elaborated to directly implement these measures into the supply chain metrics. This will be outlined in the next subchapter.

3.2   Implementing Financial Measures within Supply Chain Performance Metrics

In this subchapter, a way is outlined for implementing financial measures within the supply chain management department. For this being successful, metrics that are already common in this discipline have to be used. A widely accepted model within the supply chain management discipline is the Supply Chain Operations Reference (SCOR) model created by the Supply Chain Council (SCC) [17]. It provides an extensive framework and is organized around five primary management processes plan, source, make, deliver, and return and details them so that the processes of most supply chains can be described by standardized elements. Within every management process there are three levels of detail. A fourth level is left empty for organization-specific processes. For the purpose of this paper, the SCOR model is used to show where the financial parameters are needed to be taken into account in a greater way in order to improve the overall situation.

Performance is one component of the SCOR model besides processes, best practices and people. Performance contains the attributes reliability, responsiveness, agility, costs and asset management efficiency. Attributes cannot be measured and are used to set a strategic direction (e.g. for specific products or markets). Attributes are groupings of metrics. Metrics can be measured. This paper proposes using a new attribute that describes the financial situation 1) in the market, 2) within the supply chain and specifically 3) for the company. As shown in the previous chapters, these parameters have turned out to directly influence overall performance when included in the decision making process.

For example, in the current setting it would nearly always be beneficial to increase the accounts payable (payables outstanding) and reduce accounts receivable in order to increase the return on working capital (hierarchical structure in the SCOR-model: asset management – return on working capital – accounts payable). As shown before, this can negatively impact the situation of the suppliers which might therefore lead to higher risks of failure of a supplier. A new strategy might be to strengthen the overall supply chain and therefore reduce risks. This could have its reasons in the market situation (e.g. many smaller suppliers in a low-wage country). The strategy would make use the new "financial supply chain" attribute which encompasses e.g. a risk factor at the first level. At a second level, this risk factor is detailed in e.g. a combination of the days sales outstanding (DSO) and other factors. Balancing the DSO with the other factors would now lead to an optimal situation (whereas otherwise it would be beneficial to just increase the DSO). At the end, this could lead to a more robust supply chain. Another example is the start-up scenario Buzacott and Zhang [15] mentioned before where access to capital is limited. Following the strategy of taking "financial supply chain" attribute more into account would also lead to better inventory decisions in that case.

These are just a few examples. In the next step, the attribute would have to be elaborated in a greater detail considering various levels and analyzing the impacts and interactions. After that different case studies might have to be conducted.

4   Conclusions

The research problem has been brought to academia by several companies (in particular SMEs) who stated that they do not feel well prepared regarding financial measures within the supply chain management operations. SCF represents a powerful tool to improve supply chain performance (e.g. by releasing working capital). The paper therefore illustrates this need and creates a common understanding of SCF. It also shows current solutions in the market. In the third chapter, concepts for integrating financial concepts into the daily operations are introduced and an approach to link them to the SCOR model is outlined.

Nevertheless, SCF concepts are not easy to implement. This might be due to the fact that it is an interdisciplinary topic with several departments involved and it might have complex impacts on other measures or supply chain partners that are not always easy to foresee. Also, different objectives among the supply chain players, limited capabilities or lack of trust and transparency in the supply chain might lead to some implementation difficulties. Nevertheless, it is important to develop profound concepts that can be implemented in the daily operations. Structuring the requirements for a successful implementation of these concepts might be an important future research topic.

Also, until now an outline of the background and the need for financial measures is provided. An approach to include financial measures into the SCOR model is also given. In future research efforts, a structured catalogue of supply chain finance concepts might be developed. After that, the suggested approach has to be further detailed and case studies have to be conducted to prove positive overall performance. At the end, decision makers would be enabled to find suited metrics for their specific supply chains by selecting them from the overview according to their strategies and the indication from the SCOR model.

References

1. Institut für Demoskopie Allensbach: Studie" Stärken und Schwächen mittlerer und grosser Unternehmen im Vergleich (2011)
2. Lamoureux, J.F., Evans, T.: Supply Chain Finance: A New Means to Support the Competitiveness and Resilience of Global Value Chains (2011)
3. Global Business Intelligence: Trade and Supply Chain Finance, 3rd edn. (2012)
4. Treasury Today: Supply chain finance: the next generation. Treasury Today 1, 28–32 (2011)
5. Wagner, S.M., Locker, A.: Working Capital reduzieren. Beschaffungsmanagement-Revue de l'acheteur 9, 6–8 (2008)
6. Schneider, O.: Adding enterprise value (2009)
7. Farris II, M.T., Hutchison, P.D.: Cash-to-cash: the new supply chain management metric. International Journal of Physical Distribution & Logistics Management 32, 288–298 (2002)
8. Farris, T., Staberhofer, F., Losbichler, H.: Managing the Supply Chain Using the Cash-to-Cash Metric. RIRL 2010 (2010)
9. Losbichler, H., Rothböck, M.: Der Cash-to-cash Cycle als Werttreiber im SCM—Ergebnisse einer europäischen Studie. Controlling & Management 52, 47–57 (2008)
10. Seifert, R.W., Seifert, D.: Financing the Chain. International Commerce Review 10, 32–44 (2011)
11. Global Finance magazine: World's best supply chain finance providers (2012)
12. Yunqi, W.: Online Supply Chain Finance: Profound Changes in Financing of SMEs (2011)
13. Davies, J.: Show me the money. supplychainstandard.com. 10-11 (2010)
14. Alferink, H.: Buyer initiated non-recourse factoring of confirmed payables: A major global corporation case study. Master Thesis (2010)
15. Buzacott, J.A., Zhang, R.Q.: Inventory management with asset-based financing. Management Science, 1274–1292 (2004)
16. Protopappa, M.: Interrelating operational and financial performance measure-ments in inventory theory. EPFL (2009).
17. The Supply Chain Council Inc.: Supply Chain Operations Reference Model 10.0 (2010)

Total Cost of Ownership for Supply Chain Management: A Case Study in an OEM of the Automotive Industry

Paulo Afonso

Production and Systems Department, University of Minho, Portugal
psafonso@dps.uminho.pt

Abstract. The selection of the best suppliers is a key issue for many companies. Nevertheless, it is important to highlight that the most economical supplier may not be the one that has the lowest purchase price. The cheapest supplier is the one that represents the lowest cost to the company, after being considered various aspects of supplying, such as quality, reliability of deliveries, the history of supplier performance, its location, its financial condition, etc. The goal of this paper is to discuss the application of the methodology Total Cost of Ownership (TCO) as a tool to support supplier's selection. The case studied allowed to understand TCO in practice, to study the contribution of the various cost parameters for the TCO and to demonstrate the procedures that support the systematic application of the TCO in a worldwide company.

Keywords: Supply Chain Management, Logistics Costs, Cost Management.

1 Introduction

Nowadays, the costs with materials, parts and components are a very high expense for companies in many worldwide supply chains. Thus, supplying strategies and supplier selection are particularly important.

However, the selection of a supplier should not be made on one unique criterion, usually the price of the goods purchased. Over the past few decades several methodologies have been developed in order to examine and compare the costs associated with each supplier allowing better decisions. Many managers realized that they real intend to select the best supplier, and the cheapest may not necessarily be what sells the cheaper product. Indeed, there are other significant costs beyond the price of the material or component such as: transportation costs, costs of non-quality and non-compliance, late deliveries, costs in after-sales service, etc. For all these reasons, companies need to establish close relationships with good suppliers.

A correct model to support the selection of suppliers includes in addition to the price a wide range of quantitative and qualitative elements (Ho et al., 2010, Humphreys et al., 2003). Furthermore, the excessive focus on the acquisition cost that prevailed for many years resulted in many hidden costs or costs that have been affecting the profits of these companies without managers realized it. The failure to consider environmental factors and risks, among other factors, also had important implications in various industries.

C. Emmanouilidis, M. Taisch, D. Kiritsis (Eds.): APMS 2012, Part II, IFIP AICT 398, pp. 592–599, 2013.
© IFIP International Federation for Information Processing 2013

In this context, the purchasing function plays a critical role in the competitiveness of modern firms and supply chains. Consequently, the business world and the academia have developed ways to improve the selection process of suppliers. Dickson (1966) reported 23 criteria for selecting vendors such as quality, reliability of deliveries, historical performance and its financial position. Weber et al. (2010), report various developments in this subject, as is the case of the selection methods of suppliers. Examples of such methods are reported by Aissaoui et al. (2007), Snijders et al. (2003), de Boer et al. (2001). Among others, several techniques can be used namely, the Analytic Hierarchical Process (AHP), the Analytic Network Process (ANP), Data Envelopment Analysis (DEA) and Case-based-reasoning (CBR). Still other authors, as is the case of Bevilacqua et al. (2006), Ferrin and Plank (2002), who address the selection criteria of suppliers. Typically, the main criterion for the selection of suppliers is the purchase price, i.e. the price at which the material or part is acquired. However, the literature has been also discussing the inclusion of other monetary and nonmonetary criteria such as risk level (Weber et al., 2010).

Among the existing cost-based methodologies it is important to emphasize the importance of methods that are applicable in the final stage of the decision process such as the Life-cycle costing (LCC), Zero-based pricing (ZBP), Cost-based supplier performance evaluation and also the Total Cost of Ownership (TCO). The life-cycle costing considers the purchase price and the costs the organization incurs to use, handle and maintain, and finally get rid of a particular material, part, equipment or product (Ellram, 1995). The zero-based pricing and the cost-based supplier performance evaluation are two methods used to consider the total costs incurred with each supplier. These methods give special attention to the costs of "doing business" with a particular supplier, including costs prior to the purchase moment (Ellram, 1995).

To evaluate the a 1st Tier supplier in the automotive industry produces car radios and makes the assembly of electronic boards for various domestic and industrial applications. This company makes use of the TCO methodology for the selection of suppliers of plastic components, metal and electronic parts.

2   Total Cost of Ownership

Supplier selection strategies have been recognized as important by both the academia and the industry (Dogan and Aydin, 2011). Indeed, the high technical specialization of the firms and the consolidation of global supply chains in various industries have led to an increase of subcontracting costs, costs with subassemblies produced by suppliers instead internally, among others. de Boer et al. (2001) made a literature review of the methods which support supplier selection. According to these authors, such methodologies effectively increase the efficiency and effectiveness of the procurement processes. These methodologies take into account a greater number of criteria, in addition to the purchase price of the material, component or subassembly, allowing such decisions to be taken in terms of the long term. Supplier selection methods and tools improve the decision making process with the introduction of intangible factors such as risk. The adoption of methodologies for supplier selection, may allow eliminating redundant criteria and alternatives in the evaluation process, such as the use of audit programs. Finally, they give support for an easier communication of the differences between the alternatives, making decisions clearer if further explanations are necessary for internal control purposes as well as to manage the relationship with the different suppliers.

The TCO is a methodology developed to determine the total cost of ownership of a product or service provided by a particular supplier, through a complete investigation of the different cost items which composed the real cost of buying from a specific supplier. According to Ferrin and Plank (2002), the Total Cost of Ownership (TCO) is a methodology used in leading companies in worldwide supply chains. TCO aims to determine the true cost of buying a particular good or service from a particular supplier, accounting for it all costs associated with the purchasing activity (Degraeve et al., 2005), using the monetary quantification of all financial and non-financial attributes (Morssinkhof et al., 2011).

The TCO approach considers additional costs such as expenses on the implementation of an order, costs with searching activities and qualification of the supplier, transportation costs, insurance costs, warranties, product inspection and quality costs, replacement possibilities, downtime caused by failures, etc.

According to Dickson (1966), the main criteria to be considered in selecting a supplier are: quality, delivery, performance history, warranties and claims policies, supplier facilities and production capacity, price, technical capability, financial position, performance procedures, communication systems, reputation and position in the industry, degree of commitment to the business, management and organizational capacity, level of operational control, repair services capabilities, location, level of training and existence of reciprocal agreements.

Ferrin and Plank (2002) used a questionnaire to enumerate the major cost factors that affect the TCO of the companies surveyed. This questionnaire was sent to members of the Institute for Supply Management (ISM). In summary, these authors reported that the criteria for the selection of suppliers are divided into thirteen categories: operating costs, quality, customer-related costs, logistics, technological advantages, starting price, opportunity cost, capacity and reliability, maintenance, inventory costs, transaction costs, lifecycle costs, and others.

About 62% of firms surveyed by Ferrin and Plank (2002) reported that the TCO is used in less than 40% of the purchases. These results are consistent with the work of Ellram (1995) which states that the methodology is not widely publicized because its application is difficult. On the other hand, the results indicated that the main application of TCO (28.8% of cases) is related to the purchase of capital goods, i.e. investments and equipment purchases.

Nevertheless, it is particularly important to highlight that the TCO is particularly relevant to support decision making in terms of purchasing materials and components for the production of a large quantity of products. These cases of selecting suppliers through the TCO in the manufacturing industry are less well documented and analyzed in the literature.

TCO for "continuous delivery" of materials, component or subassemblies in a supply chain is very different and much more demanding than the total cost of ownership of an equipment (e.g. computers, printers, etc.). In these cases, TCO is essentially a lifecycle cost computation adding to the acquisition cost of the equipment, the expected amount of operation and maintenance costs in order to compare better different alternatives. This paper is about TCO on this context, i.e. to compare supplying alternatives in a manufacturing environment of generally global supply chains.

3   Case Study

The research approach used in this research fits into the type 2 case study (study of several units of analysis in one case) according to Yin (1994) classification. In this research, they were studied and analyzed three cases of application of the TCO methodology which represent the three units of analysis. In a case study, it is desirable to use the largest number of sources to ensure their reliability (Yin, 1994). In this research project, the main sources of information used were: internal documentation, records and files, interviews, direct observation and participant observation of the process of supplier selection.

Thus, in this research project it was conducted an exploratory case study in order to understand and formulate hypotheses about the conditions of operation of TCO in practice. This case study took place between February and October.

The COMPANY is located in the North of Portugal and belongs to a worldwide corporation with several companies, plants around the world and thousands of workers. The plant located in Portugal produces electronic components, namely car radios, navigation systems, appliances and boilers. The various group companies are grouped into three business units: Automotive Technology, Industrial Technology and Consumer Goods. The department of Purchasing / Project Management and Preventive Planning Purchasing Quality is responsible for various projects and functions but assumes mainly the role of "interface" between suppliers and the company. This department exists in several locations of the company around the world: in Germany, southwest Asia, China and Portugal. Although this section is located inside the Portuguese plant, it is assumed as a purchases service provider and reports directly to the central purchasing department. The section has six employees who are "driven by product", that is, each collaborator is responsible for ensuring the appointment of suppliers of all components required for each particular product, as well as to track the entire process.

4   Findings

The company has at its disposal a wide range of suppliers around the world to guarantee the diversity and volume of components needed for it large portfolio of products. When selecting the best vendor for each project the company uses a TCO computation software in which are inserted different data about the component, potential suppliers and their prices. The result of the calculation is the TCO of the component in question, which details the purchase cost, i.e. the price of the part, price of packaging, the initial cost of tools and molds, shipping costs, inventory costs, costs of appointment of supplier, quality and other costs.

To be able to use the TCO method in a daily basis, the collaborators of the department of Purchasing have access to a computation program that runs on the internet browser through the firm's intranet. This case study is very interesting, even paradigmatic, because the TCO computation model is a decision tool developed internally in the company and there are not other examples of such kind of programs documented in the literature. This model considers several and different inputs for the computation of the TCO. Attending confidentiality considerations the calculation equations and algorithms cannot be explained in detail.

The TCO tool developed in this company requires inputs of four different levels: global (at the parent company), at the business unit level (does not contain numeric values); at the level of the plant (factory); at the project level. The inputs necessary and the outputs produced by the model are summarized in eight categories as it is shown in Figure 1. After the introduction of the inputs, a sheet with detailed results for each of the first three years of the project and the overall results of the TCO by supplier is presented.

Table 1. TCO tool: inputs and outputs

Inputs	Outputs
Projetc details	Preço
Information about the supplier	Tool costs
Order costs	Packaging costs
Transportation costs	Transportation costs
Inventory costs	Inventory costs
Appointment costs	Appointment costs
Quality costs	Quality costs
Other costs	Other costs

For the overall results of the TCO it is still possible to obtain graphs where it is shown visually the weight of the different components in the final cost structure for each potential supplier. To help collaborators in the introduction of the data, there is an internal document developed by the logistics department of the company. In this document, we can found typical values for transportation costs, shipping conditions, type of inspection procedures, etc. This document contains confidential information for the company, so its contents cannot be disclosed.

However, it is important to note that, in a few cases, the selection of a supplier may consider additional aspects beyond the TCO. In some cases, the final decision may exclude suppliers with lower TCO due to various reasons such as: 1) purchasing strategies that define what is not desirable to carry out business with the supplier in question, 2) the financial rating of suppliers, which may put into question the economic viability of such alternative, 3) allocation limits defined by the business unit (e.g. a supplier cannot have more than 30% of the turnover dependent on a the business unit, or if more than 50% of suppliers sales are with companies in the group).

The TCO tool was analyzed and discussed through 3 different situations. The three cases analyzed are quite different but the results are comparable. TCO is about the consideration of indirect costs to select the best supplier. Nevertheless, direct costs remain important, i.e., the purchase price, the price of packing, tool costs, among others, have a significant contribution to the final TCO. In Case 1, the three suppliers were Portuguese firms and competed within very similar conditions, which led to the "price of parts" to be the main factor which explain the differences between suppliers. In Case 2 were surveyed four suppliers, one from Malaysia and three Portuguese. For the Portuguese suppliers the main cost drivers were the part price and the costs with the tooling, the remaining parameters originated residual values. On the other hand, the TCO of the Malaysian supplier was quite incremented by the value of shipping costs. In Case 3, two suppliers were Portuguese, one German and the last one Chinese. The results obtained through the TCO application indicated that the part price and the cost of the tool were the factors most important, despite the value of inventory and shipping costs are also considerable for the German and the Chinese suppliers. The weight of each of the cost drivers on the final TCO, in these three situations, is presented in Table 2.

Table 2. Cost items proportion on total cost

Cost itens	Case 1	Case 2	Case 3	Average
Acquisition costs	50.2	44.1	72.3	55.5
Package costs	0	0	0	0
Tool costs	43.4	54.1	14.5	37.4
Transport costs	1.5	0.1	5.7	2.4
Inventory costs	3.0	1.0	5.7	3.3
Nomination costs	0	0	0	0
Quality costs	1.8	0.6	1.7	1.4
Other costs	0	0	0	0
Total	100	100	100	100

In the three situations presented, TCO value is 1,2 to 3,1 times the purchase price of the piece and this fact demonstrates the need for a rigorous analysis of the remaining costs in the selection of suppliers. If only the selected suppliers are considered, the value of the TCO represents a lower variability: between 1.3 to 2.3 times the value of the purchase price of the part. Indeed, the complete cost of a part or component, i.e. its TCO, is much more than the immediate and direct purchase price.

It is interesting to note that in each situation studied, the supplier with the lowest TCO was always the one that showed a lower purchase cost, which does not mean that the application of the TCO methodology is unnecessary in these cases. Indeed, the realization of the TCO calculation allowed identifying costs that deserved special attention for the negotiations with the different suppliers.

For example, in Case 2, the computation of the TCO identified cost drivers that have received particular attention in the second round of negotiations, clarifying the selection of the best supplier. In Case 3, on the other hand, the application of the TCO permitted to highlight and understand the differences in between suppliers which presented direct costs of the part very similar.

5   Conclusions

The costs with the acquisition of materials and components constitute a major expenditure in many firms and a significant portion of production costs in various industries. The costs that reflect the purchasing function represent between 50% and 90% of the production cost (Weber et al., 2010, de Boer et al., 2001; Ellram and Siferd, 1998). On the other hand, the increasing complexity of products and services, the reduction of product life cycles, increased complexity of the processes in companies, the greater interconnection between customers and suppliers and other aspects make the success of a company to be very dependent of its suppliers and the relationship that they have among them (e.g. Micheli et al., 2009).

In this context, the purchasing function can contribute for higher levels of production efficiency and the competiveness of the firm, reducing business costs and therefore increasing company's profit (Dowlatshahi, 2000).

This paper illustrates the application of TCO for continuous supply, in a company that uses this methodology in a systematic and structured approach. The literature does not offer real examples of TCO in practice; thus, findings of this research project represent a contribution to the literature.

References

1. Aissaoui, N., Haouari, M., Hassini, E.: Supplier selection and order lot sizing modeling: a review. Computers & Operations Research 34, 3516–3540 (2007)
2. Bevilacqua, M., Ciarapica, F., Giacchetta, G.: A fuzzy-QFD approach to supplier selection. Journal of Purchasing & Supply Management 12, 14–27 (2006)
3. Che, Z., Wang, H.: Supplier selection and supply quantity allocation of common and non-common parts with multiple criteria under multiple products. Computers & Industrial Engineering 55, 110–133 (2008)
4. de Boer, L., Labro, E., Morlacchi, P.: A review of methods supporting supplier selection. European Journal of Purchasing & Supply Management 7, 75–89 (2001)
5. Degraeve, Z., Roodhooft, F., Van Doveren, B.: The use of total cost of ownership for strategic procurement: a company-wide management information system. Journal of the Operational Research Society, 51–59 (2005)
6. Dickson, G.W.: An analysis of vendor selection systems and decisions (1966)
7. Dogan, I., Aydin, N.: Combining Bayesian Networks and Total Cost of Ownership method for supplier selection analysis. Computers & Industrial Engineering (2011)
8. Dowlatshahi, S.: Designer-buyer-supplier interface: Theory versus practice. International Journal of Production Economics 63, 111–130 (2000)
9. Dyer, J.: Specialized Supplier Networks as a Source of Competitive Advantage: Evidence from the Auto Industry. Strategic Management Journal 17, 271–291 (1996)
10. Ellram, L., Siferd, S.: Total Cost of Ownership: A Key Concept In Strategic Cost Management Decisions. Journal of Business Logistics, 55–84 (1998)

11. Ellram, L.: Total cost of ownership: An analysis approach for purchasing. Arizona State University, Tempe (1995)
12. Ferrin, B., Plank, R.: Total cost of Ownership Models: An Exploratory Study. Journal of Supply Chain Management (2002)
13. Ho, W., Xu, X., Dey, P.: Multi-criteria decision making approaches for supplier evaluation and selection: A literature review. European Journal of Operational Research 202, 16–24 (2010)
14. Humphreys, P., Wong, Y., Chan, F.: Integrating environmental criteria into the supplier selection process. Journal of Materials Processing Technology 138(1-3), 349–356 (2003)
15. Micheli, G., Cagno, E., Giulio, A.D.: Reducing the total cost of supply through risk-efficiency-based supplier. Journal of Purchasing & Supply Management 15, 166–177 (2009)
16. Morssinkhof, S., Wouters, M., Warlop, L.: Effects of providing total cost of ownership information on attribute weights in purchasing decisions. Journal of Purchasing & Supply Management (2011)
17. Seal, W., et al.: Enacting a European supply chain: a case study on the role of management accounting. Management Accounting Research 10, 303–322 (1999)
18. Snijders, C., Tazelaar, F., Batenburg, R.: Electronic decision support for procurement management: evidence on whether computers can make better procurement decisions. Journal of Purchasing & Supply Management 9, 191–198 (2003)
19. Weber, M., Hiete, M., Lauer, L., Rentz, O.: Low cost country sourcing and its effects on the total cost of ownership structure for a medical devices manufacturer. Journal of Purchasing & Supply Management 16, 4–16 (2010)
20. Yin, R.K.: Case study research: Design and methods. Applied Social Research Methods Series, vol. 5. SAGE Publications (1994)

Greening Manufacturing Supply Chains – Introducing Bio-based Products into Manufacturing Supply Chains

David Sparling[1], Fred Pries[2], and Erin Cheney[1]

[1] The Richard Ivey School of Business, London, Canada
{dsparling,echeney}@ivey.ca
[2] University of Guelph, Guelph, Canada
fpries@uoguelph.ca

Abstract. Launching a new technology involves more than innovation within an organization. It often requires innovations in downstream firms adopting the technology and greater interaction and knowledge exchange among supply chain partners. This paper examines the introduction of new bio-based products into existing supply chains, the location of the innovations needed to successfully commercialize the product, the nature of relationships among chain members and the impact of modularization on bio-based product introductions.

Keywords: supply chain, modularity, innovation, bioproducts.

1 Introduction

The major challenges in introducing new or redesigned products are often associated with consumer acceptance. The situation is different for bio-based industrial products, where the main impacts are on companies rather than consumers and the motivations are reducing costs, oil consumption and the environmental impact of manufacturing processes and products. The main challenge is often adoption by supply chain members. Adoption may require significant innovation among supply chain partners, with greater interaction and exchange of knowledge through the chain. Success may also depend on the knowledge partners supporting the innovations through research, development and design.

An early outcome of the bio-based economy has been the construction of ethanol supply chains and investment in the capital intensive infrastructure to support them. Manufacturing supply chains are longer than fuel chains and involve more partners and products. New bio-based chemicals can often link to existing manufacturing chains, greatly reducing the investment needed to create more sustainable manufacturing chains.

This study investigates the process of greening manufacturing supply chains viewed through the lens of supply chain modularity, where inserting a bio-based chemical module (or company) into a chain can change the environmental and financial performance of the entire manufacturing chain. The study examines the innovations required to commercialize the new technologies, the location of those innovations within the chains and the nature and evolution of the interactions between innovating organizations and their supply chain partners.

C. Emmanouilidis, M. Taisch, D. Kiritsis (Eds.): APMS 2012, Part II, IFIP AICT 398, pp. 600–607, 2013.
© IFIP International Federation for Information Processing 2013

2   Literature

Concerns over the environment and energy have moved bio-based products higher on the strategic agendas of industrial supply chains. The chemical industry in particular, offers great potential for bio-based alternatives. In 2009, global chemical industry sales (excluding pharmaceuticals) were valued at about US$2.61 trillion (ICCA Review, 2009-2010). Revenue potential for what King (2010) terms *"biorefinery*-based chemicals" is estimated at US$ 10-15-billion by 2020 and projected to represent 8% of global chemical sales in 2012 (ICIS, 2010). Many different areas of science and technology overlap in bio-based chemicals creating a highly complex industry (Chotani (2000), Lorenz (2002)). While the current landscape consists primarily of smaller new bio-based technology companies, interest is growing among multinationals (King, 2010).

Although past focus was generally on innovation strategies within the firm, there is a growing recognition that successful innovation also depends on the actions taken by customers and suppliers. *Adner and Kapoor (2009)* characterize the innovation environment faced by companies as an ecosystem, where the success of an innovation depends, not only on the innovation strategies internal to the firm, but also on innovations within a firm's supply chain. They hypothesized that value creation and capture depend on the position of necessary innovations relative to the focal firm.

Innovation in business models and industry structure is as important for a sector as scientific innovation (Pisano, 2006). *Baldwin and Clark (2000)* and *Jacobides et al. (2006)* identify that industry participants can strategically re-engineer industry architecture through investment in platform technologies and *Pisano and Teece (2007)* argue that changes to industry architecture is one of two critical domains where value can be captured from innovation.

The theory of modularity, based on design theories of *Herbert Simon (1969), Christopher Alexander (1964)* and recent work by *Baldwin (2007)*, provides one lens with which to examine the introduction of bio-based technologies and products into traditional manufacturing supply chains. Commercializing some inventions may involve the simple substitution of a link in the supply chain ('drop-in' innovations), while others may require adaptation by many organizations in the supply chain. The ease with which substitutions can occur may be dependent on the modularity of the supply chain. *Baldwin and Clark (2000)* define a module as a group of tasks that are highly interrelated within the module but are only marginally related to tasks in other modules. *Baldwin (2007)* identifies and characterizes thick and thin crossing points in supply chains, suggesting thin crossing points have few, relatively simple transfers of material, energy and information and often occur between modules. Thick crossing points have numerous and/or complex transfers, high-transaction costs and can be associated with opportunistic behavior (Baldwin, 2007). The design of transactions and relationships differs systematically with the thickness of the crossing points. Spot transactions are more likely at thin crossing points, while vertical integration or formal and relational contracts designed to reduce transactions costs are more common at thicker ones.

Many of the theories on innovation, modularity and supply chains were developed in the computer industry. Bioproduct innovation differs on several dimensions. The products have longer life cycles, the objectives include greener supply chains and replacing oil, and supply chain partners include farmers and forestry companies. This study extends the concepts introduced by *Adner and Kapoor (2009)* to the bioproduct industry and particularly bio-based chemicals, examining how the nature and location of innovations affect the commercialization process for bio-based chemical innovations. It applies Baldwin's theories on the thickness of crossing points to innovation relationships in bio-based supply chains and adds consideration of timing to the discussion on modularity.

3   Methods

A case study approach was employed to study innovation in four supply chains developing new bio-based products (Figure 1). The research addressed the following hypotheses:

— H1: Introduction of a new bio-based substitute for an existing oil-based component will be more likely to succeed where the production of the bio-based substitute occurs in a highly modular organization with thin crossing points to existing supply chains and few innovations needed in the rest of the chain.
— H2: The nature of modules changes as technologies are developed. Innovating organizations must incorporate more transactions and organizations during the early stages of development of a new bio-based technology than at later stages and will exhibit differences in the thickness of its crossing points at different stages.
— H3: Introduction of a bio-based substitute will be more successful if the innovations needed to commercialize the product are located adjacent to the focal firm.

Background data for the case studies was collected using publicly available data. More detailed information on the companies was collected through semi-structured interviews with selected industry participants holding senior management positions.

4   Results

Three chains involved new to the industry bio-based chemicals and the fourth involved a bio-fibre composite material. The research found that bio-based chemical chains were typically composed of 'traditional' technology firms, with a single bio-focused firm which acted as the link between biomass production and traditional economy firms (Figure 1). The motivations for adopting bio-based products differed. For some chains the motivation was to produce more environmentally friendly products for end consumers (Chains 1 and 2). In other cases, the motivation was reducing costs (Chains 2 and 4) or supply uncertainty (Chain 3). In each chain, reducing the environmental impacts of the manufacturing processes provided an additional incentive but, by itself, sustainability did not motivate adoption.

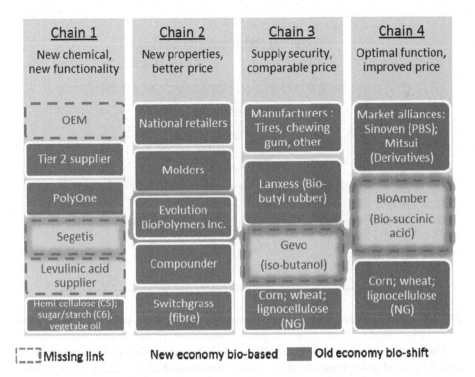

Fig. 1. Bio-based chemical supply chains   NG: Next Generation (planned)

Converting an oil-based manufacturing chain to a bio-based alternative involves two distinct sets of innovation activities. The first is primarily internal, developing bio-based substrates and adapting them to the particular needs of the chemical and manufacturing partners. The second requires innovations external to the focal firms. In the chains examined, innovations were primarily among downstream supply chain members and involved them making the process and/or product innovations needed to incorporate the bio-based alternatives. Their products often served as inputs to downstream firms, making further downstream adaptation necessary in some cases.

The location of required innovations mattered. In two of the supply chains (chains 3 & 4), the innovations required were primarily internal, as their products could act as direct substitutes for the oil-based products used by customers (Figure 2). In chain 1 the bio-based module, Segetis, introduced a new compound which required changes to the product formulations in the two subsequent downstream organizations, but not to the OEM at the end of the chain. Although the new bio-based chemical provided greater functionality, it did so at a higher cost and with more switching costs for other members of the chain. This chain has had the most significant challenges in commercializing their innovation. Chain 2 exhibited both complement (upstream) and component (downstream) challenges but because the innovations needed were in firms adjacent to the innovating firm, the challenges were more easily overcome.

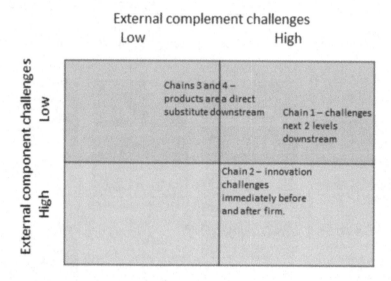

Fig. 2. Location of necessary supply chain innovations (adapted from Adner and Kapoor, 2009)

The location of the innovation challenges is important; so too is the location of the knowledge and technologies needed to overcome those challenges. Chain 2 represents a particularly interesting example of how modules adapt during development, expanding to incorporate additional capabilities needed to commercialize a new technology. The innovation was a bio-composite plastic made of switchgrass and recycled plastic for use in manufacturing small bins for hardware and small tools. A knowledge partner, a university research group external to the supply chain, was critical to commercializing the technology. The research group created different formulations for the innovating firm to test upstream with the compounder producing the bio-composite and downstream with the extruder partner manufacturing bins from the biomaterial. Fifty formulations were tested over 14 months leading to the successful launch of *bio-bins* in major retailers in Canada. Government funding supported the laboratory research, reducing transactions costs for the innovating company. Sole sourcing agreements and shared product development reduced transactions costs for the compounder, the innovating company and the downstream extrusion firm manufacturing the containers. The finished product was a direct substitute for existing plastic bins but provided retailers with a greener product offering higher margins.

The nature of the interaction between the bio-based modules and chemical/manufacturing supply chains is explored in Table 1. The modularity of the four chains was assessed by examining the costs and nature of transactions at the points where traditional economy firms interfaced with bio-modules. Overall findings were generally consistent with predictions of modularity theory. In some cases, the interactions represent thick crossing points with significant knowledge and process interactions and higher transaction costs. Thick crossing points where characterized by greater market and technology uncertainty and generally resulted in the need for more formal contractual relationships. At thin crossing points, lower transaction costs and knowledge interactions were required to commercialize the new bio-chemical products. Thin crossings were also associated with less formal contracts using spot market pricing and supply contracts. Thick crossing points were seen more in downstream relationships then upstream, where knowledge of the new biomaterial had to be passed between modules or where skills had to be temporarily incorporated to assist in commercialization, as discussed above.

Table 1. Interaction between the bioproduct innovator and the existing supply chain

	Case 1	*Case 2*	*Case 3*	*Case 4*
Innovator	Segetis	Evolution Biopolymers	Gevo	BioAmber
Product	L-ketal - Unique chemical from levulinic acid and glycerol	A biocomposite of up to 30% natural fibre and recycled plastic	Platform technology for producing bio-based iso-butanol	A bio-based succinic acid and its derivatives such as PBS and BDO
Key product features	Improved functionality as solvent, polyol, plasticizer	Lower cost, more strength and "green" footprint	Competitively priced iso-butanol	Low cost replacement - bio-succinic acid
IMPACT ON DOWNSTREAM SUPPLY CHAIN				
Knowledge user & producer must have about the other's domain	Very high. New molecule requires knowledge sharing with user.	Limited. Biocomposite resin must work in existing molding processes.	High. Exchange supports advances in chemistry and market for iso-butanol.	Very limited. Bio-succinic acid is identical to petroleum derived succinic acid.
Crossing pt	Thick	Thin	Thick	Thin
Nature of transaction between parties	Long-term supply & joint development agreements.	Purchase order	Long-term supply agreements for iso-butanol.	Exclusive and long-term supply agreements, joint development.
Transaction costs	High	Low	Moderate	Low
Strategies to reduce downstream transaction costs	Joint development agreements.	Government funded R&D center. Exclusive downstream relationships.	Investment from major customer.	Investment from customer.

Table 1. (*continued*)

IMPACT ON UPSTREAM SUPPLY CHAIN				
Knowledge user & producer must have about the other's domain	Limited. User assured of a five-carbon sugar which has been difficult to source.	Very high.	Very limited. GEVO technology will retrofit any ethanol plant.	Very limited. Feedstock is sugar (in six carbon form) and carbon dioxide.
Crossing pt	Thin	Thick	Thin	Thin
Nature of transaction between parties	Limited supply difficult sourcing; relational contract may ensure supply.	Long term supply, exclusive supplier arrangements for biomass.	Long term supply contracts, spot markets (as needed).	Long term supply contracts, spot markets as needed.
Transaction costs	Low	Moderate	High	Low
Strategies used to reduce upstream transaction costs	Consideration to back integrate into feedstock production.	Sole sourcing with upstream supplier.	Vertical integration upstream.	Co-location of new production facilities with major development partner.

Although the sample size was limited, the results affirmed H1: innovations which required fewer innovations in other firms in the supply chain were more likely to succeed. This was the case in chains 2 through 4 which were moving to successful commercialization, while chain 1 was challenged by the downstream innovations needed in the succeeding two levels. The focal firm had to deal with uncertainties of feedstock supply, in addition to the marketing and sale of a new chemical molecule that was heavily dependent on third party partners and downstream collaborators to show proof of concept at all levels of the supply chain.

Chains 2, 3 and 4 also provided confirmation for H2: each exhibited much broader modules during development, incorporating more transactions and organizations than were planned for or needed after development was completed. The innovating firm in chain 3 used vertical integration to reduce transactions costs downstream while investments by governments helped reduce transactions costs in chains 2 and 4. Both chains 2 and 3 planned to reduce their module scope once development was completed, changing their downstream crossings from thick to thin.

Results also affirmed H3: introduction of bio-based alternatives is most successful when innovations required for commercialization are located near or within the focal firm. In chain 2, the innovations required were immediately before the innovating firm and were managed during development through shared development and government support for knowledge partners. In chain 3, the innovations needed were immediately upstream, modifying an ethanol plant, and downstream, encouraging buyers to switch. The innovating firm expanded their module, vertically integrating backward during development to control the integration of their processes with ethanol production. Once the technology and processes are fully understood and stable the innovator will refocus, concentrating solely on the iso-butanol modules which can be sold or licensed to ethanol facilities. Chain 1 is a good example of how required innovations further downstream can challenge innovating companies.

5   Conclusion

The supply chains studied all illustrated the application of modularity theory to the introduction of bio-based technologies into traditional manufacturing chains. Rather than constructing entirely new chains, bio-based modules were integrated into existing chains but that integration was influenced, at least in part, by the nature and location of downstream innovations needed to commercialize the new technologies. The structure and transactions in the module and thickness of its crossing changed during development as innovation challenges were resolved. Solving the upstream and downstream innovation challenges required a relationship between the innovation process and the production processes and systems in the existing supply chains. It was also dependent on the role of partners with external knowledge.

References

1. Adner, R., Kapoor, R.: Value creation in innovation ecosystems: how the structure of technological interdependence affects firm performance in new technology generations. Strategic Management Journal 31, 306–333 (2009)
2. Alexander, C.: Notes on the synthesis of Form. Harvard University Press, Cambridge (1964)
3. Baldwin, C.L.: Where do transactions come from? Modularity, transactions, and the boundaries of firms. Industrial and Corporate Change 17, 155–195 (2007)
4. Chotani, G., et al.: The commercial production of chemicals using pathway engineering. Biochim. Biophys. Acta Mol. Cell Res. 1543, 434–455 (2000)
5. ICCA Review (2009-2010),
   http://www.icca-chem.org/ICCADocs/ICCA-review-2009-2010.pdf
6. ICIS (2010),
   http://www.icis.com/cgi-bin/mt/
   mt-search.cgi?search=McKinsey&IncluldeBlogs=148&limit=20
7. Jacobides, M.G., Billinger, S.: Designing the boundaries of the firm: from "make, buy or ally" to the dynamic benefits of vertical architecture. Organization Science 17(2), 249–261 (2006)
8. King, D.: The Future of Industrial Biorefineries. World Economic Forum, Cologny/Geneva (2010)
9. Lorenz, P., et al.: Screening for novel enzymes for biocatalytic processes: accessing the metagenome as a resource of novel functional sequence space. Curr. Opin. Biotechnol. 13, 572–577 (2002)
10. Pisano, G.: Profiting from innovation and the intellectual property revolution. Research Policy 35, 1122–1130 (2006)
11. Pisano, G., Teece, D.: 'How to capture value from innovation: shaping intellectual property and industry architecture'. California Management Review 50(1), 278–296 (2007)
12. Simon, H.A.: The Science of the Artificial. MIT Press, Cambridge (1969)

Opportunistic and Dynamic Reconfiguration of Vehicle Routing Problem Controlled by the Intelligent Product

Rodrigue Tchapnga Takoudjou[1,2], Jean-Christophe Deschamps[1,2], and Rémy Dupas[1,2]

[1] Univ. Bordeaux, IMS, UMR 5218, F-33400 Talence, France
[2] CNRS, IMS, UMR 5218, F-33400 Talence, France
{rodrigue.tchapnga-takoudjou,Jean-Christophe.Deschamps,
remy.dupas}@ims.bordeaux.fr

Abstract. The recent development of information technologies and communications as well as the miniaturization always more pushed of mecatronic components has allowed the emergence of intelligent product paradigm. An intelligent product is an instrumented product which is able to store data, to perceive its environment and to participate in decisions about its own future. The intelligent product paradigm can be used as performance lever in several sectors of the supply chain: the production and manufacturing system, warehousing, reverse logistics, etc. However, few studies exist for the application of the intelligent product paradigm to transportation problem. In this paper, we propose a methodology based on the intelligent product paradigm as well as the transshipment with the aim to show how we can improve, and optimize the transport of products in the supply chain in static or dynamic context.

Keywords: Intelligent Product, Vehicle Routing Problem, Heuristics, Transshipment.

1 Introduction

The role of transport in the economy is not any more to demonstrate. It plays a significant role in the performance of the supply chain. Because of globalization, transportation has become a more and more complex operation and presents many challenges. Indeed, the diversification of supply sources, the emergence of the practices such as the cross-dock, as well as resources sharing in the transport raises problems of intermediate reloading, and of synchronization in the transport, etc.

Because of these new practices, besides the classic problem of optimization of the costs of the transport, new problems have appeared. We can mention the problem of traceability (break of the cold chain), the calculation of the carbon footprint of a product, the lack of synchronization between the physical flow and the informational flow of a product (the vehicle is tracked but not the product), the lack of anticipation and responsiveness of the transportation system following the occurrence of an event, etc.

To solve these problems, we propose two action levers. The first one whom we propose is the transshipment. It allows optimizing the cost of collection and

C. Emmanouilidis, M. Taisch, D. Kiritsis (Eds.): APMS 2012, Part II, IFIP AICT 398, pp. 608–613, 2013.

distribution of the product in terms of number of vehicles used and total travelled distances. The second is a distributed architecture for the control of the transportation system, based on the instrumentation of the product and of the transportation in general. The aim is to propose a new control system which ensures the flexibility, robustness of the transport, and which facilitates the alignment of the informational and the physical flow for a real-time control of the transport. The expected result by the combination of these two action levers is to guarantee an overall performance of the transport of products.

2   Related Work

The rapid development of new technologies and the miniaturization of mechatronic component have allowed the emergence of the intelligent products. A recent state of the art on intelligent product paradigm as well as on its various applications on the supply chain is proposed in [1]. Among the most notable work, we can mention: the steering of the workshop by the product [2], the improvement of the management of warehouses on the basis of the use of RFID technology [3], etc. Concerning the transport, few works exist on the active or passive participation of the product in the decisions relative to its transport. One of work published on the domain is the paper [4] in which authors propose solutions facilitating the interoperability in the transport within the framework of international projects.

Concerning the transshipment, it offers the possibility to deliver a product through two vehicles at least. For instance, one vehicle picks up a load at the supplier location, drops it at a transshipment point with short storage and another vehicle carries and delivers this load to the final destination. In [5] authors propose a heuristics to solve the pickup and delivery problem with time window and transshipment (PDPT). In the literature, to author's knowledge, there is no heuristics which allows solving the PDPT in real time in which the product is active in the process of decision which concerns its transport.

3   The Pickup and Delivery Problem with Transshipment

The principle of opportunistic transshipment provides the ability for the product to use more than one vehicle before being delivered to the customer. To illustrate the advantage to practice transshipment in transportation, we provide the following example: In figure 1, two vehicles are in charge of the collection and the delivery of four products. Product "J" is to be loaded at PJ and delivered at DJ ($1 \leq J \leq 4$). If transshipment is not allowed, to delivered all the products, vehicle 1 will follow the trajectory P1, P2, D1, D2 and vehicle 2 will follow the trajectory P3, P4, D4, D3. The total distance travelled by the two vehicles is 19. If transshipment is authorized, vehicle 1 will follow trajectory P3, P4, T, D1, D3 and vehicle 2 will follow the trajectory P1, P2, T, D2, D4. The total distance travelled by the two vehicles in this case is 16. In this solution after loading product 1 and product 2 at P1 and P2, product 1 is dropped by vehicle 1 at T. After loading product 3 and 4 at P3 and P4, product 4 is dropped by vehicle 2 at T. Then, vehicle 1 reloads product 4 at T and respectively delivery product 2(4) at D2 (D4). Vehicle 2 reload product 1 at T and respectively deliver 1(3) at D1 (D3). In conclusion, for the total distance travelled, transshipment yields net saving of 16 %.

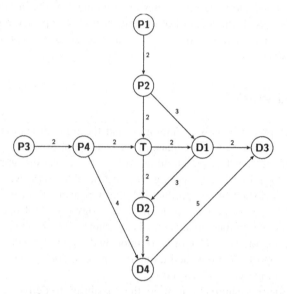

Fig. 1. Graphical representation of the problem (requests are represented by the dotted arcs)

To solve the PDPT in real time context, we have adapted the heuristic we have developed in [6] for the static case. The developed solving approach is used in a real time context; that is to say that the vehicles are moving on their routes to the customers. Position of each truck, its residual capacity and condition of products it carries are supposed to be precisely known. The overall visibility of the transportation situation allows in case of occurrence of a disturbance to quickly identify the consequence in terms of compliance of routing constraints. When a delay is observed, leading a vehicle to not respect all rendezvous with customers, the best suited vehicle is identified for recover the products of the vehicle which raise the disturbance. The real technical complexity of the proposed approach then lies in updating the graph which characterizes the transport network. Indeed, depending on the evolution of the transport situation, the customers whose demands are satisfied are removed from the graph, and the current position of the truck is considered as a new vertex of the graph. Due to lack of space, a detailed overview of the heuristic will be provided during the conference.

4   Instrumentation of the Transport

The instrumentation of the transport (figure 2) consists by means of the technology, to confer to every actor of the transport a degree of intelligence characterized by a set of properties such as memorization, perception of its environment, communication and the decision capacity. The main actors of the transport are the products (pallets and trailers), the tractor or lorry (in charge of moving trailers), customers and the transport operator that owns the vehicles fleet. To obtain in real time a permanent and continuous global vision of the transportation system, it is necessary to effectively trace and locate the products and the vehicles in real time. This supposes to have a continuous information flow issued from the product which can be described briefly in the following way: each product is tagged with an RFID chip. The chip integrates sensors and can store information. By this mechanism, the product becomes communicant. Information exchanges take place between products and a RFID reader placed in the trailer. The RFID reader in the trailer permanently scans information stored in the products. The Reader is connected to an embedded computer (smart phone) placed in the tractor cabin. The embedded terminal integrates a GPS chip to allow the localization of the vehicle and by deduction, the localization of the product. The information collected in real time by the computer is locally exploited by the vehicle to reconfigure its route, or there are sent by mobile phone to a decision maker. Once the instrumentation process of the product and of the transport has been described, we now propose a hybrid architecture that can support the distribution of the intelligence. To have a fine and global information of the situation of the transport, in addition to the instrumentation of the actors, there are two families (C1 and C2) of control points: C1 (with timestamp) - these points correspond to the visit by the truck of every customer of its route.   C2 (with variable location) - these points correspond to a periodic acquisition (by geo-localization) of the vehicle's position during its movement.

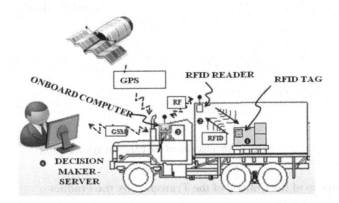

Fig. 2. The information chain

4.1   A Distributed and Decision Architecture for Transportation Systems

By considering this technical implementation, the proposed architecture of the transport system is hybrid (fig. 3). It combines the strengths of centralized and hierarchical control systems. Every product is tagged with an RFID chip which allows it to communicate with the truck which transports it. Each truck is equipped with an onboard computer in which are implemented the algorithms of calculations (heuristics and exact model) which allow the reconfiguration of its route due to the occurrence of a disturbance. Following the occurrence of a disturbance, the routes of vehicles situated in the perimeter of the disturbance are reconfigured. The reconfiguration is based on the transshipment and is made in the form of a dialogue and in a collective way between the concerned vehicles. The distribution of the algorithms of calculation towards vehicles is made in a concern of reactivity and efficiency. Indeed, the context of every disturbance is clearly establishes in real time and the precise and targeted actions are activated to bring a correction. However, this distribution of the calculation may result in a closed-optimal solution in term of cost (but not an optimal solution); what is not a handicap in the case of our application. If no action emerges from negotiations between vehicles, the server acts as an arbitrator and provides a solution (control).

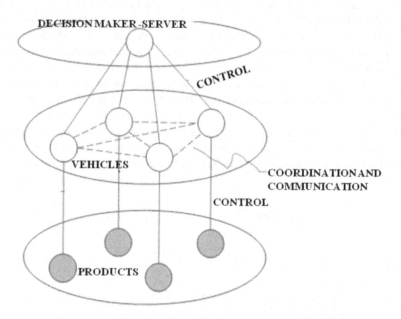

Fig. 3. Architecture of the transport system

4.2   Scenario of the Control of the Transport by the Product

A scenario of transport in which products as well as trucks are instrumented according to the process described in the previous section will be described here in the final version of the paper.

5   Conclusion

In this paper, we have worked on an opportunistic and dynamic reconfiguration of vehicle routing problem controlled by the Intelligent Product. We have showed how the global performance of the transport can be improved on several points:

- Reactivity - the disturbances are detected in real time, with a specific context. This property allows establishing an accurate correction through the distribution of intelligence between vehicles.
- Synchronization between the physical flow (the product) and the flow of information flow - the product being the carrier of its own information, this synchronization is achieved. The instrumentation of the transport such as recommended is a vector of improvement of performances in this domain.

In the following of this work, the solution proposed in a methodological way in this paper will be implemented and tested on a real case within the framework of a project[1].

Acknowledgments. This research has been supported by ANR under the grant VTT-PRODIGE (ANR-09-VTT-09-01) and is labeled by NOVALOG.

References

1. Meyer, G.G., Främling, K., Holmström, J.: Intelligent Products: A survey. Computers in Industry 60(3), 137–148 (2009)
2. McFarlane, D., et al.: Auto ID systems and intelligent manufacturing control. Engineering Applications of Artificial Intelligence 16(4), 365–376 (2003)
3. Xu, J., et al.: Comparing improvement strategies for inventory inaccuracy in a two-echelon supply chain. European Journal of Operational Research 221(1), 213–221 (2012)
4. Kärkkäinen, M., et al.: Intelligent products—a step towards a more effective project delivery chain. Computers in Industry 50(2), 141–151 (2003)
5. Mitrović-Minić, S., Laporte, G.: The pickup and delivery problem with time windows and transshipment. INFOR 44(3), 217–227 (2006)
6. Tchapnga, R., D.J.-C., Dupas, R.: An hybrid Multistart Heuristic for the Pickup and Delivery Problem with and without Transhipment. In: 9th International Conference of Modeling, Optimization and Simulation (MOSIM 2012), Bordeaux, France (2012)

---

[1] French project named PRODIGE (**ANR - VTT 2009**) funded by the French national research agency (ANR). http://anr-prodige.com/

Tactical and Operational Issues in a Hybrid MTO-MTS Production Environment: The Case of Food Production

Anita Romsdal[1], Emrah Arica[1], Jan Ola Strandhagen[2], and Heidi Carin Dreyer[1]

[1] Norwegian University of Science and Technology, Trondheim, Norway
{Anita.romsdal,heidi.c.dreyer}@sintef.no, emrah.arica@ntnu.no
[2] SINTEF Technology and Society, Trondheim, Norway
Jan.strandhagen@sintef.no

Abstract. Hybrid production environments that combine MTO and MTS strategies have emerged to enable production systems to better respond to changes in consumer and market demand. This paper discusses some of the tactical and operational production planning and control (PPC) issues involved in such hybrid production environments, using the food industry as an illustrative case. The discussion identifies MRP combined with WLC as a promising approach for incorporating MTO items into an MRP planning environment on the tactical and operational levels. Additional techniques are required to incorporate uncertainty and provide flexibility in this particular context and these should be further investigated taking different food supply chain characteristics into consideration.

Keywords: planning, control, hybrid, MTS, MTO, food.

1   Introduction

Food production is similar to process manufacturing, showing a higher complexity than discrete manufacturing (Crama et al., 2001). In addition to great attention to quality and food safety, food producers have traditionally focused on economies of scale to keep costs and prices down (van Donk et al., 2008, Verdouw and Wolfert, 2010). However, a production system as a whole should not only focus on costs but also show high flexibility in reacting to changing market conditions, fluctuating demand forecasts and actual demand (Bertrand et al., 1990). Over the past decades the food sector has therefore attempted to become more responsive by shifting from the traditional make-to-stock (MTS) approach towards applying more make-to-order (MTO) and combined MTO-MTS approaches (Crama et al., 2001, Soman et al., 2004).

The need for differentiating products and managing them differently is well recognised in literature (see e.g. Fisher, 1997, Christopher et al., 2006). However, such hybrid systems complicate the task of **production planning and control (PPC)** considerably since combining MTO and MTS in the same production system impacts on a number of tactical and operational issues and decisions - requiring companies to deal with complex trade-offs between inventory policies, number of set-ups, machine utilisation, production lead times, needs for cycle and safety stock, etc. (Soman et al.,

C. Emmanouilidis, M. Taisch, D. Kiritsis (Eds.): APMS 2012, Part II, IFIP AICT 398, pp. 614–621, 2013.
© IFIP International Federation for Information Processing 2013

2004). The purpose of this paper is therefore to **highlight and discuss some of the tactical and operational PPC issues and decisions involved in a hybrid production environment**. Particular emphasis is put on how to handle the demand uncertainty caused by the application of both MTS and MTO in the same production system.

The paper starts with a description of the study's research methodology, followed by an introduction to the empirical background. Next, PPC is defined, while the two subsequent chapters outline and discuss issues on the tactical and operational planning levels respectively. The conclusion outlines the paper's contributions and some suggestions for further research.

2   Methodology

This conceptual paper is a theoretical discussion of the tactical and operational implications of a concept involving hybrid MTO-MTS production approaches. Research on these more operational aspects of hybrid production situations is scarce since the majority of research focuses on a single type of production environment. The aim of the paper is therefore not to provide solutions to these highly complex issues, but rather to highlight and discuss some of the most critical decisions based on existing literature and the authors' experiences from industry.

The paper's theoretical base is within operations strategy, planning and control, and scheduling, and the discussion exploits and combines the advances of related production environments to provide new insights. The study focuses on the food sector as this is one of the sectors where hybrid production environments are becoming more common.

3   Food Sector Characteristics

Food supply chains deal with highly perishable goods, where rapid product and raw material deterioration significantly impacts on product quality and the amount of waste both within the supply chain and in consumer households. In addition, demand and price variability of food products is increasing, making food supply chains more complex and harder to manage than other supply chains (Ahumada and Villalobos, 2009). Food supply chain actors are faced with the challenge of supplying an ever broader variety of these perishable products to increasingly demanding customers, while at the same time moving products quickly through the supply chain and keeping costs as low as possible. Table 1 summarises some of the supply chain and logistics characteristics which are particular to the food sector.

Food production can be classified as a process industry where production of standard products is mainly continuous, with large production series, and raw materials and intermediates are accumulated and processed together in batches. The typical steps are receipt of inputs (raw materials, ingredients, packaging materials, etc.), processing, packing (where bulks are transformed to discrete products through sizing and labelling), and delivery. Typically there are three stock positions; raw materials, unpacked bulk products, and packed end products (Méndez and Cerdá, 2002, van Dam et al., 1993).

Table 1. Food supply chain characteristics (based on Romsdal et al., 2011)

Area	Characteristics
Product	• High perishability (raw materials, intermediate and finished products) • High and increasing product variety, particularly for promotions, decreasing product life cycle, high percentage of slow-moving items
Market	• Varying and increasing demand uncertainty, fairly predictable annual demand, high variation in periodic demand • Customers demand frequent deliveries and short response times
Supply	• Some supply uncertainty and variable raw material yield
Production system	• Capital-intensive technology, long set-up times, high set-up costs • Long production lead times, processes adapted to high volume, low variety, with raw materials and intermediates processed in batches

The characteristics in Table 1 show that there is increasing product variety and demand uncertainty in the food sector – which significantly increases the complexity of PPC for food producers. A **differentiation strategy** according to demand uncertainty has been suggested as a way to reduce this complexity. Kittipanya-ngam (2010) and Romsdal et al. (2012) suggest that the products that are the most difficult to plan and control should be given most focus in PPC. In this way, products with high demand uncertainty are within the "focus box" and controlled using an MTO strategy, while the remaining products are associated with an MTS strategy. This means that producers may find themselves in a situation where they need to **combine MTS and MTO approaches** within the same production system – thereby significantly complicating PPC on the tactical and operational level.

4   Introduction to Production Planning and Control (PPC)

Planning and control refers to the task of defining the structures and information upon which managers within a production system make effective decisions (Vollmann et al., 2005), and the design of the PPC system should be based on company- and industry-specific needs and characteristics (Stevenson et al., 2005).

At the highest planning level, the PPC approach is determined. The most common approaches include MTS, MTO, engineer-to-order (ETO), assemble-to-order (ATO) and mass customisation (MC). In the food sector, production systems are commonly classified as following either an MTS or an MTO strategy. In addition, ATO can be relevant in cases where the processing and packaging processes can be decoupled (Romsdal et al., 2012). However, in food processing, neither a pure MTO nor a pure MTS strategy is practical and food is therefore one of the sectors where a combined MTO-MTS approach is quite common.

At the strategic PPC level product families are formed in order to group items which can be planned and controlled using the same strategy. In addition, target service levels are set against which the performance of the production system is later evaluated. This level should also ensure that the operational capabilities meet the total load of aggregated demand for products and resources in the long run.

Operating a hybrid MTO-MTS approach brings about a number of issues involving complex trade-offs which must be thoroughly evaluated and incorporated into the lower PPC levels. The key issue is **how to deal with MTO items in the MTS schedule** – and some of the tactical and operational decision and alternative methods for dealing with these in hybrid production situations are discussed in the following chapters.

5   Tactical Level Issues

At the tactical level, the production volumes for MTS items are planned and the material planning is performed to determine the quantity and timing for components needed to produce these end-items. In a hybrid environment this level must also accommodate the uncertainty associated with the **quantity and timing** of future demand for MTO items into the material plans.

The literature contains several studies that discuss methods appropriate for tactical PPC decisions. Jonsson and Mattsson (2003) argue that the re-order point system, runout-time planning, and **material requirements planning (MRP)** methods seem to work well for making detailed materials planning decisions in an MTS environment with standardised product components produced in a batch production process. Further, they suggest a good match between MRP and the MTO environment. However, Stevenson et al. (2005) argue that MRP does not fully address the key decision support in an MTO environment since **capacity is not considered at the point of order/job entry and order release**. At the operational level, order acceptance and due date assignment are other key decisions in an MTO environment which must consider capacity. Based on the above requirements, **Workload Control (WLC)** can be appropriate since it ensures high due date adherence and considers capacity simultaneously. WLC uses a pre-shop pool of orders consisting of a series of short queues, where jobs are released if workload levels will not exceed pre-set maximum limits. Simultaneously, WLC ensures jobs do not stay in the pool too long, thereby reducing work in progress (WIP) and lead times (Stevenson et al., 2005).

However, before these methods can be applied in a hybrid MTO-MTS environment, the differences in the **production rates** in MTS and MTO environments need to be considered. The differentiation strategy described in chapter 3 is based on the majority of production being run using the MTS strategy (i.e. for products with low demand uncertainty), thus requiring a standardised method like MRP to reduce **operating costs**. In addition, MTO orders are received occasionally, requiring a focus on strict adherence to **specified due dates**. Based on this, a possible solution for the hybrid environment is to **combine the MRP method with WLC**. MRP can be used as the backbone of the system – but must be tailored and supported with some **additional techniques** so that the WLC method can be applied at the point of new MTO order entry.

In addition to the issue of dealing with MTO orders, **other potential disruptions** to schedules can occur which must be handled at the operational short-term level. Consequently, in order to ensure consistency between the tactical and operational levels, as well as to enable the combination of MRP and WLC methods, the tactical level must contain some approaches which consider such uncertainties and provide the required flexibility. Although some studies have been conducted on how to incorporate MTO products into an MTS planning environment (see e.g. Federgruen and Katalan, 1999, Soman et al., 2006), the studied approaches only considered a narrow selection of food supply chain characteristics. There is therefore a need to investigate a **broader set of techniques** that consider more of the food sector characteristics.

Different techniques exist to address uncertainties in different contexts. In general, supply chains can **buffer against uncertainty** using **inventory, capacity** and **time**. MTS environments use inventory and capacity as buffers – where safety stock is used to ensure availability when demand is greater than expected, while capacity allows for stock to be duly replenished. In MTO environments, customer orders cannot be delivered instantly and are therefore stored in the order book before they are released as production orders, thus spreading the demand variability out over time (Hedenstierna and Ng, 2011). **Safety lead time** to tackle uncertainty in timing can be a more appropriate technique than safety stocks when demand is stable (Buzacott and Shanthikumar, 1994), thus representing a useful approach for products with low perishability and low demand uncertainty. Further, **hedging** has been suggested as a useful technique for coping with internal uncertainties (Koh et al., 2002), thus representing a useful technique for products with internal error-prone characteristics such as cheese which requires maturation periods as part of the production process.

In summary, MRP in combination with WLC seems to be a promising approach for **material planning** – supported by additional techniques to accommodate uncertainties and provide flexibility. Before these techniques can be applied in practice, further investigation with regards to their ability to handle the characteristics of different product-market combinations and their interactions is needed.

6   Operational Level Issues

The operational level involves determining which product to produce next, when to produce, and how much to produce in the short term, e.g. week or day. The production orders are sequenced and scheduled on machines and other resources within the planning period, determining the set of production orders to be accomplished in the bottleneck, sequence of production orders, and production orders' run length and starting times (Soman et al., 2007).

Developing daily/weekly plans and schedules for production volumes, as well as sequencing orders on the shop floor, is not a substantially challenging task in a stable MTS environment. However, during the execution of the schedules, several types of customised orders for MTO products may be received in a hybrid production environment. Such changes may trigger the **rescheduling** of production orders and **revision of priorities** given to the shop (Jacobs, 2011).

Once required flexibility and uncertainties are accommodated at the intermediate tactical planning level, the **capacity-based WLC method** is an appropriate approach to fit MTO products into the operational schedule, while also incorporating the customer order entry level. At the point of customer order entry, the due date is set depending on the capacity status. This decision is applicable for products with long customer order lead time allowance and negotiable due dates. After the due date is known, the **order release date** is determined by deducting planned workstation lead time from the due date. Workstation lead time can be assumed stable in this highly controlled process-type environment. Depending on the existing and required workload for the new MTO order, the order is added to the sequence of MTS products being released in that period. If the **total workload exceeds the workstation load limit**, there are four available options. The preferred option is to move the order release date to the earlier periods, evaluating the available capacity until the present period. By this approach, the system nervousness and cost of rescheduling can be avoided. Products with low perishability and long customer order lead time allowances are good candidates for such forward scheduling. However, if the product perishability does not allow moving the order to earlier periods, there are three other options; to reschedule the pool of jobs at the point of order release with the aim of reducing setup costs, to increase capacity or to renegotiate the due date.

Orders are normally prioritized and sequenced according to their order release date. This is regarded as one of the advantages of WLC concepts as the performance of order release simplifies the shop floor dispatching process (Stevenson et al., 2005). However, in a food production environment this might lead to high sequence-dependant set up costs, and a sequencing rule that considers the trade-off between order priorities and set-up costs might thus generate considerable benefits.

In summary, we suggest that also at the operational level the combined MRP-WLC approach can improve the **effectiveness of schedules** in hybrid environments. The operational performance of the schedule can then be measured on its ability to meet due dates for MTO products, minimise time jobs spend in the process, reduce WIP inventory for MTS products, and minimise set-up costs and waste.

7   Conclusion

This paper has provided increased **understanding and knowledge** on the tactical and operational implications of hybrid production environments. A number of critical decisions and alternative approaches to balance the requirements of both MTS and MTO items were highlighted and discussed on a material and product level, and a combined MTS-WLC approach seems promising in addressing some of the issues. In terms of **contributions to practice**, the paper provided an overview of critical issues which companies must handle when designing PPC systems for such hybrid environments. However, **further studies** are required to investigate implications for planning and control on a resource level and how the MTS-WLC approach can be applied in practice. In addition, which PPC techniques that are appropriate for what degrees of perishability, demand uncertainty and customer order lead time allowances should be investigated. Relevant aspects to consider include differences in production lead times and maturation times, the point of variant explosion for different product families, and interdependencies between different products for instance in terms of set-up times and costs. The main **limitations** are related to the study's conceptual nature, and further research is required to investigate the appropriateness and applicability of the suggested approaches and techniques in practice.

Acknowledgements. This research was made possible by LogiNord (Sustainable Logistics in Nordic Fresh Food Supply Chains, supported by NordForsk) and SFI NORMAN (Norwegian Manufacturing Future, supported by the Research Council of Norway).

References

1. Ahumada, O., Villalobos, J.: Application of planning models in the agri-food supply chain: A review. European Journal of Operational Research 195, 1–20 (2009)
2. Bertrand, J.W.M., Wortmann, J.C., Wijngaard, J.: Production control: a structural and design oriented approach. Elsevier, Amsterdam (1990)
3. Buzacott, J., Shanthikumar, J.: Safety stock versus safety time in MRP controlled production systems. Management Science, 1678–1689 (1994)
4. Christopher, M., Peck, H., Towill, D.R.: A taxonomy for selecting global supply chain strategies. The International Journal of Logistics Management 17, 277–287 (2006)
5. Crama, Y., Pochet, Y., Wera, Y.: A discussion of production planning approaches in the process industry. In: Core Discussion Paper 2001/41. Center for Operations Research and Econometrics (CORE), Université catholique de Louvain (2001)
6. Federgruen, A., Katalan, Z.: The impact of adding a make-to-order item to a make-to-stock production system. Management Science, 980–994 (1999)
7. Fisher, M.L.: What is the right supply chain for your product? Harvard Business Review 75, 105 (1997)
8. Hedenstierna, P., Ng, A.H.C.: Dynamic implications of customer order decoupling point positioning. Journal of Manufacturing Technology Management 22, 1032–1042 (2011)
9. Jacobs, F.R.: Manufacturing planning and control for supply chain management. McGraw-Hill, New York (2011)
10. Jonsson, P., Mattsson, S.-A.: The implications of fit between planning environments and manufacturing planning and control methods. International Journal of Operations & Production Management 23, 872–900 (2003)
11. Kittipanya-Ngam, P.: Downstream food supply chain (FSC) in manufacturing firms: operating environment, firm's strategy, and configuration. PhD, University of Cambridge (2010)
12. Koh, S., Saad, S., Jones, M.: Uncertainty under MRP-planned manufacture: review and categorization. International Journal of Production Research 40, 2399–2421 (2002)
13. Méndez, C.A., Cerdá, J.: An MILP-based approach to the short-term scheduling of make-and-pack continuous production plants. OR Spectrum 24, 403–429 (2002)
14. Romsdal, A., Strandhagen, J.O., Dreyer, H.C.: Linking supply chain configuration with production strategy; the case of food production. In: 4th World P&OM Conference / 19th International Annual EurOMA Conference, Amsterdam (2012)
15. Romsdal, A., Thomassen, M.K., Dreyer, H.C., Strandhagen, J.O.: Fresh food supply chains; characteristics and supply chain requirements. In: 18th International Annual EurOMA Conference. Cambridge University, Cambridge (2011)

16. Soman, C.A., Pieter Van Donk, D., Gaalman, G.: Comparison of dynamic scheduling policies for hybrid make-to-order and make-to-stock production systems with stochastic demand. International Journal of Production Economics 104, 441–453 (2006)
17. Soman, C.A., Van Donk, D.P., Gaalman, G.: Combined make-to-order and make-to-stock in a food production system. International Journal of Production Economics 90, 223–235 (2004)
18. Soman, C.A., Van Donk, D.P., Gaalman, G.J.C.: Capacitated planning and scheduling for combined make-to-order and make-to-stock production in the food industry: An illustrative case study. International Journal of Production Economics 108, 191–199 (2007)
19. Stevenson, M., Hendry, L.C., Kingsman, B.G.: A review of production planning and control: the applicability of key concepts to the make-to-order industry. International Journal of Production Research 43, 869–898 (2005)
20. Van Dam, P., Gaalman, G., Sierksma, G.: Scheduling of packaging lines in the process industry: An empirical investigation. International Journal of Production Economics (30-31), 579–589 (1993)
21. Van Donk, D.P., Akkerman, R., Van Der Vaart, T.: Opportunities and realities of supply chain integration: the case of food manufacturers. British Food Journal 110, 218–235 (2008)
22. Verdouw, C.N., Wolfert, J.: Reference process modelling in demand-driven agri-food supply chains: a configuration-based framework. In: Trienekens, J., Top, J., Van Der Vorst, J., Beulens, A. (eds.) Towards Effective Food Chains; Models and Applications. Wageningen Academic Publishers, Wageningen (2010)
23. Vollmann, T.E., Berry, W.L., Whybark, D.C., Jacobs, F.R.: Manufacturing planning and control systems for supply chain management. McGraw-Hill, New York (2005)

A Note on the Simple Exponential Smooth Non-optimal Predictor, the Order-up-to Policy and How to Set a Proper Bullwhip Effect

Erland Hejn Nielsen

CORAL - Centre for Operations Research Applications in Logistics,
Aarhus University, Business and Social Sciences,
Department of Economics and Business,
Fuglesangs Allé 4, DK-8210 Aarhus V, Denmark
ehn@asb.dk
http://au.dk/en/ehn@asb.dk

Abstract. The literature concerning the bullwhip effect is mostly focused on determining expressions for the theoretical bullwhip measure given specific theoretical system setups, whereas it must also be of interest to deal with the problem of how in fact to make a proper choice as to a sensible bullwhip level. Such a management approach to the bullwhip phenomenon has to be of quite some importance, as the bullwhip effect on the one side definitely is a system malfunction, but on the other also an effect the size of which common intuition tells us should be possible to control. The control is based on a decision as to what variation in demand should be locally absorbed and what variation should be passed on upstream. This paper will focus on design aspects of a bullwhip control policy in order to decide on sensible trade-offs between the bullwhip level and the local inventory variability.

Keywords: The bullwhip effect, inventory variance, non-stationary demand, unobserved parameters.

1 Introduction

When digging down into the vast body of literature dealing with the bullwhip effect, it seems quite possible to get a fairly good understanding of the phenomenon on the generic level, but when it comes to the actual managerial choice of an appropriate bullwhip value, the story seems to be less decisive leaving us with an undetermined trade-off between the variation in demand that is absorbed locally into the inventory and the variation in demand that is propagated upstream in the supply chain. Somehow, such trade-off has always been at the core topic when dealing with standard production and inventory control [7] under the headings of production smoothing or production leveling. The role of forecasting in much classical production and inventory theory is often a combined one in that the forecasting mechanism also handles the production smoothing upstream. The simple exponential smoothing mechanism is one of the most popular schemes in

C. Emmanouilidis, M. Taisch, D. Kiritsis (Eds.): APMS 2012, Part II, IFIP AICT 398, pp. 622–629, 2013.

that respect and the smoothing coefficient is by experience recommended to be held within the interval 0.1 to 0.3 typically.

Any supply chain collaboration or coordination aims at balancing production smoothing with inventory control at each tier. A basic intuition tells us that the less smoothing locally the more variation is sent upstream the supply chain. So which are the controlling handles when talking about the bullwhip effect, and how should these handles be set? And do we really have this inverse relation between variation absorbed locally and variation exported upstream?

Let us consider as a starting point the discussion given by Stephen C. Graves [5], where he develops the bullwhip formula $BW = (1 + (1 - \theta)L)^2$ derived conditionally on the optimal predictor given that the demand DGP (Data Generating Process) is IMA(1,1). The optimal predictor in this case is the simple exponential smooth mechanism with the smoothing coefficient $\alpha = 1 - \theta$. In the Graves setup we are then left with the parameters θ and L, both of which are not really controllable in the short run, but given by the structure of the supply chain.

If we want to get access to the non-optimal exponential smoothing coefficient values, we need to consider bullwhip measures unconditionally. However, the unconditional variance of a non-stationary variate, as for instance a random walk (IMA(1,1) where $\theta = 0$), is infinite.

We therefore have to redefine the bullwhip measure in this case to be focused only on the amplifying signal effect on top of the (stochastic) trend movements. The traditional way to eliminate the (stochastic) trend in the classical ARIMA [1] approach is to consider the differenced data instead.

Henceforth, the bullwhip measure that will be used is then defined as

$$BW = \frac{Var(\Delta q)}{Var(\Delta D)} \tag{1}$$

where q denotes the upstream ordering and D is the demand.

The paper will be organized in the following way: In section 2 the simulation model used in this work is described and commented upon. Section 3 is devoted to mapping out the bullwhip measure as well as the inventory variation effect as a function of the simple exponential smoothing factor. Section 4 is dealing with the trade-off between absorbing demand variation in the local tier inventory and passing the variation upstream as bullwhip. Finally, section 5 presents a few concluding remarks.

2   The Supply Chain Simulation Model

The model used in order to simulate the actual bullwhip values follows tradition. Customer demand as seen by the retailer is assumed to be well described by a non-stationary time series model of the ARIMA(0,1,1) type process

$$\Delta D_t = \varepsilon_t - \theta \cdot \varepsilon_{t-1} \quad \text{where} \quad \varepsilon_t \sim \text{i.i.d. } N(0, \sigma_\varepsilon^2) \tag{2}$$

This process is covariance stationary for any value of θ, however, the MA(1)-part of the model is only invertible for values of the parameter θ between -1 and 1. Whenever $\theta=0$, the IMA(1,1) alias ARIMA(0,1,1) is equivalent to the dynamic process which is normally denoted "a random walk". As we are facing a delivery lead time L typically of a non-negligible magnitude, it is necessary to have a sound idea of the cumulative amount of demand that potentially could be executed during such a period. A measure y_t of such a lead time demand could be formalized as follows

$$\hat{D}_t(1) = \hat{D}_{t+1} = S_t = \alpha \cdot D_t + (1 - \alpha) \cdot S_{t-1}$$
$$\hat{D}_t(L) = L \cdot \hat{D}_t(1)$$

$$\hat{\sigma}_{et}^2(L) = \hat{\sigma}_\varepsilon^2 \cdot \left\{ 1 + (L - 1) \cdot \alpha^2 \right\}$$
$$y_t = \hat{D}_t(L) + z \cdot \hat{\sigma}_{et}^L$$

$$(3)$$

where $-1 < \theta < 1$ and $0 \le \alpha \le 1$. This setup represents the optimal predictor setup if $\alpha = 1 - \theta$, in terms of minimum mean square error forecast, for the IMA(1,1) process and the z-value (≥ 0) controls to some extent the "worst case" dependence as a function of the variance of the stochastic innovations of the IMA(1,1) demand process induced on the cumulative future demand.

The determination of the size and timing of orders q_t that are placed by the retailer upstream at the manufacturer can be controlled by a variety of ordering mechanisms [4], however, if we assume an order-up-to "base-stock"-policy as is often encountered in the literature (see for instance [2][3][5]) and which are basically of a make-to-order nature, q_t can be expressed as follows

$$q_t = y_t - y_{t-1} + D_t \tag{4}$$

Inventory is then simply a matter of elementary "stock-flow" bookkeeping

$$I_t = I_{t-1} - D_t + q_{t-L} \tag{5}$$

The simulation setup is a periodic time setup and 50,000 time steps (approx. steady-state) are being simulated for each combination of $\alpha = 0$ to 1 in steps by 0.02 and $\theta = 0$ to 0.9 in steps by 0.1. The optimal predictor situations $\alpha = 1 - \theta$ are singled out specifically. Demand is simulated with $D(init) = 0$ and error term Std.dev=10 and afterwards level shifted in order to be exactly non-negative. Inventory is also controlled for non-negativity. $I(init) = 5,000$ seems to do the job. z is set equal to zero throughout this paper. The actual computations are programmed and performed in the Gnu-R statistical system[6].

3   Mapping Out the Bullwhip and Inventory Variance Effect

The variance components that will be dealt with in this section are $Var(\Delta D)$, $Var(\Delta q)$ and $Var(I)$. In order for these computations to be meaningful ΔD,

Δq and I all have to be covariance stationary. ΔD complies by construction, whereas Δq and I are checked manually. For $\alpha = 0$ the inventory dynamics are defined by $I_t = I_{t-1} - D_t + D_{t-L}$ and here it seems that non-stationarity takes over resulting in $Var(I)$ approaching infinity. For $\alpha = 0$ the bullwhip effect is trivially neutral, that is $BW = 1$. However, the full BW-map turns out as follows.

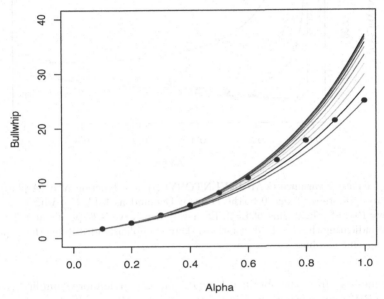

Fig. 1. Bullwhip measures as a function of α (Alpha) given $\theta = 0$ to 1 in steps of size 0.1 (the curves); Demand as IMA(1,1) with error term Std.Dev=10 and a lead time of L=3. Each bullwhip curve is θ-specific and the curve dots are indicating the $\alpha = 1 - \theta$ situations, thereby implicitly identifying the respective curves' specific θ value.

The message from the obtained BW-map is fairly simple. Irrespective the actual state of the DGP for the demand and a fixed lead time L, a smaller value of α results in a smaller bullwhip effect. Furthermore, deviations from the optimal predictor setting are almost of no consequence for small α values ($\alpha \le 0.5$) and of some consequence otherwise. This is definitely interesting from a production leveling perspective. It can furthermore be noted that the curvature of the BW-curves based on the first time differenced data is the same as the Graves ([5]) BW measure. The Graves BW measure is, however, consistently lower having a value of 16 instead of 25 for $\alpha = 1$ and $\theta = 0$. This is not surprising in that the stochasticity that works through the simple exponential smoothing mechanism has been taken completely out in the Graves setup due to the conditioning.

So being able to control the bullwhip effect by the simple exponential smoothing factor, the mirror effect on the local inventory dynamics has to be observed. The full $Var(I)$-map turns out as follows:

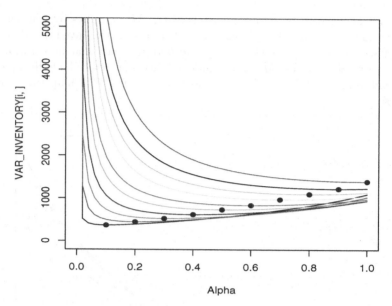

Fig. 2. Inventory variance (VAR-INVENTORY(i,)) as a function of α (Alpha) given $\theta = 0$ to 1 in steps of size 0.1 (the curves); Demand as IMA(1,1) with error term Std.Dev=10 and a lead time of L=3. Each variance curve is θ-specific and the curve dots are indicating the $\alpha = 1-\theta$ situations, thereby implicitly identifying the respective curves' specific θ value.

The message from the obtained $Var(I)$-map is a little more complicated than for the BW-map in that choosing a too low α easily results in an extremely large inventory variance implying that the local inventory is virtually out of control. Take as an example the top curve on the $Var(I)$-map with the dot corresponding to $\alpha = 1$ and thereby identifying the $\theta = 0$ curve. In this case the demand is a pure random walk and the optimal one-step-ahead predictor is the so-called naïve forecast. Even if demand is characterized by a stochastic trend, it is quite impossible to even predict whether demand goes up or down in the next period. The inventory variance is contrary to the BW measure dependent on both scale and level of noise of the demand process. In the analyzed case the optimal predictor situation implies an inventory variance of approximately 1,300, that is a standard deviation of ±36 units. If in this case we decided to choose a non-optimal but lower value of α for example 0.5, the resulting inventory variance would be approximately 1,700, that is a standard deviation of around ±41 units. Maybe not so drastic an increase, but if α is decreased to 0.3, the variance increases to 2,200, which then is a standard deviation of around ±47 units. And finally if α is decreased to 0.1, the variance increases to 5,200, which then is a standard deviation of around ±72 units. Compared to the standard deviation on demand ±10 units it is quite impressive though.

The above given example constitutes the worst case situation, but if we now turn our reasoning around and assume that we are not quite sure of the actual θ value and tend to go for a production smoothing value of α say 0.2, then we may expect the inventory variance to be somewhere between 500 and 3000, translated into standard deviations between 22 and 55. Moving up to $\alpha = 0.5$, the standard deviations must be expected to lie between 24 and 45, which is quite a reduction in the uncertainty range. On the other hand going from $\alpha = 0.2$ to $\alpha = 0.5$ the bullwhip changes from being within the interval $[2.6; 2.8]$ to being within the interval $[7.0; 8.5]$.

If we know the actual θ value from the demand DGP, we can observe that an optimal choice of $\alpha = 1 - \theta$ simply results in the minimal obtainable local inventory variance. This is quite a nice property, but it implies that the optimal prediction setup in the present case simply chooses a BW effect that is based on a maximum transference of upstream variability. This is maybe not so nice a property if the BW effect really hurts upstream. Anyway, it will clearly depend on specific trade-off considerations in given situations.

4   How to Set a Proper Bullwhip Effect

In order to decide about the choice of a "proper" bullwhip effect, here given the system's "malfunctioning" with respect to ordering, there are obviously two very different situations. One where the demand DGP parameters have been determined successfully and one where the actual parameter settings are unknown, but only known to be an IMA(1,1) structure.

The figure below is constructed based on the observation that α and BW are almost one-to-one at least for α values below 0.5. For α values above 0.5 a midpoint BW value is used.

The curves "UB Std.Dev(I)" and "LB Std.Dev(I)" represent the decision information where θ is unknown, whereas if θ is known, the "OPT Std.Dev(I)" curve represents the decision information.

Clearly, in the case of a known θ there is not much of a trade-off, but approximatively a one-to-one strictly increasing relationship between BW and $Var(I)$. But then again, there is not much of a managerial choice present in this situation.

More interesting is the situation where only the structural form is known, but none of its parameters. It must, however, be remembered that besides not knowing θ we then also do not know the size of the error of the innovation term of the demand DGP, and so any reasoning based on figure 3 is clearly only indicative as it is simulated based on a specific error term Std.Dev=10.

Nevertheless, we now have a trade-off situation with respect to the "UB Std.Dev(I)". In a worst case sense the trade-off along this curve represents a lower expected inventory variance traded against a higher BW effect and vice versa.

But maybe an interpretation that connects the range of uncertainty, to a choice of a BW effect is the really interesting angle on the subject of setting a proper BW effect. Small BW values correspond well to small α settings, but leave the local inventory with a huge uncertainty as to the actual dynamic

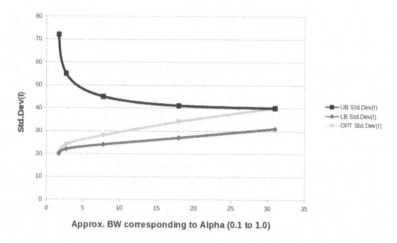

Fig. 3. BW against Std.Dev(I)-ranges.

variability. This uncertainty effect is certainly narrowed down for increasing BW values.

The question is now really - how do we value risk with respect to local inventory variance against upstream exported and amplified demand variation as expressed by the dynamics of the ordering? Clearly, this is closely related to the worst case ("UB Std.Dev(I)") trade-off against BW, but the risk element focuses more clearly on the element of gambling that is virtually always present.

5   Concluding Remarks

It is quite obvious that this work has not really given a complete answer to the posed question of how to set a proper BW effect. Still a few moments to remember have come by in that just following classical production and inventory control wisdom and setting the smoothing factor low, somewhere between 0.1 and 0.3, might be a risky business for the local inventory even if it produces a small BW effect upstream. If it was the bullwhip effect alone, α should trivially be set to zero. Now if θ is known and is low, which means that the demand process is closer to a pure random walk, then a non-optimal low α choice is really bad. We are then simply close to the "UB Std.Dev(I)" curve values. Pressing α towards zero in this situation makes things even worse in that the inventory variance goes towards infinity. So, at last and no surprise, the concrete choice of upstream bullwhip effect does in the end depend on precisely how costly unforeseen inventory and/or production activity variation is at the individual tiers in the supply chain. But the intuition that somehow there must always be a negative trade-off between the variance absorbed locally and the variance transferred up-stream seems also to be supported in the specific case studied, where demand is non-stationary and the order mechanism is of the order-up-to type, at least viewed from a certain perspective.

Acknowledgment. Initial draft versions of this work have been supported by grant no. 275-07-0094 from the Danish Social Science Research Council.

References

1. Box, G., Jenkins, G.: Time series analysis: Forecasting and control. Holden-Day, San Francisco (1970)
2. Chen, F., Drezner, Z., Ryan, J.K., Simchi-Levy, D.: Quantifying the Bullwhip Effect in a Simple Supply Chain: The Impact of Forecasting, Lead Times, and Information. J. Management Science 46(3), 346–443 (2000)
3. Chen, F., Ryan, J.K., Simchi-Levy, D.: The impact of exponential smoothing forecasts on the Bullwhip Effect. J. Naval Research Logistics 47, 269–286 (2000)
4. Disney, S.M., Lambrecht, M.R.: On Replenishment Rules, Forecasting and the Bullwhip Effect in Supply Chains. Foundations and Trends in Technology, Information and Operations Management 2(1), 1–80 (2007)
5. Graves, S.C.: A Single-Item Inventory Model for a Nonstationary Demand Process. J. Manufacturing & Service Operation Management 1(1), 50–61 (1999)
6. The, R.: Project for Statistical Computing, http://www.r-project.org/
7. Silver, E.A., Pyke, D.F., Peterson, R.: Inventory Management and Production Planning and Scheduling. John Wiley & Sons, Inc., New York (1998)

One-of-a-Kind Production (OKP) Planning and Control: An Empirical Framework for the Special Purpose Machines Industry

Federico Adrodegari[1], Andrea Bacchetti[1], Alessandro Sicco[1], Fabiana Pirola[2], and Roberto Pinto[2]

[1] Department of Mechanical and Industrial Engineering, University of Brescia, Italy
{federico.adrodegari,andrea.bacchetti}@ing.unibs.it,
a.sicco@csmt.it
[2] CELS - Department of Industrial Engineering, University of Bergamo, Italy
{fabiana.pirola,roberto.pinto}@unibg.it

Abstract. In this paper, we focus on the One-of-a-Kind Production (OKP) industry, where each product is designed and manufactured based on specific customer requirements to a large extent, according to an Engineer To Order (ETO) approach. This research has been carried out among the "SIGI-X" project, funded by the Italian Ministry of Economic Development (MISE). The paper illustrates an empirical study on the state-of-the-art of information systems supporting the leading processes in OKP companies. Through a set of 21 case studies in Italian companies producing special machines, we aim to: identify and investigate strengths and weaknesses of the main OKP business processes; analyze the ICT support and its level of integration among the different ICT solutions; identify levers for improvement, concerning organizational, methodological and informatics aspects; build a practical framework that could define and link the main processes in order to obtain a sort of guideline useful for re-engineering the processes, and laying the foundation for a new integrated ICT business template for OKP companies. The lack of support of three fundamental tasks such as project management, planning and cost control underlines that there is substantial room for improvement under the ICT support perspective. Finally, the development of an integrated IT environment to support (in particular) project management and planning activities, specifically addressed to OKP context, would help these companies to improve their performance and competitiveness.

Keywords: One-of-a-Kind Production (OKP), Engineer To Order (ETO), Special Purpose Machines Industry, Production Planning & Control (PPC).

1 Introduction

One-of-a-Kind Production (OKP) industry is characterized by a low level of repetitiveness, and each product is designed and manufactured based on customer requirements [1]. Adopting the OKP model, companies usually have to adapt managerial

C. Emmanouilidis, M. Taisch, D. Kiritsis (Eds.): APMS 2012, Part II, IFIP AICT 398, pp. 630–637, 2013.

paradigms, business models and ICT supporting tools developed for other (i.e. the repetitive) sectors. Especially from the ICT standpoint, the adaptation of existent tools leads too often to stand-alone applications and a low level of integration among different software, weakly supporting the business objectives.

In OKP environments an effective management of industrial processes, along with an efficient ICT support, may ease companies in optimizing project lead times, minimizing costs and gaining competitive advantage. For these reasons, the main aims of this paper are:

i.   to identify and investigate strengths and weakness of the main OKP business processes;
ii.   to analyse the ICT support, the level of integration among the different ICT solutions adopted and the ICT functionalities required;
iii. to build a framework that could define and link the main processes in order to obtain a guideline useful for re-engineering the processes and laying the foundation for a new integrated ICT business template for OKP companies;
iv.   to carry out a list of functionalities pertaining to the framework's distinct tasks (since one of the final aims of this research is the development of an integrated IT business solution supporting OKP companies).

In order to achieve these objectives, we carried out an empirical research in a number of leading firms in the special purpose machine sector, in which Italy is the fourth producers in the world (7,353 million euro, representing the 7.6% of the worldwide production), after China, Japan and Germany [2].

The paper structure is the following. In section two are depicted the research questions and the adopted methodology, while section three describes the main findings from the empirical research and the practical framework carried out. Conclusive remarks and directions for future research are drawn in section four.

2   Research Objectives and Methodology

The results presented in the next Section 3 of this paper are based on a *multiple case studies* empirical research, a form of quali-quantitative descriptive research that refers to the collection and presentation of detailed information about a group of companies, drawing conclusions about that group in a specific context [3]. These case studies provide an empirical body of knowledge about the state-of-the-art of information systems supporting the leading processes in OKP companies. According to the purposes of our research, the main research questions have been stated as follows:

- What are the typical OKP companies' values activities (*core activities*)?
- Which are the more and less supported ICT functionalities? What kind of ICT support is used?
- Which are the functionalities that are perceived by the companies as more critical?
- Which are the less supported processes, both in terms of managerial policies and ICT support?

Our case-study approach is based on purposive sampling rather than random sampling (see, for example, [4]). In particular, to select the companies, we adopted the judgmental sampling technique, belonging to nonprobability sampling methods that are used for many research projects and are appropriate in case of limited resources and inability to identify exactly the population members [5]. Furthermore, nonprobability sampling may be a practical choice in exploratory research, where the aim of the research is to establish whether a problem exists or not [5]. According to this technique, in our work the sample was based on the researchers' experience, knowledge of the sector and available data, considering the relevance of this kind of companies in Italy in terms of presence on the territory, the overall turnover and employment level, as well as the peaks of excellence reached by many of them in various specific sectors.

In total, 21 companies were included in the sample. Figure 1 classifies sample companies based on the number of employees and the yearly turnover. As mentioned above, these companies mainly belong to the special purpose machines industry, from CNC machine center to customized food packaging machines and automatic assembly line design and manufacturing. This information has been collected by submitting a preliminary questionnaire to these firms, concerning general information about industry, products manufactured, turnover, number of employees, and amount of investments in information and communication technology (ICT). Hence, other specific data were gathered through structured interviews until the achievement of theoretical saturation. The interviews were directed, in first instance, to the entrepreneur and, when present, to project managers and/or CIO. Whenever necessary, other managers of specific areas, such as production, logistics and purchasing were involved in the interviews. In addition, observations at the target companies and informal discussions with engineers were used to gather data, as suggested by Glesne and Peshkin [6]. Finally, the data collected through the interviews allowed to perform some cross-case analyses related to the investigated issues and reported in the remaining of the article.

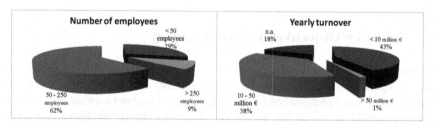

Fig. 1. Classification of target companies based on employees and turnover

3   Main Findings

3.1   Results from the Empirical Research

The analysis of the outcomes of the structured interviews is briefly summarized in this paragraph. Based on Porter's value chain [7], we classified the core activities performed by an OKP-based company into *primary* and *support activities*. Thus, we defined "quotation and order management", "technical and commercial development", "design", "purchasing", "production, assembly and testing", "delivery", "commissioning", and "after-sales service" as primary activities, and "project management", "planning", and "cost control" as support activities.

The objective of the interviews has been to analyze whether the activities are structured and governed by procedures and rules inside the companies, and to investigate their ICT support. Thus, for each of the above mentioned activities, Figure 2 shows the percentage of companies that formalizes it, while Figure 3 reports the percentage of companies that support it through the ERP system or an ERP integrated application, and through stand alone applications.

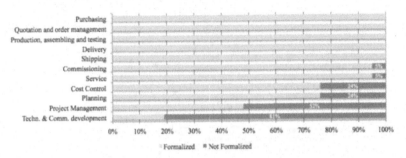

Fig. 2. Formalization level of primary and support activities

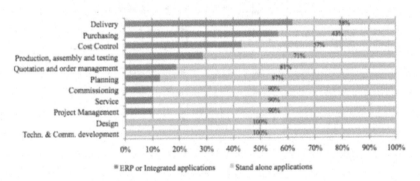

Fig. 3. ICT support of primary and support activities

Figure 2 and Figure 3 show that the primary activities are properly structured and governed by procedures and rules, and appropriately supported by ICT tools. On the contrary, the results highlight that three fundamental supporting processes ("project management", "planning" and "cost control") are not well formalized. This suggests room for improvements because these processes may be considered the core of project-based enterprises, since the high customization results in frequent changes of product design, process planning and production routines [8] and resource usage has to be carefully handled and monitored.

In addition, the interviews highlighted a scarce use and knowledge inside companies of methods to carry out project management, planning and cost control; these kinds of activities are usually driven by people expertise (generally managed by the company owner), and an on-going monitoring of order status is often missing.

3.2   The Proposed Framework and Functionalities

With the aim at supporting the development of processes and tools to fill the main gaps highlighted in the previous section, we devised a general, ideal process framework. Such a framework, graphically summarized in Figure 4, encompasses all the tasks supporting the activities described in Figure 2 and Figure 3, resulted as the most critical and less formalized for the involved sample of OKP companies. The support activities are further intertwined with other activities in an ideal flow from the request for proposal to the cost management.

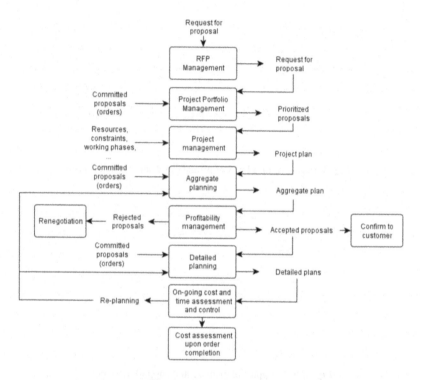

Fig. 4. Process framework

Upon the receipt of a request for proposal (RFP) from a customer, the OKP company evaluates it in order to analyse its technical feasibility, and to come up with an economic offer and an internal priority index (*RFP management*). This index allows defining the priority of each RFP in comparison with other, already committed orders, based on parameters such as the requested delivery date, the relevance of the customer, the resource requirements, the degree of similarity with other orders, and so forth. The priority index also defines the accessibility precedence to scarce resources. After this activity (also referred to as *project portfolio management*), each prioritized RFP passes to a project manager, who elaborates a project plan defining all the activities required to realize the final product, and their sequences (*project management*).

Each RFP is evaluated independently, considering the production system as empty and all the resources immediately available. In this way, the theoretical amount of resources required to realize each proposal is determined, as well as the hypothetical duration and the delivery date.

All the activities performed so far refer to RFP, and not to committed orders. Up to this point, the RFP is not yet confirmed to the customer. The subsequent step in the framework (*aggregate planning*) consists in the integration of the RFP with the already committed orders, in order to evaluate the impact of the new, potential order on the production system. Therefore, the main aim of this step is to generate an aggregate plan that incorporates the committed orders and the RFPs, considering the priority indexes, the advancement status of existing orders, the resources availability and so forth. Only after this step it is possible to evaluate and assess the impact of the RFP on the company's system through a *profitability management* step. The company can now decide whether to accept the RFP (that becomes a committed order) giving the confirmation to the customer, or reject it and return to a negotiation stage with the customer in order to change RFP's parameters such as the general requirements or the delivery date.

Once the RFP has become a committed order, it is possible to process the information at a higher detail level, performing a *detailed planning* that schedules the activities of the different phases of the whole order fulfilment process (from the design phase until delivery and commissioning) in order to drive the activities in the short-medium term. The detailed plans are then passed to each phase manager, and the *on-going cost and time assessment and control* activity is continuously performed until the product delivery to customer. This on-going monitoring can highlight the need of a re-planning, either at an aggregate or at a detailed level, which can be a consequence of internal or external time deviations or requirement changes. After the product delivery to customer, the *cost assessment after order completion* is carried out to monitor internal order performance.

Since one of the aims of this research is the development of an integrated IT business solution supporting OKP companies in dealing with multi-project management, activity planning and cost control, we firstly validated this framework with the sample companies and, then, we identified a list of IT functionalities pertaining to the framework's distinct tasks (listed in Table 1). For the sake of completeness we added also the functionalities related to cost control system setup, namely the initial definition of budget items, cost items, allocation drivers and KPI.

4   Conclusions and Further Development

Only in recent years, with the affirmation of the mass customization concept, we are assisting to a growing concern (or for some aspects, to a renovate level of interest) for the OKP model, that otherwise can count on a paucity of managerial paradigms if compared to the mass production environment.

In our research, we recognize activities (as defined in [7]) and ICT support as the pivotal elements around which the companies performance are built: therefore, we discussed the results of a multiple case studies empirical research carried out on 21

Italian companies operating in the special purpose machinery industry aiming at highlighting weaknesses and potential actionable points to improve SMEs results.

As the discussion pointed out, the lack of support of three fundamental tasks such as project management, planning and cost control underlines that there is substantial room for improvement under the ICT support perspective, where entry level solutions seems still far from compliance with OKP operations requirements, and high-end ERP solutions are out of the budget from many SMEs.

Table 1. IT functionalities

IT Functionalities			
Cost setup	Budget item definition Allocation driver definition Definition of cost items and KPI	Detailed planning	Order phases, time, constraints definition Resources assignment to activities Available capacity definition Order phases scheduling (finite capacity) Multiple detailed planning scenarios evaluation Resources loading visualization Final order activities plan visualization
RFP mngt	Budget calculation What-if analysis		
PPM	Priority criteria definition Project priority definition		
Project management	Definition of order phases and constraints Definition of time, macro-resources and responsibility Single order phases planning (considering an empty system) Risk management Order plan sharing	On-going cost and time assessment control	Check order progress Man and machine hours gathering Costs assignment to man and machine hours Costs allocation based on drivers Cost deviations calculation and analysis per single order Time deviations calculation and analysis per single order Deviations resolution suggestion Order plan adjustment Reporting (indicators)
Aggregate planning	Available capacity definition Order phases planning (finite capacity) Multiple aggregate planning scenarios evaluation Resources loading visualization Orders' plan sharing Orders' plan visualization Re-planning	Final assessment	Final cost and time deviations calculation and analysis per single order

As a result, many activities are still performed in inconsistent ways, using different ICT supporting tools (implying data redundancy and misalignment) or even manually. The development of an integrated IT environment to support (in particular) project management and planning activities, specifically addressed to OKP companies, would help these companies to improve their performance and competitiveness.

This is the reason why we developed a practical process framework that encompasses all the tasks supporting the activities resulted as the most critical and less formalized for the involved sample of OKP companies. We firstly validated this framework with the sample companies and, then, we identified a list of IT functionalities pertaining to the framework's distinct tasks.

Furthermore, besides the definition of these functionalities, one of the main contributes of this research will be the identification of methods to perform the processes under investigation in an effective way. After a scouting of literature related to project management, planning and cost control, we will come up with a list of techniques suitable to support OKP companies in their order management. Since the aim of this research is to identify methods that can be accepted and implemented by companies, the whole literature review and the final selection will be carried out considering the trade-off between adaptability to the specific context and complexity, in terms of formulation, calculation, and software requirements.

The final step of the research will be the development of an integrated IT business solution supporting OKP companies in dealing with multi-project management, planning and cost control.

Acknowledgements. The study published in this paper has been carried out among the "SIGI-X" project, funded by the Italian Ministry of Economic Development (MISE) under the "Industria2015" framework, project # M101_00015.

This work does not represent the view of the Ministry or of the "SIGI-X" consortium, and authors are solely responsible for the paper's content.

References

1. Hong, G., Xue, D., Tu, Y.: Rapid identification of the optimal product configuration and its parameters based on customer-centric product modeling for one-of-a-kind production. Computers in Industry 61(3), 270–279 (2010)
2. UCIMU: Sector report (2010) (in Italian)
3. Yin, R.K.: Case Study Research—Design and Methods, Sage, London, UK (1990)
4. Hameri, A.-P., Nihtilä, J.: Product data management-exploratory study on state-of-the-art in one-of-a-kind industry. Computers in Industry 35(3), 195–206 (1998)
5. Henry, G.T.: Practical Sampling, Sage Publications, Inc. (1990)
6. Glesne, C., Peshkin, A.: Becoming qualitative researchers. Longman, New York (1992)
7. Porter, M.: Competitive Advantage: Creating and Sustaining Superior Performance. Free Press, New York (1985)
8. Tu, Y., Dean, P.: One-of-a-kind Production. Springer, London (2011)

A Basic Study on Highly Distributed Production Scheduling

Eiji Morinaga, Eiji Arai, and Hidefumi Wakamatsu

Division of Materials and Manufacturing Science, Osaka University
{morinaga,arai,wakamatu}@mapse.eng.osaka-u.ac.jp

Abstract. Recent manufacturing systems are required to be flexible to cope with variable situation. This requirement has driven development of distributed methods of production simulation and scheduling. Recent advances in computer network technology is achieving *highly distributed manufacturing systems (HDMSs)* where each facility is computerized and manages itself autonomously by communicating with other facilities. A distributed simulation method for HDMSs was proposed. To take the full advantage of this method, scheduling problem should be also discussed. Conventional distributed scheduling methods would be inappropriate for HDMSs, since some elements perform processes for information integration and decision making and are therefore subject to heavy computational load when those methods are applied to HDMSs. This paper proposes a distributed scheduling method based on a dispatching rule where the processes for decision making are not performed by any elements but indirectly by a communication protocol.

Keywords: highly distributed manufacturing systems, distributed production scheduling, dispatching rules, agile manufacturing.

1 Introduction

Production scheduling is a key issue in realizing sophisticated manufacturing system management/operation, which is indispensable to achieve competitive manufacturing. Numerous studies have been conducted in this area for a long time in various approaches such as mathematical programming formulation[1,2], artificial intelligence[3,4], Petri nets[5] and so on. In these activities, the mainstream has been the centralized approach where the whole manufacturing system is modeled and then the optimal or a suboptimal schedule for the whole system is searched. To evaluate feasibility of the schedule in detail, production simulation is required to be performed based on the schedule. The centralized approach has been the mainstream also in production simulation area.

Recent diversified customers' needs have promoted high-mix low-volume manufacturing, and then manufacturing systems should be flexible to cope with variable situation. This requires production simulation/scheduling to be performed immediately when the situation has changed. The centralized approach is inappropriate from this point of view, since re-modeling the whole system under the

C. Emmanouilidis, M. Taisch, D. Kiritsis (Eds.): APMS 2012, Part II, IFIP AICT 398, pp. 638–645, 2013.
© IFIP International Federation for Information Processing 2013

new situation involves a heavy load. It is desirable to take the distributed approach in which the simulation/scheduling is performed by a set of local models and coordination among them. Recent development of computer network technologies is achieving *highly distributed manufacturing systems (HDMSs)*, that is, makes it achievable to equip each facility with an independent simulation model and run the models on a network so that they can communicate with each other. Production simulation for HDMSs, termed as *highly distributed (HD) simulation*, has been discussed. A framework and a time management method for this simulation with a set of models based on a master schedule was proposed[7].

To make this method beneficial enough, distributed production scheduling is also required for modification of the master schedule based on the simulation result. There have been many different kinds of distributed scheduling methods, such as auction[6] and active database scheduling. However, these methods would be inappropriate for HDMSs, since some elements such as the launcher and the database perform information integration and decision making which result in overload of the elements. Furthermore, it is desirable to carry out the scheduling in the similar framework to the HD simulation. In this paper, such type of distributed scheduling, termed as *highly distributed (HD) scheduling*[8], is discussed. This paper considers scheduling by the shortest processing time (SPT) dispatching rule, and proposes a communication algorithm for dispatching based on the architecture and mechanism of the HD simulation.

2   Highly Distributed Simulation

HD simulation[7] is carried out by a collection of autonomous on-line facility models brought together to respond to dynamic manufacturing system changes. They offer the potential of increased responsiveness and robustness compared to centralized methods. In this simulation method, each facility is equipped with a computer installed an identical model with its own data and event list, while all the computers are connected by network. The entire simulation runs by message exchanges between the models, in which each computer represents a different facility independently. By these means, engineers can save time of building models and, in addition, simulation architecture or model layout can be changed flexibly according to the real situation. As to the time management aspect, each computer manages their own data (processing time of jobs, current condition, etc) and job event list (which record the starting time of each job and the total number of jobs processed on this facility). Simulation sequence is decided by sorting of the event times within the network.

3   Highly Distributed Production Scheduling

This section describes a method of distributed scheduling based on the framework and mechanism of the HD simulation, which we call HD scheduling. The rationale behind this approach is to provide the function to modify the original master schedule immediately based on the result of the HD simulation. As a preliminary research, this paper describes a scheduling method using the SPT dispatching rule within the concept of the HD scheduling.

This research deals with a simple manufacturing scenario shown in Fig. 1(a). Materials are transported to an area one-by-one at time period a. The area is composed of a buffer and multiple machines which can do the same process but have different performance. The material arrived is assigned by the buffer to one of the machines according to the SPT dispatching rule. In the conventional method using auction technique or active databases, decisions of dispatching are made by the launcher or the database; while in the method described below, these decisions are made by message exchanges among the machines (Fig. 1(b)).

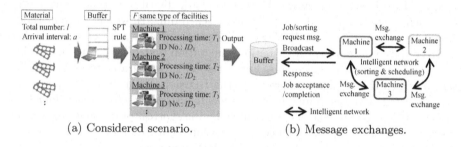

(a) Considered scenario.   (b) Message exchanges.

Fig. 1. Architecture of HD scheduling

The computer of each machine has a model of the real machine and its own processing time. At first, the models of the machines are sorted by the processing times. This phase called initial sorting is carried out by the processing flow shown in Fig. 2. Each message consists of each machine's processing time T_i, ID number ID_i (e.g. IP address in the network) and message type (in this case, 0 means that the message is sent for initial sorting). After receiving another's message, each computer analyses its message type. If its value is 0, the ith computer compares the processing time T_j with its own processing time T_i. If T_i is larger than T_j, the priority sequence number S_i (at the beginning, its value has been initialized to 1) is added by one, which means the priority decreases. If T_i is smaller than T_j, S_i remains unchanged, which results in a higher priority. If T_i equals to T_j, ID_i is compared to ID_j and then the priority is updated in the same manner. This comparison goes through every machine. When this sorting phase finished, the initial sequence of the machines for scheduling has been decided.

After the initial sorting phase, the dispatching phase starts. First of all, the buffer sends a request for processing the arrived material with its current time stamp WC to all of the machines, as shown in Fig. 3. This time the message type is 1. After sending the request, the buffer updates quantity of arrived materials Q, whose initial value is 0. Then the buffer waits for the response from all the machines and the clock of the buffer WC proceeds by one time scale a at which the next material arrives.

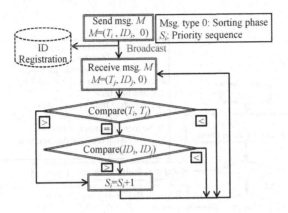

Fig. 2. Initial sorting flow

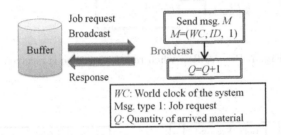

Fig. 3. Processing request from buffer

When receiving the request from the buffer, the machine having the highest priority (i.e. $S_i = 1$) sends an acceptance message back unless it is unavailable due to processing another material. Fig. 4 shows the flowchart of machines' reactions to the request. At first, each machine saves the initial priority sequence number S_i in B_i (the reason for introducing this variable will be explained later). After receiving a request message from the buffer, S_i is checked whether it equals to 1. If this is false, then the computer replies to the buffer with message type 6 which means this machine is unavailable to process the material. If S_i equals to 1, then $Flag$ is checked whether it equals to 0 which means the machine is idle and therefore available to process the material. If the $Flag$ is 1 which means the machine is working now, the computer replies to the buffer with message type 6, waits until $T_iE \geq WC \geq T_iE - a$ holds (the time at which the current processing job will finish after one time period), broadcasts its initial priority sequence number B_i and ID number ID_i with message type 3 for re-sorting among the machines, and then turns $Flag$ into 0. If $Flag$ equals to 0, the computer broadcasts B_i and ID_i with message type 2. After that this machine starts the processing, and the current time is substituted to the start time and the finished time is set to the start time added by the processing time T_i.

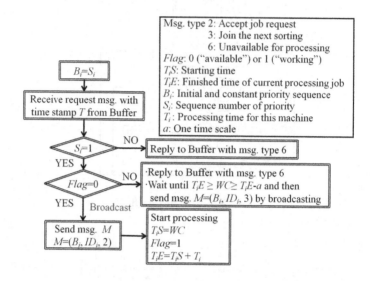

Fig. 4. Process flow when request message is received

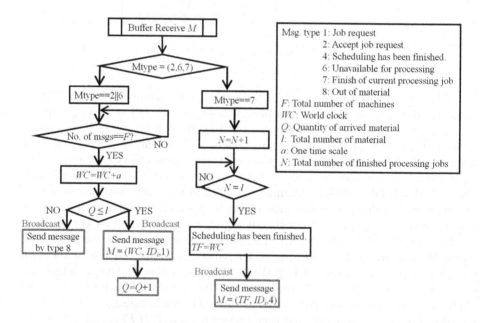

Fig. 5. Buffer's operations according to received message type

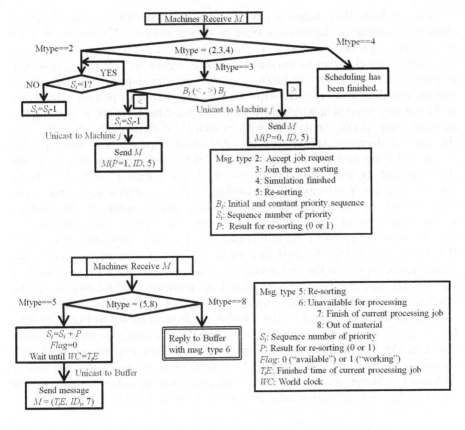

Fig. 6. Machines' operations according to received message type

In this dispatching phase, a lot of messages are broadcasted by machines. After receiving these messages, the buffer has different reaction according to the message type as shown in Fig. 5. If the message type is 2 or 6, the buffer waits until all the machines send replies (the number of replies equal to total number of the machines), increases the world clock WC by one time scale a, and then checks whether there is still any materials for processing (whether quantity of arrived materials is smaller than the total number of materials l, which has been set at the beginning of scheduling). If there is still a coming material, the buffer sends a processing request by message type 1 and increase Q by 1. If there is no more material, then the buffer sends a message of type 8 which means it is out of material now. If the message type is 7, which means one processing job has finished, then the total number of finished processing jobs N is increased by 1. After that, it is checked whether N is equal to l. If this is true, which means all the material has been processed, the buffer broadcasts a message of type 4 to notify every machine, and then this scheduling is finished.

After receiving these broadcasted messages, machines also have different operations according to the message type, as shown in Fig. 6. If the message type is 2 meaning another machine accepted the job request and started processing, the machine checks whether current value of S_i equals to 1. If this is false, the machine decreases S_i by 1 to increase its own priority sequence. By this mean, machines update their priority sequence and get chance to process a material. If the message type is 3, which means another machine joins the re-sorting, the machine compares the sender's B_j with its own B_i. If B_i is smaller than B_j, then the machine decreases the priority by subtracting 1 from S_i and send message type5 with P set as 0. If B_i is larger than B_j, then the priority sequence remains the same and the machine sends a message of type 5 with P set to 1 (to lower the rival machine's priority). If the message type is 4, which means the simulation for scheduling has finished, this machine stops running. If the machine receives a message of type 5, which is the result of re-sorting, then it updates its priority sequence and set $Flag$ to 0 (now is available for processing), waits until WC turns to T_iE (the finished time of the current processing job) and sends a message of type 7 to the buffer notifying one material has been processed. If the message type is 8, which means there is no more material for processing, the machine replys to the buffer by message type 6 (not available for processing).

These flows were applied to the scheduling problem shown in Fig. 1(a) with $l = 10, a = 1, T_1 = 4, T_2 = 2$ and $T_3 = 3$. The SPT rule brings about the schedule shown in Fig. 7. The flows were implemented on a computer, where the models communicate with each other by the local network in the computer, via coding with the C# language. Executing this code, the same schedule was successfully output, which shows fundamental feasibility of the proposed method.

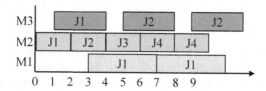

Fig. 7. The schedule obtained by the SPT rule

4   Conclusion

Recent manufacturing systems are required to be flexible to cope with variable situation. This requires production simulation/scheduling to be performed immediately when the situation has changed. The HD simulation/scheduling, where each facility is equipped with a simulation/scheduling model and can communicate with other facilities via a network, is expected to be a key technique for realization of such flexible manufacturing systems.

In this paper, a method for HD scheduling has been proposed. The simple scenario was considered where materials are transported to an area one-by-one at a constant time period and then processed by one of the facilities having different performance. In this scenario, a dispatching problem based on the SPT rule has been discussed. A framework and algorithms to achieve the dispatching by a set of elementwise models and message exchanges among them were proposed, and their feasibility was shown by a simple example.

Future works include the following issues: one is quantitive evaluation of the proposed method compared to conventional distributed and centralized methods. Another is enhancement of the proposed method to the more complex scenarios where multiple kinds of materials are transported to the area randomly, and the materials require multiple kinds of processes with transportation among the facilities. The other is development of algorithms for other dispatching rules such as the earliest-due-date rule, the minimum slack time rule, and so on.

Acknowledgement. We would like to thank Ms. Hejun Pan, who is currently with Panasonic Corporation, for her tremendous contribution, and also the members of Technical Committee on Manufacturing and Management Knowledge, The Japan Society for Precision Engineering, for their invaluable advice.

References

1. Graves, S.C.: A Review of Production Scheduling. Operations Research 29, 646–675 (1981)
2. Mendez, C.A., Cerda, J., Grossmann, I.E.: State-of-the-art review of optimization methods for short-term scheduling of batch processes. Computers and Chemical Engineering 30, 913–946 (2006)
3. Noronha, S.J., Sarma, V.V.S.: Knowledge-Based Approaches for Scheduling Problems: A Survey. IEEE Transactions on Knowledge and Data Engineerng 3, 160–171 (1991)
4. Akyol, D.E., Bayhan, G.M.: A Review on Evolution of Production Scheduling with Neural Networks. Computers & Industrial Engineering 53, 95–122 (2007)
5. Tuncel, G., Bayhan, G.M.: Applications of Petri Nets in Production Scheduling: A Review. International Journal of Advanced Manufacturing Technology 34, 762–773 (2007)
6. Kaihara, T., Fujii, N., Toide, S., et al.: Optimization Method using Combinatorial Auction for Production Scheduling with Batch Processing. Journal of Advanced Mechanical Design, Systems, and Manufacturing 4, 588–596 (2010)
7. Fujii, S., Fujii, N., Iwamura, K., et al.: A Basic Study on a Highly Distributed Simulation of Manufacturing Systems under the Ubiquitous Environment. In: Proceedings of ASME/ISCIE 2012 International Symposium on Flexible Automation, ISFA2012-7208 (2012)
8. Pan, H., Morinaga, E., Wakamatsu, H., Arai, E.: A Scheduling Method for Highly Distributed Manufacturing System. In: Proceedings of JSME Manufacturing Systems Division Conference, pp. 21–22 (2012)

A Design of Experiments Approach to Investigating the Sensitivity of the Re-order Point Method

Peter Nielsen[1], Giovanni Davoli[2], Izabela Nielsen[1], and Niels Gorm Maly Rytter[1]

[1] Department of Mechanical and Manufacturing Engineering, Aalborg University,
Fibigerstraede 16, 9220 Aalborg Oest, Denmark
{peter,Izabela,i9nr}@m-tech.aau.dk
[2] Department of Mechanical and Civil Engineering (DIMeC), University of Modena and
Reggio Emilia; via Vignolese 905, 41100, Modena, Italy
giovanni.davoli@unimore.it

Abstract. This paper investigates the re-order point inventory management models sensitivity to demand distributions, demand dependencies and lead time distributions. The investigated performance measures are four different versions of service level. The conclusion is for all measures that the single most critical aspect adversely affecting service level performance is the presence of asymmetrically distributed demand.

Keywords: Inventory management, discrete event simulation, design of experiment, demand distributions.

1 Introduction

Inventory management is a practical challenge faced by many companies across industries. Inventory management can be reduced to the single objective of maintaining the cost optimal amount of inventory on hand. However, in practice this is typically reduced to achieving a certain service level i.e. satisfying a certain percentage of demand directly from inventory. The correct service level will be situational, some schools e.g. advocated in Silver et al. (1998), that the service level is a direct trade off between various cost factors (typically holding vs. cost of stock out). Other would argue that it is determined by market requirements. Regardless of how the target service level is determined, it is possible to calculate for a given situation the amount of safety stock needed to achieve the target.

This paper presents the results from an investigation of the behavior of a simple re-order point inventory management method. The aim is to determine which factors, settings and the combination of factors influence on the achieved service level. For this purpose a simulation study is carried out using XCV software. The study is structured around a design of experiments and investigates four different service level measures and their sensitivity to four different parameters: demand distribution, correlation of demand, mean lead time and standard deviation of lead time. The aim of the study is to 1) identify which factors and settings of these that are critical regardless of

C. Emmanouilidis, M. Taisch, D. Kiritsis (Eds.): APMS 2012, Part II, IFIP AICT 398, pp. 646–653, 2013.
© IFIP International Federation for Information Processing 2013

service level measure 2) provide insight into the complexity of real life inventory management by identifying which factors interact 3) give guidelines for how to improve service level measures in practice.

The remainder of the paper is structured as follows. First, a literature review of inventory management, demand distributions and simulation studies of inventory management is presented. This is followed by a design of experiments. Third, results from a full factorial experiment are presented and discussed before final conclusions and avenues of further research are presented.

2   Literature Review

In general most methods used in practice for inventory management tend to be based on assumptions of normally independently distributed lead time demand (e.g. Silver et al. (1998), Vollmann et al. (2005). For many practical purposes this will also tend to be a reasonable assumption. However, Tadikamalla (1984) concludes that high values of Coefficient of Variance associated with asymmetrical distributions of demand lead to poor performance of inventory management techniques and that the symmetry/asymmetry of demand is critical for e.g. inventory costs (Zotteri, 2000). Bobko and Whybark (1985) find that the coefficient of variation is in fact a robust descriptor of the degree lumpiness. Tadikamalla (1984) likewise underlines that it is necessary to deviate from the assumptions of normality / symmetrical distributed (lead time) demand to achieve a satisfactory performance. Zotteri (2000) finds that the shape of the demand distribution is critical when determining the performance of inventory management methods. However, other methods (e.g. aggregation in time (Eriksen and Nielsen, 2011)) tend to be able to compensate for the asymmetry experienced. This could also indicate that there is a critical level of asymmetry of demand distribution (especially when taking into account a given lead time) that when reached will lead to poor performance. Within inventory management individual customer orders are translated into a demand rate (with a given distribution) and used for calculating re-order points, lot-sizes, timing, safety stock etc. (Silver, 1981). This is often translated into a lead time demand distribution. The shorter the lead time period, the closer the lead time demand distribution is to the actual distribution of demand. It however seems necessary to investigate to which extend inventory management techniques are sensitive to these and other parameters.

Inventory management is can be fundamentally be reduced to a combined decision of how much and when to order. In most instances this problem is reduced to taking into account (for a given cost structure; holding, ordering, stock out) four factors:

- Demand distribution (D_d) (sometimes modeled as lead time demand, in this paper modeled as the more complex daily demand)
- Correlated demand (C_d)
- Mean lead time (μ_{LT})
- Standard deviation of lead time (σ_{LT})

To investigate these factors this paper utilizes the same methods as the ones presented in e.g. Bobko and Whybark (1985) and Zotteri (2000).

3   Design of Experiments

To investigate the behavior of the re-order point method a simulation experiment is completed. The aim of the experiment is to investigate the importance of the four factors on the service level performance of the ROP. The aim is not to develop a predictive response model. A full factorial experiment with three levels is used in this paper. Four factors and three levels give 3^4 =81 combinations and thus 81 separate experiments were conducted. The three settings for the four factors are shown in Table 1.

Table 1. Overview of experimental settings of the four investigated factors

	Low (-1)	Mean (0)	High (+1)
D_d	Normal distribution, mean = 1.000 units/day, standard deviation = 300 units/day	Uniform distribution, minimum = 500 units/day, maximum = 1,500 units/day	Exponential distribution, mean = 1.000 units/day
C_d	Non correlated observations	Slightly correlated, first 4-5 lags correlated	Highly correlated
μ_{LT}	Mean = 5 days	Mean = 7 days	Mean = 9 days
σ_{LT}	CV = 0	CV = 0.1	CV = 0.2

All lead times, expect the constant values, are normal i.i.d.. The Coefficient of Variance (CV) is used to scale the variation in lead times defined as:

$$CV = \frac{\sigma_{LT}}{\mu_{LT}} \Rightarrow \sigma_{LT} = CV \times \mu_{LT} \tag{1}$$

Where μ_{LT} is the mean of the lead time and σ_{LT} is the standard deviation, so for e.g. μ_{LT} =7 days, CV=0.2 the standard deviation used is 0.2x7 days =1.4 days. All demand distributions have a mean of 1.000 units/day for both independent and dependent distributions. In the case of this experiment all factors are treated as categorical factors. This means that a linear response is not expected. It also means that it will be possible to identify not just which factors are significant for any of the four performance measures (responses) but also at which levels they are critical. This will enable a discussion of which factors should be taken into account when using a Re-order-point inventory management method in practice.

The four performance measures investigated in this paper are all service level measures. They are defined as follows:

SL1: calculated as the ratio between stock out in pieces and total demand.

SL2: calculated as the ratio between stock out in days (the sum of days when a stock out occurred) and total number of days.

SL3: calculated as the ratio between stock out in pieces and total demand during the period while at least one order is open.

SL4: calculated as 1 minus the ratio between the number of "stock out" and the total number of orders. A "stock out" is considered to have occurred when the total demand in a lead time exceeds the mean demand over the lead time.

The simulation model was developed according with the standard EOQ model for single item. A set of stochastic functions, developed in the SciLab environment, are used to generate the demand that activates the model. The simulations are conducted for a length of 1.000 days to guarantee a stable output and thus a correct estimation of the four service level measures.

4   Analysis of Results

The design and analysis of experiments have been conducted using the open source software R (r-project.org, 2012) and the package AlgDesign. The ANOVA tables for all four fitted models are presented in Table 2. The general investigation of the fitted response models show the following: QQ-plots indicate normal distributed residuals for all four models indicating a reasonable fit of models. Adjusted R2 are in the interval 0.83 to 0.90 likewise indicating a good fit of all the models. This strongly indicates that the models are valid descriptors of the behavior of the four performance measures investigated in this study.

4.1   Service Level

Table 2 shows the ANOVA of the four service level models for the models. The table includes coefficients and p-values. The values shown in Table 2 indicate firstly the coefficients and their corresponding p-values. The coefficients indicates the response difference from the baseline model where all factors assume the value -1. This means it is possible to see when there is a significant effect of a factor or combination of factors at given values. This makes it possible not only to identify which factors are significant but also on which settings they are critical.

The values shown in Table 2 indicate that there are some generic responses to given settings of the factors, furthermore it is also apparent that all four response models have significant (on a 0.05 or better level) second order interactions. This illustrates the complexity faced when doing real life inventory management, as second order interactions must apparently be considered when designing and implementing inventory management. The R^2 for the four models are respectively for SL1-4: 0.97, 0.97, 0.98 and 0.97 and adjusted R^2 are: 0.87, 0.84, 0.9 and 0.83. The high values of both R^2 and adjusted R^2 indicate a very good model fit, which is of course to be expected when all the parameters are included. The results of the factorial analysis will be split in to three parts. The first will focus on the factors and combination of factors and settings that are critical for all four service level measures. The second will focus on the individual service levels and the factors that are significant only for this particular measure. The third will focus on response models only containing main effects.

Table 2. p-values from ANOVA for SL1, SL2, SL3 and SL4 and coefficients of the fitted models. p-values emphasized with bold indicate variables significant on a better than 0.05 level. To improve readability only rows containing significant variables have been included.

	SL1		SL2		SL3		SL4	
	Estimate	Pr(>|t|)	Estimate	Pr(>|t|)	Estimate	Pr(>|t|)	Estimate	Pr(>|t|)
(Intercept)	**0.999**	**0.000**	**0.998**	**0.000**	**0.999**	**0.000**	**0.983**	**0.000**
D_d1	**-0.012**	**0.011**	**-0.012**	**0.003**	**-0.017**	**0.002**	**-0.047**	**0.003**
$D_d1{:}C_d1$	-0.009	0.099	0.004	0.398	**-0.016**	**0.017**	0.011	0.538
$D_d1{:}\mu_{LT}1$	**-0.012**	**0.036**	-0.007	0.097	-0.008	0.203	-0.025	0.167
$D_d1{:}C_d1{:}\mu_{LT}0$	0.012	0.042	0.002	0.610	**0.019**	**0.008**	-0.013	0.487
$D_d1{:}C_d0{:}\mu_{LT}1$	**0.016**	**0.012**	**0.014**	**0.008**	**0.021**	**0.005**	0.063	**0.004**
$D_d1{:}C_d1{:}\mu_{LT}1$	**0.012**	**0.042**	0.003	0.513	**0.020**	**0.007**	0.018	0.351
$D_d1{:}C_d1{:}\sigma_{LT}0$	**-0.015**	**0.016**	**-0.012**	**0.014**	**-0.019**	**0.009**	**-0.047**	**0.023**
$D_d1{:}C_d0{:}\sigma_{LT}1$	-0.011	0.066	-0.009	0.062	**-0.014**	**0.044**	-0.021	0.287
$D_d1{:}C_d1{:}\sigma_{LT}1$	**-0.012**	**0.042**	**-0.011**	**0.022**	**-0.015**	**0.033**	-0.030	0.125

In general all four SL measures are only sensitive to one main effect and that is D_d and only at the setting of 1. In all four cases the coefficient is negative for this setting of D_d, and in all cases is the setting of 0 in no way significant. Both the size of the coefficient and the significance level the demand distribution setting of 1 – indicating an asymmetrical distribution – is the largest for all four models. This strongly indicates that the asymmetrical demand distribution (supported by the fact that the other symmetrical distribution has no significant different response than the base line setting -1) is the single most significant factor in explaining lower service levels. It also strongly indicates that the re-order point method is highly sensitive to shape of the demand distribution, especially when it is skewed. Previous work by e.g. Eriksen and Nielsen (2011) and Nielsen et al. 2010 indicates that demand rates are in fact neither normal nor symmetrical distributed in practice. This underlines that this topic deserves further investigations.

Another generic significant effect is the second order interaction $D_d@1{:}C_d@0{:}\mu_{LT}@1$, indicating that demand is asymmetrically distributed, slightly correlated and lead time is long. In all four response models this combination of settings tends to increase service levels. The reason for the increase of service levels when three of the factors have these settings must be found in the central limit theorem. Under long lead times ($\mu_{LT}@1$) the asymmetrical distributed demand ($D_d@1$) will tend towards a normal distribution with low variation. However, it is interesting to note that $\mu_{LT}@1$ is not significant as a main effect, most likely because this is covered in safety stocks and calculation of these levels. A conclusion must be that to avoid the detrimental effects of a skewed demand distribution (i.e. $D_d@1$) on service levels practitioners must compensate by aggregating in time (See e.g. Fliedner (2001)). This finds support in Nielsen et al. (2010) and methods for calculating adequate aggregation horizons to achieve a satisfactory distribution of demand can be found in Eriksen and Nielsen (2011).

$D_d@1:C_d@1:\sigma_{LT}@0$ is likewise a significant second order interaction with a negative contribution in all four models. This combination of factors is for a dependently asymmetrical distributed demand with a low variation in lead time. The combination of the first two factors is not surprising as this would tend towards giving a very skewed demand distribution. However, it is difficult to establish why slightly non-constant lead time should be is significant.

Other noteworthy factors and interactions is $D_d@1:C_d@1:\sigma_{LT}@1$ that has a significant negative impact on SL1-3. This second order interaction actually indicates the almost worst case scenario. Highly correlated, asymmetrically disturbed demand, with large variation in lead times will naturally tend to lead to a lower service level. It is in fact interesting why it is not also a significant combination of factors for the fourth SL measure.

Several generic conclusions can be reached from this study. First, that asymmetrical demand distributions tend to lead to lower service levels. This is interesting since several studies of real life demand indicate that the demand faced by companies can in fact be asymmetrically distributed and also correlated in time. This also supports the findings of e.g. Zotteri (2000). Second, that to compensate for this one has to aggregate in time, in the case of inventory management this is typically achieved through longer lead times. This of course will tend to lead to higher holding costs, so here the trade-off between service and costs become critical in practice. This area deserves further study. A general problem with a full scale model with second order interactions is that there is a risk of over fitting. For this reason it could be prudent to investigate the reduced response models only including the main effects. An over view of these response models can be seen in Table 3 below.

Interestingly enough also when only main effects are considered the adjusted R^2 only drops to the range 0.60-0.78, which indicates a reasonable response model but with less precision. However, these models are interesting as they illustrate service level issues in a parameter by parameter manner. It is interesting to note that $D_d@1$ is still the single most critical factor, and that this setting reduces service level measures in all response models. It is also interesting to note that for three out of the four measures $C_d@1$ leads to a lower service level. The same goes for $\sigma_{LT}@1$ although the contribution to the service levels are for all models (SL4 exempt) quite low. It is also interesting to note that only two out of 4x4 factors set at 0 are in fact significant. Of these only $\mu_{LT}@0$ for SL4 has any significant contribution to the service level measure. This underlines that a large deviation from the assumed behavior is necessary for it to significantly affect service level performance. The combined impression is that performance primarily depends on whether or not a skewed demand distribution is present, and to some extend whether demand is highly correlated. The conclusion is again that the demand behavior is critical for the service level. A highly correlated demand will also tend to lead to demand being asymmetrically distributed in the short term, again underlying that the asymmetry of demand distributions is in fact highly critical for service level performance, regardless of which SL measure is used. It is also interesting to note from Table 3 that all deviations from the standard setting of the factors to -1 tend to lead to a negative response on all four SL measures.

Table 3. p-values from ANOVA for SL1, SL2, SL3 and SL4 and coefficients for the fitted response models only including main effects. P-values emphasized with bold indicate variables significant on a better than 0.05 level.

	SL1		SL2		SL3		SL4	
	Estimate	Pr(>|t|)	Estimate	Pr(>|t|)	Estimate	Pr(>|t|)	Estimate	Pr(>|t|)
(Intercept)	1.002	0.000	0.999	0.000	1.001	0.000	0.990	0.000
D_d0	0.000	0.829	0.000	0.737	0.000	0.838	-0.001	0.797
D_d1	**-0.017**	**0.000**	**-0.011**	**0.000**	**-0.023**	**0.000**	**-0.043**	**0.000**
C_d0	-0.002	0.158	-0.001	0.256	-0.003	0.126	-0.008	0.110
C_d1	**-0.004**	**0.001**	-0.002	0.073	**-0.006**	**0.001**	**-0.013**	**0.006**
$\mu_{LT}0$	-0.002	0.187	**-0.003**	**0.018**	0.001	0.556	**-0.010**	**0.038**
$\mu_{LT}1$	-0.001	0.310	-0.001	0.217	0.002	0.137	-0.003	0.544
$\sigma_{LT}0$	-0.001	0.255	0.000	0.663	-0.002	0.249	0.000	0.981
$\sigma_{LT}1$	**-0.003**	**0.011**	**-0.003**	**0.005**	**-0.004**	**0.015**	**-0.012**	**0.012**

5   Conclusion

The aim of the study has been to investigate which parameters are critical for a given performance criteria of a re-order point inventory model. The conclusion is that there is a significant difference in the importance of the four investigated factors depending on the performance measure. From this study it can conclusively be stated that skewed demand distribution is the single most detrimental factor with regards to service level performance. It can also be concluded that there are several second order interactions that are highly significant, underlining the fact that inventory management is in fact a highly complex problem. Furthermore the findings of the presented investigations support the conclusions reached in e.g. Tadikamalla (1984) and Zotteri (2000), namely that the asymmetry of demand distributions are in fact highly significant for the performance of inventory management methods. Based on the study it is possible to give direct conclusive guidelines for where to focus when improving service levels in real-life applications of the ROP method. Especially it should be noted that the only feasible manner to compensate for the negative effects of asymmetrically distributed demand is to aggregate in time, through a longer safety period.

The conclusion must necessarily be that the complexity of inventory management is high, since the performance of a given ROP managed system cannot be predicted solely based on the main effects affecting it. This underlines that research into the behavior of inventory management systems and their performance is in fact a topic of relevance for both researchers and practitioners.

References

1. Bobko, P.B., Whybark, D.C.: The Coefficient of Variation as a Factor in MRP Research. Decision Sciences 16(4), 420–427 (1985)
2. Brander, P., Levén, E., Segerstedt, A.: Lot sizes in a capacity constrained facility-a simulation study of stationary stochastic demand. International Journal of Production Economics 93-94, 375–386 (2005)
3. Eriksen, P.S., Nielsen, P.: Emperical order quantity distributions: At what level of aggregation do they respect standard assumptions? In: Proceedings of the International Conference on Advances in Production Management Systems, University of Stavanger (2011)
4. Fliedner, G.: Hierarchical forecasting: issues and use guidelines. Industrial Management & Data Systems 101, 5–12 (2001)
5. Lau, H.-S., Lau, A.H.-L.: Nonrobustness of the Normal Approximation of Lead-Time Demand in a (Q, R) System. Naval Research Logistics 50, 149–166 (2003)
6. Nielsen, P., Nielsen, I., Steger-Jensen, K.: Analyzing and Evaluating Product Demand Interdependencies. Computers in Industry 61(9), 869–876 (2010)
7. Pujawan, I.N., Kingsman, B.G.: Properties of lot-sizing rules under lumpy demand. International Journal of Production Economics 81-82, 295–307 (2003)
8. Silver, E.A., Pyke, D.F., Peterson, R.: Inventory Management and Production Planning and Scheduling, 3rd edn. John Wiley & Sons (1998)
9. Tadikamalla, P.R.: A Comparison of Several Approximations to the Lead Time Demand Distribution. Omega 12, 575–581 (1984)
10. Vollmann, W., Berry, D., Whybark, T.E., Jacobs, F.: Manufacturing Planning and Control for Supply Chain Management. McGraw-Hill, Singapore (2005)
11. Wijngaard, J.: On Aggregation in Production Planning. Engineering Costs and Production Economics 6, 259–266 (1982)
12. Zotteri, G.: The impact of distributions of uncertain lumpy demand on inventories. Production Planning & Control 11, 32–43 (2000)

Challenges of Measuring Revenue, Margin and Yield Optimization in Container Shipping*

Albert Gardoń[1], Peter Nielsen[2], and Niels Gorm Malý Rytter[3]

[1] Wrocław University of Economy, Komandorska 118/120, 53-345 Wrocław, Poland,
Fibigerstræde 16, 9220 Aalborg East, Denmark
Albert.Gardon@ue.wroc.pl
[2] Aalborg University, Fibigerstræde 16, 9220 Aalborg East, Denmark
peter@m-tech.aau.dk
[3] Aalborg University in Copenhagen, Lautrupvang 1A, 2750 Ballerup, Denmark
i9nr@m-tech.aau.dk

Abstract. We present in this paper some initial ideas of Revenue and Yield Management in the container shipping industry, namely a regression study of the behavior of the currently used indicator for measuring pricing and revenue performance in a leading shipping line. We consider the properties of the indicator used and discuss options of developing a better indicators of revenue or yield optimization, being either revenue or yield per available unit. At the end we also formulate implications for a future research work to be done on development of relevant measures for the industry.

Keywords: yield (revenue) management, liner shipping, transportation logistics.

1 Introduction

The aim of this paper is to provide a discussion what would constitute a reasonable measure for revenue or yield optimization in the container shipping industry. It reveals some initial ideas about Revenue (RM) or Yield Management (YM) applied in this business. The discipline of RM or YM has had widespread attention in a number of consumer oriented businesses (see [4–6] and [10]) as e.g. passenger airlines (see [3]), hotels, car rental companies and less in cargo transportation businesses for air cargo (see [9]), rail cargo, container shipping or road transport companies. Cargo businesses meet characteristics of importance for practicing RM of YM as fixed capacity, high fixed and low variable costs, time-variable or stochastic demand, segmentable markets and clients, perishable inventory or capacity and in advance selling services (see [2]). However, when addressing RM or YM in the container shipping industry, one must first realize that the industry might have similarities, but also differs from e.g. passenger and cargo airlines and their business conditions where most research and practical experience has been accumulated over many years, which makes it necessary to

---

* The Research was Conducted During the Author's Stay at Aalborg University.

C. Emmanouilidis, M. Taisch, D. Kiritsis (Eds.): APMS 2012, Part II, IFIP AICT 398, pp. 654–661, 2013.
© IFIP International Federation for Information Processing 2013

tailor solutions and measures to the particular industry in focus. This paper addresses a particular case company in container shipping and investigates options for developing measures tailored to its business needs.

The remaining part of the paper is structured in two parts. First, we investigate with use of regression analysis the behavior of the currently used measure (indicator) for revenue optimization. Next, we discuss potential alternatives for developing one more indicator better suited to its business needs. Finally, a conclusion is made on required further effort to succeed with a better profitability indicator measuring the container shipping industry.

2   Revenue Per Transported Unit and Related Behavior

The first problem faced is the manner of the business condition reporting. In the container shipping industry the dominating revenue or yield optimization measure is the average price (called *the net freight* or *the revenue*) per unit sold (e.g. FFE — Forty Foot Equivalent, i.e. the volume of a 40 feet long container or TEU — Twenty-Foot Equivalent Unit, i.e. the volume of a 20 feet long container[1]) reported every week. This is by industry standards considered to be a solid indicator of the company or market condition (see [7]). To investigate the behavior of this indicator and identifying the causes of its weekly variation we conducted a study at one of major container shipping lines. The study depended only on information about cargo type[2], transportation direction[3], client type[4] and operational region. We construct a linear regression model describing the behavior of the average net freight per FFE (Y) as the dependent variable, namely:

$$\widehat{Y}(X_1,\ldots,X_k) = \alpha_0 + \sum_{i=1}^{k} \alpha_i X_i \, ,$$

where $\widehat{Y}$ is the approximation of the average net freight per FFE (the dependent variable), $(X_i)_{i=1}^{k}$ are independent, explanatory variables and $(\alpha_i)_{i=0}^{k}$ are regression coefficients. Using only three independent variables, namely the ratio of a transported reefer and dry cargo (in FFE), the ratio of a transported cargo in the headhaul and backhaul direction (in FFE) and the ratio of a transported cargo in the most profitable (over the company average) and the least profitable (under the company average) regions (in FFE), we have explained around 85% of the weekly indicator volatility. From the study it is clear that

---

[1] Obviously 1 FFE = 2 TEU.

[2] There are two basic cargo types: *reefer* and *dry*. Reefer cargo requires containers keeping special atmosphere conditions, as low temperature, proper humidity, air circulation, which need to be pluged in. Dry cargo is shipped in ordinary containers without any additional requirements.

[3] The direction, which the greater amount of containers is shipped in, is called *the headhaul*, whereas the opposite direction is called *the backhaul*.

[4] Client types differ in companies, but usually there is a group of the most important contractors which we will call *the key clients*.

the most significant factor is the direction, because of the trade imbalances, i.e. a significantly lower demand for cargo transportation in one of directions, results in an essential number of empty containers transported in the backhaul direction. The less important has been the average region profitability, probably because of the strong inside price variation. Interestingly, replacing this variable by the amount of transported FFE's from only one properly chosen region gives a similar goodness of fit. This choice has been based on the observation that the amount of cargo shipped in this region has been almost uncorrelated with two other significant independent variables. However, both the more/less profitable

SUMMARY OUTPUT

Regression Statistics	
Multiple R	0,856548169
R Square	0,733674765
Adjusted R Square	0,72416315
Standard Error	81,64210919
Observations	59

ANOVA

	df	SS	MS	F	Significance F
Regression	2	1028271,319	514136	77,1346	8,15727E-17
Residual	56	373264,3036	6665,4		
Total	58	1401535,622			

Fig. 1. The result of a linear regression model fitting (2 variables)

regions ratio and the cargo percentage from the chosen region have got a faint business sense, therefore we have omitted these. Nevertheless, the remaining two independent variables:

$$\widehat{Y}(X_1, X_2) = \alpha_0 + \alpha_1 X_1 + \alpha_2 X_2 ,$$

i.e. the direction ratio (X_1) and the cargo type ratio (X_2) still give a satisfying goodness-of-fit which exceeds 70%, as shown in the table from Fig.1.

Unfortunately, further investigations have shown that the model fitted above for the company overall cannot be generalized for chosen parts of the business. The trouble is not only with an unstable goodness-of-fit, but in fact, similar analysis for chosen regions have given different adjusted squared Pearson correlation coefficients. In the worst case this drops even below 25%, making the model completely unuseful in that instance. Although, in some cases the fitting is improved to around 70% by addition of other independent variables, as e.g. the percentage of FFE transported from key clients. What is more, it is observed that sometimes variables which are very important for one part of the business are at the same time completely insignificant for another part. This is a serious issue, since the model is not universal one needs to make separate studies for every instance. Although this is conlcuded for only one shipping line, we assume this to be a global phenomenon similar for all companies operating in this industry. Further studies of this will focus on other aspects of the business, especially lower levels of aggregation but using reacher data sets with many additional variables, also market data as e.g. Shanghai Containerized Freight Index (SCFI), whose development is shown in Fig.2.

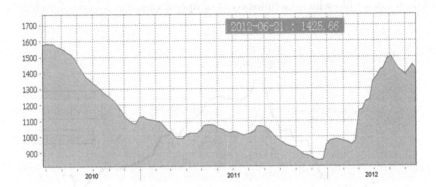

Fig. 2. Shanghai Containerized Freight Index (source: [11])

We must also add that this model is useful only in an explanatory sense, not as a predictive tool. First of all because the descriptive variables depend on the market demand and therefore are not immediately drivable by the shipping company. Besides, the values of these variables are observed only in quite short intervals, i.e. their standard deviations have been quite small, which implies the fit of the linear model could be doubtful for arguments which differ significantly from the mean values. The behavior of the indicator outside these intervals remains an open question.

3 Weaknesses of the Existing Revenue Measure

Having studied the currently used indicator we move forward to discuss what would be a better indicator for the revenue or yield optimization in this business. But what is more, and maybe the most important, the indicator mentioned in the previous section is maybe a critical parameter that cannot be omitted since it indicates market conditions, but in itself is not an adequate measure of how well the business is going. A company should not be satisfied (or dissatisfied) only because of increasing (or decreasing) prices. There should be incorporated somehow at least also such factors as e.g. the costs, the utilization (or capacity availability), i.e. the demand related to a changed service price, and the seasonality, i.e. comparison to results from previous years in a similar part of a year. This is what is done in e.g. the passenger airline industry (see [2]) and other industries further advanced in YM. Also better measures are a prerequisite for more advanced studies and prediction modelling (see [8]).

Costs could in fact be neglected if they are constant over time (something that may the case for e.g. the hotel industry), but in fact they are not. However, the freight rate is compensated for some of these changing costs in the form of surcharges, e.g. bunker surcharge (BAF), that also varies over time (see Fig.3), so an increase of prices could be caused only by a cost increase which would not improve the business results. For this reason the indicator should ideally be based on a variable which includes costs of operations, e.g. a type of yield[5].

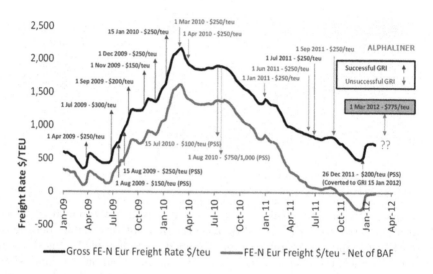

Fig. 3. Far East–North Europe spot rates (with and without bunker surcharge) vs rate increase announcements: 2009–2012 (source: [1])

Similarly, a reduction of prices does not necessarily result in worse company conditions, if at the same time the volume increases one could observe a higher total revenue, which means a better business situation due to economics of scale. An increase of the transport capacity should reduce unit costs at the same utilization which means a better yield. The conclusion despite volumes going up, means that a company in fact can have a higher revenue and due to economics of scale (with higher capacity vessels) a better total yield. However, the net freight per FFE would not show this. What is more, despite the unit price is one of the most significant variables affecting the total yield, though, a strong positive linear correlation between it and the yield is doubtful because higher prices usually imply higher yield only as long as the price increases are accepted by customers and do not result in lowering of volumes. For this reason the indicator should not be calculated just per units sold but per all capacity units available.

---

[5] The revenue after the subtraction of costs is called *the margin*, whereas *the yield* is the margin after the addition of the so-called *flow adjustment* linked to the empty containers evacuation.

Finally, in order to find out if a company has an increasing or a decreasing trend of earnings one needs to compare the results to those from analogous time from previous years. This is especially critical for the liner shipping industry, as it is highly seasonal. If the yield behaves similarly as in the same season in previous years, its increase (or decrease) in comparison to the preceding observation time does not necessarily mean it is better (or worse) at the given time. Therefore it is necessary to compensate the company condition indicator for the seasonality. There are such times in the year when the demand decreases to a half or increases twice, e.g. Chinese New Year which lasts about two weeks and occurs from the middle of January to the middle of February, depending on the year. The problem becomes one of obtating enough historical data to model accurately the seasonality. This is an industry issue, because the industry is continuously changing the network structure, routings, capacities etc., making historical analysis and comparisons difficult at best. This problem is compounded in time, so that the further back in historical observation one would like to go, the worse the problem is. This motivates the usage of relatively new data, at most a few years old. Nevertheless, if such an approach will be provided the situation will improve in time because of a constant collection of the new data pouring in.

4   The Proposed New Yield Optimization Measure

When implementing RM or YM in an industry or a company, a choice of a main measure for revenue or yield optimization must be made. In consumer oriented businesses there is a tendency to emphasize revenue, where there in cargo oriented businesses is a focus on optimizing yield instead (see [9]), as different products and services also incur different variable costs depending e.g. on routing of cargo. Additionally, in container shipping we also need to cater for flow of empty containers (flow adjustment) due to cargo imbalances, which is also important in such a company. To sum up, we have proposed a new improved business indicator which takes into account all the factors mentioned in the previous section and should describe more precisely the company condition:

$$ J_i(t) \;=\; \frac{V_i(t)}{C_i(t)} \qquad \left[\frac{\text{USD}}{\text{FFE}} \right] , $$

where t is the departure time from a crucial port in the service (the so-called bottleneck port), $V_i(t)$ is the total yield [USD] from the i-th vessel at t and $C_i(t)$ is the capacity available [FFE] on the i-th vessel at t. Incorporating the seasonality into the model we improve the indicator J to J^*:

$$ J_i^*(t) \;=\; S(t)\, J_i(t) \qquad \left[\frac{\text{USD}}{\text{FFE}} \right] , $$

where $S(t)$ [no unit] is the seasonality factor at time t.

Since the capacity on a vessel is shared usually over more than one string[6], at the first step we will focus on services. This is not a perfect approach, because

---

[6] A string is a virtual part of the network using a given amount of vessels capacity from one or more services.

the business-wise thinking is in terms of strings, but a service is a physical part of business with the precisely defined number of vessels (undertaking roundtrips), the capacity and the departure intensity. On the other hand the yield is calculated for each booking separately and the booking is linked to a string rather than to a service. The perfect solution would be a calculation of the total yield for each sea trip (port to port), taking into account the inland delivery to the first loading port, loadings and discharges and the inland delivery to the receiver. Knowing it would enable to divide the yield from each cargo not only between services, but also between strings. But it seems to be unrealistic since tracebility of costs is typically not possible for all parts of the transportation process. Therefore the idea is to begin with the simplest cases and further systematically consider the problem in a more complex way, fitting the model as good as possible to the business reality and be able to calculate the indicator for more and more parts of the business.

At the first step we want to consider the simplest case, that means to select such services which are adapted to single strings in the sense that all capacity in a bottleneck port (separatelly in each direction) belongs to only one string. The next step will be to find such services which are adapted to more than one string, but all those strings have got only one bottleneck port in this chosen service. In this instance we will need weights for the capacity division C_i over strings. This is a difficult task because the capacity on the vessel is not phisically signed for each string. What is more, it varies in time and sometimes is even exchanged by string managers. But it seems to be quite objective approach to use a discrete distribution of the slot division over strings, estimated on the basis of the historical data, for ordering the capacity available into the strings. The next step will be the calculation of the indicator for other strings which use more than one service (have got more than one bottleneck port). Now the yield V_i needs to be divided additionally between different services (different bottleneck ports). Again we need a weight for this operation. This could be the percentage of the transportation time in days of the cargo within each service. It seems to be a reasonable choice because costs depend mainly on the transportation time (fuel, ports) and, besides, time spans are easy to identify since all departure and arrival dates are known. The last step will be the choise of the time window (day, week) and the decision concerning the level of aggregation, that means the decision which strings or services should be consider jointly, e.g. a geographical accumulation.

5   Conclusions

Using this new provided indicator we would like to investigate the impact of some central steering tools on the business. The two most popular are general rate increases (GRI) and capacity changes (allocation of vessels or addition of new vessels). Until now these effects have at many instances recently been invisible when observing the mean net freight per FFE (see Fig.3). This has by industry typically been interpreted as a lack of effect of GRIs. However, this may be a faulty assumption, since the current measure is not necessarily sensitive to GRIs like a utilization based measure should be. Regarding the GRI's the possible cause could be the fact that they are maybe announced centrally, but implemented locally and local managers maintain new higher price offers very often only for a quite short time if at all, which implies the average net freight per transported FFE remains almost unchanged. Although, it is a well known fact that the GRIs causes an increased demand in the time span (several weeks) between the announcement and the implementation, which improves the company condition and should be shown by the measure. On the other hand, the capacity increase by the higher demand should lead to profit increase even though at the same time a special lower price would be offered for certain group of customers. In such case a decrease in a mean net freight per transported FFE could be observed when the company condition would be improved. And finally, we want to construct a stochastic model, in the sense of a time series or even time continuous stochastic process, for our new indicator for predictive purposes.

Acknowledgement. This research was funded by the Danish Maritime Fund, through grant no. 2011-58.

References

1. Weekly Newsletter. Alphaliner (June 2012)
2. Belobaba, P., Barnhart, C., Odoni, A.: The Global Airline Industry. John Willey and Sons Ltd., Croydon (2009)
3. Chiang, W.C., Chen, J.C.H., Xu, X.: An Overview of Research on Revenue Management: Current Issues and Future Research. International Journal of Revenue Management 1(1), 97–128 (2007)
4. Kimes, S.E.: Yield Management: A Tool for Capacity-Constrained Service Firms. Journal of Operations Management 8(4), 349–363 (1989)
5. Levinson, M.: The Box — How the Shipping Container Made the World Smaller and the World Economy Bigger. Princeton University Press, New Jersey (2006)
6. McGill, J., van Ryzin, G.: Revenue Management: Research Overview and Prospects. Transportation Science 33(2), 233–256 (1999)
7. Stopford, M.: Maritime Economics. Routledge, London (2009)
8. Talluri, K.T., van Ryzin, G.J.: The Theory and Practice of Revenue Menagement. Springer, New York (2005)
9. Yeoman, I., McMahon-Beattie, U. (eds.): Revenue Management: A practical Pricing Perspective. Palgrave Macmillan, New York (2011)
10. Zurheide, S., Fischer, K.: A simulation study for evaluating a slot allocation model for a liner shipping network. In: Böse, J.W., Hu, H., Jahn, C., Shi, X., Stahlbock, R., Voß, S. (eds.) ICCL 2011. LNCS, vol. 6971, pp. 354–369. Springer, Heidelberg (2011)
11. Chineseshipping, http://www1.chineseshipping.com.cn/en/indices/scfi.jsp

Improving Port Terminal Operations
through Information Sharing

Peter Bjerg Olesen[*], Iskra Dukovska-Popovska, and Hans-Henrik Hvolby

Centre for Logistics, Department of Mechanical and Manufacturing Engineering,
Aalborg University, Denmark
pbo@m-tech.aau.dk

Abstract. In modern industry there are well defined methods for planning and optimising the efficiency of the production. However, when looking at supply chain operations there are often problems with lack of communication and planning between nodes. By not communicating the risk of creating non-value adding work also increases as the organisations becomes less synchronised. Therefore the focus in this paper is on how information can improve the performance of a container terminal. It was found that information relating to the containers is currently not widely used. Further it was found that there are improvements to be found in terms of reducing non-value adding activities by utilising information sharing.

Keywords: Terminal operations, information sharing, waste, throughput time, case study.

1   Introduction

Businesses are becoming increasingly globalized, where each activity in the supply chain is located where the greatest value is added to the final product, which leads to increased transportation and more complex logistics. Since 1990 the global freight volume has almost doubled ([1], [2]). There is now a new growing trend towards greening of the supply chains, in order to lower the carbon footprint, which increases the use of ships as a transport mode, compared to trucks.

Typically supply chain management often focuses on customers and suppliers and not so much on how the goods are transported, and what the logistic performance is between the supply chain nodes, such as trucks, ships, trains, airplanes, shipping ports, truck terminals, airports etc. Due to the increased complexity, there is a need to focus on improving the logistic performance of the supply chain, and thereby reduce the time and cost transporting can impose.

Ports are an integral part of many supply chains, and are increasingly changing their role from being gateways, to becoming active players in the supply chain. Containers are a standardised method for handling cargo, and presents possibilities for

---

[*] Corresponding author.

C. Emmanouilidis, M. Taisch, D. Kiritsis (Eds.): APMS 2012, Part II, IFIP AICT 398, pp. 662–669, 2013.

standardising and optimising the processes within a terminal, reducing lead-time and work load. This has enabled a faster transport lead-time which then again has increased the demand for more containers and have put pressure on the supply chains and terminals, leading to an even stronger need to improve operations [2].

This change in supply chains has led to more complex transport routes, where containers often pass several transport hubs, typically going from Asia to e.g. Rotterdam and distributed further into Europe by either ship or truck. Each time a container goes through a transport hub it is subjected to a series of operations, moved from one transport type to another or to storage, e.g. waiting for a specific transport vessel with a specific destination. So in order to increase the competitiveness of the supply chain going through a specific transport hub, it is necessary to optimise the operations, reducing the lead time inside the hub as much as possible. Wang et al [3] have made an extensive analysis of port efficiency, and concludes it is far from optimal, implying the potential for optimisation is large.

This paper will focus on improving the terminal operations by reducing waste and lead-time in a container terminal through information sharing and coordination. In doing this the paper have introduced the general issues regarding port's roles in the global supply chain. Following is a description of how a terminal operates to provide a context. A case study is then introduced to support the arguments that information sharing is not widely applied and that it can have large benefits.

2   Optimising Terminal Operations

The development of ports has gone from ports just being gateways, to becoming active players in the supply chain. Beresford et al [4] reviews port development and conclude that ports need to be proactive to challenges rather that reactive, which in terms of terminal production can be faster and better customer service, by providing customers with precise information relevant to them. Ports are generally subject to incremental development going towards more integrated systems, supported by ICT. A central part of the operations taking place in a port is the movement of goods from one transport mode to another, this is called terminal operations.

A generic operation setup of a container terminal can be seen in Fig. 1 where different operation areas are presented. Stahlbock et al [5] have made a literature review that to a wide extend covers how the activities in a container terminal operates and concludes that there is need for more focus on reduction of waste and lead-time.

There are some different approaches in the literature towards optimising ports terminal operations and ports in general. Some focus on strategic development and frameworks, where the key is coordination and integration between the different actors involved with the port operations as well as other ports and transport companies ([7], [8]). These models imply that by improving the external link and cooperation, it is possible to improve the internal performance, as the tasks are done more synchronous in the supply chain. This can be difficult in practice as small ports often do not have much leverage towards the supply chains.

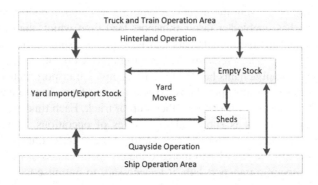

Fig. 1. Illustration of the operations areas in a generic container terminal [6]

The smaller ports can however look at their internal operations to find improvement opportunities. Paixao et al [9] builds a port development framework, based the United Nations Conference on Trade and Development's (UNCTAD's) "Port generations model". More details on UNCTAD can be found in Beresford et al [4]. Paixao et al [9] suggests to improve the operations by transforming the operations through a series of steps, starting with business process reengineering, going through just in time and lean projects ending with an agile and responsive system. Petit et al [10] also suggest the use of lean and agile principles, but segments supply and demand characteristics and attributes to different pipeline strategies, e.g. quick response and continuous replenishment. These frameworks presents an opportunity to use some of the Lean terminology and tools such as waste (muda) and kanban.

Stahlbock et al [5] suggest terminals need a more focussed approach for using ICT to plan the operations, and discuss ICT for supporting planning like seen in traditional "nuts and bolts" production systems. Stahlbock et al [11] further discuss some of the special characteristics in regards to planning and scheduling operations in terminals, such as the uncertainty of incoming containers. This lack of information is also mentioned by Kia et al [12] and Zhou et al [13]. Zhou et al [13] describes how lack of information in a dynamic supply chain reduces efficiency in each level.

The literature however lacks an empirical approach showing how to minimise waste and lead time in container terminals by using information. So this paper will through a case put focus on how information sharing can increase the throughput time of container at a terminal.

3   Case Study

The case study is based on a small/medium sized port in Denmark. The port has a wide range of activities with bulk (oil, coal, cereals) and containers as the primary ship arrivals. The port itself is also acting as landlord and infrastructure planner for companies located in the port area. All transport is handled by operators. The focus in this case will be on the container terminal operator.

The container terminal is divided into three major areas:

- A dedicated area for one container route, segmented between normal and cooling containers.
- A general container storage area for both storage and active storage for other container ship routes.
- A third area divided between specialty cargo, which cannot fit inside a normal container and then empty container storage.

According to Womack et al [14], value adding activities are activities that the customer wants (to pay for) e.g. sending a truck to the terminal, loading, unloading or forwarding goods. Waiting time and unnecessary storage is typically activities which a traditional production company tries to avoid; this line of thinking is imposed in the container terminal to make use of the terminology. Storage can in some cases be value adding, e.g. if a customer wants warehousing services, but this is not part of this papers scope.

3.1   Physical Flow

To identify the tasks which are not value adding in a container terminal, it is important to define the concepts in this context.

- Value adding activities
  - The activities the customer wants
- Non-value adding activities
  - The activities that happens because of lack of planning etc.
- Necessary activities
  - Transport and other activities which are impossible to remove but provide no value.

In this terminal the operations looks as follows: A truck arrives and waits for service by the gate and is allowed to move into the terminal and wait for a stacker to take the container. The stacker then moves the container to a storage area. From the storage area the container is picked and put onto a terminal tractor, which in turn drives under the crane that loads it onto the ship. When unloading the ship, the process is almost exactly reverse.

A process flow diagram of the container at the terminal is created in Fig 2 and activities will be analysed from a value adding perspective.

Fig 2 shows waiting time and unnecessary storage of containers that are the main culprits in reducing the lead time and resource utilisation. Also the "rework" that occur when containers are placed so they have to be moved in order to reach other containers, have a significant impact on the resource utilisation.

This amount of rework should as far as possible be avoided by ensuring that knowledge about shipment or pickup of the container is part of the planning. This would allow the operator to stack containers according to when the container is needed.

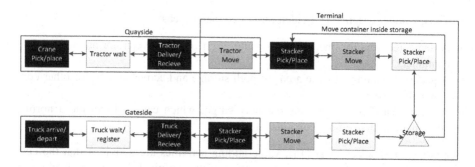

Fig. 2. Shows a simplified container flow in a small container terminal

It is not only the handling of the containers around the storage area that can be a problem. The execution of the processes also poses some pitfalls. The case terminal lists two main issues: making sure the nearest reach stacker picks up a container and making sure the stackers move optimally in relations to container placement. However it has been identified that these two issues are not the main problem at this stage. The question of how to call the nearest stacker is of course very relevant, but in order to do that other things needs to be in place in regards to coordination. With a plan for loading or unloading the ship it would be possible to assign stackers to each lift. Further the problem of storage of containers, according to the case terminal, is that they don't have any information on when a container arrives or when it is picked up, so they do not do anything to optimise this, again a clear lack of information and planning.

As a lack of information is the main reason for not making a good plan (and thereby reducing waiting time, storage, rework etc.) we will look more into the information flow in the terminal.

3.2   Information Flow

The information flow is limited today. The terminal operator only communicates on a strategic and operational level with its partners, leaving the tactical information unavailable and unused. Because of this it is not possible to coordinate the operational information to create more optimal sequences of activities. The three planning horizons; strategic, tactical and operational are based on the MPC model from Vollmann et al [15].

Instead, the information flow is directly related to the physical flow, except that execution of orders sometimes is initiated by the gate function. Containers are prior to arrival not known by the terminal, and all activities are dependent on the freight letter, that follows the container. Neither destination nor time information is available before arrival. This adds further to the possibility of lead-time delays, as there is very little coordination. Further arrival/departure time and destination of the container remains an unknown until the ship arrives and the manifest calls the container.

Another problem in terms of not having a plan or schedule for the arrival of trucks from the hinterland is that these trucks risks waiting and that the resource utilisation of the terminal can be low. This can be amplified as most trucks tend to arrive around the latest deadline, creating queues and heavy peak hours.

There is access to information about containers arriving via ship, but his information is not used, except for the ships arrival date and the number of containers. Further there is no information on containers going to or from the hinterland, except that the terminal knows that the day before ship departure the terminal is busy serving trucks.

By establishing a coordinating gate function it will be possible to put the available information to use. As the gate could allow slot times for trucks picking up or delivering containers depending on the availability on a container or the capacity of the terminal. This would also allow for planning of container placement in the storage area, reducing the amount of rework done to move containers to get to a specific one. This would be a huge improvement to the current setup.

4   Results and Discussion

It has been found in the case study, that the lack of planning and information flow is a large contributor to non-value adding activities in the terminal.

A proposal is made in order to improve the use of available information. To improve the information flow, three actions are suggested:

- Registration of containers prior to arrival
  - Destination and time information
- Time slots for trucks
- Placement of containers according to time and destination

Registration of time and destination is done in order to know where and when the container is leaving the terminal and also when they arrive. Time slots for trucks should be given prior to trucks arriving at the terminal, in order to ensure the trucks are serviced at once when arriving. And having more information about containers and their destination would allow the terminal to prepare a container for pickup by the arriving truck if the truck has to deliver a new shipment. To improve the terminal operations further the placement of the container in the storage area should be done according to departure and destination and not as now only by owner of the container. By placing the containers according to a schedule, the amount of rework and non-value adding activities would be reduced. In general it can be said about the three suggestions that they reduce some of the most obvious non-value adding activities, but in general just presenting the concept of identifying activities as being value or non-value will bring a new positive way of thinking to the terminal.

Even more important is the fact that time slots and more information would allow the terminal to level their production. As it is now the terminal has some very busy rush hours 24 hours before a ships departure. This is because there is no regulation of the input of trucks for the terminal, and then transporters tend to wait until the last minute to deliver the cargo. With time slots, this would definite become more level.

Practical implications
This paper's practical implications include showing how available information can be used at terminal operations in order to reduce the waste and improve the throughput of the container.

Research limitations/implications
The study has limitations and left questions unanswered. The findings are based on one port, and not all the findings can be generalized. The research implications are by offering an empirical case on improving efficiency by utilization of information in small ports.

Future research would include testing the hypothesis of this paper and implement the three suggestions. Also a deeper look into the operations at the terminal, to see if visual management would contribute to improving the control and execution of tasks.

References

1. United Nations Conference on Trade and Development. Secretariat: Review of maritime transport 2010. United Nations, New York (2010)
2. Notteboom, T., Rodrigue, J.-P.: Containerisation, Box Logistics and Global Supply Chains: The Integration of Ports and Liner Shipping Networks. Maritime Economics & Logistics 10, 152–174 (2008)
3. Wang, T.-F., Cullinane, K.: The Efficiency of European Container Terminals and Implications for Supply Chain Management. Maritime Economics & Logistics 8, 82–99 (2006)
4. Beresford, A.K.C., Gardner, B.M., Pettit, S.J., Naniopoulos, A., Wooldridge, C.F.: The UNCTAD and WORKPORT models of port development: evolution or revolution? Maritime Policy & Management 31, 93–107 (2004)
5. Stahlbock, R., Voß, S.: Operations research at container terminals: a literature update. OR Spectrum 30, 1–52 (2007)
6. Günther, H.-O., Kim, K.-H.: Container terminals and terminal operations. OR Spectrum 28, 437–445 (2006)
7. Brooks, M.R., McCalla, R.J., Pallis, A.A., Van der Lugt, L.M.: Coordination and Cooperation in Strategic Port Management: The Case of Atlantic Canada's Ports. Work 902, 494–1825 (2010)
8. Bichou, K., Gray, R.: A logistics and supply chain management approach to port performance measurement. Maritime Policy & Management: The Flagship Journal of International Shipping and Port Research 31, 47 (2004)
9. Paixão, A.C., Marlow, P.B.: Fourth generation ports – a question of agility? International Journal of Physical Distribution & Logistics Management 33, 355–376 (2003)
10. Pettit, S.J., Beresford, A.K.C.: Port development: from gateways to logistics hubs. Maritime Policy & Management: The Flagship Journal of International Shipping and Port Research 36, 253 (2009)
11. Stahlbock, R., Voß, S.: Vehicle Routing Problems and Container Terminal Operations – An Update of Research. In: Golden, B., Raghavan, S., Wasil, E., Sharda, R., Voß, S. (eds.) The Vehicle Routing Problem: Latest Advances and New Challenges, pp. 551–589. Springer, US (2008)

12. Kia, M., Shayan, E., Ghotb, F.: The importance of information technology in port terminal operations. International Journal of Physical Distribution & Logistics Management 30, 331–344 (2000)
13. Zhou, H., Benton Jr., W.C.: Supply chain practice and information sharing. Journal of Operations Management 25, 1348–1365 (2007)
14. Womack, J.P., Jones, D.T.: Lean thinking: banish waste and create wealth in your corporation. Simon and Schuster (2003)
15. Vollmann, T.E., Berry, W.L., Whybark, D.C., Jacobs, F.R.: Manufacturing Planning and Control Systems for Supply Chain Management: The Definitive Guide for Professionals. McGraw-Hill Professional (2004)

Perishable Inventory Challenges

Cecilie M. Damgaard, Vivi T. Nguyen, Hans-Henrik Hvolby[*],
and Kenn Steger-Jensen

Centre for Logistics, Department of Mechanical and Manufacturing Engineering,
Aalborg University, Denmark
hhh@celog.dk

Abstract. This paper is based on an exploratory research project into perishable inventory challenges in the retail industry. This paper investigates how inventory control of perishable items is managed and identifies the perishable inventory challenges. The paper includes a review of relevant literature and identification of models dealing with perishable inventory control. The paper is based on a case study in the retail industry in Denmark about how the current procedures are operating in the retail supply chain. Based on the case study and literature review it is found that product quality deterioration and the aftercare of the items in the retail stores are two important parameters in perishable inventories. Furthermore, the length of periods as well as the total cost and profit margin function of the inventory control models are does not often fit reality. Therefore there is a need for further research into models dealing with these parameters.

Keywords: Perishability, Inventory Control, Retail, Fresh Food Supply Chains.

1   Introduction

Product perishability is of major concern in many industrial sectors. Fresh food, blood products, meat, chemicals, composite materials and pharmaceuticals are all examples of perishable products that can deteriorate and become unusable after some finite time [2; 8; 15]. Other industries supplying services also deal with variety of perishable products such as airfares, hotels and concerts [1]. This complex issue supports the rationale for investigation into perishable inventory control in several industries as well as most countries.

Handlings of perishable inventories occur naturally in many practical situations. The perishable products are naturally managed in practice, as the length of the lifetime of the product defines the maximum length between the order frequency [15]. However, not many inventory control models take perishability of the products into account which is a weakness in these models. Most inventory control models assume that stock items can be stored indefinitely to meet future demands as in the case of the EOQ model. However, when dealing with perishables, the product lifetime must be taken into account in inventory models. Perishable inventory is a challenge for

---

[*] Corresponding author.

C. Emmanouilidis, M. Taisch, D. Kiritsis (Eds.): APMS 2012, Part II, IFIP AICT 398, pp. 670–677, 2013.
© IFIP International Federation for Information Processing 2013

companies both from a managerial and an operational point of view. The retail industry in Denmark deals with perishable inventory on a daily basis. The challenges arise when unsold perishable items approach their expiration date. Then management has to decide whether or not to sell the items at a lower price than expected or simply consider the remaining inventory as waste. To investigate these issues a single case study has been conducted in the Danish retail industry.

When the inventory holds the same product variant, but with different expiration dates, then the challenge occurs since the items have different quality level due to the different length of remaining shelf life. Decisions can be difficult, as the remaining items needs to be taken into account, when making replenishments. In order to ensure a higher profit, when dealing with perishable items, the shelf life must be taken into account. According to Gürler [8] a significant reduction in the cost function can be obtained by explicitly taking into account the randomness of the shelf life and the system costs differ drastically among various shelf life distributions, which imply that a precise estimation of the shelf life distribution is desirable.

This exploratory research is based on the belief that better knowledge about the products' remaining shelf life and use of this information in the inventory control can help retailer managers with better planning and less use of manual resources. Therefore, the study of the effects of a product's lifecycle are important to identify for managers and researchers alike.

In the following, an overview of the existing inventory control for perishable items is presented as well as a discussion of the ordering strategies for retailers. The paper ends up with an identification of important parameters in perishable inventories, which needs to be taken into account in perishable inventory control models.

2   Perishable Inventory Models

The literature of perishable inventory is generally divided into two; perishable inventory theory and the dynamic nature of the perishables. Together the literature discusses the impact and consequences perishable items have on inventory control models. The interest in the research literature about perishable inventory have increased over the last two decades [8], where the Nahmias [15] presented an extensive review of the relevant literature on lot-sizing problem with deteriorating and perishable items. Later several authors have contributed to the development of a number of inventory models for deteriorating items [9].

Nahmias [14] defined characteristics of a perishable item with a limited shelf life and introduced ways of using the traditional models to account for items having a limited lifetime. One way is by defining the periods according to the length of the items lifetime. An example is by using the simple EOQ model; the annual demand in the general EOQ is set to be the expected demand over a period equal to the items lifetime. This ensures that no units expire [15].

Nahmias [14] also contributed to the literature as one of the first to derive and evaluate optimal order policies for obsolescent products with shelf life greater than two periods. This was followed by an in-depth understanding of the quality deterioration of perishable items [8; 5; 4]. Pierskalla and Roach [17] addresses that issuing the oldest item first, through the FIFO principle, is the optimal policy from the perspective of the retailer, when the objective is to minimise total inventory holding cost (and waste). However, in practice this is not always controllable by retailers. Often, customers selects the latest delivered products first (especially fresh-food) thus the LIFO principle is a more realistic assumption [5].

Some authors dealing with perishable inventories suggest use of the newsvendor model, others suggest use of periodical reviews based on the items lifetime [14].Most inventory models for perishable items are based on the traditional models, which are often driven by a cost reduction focus. However, few models have a profit optimisation focus, where the price of the perishable product is an explicitly variable in the model [5]. Another model focusing on profit optimisation is the newsvendor model, which defines the possible sales opportunities and loses The objective function of the inventory control model has an impact on the outcome but also an impact on the operational level in the company. Depending on the domain of industry and the ordering strategy, there is a need to consider the objective function. A segmented overview of traditional inventory control policies is illustrated in figure 1.

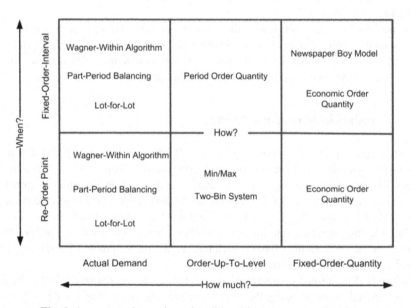

Fig. 1. A segmented overview of traditional inventory control policies

3   Ordering Strategy

Beside the elements of the traditional inventory models, some element has to be acknowledged when dealing with perishables. As perishable inventories undergo change in storage it may in time become partially or entirely unfit for consumption. The lifetime of a product is often measured in days which defines when the products become unacceptable for consumption [4]. Dealing with perishable inventories has a large impact on the inventory control model. Most inventory models assume that stock items can be stored indefinitely to meet future demands, which is not the case with perishable items [14]. Thus, the assumption of infinite shelf life for the inventoried items has originated a considerable amount of criticism to the EOQ model in the inventory lot-sizing literature [9].

A more diversified picture of strategies, which also affect the inventories, is seen when comparing high-end stores and discount stores. A general picture seems to be that high-end stores aim at customer service in terms of a broad assortment and high product availability at the expense of higher inventory investments, while discount stores aim for a limited assortment and low inventory at the expense of possible out-of-stock situations. This case study is based on both high-end stores and discount stores.

From the case study it was found that the decision-making regarding the products aftercare is based on the individual manager's perception of the characteristics of the perishable items and how the highest profit margin can be achieved.

Another challenge found in the case study is that the retailers are not able to use point of sales (POS) data to identify products that are about to reach their expiration date. Instead, many manual resources are used to identify the products, which have reached or almost reached the expiration date. This is due to the fact that the barcode used for POS identification at checkouts does not include the products expiration date. Several major challenges exist for establishing the input for calculating the order quantity:

- How to estimate the current inventory level when having products of varying lifetime stored?
- How to set the sales price for products with more or less reduced lifetime?
- How the remaining demand is affected if products with reduced lifetime are sold at a reduced price (also titled cannibalisation[1])?

3.1   Demand-Price Relation

Ferguson and Koenigsberg [5] present the mathematical function, that if the relation between demand-price is known for a given product, then the desired sales price for new and old products can be found through a linear function, based on the market potential, order quantity of new products, and inventory level of old products. If old products are sold at a discount price they might capture the entire demand share and the retailer will obtain a smaller profit margin of the product but avoid waste. Thus,

---

[1] Cannibalization is the term used when old products sold at a reduced price will lead to a reduced sale of new products [3]. If the old products are sufficiently attractive the customers may find it beneficial enough to buy the old products rather than the new products. The term originates from the literature of marketing strategy, which describe that competition among product types lead to a reduction of sales volume, sales revenue, or market share. Cannibalization can also occur when the producer or their competitors introduce new products.

the expected profit margin of a single product has to be revised by the retailer in order to recalculate the total profit. Desai [3] has further investigated the consequences of the competition of the products caused by cannibalisation. It can be interpreted from Desai's findings, that by having the right price strategy in the product differentiation of old and new products, they become substitutes of each other instead of competing for the same demand.

3.2   Quality Categorisation

The contributions which have value for the literature of perishable inventory control, are the in-depth understandings of the quality deterioration of perishable items [4; 5]. The quality of the product is a function of product life time, however there is a difference in the perception of the quality from the customer view and the retail store view. The perception of the quality is a reflection of the price the customers are willing to pay where the retail stores are speculating on determining the price. The retail stores are always seeking to mark the price as high as possible in order to gain a higher profit margin. From a retailer's point of view this is done by speculating about the customers' behaviour and perception of the quality whereas the customers consider the quality of the products from the value for money perspective.

The categorisation of the quality level is inspired by Ferguson and Koenigsberg [5], Talluri and Ryzin [19], and the retail case study. As illustrated below in figure 2 the quality level can be categorised into three main types based on the characteristics of the products, as it is believed to be representative for all product types.

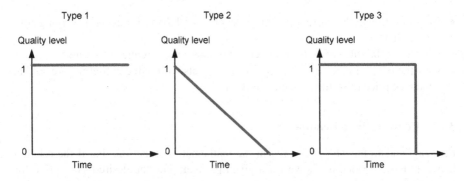

Fig. 2. Three basic quality level categorisations inspired by [5; 19]

In the first type of quality, the product maintains the same quality level, but never reaches a value of zero over time. However, the rapid changes in the market, such as season and trends, have an influence on the customers' perception of quality level of the products. Therefore, the end of the product shelf life will often be determined by the customer's perception. Type one is not affected by the time dimension and can therefore be managed from the traditional inventory models.

The second type of quality level is a product, where the quality level degrades continuously over time and at the end of the shelf life has reached the value of zero. Often, the product within this type of quality does not reach a value of zero before a replenishment of new products arrives [5]. Thus, a single product type in the retail stores can have different levels of quality on the shelves. Therefore, product quality is an important parameter in the inventory control for type two products.

The third type of quality level is where the products maintain the same quality level over time but become unusable after the expiration date. The customers' perception of quality does not decrease over time, but has no value for the customers, when the product expires at the given date. As the product can only be used before a given date, customers prefer to purchase closer to the date in order to ensure that the product will be utilised. Thus, many firms providing these product services set multiple prices for the products depending on the demand, number of remaining product, and, remaining time before expiration date. The purpose of this is to enhance the demand for purchasing in advance, in order to ensure the highest possible profit margin. Furthermore, it is also an approach the companies take in order to reduce the risk of having unsold products left. [1; 5].

3.3   Parameters in Perishable Inventory Control

Dealing with the nature of perishability in inventory control, the quality deterioration of the perishable products has to be taken into consideration together with the unsold inventory from previous periods. The reason is that the different quality levels have different values, and therefore cannot be considered the same, since the products with the lowest quality will have a lower attractiveness for some customers. Some companies meet the different quality levels by differentiating on sales prices, though this affects the profit margin. If the inventory control objective function is based in profit maximisation, then it might be beneficial to incorporate the different product qualities in the development of the inventory control model.

A major challenge is the aftercare of the unsold perishable products, as this has a great impact on the ordering policy, when finding the optimal order quantity. Many retailers, including the case company, do not have a predefined strategic decision making process describing what to do with the unsold inventory before the perishable products have almost or reached the expiration date. The consequences are; the companies do not optimize the profit gain from the potential market. The "mark down" price decision with the purpose of minimizing the loss of investment often fails due to the timing.

In the development of a perishable inventory control model some important parameters, has to be evaluated. The latter contribution is the identification of the elements: 1) demand, 2) periods, 3) quality deterioration of the perishable item, 4) the aftercare of the items including price of the new and the old perishable items and 5) total cost and profit margin function.

4   Conclusion and Further Work

The paper identifies relevant parameters which will serve as input to the further development within perishable inventory control models. They are 1) demand, 2) periods, 3) quality deterioration of the perishable item, 4) the aftercare of the items including price of the new and the old perishable items and 5) total cost and profit margin function. Furthermore, it provides a deeper understanding of the nature of perishables in the retail industry together with the identification of the importance of how the aftercare of items is conducted. It is important to acknowledge the importance of product quality and the parameter must therefore also be considered in the inventory model. Furthermore, when dealing with perishable inventory control, the pricing of products has to be taken into account. Lastly, a better aftercare of items close to expiration date will help reduce investments in inventory and ensure a better profit margin.

Further work will aim at developing a mixed model that is able to handle the time dimension of existing inventory. The case study showed that the existing models do not consider that companies have the same products with different lifetime left. Further, the options and outcome of improved information sharing in supply chains will be studied [6; 16; 18].

Acknowledgement. The authors of this paper graciously acknowledge the funding provided by NordForsk for the LogiNord *"Fresh Food Supply Chain"* project and Christopher Martin for his valuable comments in the paper writing process.

References

1. Belobaba, P., Odoni, A., Barnhart, C.: The Global Airline Industry. Wiley (2009)
2. Chakravarthy, S.R., Daniel, J.K.: A Markovian inventory system with random shelf time and back. Computers & Industrial Engineering 47, 315–337 (2004)
3. Desai, P.S.: Quality Segmentation in Spatial Markets. When Does Cannibalisation Affect Product Line Design. INFORMS Marketing Science 20(3) (2001)
4. Donselaar, K.V.: Inventory Control of Perishables in Supermarkets. International Journal of Production Economics 104(2), 462–472 (2006)
5. Ferguson, M.E., Koenigsberg, O.: How Should a Firm Manage Deteriorating Inventory? Production and Operations Management Society 16(3), 306–321 (2007)
6. Ferguson, M., Ketzenberg, M.: Information Sharing to Improve Retail Product Freshness of Perishables. Production and Operations Management 15(1), 57–73 (2006)
7. Gray, M.: Value: Operations Research and the new health care paradigm. Operations Research for Health Care 1 (2012)
8. Gürler, Ü., Özkaya, B.Y.: Analysis of the (s, S) policy for perishables with a random shelf life. IIE Transactions 40(8), 759–781 (2008)
9. Hariga, M.: A The Inventory Replenishment Problem with a Linear Trend In Demand, vol. 24(2). Pergamon Press Ltd., Saudi Arabia (1993)
10. Khouja, M.: A Note on the Newsboy Problem with an Emergency Supply Option. Journal of the Operational Research Society 47, 1530–1534 (1996)

11. Khouja, M.: The single-period (news-vendor) problem: literature review and suggestions for future research. The International Journal of Management Science 27, 537–553 (1999)
12. Minner, S., Transchel, S.: Periodic Review Inventory-Control for Perishable Products under Service-level Constraints. OR Spectrum 32(4), 979–996 (2010)
13. Moon, I., Choi, S.: The Distribution Free Newsboy Problem with Balking. Operation Research Society 46(4), 537–542 (1995)
14. Nahmias, S.: Optimal Ordering Policies for Perishable Inventory-II. Operation Research 23(4) (1975)
15. Nahmias, S.: Perishable Inventory Theory: A Review. The Univeristy of Santa Clara, California (1982)
16. Olsson, F., Tydesjö, P.: Inventory problems with perishable items: Fixed lifetimes and backlogging. European Journal of Operational Research 202, 131–137 (2010)
17. Pierskalla, W.P., Roach, C.D.: Optimal Issuing Policies for Perishable Inventory. Informs 18(11) (1972)
18. Perego, A., Perotti, S., Mangiaracina, R.: ICT for logistics and freight transportation: a literature review and research agen. International Journal of Physical Distribution & Logistics Management 41(5), 457–483 (2011)

Assessing the Impact of Management Concerns in E-business Requirements Planning in Manufacturing Organizations

John Dilworth and Ashok Kochhar

School of Engineering and Applied Science
Aston University, Birmingham, United Kingdom
a.k.kochhar@aston.ac.uk

Abstract. This paper describes the application of a model, initially developed for determining the e-business requirements of a manufacturing organization, to assess the impact of management concerns on the functions generated. The model has been tested on 13 case studies in small, medium and large organizations. This research shows that the incorporation of concerns for generating the requirements for e-business functions improves the results, because they expose issues that are of relevance to the decision making process relating to e-business. Running the model with both and without concerns, and then presenting the reasons for major variances, can expose the issues and enable them to be studied in detail at the individual function/ reason level.

Keywords: E-Business, Requirements Planning, Manufacturing, Management Concerns, Company characteristics, Supply Chain, Collaborative Working.

1 Introduction

E-business as a concept emerged around the turn of the millennium. During the intervening period, e-business (in so far as it is applied to business-to-business interaction between manufacturing and distribution organizations) seems to have become almost indistinguishable from modern thinking in Supply Chain Management.

The theory of optimization, collaboration and timely information availability seem central to supply chain management thinking [for example1, 2 and 3]. The essential point is that strategic supply chain management demands collaboration among all participants in the value chain. The real business benefits only occur when the entire supply chain is optimized. The problem is that the whole concept stands or falls by collaboration so that everyone will behave for the greater good. If it can be achieved, it may be worth doing; if it cannot for whatever reason (politics, human behavior, relative power structures, sufficient information availability) then the whole thing can be a potentially expensive failure to achieve anything worthwhile.

The e-business domain therefore deals with functionalities that not only are under the control of external organizations (for example customers and suppliers) but

C. Emmanouilidis, M. Taisch, D. Kiritsis (Eds.): APMS 2012, Part II, IFIP AICT 398, pp. 678–685, 2013.

functionalities that are only of any meaning when such organizations are working collaboratively. Any attempt to assess the relevance of e-business concepts must therefore find a way of dealing with the subjective concerns that might exist as to factors that may inhibit such collaborative working. For example buyers and sellers could use some sort of collaboration tool to upload forecasts and actual plans, and then both a given buyer and seller could go into a collaborative mode to come to a common understanding and consensus on what the seller is going to supply to the buyer. The question begged is whether this behavior is realistic taking into account politics, human behavior and the realities of business. It would seem therefore that any attempt to assist organizations with assessing the relevance of possible e-business initiatives must find a way of reflecting the impact of these "softer" issues in determining the initiatives that are likely to be practical and hence beneficial. This paper describes the development of and experience with an e-business requirements model that attempts to deal with these more subjective concerns that might exist as factors inhibiting such collaborative working.

2   An E-business Requirements Model to Deal with Concerns

There are many reported examples of "models" [4, 5, 6, 7 and 8] that find ways in which e-business activity can be categorized so that its structure can be understood. While all of these can provide useful insights into the e-business concept, an approach that dealt with specific detailed functions was felt to be required. Dilworth and Kochhar [9] proposed a systematic process that can propose at a useful level of detail the probable e-business requirements of an organization based on objective criteria. They went on to describe the creation, testing and validation of an e-business requirements specification model to provide such a systematic process. The model constructed contained all the functions relating to the process of buying, selling, or exchanging products, services, and information via computer networks.

The functions supported by the model are organised into three broad categories

- Demand Side Functions;
- Supply Side functions relating primarily to "outside" partners;
- Supply Side Functions relating primarily to "inside" the organization.

The Demand Side Functional Domains were

- Product Development and pre-production – the functions involved in communicating customer-related design and engineering information and change requests.
- Demand Management – the communications relevant to the process of creating and recording customer demand within the organization's systems.
- Supply Chain Planning – the functions involved in the process of responding to the customer's supply chain planning requirements of you as a supplier
- Outbound Logistics – the communications relevant to the dispatch of goods, to and from the customer and other external partners.

- Customer Accounting – the communications with customers or other financial organizations relating to the receiving of money for goods sold.
- Service – For those organizations that provide post sales service the functions relating to the management of remote service activity

The Supply Side "outside" functional domains were

- Product Development and pre-production – the functions involved communicating supplier-related design and engineering information and change requests.
- Supply Chain Planning – the functions involved in the process of planning what needs to be supplied by external suppliers and other partners.
- Purchasing and Procurement – the interactions relevant to the management of the supplier base and the communication of demand to the supplier.
- Inbound logistics – the communications to and from the supplier and other external partners that are relevant to the receiving of goods.
- Manufacturing – in a manufacturing "network" situation, the communications necessary between partner plants and sub contractors.
- Supplier Accounting - the communications with suppliers or other financial organizations relating to the payment of money for goods supplied
- Maintenance – the functions related to communication with external partners involved in planning and executing maintenance activity

The Supply Side "inside" functional domains were

- General Finance – includes those financial management, planning, budgeting or treasury activities conducted amongst separated groups within an organization
- Administration – administration systems managed on a centralized basis (e.g. personnel records, time recording) involving geographically dispersed groups.

3   Model Structure

A preliminary rationale (i.e. a set of reasons) was produced, based on expert knowledge and discussions with industrialists, in order to link these e-business functions to possible objective characteristics and subjective management concerns.

- Characteristics were defined as facts about the business. In principle, company characteristics are intended to be as objective and factual as possible and should be capable of being measured or counted or at least estimated to a reasonable level of accuracy. The number of customers, or the number of items dispatched per year are examples of such facts.
- Concerns are defined as the attitudes or opinions, concerning internal constraints and/or customer/supplier behavior, which can influence the relevance or practicality of e-business functions. Concerns could conceptually be thought of as being either a reason for doing something (for example the opinion of excessive current clerical activity could be a motivation for automating a clerical task), or a reason

for lack of confidence in the success of an initiative (for example suppliers are not sufficiently technologically competent).

A reasoning structure was developed to link the characteristics and concerns of the company through detailed reasoning to an overall verdict as to the overall relevance of a given function. The model thus produced was tested on a variety of case studies and was demonstrated as improving in reliability as case studies progressed. Methods were developed whereby conclusions from the model could be presented at a "management" level of detail, and whereby useful insights could be provided.

In this model the concept of management concerns was added to objective factual characteristics. Concerns were intended to address the issue of how internal attitudes or customer/supplier behavior can make or break the relevance of certain functionalities irrespective of the objective relevance or otherwise of these said functions. In the model, concerns tended to have one of two effects:

- They represent a problem that ought to be a motive for interest in an e-business function (for example excessive current clerical activity ought to be a motivation for automating a clerical task);
- They represent a problem that would tend to prevent an e-business function from being useful, or a reason for lack of confidence in the success of an initiative (e.g. our suppliers cannot cope with our e-business oriented communication with them).

Discussion of the impact of concerns uses a synthesis of the detailed results of the model that was described as an "e-business profile". This is a simple analysis of the proportion of functions triggered (in relation to the total of those possible) in each functional domain converted to a percentage score and presented visually. This provides a simplified presentation, of what are in fact very detailed results, in an accessible format.

Testing of the computerized model in 13 manufacturing organizations has shown that it can generate E-business requirements with a high level of accuracy and requires typically one man day of effort compared to months required to carry out the same task using conventional systems analysis techniques. [9]

It was possible to use these profiles to discuss in general terms the potential impact of management concerns in the achievement of e-business possibilities. Running the model both with and without taking into account the management concerns makes it possible to gain additional insight. A version without concerns potentially provides a more objective analysis, while using the version with concerns brings in more subjective factors. By analyzing the difference between the two, the potential was recognized for achieving extra insights, for example:

- What are the real needs of the organization as opposed to what can be reasonably expected to give benefits assuming current attitudes?
- Which areas of e-business are most adversely affected by current attitudes and concerns?
- How difficult might be the implementation of e-business functions?

The model run without concerns can therefore be regarded as an indication of the theoretical relevance of the functions to the organization, whereas the version with concerns represents the relevance of the functions in a practical world where theory cannot always be perfectly applied! The concept could also be used as an indication of the barriers likely to be encountered in an e-business implementation, and the consequent ease of implementation and probability of success.

4   The Impact of the Concerns across 13 Case Studies

The model has currently been used in thirteen case studies to develop the e-business requirements of manufacturing organizations. These case studies provided some interesting insights both into the potential relevance of e-business in a selection of manufacturing industry and also into the varying impact of these concerns. Figure 1, below, shows the e-business profile of a notional company representing a composite of all the case studies.

Composite profile all Case Studies

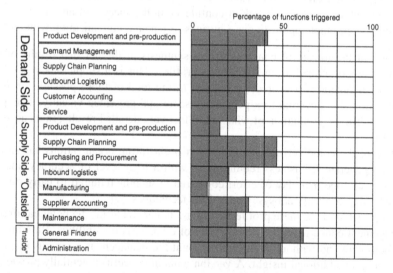

Fig. 1. Composite e-business profile

This is the full output from the model including the effect of management concerns. It shows the "average" (over all the case studies) relevance of e-business functions as predicted by the model. In the e-business profiles, the functions are organised into the three same three broad categories indicated earlier:

- Demand Side Functions;
- Supply Side functions relating primarily to "outside" partners;
- Supply Side Functions relating primarily to "inside" the organization.

In effect this composite profile represents a "league table" of popularity of e-business functions at least in so far as it affects the thirteen case studies. This is interesting primarily as a weighted assessment of e-business function relevance against the sample of British Industry that our case studies represent. The most relevant are:

- The General finance and Administration side representing activities largely internal to the organizations involved;
- The supply chain and purchasing activities oriented to the procurement of goods

On the demand side, there is a more consistent level of coverage among the functional domains. The most popular (just) e-business functions relate to Product Development with customers. For the domains of Demand Management, Supply Chain Planning and Outbound Logistics, roughly one third of the possible functions were considered relevant for the case study sample. Service functions were less triggered, but this relates more to the fact that not all the case studies provided such functions to a significant degree. Of those that did, not all managed these using remote based resources or external organizations for which electronic communication would be relevant.

On the supply side far more variability of functional coverage was encountered. The most popular functions were Supply Chain Planning, Purchasing and Procurement, General Finance and Administration. At first glance it might appear to be anomalous that the functions associated with Product Development with Suppliers were not more popular. This actually is explained by the fact that many of such functions depend on the capabilities of suppliers, and in most case studies the suppliers represented smaller, less capable organizations than the case study organizations themselves (the customers).

Manufacturing functions were by contrast the least triggered. This is perhaps to be expected because most manufacturing activity is intra rather than inter organization, but it also reflects the decreasing importance of manufacturing to some of the case study organizations. Maintenance functions were also less triggered, but this relates more to the fact that not all managed these using external organizations, for which electronic communication would be relevant.

To illustrate the impact of concerns, a second profile is provided in figure 2. The area shaded in black illustrates the additional degree of functionality that would have been considered relevant if the business concerns were ignored.

As can be seen overall, removing the concerns tended to increase the number of e-business functions that were considered relevant, but within that it is difficult to detect a pattern.

A more interesting pattern is provided by profiles that illustrate, for each case study, the e-business functions actually triggered as a percentage of all the possible e-business functions that could have been triggered. These can be visualized as an indication of an overview of the relevance of the e-business concept to each of the case studies.

Composite Concerns Profile all Case Studies

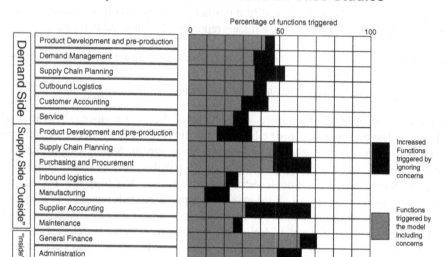

Fig. 2. Composite e-business profile with and without concerns

5   Conclusions

It can be concluded that the arguments in favor of concerns (the fact that the results are more realistic and useful) prevail against the counter-argument of undue pessimism. The key point is that the effect of these concerns in individual detailed cases can be studied at a detailed level, and therefore overridden if the effect of the concerns is unreasonable in an individual case. Having established that concerns are useful, the question arises as to whether there a value is producing results both taking concerns into account and ignoring them. Most concerns proved to be inhibitor concerns, the inclusion of which in the model tended to suppress the potential relevance of e-business functions. Excluding them would suggest that a function was relevant; including them would suggest that a concern was not relevant. For example suppose an e-business supply chain initiative is considered relevant in the absence of concerns, but concerns involving lack of support from management or lack of adequate capability of suppliers render it irrelevant. Which of these judgments is the most useful? The answer is either – depending on circumstance. The judgment including concerns could be a correct reflection of the likelihood of an organization making a success of a particular function. However the version without concerns could be an inspirational reflection of the potential for e-business in an organization providing that there was determination to address the said concerns.

Running the model both with and without concerns, and then presenting the reasons for major variances, can expose the issues and enable them to be studied in detail at the individual function/reason level. An e-business specification ignoring concerns is a useful indication of the objective relevance of the e-business functions to the organization in a reasonably concern-free world, whereas a version with concerns represents the relevance of the functions in a practical world where theory cannot always be perfectly applied! The original idea was that by exploring the difference between the two, an indication could be obtained of the significance of the difficulties of implementation of e-business functions that otherwise might have a theoretical application. Although not perfect or fully developed, it was concluded that the concept was useful in most cases in exposing some of the barriers that could inhibit an e-business implementation. It could therefore be regarded as a useful indicator of the consequent ease of implementation and probability of success.

References

1. Kehoe, D., Boughton, N.: New paradigms in planning and control across manufacturing supply chains, The utilization of Internet technologies. International Journal of Operations & Production Management 21, 582–593 (2001)
2. Horvath, L.: Collaboration: the key to value creation in supply chain management. Supply Chain Management: An International Journal 6, 205–207 (2001)
3. Reyes, P., Raisinghani, M.S., Singh, M.: Global Supply Chain management in the Telecommunications industry: The role of information technology in Integration of Supply Chain Entities. Global Supply Chain Management 5(2), 48–67 (2002)
4. Bakker, E., Zheng, J., Knight, L., Harland, C.: Putting e-commerce adoption in a supply chain context. International Journal of Operations & Production Management 28, 313–330 (2008)
5. Burn, J., Ash, C.: A dynamic model of e-business strategies for ERP enabled organizations. Industrial Management & Data Systems 105, 1084–1095 (2005)
6. Cullen, A.J., Webster, M.: A model of B2B e-commerce based on connectivity and purpose. International Journal of Operations & Production Management 27, 205–225 (2007)
7. Jackson, M.L., Sloane, A.: A model for analyzing the success of adopting new technologies focusing on electronic commerce. Business Process Management Journal 13, 121–138 (2007)
8. Stockdale, R., Standing, C.: A classification model to support SME e-commerce adoption initiatives. Journal of Small Business and Enterprise Development 13, 381–394 (2006)
9. Dilworth, A.J., Kochhar, A.K.: Creation of an e-business requirements specification model. Journal of Manufacturing Technology Management 18, 659–677 (2007)

Supporting the Design of a Management Accounting System of a Company Operating in the Gas Industry with Business Process Modeling

Nikolaos A. Panayiotou and Ilias P. Tatsiopoulos

National Technical University of Athens, School of Mechanical Engineering, Section of
Industrial Management & Operational Research, 15780 Zografos Campus, Athens, Greece
{panayiot,itat}@central.ntua.gr

Abstract. Traditional cost accounting systems are rarely capable to fully support management decision making in organizations. The design of innovative costing systems like Activity Based Costing (ABC) can offer a valuable alternative, however, their design proves to be very challenging. Although the use of business process modeling in cooperation with Activity Based Costing and Activity Based Management (ABM) has been extensively covered in the literature, few articles can be found that refer to the design of a full costing system with the use of a modeling architecture. This paper presents the use of a proposed business process modeling architecture for the design of a full hybrid traditional accounting and Activity Based Costing system of a company operating in the gas industry. The results of the study suggest that business process modeling can enhance the design of a costing system, minimize errors and maximize the acceptance level of all the stakeholders of the system.

Keywords: Business Process Modeling (BPM), Management Accounting System, Activity-Based Costing (ABC), Cost Center Accounting, ARIS.

1 Introduction

A typical traditional cost system accumulates costs by classifying them into certain categories such as labour, materials and overhead costs and then assigns these costs to cost objects [1]. Although the above approach is adequate for financial accounting purposes, it cannot always fully satisfy the needs of top management that is concerned with identifying, presenting and interpreting information for formulation strategy, planning and controlling activities, decision taking, optimizing the use of resources, disclosure to stakeholders and safeguarding assets [2]. Traditional accounting also involves the establishment of an accounting-oriented organizational view which is reflected in the organization evaluation structure [3]. This is a typical situation where accounting data only hardly reflects process-oriented organizational structures. For organizations striving to become more process-oriented, it would be both desirable and necessary to also reflect process structures within an organization's accounting model [3].

C. Emmanouilidis, M. Taisch, D. Kiritsis (Eds.): APMS 2012, Part II, IFIP AICT 398, pp. 686–692, 2013.

Business Process Modeling (BPM) has been extensively used by companies to improve their business process understanding [4]. A qualitative model that provides a graphical interpretation of the process captures the structure of a business process. The objective of qualitative process modeling is to visualize the process and to achieve a commonly agreed view of the process structure. Graphical process presentation facilitates communication between people and helps in developing a common conceptual model of what goes on in the studied process [5]. Many researchers have described objectives associated with the adoption of Business Process Management and Business Process Modeling within organizations [6-8].One popular application covered by many articles is the use of modeling in Activity Based Costing (ABC) and Activity Based Management (ABM) systems [5], [9-12]. However, few [12] emphasize on the design of a full costing system with the use of a business process modeling architecture.

The hypothesis of this paper is that Business Process Modeling can substantially assist the design of a costing system in an organization providing a number of benefits such as rational and systematic identification of cost activities, minimization of errors, improvement on the compatibility of traditional and innovative accounting concepts and maximization of acceptance from all the stakeholders of the costing system The Architecture of Integrated Information Systems (ARIS) has been used as the basis for the development of the proposed architecture, since it originates from academic research, it is well documented within the literature, and in particular it has proven its applicability and usefulness for practice. ARIS provides a framework to help dealing with the complexity of designing and implementing business processes and process aware information systems [13]. ARIS recognizes different views that provide a holistic perspective on business processes by describing "who" does "what", "how", "when" and "why". Moreover, the aspect of cost is taken into account in the framework permitting the interrelation of accounting concepts with business processes and activities. The proposed architecture is demonstrated through a case study of a company operating in the gas industry.

2   A Case Study

The company under discussion operates in the gas industry and is the leader in the national market where it operates. Among its strategic objectives is the continuous natural gas supply at competitive prices, maintaining its leading position in the domestic market, while enhancing its presence inside and outside of the national territory by developing new applications and natural gas services. The company is the immediate natural gas supplier of electricity producers, large customers with annual consumption of over 10 million m3, gas supply companies, end users in regions where gas supply companies have not yet been established and gas-powered vehicles.

The importance of costing for the company is high, as it affects important decisions concerning the procurement mix, capacity reservation in the national natural gas transmission system, scheduling, pricing of different customer categories and future investment initiatives.

2.1   Problem Definition

The existing accounting system of the company was covering the minimum needs for financial reporting but it was not adequate for the support of decision making. As a result the Sales and the Planning Divisions felt the need to maintain custom-made information systems in order to keep data needed for decisions made at a short-term and medium-term level. The existence of more than one costing systems (one formal and some others informal) caused problems in management reporting and led to inconsistent information provision to the different company divisions. In order to cover its unsatisfied needs, the company decided to design a complementary management accounting system, without affecting its existing financial-oriented accounting system. The objectives set by the new system can be summarized as follows:

- Management view of cost with accurate and adequate data in a unique way for all the divisions of the company.
- Full compatibility of the cost provided for financial accounting and management accounting.
- Rational allocation of cost to the final cost objects (customers) with the use of the appropriate cost drivers and beyond the traditional volume and turnover drivers.
- Use of the concept of cost activities in order to provide meaningful information to management.
- Improved and more detailed analysis of the sales and distribution functions.
- Cost allocation to each sector and sub-sector of the existing customers.

The design of the new system should confront with some challenging issues such as the recognition of all costing activities, the selection of the appropriate level of detail, the "bridging" of diverting views of cost provided by different departments, the identification of the existing hierarchies in the different costing dimensions and the guarantee of compatibility between the new and the old system. Taking these into account and in order to support the successful design of the new management accounting system, the adoption of an appropriate business process modeling architecture was decided.

2.2   Methodological Approach

The hybrid traditional costing and Activity Based Costing system was based on a four level hierarchy which is depicted in Figure 1. According to this, cost accumulation takes place in four levels: cost center, activity, sector/ sub-sector and cost object (customer). All four levels accumulate the same amount of cost. For example, the cost of a cost center equals the cost of activities it includes. Cost data entry must at least include the information of the corresponding activity or cost center. If cost data entry does not take place on a cost object level, cost allocation to the lower levels of the hierarchy is based on predefined cost drivers.

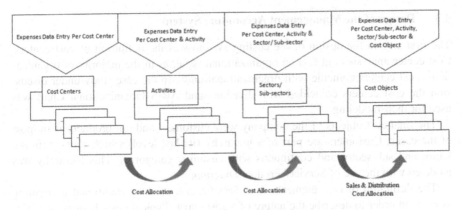

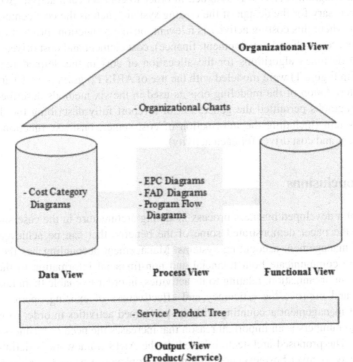

Fig. 1. Suggested Costing Approach

In order to support the design of the new costing system, a business process management architecture was constructed based on selected methods of the ARIS framework. In this framework each modeling object is defined through different perspectives (organization, function, data, process and output view). Six ARIS methods were selected for the construction of the modeling architecture covering the four of the five views of the framework. The selected methods, which are depicted in Figure 2, were interrelated and connected through the process view.

Fig. 2. Business Process Modeling Architecture

2.3   Design of the Management Accounting System

The first step in the design of the costing system was the definition of cost centers. Cost center analysis is in fact an organizational issue, as in the majority of organizations, cost centers coincide with organizational units. In the case study under discussion the cost centers coincided with divisions and ARIS Organizational Chart was used for their modeling.

The final cost objects of the company were customers and not products as in most of the cases. Customers are part of a hierarchy (its last level) which starts from the sector and sub-sector and continuous with customer categories. This hierarchy was modeled with the use of Service/ Product Diagram.

The definition of cost elements is a classification used by traditional accounting systems in order to describe the nature of a cost entry. Typical cost elements are salaries, wages, material cost, taxes, financial expenses, amortization and other costs. In order to model cost elements, the ARIS Cost Category Diagram was used.

The central concept of the designed costing system was the costing activity. The costing activities were defined in such a way that they were in fact a hierarchical decomposition of the existing cost centers in order to guarantee compatibility between the traditional accounting system and the management accounting (activity oriented) system. In order to model the activity model, the simplified Event-driven Process Chain (EPC) diagram was used. For each identified activity, a corresponding Function Allocation Diagram (FAD) was assigned in order to connect each activity with other objects necessary for the design of the costing system, such as the cost center, sector/ sub-sector where this costing activity is relevant, business function (production, sales, distribution, research and development, finance), cost element and cost driver.

All the designed algorithms for the allocation of cost in the defined four levels (depicted in Figure 1) were modeled with the use of ARIS Program Flow Charts (PF).

The interrelation of the modeling objects used in the six methods described in the above paragraphs permitted the generation of a report fully describing the designed costing system (including the information of cost center, business function, sector, cost element and cost driver for each activity).

3   Conclusions

The use of a developed business process modeling architecture in the case study presented in the paper demonstrated some of the benefits that can be achieved in the design of management accounting systems. Management accounting has the important task to communicate both financial and non-financial information to the stakeholders of an organization, relating to its activities, in order to enable them take better decisions and improve the efficiency and effectiveness of existing operations. The relation of management accounting with the performed activities in order to give full meaning to numbers is an important reason that increases the need of business process modeling. The proposed architecture based on the ARIS framework is definitely not the only way to cover business modeling needs. However, it proved to be very effective in the connection of different views of an accounting system satisfying all the stakeholders of such a system. Its effectiveness was proved, firstly by the fact that stakeholders' costing needs were satisfied (something that could not be achieved before the use of the suggested approach). Taking into account that the penetration of formal and primary activity based costing systems in Europe is very low due to existing difficulties in their acceptance, this is a good indication that the approach used for the design of the new system was effective. Secondly, it can be argued that the approach was effective because it offered useful costing functionality such as cohesively integrated views, activity orientation without losing the traditional desirable functionality and decision making support through the meaningful and flexible calculation of cost guaranteed by the integrated methods of the approach.

The most important of the benefits realized in the case study can be summarized as follows:

- Connection of the accounting view with the sales and operation view in a consistent way.
- Provision of meaningful information for decision making related to processes and activities as well as to organisational units and functional structures.
- Support of the design phase of the management accounting system enabling emphasis on the aspects that mattered.
- Generation of accurate functional specifications for the implementation of the costing system in a software.
- Provision of a structured approach for the control of the designed system and the critical review of the developed business rules for cost allocation.
- Improvement in the degree of acceptance of the new accounting system by all the stakeholders.
- Facilitation of future maintenance and improvement of the costing system in such a way that reflects real business changing practices.

The application of the suggested BPM approach for the design of other management accounting systems in the future (in the same or other sectors) is necessary in order to justify the positive results achieved in the case study presented in this paper. The design of a pure activity based costing system with the use of the suggested approach will be even more didactical and will better help in the expansion of the modeling architecture with the potential use of a larger number of views and modeling objects. Finally, the expansion of the modeling architecture in order to support the implementation phase will enhance its practical use.

References

1. Drury, C.: Management Accounting for Business Decisions, 2nd edn. Thomson Learning (2001)
2. Rama Gopal, C.: Accounting for Managers (Starting From Basics). New Age International (P) Ltd., Publishers (2009)
3. Scheer, A.-W.: Business Process Engineering, 3rd edn. Springer, Berlin (1994)

4. Laakso, T.: Performance Evaluation and Process Interventions: A Method for Business Process Development. Finnish Academy of Technology, Espoo (1997)
5. Tornberg, K., Jammsen, M., Paranko, J.: Activity-Based Costing and Process Modeling for Cost-conscious Product Design: A Case Study in a Manufacturing Company. International Journal of Production Economics 79, 75–82 (2002)
6. Davenport, T.H.: Process Innovation. Reengineering Work through Information Technology. Harvard Business School Press, Boston (1993)
7. Hammer, M., Champy, J.: Reengineering the Corporation: A Manifesto for Business Revolution. Harper Business, New York (1993)
8. Harmon, P.: Business Process Change. A Guide for Business Managers and BPM and Six Sigma Professionals, 2nd edn. Morgan Kaufmann, Burlington (2007)
9. Tatsiopoulos, I.P., Panayiotou, N.A.: The Integration of Activity Based Costing and Enterprise Modeling for Reengineering Purposes. International Journal of Production Economics 66(1), 33–44 (2000)
10. Schulze, M., Seuring, S., Ewering, C.: Applying Activity-based Costing in a Supply Chain Environment. International Journal of Production Economics 135, 716–725 (2012)
11. Baykasog, A., Kaplanog, V.: Application of Activity-based Costing to a Land Transportation Company: A Case Study. International Journal of Production Economics 116, 308–324 (2008)
12. Sonnenberg, C., Huemer, C., Hofreiter, B.: Linking Accounting and Process-aware Information Systems - Towards a Generalized Information Model for Process-oriented Accounting. In: European Conference on Information Systems (ECIS 2011), Helsinki, Finland (2011)
13. Scheer, A.-W.: ARIS – Business Process Modeling. Springer, Berlin (1999)

Base Stock Inventory Systems with Compound Poisson Demand: Case of Partial Lost Sales

M. Zied Babai[1], Ziad Jemai[2], and Yves Dallery[2]

[1] BEM-Bordeaux Management School, 680 cours de la Libération, 33405 Talence, France
mohamed-zied.babai@bem.edu
[2] Ecole Centrale Paris, Grande Voie des Vignes, 92290 Châtenay-Malabry, France
{zied.jemai,yves.dallery}@ecp.fr

Abstract. In this paper we extend earlier work that analyzes a single echelon single item base-stock inventory system where Demand is modeled as a compound Poisson process and the lead-time is stochastic. The extension consists in considering a cost oriented system where unfilled demands are lost. The case of partial lost sales is assumed. We first model the inventory system as a Makovian M/G/∞ queue then we propose a method to calculate numerically the optimal base-stock level. A preliminary numerical investigation is also conducted to show the performance of our solution.

Keywords: base-stock, compound Poisson, queuing system, service level, lost sales.

1   Introduction

Inventory control policies have been discussed extensively in the academic literature since the 1950s. A considerable amount of research has been conducted by considering the Normality assumption for modeling the demand ([6], [7], [10]). This is due to the fact that the Normal distribution is attractive from a theoretical perspective and it is also known to provide a good empirical fit to observed demand data. However, it should be noted that the normality assumption makes more sense in the context of fast moving items and in the case of intermittent demand items, such an assumption is judged to be far from appropriate [8].

Intermittent demand items are characterized by occasional demand arrivals interspersed by time intervals during which no demand occurs. As such, demand is built, for modeling purposes, from constituent elements (demand arrivals and demand sizes) that require the consideration of compound demand distributions. Compound Poisson demand processes have pretty much dominated the academic literature due to their comparative simplicity and their theoretical appeal since they may result in standard statistical distributions ([1], [4], [5], [9]). For a Poisson arrival process for example coupled with Logarithmic sizes the resulting distribution is Negative Binomial [9]. In addition, from a modeling perspective, the compound Poisson process may also

C. Emmanouilidis, M. Taisch, D. Kiritsis (Eds.): APMS 2012, Part II, IFIP AICT 398, pp. 693–698, 2013.

model the demand in the context of fast moving items by considering very low demand time intervals or equivalently a high Poisson rate.

Recently, a research work has been conducted to analyze a single echelon single item base-stock system where Demand is modeled as a compound Poisson process and the lead-time is stochastic following a General distribution [2]. In order to determine the optimal base-stock level, the authors have considered cost oriented inventory systems where unfilled demands are backordered. The backordering assumption is realistic and often considered by researchers in order to determine the optimal parameters of inventory policies. However, other interesting cases could also be considered for that purpose, such as the lost sales case under which the system assumes that an excess demand is not carried over but is lost and the total cost include a lost sales cost. This case constitutes the objective of our research work.

It should be noted that the lost sales inventory models have received far less attention from researchers than the backorder models. This is because in one hand lost sales inventory models are much less analytically tractable and in the other hand, most of the optimality results in the base-stock systems have been derived under the backorder assumption. The lack of attention to the lost sales case, especially for base-stock inventory systems under compound Poisson demand has motivated this research work. In this paper, we extend the work of [2] by analyzing the same base-stock inventory system under the lost sales case. The optimal base-stock level is determined under a cost oriented system where unfilled demands are lost.

The remainder of the paper is organized as follows. Section 2 describes the inventory system considered in the paper and provides a method that can be used to calculate the optimal base-stock level. Section 3 presents some preliminary results of the numerical investigation. We end in Section 4 with conclusions and directions for further research.

2   System Analysis

2.1   System Description and Notation

We consider a single echelon single item inventory system where the demand and the lead time are stochastic. Demand is modeled as a compound Poisson process, i.e. the inter-demand arrivals are exponentially distributed and the demand size follows an arbitrary discrete probability distribution. The focus on the discrete case is motivated by the fact that it leads to solutions that are mathematically tractable. Note that if demand sizes are continuous, the same analysis holds but summations should be replaced by their analogous integral functions. The stock is controlled according to a base-stock policy where each replenishment order is associated with a stochastic lead-time. The inventory system will be analyzed in this paper by considering a cost oriented system where unfilled demands are lost.

For the remainder of the paper, we denote by:

λ: mean demand arrival rate

X: demand size (random variable)

μ_x : mean of demand size

σ_x : standard deviation of demand size

f : probability density function of the random variable X

F : cumulative probability distribution of the random variable X

Y : lead-time (random variable)

L: mean lead-time

$I(t)$: inventory position at time t

$N(t)$: number of outstanding ordered units in the system at time t

S: order-up-to-level

h: inventory holding cost per unit per unit of time

B: unit lost sale cost per unit

X_k : the sum of k i.i.d. random variables X $(k \geq 1)$

f_k : probability density function of the random variable X_k

F_k : cumulative probability distribution of the random variable X_k $(k \geq 1)$

$(X)^+ = \max(X, 0)$

$P(x)$: probability of an event x

2.2 System Modeling and Analysis

In this paper, we assume that partial lost sales are considered, i.e. a demand can be partially satisfied from the stock on hand and the excess demand is lost. The expected total inventory cost is composed of the expected holding cost and the expected lost sales cost. It is given as follows:

$$E[C(S)] = hSp_0^{(S)} + \sum_{i=1}^{\infty} \left[h(S - X_i)^+ + B\lambda(X_i - S)^+ \right] p_i^{(S)} \tag{1}$$

which is equivalent to

$$E[C(S)] = hSp_0^{(S)} + \sum_{i=1}^{\infty} h \sum_{n=0}^{S}(S - n)f_i(n) + B\lambda \sum_{n=S+1}^{\infty}(n - S)f_i(n) \; p_i^{(S)} \tag{2}$$

where $p_i^{(S)}$ is the probability that there are $I(t) = S - X_i$ items in stock at the stationary regime. Note that analyzing the inventory level $I(t)$ is equivalent to analyzing the number of customers $N(t)$ in a Makovian M/G/∞ queue, with demand arrival rate λ_i and departure rate $\mu_i = i\mu = i\,(1/L)$, as shown in the following Markovian chain, where the state i corresponds to the number of outstanding ordered units in the system. For more details about the modeling of inventory systems by using the queuing theory, the reader is referred to [3].

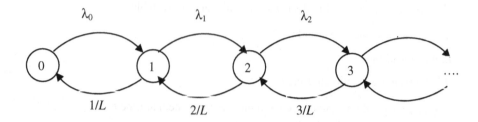

$\lambda_i = \lambda\,P(\text{the quantity of the order (i - 1) is strictly less than } S) = \lambda\,F_i(S-1)$

Thus, it is easy to show that in the stationary regime,

$$p_i^{(S)} = \frac{(\lambda L)^i}{i!}\,p_0^{(S)}\prod_{j=1}^{i-1}F_j(S-1) \quad \text{for all } i \geq 2 \tag{3}$$

where $p_0^{(S)} = 1 - \sum_{i=1}^{\infty} p_i^{(S)}$ and $p_1^{(S)} = (\lambda L)p_0^{(S)}$

The optimal base-stock level S^* should be calculated numerically such that:

$$S^* = \min\{S : E[C(S+1)] - E[C(S)] \geq 0\}$$

Where $E[C(S)]$ is given by (2) and $p_i^{(S)}$ is given by (3).

It is clear that in order to find numerically the optimal base-stock level S^*, the function $E[C(S+1)] - E[C(S)]$ should be calculated for different values of S (by using a dichotomy for example), which requires the calculation of the stationary probabilities $p_i^{(S)}$ for different values of S.

In the next section, we calculate numerically the optimal base-stock level and cost and we investigate the impact of some parameters' variation on the optimal base-stock level.

3 Numerical Investigation

For the purpose of the numerical investigation, we assume that the Poisson rate of the demand arrivals λ is varied from 0.1 to 10, which allows us to deal with demands that characterize both fast and slow moving items as it has been done by [2]. Regarding the distribution of the demand size X, in order to reduce the complexity of the of the numerical investigation, we should consider a demand size distribution that is discrete and regenerative, since in that case the distribution of the random variable X_i (the sum of i discrete demand size distributions) is of the same type, so that by knowing the type of the distribution f_i and the first two moments, the analysis is straightforward. For the purpose of this numerical investigation, we consider that demand sizes follow a Poisson distribution with $\mu_X = 10$. The results are presented by considering the case: $h = 1$, $B = 10$.

The optimal base-stock level and the optimal cost when λ is varied in $[0.1,1]$ are shown in Figure 1 which corresponds to the case of slow moving stock keeping units (SKUs). The optimal base-stock level and the optimal cost when λ is varied in $[1,10]$ are shown in Figure 3 which corresponds to the case of fast moving SKUs.

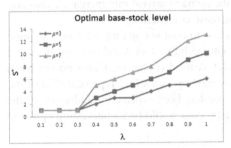 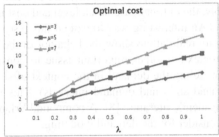

Fig. 1. Variation of the optimal base-stock level and cost in the case of slow moving SKUs

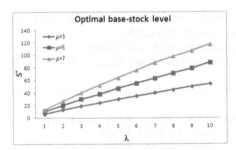 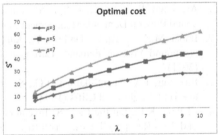

Fig. 2. Variation of the optimal base-stock level and cost in the case of fast moving SKUs

Figures 1-2 show that the optimal base-stock level is an increasing function of the demand arrival rate λ which is expected since the average demand per time unit increases which necessitates higher stock level to reduce the total cost. It should be noted that in the case of slow moving SKUs and for very low λ values, the optimal base-stock level is equal to 1 even when the average demand size increases which can be explained by the fact that the demand per time unit remains relatively low and does not necessitates more than one unit to be kept in stock. Obviously, when the demand size and the demand arrival rate increase considerably in the cases of both slow and fast moving SKUs, the optimal base-stock level and cost increase considerably.

4   Conclusions and Future Research

In this paper, we have analyzed a single echelon single item inventory system under a compound Poisson demand and stochastic lead-time. We assume that the system in controlled with a continuous review base-stock policy. Based on a Markovian M/G/∞ queue model, the optimal base-stock level is determined under a cost oriented system where unfilled demands are lost. Some preliminary numerical results, related to the optimal base-stock level and cost, have been given in the case of both slow and fast moving SKUs. The results show that in the case of slow moving SKUs and for very low λ values, the optimal base-stock level is very low. Moreover, in the cases of fast moving SKUs, when the demand size and the demand arrival rate increase considerably, the optimal base-stock level and cost increase considerably.

An interesting way to extend this research is to conduct an empirical investigation with real data to show the behavior of the optimal base-stock level and cost in such a context. Another important issue to consider is the hypothesized distribution when modeling the demand in the context of slow moving items (i.e. representation of demand sizes and demand intervals). This issue has been repeatedly addressed in the academic literature [8]. A compound Erlang process would be an interesting option to consider for the demand modeling.

References

1. Archibald, B.C., Silver, E.A. (s,S) Policies under Continuous Review and Discrete Compound Poisson Demand. Management Science 24, 899–909 (1978)
2. Babai, M.Z., Jemai, Z., Dallery, Y.: Analysis of order-up-to-level inventory systems with compound Poisson demand. European Journal of Operational Research 210, 552–558 (2011)
3. Buzacott, J.A., Shanthikumar, J.G.: Stochastic Models of Manufacturing Systems. Prentice-Hall, Englewood Cliffs (1993)
4. Cheung, K.L.: On the (S-1, S) Inventory Model under Compound Poisson Demands and i.i.d. Unit Resupply Times. Naval Research Logistics 43, 563–572 (1996)
5. Eaves, A.H.C.: Forecasting for the ordering and stock holding of consumable spare parts, Unpublished Ph.D. thesis, Lancaster University, UK (2002)
6. Silver, E.A., Pyke, D.F., Peterson, R.: Inventory management and production planning and scheduling, 3rd edn. John Wiley & Sons, Inc., New York (1998)
7. Strijbosch, L.W.G., Moors, J.J.A.: Modified normal demand distributions in (R,S)-inventory control. European Journal of Operational Research 172, 201–212 (2006)
8. Syntetos, A.A., Babai, M.Z., Lengu, D., Altay, N.: Distributional assumption for parametric forecasting of intermittent demand. Service Parts Management: Demand Forecasting and Inventory. Springer Verlag (2010)
9. Teunter, R., Syntetos, A.A., Babai, M.Z.: Determining Order-Up-To Levels under Periodic Review for Compound Binomial (Intermittent) demand. European Journal of Operational Research 203, 619–624 (2010)
10. Zipkin, P.H.: Foundations of Inventory Management. McGraw-Hill, Inc., Boston (2000)

A Concept for Project Manufacturing Planning and Control for Engineer-to-Order Companies

Pavan Kumar Sriram, Erlend Alfnes, and Emrah Arica

Norwegian University of Science and Technology, Trondheim, Norway
{Pavan.sriram,erlend.alfnes,emrah.arica}@ntnu.no

Abstract. Engineer-to-order products are customized to a particular client's specification. Planning can be a problem as the products may be large and complex especially due to uncertainties in the duration of the operations. A conceptual project manufacturing planning and control (PMPC) framework is presented in relation to typical engineer to order (ETO) companies. The existing approaches, problems, solutions, and limitations of current manufacturing planning and control (MPC) for ETO environment are discussed. This paper contributes to the development of an improved understanding and more robust definition of MPC in ETO industries, and highlights how the key challenges and the opportunities that PMPC offer in an ETO sector.

Keywords: engineer to order, project manufacturing planning and control.

1 Introduction

ETO supply networks are dynamic and hard to define, and their planning and control functionalities are frequently affected by the actions of suppliers and customers which typically may result in excessive inventories, long lead times, low customer satisfaction and poor resource allocation [5]. Due to high complexity of the products the customer are involved closely from the design to engineering phase of a product [3]. ETO companies cannot forecast due to unknown sales and product specifications for future order [5]. This type of manufacturing environment requires a modified manufacturing planning and control (MPC) method to suit the characteristics and in this paper we highlight and discuss some of the classical MPC approaches such as Kanban, Manufacturing Resource approaches' to Production Planning (MRP II) and Theory of Constrains (TOC), and also discuss techniques such as Workload Control (WLC), Constant Work In Process (CONWIP), Paired cell Overlapping Loops of Cards with Authorization (POLCA) solutions for their applicability for ETO [15]. The paper starts with a description of the methodology, followed by an introduction to the empirical background of ETO. Next, MPC is defined, while the two subsequent sections outline and discuss issues on the current MPC approaches and its limitations and Project manufacturing planning and control (PMPC) respectively. The conclusion outlines the paper's contributions and some suggestions for further research.

C. Emmanouilidis, M. Taisch, D. Kiritsis (Eds.): APMS 2012, Part II, IFIP AICT 398, pp. 699–706, 2013.

2   Methodology

This conceptual paper is a theoretical discussion of the MPC approaches applicable to an ETO environment. Research on the ETO MPC approaches situations is scarce since the majority of research focuses on a mass production environment. The paper's theoretical base is within planning and control, and the discussion exploits on improving the existing MPC system proposed by Vollmann [19] through recommendations that have been carefully identify by the literature review in the form of international journal publications, scientific textbooks, and white papers in order to capture the main challenges, approaches and solutions from previous researchers on the MPC in ETO sector. The aim of the paper is therefore not to provide solutions to these highly complex issues, but rather to highlight, discuss and develop a PMPC framework based on existing literature.

3   ETO Sector Characteristics and Requirements

ETO companies are characterized by time-limited projects related to the supply of complex equipment to third parties, and this process often includes the phases: design, manufacturing, installation, and commissioning [16] and [3] state that that the decoupling point is located at the design stage, and operate in project specific environments. According to Hicks [7] ETO products are manufactured and assembled in low volumes to satisfy individual customers' specifications. Stevenson et al., [15] agrees on this and described the production volume as batch of one to very low volume. The production volume is not mention by all authors but there is no disagreement found in literature that the production volume is low within the ETO environment. Bertrand and Muntslag [2] describe control characteristics of the ETO production situation by using the following three aspects: dynamics, uncertainty and complexity. The engineer-to order firms have to cope with strong fluctuations in mix and sales volume in the short and medium term. It is impossible to cope with these fluctuations by means of, for example, creating capacity stock because of the customer order driven production. This dynamic market situation asks for a lot of flexibility to cope with these fluctuations. Gosling and Naim [3] and Little [11] describe that flexibility is a condition for ETO firm success, an ETO company needs to deal with strong fluctuations in mix and sales volume. The second characteristics uncertainty is the difference between the amount of information required to perform a task and the amount of information already available in the organization. And in an ETO environment uncertainty is high for both the process as for the products for example in terms of specification, demand, lead times and the duration of processes [5] The third characteristic mentioned by Bertrand and Muntslag [2] is complexity and it exists because information is unknown and changes are bound to occur over time. Little [11] states that a common feature of ETO manufacturing is for the customers to change their requirements over the time of the production.

4   ETO MPC Approaches and Exiting Solutions

Classical manufacturing planning and control methods such as Material Requirement Planning, Workload Control, Drum-Buffer-Rope, Kanban and CONWIP are briefly described on the next pages. At the end of this description the characteristics of the methods are summarized in Table 2.

Material Requirements Planning (MRP) and Manufacturing Resource Planning MRP II: MRP is a periodic push-based system designed for complex production planning environments [15]. In a study of Sower and Abshire [13] was found that one-third of the manufacturing companies studied use packages such as MRP. MRP II often offers greater functionality then MRP because of the wider integration of the number of modules and company operations. According to [3] the choice of a MRP II system is often based on the wide availability. They also state that many engineer-to-order firms have tried to implement MRP II without success.

Workload Control (WLC): is a MPC method designed for highly complex production environments like job shop and MTO / ETO industry. Land and Gaalman [10] mention that WLC works particularly well in the job shop environment, reducing shop floor throughput time (SFTT) and WIP. According to Stevenson and Hendry [16] WLC originates from the concept of input and output control. The input of work to the shop floor is controlled in agreement with the capacity of work centres (the output rate) in order to regulate and maintain a stable level of WIP. The method Workload Control will not be simulated, not because it doesn't fit an engineer-to-order environment well but because this method needs to be included in the demand planning at the medium planning level horizon.

Drum-Buffer-Rope (DBR): The Theory of Constraints (TOC) is a bottleneck-oriented concept which is developed from Optimized Production Technology (OPT), as is commonly attributed to the work of Goldratt [16] The production planning and control method is now more known as the Drum-Buffer- Rope (DBR) approach. Under the TOC philosophy, the bottleneck should be scheduled at 100% utilisation because the bottleneck determines the performance of the whole production system. The bottleneck work centers are the *drums* and are used to control the workflow. The *rope* refers to "pull" scheduling at the non-bottleneck work centers. The purpose of the rope is to tie the production at each resource to the drum. The *buffers* are used to protect the throughput of the bottleneck work centers. The goal of the DBR method is to break a constraint, or bottleneck condition, and thereafter identify the next constraint. This continuous improvement process is an integral part of the TOC philosophy [19]. Wahlers and Cox [20] highlight the applicability to highly customized industries where the companies where able to reduce the lead time and improve the delivery reliability performance.

KANBAN: Kanban is a card-based production system where the start of one job is signalled by the completion of another. According to Stevenson et al. [15] there are many variations of the Kanban system but in the simplest form cards is part number specific. Kanban is not a suitable method within the engineer-to-order environment because of the routing variability, small batch size and lack of repetitions.

POLCA: POLCA is an abbreviation for Paired-cell Overlapping Loops of Cards with Authorization [18]. It is a MPC method that regulates the authorization of order progress on the shop floor in a cellular manufacturing system. POLCA controls the flow of work between production cells. The method is introduced by Suri [18] in his book on Quick Response Management (QRM). Within this management philosophy the focus is on the reduction of lead time.

CONWIP: CONWIP stands for Constant Work In Progress and is a continuous shop floor release method. The CONWIP system has been proposed in [13], and further presented in [14]. CONWIP uses cards to control the number of WIPs. For example, no part is allowed to enter the system without a card (authority). After a finished part is completed at the last workstation, a card is transferred to the first workstation and a new part is pushed into the sequential process route. Spearman et al. [13] mention that CONWIP sets a limit on the total WIP in the entire system. CONWIP and Kanban are both card systems but Kanban sets a limit on the number of jobs between every pair of adjacent stations. Rather than set a limit on the level of WIP between each step in the manufacturing process, or the entire system. Hopp and Roof [9] mention that to change the number of cards and regulates the level of WIP Statistical Throughput Control is used. This requires accurate feedback data which is difficult to provide in a complex manufacturing environment like ETO.

In table 1 all the described manufacturing planning and control methods are summarized. For each method the characteristics are summed up. It is important when using these methods to be aware of this and take it into consideration when selecting a MPC method for an engineer-to order organization.

Table 1. MPC method characteristics

MPC method	Push or Pull	Product mix	Volume	Flexibility
MRP & MRP II	Push	Stable	High	Low
WLC	Pull	Variable	High	High
DBR	Hybrid	Stable	Low	Low
Kanban	Pull	Stable	High	Low
POLCA	Hybrid	Variable	Low	High
CONWIP	Hybrid	Stable	Low	High

Based on the description and summary we can see that WLC and POLCA have some degree of relevance towards planning and control activities in an ETO and others lack the capability to meet the requirements of an ETO environment. As of now there is only one framework common to all types of manufacturing and due to issues such as demand forecast, short lead time and urgent delivery, controlling engineering change, dynamic scheduling and coordination of activities etc. calls for a modified MPC framework as even the approaches like WLC and POLCA might not be the most efficient approaches [15] to meet the overall requirement of ETO characteristics. Table 2 shows the summary of manufacturing planning and control literature in ETO reviewed. And based on the summary and discussions we propose PMPC which is described in the next section.

Table 2. Summary of manufacturing planning and control literature in ETO reviewed [16]

Topic	Author(s)	Methodology	Approaches and Solutions
Framework, problems, and implementation (MRP,ERP,and MRPII)	Jin et al. (1995)	Conceptual	Proposed a new MRP framework in ETO environment
	Bertnard and Muntslag (1993)	Literature review and conceptual	Contradiction of MRP II and ETO environment, a new framework
Web-based SCM and MPC	Kehoe and Boughton, (2001a and 2001b); Caglinao et al. (2003)	Simulation	eSCM for planning and control
Computer-aided production management issues	Hicks and Braiden, (2000)	Conceptual and simulation	MPC issues in capital goods industry, applicability of MRP II
	Gosling and Naim (2009)	Literature review	Robust definition of SCM in ETO
Overview of MPC	Gelders, (1991)	Literature review and conceptual	Review of new MPC concepts, Planning approach to monitor capacity, lead times in ETO
Integrated planning and scheduling	Little et al. (2000)	Multiple case study	MPC challenge in ETO companies , ETO planning and scheduling reference model
	Samaranayake and Toncich (2007)	Conceptual and simulation	Integrated ERP and SCM
	Caron et al. (1995)	Conceptual	Developed a project management model, Integrating manufacturing and innovative processes
	Yeo et al. (2006)	Conceptual	Managing projects in synchronization
	Rahman et al. (2003)	Literature and Conceptual	Framework to establish design and manufacturing for ETO companies

5   Project Manufacturing Planning and Control

PMPC is a modification of the well-known MPC framework developed by [19] to the project manufacturing environment. The framework illustrates the planning processes in project manufacturing and their interconnection (refer Fig. 1). The proposed framework, when implemented in an MPC environment, will act as a decision support system and can serve as a foundation of further work to be carried in this area. In project MPC, the demand management function covers the management of sales order lines and defines either project groups as "planning groups" or single projects for these orders based on the resemblance between different orders. The demand management process is carried out in collaboration with engineering management tools where preliminary design and configuration activities are performed. When the detailed engineering activities are further accomplished in time, the project schedule and tasks are updated and customized parts/ items are specified. Projects and tasks create demands for specific parts/ items, and eventually these demand items requests for resources.

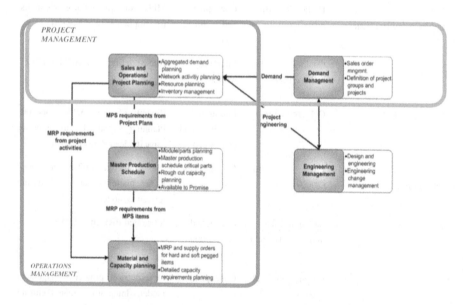

Fig. 1. Project planning and control (PMPC)

Aggregated demands planning for these main parts are done on the *sales and operations planning* function. Since the project environment requires a network of subcontractors, suppliers, and outsourcers, network activity planning, namely subcontracting and operation rates, should be identified on this overall planning function. Further a resource capacity check should be made on this level as well. Project tasks are then pegged to demand items/ parts related to each task and these demand parts/ items are also pegged to the assigned capacities. Master production scheduling is performed on modules that are defined in the product structure. This planning process is useful in project manufacturing for the planning of long lead time parts and sub-assemblies that require preproduction or need to be ordered in advance. Material requirement planning is controlled by different reservation levels that are assigned to items or item groups. Some items are project specific, some can be assigned to project groups, while some can be identified as common supply, meaning that, they can be used by all projects and project groups. When the detailed capacity is checked against the plans, the production and purchasing orders are placed.

When an engineering change request is received from the customer, project MPC system can be used to aid changes related to material management and respective adjustments on the project schedule. This can be enabled by its pegging logic. Having linked the orders with the supplies, activities, and project schedule, it facilitates change propagation of the engineering change request in an integrated and automated manner. Then, these changes can automatically adjust the project schedule by the pegging functionality which is enabling the linkage between materials and activities. Hence, the updated schedule can up-date the timing, budget, and cost, which can be either used to negotiate with the customer or for control purposes.

6   Conclusion and Future Work

ETO companies face many challenges for effective and efficient management of MPC. By means of this paper we aim to provide main contribution to theory by proposing a conceptual framework to under-stand project manufacturing planning and control. The framework will be useful for ETO companies in their ERP development and tendering practices by defining the methods and functionality that are required for efficient planning and control in ETO environments. The research has limitations due to the relatively scarce literature and lack of empirical study and evidences. However it reaches its main objective by increasing the theoretical knowledge in this field and building a framework for further study and applications. The framework will be further developed in collaboration with the Norwegian offshore supplier industry and the research projects "The Norwegian Manufacturing Future" (SFI NORMAN) and "PowerUp". The main limitations are related to the study's conceptual nature, and further research is required to investigate the appropriateness of the suggested approaches and techniques in practice.

References

1. Alderman, N., Braiden, P.M., Hills, W., Maffin, D., Thwaites, A., Vaughan, R.: Business process analysis and technological change in the capital goods industry. International Journal of Computer Applications in Technology 6, 418–427 (1998)
2. Bertrand, J.W.M., Muntslagd, R.: Production control in engineer to order firms. Int.J. Prod. Econ. 30, 3–22 (1993)
3. Braiden, P.M., Alderman, N., Thwaites, A.T.: Engineering design and product development and its relationship to manufacturing: A programme of case study research in British companies. International Journal of Production Economics 30-31, 265–272 (1993)

4. Gosling, J., Naim, M.M.: Engineer-to-order supply chain management: A literature review and research agenda. International Journal of Production Economics 122, 741–754 (2009)
5. Hicks, C., Braiden, P.: Computer-aided production management issues in the engineer-to-order production of complex capital goods explored using a simulation approach. International Journal of Production Research 38, 4783–4810 (2000)
6. Hicks, C., Mcgovern, T., Earl, C.: Supply chain management: A strategic issue in engineer to order manufacturing. International Journal of Production Economics 65, 179–190 (2000)
7. Hicks, C., Mcgovern, T., Earl, C.F.: A typology of UK engineer-to-order companies. International Journal of Logistics 4, 43–56 (2001)
8. Hicks, C., Song, D.P., Earl, C.F.: Dynamic scheduling for complex engineer-to- order products. Int. J. of Prod. Research 45(15), 3477–3503 (2007)
9. Hopp, W.J., Roof, M.L.: Setting WIP levels with Statistical Throughput Control (STC) in CONWIP production lines. International Journal of Production Research 36, 867–882 (1998)
10. Land, M.J., Gaalman, G.: Workload control concepts in job shops - a critical assessment. International Journal of Production Economics 46, 535–548 (1996)
11. Little, D., Rollins, R., Peck, M., Porter, J.K.: Integrated planning and scheduling in the engineer-to-order sector. International Journal of Computer Integrated Manufacturing 13, 545–554 (2000)
12. Sower, V.E., Abshire, R.D.: Successful implementation of advanced manufacturing technology: a cross sectional survey. International Journal of Computer Applications in Technology 16, 12–20 (2003)
13. Spearman, M.L., Hogg, G.L.: Production rates, flow times and work in process levels in a generalized pull production system. Manuscript, Department of Industrial Engineering and Management Sciences, Northwestern University, Evanstin IL, Department of Industrial Engineering, Texas A&M University (1986)
14. Spearman, M., Woodruff, D., Hopp, W.: CONWIP: a pull alternative to kanban. International Journal of Production Research 28, 879–894 (1990)
15. Stevenson, M., Hendry, L.C., Kingsman, B.G.: A review of production planning and control: the applicability of key concepts to make -to-order industry. Int. J. of Prod. Res. 43(5), 869–898 (2005)
16. Stevenson, M., Hendry, L.C.: Aggregate load-oriented workload control: A review and a re-classification of a key approach. International Journal of Production Economics 104, 676–693 (2006)
17. Sriram, P.K., Alfnes, E., Arica, E.: Manufacturing planning and control functionalities in engineer-to-order companies: an investigation of challenges and existing solutions. In: IWAMA 2012, Trondheim, Norway (2012)
18. Suri, R.: Quick Response Manufacturing. A Companywide Approach to Reducing Lead Times. Productivity Press (1998)
19. Vollmann, T.E., Berry, W.L., Whybark, D.C., Jacobs, R.F.: Manufacturing Planning and Control for Supply Chain Management (2005)
20. Wahlers, J.L., Cox, J.F.: Competitive factors and performance measurement: applying the theory of constraints to meet customer needs. International Journal of Production Economics 37, 229–240 (1994)

Practical Considerations about Error Analysis for Discrete Event Simulations Model

Giovanni Davoli[1], Peter Nielsen[2], Gabriele Pattarozzi[1], and Riccardo Melloni[1]

[1] Department of Mechanical and Civil Engineering (DIMeC), University of Modena and Reggio Emilia; via Vignolese 905, 41100, Modena, Italy
[2] Department of Production, Aalborg University, Fibigerstrede 16, DK 9220 Aalborg, Denmark
giovanni.davoli@unimore.it

Abstract. The purpose of making efficient and flexible manufacturing systems is often related to the possibility to analyze the system considering at the same time a wide number of parameters and their interactions. Simulation models are proved to be useful to support and drive company management in improving the performances of production and logistic systems. However, to achieve the expected results, a detailed model of the production and logistic system is needed as well as a structured error analysis to guarantee results reliability. The aim of this paper is to give some practical guide lines in order to drive the error analysis for discrete event stochastic simulation model that are widely used to study production and logistic system.

Keywords: discrete event, simulation model, error analysis, stochastic model.

1 Introduction

Stochastic, discrete events, simulation models are widely used to study production and logistic system. Apart from the development, one of the main problem of this approach is to perform the error analysis on the outputs of the simulation model. Simulation experiments are classified as either terminating or non-terminating as far as the goal of the simulation is concerned (Law and Kelton, 2000), (Fishman, 2000).

If we limit our interests on non-terminating simulation, the error analysis can be split into two different parts. The first part consists of individuating the initial transient period and the confidence interval of the outputs. The second part consists of estimating how the transient period and the outputs confidence interval varies when the initial model scenario is changed. The first part of the problem is widely studied, Kelton (1983-1989), Schruben (1982-1983), Welch (1982), Vassilacopoulos (1989) White (1997), and many methods are provided to determinate the transient period often related to output stability, that can be quantified in different ways. Between the proposed techniques Mean Squared Pure Error method, Mosca et al. (1985-1992), should be reminded as a practical method useful to determinate both transient period and confidence interval. On the other hand the second part of error analysis problem is not commonly addressed directly as reported in the recent work of Sandikc (2006) that tries to fill the gap for the initial transient period for simulation model addressing

C. Emmanouilidis, M. Taisch, D. Kiritsis (Eds.): APMS 2012, Part II, IFIP AICT 398, pp. 707–713, 2013.
© IFIP International Federation for Information Processing 2013

production lines. The variance of outputs confidence interval between different scenario is often faced with the hypothesis that it is normally distributed around a central value used in the reference scenario according with the basic theory of statistics (Box et al. 2013). But in many practical cases there is no evidences that this hypothesis is correct and, moreover, the significance of central value, for the reference scenario, is lost. In fact in some recent simulation handbook (Chung 2004) the advice to quantify the confidence interval for all different simulated scenario is given.

2   Purpose

The aim of this paper is to give some practical guidelines in order to drive the error analysis for discrete event stochastic simulation models. The paper is focused on the study of confidence interval variance related to the variance of simulated scenario. Nowadays, in many practical applications, the calculation potential is large enough to perform "long" simulation run in order to assure to exceed the initial transient period. Much more important is to determinate the confidence interval for the outputs in different simulated scenario, because overestimate or underestimate these confidence intervals can drive analysts towards a wrong interpretation of the results.

3   Methodology

To address the aim of the paper a quite simple discrete event simulation model is considered and the MSPE (1) is used to estimate outputs confidence interval. Then the simulation are performed according to different scenario and the variance of confidence interval is studied for different outputs.

$$MSPE_i = \frac{\sum_{j=1}^{r}(y_{ji}-Y_i)^2}{r-1} *$$ (1)

* i: day; y_{ji}: output value at day i, replication j; Y_i: output mean at day i, on r replications.

This paper is grounded on a discrete events simulation model reproducing a re-order point logistic system, in particular a single-item fixed order quantity system also known as: Economic Order Quantity (EOQ) model. The economic order quantity (EOQ), first introduced by Harris (1913), and developed by Brown (1963) and Bather (1966) with stochastic demand, is a well-known and commonly used inventory control techniques reported in a great variety of hand book, for example: Tersine (1988) and Ghiani (2004). The notation used in this paper is illustrated in table 1.

Table 1. Symbol and definitions

Symbol	Unit	Definition
N	Day	Number of days for simulation
D_i	Unit/day	Mean demand per day in units
Lt	Day	Mean lead time in day
C_o	Euro/order	Single order cost in euro
C_s	Euro/ unit*year	Stock cost in euro per unit per year
SS	Unit	Safety stocks in unit

3.1   Simulation Model

The simulation model was developed according with the standard EOQ model for single item. A set of stochastic functions, developed in SciLab environment, are used to generate the demand that activates the model. The simulation model was tested performing standard EOQ model with normal distributed demand (where σ_d is demand standard deviation) and normal distributed lead time (where σ_t is lead time standard deviation). The parameters set used in the reference scenario are illustrated in table 2.

Table 2. Used parameters set

Parameter	Set value
D_i	1.000,00
σ_d	300,00
Lt	7,00
σ_t	2,00
C_o	1.000,00
C_s	1,00
Imposed SL	0,95

To evaluate model performances, in terms of achieved service level, a set of 4 Key Performance Indicators (KPI) is defined. The used KPI are illustrated in table 3.

Table 3. Used KPI

KPI	Unit	Definition
SL1	%	1-Number of stock-out in days per day
SL2	%	1-Number of stock-out in units per day
SL3	%	1-Number of stock-out in units per day during lead time
SL4	%	1-Number of stock-out event during lead time period

3.2   Design of the Experiments

To investigate the influence of different parameters on confidence intervals four factors are considered. These four factors are:

- Demand distribution;
- Lead time distribution;
- Ratio C_o/C_s;
- SS, safety stocks.

A full factorial experiment with three levels is used in this paper. Four factors and three levels give $3^4 = 81$ combinations. For each combination a number of 5 replications were conducted for a number of 405 simulations. The three settings for the four factors are shown in table 4.

Table 4. Factors setting

	Low (-1)	Mean (0)	High (+1)
D	Normal distribution, mean = 1,000 units/day, standard deviation = 300 units/day	Uniform distribution, minimum = 500 units/day, maximum = 1,500 units/day	Exponential distribution, mean = 1,000 units/day
Lt	Normal distribution, mean = 7 day, standard deviation = 2 day	Uniform distribution, minimum = 1day, maximum = 13 day	Exponential distribution, mean = 7 day
C_o/C_s	100	1.000	1.900
SS	0 units	1.000 units	2.000 units

4   Findings

The presented experiments are evaluated in terms of stability of the results and confidence interval width for all considered KPI. The simulations are conducted for a length of 1.000 days and this guarantee the stability of outputs for all KPI. Initial transient period length varies according with different parameters set and the variance is more significant for certain KPI, as shown in figure 1.

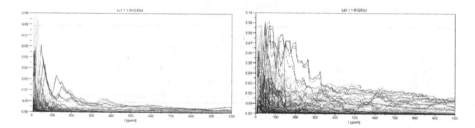

Fig. 1. MSPE for KPI SL1 and SL3

To evaluate the significance of confidence intervals the results are presented for each KPI as the ratio between half interval and the mean for each KPI. Confidence half intervals are calculated for a 95% level of significance according with (2).

$$I_{\frac{1}{2}} = Z_{\frac{\alpha}{2}} \frac{\sigma_{KPIn}}{\sqrt{r}} \quad * \tag{2}$$

* $Z_{\alpha/2}$ *normalized standard varible,* σ_{KPIn} *standard deviation for KPIn and r is replication number.*

Table 5. ANOVA test P-value results, codes: 0 '***' 0.001 '**' 0.01 '*' 0.05

Factors	LS1		LS2		LS3		LS4	
Demand distribution	3,15E-14	***	4,99E-14	***	4,85E-15	***	0,0002638	***
Lead time distribution	< 2.2e-16	***	< 2.2e-16	***	< 2.2e-16	***	0,3792613	
Safety Stocks	0,004364	**	0,013121	*	0,0001933	***	8,62E-09	***
Ratio Co/Cs	0,132156		0,126539		< 2.2e-16	***	3,49E-07	***
Demand dist.: Lead time dist.	< 2.2e-16	***	< 2.2e-16	***	4,03E-16	***	0,1436708	
Demand dist.: Safety Stocks	0,639589		0,952472		0,8427638		0,9926262	
Demand dist.: Ratio Co/Cs	0,016213	*	0,031195	*	0,0091386	**	0,0912483	
Lead time dist.: Safety Stocks	0,570304		0,801933		0,0424879	*	0,2119648	
Lead time dist.: Ratio Co/Cs	0,025063	*	0,009775	**	< 2.2e-16	***	0,1682513	
Safety Stocks: Ratio Co/Cs	0,92423		0,918936		0,9432251		0,8817591	

The ANOVA test reveals that the considered factors have different impact on confidence interval. Demand and lead time distribution have a very strong effects in comparison with the other parameters and even their interaction is important, as shown in in figure 2 for SL1.

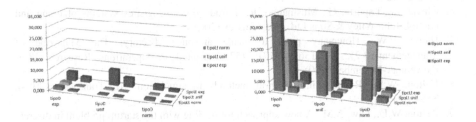

Fig. 2. Confidence half interval (min – max), in terms of %, for SL1 and SL4

5   Conclusions

The case study presented here can be used to make some practical considerations to support error analysis for discrete event simulation models. First, a "long" simulation period, in order to pass the initial transient period, is relatively easy to set, even if different behavior have been observed for different KPI. Second, the initial transient period and the related confidence interval depend in a very different way by the considered parameters. In particular, for numeric parameters, the hypothesis that confidence interval variance is normal distributed around a central value calculated in

712   G. Davoli et al.

the reference scenario is almost verified. On the other hand, when the studied parameters are not numerical, for example distribution type as in the considered case study, the confidence interval must be re-calculated in each scenario because the variance could be high and the interaction are almost unpredictable. So, in practice, the effort to check the confidence interval related to discrete event simulation should be done when the modified parameters are not simply numeric. This kind of analysis, thanks to the actual computational resource, is not prohibitive in terms of time when we manage a rather simple model.

6   Limitation and Further Work

The number of replications for each scenario provided in the DOE is fixed, a deeper study about this aspect should be investigate.

References

1. Bather, J.A.: A continuous time inventory model. J. Appl. Prob. 3, 538–549 (1966)
2. Box, G.E.P., Hunter, W.E., Hunter, J.S.: Statistics for experimenters. John Wiley & Sons (1978)
3. Brown, R.G.: Smoothing, Forecasting and Prediction of Discrete Time Series. Prentice-Hall, Englewood Cliffs (1963)
4. Chung, A.C.: Simulation Modeling Handbook – A Pratical Approach. Industrial and Manufacturing Engineering Series, Series Editor. CRC Press (2004)
5. Fishman, G.S.: Discrete Event Simulation: Modeling, Programming, and Analysis. Springer (2001)
6. Ghiani, G., Laporte, G., Musmanno, R.: Introduction to logistics systems planning and control. John Wiley & Sons Ltd., West Sussex (2004)
7. Harris, F.W.: Howmany parts to make at once. Factory, The Magazine of Management 10(2), 135–136 (1913); 152, reprinted in Operations Research 38(6) (November-December 1990)
8. Kelton, W.D.: Random initialization methods in simulation. IIE Transactions 21(4), 355–367 (1989)
9. Kelton, W.D., Law, A.M.: A new approach for dealing with the startup problem in discrete event simulation. Naval Research Logistics Quarterly 30, 641–658 (1983)
10. Law, A.M., Kelton, W.D.: Simulation Modeling and Analysis, 3rd edn. McGraw-Hill (2000)
11. Mosca, R., Giribone, P.: Teoria degli esperimenti e simulazione. Quaderni di gestione degli impianti industriali, Università di Genova (1985)
12. Mosca, R., Giribone, P., Schenone, M.: Integrated management of a bishuttle FMS using discrete/stochastic simulator. Computer-Integrated Manufacturing Systems 5(2) (1992)
13. Sandıkc, B., Sabuncuoglu, I.: Analysis of the behavior of the transient period in non-terminating simulations. European Journal of Operational Research 173, 252–267 (2006)
14. Schruben, L.W.: Detecting initialization bias in simulation output. Operations Research 30, 569–590 (1982)
15. Schruben, L.W., Singh, H., Tierney, L.: Optimal test for initialization bias in simulation output. Operations Research 31, 1167–1178 (1983)

16. Tersine, R.J.: Principles of inventory and materials management. Elsevier Science Publishing Co.,Inc., North-Holland (1988)
17. Vassilacopoulus, G.: Testing for initialization bias in simulation output. Simulation 52, 151–153 (1989)
18. Welch, P.D. A graphical approach to the initial transient problem in steady-state simulations. In: Proceedings of the 10th IMACS World Congress on Systems, Simulation, and Scientific Computation, Montreal, pp. 219–221 (1982)
19. White Jr., K.P.: An effective truncation heuristic for bias reduction in simulation output. Simulation 69(6), 323–334 (1997)

Author Index

Printed in the United States
By Bookmasters